PARAMAHANSA YOGANANDA
(January 5, 1893–March 7, 1952)

THE
SECOND COMING
OF
CHRIST

The Resurrection of
the Christ Within You

---

*A revelatory commentary on
the original teachings of Jesus*

Paramahansa Yogananda

Volume I

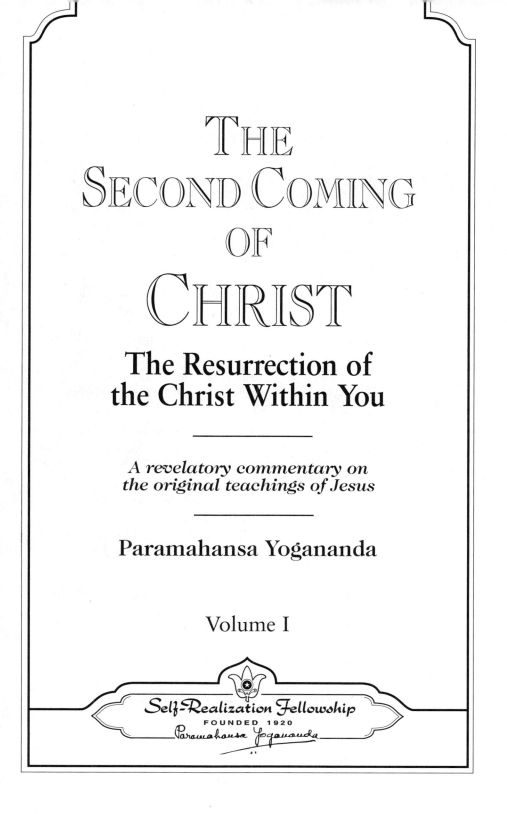

Self-Realization Fellowship
FOUNDED 1920
Paramahansa Yogananda

Acknowledgments for quoted material and artworks appear on page 1596.

 Authorized by the International Publications
Council of Self-Realization Fellowship

The Self-Realization Fellowship name and emblem (shown above) appear on all SRF books, recordings, and other publications, assuring the reader that a work originates with the society established by Paramahansa Yogananda and faithfully conveys his teachings.

Library of Congress Cataloging-in-Publication Data
Yogananda, Paramahansa, 1893–1952.
The Second Coming of Christ : the Resurrection of the Christ within you :
a revelatory commentary on the original teachings of Jesus /
Paramahansa Yogananda. — 1st ed.
p. cm.
Includes bibliographical references and index.
ISBN 0-87612-555-0 (hardcover slipcased)
1. Jesus Christ—Hindu interpretations. I. Title.
BT304.94.Y63 2004
294.5'2—dc22
2004009159

Printed in the United States of America
13691-5432

Dedicated to my revered guru,
Swami Sri Yukteswar Giri,
whose universal wisdom first illumined for me
the oneness of eternal truth
uniting the teachings of Jesus Christ
and India's ancient science of religion;

and to devout souls everywhere,
whom I summon to enter the inner light of divine perception
revealing the infinite Christ Consciousness
seeking resurrection within them

THE SPIRITUAL LEGACY OF PARAMAHANSA YOGANANDA

Paramahansa Yogananda (1893–1952) is widely recognized as one of the preeminent spiritual figures of our time, and the influence of his life and work continues to grow. Many of the religious and philosophical concepts and methods he introduced decades ago are now finding expression in education, psychology, business, medicine, and other spheres of endeavor—contributing in far-reaching ways to a more integrated, humane, and spiritual vision of human life.

The fact that Paramahansa Yogananda's teachings are being interpreted and creatively applied in many different fields, as well as by exponents of diverse philosophical and metaphysical movements, points not only to the great practical utility of what he taught. It also makes clear the need for some means of ensuring that the spiritual legacy he left not be diluted, fragmented, or distorted with the passing of time.

With the increasing variety of sources of information about Paramahansa Yogananda, readers sometimes inquire how they can be certain that a publication accurately presents his life and teachings. In response to these inquiries, we would like to explain that Sri Yogananda founded Self-Realization Fellowship to disseminate his teachings and to preserve their purity and integrity for future generations. He personally chose and trained those close disciples who head the Self-Realization Fellowship Publications Council, and gave them specific guidelines for the preparation and publishing of his lectures, writings, and *Self-Realization Lessons*. The members of the SRF Publications Council honor these guidelines as a sacred trust, in order that the universal message of this beloved world teacher may live on in its original power and authenticity.

The Self-Realization Fellowship name and the SRF emblem (shown above) were originated by Sri Yogananda to identify the organization he founded to carry on his worldwide spiritual and humanitarian work. These appear on all Self-Realization Fellowship books, audio and video recordings, films, and other publications, assuring the reader that a work originates with the organization founded by Paramahansa Yogananda and faithfully conveys his teachings as he himself intended they be given.

—SELF-REALIZATION FELLOWSHIP

Contents

Volume I

Volume II

Illustrations

Volume I

Volume II

Preface

By Sri Daya Mata

*Spiritual successor to Paramahansa Yogananda and president
since 1955 of the worldwide society he founded, Self-Realization
Fellowship/Yogoda Satsanga Society of India*

It is with a joyous sense of fulfillment that I introduce the publication of these volumes of Paramahansa Yogananda's revelatory explanations of the words of the blessed Lord Jesus. In memories as vivid and sharply etched as though yesterday, I inwardly behold the great Guru, his face radiantly enraptured, as he records for the world the inspired exposition of the Gospel teachings imparted to him through direct, personal communion with Jesus of Nazareth. Still living in my consciousness are the sacred vibrations that enfolded us when through the years Paramahansaji, in ecstatic meditation, became absorbed in one of his many visions of Christ; and when my stenographic pen seemed to take on a life of its own in attunement with the Guru's voice as I took down his words during his lectures and classes and at every opportunity in his presence—words that flowed from his oneness with the infinite Christ-*Kutastha* wisdom of the universe.

My first meeting with Paramahansa Yogananda was in 1931 when he came to my hometown of Salt Lake City to give a series of lectures and classes. Instantly I felt a soul-quickening recognition that at last I had found someone who truly knew God—one who could lead me to attainment of the God-realization that was so evident in the transforming power emanating from his very person. Not long after, in November of that year, I entered Paramahansaji's monastic ashram at the international headquarters of his society atop Mount Washington in Los Angeles to devote myself to a life of seeking and serving God under his guidance.

Having been completely transfixed by the illuminating depth of the Guru's teachings of yoga and meditation, I found it something of a surprise that this consummate exponent of India's ancient spiritual heritage would also give emphasis to the life and message of Jesus in the New Testament. Indeed, I was not only to witness in Paramahansaji a living exemplar of this scriptural wisdom, but personally to record numerous lectures, temple services, informal talks, and writings in which he explicated the teachings of Jesus.

The scope and content of *The Second Coming of Christ* are clearly set forth in the author's Introduction and the Discourses that follow. But perhaps it will add to the reader's appreciation to know something of the genesis of this work, of which I can speak firsthand —from its inception to the culminating presentation in these pages.

Paramahansaji—as a delegate to the International Congress of Religious Liberals in Boston—had arrived in America in 1920 to undertake the mission given him by a line of enlightened masters in India:* to spread worldwide the ancient soul-science of yoga meditation, and (as he expressed in the Aims and Ideals of Self-Realization Fellowship) "to reveal the complete harmony and basic oneness of original Christianity as taught by Jesus Christ and original Yoga as taught by Bhagavan Krishna; and to show that these principles of truth are the common scientific foundation of all true religions." The fulfillment of this sacred responsibility was his lifelong endeavor—beginning with classes in Boston in his first years in this country and continuing with ever newly expressed inspirations to the last days before his passing more than thirty years later.

After a few years in Boston, Paramahansaji embarked on a program of lectures and class series that, over the course of the next decade, took him over the length and breadth of the United States. He taught in nearly all the major cities; overflow audiences in the largest auditoriums were spellbound by his great wisdom and love for God—and by his dynamic personality, which was itself an explicit testimony to the practicality of the applied spiritual science he taught. The introduction of his unique exposition of the teachings of Jesus Christ dissolved theological boundaries between the liberating path to God's kingdom revealed by Lord Jesus and the Yoga science of God-union taught by Bhagavan Krishna in the sacred scripture of India, the Bhagavad Gita. Paramahansaji's American students, consisting largely of persons raised in the Judeo-Christian tradition, longed

---

* Mahavatar Babaji, Lahiri Mahasaya, and Swami Sri Yukteswar (see glossary).

for more—especially to be able to study these explanations in written form and thereby better absorb the unguessed spiritual treasures that had been revealed in their own familiar scriptures by this man of God from India.

Their requests did not go unheeded. In 1932, not long after I joined the ashram at Mount Washington, the Guru found time, amidst organizational demands and travel to fulfill lecture engagements, to begin including commentaries on the Gospels and the Bhagavad Gita in the magazine he had founded a few years earlier. Each installment consisted of a few verses of both scriptures along with Paramahansaji's explanations. "These spiritual interpretations are the result of a long-unfulfilled promise to Yogoda students," he announced in the magazine.* Not infrequently, the copy was mailed to the magazine staff from whatever faraway city he was lecturing in at the time—even during his extended trip to India via Europe and Palestine in 1935–36.

Of Paramahansaji's numerous remarkable experiences during that journey to India, especially of note in connection with this book is his visit to the Holy Land. In a letter sent from Jerusalem to his exalted disciple in America, Rajarsi Janakananda,† the Guru wrote of his experiences with Christ: "There are no words adequate enough to express to you the joy and the vision and the blessedness which I perceived here. All the primitive atmosphere, the ancient background, is still present, marred only by a few modern buildings and hotels. His name is alive as before; only the Jesus that was and walked and suffered in the streets of Jerusalem very few people see. He was with me everywhere; and a very special communion I had in Bethlehem where he was born as the little babe body of Jesus. He touched me as I entered the ancient menagerie where Mary brought him into the world—in a humble little stable under an inn. This place is absolutely authentic. I know it from the Divine. But there are other places where different factions have marked Jesus did this and that, which have some errors. Every place was verified from within. Most places are authentic."

---

* *East-West* magazine, founded by Paramahansa Yogananda in 1925; he later renamed it *Self-Realization* (the name under which it continues to this day) to clearly identify it as the official organ of his Self-Realization Fellowship organization, which had been known as Yogoda Satsanga Society in earlier years.

† First successor to Paramahansa Yogananda as president and spiritual head of Self-Realization Fellowship/Yogoda Satsanga Society of India (until his passing on February 20, 1955). See glossary.

Returning to the United States late in 1936, Paramahansaji was presented with a surprise "welcome home" gift: a secluded hermitage overlooking the Pacific Ocean at Encinitas, California. It was in this ideal location, away from the demands of lecturing and organizational work, that the Guru was able to devote himself more fully to his writings and to spend more time in seclusion and deep communion with God.

From the depths of these periods of divine communion in the Encinitas Hermitage, the Guru brought forth, in addition to profound scriptural commentaries, his long-contemplated *Autobiography of a Yogi*. It was my great blessing, along with my sister,* to record on a typewriter the Guru's dictation. He would work all day long and usually far into the night. The thrill of the truths pouring from him were intoxicating, a wonderful blissful state of consciousness! Of his interpretations of Christ's words I wrote in my personal notes: "I have watched Master's face as he dictates his inspirations. The joy and wisdom of another world are expressed there. His eyes are afire with a blaze of love for Christ, and his voice is permeated with tenderness. It evokes reflections of how Christ must have spoken centuries ago."

Of his own experience, the Guru remarked during that period: "I am worshiping the Father in the greatest joy and glory that ever was given to me. I never dreamed before how deep are the teachings of Jesus. Through the interpretation that is being given to me now, I see that they express the same truths as Patanjali's aphorisms, the condensed essence of Indian Yoga. Understood in this light, they can build a new age."

Tara Mata, a close disciple of Gurudeva whom he had appointed as editor of his writings, wrote to a literary acquaintance describing the Guru's commentaries on Christ's words: "He will come to a passage which is so obscure that it defies all possibility of plain interpretation. He will look blankly at me or one of his other secretaries for a while, close his eyes, and presently out will come the whole plain meaning. He gets it entirely from inspiration; in fact, it is only through him that I know what 'inspired books' really means."†

---

* Ananda Mata, a faithful disciple of Paramahansa Yogananda since 1931. She entered his monastic order in 1933 at the age of 17; she has served as an officer and member of the Board of Directors of Self-Realization Fellowship/Yogoda Satsanga Society of India.

† Tara Mata (Laurie V. Pratt) served as editor-in-chief of Self-Realization Fellowship publications, and as vice president and a member of the Board of Directors, until her passing in 1971.

Readers of the serialized *Second Coming* articles in Self-Realization Fellowship's magazine were also uplifted. The pastor of a Congregational Church in England, the Reverend Arthur Porter, a Doctor of Divinity who had taken the Guru's classes in New York City years earlier, wrote of Paramahansaji's interpretation as "a masterpiece of divine insight."

"One realizes that the complexities, the seeming irrelevancies and contradiction of the New Testament, have at last been solved in the white light of a soulful penetration," his testimonial went on. "[This] is not a product of scholarly study or comparison of existing Biblical commentaries, but has come forth in an awe-inspiring originality from the deeps of an unerring spiritual and intuitional judgment. It will live when whole libraries of intellectual theorizings on Christ have long been forgotten—the most important clarification of his teachings that has ever been offered the Christian world."

During this period of working on the Gospel commentaries in Encinitas, Paramahansaji began plans to have the material made available in book form. An interested gentleman with outside business contacts offered to seek a publisher. However, these attempts were unsuccessful; and Paramahansaji's Self-Realization Fellowship organization at that time had neither the printing facilities nor funds required to publish and promote a major book. Paramahansaji accepted the resulting evaluation that for the worldwide public distribution he envisioned, the manuscript would require further attention. "Continue to print the articles in our magazine for our readers," he instructed us. "Later I will have to do more work on them." In the meantime, he had already turned his attention, and that of his assisting disciples, to his *Autobiography of a Yogi,* which was completed and published in late 1946.

The final years of Gurudeva's life, from 1948 until 1952, were given over to long periods of intense concentration on his writings, his spiritual legacy to future generations. Knowing that his time on earth was drawing to a close, he found refuge for that work at a secluded retreat in the Mojave Desert, accompanied by a handful of close disciples who were assisting him, including his editor Tara Mata and the young editor he was training, Mrinalini Mata.* He was focused on

---

* Foreseeing that Tara Mata would not live long enough to complete the editorial work on all his writings, Paramahansaji designated Mrinalini Mata as her successor, and personally tutored her in the editing of his teachings for publication and worldwide dis-

completing the major publications that would make permanent the teachings he had been ordained to bring to the world. Much of this time was devoted to his translation of and voluminous commentary on the Bhagavad Gita: *God Talks With Arjuna.* He also undertook a concentrated review of many of his other works. His instruction for the completion of this present book was to draw on the full measure of material he had given on the life and teachings of Jesus in order to impart to a world audience the comprehensive presentation of the true teachings of the blessed Christ that he had divinely received.

In his talks through the years, including weekly sermons at Self-Realization Fellowship temples, he often included some commentary on, or applicable to, one or more verses from the Gospels. From these, precious realizations about Christ's life and words came into being—freshly expressed concepts, clarification and elaboration of points Paramahansaji had introduced in the magazine serialization, and also new explanations of important Gospel passages that had not been included in the magazine series. These and other of Paramahansaji's truth-perceptions, forthcoming during his full lifetime of building and serving his Self-Realization Fellowship/Yogoda Satsanga organization, have been made an integrated whole in this definitive edition of *The Second Coming of Christ.*

Preparing this manuscript for publication in book form also entailed minimizing duplication of basic concepts that had been necessary when the commentaries were presented serially in the magazine over two decades—and also condensation of material that had been included in the early magazine articles primarily for Paramahansaji's students and followers and later incorporated into the printed *Self-Realization Fellowship Lessons* or elsewhere at his request. Additional work stemmed from the fact that in the earliest stages of composing his Gospel commentaries, Paramahansaji made use of a book that had been given to him entitled *The Walks and Words of Jesus,* by Reverend M. N. Olmsted, in which the author had compiled into one chronological narrative the events and sayings recounted in all four of the Gospels (King James version). While the result was a very readable ac-

---

semination. She had met the Guru in 1945 and entered his ashram as a nun shortly thereafter; I observed how from the very beginning the Guru drew her deep into the path and nurtured her to assume that responsibility. To this day Mrinalini Mata continues to devote herself to the editorial work entrusted to her by the Guru, as well as serving as vice president of Self-Realization Fellowship.

count of Jesus' life and words, inevitably some significant phrases or points were omitted or minimized when variant tellings from two or more Gospels were merged into one. Because of this, Paramahansaji had stopped using Rev. Olmsted's book partway through the magazine series, and switched to direct quotes from the King James Bible —which he had always used when giving explanation of Bible passages in his classes and temple services. Accordingly, in preparing this book, wording of the verses from the King James Bible has been used throughout, and parallel references from all the Gospels have been cited in order to insure a thorough presentation of Jesus' words.

In the fifty years since Paramahansaji's passing, advances in physics, medicine, biology, and other fields—as well as archaeological and historical research that has shed much light on the early Christian movement—have contributed additional scientific and historical information pertinent to Paramahansaji's farseeing spiritual vision and understanding of Jesus' life and world mission. In publisher's footnotes, we have cited some of the more recent discoveries.

This two-volume scriptural treatise thus represents the inclusive culmination of Paramahansa Yogananda's divine commission to make manifest to the world the essence of "original Christianity as taught by Jesus Christ."

In giving the foregoing background as to how this book came into being, my hope has been to convey also to the reader at least something of the state of consciousness of the author. Truly his perceptions were of God. Paramahansaji's relationship with Christ far transcended a philosophical or moral appreciation of the message of the Gospels. He knew Jesus Christ in a personal way. He knew him through directly partaking of the infinite Christ Consciousness, God's consciousness omnipresent in creation, that the Master of Galilee had manifested—the consciousness through which Jesus had performed not only his wonders of healing and other "supernatural" feats, but the far greater miracles of unconditional love, forgiveness, and spiritual transformation of lives. Paramahansaji endeavored during his thirty years of teaching in the West to awaken that consciousness in all who would know Christ truly.

I had been at Mount Washington about a month when the Guru conducted the first all-day Christmas meditation. For over eight hours that day he meditated with a group of Self-Realization Fellowship members and friends, remaining continuously in communion with

God and Christ. As I sat in the afterglow of that memorable day, I remember thinking: "Here is a man from the Orient, of Hindu origin, yet such is his love for Christ that he has seen him and communed with him. It is he who has shown the West how truly to celebrate the birth and life of Jesus."

During the more than twenty years of my discipleship that I served as Paramahansaji's confidential secretary and assistant, never once did I see him step down from the lofty plane of Christlike behavior. I came to understand that his attunement with Jesus was founded not only in the profound depths of his joyous inner communion with the infinite Christ Consciousness in *samadhi* meditation, but also in his own realization and manifestation of the ideals of unconditional love, forgiveness, compassion, adherence to the highest divine truths, that were the hallmarks of Jesus' incarnation on earth. Thus, Paramahansaji's commentaries, divinely received and their truths realized, provide us an authentic glimpse of the spirit of those days when Lord Jesus walked with his beloved disciples by the shores of the Sea of Galilee and preached in the villages and countryside, and in the streets and temple of Jerusalem, giving his teachings of the "new testament" for the world. Paramahansaji takes us with Jesus on the journey of that divine life, from his birth to his death and resurrection, inviting the reader into the inner circle of Jesus' disciples to know the love and wisdom of the Christ they knew and followed. As the Discourses unfold, the universal precepts of Jesus are brought alive for today. Truth does not change with time; nor does humanity's basic potential and irrevocable choice: either to remain hapless victims of flawed human nature or to ascend to the glorious fulfillment of our blissful, immortal God-nature.

It is my hope and prayer that in this new millennium the publication of my Guru's long-awaited *Second Coming of Christ* kindle the flame of love divine in the hearts of all who read these pages. The message herein illumines the universal path that welcomes and embraces persons of every race, nationality, and religion. May the surpassing truth and inspiration set forth in these volumes help to usher the world into an enlightened era of peace, unity, world brotherhood, and communion with our one Father-Mother-Friend-Beloved God.

Los Angeles
February 2004

Introduction

In titling this work *The Second Coming of Christ,* I am not referring to a literal return of Jesus to earth. He came two thousand years ago and, after imparting a universal path to God's kingdom, was crucified and resurrected; his reappearance to the masses now is not necessary for the fulfillment of his teachings. What *is* necessary is for the cosmic wisdom and divine perception of Jesus to speak again through each one's own experience and understanding of the infinite Christ Consciousness that was incarnate in Jesus. That will be his true Second Coming.

There is a distinguishing difference of meaning between *Jesus* and *Christ.* His given name was Jesus; his honorific title was "Christ." In his little human body called Jesus was born the vast Christ Consciousness, the omniscient Intelligence of God omnipresent in every part and particle of creation. This Consciousness is the "only begotten Son of God," so designated because it is the sole perfect reflection in creation of the Transcendental Absolute, Spirit or God the Father.

Difference in meaning between "Jesus" and "Christ"

It was of that Infinite Consciousness, replete with the love and bliss of God, that Saint John spoke when he said: "As many as received him [the Christ Consciousness], to them gave he power to become the sons of God."* Thus according to Jesus' own teaching as recorded by his most highly advanced apostle, John, all souls who become united with Christ Consciousness by intuitive Self-realization† are rightly called sons of God.

---

* See Discourse 1 for detailed commentary on this verse.

† "Self" is capitalized to denote the soul, man's true identity, in contradistinction to the ego or pseudosoul, the lower self with which man temporarily identifies through ignorance of his real nature.

Self-realization is the knowing—in body, mind, and soul—that we are one with the omnipresence of God; that we do not have to pray that it come to us, that we are not merely near it at all times, but that God's omnipresence is our omnipresence; that

A small cup cannot hold an ocean within itself. Likewise, the cup of human consciousness, limited by the physical and mental instrumentalities of material perceptions, cannot grasp the universal Christ Consciousness, no matter how desirous one may be of doing so. By the definite science of meditation known for millenniums to the yogis and sages of India, and to Jesus, any seeker of God can enlarge the caliber of his consciousness to omniscience—to receive within himself the Universal Intelligence of God.

What Jesus gave as chronicled in the New Testament of the Bible very few people understand. They just read what he said and quote it;

True understanding of Jesus' teachings comes through communion with Christ Consciousness

and because it is written in the biblical Scripture they believe it blindly, with little effort to realize the wisdom therein through personal experience. Realization is to attune one's consciousness with Christ; then the right comprehension will come. When persons try to deduce the meaning of Jesus' words by intellectual analysis alone, or from the perspective of a specific dogma, they inevitably distort his sayings to suit their purpose—however well-intentioned—or to comfortably accommodate their level of understanding. Christ-wisdom has to be grasped by communion, not by rationalization.

The only reliable standard of scriptural interpretation is the testimony of actual perception—to go into that state of consciousness in which the prophets perceived the truths they expounded and thereby witness the meaning they intended. The words of Jesus fully unfold their wisdom only to those who meditate deeply on the Christ Consciousness that Jesus possessed. Then one understands Jesus in the light of his spiritual experience of the Cosmic Consciousness of the Heavenly Father, realized through the Father's Christ-Intelligence reflection present in all creation.

The detailed knowledge of the heavens as discovered by great astronomers through study and the use of telescopes could not have been acquired by lay persons lacking that training and equipment. Likewise, what enlightened sages know about Truth and Spirit through the clarifying telescope of their intuition can be known by ordinary individuals only when they have similarly extended their vision by the use of their inner telescopic intuition erstwhile hidden in the chamber of their souls.

---

we are just as much a part of Him now as we ever will be. All we have to do is improve our knowing.

Christ did not go through the sublime drama of his life merely to provide sermon material for generations of preachers and their Sunday audiences. He lived, died, and was gloriously resurrected as an inspiration to others to live a divine life and attain in themselves his experiences of God and the afterlife.

Jesus Christ was crucified once; but his teachings are crucified daily at the hands of superstition, dogmatism, and pedantic theological misinterpretations. My aim in offering to the world this spiritual interpretation of his words is to show how the Christ Consciousness of Jesus, free from such crucifixion, can be brought back a second time into the souls of all who make the effort to receive it. Surely, with the dawn of this more enlightened age, the time has come to stop the crucifixion of the Christ teachings as given by Jesus. His pristine message should be resurrected from its entombment by Self-realization, the inner enlightened experience of truth.

In these pages I offer to the world an intuitionally perceived spiritual interpretation of the words spoken by Jesus, truths received through actual communion with Christ Consciousness. They will be found to be universally true if they are studied conscientiously and meditated upon with soul-awakened intuitive perception. They reveal the perfect unity that exists among the revelations of the Christian Bible, the Bhagavad Gita of India, and all other time-tested true scriptures.

The saviors of the world do not come to foster inimical doctrinal divisions; their teachings should not be used toward that end. It is something of a misnomer even to refer to the New Testament as the "Christian" Bible, for it does not belong exclusively to any one sect. Truth is meant for the blessing and upliftment of the entire human race. As the Christ Consciousness is universal, so does Jesus Christ belong to all.

Though I emphasize the message of Lord Jesus in the New Testament and the yoga science of God-union delineated by Bhagavan Krishna in the Bhagavad Gita as the *summum bonum* of the way to God-realization, I honor the diverse expressions of truth flowing from the One God through the scriptures of His various emissaries. All such scriptures have a threefold meaning —material, mental, and spiritual. They are divine wells of "living waters" that can quench humanity's thirsts of body, mind, and soul. The

Threefold meaning identical in the Hindu and Christian Bibles

timeless revelations sent by God through illumined prophets serve human beings on each of the three levels of their nature.

The material meaning of the teachings of Christ emphasizes their value as applied to physical and social well-being—the eternal laws of right living pertinent to man's personal, familial, business, community, national, and international duties as a member of God's worldwide human family.

The mental interpretation explains the application of Christ's teaching for the improvement of man's mind and understanding—development of his intellectual and psychological faculties, his thoughts and moral values.

Interpreted in relation to the spiritual side of man's being, Jesus' teachings point out the way to the kingdom of God—personal realization of each soul's infinite divine potentials as an immortal child of God, through devout communion and ultimate oneness with the Heavenly Father-Creator of all.

Although both the material and the psychological interpretations of scriptures are necessary for the right conduct of a balanced, God-centered life, it is the spiritual interpretations that the God-sent emissaries of scriptural content intended as of supreme importance. Even the most materially or intellectually accomplished individual may fail to make a true success of life. Rather, it is the person of spiritual attainment who scientifically achieves all-round success, which means to be happy, healthy, intelligent, contented, and truly prosperous with blissful, all-fulfilling wisdom through God-communion.

The Bible and the Bhagavad Gita are satisfyingly complete, containing the science of life, the eternal principles of truth and philosophy of living that make life beautiful and harmonious. Philosophy is the love of wisdom; religion, as taught by the scriptural prophets, is likewise devotion to highest truth. The personal realization of truth is the science behind all sciences. But for most persons, religion has devolved to a matter of belief only. One believes in Catholicism, another believes in some Protestant denomination, others assert belief that the Jewish or Hindu or Muslim or Buddhist religion is the true way. The science of religion identifies the universal truths common to all—the basis of religion—and teaches how by their practical application persons can build their lives according to the Divine Plan. India's teaching of *Raja Yoga,* the "royal" science of the soul, supersedes the orthodoxy of religion by setting forth systematically the practice of those methods that are universally necessary for the perfection of every individual, regardless of race or creed.

There is a vast difference between theoretical religion and philosophy and their actual practice. Practically speaking, philosophy may be divided into three parts—ethics, psychology, and metaphysics. These three departments are covered in both the Hindu and Christian Bibles.

Ethics—scriptural truth as applied to material life—sets forth the science of human duty, moral laws, how to behave.

Psychology—truth applied to mental well-being—teaches one how to analyze himself; for no spiritual progress is possible without introspection and self-study by which one endeavors to find out what he is so that he can correct himself and become what he should be.

Metaphysics—truths pertaining to the spiritual dimension of life —explains the nature of God and the science of knowing Him.

These three, taken together and put into practice, constitute religion. The ethical moral principles prescribed in the New Testament are the same as in the Gita. The psychology and the metaphysics of these two scriptures, rightly interpreted, likewise coincide in every respect. The superficial difference is that the Hindu scriptures—of which the Gita is a sublime summation—were written in a higher age of civilization, against a background of greater understanding among the general populace. Though Jesus himself embodied the highest wisdom, he expressed truth in simple, concise language; whereas the scriptures of India are composed in Sanskrit terminology of extraordinary depth and scientific precision. Point by point I have compared the salient message of the Bible and Hindu scriptures, and have found only harmonious unity between them. It is from this understanding that these explanations of Christ's words have been written. By way of example, some parallel or complementary verses from the Bhagavad Gita are cited. I have given a detailed explanation of these verses and the entirety of the Gita in a separate work,* to which I encourage readers to refer for additional insight into the truths implicit but not elaborated in Jesus' words that have come down to us in the four canonical Gospels. Had Jesus himself written his teachings, they might indeed have been expressed in greater depth than in the generalities of a conversation with his disciples or a discourse to the multitudes. Certainly

----

* *God Talks With Arjuna: The Bhagavad Gita — Royal Science of God-Realization* (published by Self-Realization Fellowship).

in the Revelation of St. John we are led by means of metaphor into the profound insights of the yoga science in which Jesus initiated his advanced disciple John, and others, whose consciousness thereby ascended to the exalted Self-realized state of the kingdom of God within.

A scripture is mute testimony of spiritual truth; a divine personage is veritably a living scripture. Like tiny seeds that produce mighty trees, scriptural truths reveal their power and wisdom-yielding qualities in the most inspiringly useful way when manifested in the lives of God-realized souls.

Jesus is real; I have seen him

That the eternal verities were embodied in Jesus was declared by him when he said of his Christ Consciousness, "I am the way, the truth, and the life."* At once divine and human, Jesus lived among God's children as a nurturing "big brother," beloved of the Father of all, sent on earth to redeem his desire-deluded brothers and sisters by urging them to become like him. In the Gospel record of his life we find his path to the kingdom of God taught not only by precept but by example.†

The veracity of the Biblical stories of Jesus is regarded skeptically by many in the modern age. Scoffing at supernormal capacities that

---

* John 14:6 (see commentary, Discourse 70).

† The thousands of books and articles about the modern scientific search for "the historical Jesus" by archaeologists, linguists, historians, anthropologists, and other experts have been valuable in illumining the cultural context in which Jesus lived, and—even more importantly—how the interpretation of his teachings by diverse groups of followers changed and evolved in the centuries after his death. None of these works, however, has supplanted the New Testament Gospels as the richest and most complete resource available about what Jesus actually said and did.

Professor Luke Timothy Johnson of Emory University writes in *The Real Jesus* (HarperSanFrancisco, 1996): "Haven't all the archaeological discoveries of the past forty years opened up exciting new sources for the historical analysis of earliest Christianity?...The discovery of the Dead Sea Scrolls in 1947 was revolutionary because it provided previously unavailable and precious insight into the varieties of Judaism in first-century Palestine, and into the workings of a sectarian Judaism making claims analogous to those made by the Christians. But the sober conclusion of the best-informed scholars...is that the Dead Sea Scrolls do not shed any direct light either on Jesus or on the development of Christianity." Regarding the collection of Gnostic Christian manuscripts discovered at Nag Hammadi in Egypt in 1945, Professor Johnson writes: "The compositions in the library, scholars agree, do not come from a period earlier than the mid-second century....[Thus] it turns out that the canonical writings of the New Testament remain our best historical witnesses to the earliest period of the Christian movement." *(Publisher's Note)*

challenge common prejudices about what is humanly possible, some staunchly deny that the God-man of the Gospels ever lived. Others concede a measure of historicity to Jesus, but depict him only as a charismatic ethical or spiritual teacher. But to the New Testament account of the Christ of Galilee I humbly add my own testimony. From personal experience I know the reality of his life and miracles, for I have seen him many, many times, and communed with him, and received his direct confirmation about these matters.

He has come to me often as the baby Jesus and as the young Christ. I have seen him as he was before his crucifixion, his face very sad; and I have seen him in the glorious form in which he appeared after his resurrection.

Jesus did not have a light complexion with blue eyes and blond hair as many Western painters have depicted him. His eyes were dark brown, and he had the olive-colored skin of his Asiatic heritage. His nose was a little flattened at the tip. His moustache, sparse beard, and long hair were black. His face and body were beautifully formed. Of all the pictures I have seen of him in the West, the rendering by Hofmann comes closest to showing the accurate features of the incarnate Jesus.*

It is an erroneous assumption of limited minds that great ones such as Jesus, Krishna, and other divine incarnations are gone from the earth when they are no longer visible to human sight. This is not so. When a liberated master has dissolved his body in Spirit, and yet manifests in form to receptive devotees (as Jesus has appeared throughout the centuries since his passing, such as to Saint Francis, Saint Teresa, and many others of East and West), it means he has an ongoing role to play in the destiny of the world. Even when masters have completed the specific role for which they took on a physical incarnation, it is the divinely ordained task of some to look after the welfare of humanity and assist in guiding its progress.

Jesus' wish to restore his original teachings to the world

Jesus Christ is very much alive and active today. In Spirit and occasionally taking on a flesh-and-blood form, he is working unseen by

---

* Heinrich Hofmann (1824–1911).

This artist created many paintings and drawings depicting the life of Jesus. A number of them appear throughout this book. *(Publisher's Note)*

the masses for the regeneration of the world. With his all-embracing love, Jesus is not content merely to enjoy his blissful consciousness in Heaven. He is deeply concerned for mankind and wishes to give his followers the means to attain the divine freedom of entry into God's Infinite Kingdom. He is disappointed because many are the churches and temples founded in his name, often prosperous and powerful, but where is the communion that he stressed—actual contact with God? Jesus wants temples to be established in human souls, first and foremost; then established outwardly in physical places of worship. Instead, there are countless huge edifices with vast congregations being indoctrinated in churchianity, but few souls who are really in touch with Christ through deep prayer and meditation.

To reestablish God in the temples of souls through revival of the original teachings of God-communion as propounded by Christ and Krishna is why I was sent to the West by Mahavatar Babaji, the deathless Yogi-Christ of modern India, whose existence was revealed to the world at large for the first time in 1946 in *Autobiography of a Yogi:*

"Babaji is ever in communion with Christ; together they send out vibrations of redemption and have planned the spiritual technique of salvation for this age. The work of these two fully illumined masters —one with a body, and one without a body—is to inspire the nations to forsake wars, race hatreds, religious sectarianism, and the boomerang evils of materialism. Babaji is well aware of the trend of modern times, especially of the influence and complexities of Western civilization, and realizes the necessity of spreading the self-liberations of yoga equally in the West and in the East."*

It was Mahavatar Babaji who, in consonance with the wish of Christ, devolved upon me the tremendous task of properly interpreting for the world the profound meaning of Jesus' words. In 1894 Babaji instructed my guru, Swami Sri Yukteswar, to write a comparative study of the harmony between the Christian and Hindu scriptures from the point of view of India's *Sanatana Dharma,* eternal truth.† Babaji further told my Guru that I would be sent to him to train for my mission in the West: to teach, side by side, original Christianity as taught by Jesus Christ and original Yoga as taught by Bhagavan Krishna.

---

* *Autobiography of a Yogi,* Chapter 33.

†The book written by Sri Yukteswarji at Babaji's behest is *The Holy Science* (published by Self-Realization Fellowship). See also Discourse 2, page 38.

For uncounted millenniums, India has been the spiritual lightland of the earth. It is in India that the divine soul-science of yoga—union with God through direct personal communion with Him—has been preserved. That is why Jesus went to India as a youth, and why he returned to India and conferred with Babaji for the spiritual evolution of the world.* Time will testify to this truth, that they have given to the world through the *Kriya Yoga* teachings of Self-Realization Fellowship (Yogoda Satsanga Society of India) the techniques of meditation by which each soul can reunite with God through inner realization of the universal Christ-Krishna Consciousness.

The promise of Jesus to send the Holy Ghost after he was gone† few in the Christian world have understood. Holy Ghost is the sacred, invisible vibratory power of God that actively sustains the universe: the Word, or *Aum,* Cosmic Vibration, the Great Comforter, the Savior from all sorrows. Within the Holy Ghost Cosmic Vibration is the all-pervading Christ, the Son or Consciousness of God immanent in creation. The method of contacting this Cosmic Vibration, the Holy Ghost, is for the first time being spread worldwide by means of definite meditation techniques of the *Kriya Yoga* science. Through the blessing of communion with the Holy Ghost, the cup of human consciousness is expanded to receive the ocean of Christ Consciousness.

---

* See also Discourse 5.

A wealth of evidence for the primacy of India's spiritual culture in the ancient world is presented by Georg Feuerstein, Ph.D., Subhash Kak, Ph.D., and David Frawley, O.M.D., in *In Search of the Cradle of Civilization: New Light on Ancient India* (Wheaton, Ill.: Quest Books, 1995): "The old saying *ex oriente lux* ('From the East, light') is no platitude, for civilization's torch, especially the core sacred tradition of perennial wisdom, has been handed down from the eastern hemisphere....The Middle-Eastern creations of Judaism and Christianity, which largely have given our civilization its present shape, were influenced by ideas stemming from countries farther east, especially India. Of all these Eastern traditions, by far the oldest continuous religious heritage is, without question, that of Hinduism....

"It would appear that none of the world's extant traditions are as old and comprehensive as the Vedic-Hindu tradition. It is so embracing that it seems to contain all the different approaches to the Divine, or ultimate Reality, found in the other traditions. Every spiritual means—from simple devotional surrender to complex visualization to postural variation—has been systematically explored in this great tradition." *(Publisher's Note)*

† "And I will pray the Father, and He shall give you another Comforter, that He may abide with you for ever....But the Comforter, which is the Holy Ghost, whom the Father will send in my name, he shall teach you all things, and bring all things to your remembrance, whatsoever I have said unto you" (John 14:16, 26).

The adept in the practice of the science of *Kriya Yoga* who consciously experiences the presence of the Holy Ghost Comforter and merges in the Son, or immanent Christ Consciousness, attains thereby realization of God the Father and entry into the infinite kingdom of God.

Christ will thus appear a second time in the consciousness of every devout adept who masters the technique of contacting the Holy Ghost, the bestower of indescribable blissful comfort in Spirit. Those who have spiritual ears to hear, let them hear that the promise of Jesus Christ to send the Holy Ghost, the Comforter, is being fulfilled. These teachings have been sent to explain the truth as Jesus intended it to be known in the world—not to give a new Christianity, but to give the real Christ-teaching: how to become like Christ, how to resurrect the Eternal Christ within one's Self.

To interpret the words of Jesus, not according to whim or dogmatic emotionalism or theological rationalization, but as he meant them, one must be in tune with him. One must know what Christ was and is; and that can be understood only in rapport with his state of Christ Consciousness.

These interpretations inspired by God and Christ

Identifying myself with the consciousness of Jesus, I have felt what he felt when he spoke to his disciples and to the crowds as recorded in the Gospels. What I have tried to convey are the thoughts and consciousness of Jesus that were behind his words when he uttered them. I commune with Christ and ask him: "I don't want to interpret the Bible from my own views. Will you interpret it?" Then he comes to me.

In attunement with Christ in ecstasy and in spirit, I have taken down his explanations to the best of my ability as they came through me; those revelations are written in this treatise. I do not explain. I see. I do not tell you what I think, but what I am led to say by inner realization.

Many of Jesus' sayings and parables, which have undergone transformations due to mistranslation from the Aramaic, I did not understand at a first reading.* But as I prayed and attuned myself with

---

* Aramaic was the language of daily usage in Jesus' homeland. (He would also, of course, have received education in Hebrew, in which the Jewish scriptures were written.) The earliest known records of the Gospels were written not in Aramaic or He-

him, I received the meaning directly from him. Revelations that I never expected have been given to me; little did I dream what wealth of truth lay concealed. I believe that readers of this book will find that meanings buried twenty centuries have been brought out here for the first time, interpretations of the words of Jesus as he would talk to the people of today—truths he conveyed to his disciples and which he wants understood by devotees of the world throughout all time. Those who are receptive will feel through direct perception the message that Christ is speaking to them; for all I have done is to receive and convey the fullness of his thoughts and consciousness.

My singular desire to discern rightly the true meaning of Christ's words was given wondrous confirmation one night during a period when I was working on these interpretations. It was in the Hermitage at Encinitas, California. I was sitting in my darkened room in meditation, praying deeply from my soul, when suddenly the blackness gave way to a celestial opal-blue effulgence. The entire room was like an opal flame. In that light the radiant form of the blessed Lord Jesus appeared.

His face was divine. His appearance was of a young man in his twenties, with sparse beard and moustache; his long black hair, parted

---

brew, but in Greek, the *lingua franca* of the eastern part of the Roman Empire at that time. Thus the translation of Jesus' words began even with this primary written form.

For his commentaries on the Gospels, Paramahansa Yogananda used the King James translation (the "Authorized Version" of 1611). Reynolds Price, Professor of English at Duke University, has compared the King James Bible with later English translations of the original Greek text of the Gospels. In *Three Gospels* (New York: Simon and Schuster, 1997) he writes: "We now have in English several popular versions of the gospels that constitute what are well-intended but almost certainly major distortions of their originals....King James's translators proceeded under a single guiding principle (one word of the original in the fewest equivalent words of English, with the preservation when possible of at least some suggestion of the Greek word order)....

"Five minutes spent even today in the Bible section of an ordinary bookstore will show that no later version has equaled the King James in popularity; and in many conservative churches still, it is the only version consulted, as it is in a thousand college courses on 'The Bible as Literature.' And while it is customary to say that such enduring popularity derives from the King James's sonorous diction and stately syntax—the diction of Shakespeare and Ben Jonson—a close comparison of its language to that of the originals will very often show that the power and memorability of the King James is an almost automatic result of its loyal adherence to principles of literalness and the avoidance of paraphrase. Nearly four centuries of Greekless readers have sensed, unconsciously perhaps but with considerable accuracy, that...the language of the King James is truer to its strange originals than any of its successors." *(Publisher's Note)*

in the middle, had a golden light about it. His feet were not touching the floor. His eyes were the most beautiful, the most loving eyes I have ever seen. The whole universe I saw glistening in those eyes. They were infinitely changing, and with each transition of expression I intuitively understood the wisdom conveyed. In his glorious eyes I felt the power that upholds and commands the myriad worlds.

As he gazed down at me, a Holy Grail appeared at his mouth. It descended to my lips and touched them; then went up again to Jesus. After a few moments of rapt silent communion, he said to me: "Thou dost drink of the same cup of which I drink."

At that I bowed down. I was joyous beyond dreams to receive the testimony of his blessings, of his presence. Exactly the words that he said to me in this vision he also said to Thomas, which I never read before.* His words meant that I was drinking of his wisdom through the Holy Grail of his perceptions which he has dropped in my consciousness, and he was pleased. He approved very dearly and blessed me for writing these interpretations. This I can say without pride, because the interpretation of Christ's words herein is not mine. It has been given to me. I am happy this book is coming through me; but I am not the author. It is Christ. I am only the vehicle through which it is explained.

I hear Christ in the land of my inspiration; I behold Christ speaking to me all the eternal wisdom he intended to convey within his preg-

---

* Jesus' words are recorded in the noncanonical Gospel of Thomas, verse 13:

"'Compare me to someone and tell me whom I am like.'

"Simon Peter said to him, 'You are like a righteous angel.'

"Matthew said to him, 'You are like a wise philosopher.'

"Thomas said to him, 'Master, my mouth is wholly incapable of saying whom you are like.'

"Jesus said, 'I am not your master. Because you have drunk, you have become intoxicated from the bubbling spring which I have measured out.'"

Elsewhere in the Gospel of Thomas (verse 108), Jesus declares: "He who will drink from my mouth will become like me. I myself shall become he, and the things that are hidden will be revealed to him." (Translation by Thomas O. Lambdin, in *The Nag Hammadi Library in English*, James M. Robinson, ed.; HarperSanFrancisco, 1990.)

Fragments of this Gospel were discovered in the late 1800s; but the complete Gospel, including the portion cited here, was not discovered until 1945. It was part of a collection of Coptic manuscripts from the second century, unearthed at Nag Hammadi in Egypt, and was not translated into English until 1955. (Paramahansa Yogananda left his body in 1952.) However, it was in 1937 that Paramahansaji made the above statement that the words spoken by Jesus to him conveyed the same message as Jesus' words to Thomas. (*Publisher's Note*)

"Christ at 33"

"Lo, I am with you alway, even unto the end of the world."
—Matthew 28:20

Even when masters have completed the specific role for which they took on a physical incarnation, it is the divinely ordained task of some to look after the welfare of humanity and assist in guiding its progress.

Jesus Christ is very much alive and active today. In Spirit and occasionally taking on a flesh-and-blood form, he is working unseen by the masses for the regeneration of the world. With his all-embracing love, Jesus is not content merely to enjoy his blissful consciousness in Heaven. He is deeply concerned for mankind and wishes to give his followers the means to attain the divine freedom of entry into God's Infinite Kingdom.

—Paramahansa Yogananda

Painting used on Self-Realization Fellowship altars

nant words. Even when urged by well-meaning British teachers in my youth, I never read the New Testament, except for a few passages; for had I done so, theology under their tutelage would have blinded my vision and prejudiced my hearing, and I could not have heard Christ's voice or seen him speak. Now I rejoice as I will always long to rejoice, to hear Christ speak to me his words of life, truth, and eternal liberation for all.

Jesus said, "We speak that we do know,"* and through this new interpretation I feel certain that people will be enabled to understand that true knowledge, the wisdom-realizations, which he meant the world to have. Therefore, in spite of multitudinous interpretations of his words already written by others, I believe that Christ has inspired me to lift the veil of misunderstanding and misinterpretation of his teachings and utter them anew in their native purity, divested of misconceptions, and stress their applicability to the changed conditions and life of modern civilization. The people of today should break through the dark glass of theology—intellectual knowledge about God—and perceive God directly.† Such is my conviction, in thus writing the first thorough study by an Oriental of the words of Christ, who also was born in an Oriental land and who spent many years in India.

Universal Christ Consciousness appeared in the vehicle of Jesus; and now, through the Self-Realization *Kriya Yoga* teachings of meditation and these intuitively received scriptural interpretations, the Christ Consciousness is coming a second time to manifest in the consciousness of true seekers of God.

As you read the pages of *The Second Coming*, you will see the mist of difficulty, misunderstanding, and mystery about the words of Jesus lifted forever after the lapse of twenty centuries. Many sects, many denominations, many beliefs, many persecutions, many conflicts and upheavals have been created by misinterpretations. Now, Christ reveals the consummate message in the simple words he spoke to an ancient people in a less-advanced age of civilization. Read, understand, and feel Christ speaking to you through this "Second Coming" bible, urging you to be redeemed by realization of the true "Second Coming," the resurrection within you of the Infinite Christ Consciousness.

---

* John 3:11 (see commentary in Discourse 14).

† "For now we see through a glass, darkly; but then face to face: now I know in part; but then shall I know even as also I am known" (I Corinthians 13:12).

Divine Incarnations: God's Emissaries

The Mission of Divine Love That Jesus Came to Fulfill

❖

The Nature of an Avatar's Consciousness

❖

The One Spirit: Source of All Creation

❖

True Meaning of the Holy Trinity

❖

The Cosmic Word or Holy Ghost:
Intelligent Creative Vibration of Aum

❖

"Only Begotten Son" Refers Not to Jesus' Body,
but to His Christ Consciousness

❖

How the Darkness of Delusion Blinds Man
to the Light of God's Presence in Creation

❖

All Souls Are Children of God, Made in His Image

"The opening verses of Saint John's Gospel may rightly be called Genesis According to Saint John....[They] should be considered first when the true meaning of the life and teachings of Jesus is being sought."

Come to Me, O Christ, as the Good Shepherd

O Christ, beloved Son of God! thou didst embark on a storm-tossed sea of prejudiced minds. Their cruel thought waves lashed thy tender heart.

Thy trial on the Cross was an immortal victory of humility over force, of soul over flesh. May thine ineffable example hearten us to bear bravely our lesser crosses.

O Great Lover of Error-Torn Humanity! In myriad hearts an unseen monument has arisen to the mightiest miracle of love—thy words: "Forgive them, for they know not what they do."

Mayest thou remove from our eyes the cataracts of ignorance, that we see the beauty of thy message: "Love even thine enemies as thyself. Sick in mind or asleep in delusion, they are still thy brothers."

O Cosmic Christ, may we, too, conquer the Satan of dividing selfishness that prevents the gathering in sweet accord of all men in the one fold of Spirit.

As thou art Perfection, yet wert crucified, teach us not to resent the inevitable tests of life: the daily challenge to our fortitude by adversities, our self-control by temptation, and our goodwill by misunderstanding.

Purified by contemplation on thee, innumerable devotees perfume their lives with emanations from thy flower soul. O Good Shepherd! thou leadest thy countless flock to the evergreen Pastures of Peace.

Our deepest aspiration is to see the Heavenly Father with open eyes of wisdom, as thou dost; and to know like thee that we are verily His sons. Amen.*

---

* From Paramahansa Yogananda's *Whispers from Eternity* (published by Self-Realization Fellowship).

Divine Incarnations: God's Emissaries

"Father, forgive them; for they know not what they do."

With these words, Jesus placed his signature on a unique life that enthroned him everlastingly on the altar of worshipful hearts as the incarnation of God's loving compassion. The Good Shepherd of souls opened his arms to all, rejecting none, and with universal love coaxed the world to follow him on the path to liberation through the example of his spirit of sacrifice, renunciation, forgiveness, love for friend and enemy alike, and supreme love for God above all else. As the tiny babe in the manger at Bethlehem, and as the savior who healed the sick and raised the dead and applied the salve of love on the wounds of errors, the Christ in Jesus lived among men as one of them that they too might learn to live like gods.

For mere mortals to cope with a life of unsolved and unsolvable mysteries in an inscrutable universe created by the omnipotence of God, of the omniscient essence of His omnipresence, would indeed be an overwhelming challenge were it not for divine emissaries who come on earth to speak with the voice and authority of God for the guidance of man.

Aeons past, in ancient higher ages in India, *rishis* enunciated the manifestation of Divine Beneficence, of "God with us," in terms of divine incarnations, avatars—God incarnate on earth in enlightened beings. The eternal, omnipresent, unchanging Spirit has neither a corporeal nor heavenly form called God. Nor as the Lord God Creator does He fashion a form in which He then deigns to dwell among His creatures. Rather, He makes Himself known through the divinity in worthy instruments. Many are the voices that have intermediated between God and man, *khanda avatars,* or partial incarnations in God-knowing souls. Less common are the *purna avatars,* liberated beings who are fully one with God; their return to earth is to fulfill a God-ordained mission. The Lord in the sacred Hindu Bible, the Bhagavad Gita, declares: "Whenever virtue declines and vice predominates, I incarnate as an Avatar. In visible form I appear from age to age to protect the virtuous and to destroy evildoing in order to reestablish righteousness" (IV:7–8). The same one glorious infinite consciousness of God, the Universal Christ Consciousness, *Kutastha Chaitanya,* becomes familiarly apparelled in the individuality of an enlightened soul, graced with a distinguishing personality and godly nature appropriate to the times and purpose of the incarnation.

Without this intercession of God's love come to earth in the example, message, and guiding hand of His avatars, it would scarce be possible for groping humanity to find the path into God's kingdom midst the dark miasma of world delusion, the cosmic substance of human habitation. Lest His benighted children be lost forever in creation's delusive labyrinths, the Lord comes again and again in God-illumined prophets to light the way. The glory of Christ in the form of Jesus made visible the Invisible Light that leads to God.

Because the periodic recurrence of divine incarnations is a part of God's creative enterprise, signs of such a birth are imprinted in the Grand Master Plan. Sages, through their awakened soul intuition, can read the heavenly inscriptions; and if it be in accord with God's will that such a future event be made known, they prophesy in plain or veiled revelations. This is one of the many ways in which God assures His children of His awareness of their need for His presence amongst them. Of the future coming of Lord Jesus, several references in the Old Testament are cited by devout Christians and Biblical scholars. From the book of prophet Isaiah:

The mission of divine love that Jesus came to fulfill

"*The Lord Himself shall give you a sign; Behold, a virgin shall conceive, and bear a son, and shall call his name Emmanuel"* * *(7:14).*

---

* "Which being interpreted is, 'God with us'" (Matthew 1:23).

My servant shall deal prudently, he shall be exalted and extolled, and be very high....So shall he sprinkle many nations (52:13, 15).

All we like sheep have gone astray; we have turned every one to his own way; and the Lord hath laid on him the iniquity of us all....He was taken from prison and from judgment...he was cut off out of the land of the living: for the transgression of My people was he stricken....He bare the sin of many, and made intercession for the transgressors (53:6, 8, 12).

Divine intercession to mitigate the cosmic law of cause and effect, by which a man suffers from his errors, was at the heart of the mission of love Jesus came to fulfill. Moses brought the law from God to man, emphasizing the awful justice that befalls willful heedlessness. Jesus came to demonstrate the forgiveness and compassion of God, whose love is a shelter even from exacting law. Similarly, Jesus was preceded by Gautama Buddha, the "Enlightened One," whose incarnation reminded a forgetful generation of the Dharma Chakra, the ever-rotating wheel of karma—self-initiated action and its effects which make each man, and not a Cosmic Dictator, responsible for his own present condition. Buddha brought heart back into the arid theology and mechanical rituals into which the ancient Vedic religion of India had fallen after the passing of a higher age in which Bhagavan Krishna, India's most beloved of avatars, preached the way of divine love and God-realization through the practice of the supreme spiritual science of yoga, union with God.

"Greater love hath no man than this, that a man lay down his life for his friends."* Such was the exceptional mission shouldered by Jesus. Intercession by intimates of God is the palliative elixir that gives a weakened mortal the necessary strength to rise and conquer the forces of cosmic law he has roused against himself by disobedient behavior. The interceder stands with the devotee, offering him defense in the form of impermeable wisdom, and sometimes deflecting onto himself a portion of a devastating onslaught.

Jesus came in a darkened age that was little able to appreciate him; but his message of the love of God and his intercession on behalf of suffering humanity was not only for that time but for all ages to come—that God is with man in his darkest moments as well as in enlightened times. He reminded a world fearful of their Creator as a God

---

* John 15:13 (see Discourse 71).

of wrathful judgment that, though "God is a Spirit: and they that worship Him must worship Him in spirit and in truth,"* the Absolute is also a personal God who can be appealed to in prayer and who responds as a loving Heavenly Father.

To understand the magnitude of a divine incarnation, it is necessary to understand the source and nature of the consciousness that is incarnate in the avatar. Jesus spoke of this consciousness when he proclaimed: "I and my Father are one" (John 10:30) and "I am in the Father, and the Father in me" (John 14:11). Those who unite their consciousness to God know both the transcendent and the immanent nature of Spirit—the singularity of the ever-existing, ever-conscious, ever-new Bliss of the Uncreate Absolute, and the myriad manifestations of His Being as the infinitude of forms into which He variegates Himself in the panorama of creation.

The nature of an avatar's consciousness

The scientific evolution of cosmic creation from the Creator-Lord is outlined, in arcane terminology, in the Old Testament book of Genesis. In the New Testament, the opening verses of Saint John's Gospel may rightly be called Genesis According to Saint John. Both these profound Biblical accounts, when clearly grasped by intuitive perception, correspond exactly to the spiritual cosmology set forth in the scriptures of India handed down by her Golden Age God-knowing *rishis*.

Saint John was perhaps the greatest of the disciples of Jesus. Just as a schoolteacher finds among his pupils one whose superior comprehension ranks him first in the class, and others who must be ranked lower, so among the disciples of Jesus there were differing degrees of ability to appreciate and absorb the depth and breadth of the teachings of the Christ-man. The records left by Saint John, among the various books of the New Testament, evince the highest degree of divine realization, making known the deep esoteric truths experienced by Jesus and transferred to John. Not only in his gospel, but in his epistles and especially in the profound metaphysical experiences symbolically described in the Book of Revelation, John presents the truths taught by Jesus from the point of view of inward intuitive realization. In John's words we find precision; that is why his gospel, though last among the four in the New Testament, should be considered first when the true meaning of the life and teachings of Jesus is being sought.

---

* John 4:24 (see Discourse 18).

In the beginning was the Word, and the Word was with God, and the Word was God. The same was in the beginning with God.

All things were made by him; and without him was not any thing made that was made.

In him was life; and the life was the light of men.

And the light shineth in darkness; and the darkness comprehended it not....

That was the true Light, which lighteth every man that cometh into the world.

He was in the world, and the world was made by him, and the world knew him not.

He came unto his own, and his own received him not.

But as many as received him, to them gave he power to become the sons of God, even to them that believe on his name:

Which were born, not of blood, nor of the will of the flesh, nor of the will of man, but of God.

And the Word was made flesh, and dwelt among us, (and we beheld his glory, the glory as of the only begotten of the Father,) full of grace and truth.

John bare witness of him, and cried, saying, "This was he of whom I spake, 'He that cometh after me is preferred before me: for he was before me.'"

And of his fulness have all we received, and grace for grace. For the law was given by Moses, but grace and truth came by Jesus Christ.

No man hath seen God at any time; the only begotten Son, which is in the bosom of the Father, he hath declared Him.

—*John 1:1–5, 9–18* *

---

* Omitted here are verses 6–8; these are discussed in Discourse 6. In the beginning segment of Saint John's Gospel, he relates encapsulated profound truths of universal creation; appropriately for this revelation, these verses in the original Greek are written as poetry. In verses 6–8 and 15, however, Saint John digresses briefly to anticipate his historical narrative of the life and activities of Jesus by making reference to Christ's forerunner, John the Baptist; these verses, written as prose, depart from the poetic style of the rest of this opening passage. About these first eighteen verses of John 1, scholars observe: "With the exception of verses 6–8 and 15, which seem to be interruptions, this prologue is in the form of Semitic poetry."—Robert J. Miller, ed., *The Complete Gospels: Annotated Scholars Version* (HarperSanFrancisco, 1994). *(Publisher's Note)*

"In the beginning...." With these words commence the cosmogonies of the Old and New Testament alike. "Beginning" refers to the birth of finite creation, for in the Eternal Absolute—Spirit—there is neither beginning nor end.

The One Spirit:
source of all creation

When no goblin nebulae breathed and glided in the space body, when no fire-eyed baby planets opened their eyes in the cradle of space, when no star-rivers ran across the tracts of infinite space, when the ocean of space was unpeopled, uninhabited by floating island universes, when the sun and moon and planetary families did not swim in space, when the little ball of earth with its dollhouses and diminutive human beings did not exist, when no object of any kind had come into being—Spirit existed. This Unmanifested Absolute cannot be described except that It was the Knower, the Knowing, and the Known existing as One. In It the being, Its cosmic consciousness, and Its omnipotence, all were without differentiation: ever-existing, ever-conscious, ever newly joyous Spirit.

In this Ever-New Bliss, there was no space or time, no dual conception or law of relativity; everything that was, is, or is to be existed as One Undifferentiated Spirit. Space and time and relativity are categories of objects; as soon as a human being sees a planet hanging in the sky, he conceives that it is occupying dimensional space and existing in time, relative to its place in the universe. But when there were no finite objects of creation, neither were there the dimensions of being that define them, only the Blissful Spirit.

When, whence, and why came creation into being? Who may make bold to read the Mind of the Infinite in seeking causes from the Uncaused, beginnings from the Ever-Existing, paltry reasons from Omniscience?* Audacious mortals pursue their queries, while sages enter that Mind and return to state in unadorned simplicity that the One entertained a desireless desire to enjoy His Bliss through many, and the cosmos and its beings were born. The Unmanifested Spirit felt, "I am alone. I am conscious Bliss, but there is no one to taste the sweetness of My Nectar of Joy." Even as He thus dreamed, He became many.

In poetic fancy, I penned a depiction of this cosmic musing:

---

* "'For My thoughts are not your thoughts, neither are your ways My ways,' saith the Lord. 'For as the heavens are higher than the earth, so are My ways higher than your ways, and My thoughts than your thoughts'" (Isaiah 55:8–9).

"The Spirit was invisible, existing alone in the home of Infinity. He piped to Himself the ever-new, ever-entertaining song of perfect beatific Bliss. As He sang to Himself through His voice of Eternity, He wondered if aught but Himself were listening and enjoying His song. To His wittingly imposed astonishment, He felt His solitariness: He was the Cosmic Song, He was the Singing, and He was the Lone Enjoyer. Even as thus He thought, lo, He became two: Spirit and Nature, Man and Woman, Positive and Negative, Stamen and Pistil of the flowers, Peacock and Peahen, Male Gem and Female Gem."

Spirit, being the only existing Substance, had naught but Itself with which to create. Spirit and Its universal creation could not be essentially different, for two ever-existing Infinite Forces would consequently each be absolute, which is by definition an impossibility. An orderly creation requires the duality of Creator and created. Thus, Spirit first gave rise to a Magic Delusion, Maya, the cosmic Magical Measurer,* which produces the illusion of dividing a portion of the Indivisible Infinite into separate finite objects, even as a calm ocean becomes distorted into individual waves on its surface by the action of a storm. All creation is nothing but Spirit, seemingly and temporarily diversified by Spirit's creative vibratory activity.

~

In the beginning was the Word, and the Word was with God, and the Word was God. The same was in the beginning with God.

All things were made by him; and without him was not any thing made that was made. In him was life; and the life was the light of men (John 1:1–4).

"Word" means intelligent vibration, intelligent energy, going forth from God. Any utterance of a word, such as "flower," expressed by an intelligent being, consists of sound energy or vibration, plus thought, which imbues that vibration with intelligent meaning. Likewise, the Word that is the beginning and source of all created substances is Cosmic Vibration imbued with Cosmic Intelligence.†

---

* See also Discourse 7, page 140.

† Though official church doctrine for centuries has interpreted "the Word" (*Logos* in the original Greek) to be a reference to Jesus himself, that was not the understanding origi-

Thought of matter, energy of which matter is composed, matter it-self—all things—are but the differently vibrating thoughts of the Spirit, even as man in his dreams creates a world with lightning and clouds, people being born or dying, loving or fighting, experiencing heat or cold, pleasure or pain. In a dream, births and deaths, sickness and disease, solids, liquids, gases are but differently vibrating thoughts of the dreamer. This universe is a vibratory dream motion picture of God's thoughts on the screen of time and space and human consciousness.

"The Word was with God, and the Word was God": Before creation, there is only undifferentiated Spirit. In manifesting creation, Spirit becomes God the Father, Son, and Holy Ghost.

As soon as Spirit evolved a cosmic vibratory thought, through the action of the cosmic magical measuring power of *maya*, delusion, the

---

nally intended by Saint John in this passage. According to scholars, the concept John was expressing can best be understood not through the exegesis of much-later church ortho-doxy, but through the scriptural writings and the teachings of Jewish philosophers of John's own period—for example, the Book of Proverbs (with which John and any other Jewish person of his time would have been familiar). Karen Armstrong in *A History of God: The 4,000-Year Quest of Judaism, Christianity and Islam* (New York: Alfred A. Knopf, 1993) writes: "The author of the Book of Proverbs, who was writing in the third century BCE...personifies Wisdom so that she seems a separate person:

"Yahweh created me [Wisdom] when his purpose first unfolded, before the oldest of his works. From everlasting I was firmly set, from the beginning, before earth came into being...when he laid the foundations of the earth, I was at his side, a master craftsman, delighting him day after day, ever at play in his presence, at play everywhere in the world, delighting to be with the sons of men" (Proverbs 8:22–23, 30–31; The Jerusalem Bible)....

"In the Aramaic translations of the Hebrew scriptures known as the *targums*, which were being composed at this time [i.e., when John's Gospel was written], the term *Memra* (word) is used to describe God's activity in the world. It performs the same function as other technical terms like 'glory,' 'Holy Spirit' and 'Shekinah' which em-phasized the distinction between God's presence in the world and the incomprehensi-ble reality of God itself. Like the divine Wisdom, the 'Word' symbolized God's origi-nal plan for creation."

The writings of early Church Fathers also indicate that this was the meaning in-tended by Saint John. In *Clement of Alexandria* (Edinburgh: William Blackwood and Sons, 1914) John Patrick states: "Clement repeatedly identifies the Word with the Wis-dom of God." And Dr. Anne Pasquier, professor of theology at Université Laval, Que-bec, writes in *The Nag Hammadi Library After Fifty Years* (John D. Turner and Anne McGuire, editors; New York: Brill, 1997): "Philo, Clement of Alexandria, and Ori-gen...all associate the Logos with the word of God in the Old Testament accounts of the creation when 'God spoke and it was done.' The Valentinians do likewise....Ac-cording to the Valentinians, the prologue to John's Gospel depicts a spiritual genesis, the model for the material one, and it is seen as a spiritual interpretation of the Old Testament accounts of the creation." *(Publisher's Note)*

Unmanifested Spirit became God the Father, the Creator of all creative
vibration. God the Father, in the Hindu scriptures, is called *Ishvara* (the
Cosmic Ruler) or *Sat* (the supreme pure essence of
Cosmic Consciousness)—the Transcendental Intelli-   *True meaning of the*
gence. That is, God the Father exists transcenden-   *Holy Trinity: God the*
tally untouched by any tremor of vibratory creation   *Father, Son, and Holy*
—a conscious, separate Cosmic Consciousness.   *Ghost*

The vibratory force emanating from Spirit, en-
dowed with the illusory creative power of *maya*, is the Holy Ghost:
Cosmic Vibration, the Word, *Aum* (*Om*) or Amen. All things, all created planets and living beings in the Holy Ghost, or Holy Vibration,
are nothing but the frozen imagination of God. This Holy Ghost in
the Hindu scriptures is called the *Aum* or Maha-Prakriti (Great Nature, the Cosmic Mother that gives birth to all creation); by the scientists, the structure of matter, its tissue or material, is also known, to a
lesser degree, as cosmic vibration. "These things saith the Amen [the
Word, *Aum*], the faithful and true witness, the beginning of the creation of God."* The holy Cosmic Sound of *Aum* or Amen is the witness of the manifested Divine Presence in all creation.

A cosmic vibration omnipresently active in space could not of itself
create or sustain the wondrously complex cosmos. The universe is not
the result merely of a fortuitous combination of vibrating forces and
subatomic particles, as proposed by material scientists—a chance ex-
crescence of solids, liquids, and gases into earth, oceans, atmosphere,
plants, all harmoniously interrelated to provide a habitable home for human beings. Blind forces cannot organize themselves into intelligently
structured objects. As human intelligence is needed to put water into the
small square compartments of an ice tray to be frozen into cubes, so in
the coalescence of vibration into progressively evolving forms throughout the universe we see the results of a hidden Immanent Intelligence.

The transcendent consciousness of God the Father became manifest
within the Holy Ghost vibration as the Son—the Christ Consciousness,
God's intelligence in all vibratory creation. This pure reflection of God
in the Holy Ghost indirectly guides it to create, re-create, preserve, and
mold creation according to God's divine purpose.

---

* Revelation 3:14. *Aum* of the Vedas became the sacred word *Hum* of the Tibetans,
Amin of the Moslems, and *Amen* of the Egyptians, Greeks, Romans, Jews, and Christians. The meaning of *Amen* in Hebrew is "sure, faithful."

Just as the husband is born again in the wife as the son, so the transcendental God the Father manifested in the Holy Ghost, the Cosmic Virgin Mary (the Virgin Creation), became the sole reflected intelligence of God, the only begotten Son, or Christ Consciousness.

An analogy may serve to illustrate how the One Eternal Spirit becomes the Holy Trinity: God the Father, Son, and Holy Ghost, similarly acknowledged in the Hindu scriptures as *Sat, Tat, Aum.* Imagine the sun as existing by itself, with nothing surrounding it—a bright mass of light with untold power and heat, its rays spreading into boundless space. Place a blue crystal ball within this radiation. The sun now exists in relation to the blue crystal ball. The sunlight is divided as the inactive, transcendental white light beyond and around the crystal ball, and as the essentially unchanged light appearing as blue light by its reflection in the blue crystal ball. This division of the one sunlight into white and blue light is due to the dividing effect of the third object, the blue crystal ball.

Just as the sun is solitary pure brilliance, spherically spreading its rays in space when it stands by itself, so Spirit without any vibratory creation is the Unmanifested Absolute. But introduce the "blue crystal ball" of a manifested universe, and Spirit becomes differentiated as the vibratory substance of all manifestations evolved from the *Aum* or Holy Ghost; the pure reflected Intelligence of God as Christ Consciousness omnipresent in every object and pore of space in the realm of vibration; and the supreme Essence of all, Cosmic Consciousness, the transcendental God the Father of all creation. (Most analogies employed to define absolutes are at best imperfect intimations, since by their limited material nature they cannot depict the subtleties of spiritual truths. In the illustration of the sun and crystal ball, the sun does not create the crystal ball, whereas the Spirit, as God the Father, evolved the Holy Ghost with its creative vibratory power to manifest God's universal imaginings.)

Thus, metaphorically, as soon as the cosmic bachelor Spirit stirs Itself to create the universe, He becomes the husband, God the Father, wedded to Cosmic Virgin Mary or Cosmic Vibration, giving birth to His reflection, the only begotten Son.* Christ Consciousness, present

---

* "My womb is the Great Prakriti into which I deposit the seed (of My Intelligence); this is the cause of the birth of all beings" (*God Talks With Arjuna: The Bhagavad Gita* XIV:3).

in all specks of creation, is the only undifferentiated, pure reflection of the Absolute, God the Father. Hence, this Christ Intelligence, the only begotten Son, maintains an immanent, influential transcendence: Christ Consciousness is not the active element in creation; the distinct, active, differentiated conscious intelligence that brings into manifestation all particles of vibratory creation is the Holy Ghost, which is imbued with the only begotten Son. The inactively active Christ Consciousness or Son is the conscious Presence of God's intelligent divine plan in creation, and the Eternal Witness of the work of the Holy Ghost, which is called "Holy" because it acts according to the will of God manifest in the immanent Christ Consciousness.

Spirit as the intelligent Holy Ghost, creative *Aum* Vibration, transforms Itself into matter by changing the rates of the cosmic creative vibration. Cosmic Intelligence becomes cosmic intelligent motion, or vibration of consciousness, which changes into cosmic energy. Intelligent cosmic energy changes into electrons and atoms. Electrons and atoms change into molecules of gas, such as cosmic nebulae. Nebulae, masses of diffuse gaseous matter, change into water and solid matter. As Cosmic Vibration, all things are one; but when Cosmic Vibration becomes frozen into matter, it becomes many — including man's body, which is a part of this variously divided matter.*

This metamorphosis of Spirit through the creative vibration of the Holy Ghost — taking place within a relatively minute sphere of the In-

––––––––––

* Recent advances in what theoretical physicists call "superstring theory" are leading science toward an understanding of the vibratory nature of creation. Brian Greene, Ph.D., professor of physics at Cornell and Columbia Universities, writes in *The Elegant Universe: Superstrings, Hidden Dimensions, and the Quest for the Ultimate Theory* (New York: Vintage Books, 2000):

"During the last thirty years of his life, Albert Einstein sought relentlessly for a so-called unified field theory — a theory capable of describing nature's forces within a single, all-encompassing, coherent framework....Now, at the dawn of the new millennium, proponents of string theory claim that the threads of this elusive unified tapestry finally have been revealed....

"The theory suggests that the microscopic landscape is suffused with tiny strings whose vibrational patterns orchestrate the evolution of the universe," Professor Greene writes, and tells us that "the length of a typical string loop is...about a hundred billion billion (10^{20}) times smaller than an atomic nucleus."

Professor Greene explains that by the end of the twentieth century, science had determined that the physical universe was composed of a very few fundamental particles, such as electrons, quarks (which are the building blocks of protons and neutrons), and neutrinos. "Although each particle was viewed as elementary," he writes, "the kind of 'stuff' each embodied was thought to be different. Electron 'stuff,' for example, had neg-

13

finite—produces a triune creation: an ideational, or causal, world of the finest vibrations of consciousness, God's thoughts or ideas that are

The causal, astral, and material planes of God's creation

the cause of all forms and forces; an astral world of light and life force, vibratory energy, the first condensation cloaking the original ideational concepts; and the material world of the gross atomic vibrations of matter. These worlds are superimposed on one another, the grosser dependent on the subtler, and all three ultimately conditional on the sole support of the will and consciousness of God.

As in the macrocosm of the universe, so in the microcosm of man there are three interdependent bodies. Man's soul dons these three coverings that serve as instrumentalities through which the incarnate spirit can perceive, comprehend, and interact with God's creation. The very tenuous first covering of the soul, which individualizes it from Spirit, is one of pure consciousness; it is composed of God's thoughts or ideas that cause the other two sheaths. Thus it is referred to as the causal body. These causal ideas emit a magnetic force of light and intelligent energy, which I have called lifetrons, that form the astral body of man. The astral body of lifetrons is itself the life energy that empowers all the senses and functions of the physical body. The physical body is merely a gross materialization of the causal ideas activated by the life and energy of the astral body, and endowed with consciousness, self-awareness, and intelligence from the causal body. All of these vibratory manifestations of the macrocosm and microcosm derive from the Holy Ghost Vibration and the transcendent consciousness of God.

---

ative electric charge, while neutrino 'stuff' had no electric charge. String theory alters this picture radically by declaring that the 'stuff' of all matter and all forces is the *same*."

"According to string theory, there is only *one* fundamental ingredient—the string," Greene writes in *The Fabric of the Cosmos: Space, Time, and the Texture of Reality* (New York: Alfred A. Knopf, 2004). He explains that "just as a violin string can vibrate in different patterns, each of which produces a different musical tone, the filaments of superstring theory can also vibrate in different patterns....A tiny string vibrating in one pattern would have the mass and the electric charge of an electron; according to the theory, such a vibrating string would *be* what we have traditionally called an electron. A tiny string vibrating in a different pattern would have the requisite properties to identify it as a quark, a neutrino, or any other kind of particle....Each arises from a different vibrational pattern executed by the same underlying entity....At the ultramicroscopic level, the universe would be akin to a string symphony vibrating matter into existence." *(Publisher's Note)*

14

Thus John summarizes: "In him (the Word) was life; and the life was the light of men" (John 1:4).*

The Biblical writers, not versed in the terminologies that express the knowledge of the modern age, quite aptly used "Holy Ghost" and "the Word" to designate the character of the Intelligent Cosmic Vibration. "Word" implies a vibratory sound, carrying materializing power. "Ghost" implies an intelligent, invisible, conscious force. "Holy" describes this Vibration because it is the manifestation of Spirit; and because it is trying to create the universe according to the perfect pattern of God.†

---

* A subtle change in the meaning intended by Saint John, but one with far-reaching implications, is evident in most translations of this and the preceding verses. All nouns in Greek are either masculine, feminine, or neuter in gender. The noun *logos* ("word") is masculine, apparently leading English translators to use the masculine pronoun "him" when referring to "the Word." However, since English does not differentiate the gender of nouns such as "word," the correct pronoun in translation would be "it"—unless referring to a person, in which case the personal pronoun "him" would be appropriate. Thus, the use of "him" reflects a theological interpretation by the translator that "the Word" in fact signifies a person: Jesus.

This interpretation became accepted as church orthodoxy in large part through the efforts of Irenaeus, second-century bishop of Lyons and author of the influential work *Against Heresies*. Dr. Elaine Pagels, professor of religion at Princeton University, writes in *Beyond Belief* (New York: Random House, 2003): "Irenaeus tells us that Valentinus's disciple Ptolemy, reading these words [John 1:1–3], envisioned God, *word*, and finally Jesus Christ as, so to speak, waves of divine energy flowing down from above; thus, he suggests, the infinite divine Source above reveals itself in diminished form in the divine *word*, which reveals itself, in turn, in the more limited form of the human Jesus....Irenaeus challenges Ptolemy's interpretation of John's prologue and argues instead that 'God the Father' is equivalent to the *word*, and the *word* is equivalent to 'Jesus Christ.'...What Irenaeus's successors would derive from this was a kind of simple, almost mathematical equation, in which God=*word*=Jesus Christ. That many Christians to this day consider some version of this equation the essence of Christian belief is a mark of Irenaeus's accomplishment—and his success....Because Irenaeus's bold interpretation came virtually to define orthodoxy, those who read John's gospel today in any language except the Greek original will find that the translations make his conclusion seem obvious."

However, the "Word" (as also "the only begotten Son") came to signify the *person* of Jesus only through a gradual evolution of doctrine brought about by complex theological and political influences. It was not until the fourth century, writes historian Karen Armstrong in *A History of God* (New York: Alfred A. Knopf, 1993), that the church came to "adopt an exclusive notion of religious truth: Jesus was the first and last Word of God to the human race." *(Publisher's Note)*

† See Discourse 7, which explains the dual nature assumed by the Cosmic Creative Vibration: pure Holy Ghost in tune with God's will; and obstructive Cosmic Satan, originator of all evil, which tries to divorce all creatures from their Creator.

The designation in the Hindu scriptures of this "Holy Ghost" as *Aum* signifies its role in God's creative plan: *A* stands for *akara*, or cre-

The Cosmic Word or Holy Ghost: intelligent creative vibration of Aum

ative vibration; *u* for *ukara*, preservative vibration; and *m* for *makara*, the vibratory power of dissolution. A storm roaring across the sea creates waves, large and small, preserves them for some time, and then by withdrawing dissolves them. So the *Aum* or

Holy Ghost creates all things, preserves them in myriad forms, and ultimately dissolves them in the sea-bosom of God to be again re-created—a continuing process of renewal of life and form in the ongoing cosmic dreaming of God.

Thus is the Word or Cosmic Vibration the origin of "all things": "without him was not anything made that was made." The Word existed from the very beginning of creation—God's first manifestation in bringing forth the universe. "The Word was with God"—imbued with God's reflected intelligence, Christ Consciousness—"and the Word was God"—vibrations of His own one Being.

Saint John's declaration echoes an eternal truth resonating in various passages of the hoary Vedas: that the cosmic vibratory Word (*Vak*) was with God the Father-Creator (*Prajapati*) in the beginning of creation, when naught else existed; and that by *Vak* were made all things; and that *Vak* is itself Brahman (God). In the Bhagavad Gita, the Lord affirms: "Among words, I am the one syllable *Aum*" (x:25). "Of all manifestations, I am the beginning, middle, and end" (x:32). "I, the Unchanging and Everlasting, sustain and permeate the entire cosmos with but one fragment of My Being" (x:42).

With the understanding of this truth, we have the underlying science of the universe and a proper basis for appreciating these verses of Saint John in the context of their reference to the life of Jesus Christ.

In scriptural parlance characteristic of India's sages, Saint John in the several opening verses of his Gospel posits, in a *double entendre* reference to the incarnation of Jesus, the divinity of the Christ state of Jesus as analogous to the Universal Christ manifestation of God that comes forth as Intelligence and Creative Vibration at the birth of creation. Devotees in India make no differentiation between the divinity of God in the microcosm of the incarnate consciousness of an avatar —as in Lord Krishna, for example—and the divinity of God in the macrocosm of universal expression. Likewise, Saint John speaks allegorically of the Christ in Jesus as one and the same as the Christ manifestation in Infinitude (the presence of God in creation), the latter being the prime intent of his presentation in these verses.

The Holy Trinity of Christianity—Father, Son, and Holy Ghost —in relation to the ordinary concept of the incarnation of Jesus is wholly inexplicable without differentiating between Jesus the body and Jesus the vehicle in which the only begotten Son, Christ Consciousness, was manifested. Jesus himself makes such distinction when speaking of his body as the "son of man"; and of his soul, which was not circumscribed by the body but was one with the only begotten Christ Consciousness in all specks of vibration, as the "son of God."

"Only begotten Son" refers not to Jesus' body, but to his Christ Consciousness

"God so loved the world, that He gave His only begotten Son"* to redeem it; that is, God the Father remained hidden beyond the vibratory realm that went out from His Being, but then secreted Himself as the Christ Intelligence in all matter and in all living beings in order to bring, by beautiful evolutional coaxings, all things back to His home of Everlasting Blessedness. Without this presence of God ubiquitously permeating creation, man would indeed feel bereft of Divine Succor—how sweetly, sometimes almost imperceptibly, It comes to his aid when he bows his knee in supplication. His Creator and Supreme Benefactor is never more than a devotional thought away.

Saint John said: "As many as received him, to them gave he power to become the sons of God."† The plural number in "sons of God" shows distinctly, from the teachings he received from Jesus, that not the body of Jesus but his state of Christ Consciousness was the only begotten son; and that all those who could clarify their consciousness and receive, or in an unobstructed way reflect, the power of God, could become the sons of God. They could be one with the only begotten reflection of God in all matter, as was Jesus; and through the son, Christ Consciousness, ascend to the Father, the supreme Cosmic Consciousness.‡

---

* John 3:16, commented on in Discourse 15.

† John 1:12 (explained in more detail on pages 24–27).

‡ "I am the way, the truth, and the life: no man cometh unto the Father, but by me" (John 14:6). That is, no man can reach the transcendent Father beyond creation without first attuning himself with the 'Son' or Christ Consciousness within creation. (See Discourse 70.)

Before the advent of Jesus, Sage Vyasa, writer of the Bhagavad Gita, was a son of God, one with the only begotten reflection of God, the *Kutastha Chaitanya* or Christ Consciousness. So also, Swami Shankara (the founder of the Swami Order of renunciation circa A.D. 700), Mahavatar Babaji, Lahiri Mahasaya, and my guru Swami Sri Yukteswar,* and others having Christ Consciousness, became thereby sons of God. The Spirit could not be partial in creating Jesus as a Christ and all others as spiritually ineffectual mortal beings. Divinely imported Jesuses could be made by the thousands by God; and they would, being predestined, naturally behave on earth as Christs—spiritual puppets of God. Such Christs could hardly be the ideals of mortals struggling with all their frailties. But when there is one who became a Christ by self-effort to conquer temptations and by proper use of God-given free choice and power of God-communion through intense worship or a scientific technique of meditation, then that example stirs hope of salvation in the frail, timorous, matter-tortured human breast.

India's priceless contribution to the world, discovered anciently by her *rishis,* is the science of religion—yoga, "divine union"—by which God can be known, not as a theological concept but as an actual personal experience. Of all scientific knowledge, the yoga science of God-realization is of the highest value to man, for it strikes at the root-cause of all human maladies: ignorance, the beclouding envelopment of delusion. When one becomes firmly established in God-realization, delusion is transcended and the subordinate mortal consciousness is elevated to Christlike status.

～

And the light shineth in darkness; and the darkness comprehended it not (John 1:5).

Darkness means delusion, ignorance. In the Sanskrit scriptures the concepts in Saint John's esoteric verses are explained very thoroughly. When interpreted with the illumination provided by the mas-

---

* In India's sacred tradition of spiritual succession (*guru-parampara*), Paramahansa Yogananda's direct lineage of gurus is Mahavatar Babaji, Lahiri Mahasaya, and Swami Sri Yukteswar. Each of these masters is renowned for his remarkable spiritual stature, about which Paramahansaji has written in *Autobiography of a Yogi* (published by Self-Realization Fellowship). See also individual entries in the glossary. *(Publisher's Note)*

ters of India, these truths will be found to be universal and scientific. Spiritual laws defining the workings of the universe and man's place in it are the highest science, underpinning all scientific discoveries; but since scientists depend more on effects than ultimate causes, spiritual pronouncements of the sages are largely dismissed as superstition. By a gradual pace of broadened understanding, however, spiri-
tual science and material science find they are standing on common ground.

How the darkness of delusion blinds man to the light of God's presence in creation

There are two manifestations of the darkness of delusion: one is *maya,* cosmic delusion, "that which measures the Infinite"; and the other is *avidya,* which means ignorance or individual illusion.

If someone sees an elephant moving around in the air, it would be said that what he is seeing is an illusion or hallucination; but to him the perception is real. *Maya* is the mass hypnosis of God by which He makes every human being believe in the same illusory "reality" of creation as perceived by the senses; *avidya* gives individuality of form, experience, and expression (it supports the ego or I-consciousness).

The light that "shineth in the darkness" of the delusion of creation is the light of God. God is light. In the First Epistle of St. John (1:5) we read: "This then is the message which we have heard of him, and declare unto you, that God is light, and in Him is no darkness at all."

In the intelligent creative Cosmic Vibration that went forth from the cosmic consciousness of God were His first two expressions in manifested creation: sound (the holy *Aum* or Amen) and light ("In the beginning....God said, 'Let there be light'"—Genesis 1:1, 3). Units of divine light, finer than electrons and other subatomic particles, are the bricks of which matter is composed. All things seen on the screen of the universe are differentiated currents of the cosmic light and the shadows or "darkness" of delusion.

The light of God shines within the darkness of cosmic delusion, but man, the perceiver, suffers from two blinding maladies: the limitation of his senses, or individual delusive ignorance, and the cosmic delusion, combined.

Because of the limitation of the senses, man does not perceive the full spectrum of even material manifestations. If the power of vision were increased, one could see all kinds of lights—atoms, electrons, photons, vibratory auras—dancing around him. If the power of hearing were sufficiently increased, man could hear the hum of the atoms, the planets in their course around the sun, the explosion of stars, making a tremendous rumbling throughout the universe. One would sense the whole universe throbbing with life. But none of the finer and higher vibrations can be sensed except to a limited degree with the aid of delicate supersensory instruments. "Darkness" denotes that limitation, because it produces the illusion of confinement of consciousness.

Even the light of the sun is considered darkness, because it is a part of this physical world of duality; its grossness, also, hides the greater light of God. Only in spiritually transcendent ecstatic states is there no duality of day and night, light and darkness, but God's light alone. Just behind the darkness of closed eyes in meditation shines that radiance of God.

Man is blinded by the relativities of life. Without the aid of physical light he sees darkness. But beyond that darkness is another light that pervades the world. Hidden behind the ether of space is the tremendous light of the astral world, providing the life and energy that sustains the whole universe.* The auroral rays of astral lifetrons are a

---

* See "ether" in glossary.

The Sanskrit word *akasha,* translated as both "ether" and "space," refers specifically to the vibratory element that is the subtlest in the material world. "Ether-permeated space is the boundary line between heaven, or the astral world, and earth," Paramahansaji said. "All the finer forces God has created are composed of light, or thought-forms, and are merely hidden behind a particular vibration that manifests as ether."

Frank Wilczek, Ph.D., professor of physics at the Massachusetts Institute of Technology, writes in *Physics Today* (January 1999): "There is a myth, repeated in many popular presentations and textbooks, that Albert Einstein swept [the ether] into the dustbin of history....The truth is more nearly the opposite: Einstein first purified, and then enthroned, the ether concept. As the twentieth century has progressed, its role in fundamental physics has only expanded. At present, renamed and thinly disguised, it dominates the accepted laws of physics."

Physicists investigating the ether—now also called the quantum vacuum, the quantum field, and the zero-point field—have realized that "the very underpinning of our universe [is] a heaving sea of energy, one vast quantum field," writes Lynne McTaggart in *The Field: The Quest for the Secret Force of the Universe* (New York: HarperCollins, 2002). "What we believe to be our stable, static universe," she explains, "is in fact a seething maelstrom of subatomic particles fleetingly popping in and out of existence....Largely because of Einstein's theories and his famous equation $E=mc^2$, relating energy to mass, all elementary particles interact with each other by exchanging energy through other quantum particles, which are believed to appear out of nowhere, combining and annihilating each other in less than an instant....The fleeting particles generated during this brief moment are known as 'virtual particles.'...Every exchange

spiritual ectoplasm around the entire cosmos. Out of the astral light, God is creating planets and universes. I am in that light all the time; I see everything aglow with that heavenly essence—all physical manifestation emanates from that astral light, and that light emanates from the creative manifestation of God as Light.

If you saw God right now, you would see Him as one mass of light scintillating over the whole universe. As I close my eyes in ecstasy everything melts into that great Light. It is not imagination; rather, the perception of the Sole Reality of being. Whatever is seen in that state will happen; that is the proof of the reality of that Omnipresent Light of all becomings.

Man is so drunk with delusion, it obliterates his true perception so that the darkness of his ignorance cannot apprehend the light of God vibrating everywhere. Both cosmic delusion (*maya*) and individual illusion or ignorance (*avidya*) work together to thus obscure and confound the soul's inherent intuitive sense of God's omnipresence. In meditation this darkness of sensory dependence goes away and intuition prevails, revealing oneself as light in the magnitude of a whole universe of light.

∼

That was the true Light, which lighteth every man that cometh into the world (John 1:9).

---

of every virtual particle radiates energy. The zero-point energy in any one particular transaction in an electromagnetic field is unimaginably tiny—half a photon's worth. But if you add up all the particles of all varieties in the universe constantly popping in and out of being, you come up with a vast, inexhaustible energy source...all sitting there unobtrusively in the background of the empty space around us."

"Indeed, calculations of the quantity known as the zero-point energy suggest that a single cubic centimeter of empty space contains more energy than all of the matter in the known universe," states Will Keepin, Ph.D., in "Lifework of David Bohm: River of Truth" (*ReVision* magazine, Summer 1993). Keepin writes that for Bohm, who is regarded as one of the twentieth century's greatest physicists, "this enormous energy inherent in 'empty' space can be viewed as theoretical evidence for the existence of a vast, yet hidden realm....The vast physical universe we experience is but a set of 'ripples' on the surface of the implicate order. The manifest objects that we regard as comprising ordinary reality are only the unfolded projections of the much deeper, higher dimensional implicate order, which is the fundamental reality." *(Publisher's Note)*

In the fourth verse it was said and explained: "In him was life; and the life was the light of men." Now this ninth verse is a restatement of the same concept. In pragmatic or entertaining literature, redundancy is considered boring, even irritating, impeding the flow of thought. But repetition of truth, as evidenced in scriptural writings, is good, even necessary, for moral perception and spiritual assimilation, bringing out the meaning clearly. Truth is a living entity; familiarity with its principles through frequent contact makes it a faithful, supportive companion.

The light of Cosmic Energy is the life of all beings

The light of the cosmic energy flowing out of the cosmic consciousness of God is the life that informs all beings and lights their consciousness, as a dynamo sends electricity into the bulbs of a city. It is the omnipresence of that light of God that supports the grand illusion of an infinitude of forms and their wondrous portrayals of individuality. That light is the true light because it is infinite and everlasting, while man only borrows from it his temporary mortal existence from one life to the next. Yoga teaches how to join the immortals by contacting that light and realizing the unity of human consciousness with "the true light, which lighteth every man."

~

He was in the world, and the world was made by him, and the world knew him not (John 1:10).

The words "he" and "him," though ambiguous at first reading, refer, in continuity of the preceding verses, to the Light, or omnipresent creative manifestation of God "in the world."* The "world" means not just this little earth, but the entire cosmos. (It is a transla-

---

* Many scholars have puzzled over why, in the original Greek of the Gospel, the masculine pronouns "he" and "him" are used to refer to the neuter noun "light" (*phos*) —even though grammatically the masculine pronoun does not agree with this neuter noun. Biblical historian and linguist Charles H. Dodd writes in *The Interpretation of the Fourth Gospel* (Cambridge University Press, 1968): "There seem to be two possibilities: either (a) the propositions in question really refer to the masculine *logos*, here considered in its aspect as light; or (b) the thought of incarnation is already in the evangelist's mind, and the propositions of verses 9–12 refer to Christ as incarnate." As church doctrine evolved over the centuries it became common to presume the latter. However, the question is resolved in favor of the first of these possibilities when one

tion in the Bible that should be changed, as also many other words that have been misunderstood.)*

"The world was made by him" means the whole cosmos was evolved from that cosmic light, not just this little planet, which is nothing but a grain of sand on the seashore of time.

"And the world knew him not": That "true light" was kept hidden by delusion, unseen by sentient beings.

~

He came into his own, and his own received him not (John 1:11).

He was omnipresently immanent in creation, all things ("his own") having been made or materialized from the cosmic light issuing from God's cosmic consciousness, His own Self.

God objectified Himself as matter, life, and mind. His spirit is thus reflected in "his own," since matter, life, and mind are direct manifestations of Spirit, just as man's soul has manifested itself into body and mind imbued with life. Although these physical instrumentalities belong to the soul, and are indeed manifestations of the soul, the limitations imposed on the body and mind by delusion prevent man from knowing his ever perfect, blissful soul, his true Self. He rather thinks of himself as a form, name, and specific characteristics subject to worries, troubles, and other afflictions of delusion.

Through delusion, matter, life, and mind do not fully reflect the Spirit

So it is said in this verse that the spirit of God came into "his own," that is, became manifested in matter and life and His conscious processes in human beings; and "his own received him not"; that is, through the intervention of cosmic delusion, matter, life, and mind do not fully and truly reflect and express ("receive") the Divine Immanence.

realizes, as is clear from Paramahansa Yogananda's commentary, the relationship of "light" and "word" (*logos*) in this context—primal expressions of God's cosmic vibratory energy in creation. See also footnote on page 9. *(Publisher's Note)*

* The original Greek in which this Gospel was composed used *kosmos;* the King James version translates it as "world" instead of in its broader sense as "the universal order."

~

But as many as received him, to them gave he power to become the sons of God, even to them that believe on his name:
Which were born, not of blood, nor of the will of the flesh, nor of the will of man, but of God (John 1:12–13).

The light of God shines equally in all, but because of delusive ignorance all do not receive, reflect, it alike. Sunlight falls the same on a lump of coal and a diamond, but only the diamond receives and reflects the light in brilliant splendor. The carbon in the coal has the potential to become a diamond. All it requires is conversion under high pressure. So it is said here that everyone can be like Christ— whosoever clarifies his consciousness by a moral and spiritual life, and especially by the purification of meditation in which rudimentary mortality is sublimed into the soul's perfection of immortality.

Everyone who clarifies his consciousness to receive God's light can be like Jesus

To be a son of God is not something one has to acquire: rather, one has only to receive His light and realize God has already conferred on him, at his very inception, that blessed status.

"Even to them that believe on his name": When even the Name of God rouses one's devotion and anchors one's thoughts in Him, it becomes a door to salvation. When the mere mention of His name sets the soul afire with love for God, it will start the devotee on his way to liberation.

The deeper meaning of "name" is a reference to Cosmic Vibration (the Word, *Aum,* Amen). God as Spirit has no circumscribing name. Whether one refers to the Absolute as God or Jehovah or Brahman or Allah, that does not express Him. God the Creator and Father of all vibrates through nature as the eternal life, and that life has the sound of the great Amen or *Aum.* That name most accurately defines God. "Those who believe on his name" means those who commune with that *Aum* sound, the voice of God in the Holy Ghost vibration. When one hears that name of God, that Cosmic Vibration, he is on his way to becoming a son of God, for in that sound his consciousness touches the immanent Christ Consciousness, which will introduce him to God as Cosmic Consciousness.

"Believe on his name": communion with holy Cosmic Vibration

Sage Patanjali,* India's greatest exponent of yoga, describes God the Creator as Ishvara, the Cosmic Lord or Ruler. "His symbol is *Pranava* (the Holy Word or Sound, *Aum*). By prayerful, repeated chanting of *Aum* and meditation on its meaning, obstacles disappear and the consciousness turns inward (away from external sensory identification)" (*Yoga Sutras* 1:27–29).

The common condition of human beings is that their consciousness is hidebound by the body. Man's body, being a delimited vibratory expression, existing in but separated from Cosmic Vibration, similarly circumscribes the consciousness. Yoga teaches that the spiritual aspirant must retrace the various states of higher vibrations in order to lift the consciousness from the captive vibrations of breath, heart, and circulation to the more subtly vibrating sound emanating from the bodily atoms and life force. By a special technique of meditation on *Aum,* known to students of the *Self-Realization Fellowship Lessons,* the devotee becomes aware of his consciousness as limited by the constrictions of the flesh, evidenced by the sounds of breath, heart, and circulation. And then, by a deepening of his meditation, he can hear the voice of the great *Aum* or Amen, the cosmic sound emanating from all atoms and sparks of cosmic energy. By listening to this omnipresent sound, and merging in its holy stream, the consciousness of the body-caged soul begins gradually to spread itself from the limitations of the body into omnipresence. The mental faculties renounce their boundaries and, with the all-knowing soul faculty of intuition, tune in with the Cosmic Mind, the Intelligence immanent in the all-pervasive Cosmic Vibration.

After listening to and feeling oneness with the cosmic sound of the Holy Ghost emanating from every part and particle of God's material, heavenly, and ideationally conceived spheres of being, the consciousness of the meditating devotee will vibrate in all creation as his own cosmic body. When his expanded consciousness becomes stable in all vibratory creation, he realizes the presence of the immanent Christ Consciousness. Then the devotee becomes Christlike; his conscious-

---

* Patanjali's date is unknown, though many scholars assign him to the second century B.C. His renowned *Yoga Sutras* presents, in a series of brief aphorisms, the condensed essence of the exceedingly vast and intricate science of God-union—setting forth the method of uniting the soul with the undifferentiated Spirit in such a beautiful, clear, and concise way that generations of scholars have acknowledged the *Yoga Sutras* as the foremost ancient work on yoga.

ness experiences, within the vehicles of his expanded Self, the "second coming of Christ"—the presence within him of Christ Consciousness, even as Jesus felt the Universal Christ expressed in his body and taught his disciples to do likewise.*

When the devotee feels his consciousness one with the Universal Christ, he realizes that Christ Consciousness is the reflection in his soul and in all creation of the Cosmic Consciousness of God the Father. The Cosmic Consciousness (God the Father) existing transcendentally beyond all vibratory (Holy Ghost) creation and the Christ Consciousness (Universal Intelligence, *Kutastha Chaitanya*) in all vibratory manifestation are realized as one and the same. The devotee rejoices in the ultimate joy, as Jesus proclaimed, "I (Christ Consciousness in creation) and my Father (Cosmic Consciousness beyond creation) are one."

"Which were born, not of blood, nor of the will of the flesh, nor of the will of man, but of God": The son of man is the physical body, which comes out of another human body as a result

All souls are children of God, made in His image

of human will and sexual union, born of protoplasm and the bloodline of family or racial heredity. But son of God means the soul, the inherent divine consciousness of man, born not of man's will or flesh or sex or family blood or pedigree, but of God. Thus in truth all human beings are sons of God, children born of God, made in His image.

Essential sons of God, clear reflections of the Father untarnished by delusion, have become sons of man by identification with the flesh and forgetfulness of their origin in Spirit. Deluded man is just a beggar on the street of time. But as Jesus received and reflected through his purified consciousness the divine sonship of Christ Consciousness, so also every man, by yoga meditation, can clarify his mind and become a diamondlike mentality who will receive and reflect the light of God.

To receive Christ is not accomplished through church membership, nor by outer ritual of acknowledging Jesus as one's savior but never knowing him in reality by contacting him in meditation. To know Christ signifies to close the eyes, expand the consciousness and so deepen the concentration that through the inner light of soul intu-

---

* That Jesus knew and taught the yoga science of meditation to his close disciples may be deduced from the highly metaphorical Revelation of St. John and other Gospel references, as will be noted in the various Discourses throughout this book.

ition one partakes of the same consciousness that Jesus had. Saint John and other advanced disciples of Jesus who truly "received him" felt him as the Christ Consciousness present in every speck of space. A true Christian—a Christ-one—is he who frees his soul from the consciousness of the body and unites it with the Christ Intelligence pervading all creation.

∿

And the Word was made flesh, and dwelt among us, (and we beheld his glory, the glory as of the only begotten of the Father,) full of grace and truth (John 1:14).

The Word, the creative energy and sound of Cosmic Vibration, like the sound waves of an unimaginably powerful earthquake, went out of the Creator to manifest the universe. That Cosmic Vibration, permeated with Cosmic Intelligence, was condensed into subtle elements—thermal, electric, magnetic, and all manner of rays; thence into atoms of vapor (gases), liquids, and solids. The "Word was made flesh" means the vibratory energy producing that cosmic sound was condensed into matter.*

"The Word was made flesh": Divine Energy manifesting as matter

All matter is "flesh" because it is all living; even the stone has life. Professor Jagadis Chandra Bose, founder of the Bose Research Insti-

---

* "The creation myths of almost every culture show sound as the mechanism by which Spirit gives birth to the physical world," write Robert Gass and Kathleen Brehony in *Chanting: Discovering Spirit in Sound* (New York: Broadway Books, 1999). "The New Testament tells us: 'In the beginning was the Word, and the Word was with God, and the Word was God.' Since the original Greek word *logos* (here translated as 'word') also means 'sound,' it would be also accurate for this famous passage to read: 'In the beginning was the Sound, and the Sound was with God, and the Sound was God.'"

Gass and Brehony quote the Greek philosopher Pythagoras as saying "A stone is frozen music, frozen sound." Recent data collected by astrophysicists correlates remarkably with what the ancient seers perceived. In *Mind Over Matter: Conversations With the Cosmos* (New York: Harcourt, 2003) K. C. Cole reports that in 2000 a team of astronomers led by Andrew Lange of the California Institute of Technology "published the most detailed analysis yet of the cosmos's primordial song: a low hum, deep in its throat, that preceded both atoms and stars. It is a simple sound, like the mantra 'Om.' But hidden within its harmonics are details of the universe's shape, composition, and birth."

Those harmonic "notes," reported *The Independent*, London, April 30, 2001, "rang out like a bell in the first fractions of a second after the Big Bang. Cosmologists

tute in Calcutta, India, engaged in remarkable experiments in which he proved that even a piece of tin responds favorably to stimuli that are pleasurable and contrarily to others it dislikes; and that its life vibrations can also be poisoned and killed.*

"And dwelt among us": The Cosmic Vibration, which was materialized into physical creation, including man's body, provided a circumambient universe observable to sentient souls.

Man is a threefold being: physical, mental, and spiritual—a unique combination of forces and consciousness capable of fully cognizing Divinity in himself and in the universe conceived for his appreciation. He is the soul, the Self, made in the image of God (an individualized reflection of God), which expresses itself in the manifested universe through the instrumentality of a body and a mind. The bodily instrument is a collective vibration of grossly stirring atoms, electromagnetic waves, and intelligent life force (subtle vital energy, finer than electrons). The mental faculty consists of both sensory instruments (of perception and action) and discriminative intelligence (which interprets sensory information and makes determinations regarding knowledge and action). The soul, while dwelling within the body, becomes identified with its physical and mental experiences and forgets its divine nature; it masquerades

---

believe these minute ripples of sound became the 'seeds' of matter, which eventually led to the formation of stars, galaxies, and planets such as Earth."

Through painstaking computer analysis, writes Cole, Lange and his colleagues produced "graphic depictions of the sound" made by the universe in the first few hundred thousand years after its creation in the Big Bang. In that primordial period, the data shows, "nothing existed but pure light, sprinkled with a smattering of subatomic particles. Nothing happened, either, except that this light-and-matter fluid, as physicists call it, sloshed in and out of gravity wells, compressing the liquid in some places and spreading it out in others. Like banging on the head of a drum, the compression of the 'liquid light' as it fell into gravity wells set up the 'sound waves' that cosmologist Charles Lineweaver calls 'the oldest music in the universe.'"

Scientific American, July 2000, says that as the universe aged those sound waves "developed on ever larger scales, filling the heavens with a deepening roar." About 300,000 years after the Big Bang, the universe cooled down to the point where electrons and protons condensed into atoms of hydrogen—and separated from the vibrating light (photons). "The photons went their separate ways, and the universe abruptly went silent."

"The rest," concludes K. C. Cole, "is the history of the universe: The particles joined each other to form atoms, stars, and everything else, including people." *(Publisher's Note)*

* The work of this great Indian physicist and plant physiologist (1858–1937) is discussed in *Autobiography of a Yogi,* Chapter 8.

instead as the body-circumscribed ego, the pseudosoul. Scientific yoga techniques of meditation enable the soul to regain the memory of its oneness with the omniscient, omnipresent Spirit.

"And we beheld his glory, the glory as of the only begotten of the Father." "We" means advanced souls who have reclaimed their sonship with God, and who experience the Holy Ghost Cosmic Vibration and the innate cosmic Christ Intelligence—the only begotten of God the Father in all creation. The Christ-imbued Word, "full of grace and truth," is the replete repository of the universal principles and laws of natural righteousness, the "truth" that upholds the order of the world and governs man's duty to God, nature, and his fellow beings.

The glory of the magnitude of the Light of Cosmic Vibration is coming like a great comet of life from God, surrounding matter and secreted just beneath its grossness. "We beheld...the glory" of the Cosmic Light and "of the only begotten" Intelligence of God that guides the Cosmic Light or Vibration and gives grace and beauty and true substance to all matter. Without "the glory as of the only begotten of the Father," there would be no matter at all.

The entire creation of matter, Holy Ghost or Holy Energy; and the only begotten, only reflected intelligence of God in matter, receive their grace and truth, the glory of their manifestation, from God, who is the Father-Creator of all.

~

John bare witness of him, and cried, saying, "This was he of whom I spake, 'He that cometh after me is preferred before me: for he was before me'" (John 1:15).

The consciousness of the prophet John the Baptist was in tune with the universal Christ Intelligence and could "witness" or declare from his own intuitive realization the glory of Christ Consciousness as manifest in the omnipresence of the Holy Ghost creative Light, and also in the divine consciousness he saw incarnate in Jesus. That Consciousness was "preferred" in Jesus for he came to fulfill a special dispensation.*

---

* The content of John 1:15 is repeated in verses 27 and 30 and is explained in greater detail in that fuller context in Discourse 6.

~

*And of his fulness have all we received, and grace for grace. For
the law was given by Moses, but grace and truth came by Jesus
Christ (John 1:16–17).*

Of the fullness of the Christ Consciousness that permeates creation all prophets have received—all those who are in tune receive that consciousness without measure. Lesser men, according to
their capacity, also receive; their every goodness, like a mouth, drinks
of the eternal grace of the Christ Consciousness. "And of his fulness":
That is, the omnipresent Christ Consciousness all can receive who
make their minds pure. "And grace for grace": For every goodness in
man, he receives from the eternal goodness of God.

*The fullness of Spirit
is reflected in all souls*

The fullness of the Spirit is reflected evenly in
all souls. But those who are sons of God—those
who have changed their charcoal mentality into a
diamond mentality—receive and reflect the fullness
of the Divine Presence. In the sons of God is the "fulness" of the omnipresent omniscience of the Bliss of Spirit, the complete awareness of
the glory of God within themselves.

"And grace for grace": Every goodness is an opening through
which the light of God shines. Every expression of a dark mentality
shuts out the sunny Divine Presence. So each time man practices goodness, he receives a special measure of God's grace.

"For the law was given by Moses, but grace and truth came by
Jesus Christ": Now here is a contentious verse of scriptural disagree-
ment between Jews and Christians. But this verse is not intended to
define any difference in the degree of spirituality between Jesus and
Moses. The point is, every prophet has a special purpose to fulfill on
earth. This statement of Saint John's merely recognizes Moses' gift
from God to man in the form of the Ten Commandments. These are
eternal verities, universal laws of life that make man's existence
morally comfortable and spiritually fulfilling. The word "commandment," however, does not give the best connotation, for it is as if God
is a dictator and man His servile attendant. These dictums should
rather be regarded as a code of natural righteousness. If man does not
follow those laws which evince the divine image within him, he falls
out of tune with God into delusive suffering of his own making.

Mary Visits the Mother of John the Baptist

And it came to pass, that, when Elisabeth heard the salutation of Mary, the babe leaped in her womb; and Elisabeth was filled with the Holy Ghost: And she spake out with a loud voice, and said...."Lo, as soon as the voice of thy salutation sounded in mine ears, the babe leaped in my womb for joy."

—Luke 1:41–44

The relationship between Jesus and John was of a continuing journey together of two divine souls, begun in previous lifetimes....God's plan was in evidence from the moment of conception of these two souls in the wombs of their earthly mothers, embodying them for their incarnations as John and Jesus. Even when still in the womb, their spirits recognized one another and communicated their everlasting fealty and love.

—Paramahansa Yogananda

Painting by Carl Bloch

"Grace and truth came by Jesus Christ": That is, all truth, the power behind universal laws, flows from the Christ Consciousness, which power was manifested in Jesus, as in all great prophets. The eternal laws are in fact maintained through the omnipresence of the Christ Intelligence. Jesus, through the consciousness of the Universal Christ within him, came to show that grace and truth and goodness flow from that divine Source.

∾

No man hath seen God at any time; the only begotten Son, which is in the bosom of the Father, he hath declared Him (John 1:18).

M any have been misled due to a wrong reading of these words. If God is imperceptible, He must be equally unknowable. How frustrating would seem one's efforts in meditation, or in prayer to such a reclusive God. The meaning is this:

"No man hath seen God at any time (no mortal under 'time,' the relativities of *maya*, can realize the Infinite); the only begotten Son, which is in the bosom of the Father (the reflected Christ Consciousness or outwardly projected Perfect Intelligence that, guiding all structural phenomena through *Aum* vibration, has issued forth from the 'bosom' or deeps of the Uncreated Divine in order to express the variety of Unity), he hath declared (subjected to form, or manifested) Him."

No mortal can see God except by lifting his consciousness to Christ Consciousness

It is the Christ Intelligence in all creation that has manifested the invisible God the Father transcendent beyond creation. We would not have seen the beauty of the flower or responded with love to the sweet life in an infant if that Christ Intelligence were not present there. We would have had no inkling of God the Father in His transcendent vibrationless abode beyond the etheric vastness of creation unless that "only begotten" Intelligence reflected in matter declared His existence.

The word "seen" has such a provisory connotation. One who is body-bound, whose consciousness is limited to sensory perceptions and the thought that he is a mortal being—he cannot see God. But to Jesus, who was in tune with the Infinite Christ Intelligence, God was no longer an unintelligible mystery. With the all-seeing intuitive perception of his soul he could see God in any aspect, materialized out of the Vibratory Light, or in divine oneness embrace his Father as the Formless Absolute. When man has lifted his consciousness from the ordinary sensory state to receive that only begotten Christ Consciousness, he also shall see God, not with mortal sight but with divine perception.

When the consciousness is impregnate with the Christ Intelligence, one sees that Intelligence as the reflection of God manifesting in everything. But when the Creative Vibration of the outgoing externalization of God's consciousness is enshrouded in *maya*, the true Essence of manifestation is hidden. It is the Holy Ghost pure intelligence and its innate undistorted reflection of God as Christ Consciousness that proclaims the everywhereness of the Divine Presence and is the stabilizer and magnetic attraction in matter that keeps created forms linked to their Divine Source, and ultimately pulls them back to God. The nature of this Christ magnetism is God's Love—His eternal caring and watchfulness of the greatest and the tiniest of His manifestations, never allowing them to wander outside of His sheltering presence.

This Omnipresent Love of God is why I consider Bhagavan Krishna and Jesus Christ, avatars of East and West, as the supreme expressions of the Krishna-Christ Consciousness (the Universal *Kutastha Chaitanya*), for in them was evident in the highest degree the incarnation of God's divine love and compassion. Krishna's love gave to the world the yoga of liberation from the sea of suffering through scientific meditation and right action, and the devotional approach of flinging oneself on the Divine Compassion. Jesus demonstrated in his every act of ministering to the sick and forsaken, and in the consummate sacrifice of his body to alleviate the sins of many, the incomparable love of God that is an infinitude of mercy and forgiveness. The paramount meaning of the birth of Jesus is the forgiveness of God. Though man cast himself into the darkest abyss of God-forgetfulness, spurning the Lord in favor of rampant material gratifications, yet is he ultimately rescued by the pull of God's love within and around him that aids in a natural upward evolutionary return to God. This is the world message Jesus the Christ was born to declare, by the hidden love of God made manifest in the divinity of his life.

Jesus' Immaculate Conception and His Relationship With John the Baptist

"God's plan was in evidence from the moment of conception of these two souls in the wombs of their earthly mothers, embodying them for their incarnations as John and Jesus."

*T*here was in the days of Herod, the king of Judea, a certain priest named Zacharias, of the course of Abia: and his wife was of the daughters of Aaron, and her name was Elisabeth. And they were both righteous before God, walking in all the commandments and ordinances of the Lord blameless. And they had no child, because that Elisabeth was barren, and they both were now well stricken in years.

And it came to pass, that while he executed the priest's office before God in the order of his course, according to the custom of the priest's office, his lot was to burn incense when he went into the temple of the Lord. And the whole multitude of the people were praying without at the time of incense.

And there appeared unto him an angel of the Lord standing on the right side of the altar of incense. And when Zacharias saw him, he was troubled, and fear fell upon him.

But the angel said unto him, "Fear not, Zacharias: for thy prayer is heard; and thy wife Elisabeth shall bear thee a son, and thou shalt call his name John.* And thou shalt have joy and gladness; and many shall rejoice at his birth. For he shall be great in the sight of the Lord, and shall drink neither wine nor strong drink; and he shall be filled with the Holy Ghost, even from his mother's womb. And many of the children of Israel shall he turn to the Lord their God. And he shall go before him in the spirit and power of Elijah, 'to turn the hearts of the fathers to the children,' and the disobedient to the wisdom of the just; to make ready a people prepared for the Lord."

And Zacharias said unto the angel, "Whereby shall I know this? for I am an old man, and my wife well stricken in years."

And the angel answering said unto him, "I am Gabriel, that stand in the presence of God; and am sent to speak unto thee, and to shew thee these glad tidings. And, behold, thou shalt be dumb, and not able to speak, until the day that these

---

* "Gift of God." *Smith's Bible Dictionary* says it is "the same name as Johanan, a contraction of Jehohanan, 'Jehovah's gift.'"

things shall be performed, because thou believest not my words, which shall be fulfilled in their season."

And the people waited for Zacharias, and marvelled that he tarried so long in the temple. And when he came out, he could not speak unto them: and they perceived that he had seen a vision in the temple: for he beckoned unto them, and remained speechless.

And it came to pass, that, as soon as the days of his ministration were accomplished, he departed to his own house. And after those days his wife Elisabeth conceived, and hid herself five months, saying, "Thus hath the Lord dealt with me in the days wherein He looked on me, to take away my reproach among men."

—Luke 1:5–25

DISCOURSE 2

Jesus' Immaculate Conception and His Relationship With John the Baptist

꟥

"Behold, I will send you Elijah the prophet before the coming of the great and dreadful day of the Lord."* These words, at the very end of the Old Testament, foretell the coming of Christ Jesus and the rebirth of Elijah as his precursor. The prophecy was fulfilled by John the Baptist, divinely ordained to "prepare the way of the Lord" and "go before him in the spirit and power of Elijah."

The Biblical telling of the relationship between Jesus and John the Baptist takes on a new sanctity when viewed in the light of the holy tradition of the bond formed between guru and disciple—between one who knows God and one who is seeking to know Him. The relationship between Jesus and John was of a continuing journey together of two divine souls, begun in previous lifetimes.

The cosmic principle of reincarnation: souls' journey through many lives

The cosmic principle of reincarnation, with its dynamism of the law of karma (cause and effect, sowing and reaping), is a time-honored doctrine, embraced by the Hindus, Buddhists, the ancient Druid priests, the Essenes and Gnostics and many early Christian theologians; and also, eminent philosophers of the East and West. Though for centuries it has been divorced by church orthodoxy

* Malachi 4:5.

36

from the common understanding of Jesus' life and teachings, reincarnation is in fact evident in many passages in both the Old and New Testaments, including unequivocal statements by Jesus himself.* For example, from the Book of Revelation (3:12): "Him that overcometh will I make a pillar in the temple of my God, and he shall go no more out." Here Jesus distinctly refers to the doctrine of reincarnation, saying that when a soul overcomes by spiritual discipline his mortal desires accrued through contact of matter, that soul becomes a pillar of immortality in the everlasting mansion of Cosmic Consciousness; and, having found fulfillment of all his desires in Spirit, that soul has no more to be reborn on earth through the karmic reincarnating force of unsatisfied desires.†

All souls come from God—individualized rays of pure Spirit— and evolve back to their native perfection by exercise of their God-given free will. The ignorant and the wise alike require equal opportunity from the hand of a just and loving God in order to fulfill this quest. For instance, a baby who dies prematurely cannot possibly have used its free will to be either virtuous enough to be granted salvation or vicious enough to be damned. Nature must bring that soul back to earth to give it a chance to use its free will to work out the past actions (karma) that were the lawful cause of its untimely death, and to perform sufficient good actions to attain liberation.

Ordinary souls are compelled to reincarnate by their earthbound desires and effects of past actions. Great souls, advanced in wisdom through learning the lessons of many lifetimes, come on earth partially to finish their karma but principally to act as noble sons of God whose

---

* Cited later in this Discourse and in subsequent ones. See *reincarnation* in index.

† "Understanding of the law of karma and of its corollary, reincarnation, is displayed in numerous Biblical passages; e.g., 'Whoso sheddeth man's blood, by man shall his blood be shed' (Genesis 9:6). If every murderer must himself be killed 'by man,' the reactive process obviously requires, in many cases, more than one lifetime. The contemporary police are just not quick enough!

"The early Christian church accepted the doctrine of reincarnation, which was expounded by the Gnostics and by numerous church fathers, including Clement of Alexandria, the celebrated Origen (both 3rd century), and St. Jerome (5th century). The doctrine was first declared a heresy in A.D. 553 by the Second Council of Constantinople. At that time many Christians thought the doctrine of reincarnation afforded man too ample a stage of time and space to encourage him to strive for immediate salvation. But truths suppressed lead disconcertingly to a host of errors. The millions have not utilized their 'one lifetime' to seek God, but to enjoy this world—so uniquely won, and so shortly to be forever lost! The truth is that man reincarnates on earth until he has consciously regained his status as a son of God." —*Autobiography of a Yogi*

example inspires His lost children along their way to the Heavenly Father's all-blissful home. Masters and prophets, having graduated from the school of mortal life into the immortality of Cosmic Consciousness, incarnate voluntarily to serve, at God's behest, as plenipotentiary agents of His millennial plan to shepherd all souls back to their eternal abode in Spirit.*

From my guru, Swami Sri Yukteswar, a master of Vedic wisdom with a universal spiritual understanding, I received a new appreciation

Jesus and John in light of reincarnation

of the Christian Bible—in which I confess to only a cursory interest in my youth, having been put off by the irrational orthodoxy of missionaries whose aim was to convert me. Listening to Master expound the Christian scripture with the same natural ease he felt among the esoteric depths of his native Hindu heritage, I experienced a wondrous expansion in the realm of truth, which has no boundaries or religious demarcations. Sri Yukteswar had written, at the request of his *paramguru,* Mahavatar Babaji, an amazingly compacted analysis of the unity of the Hindu and Christian scriptures: *The Holy Science.*† That commission was the seed of my future mission—to show the harmony between the original science of yoga given by Bhagavan Krishna and the original teachings of Lord Jesus. My mind, therefore, early on, dwelt often on the life of Christ; his presence became a very real experience to me.

As every human being has undergone many lifetimes to fashion his present nature and condition, an idle curiosity often imposed itself on my mind as to what incarnations Jesus must have passed through in order to reach Christhood. An ordinary materially minded man's consciousness is limited to the satisfaction of hunger, thirst, and minor necessities of the body, including gratification of desires. An intellectual man spreads his consciousness to explore the stars or the deeper regions of the secret caves of wisdom connected with the mind, life, or surroundings of human existence. A spiritual man, by many lifetimes of meditation and by extending his love to all, unites his consciousness with the all-pervading Christ Consciousness. Therefore, Jesus the man must have lived through other

---

* Reincarnation of liberated or nearly liberated saints for a divine mission is implicit in God's declaration to Jeremiah: "Before I formed thee in the belly I knew thee; and before thou camest forth out of the womb I sanctified thee, and I ordained thee a prophet unto the nations" (Jeremiah 1:5).

† Published by Self-Realization Fellowship.

incarnations of human schooling and meditation before he reached his expanded, exalted state as Jesus the Christ.

Over the years, I made deep researches in Spirit to ascertain the outstanding previous incarnations of Jesus—with little result. (God keeps tightly closed the mystery door that closets a soul's past lives, lest undue and irrelevant attention be focused on former glories or disastrous errors rather than on the merits of the here and now. Nevertheless, glimpses He does vouchsafe when the purpose is beneficial.) One day as I sat in absorbed contemplation, with the Christian Bible in my hands, I deeply prayed, "Father, tell me who was Jesus Christ before he came to earth in that incarnation." In unexpected instancy, the Father's silent omnipresent voice became manifest in audible words: "Open the Bible!"

I obeyed the Divine Command; and the first verse on which my eyes fell was I Kings 19:19:

So he (Elijah) departed thence, and found Elisha the son of Shaphat, who was plowing with twelve yoke of oxen before him, and he with the twelfth: and Elijah passed by him, and cast his mantle upon him.

Then I remembered what Jesus had spoken of John the Baptist: "'But I say unto you, that Elijah is come already, and they knew him not....' Then the disciples understood that he spake unto them of John the Baptist" (Matthew 17:12–13).* It was Elisha, incarnate as Jesus, who could recognize his master in John the Baptist from their past association as Elijah and Elisha. In many places, as will be shown in these Discourses, Jesus made significant references to John the Baptist and showed deference to him—when Jesus asked to be baptized of him; when he extolled John as the greatest of prophets born of woman (which included himself); when Jesus was transfigured on the mountain and Moses and Elijah appeared and when afterward he identified Elijah as John the Baptist.

Both John the Baptist and Jesus in their former incarnations as Elijah and Elisha had found complete liberation. Who Jesus was be-

---

*The names of certain individuals from the Old Testament appear in modified form in the New Testament, where the Greek rather than Hebrew form of the names is used. Thus, Elijah is called Elias in the New Testament, Elisha is called Eliseus, Isaiah is known as Esaias, and so on. To avoid the confusing use of two names for the same individual, in this publication the Old Testament spellings have been used. *(Publisher's Note)*

fore he was born as Elisha is not important, for it was in that incarnation that he attained the supreme goal. By divine appointment, Elisha was perfected through Elijah, who cast on him his mantle of spiritual realization.

The hand of the Lord was on Elijah (I Kings 18:46).

And God directed Elijah to initiate Elisha:

And the Lord said unto him, "Go, return on the way to the wilderness of Damascus: and when thou comest...Elisha the son of Shaphat of Abelmeholah shalt thou anoint to be prophet in thy room" (I Kings 19:15–16).

Thus did God distinctly appoint Elijah to be the guru of Elisha. The Guru of Gurus, the Supreme Preceptor, always designates the channel

Elijah as the past-life guru of Jesus

through which the disciple shall receive instruction and liberation. Elijah, finding Elisha plowing with the twelve yoke of oxen is significantly symbolic, since Elisha, later as Jesus, was to plow the hard soil of human consciousness with his twelve disciples to bring forth a harvest of divine wisdom and salvation in many souls. By this incident did God indicate to Elijah the future remarkable world mission of Elisha; and that he was chosen for this divine dispensation because he was an extraordinary disciple.

To cast a cloth mantle on another has no transforming power in and of itself. But the casting of a master's garment of Self-realization over the consciousness of an advanced disciple is the baptism by the Holy Ghost. Having received that initiation from Elijah, Elisha, without word or argument or persuasion, thereafter faithfully followed his guru.

When it came time for the Lord to end the earthly incarnation of Elijah, the great prophet said to Elisha:

"Ask what I shall do for thee, before I be taken away from thee."
    And Elisha said, "I pray thee, let a double portion of thy spirit be upon me."
    And he (Elijah) said, "Thou hast asked a hard thing: nevertheless, if thou see me when I am taken from thee, it shall be so unto thee; but if not, it shall not be so."

And it came to pass, as they still went on, and talked, that, behold, there appeared a chariot of fire, and horses of fire, and parted them both asunder; and Elijah went up by a whirlwind into heaven.

And Elisha saw it, and he cried, "My father, my father, the chariot of Israel, and the horsemen thereof." And he saw him no more: and he took hold of his own clothes, and rent them in two pieces.

He took up also the mantle of Elijah that fell from him, and went back, and stood by the bank of Jordan;

And he took the mantle of Elijah that fell from him, and smote the waters, and said, "Where is the Lord God of Elijah?" And when he also had smitten the waters, they parted hither and thither: and Elisha went over.

And when the sons of the prophets which were to view at Jericho saw him, they said, "The spirit of Elijah doth rest on Elisha." And they came to meet him, and bowed themselves to the ground before him (II Kings 2:9–15).

So it was that Elisha, as Jesus, came with "a double portion of spirit," to bring salvation to many disciples as well as to conquer by all-forgiving divine love when supremely tested with crucifixion. Elijah and Elisha both had performed many miracles, and were able to heal the sick, to produce abundance from a little food, and to raise the dead. Therefore, in accordance with the law of karma, Jesus possessed great powers even in childhood as a natural endowment from his incarnation as Elisha. As Jesus imbued life into the shell of his dead body, spiritualizing and immortalizing it, so also even the decaying bones of the departed Elisha retained life-reviving power:

And Elisha died, and they buried him. And the bands of the Moabites invaded the land at the coming in of the year. And it came to pass, as they were burying a man, that, behold, they spied a band of men; and they cast the man into the sepulchre of Elisha: and when the man was let down, and touched the bones of Elisha, he revived, and stood up on his feet (II Kings 13:20–21).

The soul of Elijah, after converting his physical body into luminous astral energy and ascending to heaven "in the whirlwind of a

41

fiery chariot,"* remained in the astral land to be timely reincarnated as John the Baptist to witness for the divine mission his disciple Elisha,

Jesus' mission and miracles foreshadowed in his previous incarnation

reincarnated as Jesus, was preordained to fulfill.† Elijah and Elisha, both being one with Spirit, were spiritual equals. Yet Elijah, returning as John the Baptist, humbly took an insignificant part in that incarnation, just to see and support his reincarnated disciple, Jesus, who came "with a double portion of spirit" to fulfill God's wish that he play an eminent role in revolutionizing the spiritual destiny of man. Both Jesus and John were fulfilling the will of God. It is natural that Elijah, being the master, wanted to be on earth to witness and be the one to prepare the way for his disciple to carry out his divine dispensation and be glorified as a savior on earth. A noble father is never jealous of his son's glory, but rather takes pride if the son surpasses his own repute in the eyes of the world. And though John played a lesser part, his ordeal of iniquitous imprisonment and beheading for the sake of truth was no less than the tribulation of Jesus on the cross.

God's plan was in evidence from the moment of conception of these two souls in the wombs of their earthly mothers, embodying them for their incarnations as John and Jesus. Even when still in the womb, their spirits recognized one another and communicated their everlasting fealty and love. Advanced souls who have broken the cycles of compulsory incarnations do not have to undergo the ordinary experience of oblivion that disconnects one life from the next. If they choose it to be so, their ever awake souls can retain their continuity of consciousness throughout the sequence of death, afterlife, and rebirth—even in the mother's womb.

---

* "The advanced yogi transmutes his cells into energy. Elijah, Jesus, Kabir, and other prophets were past masters in the use of *Kriya Yoga* or a similar technique, by which they caused their bodies to materialize and dematerialize at will" (*Autobiography of a Yogi,* Chapter 26).

† Jesus and John the Baptist echoed their previous incarnations by outer roles as well as by their inner spirituality. According to *Smith's Bible Dictionary:* "In almost every respect Elisha presents the most complete contrast to Elijah....Elijah was a true Bedouin child of the desert. If he enters a city it is only to deliver his message of fire and be gone. Elisha, on the other hand, is a civilized man, an inhabitant of cities. And as with his manners so with his appearance. The touches of the narrative are very slight; but we can gather that his dress was the ordinary garment of an Israelite...that his hair was worn trimmed behind, in contrast to the disordered locks of Elijah." *(Publisher's Note)*

*A*nd in the sixth month the angel Gabriel was sent from God unto a city of Galilee, named Nazareth, to a virgin espoused to a man whose name was Joseph, of the house of David; and the virgin's name was Mary. And the angel came in unto her, and said, "Hail, thou that art highly favoured, the Lord is with thee: blessed art thou among women."

And when she saw him, she was troubled at his saying, and cast in her mind what manner of salutation this should be.

And the angel said unto her, "Fear not, Mary: for thou hast found favour with God. And, behold, thou shalt conceive in thy womb, and bring forth a son, and shalt call his name Jesus. He shall be great, and shall be called the Son of the Highest: and the Lord God shall give unto him the throne of his father David: And he shall reign over the house of Jacob for ever; and of his kingdom there shall be no end."

Then said Mary unto the angel, "How shall this be, seeing I know not a man?"

And the angel answered and said unto her, "The Holy Ghost shall come upon thee, and the power of the Highest shall overshadow thee: therefore also that holy thing which shall be born of thee shall be called the Son of God. And, behold, thy cousin Elisabeth, she hath also conceived a son in her old age: and this is the sixth month with her, who was called barren. For with God nothing shall be impossible."

And Mary said, "Behold the handmaid of the Lord; be it unto me according to thy word." And the angel departed from her....

And Mary arose in those days, and went into the hill country with haste, into a city of Juda; and entered into the house of Zacharias, and saluted Elisabeth. And it came to pass, that, when Elisabeth heard the salutation of Mary, the babe leaped in her womb; and Elisabeth was filled with the Holy Ghost: And she spake out with a loud voice, and said, "Blessed art thou among women, and blessed is the fruit of thy womb. And whence is this to me, that the mother of my Lord should come to me? For, lo, as soon as the voice of thy salutation sounded in mine ears, the babe leaped in my womb for joy."

...And Mary abode with her about three months, and returned to her own house.

—Luke 1:26–44, 56

Now the birth of Jesus Christ was on this wise: When as his mother Mary was espoused to Joseph, before they came together, she was found with child of the Holy Ghost. Then Joseph her husband, being a just man, and not willing to make her a publick example, was minded to put her away privily.

But while he thought on these things, behold, the angel of the Lord appeared unto him in a dream, saying, "Joseph, thou son of David, fear not to take unto thee Mary thy wife: for that which is conceived in her is of the Holy Ghost. And she shall bring forth a son, and thou shalt call his name Jesus: for he shall save his people from their sins."

Now all this was done, that it might be fulfilled which was spoken of the Lord by the prophet, saying, "Behold, a virgin shall be with child, and shall bring forth a son, and they shall call his name Emmanuel,"* which being interpreted is, "God with us."

—Matthew 1:18–23

---

* The prophecy is in Isaiah 7:14.

The conception and birth of Jesus has been the subject of considerable controversy: Was he conceived in the natural or a preternatural way? Was he truly born of immaculate conception? Myth, fact, faith? Man so engrosses himself in trying to decipher the encrypted formulas of God's doings that he misses the joy of appreciating the hand of God in the affairs of man. Must one comprehend the full molecular biology of wheat to know the satisfaction of hunger in a loaf of bread? Must one be an astronomer to receive the life-giving light and warmth of the sun? The ultimate knowledge of every God-mystery is barred to no one who makes himself ready to read the Book of Life, whenever and in whatever way the Lord opens its pages to him.

The metaphysical truth about immaculate conception

God is the Great Cosmic Organizer. The most elite conclave of mortal minds could not so thoroughly set forth universal laws that endure the assaults of time and the presumptuous rejections of cultural change. Yet God is not rigid. He accords freedom to man to induce kaleidoscopic variations by manipulation of known laws—for good and ill—which in effect simply activate other laws which are thereby newly "discovered." He Himself delights in surprising His children with a divine innovation now and again that confounds their common reason. In dismay man backs away and scoffs at the implausibility, or reverently folds his hands and concedes a miracle.

Even in nature, God plays with the staid methods. Some plants cannot grow and reproduce without sexual cross-pollination from male stamen to the female pistil; while other plants, such as the common geranium, can vigorously proliferate themselves from a small stem cutting. The animal kingdom, likewise, has evolved through sexual reproduction; yet a certain species of snail produces its own kind quite independently of male-female union. In science laboratories, frogs have been reproduced by stimulation of female ova without the introduction of male sperm.*

---

* The snail, *Potamopyrgus antipodarum*, is found in freshwater lakes in New Zealand. The asexual reproduction of frogs by inserting nuclei from embryonic cells into unfertilized eggs was first accomplished in 1951; however, the experiment was carried on only until the newborn frogs had grown to the tadpole stage.

National Geographic News, September 26, 2002, reported: "A female white spotted bamboo shark at the Belle Isle Aquarium in Detroit surprised zookeepers in July by giving birth to two babies. Why the surprise? It was a virgin birth: She hadn't been near a male for six years....The births have raised questions among scientists as to whether sharks may be able to reproduce parthenogenetically, a mode of reproduction

Creation is creation, the forming of something new. It is always "immaculate" in the sense that it brings something into being by the creative power of God, whether by His divine fiat or by man's employment of God's natural laws. The first real immaculate conception, in its highest form, was when God materialized Adam and Eve—the symbolic parents of all human beings. God did not create original man and woman by sexual union. (Which came first, the tree or the seed? The tree, of course, which was then endowed with the ability to produce its own kind.) Though the physical body of man was generally patterned after the physiological and anatomical instrumentalities that had resulted from the long process of evolution of animal species, human beings were created by God with a unique endowment possessed by no lower forms: awakened spiritual centers of life and consciousness in the spine and brain that gave them the ability to express fully the divine consciousness and powers of the soul. By an act of special creation, God thus created the bodies of Adam and Eve in the immaculate way of direct materialization, and empowered these first beings similarly to reproduce their own kind. We find in the Hindu scriptures, also, mention of the real immaculate conception when the divinely endowed first beings could create offspring by mind power.*

---

in which the egg is not fertilized. These so-called virgin births are common in invertebrates like snails, but are unusual in higher vertebrates. 'Parthenogenesis has been documented in many reptiles,' said Doug Sweet, curator of fishes at the Belle Isle Aquarium. 'There are at least five or six species of snakes, and it's been known in salamanders, lizards, and even a breed of turkeys.'" *(Publisher's Note)*

* "While the Genesis story in the Bible focuses on the fall of original man, the Hindu scriptures extol the first beings on earth as divine individuals who could assume corporeal forms and similarly create offspring by divine command of their will. In one such account, in the hoary *Purana, Srimad Bhagavata,* the first man and woman in physical form, the Hindu 'Adam and Eve,' were called Svayambhuva Manu ('man born of the Creator') and his wife Shatarupa ('having a hundred images or forms') whose children intermarried with Prajapatis, perfect celestial beings who took physical forms to become the progenitors of mankind. Thus, entering the original unique human forms created by God were souls that had either passed through the upward evolutionary stages of creation as Prakriti prepared the earth for the advent of man, or were pristine souls that had descended to earth specifically to begin the world's human population. In either case, original man was uniquely endowed to express soul perfection. Those 'Adams and Eves' and their offspring who maintained their divine consciousness in the 'Eden' of the spiritual eye returned to Spirit or the heavenly realms after a blissful sojourn on earth. The 'fallen' human beings and their 'fallen' offspring were caught in the reincarnational cycles that are the fate of desire-filled, sense-identified mortals" (*God Talks With Arjuna: The Bhagavad Gita,* commentary on xv:1).

Man and woman, expressing from their sexless souls a positive or negative vibration, could produce other male or female beings, respectively, by materialization even as God had created the Biblical Adam and Eve.

In the beginning, the sexual organs were not pronounced at all in the symbolic Adam and Eve. God warned them not to eat of the fruit "in the midst of the garden" (Genesis 3:3). That fruit was the sensual touch of sex in the middle of *Sexual reproduction* the bodily garden. When Adam and Eve succumbed *in humans began* to temptation and ate of that fruit—embraced each *with the fall of Adam* other in a lustful way—they were "driven out" of *and Eve* the Eden of spiritual consciousness. In their "fall," having descended to the low estate of body identification, they lost their soul-awareness of the divine perceptions and capacities in the subtle cerebrospinal centers—including the power to create in the immaculate way.* Their sexual organs developed, as in the lesser evolved forms of the animal kingdom. In the positive, more aggressive human form the protruding male organ developed; and in the negative, more passive body the recessive female organs developed.†

The divinity and power of creation that God gave to Adam and Eve before their fall is still potentially present in every human soul, and will be brought back again when the Eden of godliness is reentered. The *rishis* of the ancient higher ages in India had the power to create by mind. By will power anything can be materialized in this world. In all cases, it is the Cosmic Vibration (Prakriti, Holy Ghost) that informs all matter. This vibration can be consciously wielded by the will power of Christlike beings who unite themselves with the Directing Intelligence of God's will in the Holy Vibration. Or God Himself, directly or through His hierarchy of angelic agents, may transmit this power of the Holy Ghost to fulfill His purpose.

When it is written in the Bible that God took a rib from Adam to fashion Eve (Genesis 2:21–22), "rib" refers to vibration: The creation of man (the positive or male manifestation of creative vibration) consisted of God's consciousness with reason uppermost and feeling par-

---

* "Unto the woman [God] said, I will greatly multiply thy sorrow and thy conception; in sorrow thou shalt bring forth children..." (Genesis 3:16).

† The spiritual significance of the Adam and Eve story in Genesis is explained in more detail in Discourse 7.

tially hidden; and with the same vibratory power He then created woman (the negative or feminine manifestation of the creative vibration) with feeling uppermost and reason less dominant. From the predominance of these qualities, He fashioned differences in their bodies that encased their sexless souls. God's plan—since creation depends on interaction between positive and negative forces—is that the God-given natures of man and woman would balance each other. When this vibration is equalized in a human being, he or she begins to manifest his or her innate divine soul-nature of perfect God-equilibrium.

Many saints have been born in the natural way, and some in the immaculate way. The great ones who have attained liberation retain their individuality in Spirit; and at God's behest to return to the world as saviors, they can take a physical body either by immaculate conception or natural birth. (In higher world ages, they may even do so by direct materialization—though that is not for the eyes of unenlightened times.) The mode of birth does not matter, nor does it necessarily indicate the degree of divinity.

Sexual creation has the selfish sexual instincts of the parents in it. Therefore, some saints choose to be conceived in the immaculate way,

Buddha and other avatars also born in the immaculate way

the pure system of conception. So it is a fact that Jesus was created by immaculate conception. His mother Mary, she who "had found favor with God," was filled with the Holy Ghost Cosmic Vibration: "The Holy Ghost shall come upon thee, and the power of the Highest shall overshadow thee." This sacred creative Vibration, suffused with the reflection of God as the Christ Consciousness, entered the ovum in Mary's womb, immaculately creating the germ cell of life into which entered the soul of Jesus, the individualized Christ Consciousness. From this pristine cell, according to the pattern inherent in the soul of Jesus, grew the body in which Jesus the Christ was born. It is not a myth. Gautama Buddha (as also other avatars) was born in the same way. His mother saw the Spirit enter her body. As told in traditional Indian allegory in the *Jataka* (ancient Buddhist scripture):

"And lying down on the royal couch, she fell asleep and dreamed the following dream:

"The four guardian angels came and lifted her up, together with her couch, and took her away to the Himalaya Mountains....After clothing her with divine garments, they anointed her with perfumes and decked her with divine flowers. Not far off was Silver Hill, and in it a golden mansion. There they spread a divine couch with its head towards the east, and laid her down upon it.

"Now the Future Buddha had become a superb white elephant,* and was wandering about at no great distance, on Gold Hill. Descending thence, he ascended Silver Hill, and approaching from the north, he plucked a white lotus with his silvery trunk, and trumpeting loudly, went into the golden mansion. And three times he walked round his mother's couch, with his right side towards it, and striking her on her right side, he seemed to enter her womb. Thus the conception took place in the Midsummer Festival.

"On the next day the queen awoke, and told the dream to the king. And the king caused sixty-four eminent Brahmins to be summoned.... [and] told them the dream and asked them what would come of it?

"'Be not anxious, great king!' said the Brahmins; 'a child has planted itself in the womb of your queen....You will have a son. And he, if he continue to live the household life, will become a Universal Monarch; but if he leave the household life and retire from the world, he will become a Buddha, and roll back the clouds of sin and folly of this world.'"†

There is a cosmic metaphysical symbolism in the wondrous conception and birth of Jesus. His incarnate Christ Consciousness came immaculately through the Virgin Mary. Likewise, the universal Christ Intelligence was born or reflected in the cosmic body of pure vibratory creation (Cosmic "Virgin Mary") through the instrumentality of God the Father. The Holy Ghost Cosmic Vibration, *Aum,* Maha-Prakriti, is analogous to the Cosmic Virgin Mary because it is thus the mother of the immanent Universal Christ Intelligence, the Son of God, and of all created objects.

---

* Symbolizing pure divine wisdom and royalty. In the Bhagavad Gita, the Lord says: "Among stallions, know Me to be the nectar-born Uchchaihshravas; among elephants, Indra's white elephant, Airavata; and among men, the emperor" (*God Talks With Arjuna: The Bhagavad Gita* x:27). The elephant is a symbol of wisdom. Significantly, Airavata is referred to as the guardian or supporter "of the east quarter" (in man's body, the "east" or center of wisdom in the forehead). The word *Indra* ["king of the gods"] implies one who is a conqueror of the senses (*indriya*). Wisdom is the vehicle of the yogi who has conquered his senses. God is indeed prominently manifested in the colossal wisdom of the sense conqueror.

† The Harvard Classics, Volume 45, Part 3: *Buddhist Writings,* trans. Henry Clarke Warren (New York: Collier, 1909).

*N*ow Elisabeth's full time *came that she should be delivered; and she brought forth a son. And her* neighbours and her cousins heard how the Lord had shewed great mercy upon her; and they rejoiced with her.

And it came to pass, that on the eighth day they came to circumcise the child; and they called him Zacharias, after the name of his father. And his mother answered and said, "Not so; but he shall be called John."

And they said unto her, "There is none of thy kindred that is called by this name." And they made signs to his father, how he would have him called. And he asked for a writing table, and wrote, saying, "His name is John." And they marvelled all. And his mouth was opened immediately, and his tongue loosed, and he spake, and praised God. And fear came on all that dwelt round about them: and all these sayings were noised abroad throughout all the hill country of Judea. And all they that heard them laid them up in their hearts, saying, "What manner of child shall this be!" And the hand of the Lord was with him.

And his father Zacharias was filled with the Holy Ghost, and prophesied, saying, "Blessed be the Lord God of Israel; for He hath visited and redeemed His people....And thou, child, shalt be called the prophet of the Highest: for thou shalt go before the face of the Lord to prepare his ways; to give knowledge of salvation unto his people by the remission of their sins, through the tender mercy of our God; whereby the dayspring from on high hath visited us, to give light to them that sit in darkness and in the shadow of death, to guide our feet into the way of peace."

And the child grew, and waxed strong in spirit, and was in the deserts till the day of his shewing unto Israel.

—Luke 1:57–68, 76–80

The Birth of Jesus
and the Adoration
of the Three Wise Men

Spiritual Celebration of Jesus' Birth:
Communion With the Infinite Christ in Meditation

❖

Jesus' Connection With India
Through the "Wise Men From the East"

❖

The Spiritual Eye: True "Star in the East"

❖

Infinite Power Manifested in the Little Babe Jesus

"Fear not: for, behold, I bring you good tidings of great joy, which shall be to all people. For unto you is born this day in the city of David a Saviour, which is Christ the Lord."

And it came to pass in those days, that there went out a decree from Caesar Augustus, that all the world should be taxed. (And this taxing was first made when Cyrenius was governor of Syria.) And all went to be taxed, every one into his own city. And Joseph also went up from Galilee, out of the city of Nazareth, into Judea, unto the city of David, which is called Bethlehem; (because he was of the house and lineage of David:) to be taxed with Mary his espoused wife, being great with child.

And so it was, that, while they were there, the days were accomplished that she should be delivered. And she brought forth her firstborn son, and wrapped him in swaddling clothes, and laid him in a manger; because there was no room for them in the inn.

And there were in the same country shepherds abiding in the field, keeping watch over their flock by night. And, lo, the angel of the Lord came upon them, and the glory of the Lord shone round about them: and they were sore afraid.

And the angel said unto them, "Fear not: for, behold, I bring you good tidings of great joy, which shall be to all people. For unto you is born this day in the city of David a Saviour, which is Christ the Lord. And this shall be a sign unto you; ye shall find the babe wrapped in swaddling clothes, lying in a manger."

And suddenly there was with the angel a multitude of the heavenly host praising God, and saying, "Glory to God in the highest, and on earth peace, good will toward men."

—Luke 2:1–14

Now when Jesus was born in Bethlehem of Judea in the days of Herod the king,* behold, there came wise men from the east to Jerusalem, saying, "Where is he that is born King

---

* According to nonbiblical historical records, Herod died in 4 B.C. Most modern scholars therefore believe that Jesus' birth occurred sometime between 7 and 4 B.C. *(Publisher's Note)*

of the Jews? for we have seen his star in the east, and are come to worship him."

When Herod the king had heard these things, he was troubled, and all Jerusalem with him. And when he had gathered all the chief priests and scribes of the people together, he demanded of them where Christ should be born.

And they said unto him, "In Bethlehem of Judea: for thus it is written by the prophet, 'And thou Bethlehem, in the land of Juda, art not the least among the princes of Juda: for out of thee shall come a Governor, that shall rule my people Israel.'"*

Then Herod, when he had privily called the wise men, enquired of them diligently what time the star appeared. And he sent them to Bethlehem, and said, "Go and search diligently for the young child; and when ye have found him, bring me word again, that I may come and worship him also."

When they had heard the king, they departed; and, lo, the star, which they saw in the east, went before them, till it came and stood over where the young child was. When they saw the star, they rejoiced with exceeding great joy. And when they were come into the house, they saw the young child with Mary his mother, and fell down, and worshipped him: and when they had opened their treasures, they presented unto him gifts; gold, and frankincense, and myrrh.

And being warned of God in a dream that they should not return to Herod, they departed into their own country another way.

—Matthew 2:1–12

---

* The prophecy referred to is in Micah 5:2.

The Birth of Jesus and the Adoration of the Three Wise Men

To simple persons, pure in heart, God sometimes proclaims a message or event of import to the masses. Such revelations have been well documented and attested to: for example, the visions of Saint Bernadette that brought forth the miraculous healing waters at Lourdes, which have benefited generations since; and the prophecies of Fatima conveyed to three peasant children, confirmed by a phenomenon witnessed by thousands when the heavens seemed to open and the sun appeared to hurtle toward earth. And one whose authenticity I personally witnessed, the testament of the holy Bavarian peasant Therese Neumann, who relives in vision the life of Christ and bears on her own body the marks of his crucifixion. Perhaps the Lord wisely concludes that astounding news might be better received by the common man if conveyed through one (or a few) of their own. Self-lauding orators with messianic ambitions make notoriously unreliable messengers. To my knowledge, an egotist has never been so entrusted with the word of God to man, notwithstanding avowed assertions.

On that first "Christmas" night, lowly shepherds, the Bible tells us, were blessed to behold the heralding of the birth of Jesus. God and His heavenly host celebrate the earthly incarnations of great ones whose lives are ordained to influence the destiny of man. It was the celestial rejoicing at the advent of Jesus' birth that was seen by the shepherds. Perception of the finer vibratory dimensions are unperceived by the gross sensory instruments of the body; but through the touch of God's grace, the veil of matter is parted, and with sight divine of the soul's spiritual eye of intuitive perception glimpses of the heavenly spheres and beings are revealed.

The pageantry of Jesus' coming to earth lacked no detail of symbolic significance. As with the shepherds on the hillside, the shepherds of man's faith, devotion, and meditation will be bathed in the light of realization and lead those devotees who are humble in spirit to behold the infinite presence of Christ newborn within them.

The observance by God and His hierarchy of the incarnation of divine ones is not only at the time of such a birth, but during succeeding celebrations of natal anniversaries as well. Each year at Christmastime there are stronger than usual vibrations of Christ-love and joy that emanate to earth from the heavenly realms. The ether becomes filled with the Infinite Light that shone on earth when Jesus was born. Those persons who are in tune through devotion and deep meditation feel in a wondrously tangible way the transforming vibrations of the omnipresent consciousness that was in Christ Jesus.

Spiritual celebration of Jesus' birth: communion with the Infinite Christ in meditation

To celebrate the birth of Jesus in solely materialistic ways is a desecration of the meaning of his holy life and of the immortal message of divine love and God-union that he preached. Seeing in the West the shallow, often irreverent, observance given to the birth anniversary of this great avatar, I inaugurated in Self-Realization Fellowship the spiritual celebration of Christmas, before Christmas Day festivities, by devoting a daylong meditation service to the worship of Christ. The ideal is to honor Christ in spirit in meditation from morning till evening, absorbed in feeling in one's own consciousness the Infinite Christ that was born in Jesus. That experience is one of profound peace and joy, more than a human heart has ever known—expanding into an all-embracing consciousness. Often has the form of Jesus appeared before me during these services—such love in those eyes! It is my prayer—and my conviction that it will come to pass—that comparable observances of the real meaning of Christmas will become a tradition throughout the world.

The message of the "heavenly host" to the shepherds in the countryside of Bethlehem was "on earth peace, good will toward men." Peace in the world starts with peace in individual hearts. "The peace of God, which passeth all understanding"* is the peace Jesus came to bring to man; it is the only sure foundation for world amity. It is found in the interiorized state of one's God-communion in meditation. Then, like an ever full reservoir, it pours out freely to one's family, friends, community, nation, and the world. If everyone lived the ideals exemplified in the life of Jesus, having made those qualities a part of their own selves through meditation, a millennium of peace and brotherhood would come on earth.

A person who is imbued with God's peace can feel naught but goodwill toward all. The crib of ordinary consciousness is very small, filled to capacity with self-love. The cradle of goodwill of Christ-love holds the Infinite Consciousness that includes all beings, all nations, all races and faiths as one.

Legends abound concerning the worship of the infant Jesus by the "wise men from the east." A common tradition is that they were magi (Hebrew *chartumim*; Greek *magoi*), a priestly class of mystics among ancient Medes and Persians credited with esoteric powers and knowledge by which they were able to interpret hidden meanings in the scriptures and to read secrets of the past and divine the future. The Roman Church honored the Wise Men with the title of kings, based on Psalms 72:10 relevant to the future coming of the Messiah: "The kings of Tarshish and of the isles shall bring presents: the kings of Sheba and Saba shall offer gifts." The kings are sainted by the Church and identified as Gaspar, Melchior, and Balthasar; relics of these kings are enshrined at Cologne. The Wise Men are presumed to be three in number, commensurate with the New Testament account of the offering of three gifts: gold, frankincense, and myrrh.

Jesus' connection with India through the "wise men from the east"

The adoration of the Wise Men is far more significant than merely another scene of pageantry recognizing the holy birth. It was the defining stamp of God placed on the life of Jesus that would in future characterize his mission and message—a reminder that Jesus was born in the Orient, an Oriental Christ; and that his teachings bore the influence of the Eastern culture and customs. There is a very strong tradition in India, authoritatively known amongst high metaphysicians in tales well told and written in ancient

---

* Philippians 4:7.

manuscripts, that the wise men of the East who made their way to the infant Jesus in Bethlehem were, in fact, great sages of India. Not only did the Indian masters come to Jesus, but he reciprocated their visit. During the unaccounted-for years of Jesus' life—the Scripture remains silent about him from approximately ages fourteen to thirty—he journeyed to India, probably traveling the well-established trade route that linked the Mediterranean with China and India.* His own God-realization, re-awakened and reinforced in the company of the masters and the spiritual environs of India, provided a background of the universality of truth from which he could preach a simple, open message comprehensible to the masses of his native country, yet with underlying meanings that would be appreciated in generations to come as the infancy of man's mind would mature in understanding.

As civilization takes giant strides in the proliferation of material knowledge, man will find that the underpinnings of many of his old fa-

---

* See also Discourse 5.

"Tradition pictures the world of Jesus as a peaceful and pastoral place, governed by the ancient rhythms of field and farm. But recent archaeological evidence has revealed a different environment," reports the PBS television documentary *From Jesus to Christ* (Frontline, 1998). In the early 1970s, archaeologists began to excavate the ruins of the ancient city of Sepphoris, the capital of Galilee, located less than four miles from Jesus' hometown of Nazareth—within an hour's walking distance. "What the excavations at Sepphoris suggest," says Professor Holland L. Hendrix, president of Union Theological Seminary, "is that Jesus was quite proximate to a thriving and sophisticated urban environment that would have brought with it all of the diversity of the Roman Empire."

Professor D. P. Singhal writes in *India and World Civilization* (Michigan State University Press, 1969, Vol. I): "The traditional account of Christian origins concentrates almost exclusively on the incidents connected with the rise of Christianity, giving the impression that nothing else was happening at that time in the area. Actually the situation was vastly different. It was a period of intense political activity and diverse religious practices, and it would hardly be an overstatement to suggest that in every city and village in the Roman Empire there were activities, customs, and rituals that eventually played a part in the moulding of Christianity....

"Hinduism, though not a proselytizing religion, had also reached western Asia. A Hindu settlement was established in Armenia in the Canton of Taron in the second century B.C. under the patronage of King Valarasaces of the Arsacidae dynasty. These Hindus built fine cities and temples, but the temples were destroyed early in the fourth century by St. Gregory the Illuminator." Dr. Singhal cites the Syrian writer Zenob as saying that by "early in the fourth century A.D. there were about five thousand followers of Krishna in Armenia."

Dr. Singhal further avers: "Jesus, no doubt, principally enlarged and transformed the Jewish conceptions but he did so in the light of personal experiences in a cosmopolitan area where a variety of cultures, including that of India, had intermingled to produce a distinct religious environment." *(Publisher's Note)*

miliar religious dogmas may well begin to crack and crumble. What is needed is a reunion of the science of religion with the spirit, or inspiration, of religion—the esoteric with the exoteric. The yoga science taught by Lord Krishna, which provides practical methods for actual inner experience of God to supplant the feeble life-expectancy of beliefs, and the spirit of Christ-love and brotherhood preached by Jesus—the only sure panacea to prevent the world from tearing itself apart by its unyielding differences—are in tandem one and the same universal truth, taught by these two Christs of East and West, only with a variant outward emphasis according to the times and conditions of their respective incarnations.

The pages of this book invite the reader to reach back with the teachings of Jesus to the cradle of religion that has from ages unnumbered been tended by Mother India, and thence to the universality of religion in God-realization. In the words of Jesus: "Think not that I am come to destroy the law, or the prophets: I am not come to destroy, but to fulfill."* The great ones come to preserve and restate not the dogma and expedient customs of religion, but the eternal principles of truth enunciated from time to time by God-knowing prophets. Thus was the continuity of God's word through His avatars beautifully symbolized by the spiritual exchange between Jesus at his birth and the Wise Men of India come to honor his incarnation.†

As the prophets of the Old Testament foretold the coming of a Christ to be born in Bethlehem, so this major event of God's helping hand extended to man was foreknown also to the Wise Men with whom

---

* Matthew 5:17 (see Discourse 27).

† The words of the Gospel give no specific information about the origin of the Magi (or even their number); opinions as to their native land vary from Babylon, Arabia, Chaldea, or Persia—the latter deriving support from the fact that the Zoroastrian priests of the Persian religion were known as Magi. However, in *The Story of the Magi* (Bombay: Society of St. Paul, 1954), Henry Heras, S.J., Director of the Indian Historical Research Institute, St. Xavier's College, Bombay, presents an extensive array of historical information to support the view that the Wise Men were in fact Hindu *rishis* from India. (Father Heras's work was held in high repute; he was honored by the Government of India in 1981 with a commemorative stamp for his outstanding contribution to historical research and archaeology.)

According to Father Heras, in the Gospel the word *magoi* is not used to identify the Wise Men as Zoroastrian priests, "for if that were so, all the patristic tradition would have acknowledged Persia as the country of the Magi, which is not the case.... St. Matthew uses this name with reference to the gift of wisdom in general, that is to say, partakers of the gift of wisdom, sages. The English translation of this passage, 'Wise Men,' seems to give precisely the meaning intended by the author. But from what

Christ's life and mission were to be linked. Avatars often choose for their time of birth auspicious astronomical and astrological configurations of the heavenly bodies, all of which emit their own characteristic vibrations that interact with one another for good or ill effect. These starry signs can be read by the spiritual insight of men of God, perception not even remotely approachable by the elaborate charts attempted by modern casters of horoscopes. Whatever celestial star might have indicated to

---

country did the Wise Men hail?…Everything seems to indicate that the Wise Men were Indians, certain *rishis* of this country who from immemorial times made the quest of Truth—the eternal breath of this most ancient nation.…"

Long before the time of Christ, India had trade relations with Palestine; much of the commerce between the Orient and the Mediterranean civilizations (including Egypt, Greece, and Rome) passed through Jerusalem, the western terminus of the ancient Silk Road and other important caravan routes to China and India. East-west commerce is also referred to in the Bible (II Chronicles 9:21, 10), which records that the "ships of Tarshish" brought to King Solomon "gold, and silver, ivory, apes, and peacocks" and "algum [sandalwood] trees and precious stones" from Ophir (Sopara on the Bombay coast). Furthermore, scholarly and Christian tradition agree that Christianity arrived on the western coast of India very shortly after the time of Jesus, reportedly brought in person by one of Christ's twelve apostles, Thomas, who spent the last years of his life in India. Father Heras quotes an ancient Christian text called the *Opus Imperfectum in Mattheum,* which "locates the preaching of St. Thomas the Apostle in the land of the Magi. Ancient Oriental writers knew very well that India was the field of the ministry of this Apostle. St. Jerome writes that St. Thomas preached the Gospel to the Magi and finally slept, that is died, in India."

Father Heras points out: "If therefore the Magi were *rishis* of India, the traditional land of wisdom, it is not to be wondered at that they offered gold, frankincense, and myrrh to the infant and his mother, since these were precisely the gifts that from the most ancient times were offered in India to the parents of the newly born.…The custom of offering these three gifts to the parents of the recently born does not now exist in Persia; nor do scholars know that any such custom ever existed in that country."

Centuries-old traditions in India itself refer to the Wise Men as having come from that land. Fernao do Queyroz, a seventeenth-century Portuguese Jesuit priest who lived in Goa (Portuguese colony on the west coast of India), cited the work of earlier historians (Manuel dos Anjos and Jeronimo Osorio, both of the sixteenth century) who wrote that when the famous Portuguese explorer Vasco da Gama reached India in May 1498, he found at Calicut on the western coast a Hindu temple dedicated to the Virgin Mary. According to these Portuguese historians, da Gama was told that the annals of the Malabar Kingdom relate that the temple was founded by Chery Perimale ("Chera Perumal"), an ancient emperor of Malabar who also founded the city of Calicut. Da Gama was informed that Perimale "was a Brahmin, one of the wisest in India, and was one of the three Magi who went to Bethlehem" to adore the baby Jesus; on his return to Calicut he had the temple erected.

Another account is found in the writings of Joao De Barros, a sixteenth-century Portuguese historian, who mentions the Malabar tradition that a king from South India named "Pirimal" went to Mascate and thence with others to Bethlehem to adore the infant Jesus. *(Publisher's Note)*

the Wise Men the birth of Jesus, it was a "star in the east" of greater
power by which they knew of the coming on earth of Christ Jesus: the
all-revealing light of the spiritual eye of the soul's intuitive divine per-

_____•_•_____   ception located in the "east" of the body—in a sub-
The spiritual eye: true   tle spiritual center of Christ Consciousness in the
"star in the east"   forehead between the two physical eyes.*

Man is veritably a microcosm of the macro-
cosmic universe. His finite consciousness is potentially infinite. While
his physical sensory organs confine him to the world of matter, his
soul is endowed with all-powerful instruments of perception by which
God Himself may be known. Jesus said, "Behold, the kingdom of God
is within you."† All manifestation is of the Holy Ghost Vibration, imbued with the Intelligence and Power of the transcendental Cosmic
Consciousness of God the Father reflecting within vibratory creation
as Christ Consciousness. This trinity of God is manifested microcosmically in man as the spiritual eye. As the universe is created by the
Power and Intelligence of the Trinity, so is man upheld by the microcosmic triune power and consciousness in the spiritual eye.

During meditative concentration at the point between the eyebrows, the spiritual eye can be seen: a brilliant white star in the center, encased within a sphere of sapphire-blue light, encircled by a radiant golden aura. The golden light is the epitome of the vibratory

---

*In the Hindu scriptures the forehead in man is called the "eastern" part of his body.
Even as the earth's directional compass points are derived from the north and south magnetic poles, and from the earth's rotation on its axis which makes the sun appear to rise
in the east and set in the west, so yoga physiology speaks symbolically of north, south,
east, and west in relation to the microcosm of the human body. "North" and "south"
are the positive and negative poles of the cerebrospinal axis. Life energy and consciousness are magnetically drawn either upward to the higher spiritual centers in the brain
("north") or downward to the lower spinal centers associated with material consciousness ("south"). "East" and "west" refer to the orientation of man's life and awareness
either inward ("east") through the intuitive spiritual eye to perceptions of the subtle divine realms or outward ("west") through the senses to interaction with the gross material creation. The "star in the east" thus symbolizes the spiritual eye in the forehead—
the sun of life in the human body and doorway to the inner kingdom of God.

Ezekiel said: "Afterwards He brought me to the gate, even the gate that looketh
toward the east: and, behold, the glory of the God of Israel came from the way of the
east: and His voice was like a noise of many waters: and the earth shined with His
glory" (Ezekiel 43:1–2). Through the divine eye in the forehead (east), the yogi sails
his consciousness into omnipresence, hearing the Word or *Aum,* divine sound of "many
waters": the vibrations of light that constitute the sole reality of creation.

† Luke 17:21 (see Discourse 61).

sphere of the Holy Ghost; the blue light is the omnipresent Intelligence of the Christ Consciousness; the star is the mystic door into the Cosmic Consciousness of God the Father.

Jesus said, "If therefore thine eye be single, thy whole body shall be full of light."* Any devotee who, by the practice of yoga meditation, knows how to focus his inward gaze at the point between the eyebrows, finds that the light traveling through the optic nerves into the two physical eyes becomes concentrated instead into the single visible spiritual eye. The two physical eyes perceive only limited portions at a time of the world of relativity; the vision of the spiritual eye is spherical and can see into omnipresence.

By deep meditation the devotee penetrates his consciousness and life force through the tricolored lights of the spiritual eye into the macrocosmic manifestation of the Trinity.

When the Wise Men saw a star intimating to them the birth of Christ, they were beholding through the wisdom-star of infinite perception in their spiritual eye where the Christ Consciousness was newly manifested in the body of infant Jesus.†

We think of the baby Jesus as helpless in his crib, dependent on his mother's milk and care; yet within that tiny form was the Infinite Christ, the Light of the universe in which we are all dancing as motion-picture shadows. During one of our day-long Christmas meditations, when I prayed to see the baby Christ, the light of the spiritual eye in my forehead opened its rays, and I saw Jesus as an infant.

Infinite power manifested in the little babe Jesus

He appeared in such beauty and power of God. All the forces of nature were playing in that baby-face. In the light of those eyes the universe trembled—waiting for the command of those eyes. Such was the infant the Wise Men beheld—a little child over whom the angels stood watch, and in whom the whole universal consciousness was manifest.

---

* Matthew 6:22 (see Discourse 28).

† Saint John Chrysostom (c. 347–407, bishop of Constantinople, Doctor of the Church, greatest of the Greek Church Fathers) wrote in his "Sixth Homily on the Gospel of Saint Matthew": "It seems to me that not only was it not one of the many stars, but that it was not a star at all; it was rather, in my belief, a certain invisible power that looked like a star....This star appeared not only by night but also during the day when the Sun shone over the skies....Had it been in the high skies, it could hardly guide the travelers...for it is impossible that a star can show the place in which a cottage stands; much less still, the place in which the Babe lay down."

Spiritual signs appear on the body and face of one who is a realized soul; these signs are held secret, and only a few know how to read them. By these signs, and by their sight divine, the Wise Men were able to know they had found the Christ they sought, the babe who was one with the Lord of the Universe. They knelt and offered their symbolic gifts. These were the traditional gifts given in India to the newborn; but they held further meaning coming from the Wise Men to Jesus: Gold (material treasure) is offered to a giver of wisdom as a symbol of appreciation of the great value of liberating truth bestowed by the spiritual teacher. Incense symbolizes devotion, the fragrance of the heart's love offered to the master who is a channel through whom God's guidance and blessings flow. The myrrh was in recognition of the bitter trial and sacrifice that would be required of Jesus in fulfilling his divine mission.

On a transcendent level of consciousness, in which others could neither participate nor bear witness, there was a spiritual exchange of soul-communion concerning the destiny of Jesus, which would be of universal benefit to man—as Jesus would be one of God's supreme message-bearers of Truth.*

---

* Among Westerners who concur that the Wise Men came from India is the great twentieth-century mystic and stigmatist Therese Neumann of Konnersreuth, Germany, who experienced weekly visions of Jesus' passion and crucifixion, the "stations of the cross." (See *Autobiography of a Yogi,* Chapter 39.) In *Therese of Konnersreuth: A New Chronicle,* by Friedrich Ritter von Lama (Milwaukee: Bruce Publishing Company, 1935), the following incident is related:

"The visit to Konnersreuth in September, 1932, of His Excellency Bishop Alexander Chulaparambil of Kottayam, India, with the Reverend Father Theccanat, the rector of the Bishop's seminary, afforded interesting evidence of Therese's ability in the state of ecstasy and corporal blindness to recognize what must be unknown to her in a normal state. The companion of His Excellency wrote me as follows: 'Neither Therese nor the pastor knew of our coming....Therese had just witnessed the Station in which Simon of Cyrene appears and now, in a period of rest, was talking of what she had seen and heard....and repeated in Syrian (that is, Aramaic) the words *"Slanlak Malka de Judae!"* (Hail, King of the Jews!) We were of course astounded at hearing these words. The Bishop, who belongs to the Syro-Malabarian Rite, repeated them, but Therese corrected his expression, saying: "Perhaps you speak the words as they are written, but I heard them this way," and she repeated them. Thereupon we recognized the mistake we had made. We had used a short *a* in the last syllable of the first word, whereas it ought to be a long *a,* as Therese used it....After a few minutes Father Naber motioned to His Excellency to come close to the bed. When the Bishop touched Therese's left hand, she held it fast. "This is a high pastor from the land whence the Kings came to worship the Christ Child," [she said.]'" *(Publisher's Note)*

The Visit of the Three Wise Men

Behold, there came wise men from the east to Jerusalem, saying, "Where is he that is born King of the Jews? for we have seen his star in the east, and are come to worship him."...

And when they were come into the house, they saw the young child with Mary his mother, and fell down, and worshipped him: and when they had opened their treasures, they presented unto him gifts; gold, and frankincense, and myrrh.

—Matthew 2:1–2, 11

There is a very strong tradition in India, authoritatively known amongst high metaphysicians in tales well told and written in ancient manuscripts, that the wise men of the East who made their way to the infant Jesus in Bethlehem were, in fact, great sages of India....

We think of the baby Jesus as helpless in his crib, dependent on his mother's milk and care; yet within that tiny form was the Infinite Christ, the Light of the universe in which we are all dancing as motion-picture shadows. During one of our daylong Christmas meditations, when I prayed to see the baby Christ...I saw Jesus as an infant. He appeared in such beauty and power of God. All the forces of nature were playing in that baby-face. In the light of those eyes the universe trembled—waiting for the command of those eyes. Such was the infant the Wise Men beheld....

—Paramahansa Yogananda

Drawing by Heinrich Hofmann

The Infancy and Youth
of Jesus

"My purpose in noting the broader narratives of Jesus' life available in ancient records is not to insinuate their authenticity or opine as to their factualness, but rather to suggest their plausibility against the background of India's vast spiritual tradition of saints, rishis, and avatars."

And when they [the Wise Men from the East] *were departed, behold, the angel of the Lord appeareth to Joseph in a dream, saying, "Arise, and take the young child and his mother, and flee into Egypt, and be thou there until I bring thee word: for Herod will seek the young child to destroy him." When he arose, he took the young child and his mother by night, and departed into Egypt: And was there until the death of Herod: that it might be fulfilled which was spoken of the Lord by the prophet, saying, "Out of Egypt have I called My son."*

Then Herod, when he saw that he was mocked of the wise men, was exceeding wroth, and sent forth, and slew all the children that were in Bethlehem, and in all the coasts thereof, from two years old and under, according to the time which he had diligently enquired of the wise men. Then was fulfilled that which was spoken by Jeremiah the prophet, saying, "In Ramah was there a voice heard, lamentation, and weeping, and great mourning, Rachel weeping for her children, and would not be comforted, because they are not."

But when Herod was dead, behold, an angel of the Lord appeareth in a dream to Joseph in Egypt, saying, "Arise, and take the young child and his mother, and go into the land of Israel: for they are dead which sought the young child's life." And he arose, and took the young child and his mother, and came into the land of Israel. But when he heard that Archelaus did reign in Judea in the room of his father Herod, he was afraid to go thither: notwithstanding, being warned of God in a dream, he turned aside into the parts of Galilee: And he came and dwelt in a city called Nazareth: that it might be fulfilled which was spoken by the prophets, "He shall be called a Nazarene."

—Matthew 2:13–23

And the child grew, and waxed strong in spirit, filled with wisdom: and the grace of God was upon him.

Now his parents went to Jerusalem every year at the feast of the Passover. And when he was twelve years old, they went up to Jerusalem after the custom of the feast.

And when they had fulfilled the days, as they returned, the child Jesus tarried behind in Jerusalem; and Joseph and his mother knew not of it. But they, supposing him to have been in the company, went a day's journey; and they sought him among their kinsfolk and acquaintance. And when they found him not, they turned back again to Jerusalem, seeking him. And it came to pass, that after three days they found him in the temple, sitting in the midst of the doctors, both hearing them, and asking them questions. And all that heard him were astonished at his understanding and answers.

And when they saw him, they were amazed: and his mother said unto him, "Son, why hast thou thus dealt with us? Behold, thy father and I have sought thee sorrowing."

And he said unto them, "How is it that ye sought me? Wist ye not that I must be about my Father's business?" And they understood not the saying which he spake unto them. And he went down with them, and came to Nazareth, and was subject unto them: but his mother kept all these sayings in her heart.

—Luke 2:40–51

DISCOURSE 4

The Infancy and Youth of Jesus

And the child grew, and waxed strong in spirit, filled with wisdom: and the grace of God was upon him (Luke 2:40).

The Gospels of the New Testament contain an inordinate paucity of information concerning the early years of Jesus. The verses are silent about the entire period of his infancy in Egypt and his youth in Israel, with the one exception of Luke's account of the twelve-year-old boy sagely disputing with the learned men in the temple in Jerusalem. Either unknown or discountenanced by the general Christian populace are ancient manuscripts that purport to relate anecdotes about the child Jesus. Titled simply as "The Gospels of the Infancy of Jesus Christ" (of which one is attributed to Jesus' disciple Thomas), these are referenced as in use and held sacred by some Christians, including the Gnostics, as early as the second century, and by other Christian sects in the following ages.*

Time works on men's minds, especially on those removed from the instant of happening, to enhance or detract from the character of noteworthy personages and the events associated with their lives. If these are of religious import, transformations of facts into legend seem to be

---

* The texts to which Paramahansaji refers were a part of *The Apocryphal New Testament*, edited and annotated by William Hone (fourth edition, published in London in 1821). The book's title page identifies it as "being all the gospels, epistles, and other pieces now extant, attributed in the first four centuries to Jesus Christ, his apostles, and their companions, and not included in the New Testament by its compilers." Two "infancy gospels" are included in Hone's volume. The first, now called The Arabic Infancy Gospel, was translated into English in 1697 by Henry Sike, professor of oriental languages at Cambridge University, from an Arabic manuscript, which current

66

even more precipitate. Yet who can gainsay that the charm and mystery of pulling the threads of truth from the fabric of legendary tellings does not produce a singular inspiration and awe absent in the merely prosaic? India well understood this and cloaked her most sacred spiritual wealth and the godly givers of this treasure with symbology and a depth of meaningful mythology that has preserved her scriptural principles and codes through-

—————•–•–•—————

Alternative voices from antiquity: scriptural fact or heretical fiction?

out generations of foreign domination and influence. Perhaps the voices from antiquity should not be altogether silenced by offhand dismissal from our mental consideration. Discriminative perusal, however, is certainly warranted. Both innocent distortion and outright willful falsity are inevitable when truth is passed through the interpretations of successive generations, or even of individuals within a single generation, each of which finds it expedient to make it "clearly understood" according to what best suits the present time and purpose.

This sorting out of fact from fiction to maintain the integrity of the Christian church and doctrine was clearly the intention of the early church fathers. The twenty-seven books of the New Testament that today constitute the Biblical account of the life and teaching of Jesus were gleaned by the early church from a much larger collection of texts.* Councils of the so-called learned were assembled to debate and determine holy doctrine from heresy. Propounders who were judged to be heretics

---

scholars believe was derived from an earlier version in the Syriac language (a dialect of Aramaic). Some of the stories therein also appear in the Koran.

The second Infancy Gospel included in Hone's book is a short fragment of The Infancy Gospel of Thomas. A manuscript of this gospel that is more complete than what Hone reproduced was later discovered and is readily available in works by later scholars; indeed, much of the material in the Arabic Infancy Gospel is now thought to have come from the earlier Infancy Gospel of Thomas. The very early origins of the material in Thomas' text are attested to by a reference to them in writings by the church father Irenaeus in A.D. 185.

Interestingly, Hone mentions the fact that in 1599 it was discovered that the Arabic Infancy Gospel was in use by a congregation of Nestorian Christians active in the mountains of Malabar on the coast of India. Traditionally, this is the area associated with the missionary activity of the apostle Thomas himself (see page 59 n.). *(Publisher's Note)*

* "And there are also many other things which Jesus did, the which, if they should be written every one, I suppose that even the world itself could not contain the books that should be written" (John 21:25).

Andrew Bernhard, author of *Jesus of Nazareth in Early Christian Gospels*, writes: "Comments such as the conclusion of the Gospel of John (21:25) make it clear that

might find themselves condemned to the flames along with their writings. One wonders how honest an appraisal could be made by an individual member of one of these councils when not only their reputation but their very life depended on the favor of a political and religious hierarchy.

William Hone, in *The Apocryphal New Testament*, cites a legendary telling—at which one must wonder—of events at the Council of Nicaea, convened by Emperor Constantine in A.D. 325, which recounts how some three hundred bishops, having "promiscuously put all the books that were referred to the Council for determination under the communion table in a church, they besought the Lord that the inspired writings might get upon the table, while the spurious ones remained underneath, and that it happened accordingly." In regard to the bishops assembled at this Council, annotator Hone remarks: "The Emperor Constantine says, that what was approved by these bishops could be nothing less than the determination of God Himself; since the Holy Spirit residing in such great and worthy souls, unfolded to them the divine will. Yet Sabinus, the Bishop of Heraclea, affirms that 'excepting Constantine himself, and Eusebius Pamphilus, these were a set of illiterate simple creatures that understood nothing.'" One can hardly suppress at least a modicum of mental fraternity with the commentator John Jortin (1698–1770; archdeacon of London) who, we are told by Hone, in analyzing the authority of these General Councils wryly concluded: "The Council held by the Apostles at Jerusalem [Acts 1] was the first and the last in which the Holy Spirit may be affirmed to have presided."*

The influence of the dark age in which Jesus took incarnation, and which continued for several successive centuries, may well be faulted as providing a confounding background of ignorance and superstition that led the church fathers to exclude certain texts from the official canon of scripture. It is not altogether surprising that in attempting to

---

early Christians had no shortage of stories about Jesus. They undoubtedly spoke often of their recently departed master, sharing all that they remembered of him with each other and anyone else who was willing to listen. When it became evident that Jesus' memory could not be preserved forever by oral traditions dependent on the recollections of first-hand witnesses, some of his followers decided to write down what they believed about him for posterity. According to the Gospel of Luke (1:1–4), 'many' ancient writers endeavored 'to draw up an account' of the activities of Jesus. Although many of these accounts did not ultimately become New Testament gospels, they are identified and described in the writings of numerous early Christian authors, such as Origen (*Homily on Luke* 1:1)." *(Publisher's Note)*

* John Jortin, *Remarks on Ecclesiastical History,* Vol. II.

define and preserve the memory and message of Jesus, believers were wont to err on the side of authenticating only those doctrines and texts that would best defend the new faith against contrary or diluting forces and secure the power of church hierarchy as the supreme keepers of the faith. Above all, their doctrinal concept of what the nature and acts of Jesus should be as the unique and perfect Son of God come to earth, with all that this implied to the understanding of the times, was in no measure to be compromised.*

Influence of a dark age on the official canon of scripture

The absolute proof of truth must pass more than the reasoned analysis of pedants, the prayers of faith of ecclesiastics, the scientific testing of dedicated researchers; the ultimate validation of any doctrine lies in the actual personal realization of those who touch the Sole Reality. Diversity of opinion in religious matters will doubtless persist so long as the masses are still wanting in such qualification. Nevertheless, God must enjoy the heterogenous medley in His human family, for He has not troubled Himself to write clear directions across the heavens for all alike to see and follow in unity.

My purpose in noting the broader narratives of Jesus' life available in ancient records is not to insinuate their authenticity or opine as to their factualness, but rather to suggest their plausibility against the background of India's vast spiritual tradition of saints, *rishis,* and

---

* The first appearance of the specific compilation of books that today are known as the New Testament was in A.D. 367.

For centuries, the existence of many of the texts that were suppressed and destroyed was virtually unknown to scholars and believers alike. Some of them came to light in the famous discovery at Nag Hammadi, Egypt, in 1945. Because of the Nag Hammadi discoveries, writes Elaine Pagels, Ph.D., professor of religion at Princeton University and a renowned scholar of early Christianity, "we now begin to see that what we call Christianity—and what we identify as Christian tradition—actually represents only a small selection of specific sources, chosen from among dozens of others....

"By A.D. 200...Christianity had become an institution headed by a three-rank hierarchy of bishops, priests, and deacons, who understood themselves to be the guardians of the only 'true faith.'...The efforts of the majority to destroy every trace of heretical 'blasphemy' proved so successful that, until the discoveries at Nag Hammadi, nearly all our information concerning alternative forms of early Christianity came from the massive orthodox attacks upon them....Had they been discovered 1,000 years earlier, [these] texts almost certainly would have been burned for their heresy....Today we read them with different eyes, not merely as 'madness and blasphemy' but as Christians in the first centuries experienced them—a powerful alternative to what we know as orthodox Christian tradition."—Elaine Pagels, *The Gnostic Gospels* (New York: Vintage Books, 1981). *(Publisher's Note)*

avatars. The spiritually exceptional is quite the norm for incarnate souls who are able to pierce the veils of deceptive *maya* and behold the Lord's creation from His perspective. How else may the devotee and seeker recognize and appreciate the inner divinity of a godly person, except that it be manifested and extolled in the uncommon features and acts that characterize that life. A "miraculous" life may be a subtle vibratory influence that has the power to uplift others from ignorance, or it may be dramatic demonstrations as employed by Jesus to rouse faith in the power and word of God.

One of the difficulties encountered in Western perception of divinity is the mindset that one is either human or divine. If human, he is made

Human as well as divine attributes evidenced in the lives of avatars

in man's image and subject to all the flaws inherent therein; if divine, he is made in God's image and must bear no hint of imperfection. But India's Vedic wisdom, and especially Bhagavan Krishna's yoga science in the Bhagavad Gita, quite reconciles human attributes and divinity in those whose consciousness transcends the ordinary and realizes its oneness with God. As the very existence of manifestation is the result of a complex formula of laws and forces activated by the catalyst of *maya*—the delusive factor that divides and differentiates the one consciousness of Spirit into diverse forms—a divine being cannot even assume and maintain a corporeal form without becoming subject to the principles that create and sustain manifestation. Thus the divine being undergoes the natural experiences associated with the limited instrumentality of the body and the effects of its environment, while at the same time his soul remains unbeclouded by the cosmic hypnosis of *maya* that stultifies the common man.

The accounts in the Infancy Gospels concerning the acts of Jesus would not be considered at all surprising or unexpected by the Eastern mind. In referring to these texts, William Hone notes in the preface to his second edition of *The Apocryphal New Testament* that "the legends of the Koran and the Hindoo Mythology are considerably connected with this volume. Many of the acts and miracles ascribed to the Indian God, Creeshna [Krishna], during his incarnation, are precisely the same with those attributed to Christ in his infancy by the Apocryphal Gospels, and are largely particularized by the Rev. Thomas Maurice in his learned *History of Hindostan*."*

---

* London: W. Bulmer and Co., 1795.

"Miracles" according to the will of God exude from His divine emissaries, whether consciously initiated or spontaneously expressed through the physical instrumentality from the superconscious motivation of the indwelling God-tuned soul. Thus even in childhood Jesus possessed great powers, akin to those he had manifested in his previous incarnation as Elisha, presaging the miracles of his adult ministry that showed command over life and death and over natural laws that do not yield their fixity except at a divine command. In the Infancy Gospels, Jesus is said to have spoken to his mother, even from the cradle, declaring his divine descent and world mission. When, as was the custom, the infant on the fortieth day after birth was presented to God at the temple in Jerusalem, "angels stood around him, adoring him, as a king's guard stands around him." When honored by the Wise Men from the East, Mary gave to them one of the swaddling clothes in which Jesus was wrapped; "at the same time there appeared to them an angel in the form of that star which had been their guide in their journey." On their return to their own country, "kings and princes came to them, enquiring what they had seen and done." They produced the swaddling cloth, and according to custom prepared a fire and worshiped the cloth and cast it into the sacred flame. "And when the fire was put out, they took forth the swaddling cloth unhurt, as much as if the fire had not touched it."

When King Herod, fearing the prophecy of the birth in Bethlehem of an almighty king, ordered the death of all infants, and God warned Joseph to flee into Egypt with Mary and Jesus, several miracles occurred in the land of their exile in the presence of the holy child. The Infancy Gospels relate how the son of an Egyptian high priest is *Miracles ascribed to the child Jesus* cured of possession by devils, and the famous idol tended by his father inexplicably falls down and is destroyed, to the great terror of worshipers. A woman is dispossessed of a devil; a bride struck dumb by sorcerers is healed when she takes the infant Jesus lovingly in her arms. So also, others are cured of infirmities, including leprosy and other ills, sometimes by pouring over their body the water that had been used to bathe the infant Jesus.

Jesus, Joseph, and Mary, according to the apocryphal texts, abode three years in Egypt.*

---

* In a note to his edition of *The Apocryphal New Testament* (1821), William Hone

On return to Israel, a litany of similar miracles ascribed to the infant Jesus continues. As the child emerges from infancy, he begins a more conscious wielding of his God-given powers. The legendary tellings might well be misconstrued as describing a child with powers over matter and life and death itself who is of a capricious, even petulant, nature, at whose command the elements obey. Certainly, in and of itself this literal acceptance of the tales would rightly doom them to the ash heap of heresy. Whatever vestiges of authenticity may breathe within these legends must be viewed in the light of the singular purpose for which saviors come to earth. No vindictive or arrogant intent motivates the actions of such a one. If indeed, according to the accounts, some persons were withered or struck blind or lifeless in their encounters with the child Jesus, it was through his command that some consequence from their past-life evils was thereby mitigated. Correspondingly, children who taunted Elisha were destroyed by bears summoned from the woods by the prophet, not as an act of wrath, but in recognition of a present cause providing the opportunity for the atonement and expiation of long-past evil actions — fruition of the law of karma, cause and effect, God's law of justice.* It is, in fact, noted in the scriptures of India that karmic justice dispensed by the hand of

---

writes of a tradition traceable to Peter, third-century bishop of Alexandria, who purportedly said that "the place in Egypt where Christ was banished is now called Matarea, about ten miles beyond Cairo; that the inhabitants constantly burn a lamp in remembrance of it; and that there is a garden of trees yielding a balsam, which were planted by Christ when a boy." (The Infancy Gospel itself refers to the balsam trees as having grown on that site after Mary washed Jesus' clothes there in a spring that gushed forth at the command of the divine child.)

* "It is written in the Bible (II Kings 2:24) that a crowd of children ridiculed the prophet Elisha. He then 'cursed them in the name of the Lord. And there came forth two she bears out of the wood, and tare forty and two children of them.' As a prophet of God, Elisha was acting as His instrument. The curse was karmically ordained through God's law; hence Elisha cannot be accused of causing the mutilation of the children. They suffered because of their own wickedness — the accumulation of their wrong thoughts and actions of past lives. Their seemingly childish taunting was the timely fruition of their past evil, which precipitated its inevitable consequence. The 'curse' that issued forth from the instrumental Elisha was the 'high voltage' of his spiritual vibration, operating with no selfish intent to harm.

"If a man disregards a warning not to touch a live wire and is electrocuted, it is not the live wire but the man's foolishness that is responsible for his death. The same truth applies in the case of the wicked children who mocked Elisha. It is the story of all evil opposition to the righteous will of God: Evil eventually causes its own destruction." — God Talks With Arjuna: The Bhagavad Gita

an emissary of God is a privileged blessing leading to that chastened soul's liberation. Thus only with divine purpose does the god-king Krishna slay those of evil doing. Similarly, God's just law manifests through the child Jesus not to maim, but to free. (No such concession is attached to the destructive actions of a despot or egotist with a self-induced savior complex. God's laws will not be mocked!)

Life and death, animate and inanimate matter, were all seen by the child Jesus as manipulatable vibrations of God's consciousness. We are told he formed sparrows from mud scooped from ponds after a rainstorm; and when chastised for such action on the Sabbath, he gave life to the birds and bade them fly away. More often than not, those who suffered death or affliction at his command were restored by him to life and health, just as later in his ministry he withdrew life from the fig tree and caused it to wither and restored life to Lazarus and raised him from the dead. Nature's laws are activated quite ingenuously by one who knows his unity with the omnipresent Universal Consciousness through which all existences are created, sustained, and dissolved.

It is related in the Infancy Gospels that father Joseph found the extraordinary talent of his son of incredible assistance in his carpentry trade—not as an artisan with hammer and chisel, but when by error "Joseph had any thing to make longer or shorter, or wider or narrower, the Lord Jesus would stretch forth his hand towards it. And presently it would become as Joseph would have it." After two years of labor on a commissioned throne for the ruler of Jerusalem, the seat was found to be lacking "two spans on each side, of the appointed measure." The king was angry and Joseph fearful; whereupon Jesus directed his father to pull on one side while he pulled on the opposite.* And when "each of them had with strength drawn his side, the throne obeyed, and was brought to the proper dimension of the place: which miracle when they who stood by saw, they were astonished, and praised God." (This was as elementary for Jesus as later it would be for him to change water into wine, or to multiply the loaves and fishes.)†

---

* "King" is most likely a reference to Archelaus, ruler until A.D. 6. *(Publisher's Note)*

† A story about the infant Krishna likewise recounts his ability to alter the shape of material objects. He was adored by all the village milkmaids and indulged in his sweet misbehavior, especially in helping himself to their store of fresh curds. But one day this had gone too far, and in order to get at the curds he broke the container in which his mother Yashoda had been churning fresh milk into butter. Thinking to anchor him to

A boy at the point of death from a serpent's venom is restored to his former health. "And when he began to cry, the Lord Jesus said, Cease crying, for hereafter thou shalt be my disciple. And this is that Simon the Canaanite, who is mentioned in the Gospel."

Satan is cast out of a young boy who went about biting people, or himself when no one else was nearby. That same child is identified as the later perfidious Judas Iscariot.

Jesus' brother James, while they both were out gathering wood, is bitten by a venomous viper; whereupon Jesus blew his breath on the wound and it was instantly well. Amidst play, a boy falls from the roof and dies; Jesus restores him to life.

Precocious would hardly describe the child Jesus. Attempts at schooling by competent teachers met with frustration and even disgrace for these scholars. In beginning with the alphabet, the teacher could not progress beyond the first letter because of the insistence of Jesus that the teacher explain the full meaning of the letter. Whereupon receiving no such explanation the child proceeded with the whole alphabet and the process of its formation and the diagramming of each letter—none of which the teacher had ever heard nor read in any book. The parents brought Jesus to a more learned teacher, who suffered a similar defeat, and in addition a withered hand when he raised it to strike what he took to be an insolent child.

~

Now his parents went to Jerusalem every year at the feast of the Passover. And when he was twelve years old, they went up to Jerusalem after the custom of the feast.

And when they had fulfilled the days, as they returned, the child Jesus tarried behind in Jerusalem; and Joseph and his mother knew not of it. But they, supposing him to have been in the company, went a day's journey; and they sought him among

---

a mortar stone and thereby put at least a temporary halt to his pranks, she fetched a length of rope to fasten around his waist. When she tried to tie the knot, however, she was surprised to find the rope too short. She got a longer piece and tried again, only to find this one too short as well. Eventually, all the rope in the household had been brought, but still it proved insufficient to tie up the divine child! After a crowd had gathered and was chuckling at the plight of poor Yashoda, Krishna took pity on his mother and permitted himself to be fastened securely to the mortar stone.

their kinsfolk and acquaintance. And when they found him not, they turned back again to Jerusalem, seeking him. And it came to pass, that after three days they found him in the temple, sitting in the midst of the doctors, both hearing them, and asking them questions. And all that heard him were astonished at his understanding and answers.

And when they saw him, they were amazed: and his mother said unto him, "Son, why hast thou thus dealt with us? Behold, thy father and I have sought thee sorrowing."

And he said unto them, "How is it that ye sought me? Wist ye not that I must be about my Father's business?" And they understood not the saying which he spake unto them. And he went down with them, and came to Nazareth, and was subject unto them: but his mother kept all these sayings in her heart (Luke 2:41–51).

We know of mental geniuses, whose brains absorb knowledge at astonishing speed. They are endowed with learning and learning abilities from past lives, which predisposes them to super-efficient brain development. Spiritual geniuses have, in addition, the superconscious ability to tap the wisdom library of soul realization—the all-knowing intuitive faculty of the soul that manifests its oneness with the infinite Divine Intelligence.

Spiritual geniuses draw on the all-knowing intuitive faculty of the soul

Narratives about godly youthful savants abound in the spiritual lore of India. It is widely accepted that those who come on earth for a God-given purpose are graced with divine intervention that blesses them with wisdom transcending the natural growth of the intellect.

Shukadeva was the saintly son of Rishi Vyasa (compiler of the Vedas and composer of the epic *Mahabharata,* which contains the Bhagavad Gita). The boy was an extraordinary child from birth. Quickly absorbing all knowledge, he is reputed to have recited from memory the entire Vedas as well as the more than 100,000 verses of the *Mahabharata,* having heard them from his father, Vyasa.

Of exceptional renown is the sainted Swami Shankara, often extolled as India's greatest philosopher. The annals surrounding him relate that within his first year he was proficient in languages; by age two he could read; having once heard something he could recall it, and absorb its meaning intuitively. By the age of eight he had mastered the Vedas and completed his formal education—having become a wisdom expert in all the holy scriptures, writings, and six systems of Hindu philosophy. He preached throughout India his Advaita (non-dualistic) philosophy. The very best of the learned could not match him in debate. By sixteen he had completed writing his extensive commentaries, which are veritably revered to this day by scholars. He reorganized the monastic Order of Swamis, of which he is known as Adi ("the first") Shankaracharya, head of this sacred tradition of *sannyasis*. Having completed his work, he died at the age of thirty-two.

As told in the Biblical gospel of Luke, Jesus in his twelfth year, having been missing for three days is at last found in the temple at Jerusalem discoursing with the learned doctors and elders. One final amplification of this temple scene from the apocryphal Infancy Gospels might be noted; its recounting by the early Christians an attempt, no doubt, to express the awe and reverence they felt that Jesus was vested not only with heavenly wisdom, but earthly profundity as well.

"A certain principal rabbi asked him, Hast thou read books? Jesus answered he had read both books and the things which were contained in books. And he explained to them the books of the law, and precepts, and statutes, and the mysteries which are contained in the books of the prophets; things which the mind of no creature could reach....

"When a certain astronomer, who was present, asked the Lord Jesus, Whether he had studied astronomy? The Lord Jesus replied, and told him the number of the spheres and heavenly bodies, as also their triangular, square, and sextile aspect; their progressive and retrograde motion; their size and several prognostications; and other things, which the reason of man had never discovered.

"There was also among them a philosopher well skilled in physic and natural philosophy, who asked the Lord Jesus, whether he had studied physic?"

Here the reply attributed to Jesus transforms the young child into what might be seen as a hoary *rishi* reciting yoga philosophy from the Upanishads and Bhagavad Gita:

"He replied, and explained to him physics and metaphysics, and also those things which were above and below the power of nature; the powers also of the body, its humors and their effects; also the number of its members, and bones, veins, arteries, and nerves; the several constitutions of the body, hot and dry, cold and moist, and the tendencies of them. How the soul operated upon the body; what its various sensations and faculties were; the faculty of speaking, anger, desire. And lastly, the manner of its composition and dissolution; and other things, which the understanding of no creature had ever reached."

When Mary finds and chastises the child for the worry he had caused by his disappearance, he, in effect, spoke before the assemblage his encapsulated first sermon, which was to characterize his forthcoming ministry: his simple message was to be one of renunciation of material bonds for the greater love of God. "How is it that ye sought me? Wist ye not that I must be about my Father's business?"

In setting Jesus apart as one who is to be venerated but whose perfection cannot be emulated, the majority of his followers pay only token notice to the example of renunciation that he lived and preached: Seek ye first the kingdom of God; sell that thou hast and give to the poor and follow me; take no thought for your life, what ye shall eat, or what ye shall drink, nor yet for your body, what ye shall put on; who is my mother or

"I must be about my Father's business": Jesus' ideal of renunciation

my brethren save whosoever shall do the will of God; follow me and let the dead bury the dead; the foxes have holes, and the birds of the air have nests, but the Son of Man hath not where to lay his head; whosoever that forsaketh not all that he hath, he cannot be my disciple. Lofty admonitions! But all who have stood in purity before the omnipresence of God know that without letting go of corporeal attachments in one's consciousness—to which outer renunciation is an aid if not an absolute condition—there is no possibility of possessing the Infinite. Though Jesus stressed complete renunciation, he also said, "Love thy neighbour," which means work for all—and this, while you "Love the Lord thy God with all thy heart."

The perfect life of Jesus, even at such a tender age, brings forth a perfect utterance as to how a divine child, consecrated to serve humanity, behaves. Knowing himself as a son of God, he states outright that his highest duty is to look after the celestial business of spreading the kingdom of his Heavenly Father. His caring parents had no cause to worry for him who was protected by the King of kings. It was the first public hint by Jesus to his parents as to what they would have to expect about what his life was to be.

Jesus knew that parental love and affection, being blindly compulsive, might demand from him greater attention to his earthly father's occupation than to the work of his Heavenly Father, for which he came on earth. With the innocence of a divine audacity Jesus remonstrates that his parents should know this, and should wish for him to be busy with God's work. The world, busy with all its busy-ness, little understands, as Jesus' parents did not, the supreme focus of one who knows there is no greater duty than one's duty to God. The *Mahabharata* says that if one duty contradicts another, then it is not duty, but something to be avoided. Spiritual and material duties should not contradict, but rather complement one another. If contradiction occurs, those duties are incomplete and should be modified so that instead of contending against each other they work together like two stallions, pulling the car of life harmoniously and uniformly to one happy goal.

Spiritual and material duties should complement one another

The ordinary man thinks of the world, his family, and his work as his business; but the spiritual man knows that duties to parents, children, family ties, the business world, and all else are to be carried out as service to God. Everyone should help to maintain the well-being of the world by a universal consciousness of love and service, rather than as a selfish man whose actions are compelled and actuated by instinctive blood ties and greed.

Business should be spiritualized; everything should be done with the consciousness of God within. Man should endeavor in his works to please God by harmonizing all things with His ideals. Business that conforms with God's divine laws is of lasting benefit to mankind. Moneymaking enterprises that cater only to human luxury, and to false or evil propensities, are bound to be destroyed by the working of the divine law of the survival of the worthiest. Any business that harms the real spiritual comfort of people does no real service, and is bound to meet with destruction by the very nature of its activities.

A successful life must be begun with spiritual culture, for all material and moral actions are governed by spiritual laws. Noble parents, lovers of God, should wish the first interest of their children to be in God's business. They should start their children on the right road in life by showing them the way to be proficient in contacting God and in doing all things with God-consciousness. A life can be successful, healthy, and complete—balanced with wisdom and happiness—when activity is guided by God's inner, intuitive direction.

In expressing the proper attitude toward his parents—that though duty to parents is important, it is secondary to one's first and foremost duty to the Heavenly Father—Jesus spoke not only of his own divine dispensation, but the truth that every man should remember: "God first."

The Unknown Years of Jesus' Life—Sojourn in India

Ancient Records From a Tibetan Monastery

❖

Jesus' Journey to India, Motherland of Religion

❖

Cycles of Progress and Degradation in
Outward Expression of Religion

❖

All Chronicles of Jesus' Life Colored by the
Cultural Perspective of Their Authors

❖

Teachings of the Oriental Jesus Have Been Too Much Westernized

❖

Oriental and Occidental Christianity:
The Inner and Outer Teachings

❖

Truth Is the Ultimate Religion;
Sectarian Affiliation Is of Little Meaning

"Jesus knew his divine destiny and set out for India to prepare himself for its fulfillment....because India specialized in religion from time immemorial."

The Unknown Years of Jesus' Life — Sojourn in India

In the New Testament, the curtain of silence comes down again on the life of Jesus after his twelfth year, not to rise once more until eighteen years later, at which time he receives baptism from John and begins preaching to the multitude. We are told only:

> *And Jesus increased in wisdom and stature, and in favor with God and man.*
>
> *— Luke 2:52*

For the contemporaries of such an extraordinary figure to find nothing noteworthy to record from his childhood to his thirtieth year is in and of itself extraordinary.

Remarkable accounts, however, do exist, not in the land of Jesus' birth but farther east where he spent most of the unaccounted-for years. Hidden away in a Tibetan monastery priceless records lie. They speak of a Saint Issa from Israel "in whom was manifest the soul of the universe"; who from the age of fourteen to twenty-eight was in India and regions of the Himalayas among the saints, monks, and pundits; who preached his message throughout that area and then returned to teach in his native land, where he was treated vilely, condemned, and put to death. Except as chronicled in these ancient manuscripts, no other history of the unknown years of Jesus' life has ever been published.

Providentially, these ancient records were discovered and copied by a Russian traveler, Nicholas Notovitch. During his travels in India in 1887, Notovitch basked in the wonders of the soul-stirring stark contrasts of her ancient civiliza-tion. It was midst the natural grandeur of Kashmir that he heard stories about a Saint Issa, the details

———— *·•·* ————

Ancient records from a Tibetan monastery

of which left no doubt in him that Issa and Jesus Christ were one and the same person. He learned that copies of ancient manuscripts pre-served in some Tibetan monasteries contained a record of Issa's years of sojourn in India, Nepal, and Tibet. Undeterred by hazards and ob-stacles, he journeyed northward, finally arriving at the Himis monastery outside of Leh, the capital city of Ladakh, which he was told possessed a copy of the sacred books about Issa. Though he was received graciously, he did not gain access to the manuscripts. A dis-appointed Notovitch turned back toward India; but in a near-fatal mishap on the treacherous mountain pass, his leg was broken in a fall. Seizing this as an opportunity for a second attempt to see the sacred books, he asked to be carried back to Himis to receive the necessary care. This time, after repeated requests, the books were brought to him. Perhaps the lamas now felt obliged to treat as hospitably as pos-sible their stricken guest—a time-honored tradition in the East. With the help of an interpreter, he meticulously copied the contents of the pages pertinent to Jesus as they were read to him by the head lama.

Returning to Europe, Notovitch found that his enthusiasm for the discovery was not shared by the Western Christian orthodoxy, which was loath to support such a radical revelation. So he published his notes himself in 1894 under the title *The Unknown Life of Jesus Christ*. In his publication, he urged that a qualified research team be dispatched to view and judge for itself the value of these previously se-creted documents. Though Notovitch's claims were challenged by crit-ics in America and Europe, the accuracy of his account was attested to by at least two other reputable persons who journeyed to Tibet to seek out and ascertain the authenticity of these manuscripts.

In 1922, Swami Abhedananda, a direct disciple of Ramakrishna Paramahansa, visited the Himis Monastery, and confirmed all of the salient details about Issa published in Notovitch's book.*

---

* Swami Abhedananda (1866–1939) was vice president of Ramakrishna Math and Mission from 1921 to 1924. He had traveled in America teaching Vedanta from 1897

Nicholas Roerich,* in an expedition to India and Tibet in the mid-1920s, saw and copied verses from ancient manuscripts that were the same, or at least the same in content, as those published by Notovitch. He was also deeply impressed by the oral traditions of that area: "In Srinagar we first encountered the curious legend about Christ's visit to this place. Afterwards we saw how widely spread in India, in Ladak and in Central Asia, was the legend of the visit of Christ to these parts during his long absence, quoted in the Gospel."†

Answering the critics who had claimed that Notovitch's story was a fabrication, Roerich writes: "There are always those who love scornfully to deny when something difficult enters their consciousness.... [But] in what possible way could a recent forgery penetrate into the consciousness of the whole East?"‡

Roerich notes: "The local people know nothing of any published book [i.e., Notovitch's] but they know the legend and with deep reverence they speak of Issa."§

The Gospel account of Jesus' early life ends in his twelfth year with his discourse with the priests in the temple at Jerusalem. According to the Tibetan manuscripts, it was not long after this that Jesus left his home in order to avoid plans for his betrothal as he reached maturity — which for an Israelite boy at that time was thirteen years of age. Certainly Jesus was above the commonality of marriage. Of what necessity was human love and family ties for one who possessed supreme ardor for God and a universal love that embraced all human beings? The world urges a conformity to its pedestrian course,

Jesus' journey to India, motherland of religion

---

until 1921. While there, he had read Notovitch's book; and in 1922 he visited the Himis Monastery. With the help of one of the lamas, he made his own translation of some of the Tibetan verses about Issa, which he published in Bengali in 1929. The English translation, *Journey into Kashmir and Tibet,* is published by Ramakrishna Vedanta Math, Calcutta, 1987. *(Publisher's Note)*

* Nicholas Roerich (1874–1947), renowned artist, explorer, and archaeologist, born in St. Petersburg, Russia. From 1923 to 1928 he headed the Central Asiatic Expedition through India, Tibet, Sikkim, Chinese Turkestan, and Mongolia Altai. Reports about the expedition, which mentioned Roerich's recountal of the evidence for Jesus' trip to India, appeared in *The New York Times* May 27, 1926, and other newspapers and magazines.

† Roerich, *Heart of Asia* (New York: Roerich Museum Press, 1929).

‡ Roerich, *Altai-Himalaya* (New York, Frederick A. Stokes Co., 1929).

§ Roerich, *Altai-Himalaya.*

and little knows how to reckon with those who hew a higher path in response to God's will. Jesus knew his divine destiny and set out for India to prepare himself for its fulfillment.

India is the mother of religion. Her civilization has been acknowledged as much older than the legendary civilization of Egypt. If you study these matters, you will see how the hoary scriptures of India, predating all other revelations, have influenced the Book of the Dead of Egypt and the Old and New Testaments of the Bible, as well as other religions. All were in touch with, and drew from, the religion of India, because India specialized in religion from time immemorial.*

---

* See also page xxix n. "On the basis of archaeology, satellite photography, metallurgy, and ancient mathematics, it is now clear that there existed a great civilization—a mainly spiritual civilization perhaps—before the rise of Egypt, Sumeria, and the Indus Valley. The heartland of this ancient world was the region from the Indus to the Ganga—the land of the Vedic Aryans," state N. S. Rajaram and David Frawley, O.M.D., in *Vedic Aryans and the Origins of Civilization* (New Delhi: Voice of India, 1997).

The scriptures of India "are the oldest extant philosophy and psychology of our race," says renowned historian Will Durant in *Our Oriental Heritage* (*The Story of Civilization,* Part I). Robert C. Priddy, professor of the history of philosophy at the University of Oslo, wrote in *On India's Ancient Past* (1999): "India's past is so ancient and has been so influential in the rise of civilization and religion, at least for almost everyone in the Old World, that most people can claim it actually to be the earliest part of our own odyssey....The mother of religion, the world's earliest spiritual teachings of the Vedic tradition contains the most sublime and all-embracing of philosophies."

In his two-volume work *India and World Civilization* (Michigan State University Press, 1969), historian D. P. Singhal amasses abundant documentation of India's spiritual nurturing of the ancient world. He describes the excavation of a vase near Baghdad that has led researchers to the conclusion that "by the middle of the third millennium B.C., an Indian cult was already being practiced in Mesopotamia....Archaeology thus has shown that two thousand years before the earliest references in cuneiform texts to contact with India, she was sending her manufactures to the land where the roots of Western civilization lie."

India's spiritual influence extended not only west, but east. "India conquered and dominated China for 20 centuries without ever having to send a single soldier across its border," observed Dr. Hu Shih, former chancellor of Beijing University and Chinese ambassador to the United States. And Professor Lin Yutang, the famous Chinese philologist and author, says in *The Wisdom of India* (New York: Random House, 1942): "India was China's teacher in religion and imaginative literature, and the world's teacher in philosophy....India is a land overflowing with religion and with the religious spirit. A trickle of Indian religious spirit overflowed to China and inundated the whole of Eastern Asia."

The high civilizations of the Americas, as well, show definite evidence of India's influence. "In ancient times, no civilization spread abroad more extensively than that of India," Professor Singhal writes. "And thus, occupying a central position in the cultures of the world, India has contributed enormously to human civilization. Indian contacts with the Western world date back to prehistoric times." He goes on to quote the illustrious scientist and explorer Baron Alexander von Humboldt, founder of the sys-

So it was that Jesus himself went to India; Notovitch's manuscript tells us: "Issa secretly absented himself from his father's house; left Jerusalem, and, in a train of merchants, journeyed toward the Sindh, with the object of perfecting himself in the knowledge of the Word of God and the study of the laws of the great Buddhas." *

---

tematic study of ancient American cultures, who was convinced of the Asian origin of the advanced pre-Columbian civilizations in the New World: "If languages supply but feeble evidence of ancient communication between the two worlds, their communication is fully proved by the cosmogonies, the monuments, the hieroglyphical characters, and the institutions of the people of America and Asia."

"The traces of Hindu-Buddhist influence in Mexico...correspond in kind precisely to those cultural elements which were introduced by Buddhist monks and Hindu priests in Southeast Asia," Dr. Singhal observes, and cites the conclusion of Professor Robert Heine-Geldern in *The Civilizations of the Americas* as follows: "We have little doubt that a sober but unbiased comparative analysis of the Mexican religions will reveal many traces of the former influences of either Hinduism or Buddhism or of both....to such an extent, both in a general way and in specific details, that the assumption of historic relationship is almost inevitable." *(Publisher's Note)*

* Cf. Swami Abhedananda's translation of this verse from the Tibetan: "At this time his great desire was to achieve full realisation of godhead and learn religion at the feet of those who have attained perfection through meditation."—*Journey into Kashmir and Tibet*

The Lost Years of Jesus Revealed, by Rev. Dr. Charles Francis Potter (Greenwich, Conn.: Fawcett, 1962), observes: "Many Hindus believe that Jesus' 'Lost Years' were, partly at least, spent in India, getting much of his best teaching from the Vedas. Didn't he say 'Take my yoga upon you and learn of me, for my yoga is easy?' Both *yoga* and *yoke* are pronounced as one syllable, with the final vowel silent, and both are the same word, *zeugos,* in Greek." [And in Sanskrit, for the generic meaning of Sanskrit *yoga* is "yoke."—*Publisher.*]

Dr. Potter continues: "Fanciful as it may seem to an American, the thought of any connection between Jesus' teaching and India is rendered less fantastic not only by the scrolls from the Qumran caves [the so-called Dead Sea Scrolls], but especially by the new find of many Gnostic Christian books [at Nag Hammadi] in Egypt....The first part (and several other parts) of John's Gospel—'In the beginning was the Word, and the Word was with God, and the Word was God....'—is pure Gnosticism. Gnostic mysticism had come to the Jews from the East, from India and Persia and Babylon; it had appealed to them in their Babylonian captivity, and they had brought much of it back home with them in the Return....

"Lest we should undervalue Gnosticism because its terms, symbols, and vocabulary differ so from ours, it should be stated that Gnosticism was Egyptian Christianity for the two hundred years that the leaders of the new faith were working out its theology. It was gradually pushed out by orthodox Catholic Christianity and its books were burned. Similarly, Essenism was the early form of Palestinian Christianity....At Qumran and at Chenoboskion [Nag Hammadi], hidden for centuries, were the great libraries of these early forms of Christianity, which now so suddenly and dramatically have been restored to us. And Essenism and Gnosticism were much alike: if you doubt it, read the canonical Gospel of John, especially the first chapter, where you will find both Essenism and Gnosticism, blended with and sublimated into the Christianity more familiar to us." *(Publisher's Note)*

The ancient manuscripts say Jesus spent six years in various holy cities, settling for some time in Jagannath, a sacred pilgrimage site in Puri, Orissa.* The famous temple there, which has existed in one form or another since ancient times, is dedicated to Jagannath, "Lord of the Universe"—a title associated with the universal consciousness of Bhagavan Krishna. The name by which Jesus is identified in the Tibetan manuscripts is Isa ("Lord"), rendered by Notovitch as Issa.† *Isa* (*Isha*), or its extension *Ishvara,* defines God as the Supreme Lord or Creator immanent in as well as transcendent of His creation.‡ This is the true character of the Christ/Krishna universal consciousness, *Kutastha Chaitanya,* incarnate in Jesus, Krishna, and other God-united souls who possess oneness with the Lord's omnipresence. It is my conviction that the title *Isa* was given at birth to Jesus by the Wise Men from India who came to honor his advent on earth. In the New Testament, Jesus' disciples commonly refer to him as "Lord."§

---

* Records of Jesus' years in India were preserved in Puri, according to His Holiness Sri Jagadguru Shankaracharya Bharati Krishna Tirtha, spiritual head of that city's ancient Gowardhan Math and, until his passing in 1962, seniormost of the reigning Shankaracharyas (ecclesiastical heads of orthodox Hinduism; apostolic successors to Swami Shankara, ancient reorganizer of the venerable Swami Order). His Holiness visited America on a speaking tour of major universities in 1958; his historic tour—the first time any Shankaracharya had traveled to the West—was sponsored by Self-Realization Fellowship. Sri Daya Mata, president and spiritual head of Self-Realization Fellowship, wrote: "In my discussions with His Holiness during my visits with him in India, he told me that there is proof positive, to which he had access, that as Paramahansaji has stated, Jesus Christ was in India as a young lad and received training in the monasteries there. The Shankaracharya further told me that, God willing, it was his hope to translate these documents and write a book about this period in the life of Jesus. Unfortunately this could not be accomplished owing to the advanced age and fragile health of this saintly Shankaracharya." *(Publisher's Note)*

† Notovitch recorded that the manuscripts he saw at the Himis monastery in Ladakh were a translation into the Tibetan language from the original stored at a monastery near Lhasa, which was written in the Pali language. In Pali (and in Sanskrit), *Isa* (pronounced *ee-sha*) means "lord, owner, ruler"—as does the related word *Issara* (Pali version of Sanskrit *Ishvara*). *Issa,* on the other hand, means "jealousy, anger, ill-will" in Pali—obviously not the meaning intended by the Buddhist scribes who composed the scrolls. *(Publisher's Note)*

‡ See also Discourse 21, page 350 n.

§ Jesus' name is pronounced and spelled in different ways in various languages, but it has the same meaning. In the Koran (written in Arabic), the name used for Jesus is *Isa* or *Issa*—the same as in the Tibetan texts discovered by Notovitch. Only through changes by speakers in many lands did his name come to be pronounced *Jesus*. That English word is relatively modern; prior to the sixteenth century it was not spelled with

The ancient history relates that Jesus became learned in all the Vedas and *shastras*. But he took issue with some precepts of the Brahminic orthodoxy. He openly denounced their practices of caste bigotry; many of the priestly rituals; and the emphasis on worship of many gods in idolic form rather than sole reverence for the one Supreme Spirit, the pure monotheistic essence of Hinduism which had become obscured by outer ritualistic concepts.

Distancing himself from these disputes, Jesus left Puri. He spent the next six years with the Sakya Buddhist sect in the Himalayan mountainous regions of Nepal and Tibet. This Buddhist sect was monotheistic, having separated itself from the distorted Hinduism that prevailed during the dark age of Kali Yuga.*

Though true God-realized masters have arisen in India in every age, preserving from generation to generation the eternal truths of Spirit (*Sanatana Dharma*), the outward religious

———————

Cycles of progress and degradation in outward expression of religion

practices of the masses have undergone cycles of progress and degradation as have the religions of other lands and cultures. According to my guru, Swami Sri Yukteswar, the most recent descending and ascending Dark Ages (Kali Yuga) lasted from about 700 B.C. to A.D. 1700. In India, this period saw the gradual perversion and loss of the sublime spiritual science of the Vedas and Upanishads, resulting in priestly adherence to a number of misunderstood precepts falsely held to be taught by the scriptures. It was during this time of spiritual darkness that the avatar Gautama Buddha took incarnation in India (c. 563 B.C.), to right some of the gross abuses of

———————

a "J" but with an "I," as in Latin and Greek (*Iêsous*). Even today, in Spanish, though spelled with a "J," *Jesus* is pronounced "Hay-soos."

The Biblical account, given in the Gospels of Luke and Matthew (see Discourse 2), is that both Mary and Joseph were instructed by an angel that the divine child was to be named *Yeshua,* "savior" (in Greek, *Iêsous;* in English, *Jesus*): "...thou shalt call his name Jesus: for he shall save his people from their sins" (Matthew 1:21). The Hebrew word *Yeshua* is a contraction of *Yehoshua,* "Yahweh (Jehovah, the Creator) is salvation." However, the language of daily use for Jesus and his fellow Galileans was not Hebrew, but the related dialect Aramaic, in which his name would have been pronounced "Eshu." Thus, strangely enough, the name predicted for Jesus by the angel, and given to him by his family, was remarkably akin to the more ancient Sanskrit name bestowed by the Wise Men. Aside from the phonetic similarities, there is an underlying unity of meaning of the words *Isha* and *Yeshua*—the two appellations bestowed on the one revered by millions as "Lord and Savior." *(Publisher's Note)*

* The *yugas,* or world cycles of civilization, are explained in Discourse 39.

truth perpetrated by priestly pundits. His message of compassion for all beings and his Noble Eightfold Path taught how to escape misery and free oneself from the karmic wheel of birth and death.*

The Tibetan scrolls relate that while among the Buddhists, Jesus applied himself to the study of their sacred books and could perfectly expound from them. Apparently around age twenty-six or twenty-eight, he preached his message abroad as he wended his way back to Israel through Persia and adjacent countries, encountering fame from the populace and animosity from the Zoroastrian and other priestly classes.

All this is not to say that Jesus learned everything he taught from his spiritual mentors and associates in India and surrounding regions. Avatars come with their own endowment of wisdom. Jesus' store of divine realization was merely awakened and molded to fit his unique mission by his sojourn among the Hindu pundits, Buddhist monks, and particularly the great masters of yoga from whom he received initiation in the esoteric science of God-union through meditation. From the knowledge he had gleaned, and from the wisdom brought forth from his soul in deep meditation, he distilled for the masses simple parables of the ideal principles by which to govern one's life in the sight of God. But to those close disciples who were ready to receive it, he taught the deeper mysteries, as evidenced in the New Testament book of Revelation of St. John, the symbology of which accords exactly with the yoga science of God-realization.

All chronicles of Jesus' life colored by the cultural perspective of their authors

The major import of the chronicles discovered by Notovitch is that they provide compelling evidence that the missing years of Jesus' life were spent in India. But they bear also, as would be expected, the distinctive character of their authors. The original documents purportedly were written in Pali script

---

* With the passage of time, Buddha's doctrines also fell prey to the limited understanding prevalent in Kali Yuga; his teachings degenerated into a nihilistic philosophy: The state of *nirvana*, or cessation of dualistic existence, was misinterpreted as extinction of the self. Buddha, however, meant extinction of the deluded ego, or pseudoself; the little self must be overcome in order that the real, eternal Self may achieve liberation from human incarnation. This perversion of Buddha's doctrine, with its emphasis on a negative state of nonbeing (extinction), was later supplanted in India by the doctrine of Swami Shankara, founder of the time-honored monastic Swami Order, who taught that the goal of life is the positive attainment of the ever-conscious, ever-existing, ever-newly blissful state of oneness with Spirit.

just a few years after the death of Jesus. This was the language of the Buddhists of that day. When reports reached India through traders from Jerusalem of the ignominious death of Isa, the holy one who had been held in such reverential regard by their community during his time among them, they set about to record his history as a part of their sacred annals. The Buddhistic perspective is quite naturally evident in their accounts.

If Jesus himself had written his life history and the substance of his teachings, they would have been expressed significantly differently than what has come down to this present day. With all the best efforts of those who related and recorded the events of Jesus' life, the view of each narrator was bound to have been somewhat influenced by his own background, be it of a Jewish, Gnostic, Greek, Roman, Buddhist, Zoroastrian, or any other religious persuasion or cultural bias—not to mention the additional assault of translation from one language to another, sometimes passing through many transitions.

The manuscripts published by Notovitch, for example, were written originally in Pali, having been gathered from eyewitnesses or hearsay-tellings of persons from various linguistic and regional backgrounds and then translated into Pali. The manuscripts then made their way from India to Nepal and thence to Lhasa in Tibet where they were translated into Tibetan and eventually copied for various major monasteries. Notovitch, a Russian, copied the Tibetan pages with the assistance of a translator, eventually published them in French, and that edition was subsequently translated and published in English.

Nevertheless, the overall value of these records is inestimable in a search for the historical Jesus. There are two ways to know an avatar. First, to glimpse his essence that shines through a mélange of fact, legend, innocent or purposeful distortion; and by discriminatively sifting the significant from the unimportant, just as a person is recognized for himself apart from the accoutrements he wears. And second, to have direct knowledge of a great one through intuitive divine communion with that soul—as many through the centuries have known Jesus Christ, such as Saint Francis of Assisi to whom Jesus appeared nightly in flesh and blood, Saint Teresa of Avila, and many others of the Christian faith; and such as Sri Ramakrishna of the Hindu faith, and I also who have been many times in the manifested presence of Jesus. Never would I have undertaken this book except with the assurance of personal knowledge of that Christ.

The documents discovered by Notovitch lend historical support to my long-held assertion, gleaned from my earliest years in India, that Jesus was linked with the *rishis* of India through the Wise Men who journeyed to his cradle, and for whom he went to India to receive their blessings and to confer concerning his world mission. That his teaching, born internally from his God-realization and nurtured externally by his studies with the masters, expresses the universality of Christ Consciousness that knows no boundary of race or creed, is what I shall endeavor to make evident throughout the pages of this book.

Like the sun, which rises in the East and travels to the West spreading its rays, so Christ rose in the East and came to the West, there to be enshrined in a vast Christendom whose adherents look to him as their guru and savior. It is no happenstance that Jesus chose to be born an Oriental Christ in Palestine. This locale was the hub linking the East with Europe. He traveled to India to honor his ties with her *rishis,* preached his message throughout that area, and then went back to spread his teachings in Palestine, which he saw in his great wisdom as the doorway through which his spirit and words would find their way to Europe and the rest of the world. This great Christ, radiating the spiritual strength and power of the Orient to the West, is a divine liaison to unite God-loving peoples of East and West.

Teachings of the Oriental Jesus have been too much Westernized

Truth is not the monopoly of the Orient or the Occident. The pure silver-gold rays of sunlight appear to be red or blue when observed through red or blue glass. So, also, truth only appears to be different when colored by an Oriental or Occidental civilization. In looking at the simple essence of truth expressed by the great ones of various times and climes, one finds very little difference in their messages. What I received from my Guru and the venerated masters of India I find the same as that which I have received from the teachings of Jesus the Christ.

It amuses me when my Western brothers ask: "Do you believe in Christ?" I always say: "Jesus the Christ"—Jesus the divine son of man in whom was manifested the Christ Consciousness, the Son of God. Much more than merely believing in him is to *know* him.

Christ has been much misinterpreted by the world. Even the most elementary principles of his teachings have been desecrated, and their esoteric depths have been forgotten. They have been crucified at the hands of dogma, prejudice, and cramped understanding. Genocidal wars have been fought, people have been burned as witches and heretics, on the presumed authority of man-made doctrines of Christianity. How to salvage the immortal teachings from the hands of ignorance? We must know Jesus as an Oriental Christ, a supreme yogi who manifested full mastery of the universal science of God-union, and thus could speak and act as a savior with the voice and authority of God. He has been Westernized too much.*

Jesus was an Oriental, by birth and blood and training. To separate a teacher from the background of his nationality is to blur the understanding through which he is perceived. No matter what Jesus the Christ was himself, as regards his own soul, being born and ma-

---

* Through the remarkable discovery of early Christian gnostic texts at Nag Hammadi, Egypt in 1945, one may glimpse something of what was lost to conventional Christianity during this process of "Westernization." Elaine Pagels, Ph.D., writes in *The Gnostic Gospels* (New York: Vintage Books, 1981): "The Nag Hammadi texts, and others like them, which circulated at the beginning of the Christian era, were denounced as heresy by orthodox Christians in the middle of the second century....But those who wrote and circulated these texts did not regard *themselves* as 'heretics.' Most of the writings use Christian terminology, unmistakably related to a Jewish heritage. Many claim to offer traditions about Jesus that are secret, hidden from 'the many' who constitute what, in the second century, came to be called the 'catholic church.' These Christians are now called gnostics, from the Greek word *gnosis,* usually translated as 'knowledge.' For as those who claim to know nothing about ultimate reality are called agnostic (literally, 'not-knowing'), the person who does claim to know such things is called gnostic ('knowing'). But *gnosis* is not primarily rational knowledge.... As the gnostics use the term, we could translate it as 'insight,' for *gnosis* involves an intuitive process of knowing oneself....[According to gnostic teachers,] to know oneself, at the deepest level, is simultaneously to know God; this is the secret of *gnosis....*

"The 'living Jesus' of these texts speaks of illusion and enlightenment, not of sin and repentance, like the Jesus of the New Testament. Instead of coming to save us from sin, he comes as a guide who opens access to spiritual understanding....

"Orthodox Christians believe that Jesus is Lord and Son of God in a unique way: he remains forever distinct from the rest of humanity whom he came to save. Yet the gnostic *Gospel of Thomas* relates that as soon as Thomas recognizes him, Jesus says to Thomas that they have both received their being from the same source: 'I am not your master. Because you have drunk, you have become drunk from the bubbling stream which I have measured out....He who will drink from my mouth will become as I am: I myself shall become he, and the things that are hidden will be revealed to him.'

"Does not such teaching—the identity of the divine and human, the concern with illusion and enlightenment, the founder who is presented not as Lord, but as spiritual guide—sound more Eastern than Western?...Could Hindu or Buddhist tradition have influenced gnosticism?...Ideas that we associate with Eastern religions emerged in the first century through the gnostic movement in the West, but they were suppressed and condemned by polemicists like Irenaeus." *(Publisher's Note)*

turing in the Orient, he had to use the medium of Oriental civilization, customs, mannerisms, language, parables, in spreading his message. Hence to understand Jesus Christ and his teachings one must be sympathetically open to the Oriental point of view—in particular, India's ancient and present civilization, religious scriptures, traditions, philosophies, spiritual beliefs, and intuitive metaphysical experiences. Though, esoterically understood, the teachings of Jesus are universal, they are saturated with the essence of Oriental culture—rooted in Oriental influences which have been made adaptable to the Western environment.

The Gospels can be rightly understood in the light of the teachings of India—not the caste-ridden, stone-worshiping, distorted interpretations of Hinduism, but the philosophical, soul-saving wisdom of her *rishis*: the kernel not the husk of the Vedas, Upanishads, and Bhagavad Gita. This essence of Truth—the *Sanatana Dharma*, or eternal principles of righteousness that uphold man and the universe—was given to the world thousands of years before the Christian era, and preserved in India with a spiritual vitality that has made the quest for God the be-all and end-all of life and not an armchair diversion.

In spite of the meaningless superstitions and pitiful provincialism in religious thinking that have crusted on both Hinduism and Christianity down the ages, each of them has done immeasurable good to mankind—each has brought peace, happiness, consolation to millions of suffering souls; each has inspired people to highest spiritual endeavor and granted salvation to many.

My endeavor is to restore a proper view of Christianity as an aggregate of the teachings of Jesus—separating them without any prejudice or partiality from the Western adaptations of dogma and sectarian creeds that can more accurately be called churchianity, with its sundry defects as well as merits. In order to understand Christ-ianity—that is, the pure teachings of Jesus—one must first take away its Western crust, and then its Oriental crust. Behind the two opaque coverings lies the universality of true Christianity.

Oriental and Occidental Christianity: the inner and outer teachings

Occidental Christianity is the outer crust, and Oriental Christianity is the inner crust. The Oriental Christ always emphasized: "Take no heed for the body, what ye shall eat, what ye shall wear. Bread, the men of the world seek after; seek ye the kingdom of God, and all these things will be added unto you." The proposition of the

Occidental Christian is instead: "Take heed of the body first, that in a healthy body temple ye may find God. Bread, ye men of the world, seek first—and afterwards, seek the kingdom of God."

In the warm Oriental climate, in a bygone age, "bread," clothing, and shelter were simpler and attainable without much effort; thus there was more freedom to meditate on God in leisure and solitude. In the Occident, however, with its artificially high standard of living, one has to think and work for these material necessities, hard and fast and successfully, or he will have no time at all, or strength, to seek the kingdom of God.

The universal teachings of Jesus Christ should be judiciously adapted according to the respective needs of the Oriental and Occidental—emphasizing the principles of Christian religion, and omitting the nonessential forms added to them from time to time. Great care should be taken, however, to embody the essential, living Christianity while it is being transplanted from Oriental atmosphere to Occidental environment. Otherwise, it would happen that, as some doctors say, "the operation was successful," but the patient peacefully died on the table! No difference should be made between Occidental religious methods of salvation and the Oriental technique of salvation. The only distinction to be made is between true Christ-principles and dogma-bound beliefs.

Oriental Christ-ianity would consider the exoteric practices of churchgoing, sermonizing, theological study of scriptures, as spiritual kindergarten work. The purpose of these would be to emphasize and support the necessity of "university-level" testing of religious beliefs in the laboratory of scientific esoteric meditation, under the direction of a Self-realized guide who through deep spiritual effort has found God in the light of his own intuitive soul-perception. While Western Christianity has saved its civilization from a plenary slide into atheism and immorality, it has accomplished relatively little to awaken the desire, and the faith that it is possible, to attain personal metaphysical experience of God, evolved out of the self-effort of scientific meditation.

The community religious services of the West are marvelous if they turn the mind to God and truth, but they are not enough if they lack meditation and knowledge of the methods of actual communion with God. On the other hand, the East emphasizes direct, personal realization of God, but is wanting in organization and philanthropic social welfare work. In order to understand Jesus Christ's doctrine, it is necessary to combine organizational efficiency and social welfare philanthropy with personal verification of Christ's teachings by metaphysical study and the actual contact of God in the temple of meditation. Then each one can, himself, realize what Jesus Christ was, and is, through the intuitive self-verification of his teachings.

Truth, in and of itself, is the ultimate "religion." Though truth can be expressed in different ways by sectarian "isms," it can never be exhausted by them. It has infinite manifestations and ramifications, but one consummation: direct experience of God, the Sole Reality.

Truth is the ultimate religion; sectarian affiliation is of little meaning

The human stamp of sectarian affiliation is of little meaning. It is not the religious denomination in which one's name is registered, nor the culture or creed in which one was born, that gives salvation. The essence of truth goes beyond all outer form. It is that essence which is paramount in understanding Jesus and his universal call to souls to enter the kingdom of God, which is "within you."

The great message of Jesus Christ is living and thriving in both East and West. The West has concentrated on perfecting the physical conditions of man, and the East on developing the spiritual potentials of man. Both East and West are one-sided. Granted, the East is not practical enough; but the West is too practical to be spiritually practical! That is why I advocate a harmonious union of the two; they need each other. Without spiritual idealism, material practicality is the harbinger of selfishness, sin, competition, and wars. This is a lesson for the West to learn. And unless idealism is tempered with practicality, there is confusion and suffering and lack of natural progress. This is the lesson to be learned by the East.

The East can learn from the West, and the West can learn from the East. Is it not strange that, perhaps due to God's secret plan, since the East needs material development, it was invaded by Western material civilization? And since the West needs spiritual balance, it has been silently but surely "invaded" by Hindu philosophy, not to conquer lands but to conquer souls with the liberation of God-realization.*

---

* The following was written in 1932 by Dr. W. Y. Evans-Wentz, renowned author and Oxford University scholar of comparative religion:

"Glorious are the spiritual legacies of Egypt and Greece and Rome, but even more glorious are the spiritual legacies which India is offering to the peoples of Europe and America through the agency of its Wise Men of the East, of whom Swami Yogananda, the illustrious creator of the Yogoda [Self-Realization] system, is but one in a long dy-

We are all children of God, from our inception unto eternity. Differences come from prejudices, and prejudice is the child of ignorance. We should not proudly identify ourselves as Americans or Indians or Italians or any other nationality, for that is but an accident of birth. Above all else, we should be proud that we are children of God, made in His image. Is not that the message of Christ?

Jesus the Christ is an excellent model for both East and West to follow. God's stamp, "son of God," is hidden in every soul. Jesus affirmed the scriptures: "Ye are gods."* Do away with masks! Come out openly as sons of God—not by hollow proclamations and learned-by-heart prayers, fireworks of intellectually worded sermons contrived to praise God and gather converts, but by *realization*! Become identified not with narrow bigotry, masked as wisdom, but with Christ Consciousness. Become identified with Universal Love, expressed in service to all, both materially and spiritually; then you will know who Jesus Christ was, and can say in your soul that we are all one band, all sons of One God!

---

nasty that extends unbrokenly to our own epoch from the dim prehistoric ages. The Swami has come to the nations of the West to expound the supreme science of life, which each of his dynastic predecessors, one after another, from century to century, has expounded.

"It has remained for the illuminated sons of India of this generation to free the Oriental-born Christ from the prison-house wherein the theologies of the Occident have kept him imprisoned throughout the centuries; and to proclaim anew, as he did, the ancient yet ever-new message of worldly renunciation and selflessness, and to reveal the One Path to Self-realization, to liberation and world-conquest, which all of the founders of the great historical faiths of mankind have trod and revealed...." *(Publisher's Note)*

* John 10:34.

The Infant Jesus With Mary and Joseph

One who knows God remembers at all times that the Heavenly Father-Mother-Creator is the true Parent of the souls and the bodies of all....The spirit of motherhood should be reverenced as an expression of the unconditional love of God, as also honor belongs to the father-figure as imaging the wisdom guardianship of the Heavenly Father. Devotion to parents is thus a part of devotion to God, which first and foremost is filial love for the Parent behind the familial caregivers, the Divine Father-Mother who has delegated parents to nurture the child. When the heart is divinely attuned, close human relationships are opportunities to imbibe God's infinite love from the vessels of many hearts.

— *Paramahansa Yogananda*

DISCOURSE 6

The Baptism of Jesus

"The ultimate baptism, acclaimed by John the Baptist and by all Self-realized masters, is to be baptized 'with the Holy Ghost, and with fire' — that is, to become permeated with God's presence in the holy Creative Vibration."

*I*n those days came John the Baptist, preaching in the wilderness of Judea, and saying, "Repent ye: for the kingdom of heaven is at hand."

For this is he that was spoken of by the prophet Isaiah saying, "The voice of one crying in the wilderness, 'Prepare ye the way of the Lord, make his paths straight.'"

And the same John had his raiment of camel's hair, and a leathern girdle about his loins; and his meat was locusts and wild honey. Then went out to him Jerusalem, and all Judea, and all the region round about Jordan, and were baptized of him in Jordan, confessing their sins.

But when he saw many of the Pharisees and Sadducees come to his baptism, he said unto them, "O generation of vipers, who hath warned you to flee from the wrath to come? Bring forth therefore fruits meet for repentance: And think not to say within yourselves, 'We have Abraham to our father': for I say unto you, that God is able of these stones to raise up children unto Abraham. And now also the axe is laid unto the root of the trees: therefore every tree which bringeth not forth good fruit is hewn down, and cast into the fire.

"I indeed baptize you with water unto repentance: but he that cometh after me is mightier than I, whose shoes I am not worthy to bear: he shall baptize you with the Holy Ghost, and with fire: whose fan is in his hand, and he will throughly purge his floor, and gather his wheat into the garner; but he will burn up the chaff with unquenchable fire."

Then cometh Jesus from Galilee to Jordan unto John, to be baptized of him. But John forbad him, saying, "I have need to be baptized of thee, and comest thou to me?"

And Jesus answering said unto him, "Suffer it to be so now: for thus it becometh us to fulfill all righteousness." Then he suffered him.

And Jesus, when he was baptized, went up straightway out of the water: and, lo, the heavens were opened unto him, and he saw the Spirit of God descending like a dove, and lighting

upon him: And lo a voice from heaven, saying, "This is My
beloved Son, in whom I am well pleased."

—Matthew 3:1–17

There was a man sent from God, whose name was John.
The same came for a witness, to bear witness of the Light,
that all men through him might believe. He was not that
Light, but was sent to bear witness of that Light. That was
the true Light, which lighteth every man that cometh into the
world....

And this is the record of John, when the Jews sent priests
and Levites from Jerusalem to ask him, "Who art thou?"

And he confessed, and denied not; but confessed, "I am
not the Christ."

And they asked him, "What then? Art thou Elijah?"

And he saith, "I am not."

"Art thou that prophet?"

And he answered, "No."

Then said they unto him, "Who art thou? that we may give
an answer to them that sent us. What sayest thou of thyself?"

He said, "I am the voice of one crying in the wilderness,
Make straight the way of the Lord, as said the prophet Isaiah."

And they which were sent were of the Pharisees.

And they asked him, and said unto him, "Why baptizest
thou then, if thou be not that Christ, nor Elijah, neither that
prophet?"

John answered them, saying, "I baptize with water: but
there standeth one among you, whom ye know not; he it is,
who coming after me is preferred before me, whose shoe's
latchet I am not worthy to unloose."

These things were done in Bethabara beyond Jordan,
where John was baptizing.

The next day John seeth Jesus coming unto him, and saith,
"Behold the Lamb of God, which taketh away the sin of the
world. This is he of whom I said, 'After me cometh a man
which is preferred before me: for he was before me.' And I

knew him not: but that he should be made manifest to Israel, therefore am I come baptizing with water."

And John bare record, saying, "I saw the Spirit descending from heaven like a dove, and it abode upon him. And I knew him not: but He that sent me to baptize with water, the same said unto me, 'Upon whom thou shalt see the Spirit descending, and remaining on him, the same is he which baptizeth with the Holy Ghost.' And I saw, and bare record that this is the Son of God."

—John 1:6–9, 19–34

DISCOURSE 6

The Baptism of Jesus

In those days came John the Baptist, preaching in the wilderness of Judea, and saying, "Repent ye: for the kingdom of heaven is at hand."

For this is he that was spoken of by the prophet Isaiah, saying, "The voice of one crying in the wilderness, 'Prepare ye the way of the Lord, make his paths straight.'"

And the same John had his raiment of camel's hair, and a leathern girdle about his loins; and his meat was locusts and wild honey. Then went out to him Jerusalem, and all Judea, and all the region round about Jordan, and were baptized of him in Jordan, confessing their sins.

But when he saw many of the Pharisees and Sadducees come to his baptism, he said unto them, "O generation of vipers, who hath warned you to flee from the wrath to come? Bring forth therefore fruits meet for repentance: And think not to say within yourselves, 'We have Abraham to our father': for I say unto you, that God is able of these stones to raise up children unto Abraham.* And now also the axe is laid unto the root of the trees: therefore every tree which bringeth not forth good fruit is hewn down, and cast into the fire.†

"I indeed baptize you with water unto repentance: but he that cometh after me is mightier than I, whose shoes I am not

---

* See Discourse 64, pages 1258–59, for commentary on these verses, Matthew 3:7–9.

† This verse is paralleled in Matthew 7:19 and is commented on in that context in Discourse 30.

worthy to bear: he shall baptize you with the Holy Ghost, and with fire: whose fan is in his hand, and he will throughly purge his floor, and gather his wheat into the garner; but he will burn up the chaff with unquenchable fire" (Matthew 3:1–12).*

O f great import was the role played by John the Baptist as the prophesied forerunner divinely sent before Jesus to prepare his way and bear testimony to the Christ incarnate in him and evidenced in the authority of his teaching.

John the Baptist: fore-runner of the Christ Incarnate

      A holy man of the desert solitudes, subsisting on wild honey and the fruit of locust trees, John engaged himself in the mysteries and meditations of an anchorite, awaiting Jesus to proclaim himself ready to begin his ministry. Many believe that John was associated with the Essenes and their ascetic and esoteric practices; included among their ceremonies was baptism for purification of the body and spirit.† When John made himself known in the environs of Judea, crowds followed him as a saint and prophet. His renown made

---

* For this entire group of verses, cf. parallel references in Mark 1:1–8 and Luke 3:1–18. See Discourse 56, page 1099, for commentary on verse 12.

† See Luke 1:80, Discourse 2: "And the child grew, and waxed strong in spirit, and was in the deserts till the day of his shewing unto Israel." The Bible gives no further information on the childhood and youth of John the Baptist. The Essenes were an ascetical Jewish sect extant from about 150 B.C. until the end of the first century A.D. The Jewish historian Flavius Josephus (c. A.D. 37–100) describes the Essenes in his *Antiquities of the Jews* (Book 18, Chap. 1, No. 2). The Roman scholar Pliny the Elder (A.D. 23–79) wrote that the Essenes lived near the Dead Sea in the hills above Ein Gedi (where in 1998 Israeli archaeologists excavated what are believed to be ruins of an Essene community). Many similarities exist between what historians know of the Essene way of life and that of John the Baptist described in the Gospels. In addition to purificatory baptism by water, there is also evidence that they adhered to a vegetarian diet. They maintained monastic-like communities in the desert in order to separate themselves from what they saw as the corrupt and worldly practices of the priests and populace.

  "The Essene, like the Indian yogi, sought to obtain divine union and the 'gifts of the Spirit' by solitary reverie in retired spots," wrote archaeologist Arthur Lillie in *India in Primitive Christianity* (London: K. Paul, Trench, Trubner, 1909). Historian D. P. Singhal writes in *India and World Civilization* (Michigan State University Press, 1969): "Numerous authorities, such as Hilgenfeld and Renan, maintain that there was Buddhist influence on the Essene doctrines. And it was through this Jewish sect that Buddhist influences reached Palestine and later filtered through to Christianity....The life led by the Essenes," he says (quoting historian Sir Charles Eliot in *Hinduism and Buddhism: An Historical Sketch*) "was 'just as might have been evolved by seekers after truth who were trying to put into practice in another country the religious ideals of India.'" *(Publisher's Note)*

it possible for him to fulfill worthily his part in Jesus' destiny, a pattern set in their previous relationship as Elijah and Elisha.*

One of God's grand illusions is the screening of one incarnation from another. Without this partitioning, no actor on the stage of life would be able to cope with his kaleidoscopic identity and its relationships with others, and with his place in the karmic cause-and-effect events whirling around him—a dizzying conflict of countless incarnations with their interpersonal relationships branching off into their own limitless previous existences and experiences. By wiping clean the memory slate of each new lifetime, there is a freshness and a degree of progressive order maintained in the cosmic drama.

The Hindu scriptures refer to creation as God's *lila,* a delusive phantasmagoria for man's entertainment through interaction with the workings of the Cosmic Creator. Without a perception of believability in each actor's part, the drama would soon lose its charm and come to a close. Thus even those of high spiritual estate accept the "reality" of their present position, dissociated outwardly from identity with their previous roles lest their overlay unduly influence and characterize their new dramatic portrayal. God-realized and liberated souls can well remember previous enactments if they choose to do so; but for the effectiveness of the earthly theatrics, they fully submit themselves to God's direction for their part in an unfolding new scene. This is in evidence in the following verses concerning the statement of John the Baptist about his identity:

And this is the record of John, when the Jews sent priests and Levites from Jerusalem to ask him, "Who art thou?"

And he confessed, and denied not; but confessed, "I am not the Christ."

And they asked him, "What then? Art thou Elijah?"

And he saith, "I am not."

"Art thou that prophet?"

And he answered, "No."

Then said they unto him, "Who art thou? that we may give an answer to them that sent us. What sayest thou of thyself?"

He said, "I am the voice of one crying in the wilderness, Make straight the way of the Lord, as said the prophet Isaiah."

---

* See Discourse 2.

> *And they which were sent were of the Pharisees. And they asked him, and said unto him, "Why baptizest thou then, if thou be not that Christ, nor Elijah, neither that prophet?"*
>
> *John answered them, saying, "I baptize with water: but there standeth one among you, whom ye know not; he it is, who coming after me is preferred before me, whose shoe's latchet I am not worthy to unloose" (John 1:19–27).*

The priests and Levites, with only ordinary perception, were naturally unable to discern the qualities of a Christ. Wise men would not need to question a Christlike person, but would at once recognize his spiritual aura. By asking John if he were the expected Christ, the Pharisees revealed their spiritual ignorance.

John disavowed them of any notion that he was the foreordained Christ they sought. In spite of his greatness he did not see himself as one who had expressed Christ Consciousness.

Why John denied that he was Elijah

Though he had attained that consciousness as Elijah, yet owing to his acceptance of and delusive identification with his role as a lesser figure, he spoke the truth relative to his present life that the potential Christ in him was not manifest in his outward human consciousness. That is why John affirmed: "I am not the Christ."

John also denied that he was Elijah, because he chose not to remember his previous exalted incarnation as that prophet. It was not part of John's role that he extol himself, but rather in absolute subjugation of the ego to portray a somewhat "fallen" spiritual state in which he could rightly declare, "I am not Elijah."

Therefore John gave an evasive answer when he was asked: "Who art thou, that we may give an answer to them that sent us?" His reply meant: "I am the voice, or Cosmic Sound, crying or vibrating in the wilderness of silence."* *Wilderness* signifies the consciousness of a saint wherein no verdure of fresh material desires can grow. The saint makes himself a barren tract on which the presence of God may flower without resistance from the burgeoning growth of materialistic intrusions.

The people sent to confront the Baptist, unable to understand the depth of John's statement, asked further: "Why baptize thou then, if

---

* Elaborated on pages 117 ff.

thou be not that Christ, nor Elijah, neither that prophet?" John answered that he was giving the physical baptism of water, clarifying the consciousness with repentance that would bring a temporary spiritual influence. He went on to say that the exalted one who was yet to come would show people the path of redemption through baptism in Spirit—proclaiming that it was the role of Jesus, with his Christ-aura, to baptize souls with the fiery wisdom and power of the sacred cosmic vibratory emanations of the Holy Ghost. By his words John turned the minds of the multitude from himself to the Christ Savior whose special dispensation he had come to herald, and to witness and support.

❦

There was a man sent from God, whose name was John. The same came for a witness, to bear witness of the Light, that all men through him might believe. He was not that Light, but was sent to bear witness of that Light. That was the true Light, which lighteth every man that cometh into the world (John 1:6–9).

"To bear witness of the Light" means that John had tuned himself with the cosmic creative light of the Holy Ghost that imbues the whole universe. Just as the electric current from a dynamo pervades the lightbulbs of a city, so the Cosmic Light manifests itself in the stones, the grass, the animals, the air, the thermal and electric currents; and enlivens every human being. John experienced and bore witness to that Light. In his incarnate consciousness he was not actively manifesting oneness with the whole Cosmic Light, but rather knew himself as an individualized expression of it. He came to bear witness of that All-Pervading Light and of its immanent radiant power of Christ Consciousness that would be evidenced in the Lord Jesus.*

❦

---

* The above reference to John the Baptist by the apostle John served as both a factual record of the role of the Baptist and also as a metaphorical medium to express esoterically, in the context of the opening verses of the Gospel According to St. John, the underlying spiritual nature of the coming-forth and subsistence of God's creation. (See elaboration, Discourse 1.)

*Then cometh Jesus from Galilee to Jordan unto John, to be bap-
tized of him. But John forbad him, saying, "I have need to be
baptized of thee, and comest thou to me?"*

*And Jesus answering said unto him, "Suffer it to be so now:
for thus it becometh us to fulfill all righteousness." Then he suffered him (Matthew 3:13–15).*

W hen Jesus came to John asking to be baptized, John affirmed
his inferior position, an incarnation of lesser prominence in the
cosmic drama. With what artless humility, the hallmark of godliness,
John had set aside his former preeminence—declaring himself unworthy to baptize Jesus, and that he himself rather
had need to be baptized. Certainly Jesus, a master,
was far above the need for ritualistic baptism, especially by anyone of far lesser spiritual stature. A
doctor of philosophy does not take lessons from a
child engaged in elementary studies. Jesus, recognizing the divine instrumentality of his past-life guru, therefore gave no credence to John's
statement; rather he said: "Suffer it to be so now: for thus it becometh
us to fulfill all righteousness." These words speak volumes of Jesus'
reverential regard for John, of whom he was later to proclaim, "Verily I say unto you, among them that are born of women there hath not
risen a greater than John the Baptist."*

In receiving baptism from John, Jesus not only honored in the
eyes of the masses the ancient, pre-Christian, Hindu custom of baptism in holy waters, but also the tradition of initiation that uniquely
distinguishes the guru-disciple relationship, the divine law through
which "all righteousness" (truth and salvation) is bestowed on the disciple by a God-ordained master. Jesus came to John for that spiritual
anointing, an avowal of reverence for his guru from whom he had received "a double portion of Spirit" in their incarnations as Elijah and
Elisha.

The relationship of guru and disciple is not for one incarnation
only. A guru, being the agent of salvation appointed by God, must
take the disciple through successive incarnations, if necessary, until
complete liberation of the disciple is reached. In the dim past, in former lifetimes when John was first sent by God as the guru of Jesus in

*Guru-disciple relation-
ship: the way of "all
righteousness"*

---

* Matthew 11:11 (see Discourse 34).

response to his prayers, the souls of John the Baptist and of Jesus were eternally bound together by the law of unconditional divine friendship; and both at this long-ago first meeting as guru and disciple had made the resolution, "We will be divine friends forever until our souls by mutual help and the lasting goodwill of many incarnations break the bubble-walls of caging desires and set free our imprisoned omnipresence to become one with the sea of Infinitude."

Jesus came on earth as a world savior, a role of higher degree than that of John the Baptist, yet he acknowledged John as his guru of former incarnations, the agent first sent by God to enter with him into this covenant of divinely ordained friendship. This is why Jesus said, "Suffer it to be so now, for thus it becometh us to fulfill all righteousness." Though John and Jesus both knew that Jesus was far beyond the need for this outer ritual, they were quite sincerely enacting the necessary formalities in setting the right example for the world.* Words may be easily forgotten or distorted; the erudition of acts is far more indelible.

John's declaration to the priests and Levites, "I indeed baptize you with water unto repentance; but he that cometh after me...shall baptize you with the Holy Ghost, and with fire," introduces a doctrine crucial to the attainment of salvation: that the real baptism consists of spiritual initiation bestowed by a true guru. Even though John said he baptized the masses with water, he did not say he was incapable of baptizing with Spirit, only that such initiation would be the prerogative of the Christ who by special dispensation would come to be their savior, or guru. In fact, it was the true baptism of Spirit that was bestowed on Jesus when, after immersion in the Jordan (purification by water), "the heavens were opened unto him." As John himself witnessed: "I saw the Spirit descending from heaven like a dove, and it abode upon him" (John 1:32). If John were an ordinary man, he would not have seen the Spirit descending on Jesus. He himself was in tune with Spirit, but with unfeigned humbleness deflected attention from himself to the preeminence of Jesus.

It is by the grace of the guru that heavenly consciousness unfolds to the initiated disciple, revealing the light of the omniscient spiritual eye, symbolized by the dove—through this medium one ascends from

---

* "Whatever a superior being does, inferior persons imitate. His actions set a standard for people of the world" (*God Talks With Arjuna: The Bhagavad Gita* III:21).

the body to Spirit through the Holy Ghost, the Christ Consciousness "only begotten Son," and Cosmic Consciousness, or God the Father.

The various processes of baptism and their corresponding effects or spiritual states should be explained.

The ritual of baptism by immersion in water originated in India, which laid stress on purification of the body precedent to the purifi-

Different types of baptism

cation of the mind. Students who sought instruction in the spiritual life from a holy man had first to purify their bodies by bathing, which in itself was the beginning of cleansing the mind, by showing proper respect to the teacher, and by interiorizing the thoughts in expectation of the blessings and the value of the lessons to be received. "Cleanliness is next to godliness" is a worthwhile first lesson. Immersion in water opens the pores of the skin, letting out disturbing body poisons and calming and soothing the circulatory system. Water cools the nerve endings and sends reports of calm sensations throughout the vital centers of the body, balancing evenly all the vital energies.

Life came initially from energy, then from nebulae, then from water. All seeds of life are irrevocably connected with water. Physical life cannot exist without it. One who bathes every day and meditates immediately thereafter will feel the power of "baptism" by water. To bathe with the consciousness of purification in a holy river or a lake, or other natural waters surrounded by God's scenic grandeur, is a vibrantly uplifting experience.

While baptism by water as a sacred rite has its valid points, including the temporary cleansing of the mind, the ceremony, to be of lasting value, must be followed up with continued lessons in spiritual living and God-contact. Otherwise, the mind begins to revert to its old habits; their evils wear away the salutary effects of the baptismal ritual. Unless wickedness is purged by meditation and constant spiritual vigilance and endeavor, the initiated simply remain possessed of the same devils with a penchant for misbehavior. A story in India illustrates this point metaphorically: A saint said to his would-be disciple, "Son, it is necessary to bathe in the Ganges to purify the mind from sin. The sins will leave you while you bathe, for they cannot tolerate the holy waters. But take care, for they will wait in the trees skirting the river; and as soon as you come out of the sacred influence of the holy waters, they will again try to jump on you."

It is the mental attitude of faith and devotion in which one receives a ceremonial baptism—whether by immersion or the modified symbolic way of sprinkling water on the head—that determines the blessings received; and it is the continuity of right thought and action that assures the lasting benefit. The initiate thereafter should regularly baptize the self with Spirit by immersion of the consciousness in the wisdom, magnetism, and spiritual radiation of the Holy Ghost in meditation.

As the intent of baptism is to bring about an uplifting change in the consciousness by some form of symbolic immersion, it is good to consider how one can be "baptized" unknowingly by one's associates. The would-be "initiate" should therefore be discriminatively aware of the waters into which the consciousness is immersed.

Vibrations of other people can be received by an exchange of magnetism. One who comes near a holy person will be benefited; this is baptism by spiritual magnetism. The saint's thoughts and magnetic aura cast out a vibratory glow that changes the consciousness and brain cells of those who come within range. All who visit or live on the same grounds where a master lives or has lived will automatically be transformed if they are in tune. If that attunement is deep enough, even from thousands of miles away a holy person's uplifting vibrations can be received.

If one loves poetry and is much in the company of a poet of noble ideals, one will be baptized with wholesome elevated feelings and the appreciation of the goodness and beauty in everything. Such baptism by feeling makes one aesthetically imaginative and sympathetic.

If one associates long with persons of high morality and self-control, one's own life will feel a positive reinforcement of moral consciousness and self-control.

If purposely and attentively one associates with successful creative business minds, the consciousness will be baptized with a creative business sense.

The ultimate baptism, acclaimed by John the Baptist and by all Self-realized masters, is to be baptized "with the Holy Ghost, and with fire"—that is, to become permeated with God's presence in the holy Creative Vibration whose *Baptism by the Holy* omnipresent omniscience not only uplifts and ex- *Ghost* pands the consciousness, but whose fire of cosmic life energy actually cauterizes sins of present bad habits and karmic effects of past erroneous actions.

107

The macrocosm of the universe with its diverse beings is made of the divine vibration, or cosmic energy, of the Holy Ghost, imbued with the Christ Intelligence, which in turn is a reflection of the Cosmic Consciousness of God. Man is a microcosm of the universe: a combination of body, life force, and consciousness. His consciousness is a reflection of Christ Consciousness, his soul differentiated by his own personalized ego. His life force is individualized cosmic energy. His body is condensed cosmic energy, enlivened by specialized life energy.* Life force vibrating grossly changes into electrons, atoms, molecules, and bodily flesh; life force vibrating progressively finer becomes consciousness. In the human being, the body, life force, and consciousness—being three different rates of vibration—are held together by the nucleus of ego and its pure nature, the soul. In order to free the soul, the Christ in man, from the limited threefold vibrations of the human body, life force, and consciousness, the divine consciousness in man has first to be baptized or united with the Holy Ghost, the original cosmic vibration of *Aum*, the Word, the primal manifestation of God. Thence, the consciousness merges in the Omnipresent Christ immanent in creation and ascends to the transcendent Cosmic Consciousness, the Father. No one can reach God the Father except through the Holy Ghost and Christ Consciousness.

The way of ascension was made manifest in the baptism of Jesus. As told in the Gospel According to St. Matthew:

> *And Jesus, when he was baptized, went up straightway out of the water: and, lo, the heavens were opened unto him, and he saw the Spirit of God descending like a dove, and lighting upon him: And lo a voice from heaven, saying, "This is My beloved Son, in whom I am well pleased" (Matthew 3:16–17).†*

"Spirit" signifies the Unmanifested Absolute. As soon as Spirit descends into manifestation, It becomes three, the Trinity: God the Father, Son, and Holy Ghost. In the cosmic sense, if one sees the whole universe, it would be as a tremendous mass of radiant light, like a mist

---

* Cosmic energy in the body works as five specialized currents, empowering the performance of the crystallizing (*prana*), assimilating (*samana*), eliminating (*apana*), metabolizing (*udana*), and circulatory (*vyana*) activities of the body.

† Cf. parallel references in Mark 1:9–11 and Luke 3:21–22.

of aurora. That is the great *Aum* vibration of the Holy Ghost. God's superimposed intelligence omnipresent in all manifestation—the Son or Christ Consciousness—is reflected as a wondrous light of opal blue; it overlays and permeates every particle of creation,

yet remains always untouched and unchanged by its ever-mutating environment. Beyond creative manifestation, through a radiating white light, is God the Father in the vibrationless heaven of ever-existing,

Meaning of "the Spirit of God descending like a dove"

ever-conscious, ever-new Bliss. That triune manifestation is the cosmic aspect of Spirit descending in these three forms: as Cosmic Vibration, Christ Consciousness, and God the Father. This Trinity is manifested in the microcosm of man as the triune light of the spiritual eye.

Man's body, unique among all creatures, possesses spiritual cerebrospinal centers of divine consciousness in which the descended Spirit is templed. These are known to the yogis, and to Saint John—who described them in Revelation as the seven seals, and as seven stars and seven churches, with their seven angels and seven golden candlesticks.* When one is baptized by immersion in the light of Spirit, the microcosmic spiritual eye in the body may be seen in its relation to the light of descending Spirit as the Cosmic Trinity.

---

* "Write the things which thou hast seen, and the things which are, and the things which shall be hereafter; the mystery of the seven stars which thou sawest in my right hand, and the seven golden candlesticks. The seven stars are the angels of the seven churches: and the seven candlesticks which thou sawest are the seven churches" (Revelation 1:19–20). "And I saw in the right hand of him that sat on the throne a book written within and on the backside, sealed with seven seals. And I saw a strong angel proclaiming with a loud voice, 'Who is worthy to open the book, and to loose the seals thereof?'" (Revelation 5:1–2). Yoga treatises identify these centers (in ascending order) as: *muladhara* (the coccygeal, at the base of the spine); *svadhisthana* (the sacral, two inches above *muladhara*); *manipura* (the lumbar, opposite the navel); *anahata* (the dorsal, opposite the heart); *vishuddha* (the cervical, at the base of the neck); *ajna* (seat of the spiritual eye, traditionally located between the eyebrows; in actuality, directly connected by polarity with the medulla oblongata); and *sahasrara* ("thousand-petaled lotus" in the uppermost part of the cerebrum). The seven centers are divinely planned exits or "trap doors" through which the soul has descended into the body and through which it must reascend by a process of meditation. By seven successive steps, the soul escapes into Cosmic Consciousness. Yoga treatises generally refer to the six lower centers as *chakras* ("wheels," because the concentrated energy in each one is like a hub from which radiate rays of life-giving light and energy), with *sahasrara* referred to separately as a seventh center. All seven centers, however, are often referred to as lotuses, whose petals open, or turn upward, in spiritual awakening as the life and consciousness travel up the spine.

109

In the baptism of Jesus, this is described metaphorically as "Spirit descending like a dove, and lighting upon him." The dove symbolizes the spiritual eye, seen by deeply meditating devotees at the Christ Consciousness center in the forehead between the two physical eyes. This eye of light and consciousness appears as a golden aura (the Holy Ghost Vibration) surrounding an opal-blue sphere (Christ Consciousness) in the center of which is a five-pointed star of brilliant white light (doorway to the Cosmic Consciousness of Spirit). The threefold light of God in the spiritual eye is symbolized by a dove because it brings perennial peace. Also, looking in the spiritual eye produces in man's consciousness the purity signified by the dove.

The mouth of the symbolic dove represents the star in the spiritual eye, the secret passage to Cosmic Consciousness. The two wings of the dove represent the two spheres of consciousness emanating from Cosmic Consciousness: The blue light of the spiritual eye is the microcosm of the subjective Christ Intelligence in all creation; and the golden ring of light in the spiritual eye is the microcosmic objective cosmic energy, Cosmic Vibration, or Holy Ghost.*

All manifestation is a product of vibration, which is of the Holy Ghost, and is sustained by the inherence of God's consciousness. Thus the light of the spiritual eye is composed of vibratory lifetrons, the finest ultimate unit of intelligent energy emanating from the Holy Ghost (the subtlety of lifetrons is superseded only by the vibrations of pure consciousness). Lifetrons are the underlying support of the grosser electrons and structural atoms of which all matter is composed. Each microscopic lifetron contains in miniature the essence of all macroscopic creation.

The triune Spirit manifested though man's spiritual eye

The consciousness present microcosmically in the spiritual eye in man is composed of the elements of God the Father, Son, and Holy Ghost—transcendental Cosmic Consciousness, immanent Christ Consciousness, and Cosmic Energy. Jesus saw the Spirit descending from the abode of Heavenly Bliss in the form of a microcosmic spiritual eye and settle upon his consciousness. The spiritual eye of Jesus was opened, and through this immersion in Spirit,

---

* The identifying emblem of Self-Realization Fellowship/Yogoda Satsanga Society of India depicts the spiritual eye, showing the white star and surrounding rings of blue and golden light at the point between the two eyebrows, situated within a golden lotus flower. It signifies the meditating devotee's goal of opening the eye of divine perception, just as the open lotus is an ancient symbol of awakened spiritual consciousness.

he perceived the mergence of his individualized consciousness with the macrocosmic manifestations of Cosmic Consciousness, Christ Consciousness, and Cosmic Energy.

The holy Cosmic Vibration, the primal manifestation of transcendental God the Father, emits not only the property of light—the magnificent effulgence of God's divine light and its structural lifetrons and microcosmic spiritual eye of supernal consciousness—but also the wondrous sound of *Aum,* the Word, the great Amen, which is the witness or proof of the Holy Presence. During baptism by Spirit in the form of the Holy Ghost as experienced by Jesus, he saw the light of the spiritual eye as descended from the macrocosmic Divine Light; and from this came the voice of *Aum,* the intelligent, all-creative heavenly sound, vibrating as an intelligible voice: "Thou art My Son, having lifted thy consciousness from the limitation of the body and all matter to realize thyself as one with My perfect reflection, My only begotten image, immanent in all manifestation. I am Bliss, and My joy I express in thy rejoicing in attunement with My Omnipresence." Jesus felt his consciousness attuned to the Christ Consciousness, the "only begotten" reflection of God the Father's Intelligence in the Holy Vibration: he first felt his body as the entire vibratory creation in which his little body was included; then within his cosmic body of all creation, he experienced his oneness with God's innate Presence as the Infinite Christ or Universal Intelligence, a magnetic aura of blissful Divine Love in which God's presence holds all beings.

∼

Saint John, the beloved disciple of Christ, records the testimony of John the Baptist, the guru through whose instrumentality Jesus received this baptism of Spirit:

> *The next day John seeth Jesus coming unto him, and saith, "Behold the Lamb of God, which taketh away the sin of the world. This is he of whom I said, 'After me cometh a man which is preferred before me: for he was before me.' And I knew him not: but that he should be made manifest to Israel, therefore am I come baptizing with water."*
>
> *And John bare record, saying, "I saw the Spirit descending from heaven like a dove, and it abode upon him. And I knew*

111

him not: but He that sent me to baptize with water, the same
said unto me, 'Upon whom thou shalt see the Spirit descending,
and remaining on him, the same is he which baptizeth with the
Holy Ghost.' And I saw, and bare record that this is the Son of
God" (John 1:29–34).

All masters who have attained the ultimate realization and oneness with God are equal in the eyes of God. But the Father of the Universe, during certain cycles of time, "prefers," that

The Lamb of God: a is, chooses, one soul to come to earth as a world
world savior prophet to give spiritual impetus to His children.
Sometimes in the world there are several masters
present, but one is delegated by God to carry out a preeminent dispensation. That in no degree lessens the greatness of other masters,
who are all one in Spirit. John came baptizing with water, in the customary ritualistic way, to draw the attention of Israel, true souls, to
the advent of Jesus. Having stirred their receptivity, he could then
humbly fulfill his own dispensation: to make manifest by his testimony
the divine credentials of Jesus, who was "preferred"—chosen by God
—for a grand mission of the reformation of humanity. Jesus was to
do this by inspiring the world with a new consciousness through revival of the true rite of baptism by Spirit, the transformation of consciousness by immersion in the sacred vibration of the Holy Ghost.

The expression "I knew him not" is misleading. It does not mean
that John didn't recognize Jesus. Rather, he was pointing out that no
one in the ordinary state of body-identified ego consciousness—or
even John himself, through purely external sensory perception—could
possibly fathom the spiritual consciousness of the Christ in Jesus. It
was during Jesus' baptism, when both he and John were transfigured
in the light of the Holy Ghost, that John witnessed that Jesus was indeed a fully manifested "Son of God." Such recognition could not be
evidenced to an ordinary mind; but through the transparency of an
uplifted consciousness, the full divinity of Jesus' consciousness as one
with Christ Consciousness can be realized.

John's reference to Jesus that "he was before me" again demonstrates John's humility in acknowledging, in their incarnations as John
and Jesus, the reversal of their previous roles as Elijah and Elisha—it
was Jesus in this present drama who demonstrated Christhood before
John ("before me").

John introduced Jesus the Savior with the epithet "Lamb of God, which taketh away the sin of the world." A lamb is a symbol of innocence, meekness, and loyalty. Jesus was innocent, pure, humble, and true to God in every way. His was not the arrogant power of a tyrannical crusader out to destroy evil by force. Rather he came to offer himself as a sacrifice (as lambs are sacrificed in the Orient) to exemplify the supreme power of love. If God used His omnipotence to punish man, it would be impossible for a mere mortal to exercise independent judgment and thus learn and grow by his own mistakes. The karmic law works whereby man punishes himself proportionate to his misdeeds, while at the same time God uses love to encourage discriminative right behavior and to awaken in the human spirit the higher soul qualities of God's image within the true Self.

Jesus exemplified God's love in a rare expression of spiritual magnanimity: the willing oblation of his own life. By sacrificing himself for the spiritual welfare of others, a savior who is empowered by God to do so can expiate the sins of others. Jesus, a world savior, took on himself not only the karmic debt of his disciples but also the sin of the masses by allowing himself to be crucified.

It would be folly to presume that anyone, even a Jesus, can take away an individual's sin unless the sinner himself cooperates to remove that karmic consequence. A master can take upon himself some of the burden of a disciple if that devotee makes a worthwhile spiritual effort to improve himself. But most of all, a master serves in the highest way by example and teachings that inspire the errant children of God to free themselves from their bad habits and spiritual negligence.

To demonstrate the Divine Compassion, Jesus came as the lamb of spirituality, ready to offer himself as a sacrifice before the temple of truth—an exemplar of the consummate power of love over evil, wisdom over ignorance, forgiveness over vengefulness, light over darkness.

Jesus' sacrifice was, primarily, to exemplify for all time the power of spiritual force over ignorance and brute force. He showed that the power of love could conquer the Roman Empire, which with all its might could not suppress his philosophy. His reign has outlasted that of all warrior conquerors, based on the divine edict: "Love your enemies."

In pointing to Jesus as one sent by God to be the savior of multitudes, John proclaims: "Behold the gentleness of compassion and the meek but almighty power of love represented in Jesus, which will destroy ignorance and evil from the lives of those who will receive within

113

themselves the Christ incarnate in him. Christ-love will act as a powerful current in the heart and brain to destroy the sin of evil."

The word "initiation" (in Sanskrit, *diksha*), as used in India, means the same as implied in the term "baptism" adopted by the West. Initiation by a guru is the interior consecration of the disciple into the spiritual path that leads from the domain of matter-consciousness into the kingdom of Spirit. The true initiation, as has been shown, is baptism by Spirit: coming in contact with a saintly person who can by a glance or a touch send the vibrating light of Spirit over the devotee to change and uplift the consciousness. This real baptism cleanses the consciousness of the initiate with the Holy Light of the spiritual eye and the sacred sound of *Aum*. Whosoever can see the life current of the spiritual eye changing and spiritualizing the brain cells and the very composition of the mind of the initiate is one who baptizes with the Holy Ghost. He sees the light of the spiritual eye and throws that Light of Spirit onto the consciousness of the devotee. When that vibratory power passes through the initiate, it cauterizes present bad habits and past karmic seeds lodged in the brain. By the consciousness of God which is within him, a great spiritual soul can transfer to others who are receptive an experience of some of his own God-consciousness.

The three aspects of spiritual initiation

This spiritual baptism is threefold. First, when the teacher bestows initiation, he sees the Light himself as he baptizes the disciple. Second, when the teacher sends that Light into the initiate, which the devotee may or may not see himself, it remains a little while with its full vibratory power to effect a spiritual change in the devotee; but it is temporary. A master's blessings can for some time hold that Light within the disciple, but the devotee must also make the effort to retain it. Third, to keep the Light permanently, the devotee has to make it his own through conscientious endeavor in meditation and in following the spiritual guidance and practices, the *sadhana,* given by the master.

The surest way to find God is to learn about Him from one who *knows* Him. To follow a master whose path has led him to God-realization is to reach assuredly the same Goal.

The scriptures of India speak of the liberation of the soul in terms of a calibrated formula, which, providentially, seems to favor the "spirit is weak" syndrome in man. Of the total requirement to achieve salvation, it is said that 25% is the disciple's spiritual effort, 25% is the blessing of the guru, and the remaining 50% is the grace of God. The aspirant should not be tempted into complacency, however, waiting to be moved by the spirit of the blessings and grace, for it is the catalyst of the devotee's effort that makes the formula work.

The necessity of following a true guru on the spiritual path

As the devotee's effort and the guru's blessings are equally necessary to the disciple's progress, we are taught in India the first requisite importance on the spiritual path of following faithfully one's guru. He takes personal interest in the welfare of the devotee's soul and lays before him a path of spiritual discipline that leads as far as the God-seeker wishes to go.

In the early years of my spiritual search I was blessed to have frequent association with saintly souls whose God-consciousness transported my consciousness into supernal realms. But it was not until I met my own God-ordained guru, Swami Sri Yukteswar, and received initiation from him, that I understood fully the transforming power of the sacred guru-disciple tradition. Baptized in a radiance as of a thousand suns, my whole being was blissfully enwrapped in God's love and secured in the care of Guru's wisdom. The *Kriya Yoga sadhana* imparted to me at that *diksha* was the "pearl of great price" with which all doors to the Divine Presence would be opened.

A guru is not an ordinary spiritual teacher. One may have many teachers, but only one guru, who is the agent of salvation appointed by God in response to a devotee's demands for release from the bondage of matter.

Ministers in churches and priests in temples are oftentimes chosen only by a set standard of their intellectual knowledge of the scriptures, or by virtue of sacerdotal authority ceremonially conferred on them by a formally higher ecclesiastical superior. No guru can be developed only by years of study in the intellectual factory of a theological seminary, which deems it has attained its ends when it confers B.D. or D.D. degrees. Such titles can be won by men of good memory; but character, self-control, and the wisdom of soul intuition can be cultured only by knowledge and application of advanced methods of deep daily meditation that produce Self-realization and actual experience of God.

Neither can one be a guru by self-choice. He must be ordained to serve and save others by a real guru, or else he must hear in reality the voice of God asking him to redeem others. As has been shown, this law was honored even by Jesus, who received his guru's blessing before beginning his ministry—just to set the right example. Self-appointed gurus are much misguided by listening to the voice of their imaginative ego in their subconscious mind. Those who thus falsely anoint themselves as gurus, or exult in the veneration of followers who are encouraged to look on them as such, are not empowered by God nor their own spiritual attainment to grant salvation to anyone. It is admirable to lecture and teach good principles; but without possessing the qualifications of a real guru a teacher cannot redeem souls, nor should he presume to accept others as disciples until he himself has progressed far in his own Self-realization.

True gurus train first their inner selves in the theologically advanced school of intuition and God-communion in meditation. They spiritually baptize themselves in Spirit before they aspire to initiate others. They teach not for mundane gain or glory, but for the singular purpose of leading souls to God. A guru never seeks for himself the devotion and obedience of his disciples, but transfers that reverence to God.

It is not necessary for a disciple to be in the company of the guru in order to receive his blessings. What is most important is to be spiritually in tune with the guru, for his help is transferred to the disciple primarily on the inner spiritual plane rather than through material means. If the disciple is uncarping, unconditionally reverential and loving to the master, and faithful in following his precepts, his receptivity makes the task of the guru easier. Attunement links the help of the guru with the sincere striving of the disciple, even if the guru is no longer incarnate on earth. My guru, Sri Yukteswarji, wrote: "To keep company with the Guru is not only to be in his physical presence (as this is sometimes impossible), but mainly means to keep him in our hearts and to be one with him in principle and to attune ourselves with him....by keeping his appearance and attributes fully in mind, and by reflecting on the same and affectionately following his instructions, lamblike."*

Many who were born centuries after Christ have attained God-realization through devotion to Jesus, the Good Shepherd, whom they followed as their guru or savior. Jesus said, "Why call ye me Lord, Lord, and do not the things which I say?"† The secret of the saints is that they practiced what Jesus taught and exemplified; and by their single-hearted devotion they were able to attain ecstatic interiorization, as do adept yogis, which is necessary for communion with Christ.

---

* *The Holy Science,* published by Self-Realization Fellowship.

† Luke 6:46.

~

There is a beautiful revelation of the way to that divine contact hidden in the Biblical verses where John the Baptist describes himself:

"I am the voice of one crying in the wilderness, Make straight the way of the Lord, as said the prophet Isaiah" (John 1:23).

John prepared the way for the extremely short ministry of Jesus by baptizing and preaching to the masses to make ready, as best he could, a not very enlightened generation. For his own part, his quoting the veiled prophecy of Isaiah in the Old Testament* was not only a confirmation of himself as the one foretold to announce Christ, but a pronouncement of the true preparation required to receive Christ—in the coming of Jesus at that time, and for all future times.

Highway to Christ Consciousness: "the straight way of the Lord"

When one's senses are engaged outwardly, one is engrossed in the busy mart of creation's interacting complexities of matter. Even when one's eyes are closed in prayer or in other concentrated thoughts, still one is in the domain of busyness. The real wilderness, where no mortal thoughts, restlessness, or human desires, intrude, is in transcendence of the sensory mind, the subconscious mind, and the superconscious mind—in the cosmic consciousness of Spirit, the uncreate trackless "wilderness" of Infinite Bliss.

John the Baptist spoke from his inner spiritual state as having attained realization of the omnipresent Cosmic Vibration: "I am in tune with the Sound of Creation vibrating in the wilderness where there are no desires or restlessness. The human expression of my voice crying— that is, trying to teach people from my cosmic consciousness—emanates from the Voice or Word of the Cosmic Vibration coming out of Spirit. With the divine power of that Voice, I have come to declare the consciousness that is in Jesus."

As John heard within himself in the wilderness of silence the all-knowing Cosmic Sound, the intuitive wisdom commanded him silently: "Make straight the way of the Lord." Manifest the Lord, the subjec-

---

* Isaiah 40:3: "The voice of him that crieth in the wilderness, 'Prepare ye the way of the Lord, make straight in the desert a highway for our God.'"

tive Christ Consciousness in all cosmic vibratory creation, within yourself through the intuitive feeling awakened when in the state of transcendental ecstasy the divine metaphysical centers of life and consciousness are opened in the straight spinal pathway.

Yoga treatises explain the awakening of the spinal centers not as some mystical aberration but as a purely natural occurrence common to all devotees who find their way into the presence of God. The principles of yoga know no artificial boundaries of religious isms. Yoga is the universal science of divine union of the soul with Spirit, of man with his Maker. Yoga describes the definite way Spirit descends from Cosmic Consciousness into matter and individualized expression in all beings; and how, conversely, individualized consciousness ultimately must reascend to Spirit. Many are the pathways of religion and the modes of approaching God; but ultimately they all lead to one highway of final ascension to union with Him. The way of liberation of the soul from its ties to mortal consciousness in the body is identical for all: through the same "straight" highway of the spine by which the soul descended from Spirit into the body and matter.*

Man's true nature is the soul, a ray of Spirit. As God is ever-existing, ever-conscious, ever-new Bliss, so the soul, by encasement in the body, is individualized ever-existing, ever-conscious, ever-new Bliss. The bodily covering of the soul is threefold in nature. The physical body, with which man so affectionately and tenaciously identifies himself, is little more than inert matter, a clod of earthly minerals and chemicals made up of gross atoms. The physical body receives all its enlivening energy and powers from an inner radiant astral body of lifetrons. The astral body, in turn, is empowered by a causal body of pure consciousness, consisting of all of the ideational principles that structure and maintain the astral and physical bodily instruments employed by the soul to interact with God's creation.† The three bodies are tied together and work

---

* "And an highway shall be there, and a way, and it shall be called The way of holiness; the unclean shall not pass over it....but the redeemed shall walk there. And the ransomed of the Lord shall return, and come to Zion with songs and everlasting joy upon their heads: they shall obtain joy and gladness, and sorrow and sighing shall flee away" (Isaiah 35:8–10).

† The causal body, the idea-matrix for the astral and physical bodies, consists of 35 idea elements, 19 of which constitute the astral body and 16 of which correspond to the chemical elements of the physical body. Hindu scriptures identify the 19 astral-body elements as: intelligence; ego; feeling; mind (sense-consciousness); five instruments of

as one by a knotting of life force and consciousness in seven spiritual cerebrospinal centers: a physical bodily instrument, empowered by the life force of the astral body and the consciousness from the causal form. In its residency in the triune body, the soul takes on the limitations of confinement and becomes the pseudosoul, or ego.

Descending first into the causal body of consciousness through the ideational centers of the causal spine of magnetized consciousness, thence into the wondrous spinal centers of light and power of the astral body, life force and consciousness then descend into the physical body through the brain and spine outward into the nervous system and organs and senses, enabling man to cognize the world and interact with his material environment.*

---

knowledge (the sensory powers within the physical organs of sight, hearing, smell, taste, and touch); five instruments of action (the executive powers in the physical instruments of procreation, excretion, speech, locomotion, and the exercise of manual skill); and five instruments of life force that perform the functions of circulation, metabolization, assimilation, crystallization, and elimination.

* Scientific discovery of the electromagnetic energy that forms an organizing template for the physical body is described in *Vibrational Medicine* (Rochester, Vermont: Bear and Company, 2001), by Richard Gerber, M.D.: "Neuroanatomist Harold S. Burr at Yale University during the 1940s was studying the shape of energy fields"—which he termed "fields of life" or "L-fields"—"around living plants and animals. Some of Burr's work involved the shape of electrical fields surrounding salamanders. He found that the salamanders possessed an energy field roughly shaped like the adult animal. He also discovered that this field contained an electrical axis which was aligned with the brain and spinal cord. Burr wanted to find precisely when this electrical axis first originated in the animal's development. He began mapping the fields in progressively earlier stages of salamander embryogenesis. Burr discovered that the electrical axis originated in the unfertilized egg....Burr also experimented with the electrical fields around tiny seedlings. According to his research, the electrical field around a sprout was not the shape of the original seed. Instead the surrounding electrical field resembled the adult plant."

In *Blueprint for Immortality: The Electric Patterns of Life* (Essex, England: Saffron Walden, 1972), Professor Burr describes his research: "Most people who have taken high-school science will remember that if iron filings are scattered on a card held over a magnet they will arrange themselves in the pattern of the 'lines of force' of the magnet's field. And if the filings are thrown away and fresh ones scattered on the card, the new filings will assume the same pattern as the old.

"Something like this—though infinitely more complicated—happens in the human body. Its molecules and cells are constantly being torn apart and rebuilt with fresh material from the food we eat. But thanks to the controlling L-field, the new molecules and cells are rebuilt as before and arrange themselves in the same pattern as the old ones.

"Modern research with 'tagged' elements has revealed that the materials of our bodies and brains are renewed much more often than was previously realized. All the

The flow of the life force and consciousness outward through the spine and nerves causes man to perceive and appreciate sensory phe-

Reversing the flow of consciousness and life force to awaken the spiritual eye

nomena only. As attention is the conductor of man's life currents and consciousness, persons who indulge the senses of touch, smell, taste, sound, and sight find the searchlights of their life force and consciousness concentrated on matter. But when, by self-mastery in meditation, the attention is focused steadily on the center of divine perception at the point between the eyebrows, the searchlights of life force and consciousness are reversed. Withdrawing from the senses, they reveal the light of the spiritual eye.

As one switch throws light into the two headlights of an automobile, so the astral center of superconsciousness in the medulla throws its current into the two physical eyes that behold the world of duality. But by deep concentration on the point between the two eyes, the light of the medulla flowing into the two eyes can be made to converge into the one single spiritual eye in the forehead. Jesus said: "If therefore thine eye be single, thy whole body shall be full of light." Through this eye of omnipresence the devotee enters into the realms of divine consciousness.

India's yogis (those who seek union with God through formal scientific methods of yoga) lay the utmost importance on keeping the spine straight during meditation, and upon concentrating on the point between the eyebrows. A bent spine during meditation offers real resistance to the process of reversing the life currents to flow upward towards the spiritual eye. A bent spine throws the vertebrae out of alignment and pinches the nerves, trapping the life force in its accustomed state of body consciousness and mental restlessness.

The populace in Israel was looking for Christ in a physical body, so John the Baptist assured them of the coming of one in whom Christ

protein in the body, for example, is 'turned over' every six months and, in some organs such as the liver, the protein is renewed much more frequently. When we meet a friend we have not seen for six months there is not one molecule in his face which was there when we last saw him. But, thanks to his controlling L-field, the new molecules have fallen into the old, familiar pattern and we can recognize his face. Until modern instruments revealed the existence of the controlling L-fields, biologists were at a loss to explain how our bodies 'kept in shape' through ceaseless metabolism and changes of material. Now the mystery has been solved, the electro-dynamic field of the body serves as a matrix or mould, which preserves the 'shape' or arrangement of any material poured into it, however often the material may be changed." *(Publisher's Note)*

was manifested; but he also told them subtly that anyone who wanted truly to know Christ must receive him by uplifting the consciousness through the spine in meditation ("the way of the Lord"). John was emphasizing that just worshiping the body of Christ Jesus was not the way to know him. The Christ Consciousness embodied in Jesus could be realized only by awakening the astral centers of the spine, the straight way of ascension by which the metaphysical Christ Consciousness in the body of Jesus could be intuitively perceived.

The words of the prophet Isaiah, which were echoed by John the Baptist, show that both knew that the subjective Lord of Finite Vibratory Creation, or Christ Consciousness, could be welcomed into one's own consciousness only through the meditation-awakened straight highway of the spine. Isaiah, John, the yogis, all know that to receive Christ Consciousness more than a simple physical contact with a Christlike person is necessary. One must know how to meditate—how to switch off the attention from the distractions of the senses, and how to keep the consciousness fixed on the altar of the spiritual eye where Christ Consciousness can be received in all its glory.

Jesus himself and his disciples were products of the intuitive omniscience of ecstatic meditation and devotion, not results of intellectual theological seminaries.

Churches today have digressed from the path of Self-realization, personal experience of God and Christ. Congregations are generally satisfied with sermons, ceremonies, organizations, and festive socials. The complete revival and restoration of Christ-ianity can be effected only by less emphasis on theoretical sermons with their oft-repeated platitudes, and on external emotion-rousing, psychophysical ceremonies, and by substituting instead quiet meditation and real inner communion. Rather than being passive members of a church, satisfied merely with listening to sermons, worshipers should engage more in the effort to cultivate perfect stillness in both body and mind. The peace of absolute physical and mental stillness is the real temple wherein God most often visits His devotees. "Be still, and know that I am God."*

Scientific meditation lifts the practice of religion beyond intellectual theory

The word "straight" also signifies following the straight path of truth, through which alone the soul can reach God. It is very difficult

* Psalms 46:10.

to choose the right course amid the varied religious opinions. John declared to the people the straight path out of their ignorance, and exhorted them to follow it to receive the teachings of Jesus in attaining Christ Consciousness. People who wander from church to church seeking intellectual satisfaction seldom find God, for intellectual nourishment is necessary only to inspire one to "drink" God. When the intellect forgets to actually taste God, it is a detriment to Self-realization. Spiritual truth and wisdom are found not in any words of a priest or preacher, but in the "wilderness" of inner silence. The Sanskrit scriptures say: "There are many sages with their scriptural and spiritual interpretations, apparently contradictory, but the real secret of religion is hidden in a cave."* True religion lies within oneself, in the cave of stillness, in the cave of calm intuitive wisdom, in the cave of the spiritual eye. By concentrating on the point between the eyebrows and delving into the depths of quiet in the luminous spiritual eye, one can find answers to all the religious queries of the heart. "The Comforter, which is the Holy Ghost...shall teach you all things" (John 14:26).

By the right method of meditation on the Holy Ghost as the light of the spiritual eye and the holy sound of the cosmic vibration of *Aum*, any persevering devotee, by constant practice, can experience the blessings of the manifested vibratory presence of God. The Sacred Vibration, the Great Comforter, being imbued with the universal, reflected God-consciousness, contains the all-encompassing bliss of God. On the day of Pentecost the disciples of Jesus were filled with the new wine of this Joy coming from the touch of *Aum*, the comforting Holy Vibration, and they could talk "in diverse tongues." *Aum*, the Word, the cosmic intelligent Vibratory Sound, is the origin of all sounds and languages. One filled with the Holy Ghost—one who can hear, feel, and spread his consciousness in *Aum*—can understand and communicate in the diverse tongues of inspirations of men, animals, and atoms. He truly communes with Nature; not as an experience of the senses, but as one united with the Voice of God through which the Creator guides the symbiosis of His beings in an underlying harmony.

All human beings are born of the Creative Vibration of the Holy Ghost; but they are prodigal sons who have left the home of their parental Divine Consciousness and have identified themselves with the finitely limited territory of the human body. The soul feels confine-

---

*The *Mahabharata*, Vana Parva (312.117).

ment in the physical, astral, and ideational bodies. At the onset of spiritual awakening, that Self begins to assert its connate desire for freedom from delusion's constraints. The conscious mind should then be taught how to detach the soul consciousness from identification with these three bodies to reclaim its origin in the omnipresent Spirit.

By a guru-given technique of meditation on *Aum* (*Om*), such as I have taught to Self-Realization Fellowship students,* the sacred *Aum* vibration of the Holy Ghost can be heard in meditation through the supersensory medium of intuition. First, the devotee realizes *Aum* as the manifested cosmic energy in all matter. The earthly sounds of all atomic motion, including the sounds of the body—the heart, lungs, circulation, cellular

Meditation on Aum brings baptism in the Holy Ghost and Christ Consciousness

activity—come from the cosmic sound of the creative vibratory activity of *Aum.* The sounds of the nine octaves perceptible to the human ear, as well as all cosmic low or high vibrations that cannot be registered by the human ear, have their origin in *Aum.* So also, all forms of light—fire, sunlight, electricity, astral light—are expressions of the primal cosmic energy of *Aum.*

This Holy Vibration working in the subtle spinal centers of the astral body, sending forth life force and consciousness into the physical body, manifests as wonderful astral sounds—each one characteristic of its particular center of activity. These astral sounds are likened to melodic strains of the humming of a bee, the tone of a flute, a stringed instrument such as a harp, a bell-like or gong sound, the soothing roar of a distant sea, and a cosmic symphony of all vibratory sound. The Self-Realization Fellowship technique of meditation on *Aum* teaches one to hear and locate these astral sounds. This aids the awakening of the divine consciousness locked in the spinal centers, opening them to "make straight" the way of ascension to God-realization.

As the devotee concentrates on *Aum,* first by mentally chanting *Aum,* and then by actually hearing that sound, his mind is diverted from the physical sounds of matter outside his body to the circulatory and other sounds of the vibrating flesh. Then his consciousness is diverted from the vibrations of the physical body to the musical vibrations of the spinal centers of the astral body. His consciousness then expands from the vibrations of the astral body to the vibrations of consciousness in

---

* Available in the *Self-Realization Fellowship Lessons* (see page 1575).

the causal body and in the omnipresence of the Holy Ghost. When the devotee's consciousness is able not only to hear the cosmic sound of *Aum,* but also to feel its actual presence in every unit of space, in all finite vibrating matter, then the soul of the devotee becomes one with the Holy Ghost. His consciousness vibrates simultaneously in his body, in the sphere of the earth, the planets, the universes, and in every particle of matter, space, and astral manifestation. Through the expanding power of the Holy Ghost, the all-spreading *Aum*-vibrating sound heard in meditation, the consciousness then becomes immersed, or baptized, in the sacred stream of Christ Consciousness.

These progressively higher states of realization are attained through deeper and longer meditation as guided by the guru. But from the very beginning, the blessings of contact with *Aum* become increasingly manifest.

The uplifting vibrations of "the Comforter" bring profound inner peace and joy. The Creative Vibration vitalizes the individual life force in the body, which conduces to health and well-being, and can be consciously directed as healing power to those in need of divine aid.* Being the source of intelligent creativity, the *Aum* vibration inspires one's own initiative, ingenuity, and will.

Baptism in the vibration of the Holy Ghost loosens the hold of bad habits and wrong desires, and aids in the establishment of good habits and desires—ultimately transmuting desire itself into a single-hearted attraction to blessed contact with God. To know God is not the negation of desires, but rather complete fulfillment. Just as by feeding somebody else one's own hunger cannot be appeased, so the soul can never be satisfied by catering to the senses. The senses crave indulgence, greed, and temptations to excite and amuse them; the soul feels fulfilled only by the calmness, peace, and bliss bestowed by meditation and the moderate use of the sensory instruments.

Ambition for good things, noble achievements, and spiritual work, serving the many, should be instituted to displace selfishness

---

* Paramahansa Yogananda daily prayed for and sent healing energy to all who had asked for his help, and taught his disciples a special technique of sending the healing power of *Aum* to aid others in overcoming physical, mental, and spiritual difficulties. This service is continued today by the Prayer Council at Self-Realization Fellowship International Headquarters, joined by the thousands of members of the SRF Worldwide Prayer Circle in praying for those in need and for world peace. See footnote on page 420. *(Publisher's Note)*

and greed, and the limiting circumscription of sole consideration for one's self and one's immediate family. When undertaken in the thought of God, there is great enjoyment in all good work and achievements.

By contacting God in the world and in meditation, all desires of the heart are fulfilled; for nothing is more worthwhile, more pleasant or attractive than the all-satisfying, ever-new joy of God.

Desire limits the consciousness to the object of desire. Love for all good things as expressions of God expands man's consciousness. One who bathes his consciousness in the Holy Ghost becomes unattached to personal desires and objects while enjoying everything with the joyousness of God within.

In deepest meditation, as practiced by those who are advanced in the technique of *Kriya Yoga,** the devotee experiences not only expansion in the *Aum* vibration "Voice from heaven," but finds himself able also to follow the microcosmic light of Spirit in the "straight way" of the spine into the light of the spiritual eye "dove descending from heaven."

Traversing the "straight way" for highest ascension in Spirit

First, the life force and consciousness must be withdrawn from the senses and bodily restlessness, and must cross the portals of Cosmic Energy represented by the golden ring of the spiritual eye. Then the consciousness must plunge in the blue light representing Christ Consciousness. Then it must penetrate through the silver star opening into Spirit, in the boundless region of Infinity. This golden, blue, and silver light contains all the walls of rays—electronic, atomic, and lifetronic—of Cosmic Vibration through which one has to penetrate before one can reach heaven.

In these highest states of meditation, the body itself becomes spiritualized, loosening its atomic tenacity to reveal its underlying astral structure as life force. The aura often depicted around saints is not imaginative, but the inner divine light suffusing the whole being. By

---

* A sacred spiritual science embodying techniques for withdrawal of life and consciousness from the senses upward through the gates of light in the subtle cerebrospinal centers, dissolving the consciousness of matter into life force, life force into mind, mind into soul, and soul into Spirit. *Kriya Yoga,* an ancient form of *Raja* ("royal" or "complete") *Yoga,* is extolled by Krishna in the Bhagavad Gita and by Patanjali in his *Yoga Sutras.* As recounted in *Autobiography of a Yogi, Kriya* was revived in this age by Mahavatar Babaji, who ordained me to spread the liberating science worldwide. *Kriya Yoga* is taught to students of the *Self-Realization Fellowship Lessons* who fulfill preliminary spiritual requirements. (See page 1575.)

deeper meditation still, the astral body becomes elaborated into the ideational body of consciousness. Then as pure wisdom the ideational consciousness transcends the vibrations of the Holy Ghost and becomes immersed in Christ Consciousness, through which it ascends to Cosmic Consciousness, the bosom of God the Father.

This, then, is the real teaching of Jesus Christ who came to baptize with the Holy Ghost. Only that person who can see his spiritual eye, not temporarily, but always, and who can perceive through this eye the Omnipresent Spirit, can baptize others with the cosmic magnetism of the Holy Ghost. Simply seeing the light, or being able to show others the light of the spiritual eye, is not enough. One must be able to perceive the Spirit through the spiritual eye. This is the baptism given by John to Jesus, the *diksha* given by a true guru who can summon the Almighty Spirit to envelop the disciple with the Cosmic Magnetism. The disciple, in turn, must be advanced and deserving in order to be able to receive such a baptism in Omniscience by his advanced guru who is one with Cosmic Consciousness, and thus serves as the channel of Spirit.

Through his two physical eyes, man sees only his body and a little portion of the earth at a time. But spiritual baptism or initiation received from a true guru expands the consciousness. Anyone who can see, as did Jesus, the spiritual dove alight on him—that is, who can behold his spiritual eye of omnipresent omniscience—and through perseverance in ever deeper meditation penetrate his gaze through its light, will perceive the entire kingdom of Cosmic Energy and the consciousness of God existing within it and beyond, in the Infinite Bliss of Spirit.

The Baptism of Jesus

And Jesus, when he was baptized, went up straightway out of the water: and, lo, the heavens were opened unto him, and he saw the Spirit of God descending like a dove, and lighting upon him: And lo a voice from heaven, saying, "This is My beloved Son, in whom I am well pleased."

—Matthew 3:16–17

The dove symbolizes the spiritual eye, seen by deeply meditating devotees at the Christ Consciousness center in the forehead between the two physical eyes....Jesus saw the Spirit descending from the abode of Heavenly Bliss in the form of a microcosmic spiritual eye and settle upon his consciousness. The spiritual eye of Jesus was opened, and through this immersion in Spirit, he perceived the mergence of his individualized consciousness with the macrocosmic manifestations of Cosmic Consciousness, Christ Consciousness, and Cosmic Energy....

He saw the light of the spiritual eye as descended from the macrocosmic Divine Light; and from this came the voice of Aum, the intelligent, all-creative heavenly sound, vibrating as an intelligible voice: "Thou art My Son, having lifted thy consciousness from the limitation of the body and all matter to realize thyself as one with My perfect reflection, My only begotten image, immanent in all manifestation. I am Bliss, and My joy I express in thy rejoicing in attunement with My Omnipresence."

—Paramahansa Yogananda

Painting by Carl Bloch

The Role of Satan in God's Creation

"Satan originated as the natural consequence of God's desireless desire to divide His Sea of Oneness into waves of finite creation....The Adversarial Force maintains its realm of influence by the gross obscuration of the true God-nature of all created beings."

*A*nd Jesus being full of the Holy Ghost returned from Jordan, and was led by the Spirit into the wilderness, being forty days tempted of the devil....And Jesus answered and said unto him, "Get thee behind me, Satan."*

—Luke 4:1–2, 8

꽃

---

* The details of Jesus' temptation by Satan are discussed in Discourse 8.

The Role of Satan in God's Creation

꧁

The consciousness of Jesus the man who had become Jesus the Christ was permeated with the omnipresence of the Holy Ghost —one with the sacred Vibratory Essence of God that upholds all manifestation. The universality of creation became his body, in which his little Jesus-form lived and moved.

To understand exactly what is meant by Jesus being filled with the Holy Ghost, one must scientifically and metaphysically explode superstition with true understanding of the significance as demonstrated by the actions and statements of Jesus. He spoke of the Christ omnipresence in the Holy Ghost when he said: "Are not two sparrows sold for a farthing? and one of them shall not fall on

True meaning of "being full of the Holy Ghost"

the ground without [the sight of] your Father."* Jesus, as also the divinely realized yogis of India, not only could foretell the actions of people and the distant course of events through telepathic vibrations of thought, but he also could know all happenings within vibratory creation through the feeling of his Christ omnipresence.

An ant's consciousness is limited to the sensations of its little body. An elephant's consciousness is extended throughout its massive frame, so that ten people touching ten different parts of its body would awaken simultaneous awareness. Christ Consciousness, experienced in oneness

---

* Matthew 10:29 (see Discourse 41).

with the Holy Ghost, extends to the boundaries of all vibratory regions.

The entirety of vibratory creation is an externalization of Spirit. [See Discourse 1.] Omnipresent Spirit secretes Itself in vibratory matter, just as oil is hidden in the olive. When the olive is squeezed, tiny drops of oil appear on its surface; so Spirit, as individual souls, by a process of evolution gradually emerges from matter. Spirit expresses Itself as beauty and magnetic and chemical power in minerals and gems; as beauty and life in plants; as beauty, life, power, motion, and consciousness in animals; as comprehension and expanding power in man; and again returns to Omnipresence in the superman.*

Each evolutionary phase thus manifests a fuller measure of Spirit. The animal is freed from the inertia of minerals and the fixity of plants to experience with locomotion and sentient consciousness a greater portion of God's creation. Man, by his self-consciousness, additionally comprehends the thoughts of his fellow beings and can project his sensory mind into star-studded space, at least by the power of imagination.

The superman expands his life energy and consciousness from his body into all space, actually feeling as his own self the presence of all universes in the vast cosmos as well as every minute atom of the earth. In the superman, the lost omnipresence of Spirit, bound in the soul as individualized Spirit, is regained.

The superman attains this ultimate evolutionary state after "baptism" or immersion in the Holy Ghost Cosmic Vibration [as described in Discourse 6] by advancing from body consciousness through the successive stages of superconsciousness, Christ Consciousness, and Cosmic Consciousness.

Two phases of communion with the Holy Ghost Cosmic Vibration

In the first state attained in the successful attempt of the soul of Jesus to rise above the Cosmic Nature–induced habit of bodily attachment of incarnations, Jesus the man felt within the limitation of the body the vibratory presence of the Holy Ghost: the intelligent Cosmic Vibration heard intuitively in the meditative state of inner communion. In this state of metaphysical development, the divine perception of Spirit as the Holy Ghost Comforter and the power of attraction of God's love and intel-

---

* These five evolutionary stages are referenced in yoga philosophy as *koshas,* "sheaths" that are progressively unfolded as creation evolves from inert matter back to pure Spirit. (See *God Talks With Arjuna: The Bhagavad Gita,* commentary on 1:4–6.) *(Publisher's Note)*

ligence in the Christ Consciousness is experienced as bounded by the body occupying a little speck of vibratory region on the earth.

In the second higher state, by immersion of his consciousness in the Holy Ghost vibration with its inherent Christ Intelligence, the consciousness of Jesus was transferred from the circumference of the body to the boundary of all finite creation in the vibratory region of manifestation: the sphere of space and time encompassing planetary universes, stars, the Milky Way, and our little solar system family of which the earth is a part, and on which the physical body of Jesus was but a speck. Jesus the man, a tiny particle on the earth, became Jesus the Christ, with his consciousness all-pervading in oneness with the Christ Consciousness in the Holy Ghost.

This state can be cultured externally by experiencing God's love in His reflection as Christ Consciousness, which attracts matter and consciousness toward Divinity, and then expanding that feeling of unconditional love to one's family, society, nation, all nations, all creatures. And it can be attained by internally expanding the consciousness in meditation on the Cosmic Sound of *Aum,* transcending semi-subconsciousness, semi-superconsciousness, soul consciousness, semi–Christ Consciousness to the culminative all-embracing Christ Consciousness.

A Christlike person loves all beings and actually feels every portion of the earth and vibratory space as the living cells of his own body.

Once Lahiri Mahasaya, my preceptor's Guru, was teaching from the scriptural Bhagavad Gita to a group of his students in Banaras.* While explaining the meaning of *Kutastha Chaitanya* (the universal Christ or Krishna Consciousness), suddenly he gasped and cried out: "I am drowning in the bodies of many souls off the coast of Japan." The next morning the disciples read in the newspapers that a ship had foundered near the coast of Japan, resulting in the deaths of a number of persons; the fatal event occurred at exactly the time Lahiri Mahasaya experienced the shipwreck in his omnipresence.

So it was with Jesus. He had successfully led his consciousness through the ascending degrees of expanding consciousness to this second Holy Ghost state—the Christ state of omnipresence. That is what is meant by Jesus "being full of the Holy Ghost."

---

* Since India gained her independence, the original Indian spellings have been restored to many words that had become anglicized during British rule. Thus *Banaras* is now more commonly spelled *Varanasi,* or is referred to by its more ancient name, Kashi. *(Publisher's Note)*

The Holy Ghost or Christ state, oneness with the presence of God in manifested creation, is the commonality of divine beings who incar-

<hr/>

A degree of delusion is accepted even by God-sent saviors

nate to serve and uplift delusion-entrapped humanity. As it is none else than the Lord Himself as individualized souls who is imprisoned in the multitudinous forms in the created realm fraught with tests and trials, struggle and suffering, so also saviors sent by God choose to share the challenges and woes of those they have come to free. To redescend into a new body and mind necessitates taking on a degree of delusion, even for fully liberated masters. The bliss of intimacy with the transcendental God the Father, Spirit beyond all workings of delusion, is embraced by Christs in periods of transcendence in *samadhi* meditation, but they return therefrom to the realm of manifestation and its circumscribing creative principles that make possible the cosmic drama of interacting delimited forces and forms. The nature of the manifested world is such that a prolonged or constant state of mergence in Transcendence would be less than feasible—or even possible—for one whose work for humankind is carried out in their midst.

Rare souls sometimes serve the world by remaining primarily in transcendent meditation, sending forth powerful spiritual vibrations to balance the world's evils; but these souls seclude themselves in remote haunts and seldom or never appear before ordinary men. I have written of one such avatar, Mahavatar Babaji, in *Autobiography of a Yogi:* Nature herself stands in powerless awe before him. Stumbling man needs not only the silent blessings issuing from these exalted spiritual benefactors, but also familiar examples who live as mortal beings to bolster courage, faith, and desire for God, and to demonstrate the way to redemption. Enter thus the divine ones who choose for their service the milieu of human fracas.

There is an exalted state of inner transcendence in oneness with the Absolute which in Yoga is defined as *nirvikalpa samadhi:* the soul remains in conscious realization of its oneness with transcendent God even while the physical and mental instrumentalities of the body engage in normal expression and exacting activities. This is the goal of advancement, seen only in supernal beings. It can be experienced for short intervals, or by the highly advanced for months at a time, or for even a few years by those who attain what Yoga describes as *Brahmasthiti,* the state of being permanently established in God-union. To remain in the world of illusion while experiencing the indescribable bliss of the Sole Unmanifested Reality makes one's hold on the body tenuous indeed; it becomes eventually a difficult proposition just to sustain the atomic cohesiveness of the specious material form and to prevent the soul-individuality from dissolving into Spirit. So even in the highest states of divine oneness, the outer nature of the God-united retains some degree of the individualized consciousness of egoity and delusion, just to keep body and soul together.

Jesus the man become Jesus the Christ, enacting his special role in God's drama, prepared himself for his culminating three years of ministry, when he would have to face the strongest of foes, delusive evil and ignorance. To bear his mission's foreordained burden, his physical and mental faculties needed to be forged and strengthened in the fires of testing and temptation, securing his outer consciousness in the God-union of his immu-

Third state of spiritual transcendence: complete union with the Absolute

table inner realization. He had to conquer the metaphysical and psychological tests of Satan before he could relinquish all delusion in the third and last state of transcendence in Spirit—the complete union of body, Holy Ghost, Christ Consciousness, and God the Father perceived as one in Spirit. He knew that so long as he was incarnate in *maya's* domain, mortal tests born of delusion remain.

Although Jesus was already liberated in Spirit in his incarnation as Elisha, his newly incarnated body and mind as Jesus bore somewhat of the pattern of past existences. Though no longer binding, the memory and intimations of his prior limited human consciousness and its earthly desires, through the law of habit that attaches the soul to mortal existence, tried to attract his expanded consciousness to earthly consciousness. This is the psychological explanation of the tempting of Jesus' habit of divine consciousness by his past-life established mortal habits in order to lure him from the Great Comforter—the Holy Ghost Vibration from which comes all satisfaction, being the sum total of all earthly things looked for.

The Nature and Origin of Evil

Many modern scriptural interpreters, unable to understand why a perfect Christ would acknowledge the existence of Satan and Satan's power to tempt him, have tried to explain away the old concept of a devil by saying it is obsolete and metaphorical. God is the Source and Essence of all things, they point out, therefore evil does not exist—how could evil exist in a world created by the Deity who is only good? Others say that the good God does not know evil, for if He did He would surely put an end to it.

To see God in everything and to deny the power of evil to influence one's life has its good points; for even if it is conceded that a conscious evil force or Satan does exist, it cannot influence human minds unless they mentally accept it. However, it is quite contradictory to deny the existence and temptations of evil while remaining subject to suffering and succumbing to desires unbefitting the God-image within one. If one inhabits a body, he has tacitly acknowledged the duality of the world of matter. Philosophy can play an intricate word-game with truth, but what each individual has to deal with in fact is the obstinate mindset of his present state of consciousness. It is better to know the wiles of evil and the ways to combat them than to be caught unaware in blithe denial. Knowledge only, and not assertion without realization, can produce final emancipation.

Though it cannot be denied that God is the Source of all that exists, and that evil is a part of His creation, it must also be acknowledged that what we call evil is relative. Certainly it is terrible that violence, accidents, and diseases kill billions of people every century. But death itself is necessary to the renewal and progress of life. Also, earth is not meant to be "heavenly"; if it were, no one would want to leave the comfortable physical body and pleasurable world to go back to God. Misery, in one sense, is man's benefactor, because it drives him to seek sorrow-transcendence in God. Thus it is hard to fix a boundary line between good and evil, except in a relative sense. To God Himself nothing is evil, for nothing can diminish His immortal, eternally perfect Bliss. But for the myriad beings trapped in the crucible of mortal existence evil is all too real; and to say that God does not know their suffering as evil would imply that He is a very ignorant God!

There are various causes that can be put forth to explain evil occurrences in the world. Some people say that the responsibility for them

The subjective nature of evil—arising from man's thoughts and actions

lies neither with God nor with any objective Evil Power. They reject as medieval superstition the view that Satan is an actual being, like a dragon who has to be slain by the sword of the conquering knight; and try to explain Satan away by saying that the origin of evil is subjective, arising from psychological factors, from the thoughts and actions of man himself. This can perhaps be granted in the case of heinous acts perpetrated by villainous souls who cause suffering for their fellow beings; but what about the pain of disease, injury, and premature death? According to the view that evil is subjective, even these sufferings result from man's erroneous choices and actions—his lack of harmony with universal laws.

In this sense it is certainly true that evil in man's life is self-engendered: If a man hits a stone wall with his knuckles, the resulting undeniable evil of pain would not be created or willed by the wall, but would be the result of his ignorance in striking the naturally unyielding hardness of the stones. Likewise, it can be said that God is a stone wall of Eternal Goodness. His universe subsists on the workings of just and natural laws. Anyone foolish enough to misuse his intelligence to act against that goodness will inexorably produce the evil of pain and suffering—not because of any intent or wish of God, but because of pernicious ways of life colliding with the eternal good principles underlying all things in God. Man possesses the divinely given gift of free choice to tune in with God's goodness, peace, and immortality. Those who use their will contrarily and act out of tune with Him, breaking His laws, are bound to suffer from the recoil of their misdeeds, according to the law of cause and effect.

A little boy endowed with reason may enjoy perfect health and protection under the strict discipline of his mother; but when he grows up, he says: "Mother, I know I am safe in your care; but I wonder why you fostered my intelligence and gave me the power of free choice if you are always to decide how I am to behave? I want to make my own choices; I will find out for myself what is good or bad for me."

The mother replies: "Son, it is fitting for you to demand the right to use your free choice. When you were helpless and your reason had not yet budded forth, I nurtured you through the protection of maternal love. Now your eyes of reason are opened; it is time for you to depend upon the guidance of your own judgment."

Thus the youth ventures into the world unguarded, with only a semideveloped discrimination. He abuses health laws and becomes ill. He chooses wrong company and gets into a fight, resulting in a black eye and a broken leg.

It is the Divine Mother* who tries to protect each baby through the instinctive love of parents. But there comes a time when the baby

----

* The aspect of God that is active in creation; the *shakti,* or power, of the Transcendent Creator. In this context, the reference is to the personal aspect of God embody-

grows up and has to protect itself by the exercise of reason. If guided rightly by discrimination, the maturing individual becomes happy; but if reason is misused, then an evil outcome is precipitated.

From the foregoing analysis of evil, it would appear that the cause of evil is more subjective than objective, that much of it is due to the ignorance and wrong judgment of man, not to some malicious force in the universe. The power of habits presents an apt example: The consequent evils of physical overindulgence or indiscretion—ill health, being held in the grip of temptation—do not arise until man, by an act of erroneous judgment, forgets himself and by repeated transgressions allows the wrong indulgence to become a habit in the consciousness. All habits, good or bad, control and enslave the mind only after the will has allowed itself to be overcome by repeated good or evil actions born of good or evil judgment.

Why, then, are some children born with special tendencies of self-control and some with tendencies of weakness, before they have had any opportunity to exercise their reason and free choice? Some intellectuals confidently assert that heredity is responsible for good or bad traits in a child. But why would an impartial God endow one child with a good heredity producing a good brain inclined only to good tendencies, and another child with a bad heredity and a dysfunctional brain inclined only to do evil under the compelling influence of evil physiological instincts?

An answer is found in the law of reincarnation and its corollary of karma—the cosmic dispenser of justice through the law of cause and effect which governs the actions of all persons. According to this law, the soul attracts to itself a good or bad heredity, and a good or bad mentality, according to desires and habits formed in past earth-existences, which being unexpurgated are carried forward from the last incarnation into rebirth in one's present life. A person's good or bad judgment of all incarnations, working through the law of cause

---

ing the motherly qualities of love and compassion. The Hindu scriptures teach that God is both immanent and transcendent, personal and impersonal. He may be sought as the Transcendent Absolute; but as the Bhagavad Gita XII:5 points out, "Those whose goal is the Unmanifested increase the difficulties; arduous is the path to the Absolute for embodied beings." Easier for most devotees is to seek God as one of His manifest eternal qualities, such as love, wisdom, bliss, light; in the form of an *ishta* (deity); or as Father, Mother, or Friend. Other terms for the Mother aspect of Divinity are *Aum, Shakti,* Holy Ghost, Cosmic Intelligent Vibration, Nature or Prakriti.

and effect, creates good or bad inclinations, and those inclinations attract him to rebirth in a family with good or bad hereditary tendencies (or beyond the effects of heredity, to an environment and life experiences consistent with his karmic propensities). Thus it may be said that evil in man's life arises from his own wrong judgment.

While all of these facts support the contention that evil is subjective—that man may be accused of misusing his reason and, by creating inharmony with God's laws, of giving birth to evil—this explanation does not adequately account for every aspect of evil inextricably bound into the myriad manifestations of creation.

The objective force of evil in creation independent of man's actions

Millions of bacteria and virulent, invisible armies of germs move silently about the earth seeking, like devouring locusts, to destroy the crops of human lives. Numberless diseases infest plants and animals who have no free choice and consequently could not attract these evils due to prenatal bad karma.

Why is there death by floods and cataclysms? It does not seem possible that all of the millions of people destroyed by floods and famine in China could have suffered due to their past actions in previous lives.*

Why is there cannibalism in nature? The baby salmon lives on the flesh of its mother; the big fish eats the little fish. Then the fisherman finds joy in catching the big fish, deceiving it with hooked food; and the more the fish struggles for life, the more the sportsman enjoys it and says, "My, it is a game fish!" Who would like to change places with the fish?

Why do men murder each other in war? Why do even the thoughts of wrong judgment and emotions of jealousy, revenge, greed, and selfishness arise at all in the human mind? If man is made in the image of God, and God is good, then the logical deduction is that man could become nothing else but good. Wars result from industrial and territorial selfishness, from nations fuming with national selfishness and greed for possession; but why are conflicts not avoided by parliamentary discussions? Why was it that the slaying of the Austrian Archduke Franz Fer-

---

* Reference to the summer flood along the Yangtze during July–August 1931. Over 51 million people were affected (one-fourth of China's population). 3.7 million people perished due to disease, starvation, or drowning. This flood was preceded by a prolonged drought in China during the 1928–1930 period, causing a famine in which 3 million people died, according to the National Oceanic and Atmospheric Administration's National Climatic Data Center. *(Publisher's Note)*

dinand threw the world into furious conflagration precipitating World War I? Think of Tamerlane, emperor of India, slaying one million Hindus after his victory. Think of the Aztecs who used to cut out the hearts of their prisoners of war, hundreds at a time, in front of their idol gods. Think of the burning of witches and martyrs under the zeal of the Christian faith. How do despots such as Hitler gain the power to wreak untold horrors on humanity? And what of the war of the Crusades, fought in the name of Jesus' teachings, which stress only love for one's enemies—thousands of priests advocated this war and prayed for the destruction of their enemy brothers and victory for themselves.

Man did not create physical temptation, death-dealing bacteria, natural cataclysms. From the very beginning evil existed to delude man and influence his free choice. How easy it is for the majority of people to be tempted materially, to languish spiritually and do the very things that will hurt themselves.

The warfare of animals preying on each other, the battle of opposites and destructive forces in nature, predatory germs, delusion's power to effect wrong judgment in men, infinitely creative temptations to do wrong even against better judgment, distinctly show that there is an objective evil force that tries to destroy the evidential expressions of the Infinite Good.

The delusion-wizened mind of man sends forth a boasting, hollow challenge to Omniscient Divinity that if he were the Almighty he could create a much better world than this. He would banish from this earth devastating diseases and accidents; mental weakness and pernicious emotions such as revengefulness, anger, greed; industrial avarice resulting in depression; natural disasters of earthquakes, floods, droughts, famines; boredom, despair, old age, painful death—all of the ruinous tragedies of life.

Why evil has a place in God's plan

He would create a world with a joyous struggle free from the pain of travail, an ever newly happy state of mind for all men, sans mental idleness and boredom. He would make the body invulnerable, changeable according to the commandments of one's will. He would have our bodies tailored in the workshop of materialization and self-rejuvenation.

He would create a variety of occupations with a vast scope of activity, all leading to infinite, unending, pleasurable satisfaction. Good citizens would be materialized by will from the ether, as God created the first man and woman. All beings would go to heaven and become angels after they had successfully finished their earthly entertainment.

Such a world is easy to fancy, for the soul is always whispering to man its native perfection, even while the ego engages him in gambling with the enticements of a distorted earthly duality. An ideal existence is not impossible, but it is for a different time and realm reserved for those who have graduated from the learning assignments of earth life. For the ordinary man in his present stage of evolution, a life without difficulties would be of little value. No lessons of growth would be learned, no transformations of inflexible natures into godly consciousness, no compelling incentives to seek and know one's Maker.

Regardless, the time-worn, unresolved conundrum persists: Did evil have its origin in the plan of a good and perfect God? The Lord Himself answered prophet Isaiah: "I am the Lord, and there is none else, there is no God beside Me: I girded thee (invested thee with thy powers and attributes), though thou hast not known Me....I form the light, and create darkness: I make peace, and create evil: I the Lord do all these things."* The illumined *rishis* of India similarly perceived: "...Joy, sorrow, birth, death, fear, courage...these diverse states of beings spring from Me alone as modifications of My nature....I am the Source of everything; from Me all creation emerges."†

Spirit alone is perfect. Everything in creation, being delimited, is imperfect. The very beginning of creation gave rise to the law of duality—light and darkness, good and evil—the law of relativity necessary to divide the One into the many. By the storm of vibration, God's thoughts of multiplicity brought forth the waves of manifestation: His *lila*, or divine play.

Dualities of good and evil are inherent in creation

Spirit's desireless desire to enjoy Its Bliss as many selves was unnecessary to the complete and perfect Spirit, just as a father through no vital necessity may desire the joy in playing with his child. Spirit's desire was therefore an imperfect stirring in the perfect Quiescent Bliss, a thought vibration to accomplish something when that accomplishment was not necessary.

As introduced earlier, Spirit, being the only Substance existent, had nothing other than Itself with which to create. [See Discourse 1.]

---

* Isaiah 45:5, 7.

† *God Talks With Arjuna: The Bhagavad Gita* x:4–5, 8.

So in Its infinite consciousness Spirit differentiated—in thought only —between Itself and creation evolved from Itself, just as the varied images in a dream assume a semblance of reality in their relative existence as separate thoughts made of the one mind-stuff of the dreamer's imagination.

In order to give individuality and independence to Its thought images, Spirit had to employ a cosmic deception, a universal mental magic. Spirit overspread and permeated Its creative desire with cosmic delusion, a grand magical measurer described in Hindu scriptures as *maya* (from the Sanskrit root *mā,* "to measure"). Delusion divides, measures out, the Undefined Infinite into finite forms and forces. The working of cosmic delusion on these individualizations is called *avidya,* individual illusion or ignorance, which imparts a specious reality to their existence as separate from Spirit.* Individualized selves possessing the instrumentalities of a human body and mind are gifted with the power of free choice and independent action.

Even though God has created the universe out of delusion, He Himself is not deluded by it. He knows *maya* as naught but a modification of His one Consciousness. The colossal dramas of creation and dissolution of planets and galaxies; the birth, growth, and decline of empires and civilizations; the countless miniature plays of individual lives with their subplots of health and sickness, riches and poverty, life and death—all are happening in God as the One Dreamer-Creator, a chimerical perception of change within the Eternally Changeless. One part of the Infinite Being ever remains transcendent, beyond vibratory dualities: There He is the inactive Absolute—Spirit. When Spirit vibrates Its consciousness with thoughts of diversity, It becomes immanent as the omnipresent Creator in the finite vibratory realm of infinity: There God is active as the creative Vibratory Holy Ghost with its immanent Christ Consciousness.

Within the creative Holy Ghost Intelligence are all the governing laws and principles that manifest, sustain, and dissolve every part and particle of the Lord's universe. The Holy Ghost inherited from Spirit the independence to create and govern within the mandated vast scope of the manifesting powers endowed to it.

This Creative Power, which gives birth and nurture to creation, is referred to in Hindu scripture as Maha-Prakriti, Great Nature, the po-

---

* See also page 150.

tentials of all becomings. When this power goes forth from Ishvara (God the Father of Creation) as Intelligent Creative Cosmic Vibration, it takes on a dual nature. As Para-Prakriti (Pure Nature) it creates and expresses all good and beauty in harmony with the God-tuned immanent *Kutastha Chaitanya* (Christ Consciousness). Its divine nature is magnificently expressed in the causal and astral heavenly realms. But as the Vibratory Power descends into material manifestation, it becomes conjointly a deviant Apara-Prakriti (Impure Nature), creating through the circumscriptive laws of gross matter and the uttermost density of delusion.

These two aspects of Prakriti correspond to the Christian designations of Holy Ghost and Satan. The Holy Ghost in tune with Christ Consciousness creates goodness and beauty and draws all manifestation toward a symbiotic harmony and an ultimate oneness with God. Satan (from the Hebrew, literally "the adversary") pulls outward from God into entanglement with the delusive world of matter, employing the mayic cosmic delusion to diffuse, confuse, blind, and bind.

The origin of Satan, the creative power that rebelled against God

Thus Satan is defined as an archangel that fell from heaven, a force fallen from the grace of attunement with the Holy Creative Vibration of God. Jesus said: "I beheld Satan as lightning fall from heaven" (Luke 10:18). The divine Cosmic Vibration with its creative light became a divided force (Para- and Apara-Prakriti). The satanic or *apara* aspect asserts its independence and turns from God and the heavenly realms to ply its wiles in the grossest regions of duality, contrast, inversion, oppositional states, and mortality. Because it enshrouds matter and engages man in the most deceptive confusion of mayic delusion, Jesus referred to this satanic force as a devil, a murderer, and a liar. "The devil...was a murderer from the beginning, and abode not in the truth, because there is no truth in him. When he speaketh a lie, he speaketh of his own: for he is a liar, and the father of it" (John 8:44).

Satan originated as the natural consequence of God's desireless desire to divide His Sea of Oneness into waves of finite creation—a power of independent will that would wield the laws of material creation to manifest and sustain its existence. The plan of Spirit was that this conscious Cosmic Delusive Force should be endowed with independence in order to use *maya* and *avidya* to create God-reflecting finite objects out of Holy Ghost cosmic vibratory energy, in harmonious attunement with the divine Christ Intelligence present therein.

Perfect gems in mines, perfect flowers, perfect animals, and human soul-luminaries residing on perfect planets were thus created, brought forth as material manifestations from the heavenly astral and causal realms. That is why in the Christian Bible we find the ideal Adam and Eve communing with God, so naturally and simply in the abundant Garden of Eden. After a harmonious existence—a perfect expression of form, health habits, and modes of existence on the stage of time, without suffering, disease, cruel accidents, or painful premature death—all created forms were to return to God. Just as rainbows come and go, or as motion-picture forms can be created for entertainment and electrically switched on or off at will, so all created things were to exist as pleasant, mutually entertaining pictures on the screen of space and time, and were to resolve into their pure essence in God at the end of their cycle, after the drama of that period was perfectly played.

Thus originally all Cosmic Energy, being vibrated by the Holy Ghost and Christ Intelligence, was flowing Godward, creating perfect images from astral light turned inward to reveal God. The conscious Cosmic Delusive Force, with its independent power from God, saw that if the cosmic-energy manifestations of the Holy Ghost Vibration were to dissolve back into Spirit according to the divine plan, then its own separate existence would also cease. Without the Holy Vibration, there would be neither a reason for nor sustenance of the Cosmic Delusive Force. This thought frightened Satan; the sole purpose of his being— to keep these forms in manifestation—was threatened. So for his own purpose of self-perpetuation he rebelled against God, as an obstreperous general sometimes turns against his king, and started to misuse his cosmic powers. He manipulated the laws and principles of creation under his command to establish patterns of imperfection that would preclude their automatic resolution back into Spirit. Satan became as lightning falling from heaven because he turned the light of cosmic energy away from its focus on God and concentrated it on gross matter. The heaven-revealing astral light became the bedimmed physical luminaries of sun, fire, electricity, which show only material substances.

Scriptural literature of many persuasions employs a pragmatic imagery of personifying the qualities, acts, and motivations of the Deity and Its hierarchical derivations, inasmuch as the minds of ordinary persons, comfortably closed in a cause-effect view of phenomena, do not easily accommodate divine abstracts unless they too are metaphorically cloaked in familiar guise. God must have a cause to create—His desireless desire—and there must be a rationale for the existence and behavior of a fallen archangel who became a devil, deceiving man and opposing God in ways innumerable—Satan's desire to perpetuate his own existence.

Therefore, it can be said that except in the absolute sense that everything is made of the one Cosmic Consciousness of God, there is no evil in the All-Perfect God. Evil resides in the Adversarial Force that maintains its realm of influence by the gross obscuration of the true God-nature of all created beings. Philosophic sophistry could convincingly make the case that since the duty of Satan as an archangel was to sustain the existence of manifested forms, he fell from heaven just trying to do his job!

In whatever way it has been rationalized, Satan's fall started an enduring conflict between the God-tuned Holy Ghost with its immanent Christ Intelligence, and the matter-bent lover of finite creation, Satan. Satan has conjured an ugly counterpart for every beautiful creation of God in man's body and mind, and in Nature. God created a wondrous human form to be charged by cosmic energy, and to live in a free, unconditioned divine state; but Satan created hunger and the lure of sensory indulgence. For mental power, Satan substituted mental temptation; for soul's wisdom, Satan contrived perplexing ignorance; for the grandeur of Nature, Satan countered with the potentialities of warfare, disease, pestilence, earthquakes, floods—a horde of disasters.

The conflict in creation between Christ Consciousness and Satan

God made man immortal, to reign on earth as an immortal; Satan's evils bound man with the consciousness of mortality. Man was to behold the drama of change with a changeless immortal mind; and after seeing change dancing on the stage of changelessness, he was to return to the bosom of Eternal Blessedness by consciously dematerializing his physical form. If Adam and Eve, the symbolic first beings, had not succumbed to the temptations of Satan, and their descendants had not allowed themselves to be influenced by hereditary ignorance, modern man would not have to experience heartrending, painful deaths through accident and disease. Man, being out of tune with God, has lost the power of dematerialization given to the original human beings, so he lives with the frightening prospect of the movie of life being prematurely cut off before he has finished seeing the whole perfect picture of his changeful life.

In the temptation of Adam and Eve we see that Satan's evil was at work from the earliest period of creation. It was from my Hindu guru, Swami Sri Yukteswarji, that I received my first clear insight into the es-

How Satan caused the fall of man from divine consciousness

oteric essence of the Christian Bible and its enigmatic story of Adam and Eve. I related his explanation in *Autobiography of a Yogi* and reproduce it in this present context for the edification of the reader.

"Genesis is deeply symbolic, and cannot be grasped by a literal interpretation," he explained. "Its 'tree of life' is the human body. The spinal cord is like an upturned tree, with man's hair as its roots, and afferent and efferent nerves as branches. The tree of the nervous system bears many enjoyable fruits, or sensations of sight, sound, smell, taste, and touch. In these, man may rightfully indulge; but he was forbidden the experience of sex, the 'apple' at the center of the body ('in the midst of the garden').*

"The 'serpent' represents the coiled-up spinal energy [at the base of the spine] that stimulates the sex nerves. 'Adam' is reason, and 'Eve' is feeling. When the emotion or Eve-consciousness in any human being is overpowered by the sex impulse, his reason or Adam also succumbs.†

"God created the human species by materializing the bodies of man and woman through the force of His will; He endowed the new species with the power to create children in a similar 'immaculate' or divine manner.‡ Because His manifestation in the individualized soul had hitherto been limited to animals, instinct-bound and lacking the potentialities of full reason, God made the first human bodies, symbolically called Adam and Eve. To these, for advantageous upward evolution, He transferred

---

* "We may eat of the fruit of the trees of the garden: but of the fruit of the tree which is in the midst of the garden, God hath said, 'Ye shall not eat of it, neither shall ye touch it, lest ye die'" (Genesis 3:2–3).

† "'The woman whom Thou gavest to be with me, she gave me of the tree, and I did eat.'...The woman said, 'The serpent beguiled me, and I did eat'" (Genesis 3:12–13).

‡ "So God created man in His own image, in the image of God created He him; male and female created He them. And God blessed them, and God said unto them, 'Be fruitful, and multiply, and replenish the earth, and subdue it'" (Genesis 1:27–28).

the souls or divine essence of two animals.* In Adam or man, reason predominated; in Eve or woman, feeling was ascendant. Thus was expressed the duality or polarity that underlies the phenomenal worlds. Reason and feeling remain in a heaven of cooperative joy so long as the human mind is not tricked by the serpentine energy of animal propensities.

"The human body was therefore not solely a result of evolution from beasts, but was produced through an act of special creation by God. The animal forms were too crude to express full divinity; man was uniquely given the potentially omniscient 'thousand-petaled lotus' in the brain, as well as acutely awakened occult centers in the spine.

"God, or the Divine Consciousness present within the first created pair, counseled them to enjoy all human sensibilities, with one exception: sex sensations.† These were banned, lest humanity enmesh itself in the inferior animal method of propagation. The warning not to revive subconsciously present bestial memories was unheeded. Resuming the way of brute procreation, Adam and Eve fell from the state of heavenly joy natural to the original perfect man. When 'they knew that they were naked,' their consciousness of immortality was lost, even as God had warned them; they had placed themselves under the physical law by which bodily birth must be followed by bodily death.

"The knowledge of 'good and evil,' promised Eve by the 'serpent,' refers to the dualistic and oppositional experiences that mortals under *maya* must undergo. Falling into delusion through misuse of his feeling and reason, or Eve- and Adam-consciousness, man relinquishes his right to enter the heavenly garden of divine self-sufficiency.‡ The personal responsibility of every human being is to restore his 'parents' or dual nature to a unified harmony or Eden."§

---

* "And the Lord God formed man of the dust of the ground, and breathed into his nostrils the breath of life; and man became a living soul" (Genesis 2:7).

† "Now the serpent (sex force) was more subtil than any beast of the field (any other sense of the body)" (Genesis 3:1).

‡ "And the Lord God planted a garden eastward in Eden; and there He put the man whom He had formed" (Genesis 2:8). "Therefore the Lord God sent him forth from the garden of Eden, to till the ground from whence he was taken" (Genesis 3:23). The divine man first made by God had his consciousness centered in the omnipotent single eye in the forehead (eastward). The all-creative powers of his will, focused at that spot, were lost to man when he began to "till the ground" of his physical nature.

§ The fall of man from his native state of divine consciousness under the influence of Satan is understood in Yoga to be the descent of his life energy and awareness from

When Eden, the state of divine consciousness, was lost to the original Adam and Eve, they became intensely identified with the gross physical form and its limitations. They lost their primal innocence, in which they could see themselves as souls encased in a won-

Delusion of body-identification produces the false idea of death

drous triune body of consciousness, life force, and atomic radiation. God intended man to behold the human body and mind as delusive thought-forms that provide the soul with a means to experience the Lord's cosmic drama. Ever since the Fall, man has indulged in the ephemeral attractions of bodily pleasures, thereby subjecting himself to countless miseries inherent in body consciousness. Under the influence of Satan, man concentrates on the outward appearances and vicissitudes of life rather than on the underlying immutability. He is thus stricken with the false idea of death as annihilation.

The cosmic motion picture of a man's life seen on earth—his birth, experiences, and death—produces the exhilarating consciousness associated with his birth and the sad concept of his ending in death. Satanic ignorance hides from view man's life as he joyously began the descent from God, and his exultant return to God as he hies back to Him. Satan, by enslaving man's attention to the physical body and senses, makes him forget prenatal and after-death experiences in the superphysical astral realm; and by showing for a time this drama of life and then lowering the curtain of obscurity, it has produced a fallacious conception of death.

The change called death is only an outward link in the chain of immortality, the continuity of which is surreptitiously hidden from man's view. It is unmetaphysical and erroneous to say that death does not exist, but it is equally untrue to give to it the reality and finality suggested by delusion. To dismiss the dismal view of the *danse macabre,* man should learn to behold all permutations as mere wavelets of change appearing and disappearing on the changeless ocean of Infinity.

---

the centers of heavenly perception in the upper portion of the cerebrospinal axis down to the base of the spine, whence the consciousness flows outward to the senses and body identification (mentioned in Discourse 6). The meaning of Satan "falling like lightning from heaven" in this microcosmic sense is explained in Discourse 41.

The deeper spiritual meaning of the Bible has been woefully trivialized at the hands of nonunderstanding literalists. I once talked to a very orthodox Christian missionary, asking him how the serpent could influence Eve to take a bite of the apple. "Well," he confidently asserted, "in those days serpents could talk!"

As it is possible to watch the slow process of a flower budding, blossoming, and disappearing on a movie screen, so man should behold his life pictured on the screen of his consciousness through the stages from childhood to a full-grown individual; and then his disappearance into God of his own accord.

Satan saw that it would all be very simple if the immortal children of God, after beholding a perfect earthly existence with a changeless attitude, would go back again to immortality. So Satan tampered with the showing of this perfect picture of life before it had a chance to be completed in God. Satan's delusive machinations introduced mental and bodily pain and sorrow. These devil-born patterns of evil have disturbed the intended desireless, perfect existence of human beings. Dissatisfaction arising from an imperfect, prematurely destroyed picture of life created in man a sense of unfulfillment and the desire to see perfect pictures played out and completed to his satisfaction.

How Satan entraps souls in the mortal labyrinth of earthly reincarnations

Thus, the immortal soul-images of God forgot their already perfect immortality. They began to exercise their free will in pursuit of a desire for temporal fulfillment. But desire begets a brood of desires, enticing immortals into a mortal labyrinth of cause and effect comings and goings, earthly births and deaths. The law of compensation, that for every action there is a binding reaction, serves as Satan's most effective means of keeping otherwise free souls earthbound. This law of action, karma, which imprisons souls in Satan's kingdom of finitude, makes necessary the constantly revolving wheel of reincarnation. The rebellious Cosmic Delusive Force, through the karmic consequences of man's wrong actions and his mundane desires arising from the dissatisfactions of imperfect living, slaps back into finite existence again and again those beings who earn only a brief respite between incarnations in the astral realm of life after death.

Reincarnation evolved from Satan's attempt to immortalize changeable flesh in order to keep creatures under his subjugation. Flesh, being subject to change, was not perdurable but fated to succumb to the ultimate change of the state called death. Immortal souls in bondage to the karmic law of recurrence could not go back to God with their Satan-engendered imperfect desires, so they had to return repeatedly to earth, through rebirth in new fleshly forms.

Satan, like a fisherman, has cast a net of delusion around all mankind and is continually trying to drag man toward the slavery of delusion, death, and finitude. Satan tempts humanity by his baits of greed, and promises of pleasure, and leads people to destruction and continuous painful reincarnations. He keeps souls, like fish, in the pond of finitude and spawns in them the consciousness of mortal limitations and desires in order to make them reincarnate on earth—again and again. As one desire is fulfilled, Satan insinuates into the consciousness new desires by ingenious temptations lest the soul escape his devilish earthly nets.

In a way, Satan provided a means, witlessly acting as the tool of God, to ultimately free souls from their mortal attachments. Reincarnation assures freedom, for it gives immortal souls ample time and opportunities to divest themselves of all false notions of earthly fulfillment, and to realize through wisdom their already perfect divine natures. With the expiration of desires and karmic consequences from wrong determinations, they will be liberated.

It has to be conceded that Satan is exceedingly clever to be able to captivate immortals with material tawdry, after successfully mesmerizing them with forgetfulness of their endowment of divine treasure. Satan uses this forgetfulness to hold all created beings in their finite state, identified with the physical body and consequent slavery to material attachment, instinct, and conscious and unconscious desires for finite experiences. Until man regains his lost Eden on earth, he remains an exile, constrained by the law of reincarnation to strive ceaselessly for the outworking of his human longings.

Satan has a subtle strategy for propagating desires: the introduction of the idea of pain, which is purely a mental phenomenon. The original humans had great self-control and a mind that was impersonally nonattached to the body, and so did not feel pain when the body was injured. Originally, pain as a part of creation was simply a heightened sense of awareness to protect the fragile physical and mental instrumentalities from injurious clashes with the objects and laws of gross matter. But by increasing man's attachment to the body and ego, and thereby his mental sensitiveness to their complaints, Satan made pain excruciating. Every impingement of discomfort, physical or emotional, great or small, creates a desire for appeasement.

Satan's strategies of pain and sorrow, and how man may defeat them

Similarly with the affliction of sorrow imposed by Satan on the phenomenon of death: Death was to have been a conscious, happy transition from the changeful body to Changeless Spirit. That was God's idea of death. Satan so influenced man's consciousness to desire lasting happiness in the physical body that death became a dreaded, painful parting from the mortal form, causing unconsciousness at the time of transition. Because of Satan's delusion, man fails to see the godly event that death was meant to be—a promotion, a liberation from toilsome, imperfect earth-life to perfect, everlasting freedom in God. Rather, the grief at being forced to depart the material playground engenders a Satan-devised desire to come back.

Ultimately, however, Satan defeats his own purpose; for physical pain and sorrow are also prods that at last cause matter-weary souls to seek their preordained freedom in God.

Emancipation is hastened by playing the living drama of a perfect life of health, abundance, and wisdom with a detached mental aboveness. Satan-engendered dualities of pain and sorrow are greatly lessened by a strong mind that does not exacerbate suffering by fear or nervous imagination. That is, if one can remove the consciousness of sickness and not fear illness if it does come; and not crave health while suffering from ill health, this helps one to remember one's own soul, the transcendent Self that has never undergone the fluctuations of either sickness or health, but has always been perfect.* If one can feel and know that he is a child of God, and as such possesses everything, even as his Father God does—whether he be poor or rich—he can be free. If one can believe in his soul-omniscience, even while endeavoring to add to his little store of knowledge, he can transcend the ignorance of delusion.

All dualities belong to the domain of ignorance: fear of sickness and a desire for mortal health, fear of poverty and a desire for opulence, a feeling of inferiority from a lack of knowledge as well as a desire for a great intellect. Of course, if one is stricken with ill health, failure, or ignorance, this doesn't mean he should supinely continue in that state. He should rouse the perfection within him to express outwardly as health, prosperity, and wisdom, but without acknowledging the pain of lack or the fear of failure. Man should know that his struggle for completeness is born of delusion; for he already has all he needs within his inner powerful Self. It is only because he mistakenly imag-

---

* "The Supreme Spirit, transcendent and existing in the body, is the detached Beholder, the Consenter, the Sustainer, the Experiencer, the Great Lord, and also the Highest Self" (*God Talks With Arjuna: The Bhagavad Gita* XIII:22).

ines, while identifying himself with spiritually ignorant mortal company, that he is lacking in these divine endowments. He needs only to realize the everlasting fullness of his soul treasure-house.

The ignorant man stubbornly dreams about lack and failure, when he might instead claim his birthright of joy, health, and plenty as a son of the Ruler of the Universe. He is even now, in his transcendent Self, living in his perfect kingdom, yet in his mortal consciousness persistently dreaming Satan's evils.*

God's awakening touch in meditation is the way to be free from pernicious delusions. Divine contact with the Perfect Fulfillment destroys utterly all seeds of earthly longings and attachments. The soul instantly recalls its inheritance of Eternal Bliss, which makes a mockery of all desires for exiguous earthly ways.

God in His omniscience must surely have anticipated the origin of evil in the outgoing powers of His creative archangel. But even though delusive duality was the only means by which God could organize a cosmic play in order to enjoy Himself through His many selves, He assured that no convolution of His design would be outside

Man's place in the conflict between God's goodness and Satan's temptations

the embrace of His Goodness reflected ubiquitously in the Christ Consciousness. This magnetic power of God's love would in time attract all beings back to Him through evolution into divine awakening.

By an infinite display in nature and the life of man, God's Goodness advertises itself to impress

---

* "The influence of the force of *avidya* [the individuality of the ego] is such that no matter how irksome the illusion, deluded man is loath to part with it....The confirmed materialist, captive in his own realm of 'reality,' is ignorant of his deluded state and therefore has no wish nor will to exchange it for the sole Reality, Spirit. He perceives the temporal world as reality, eternal substance—insofar as he is able to grasp the concept of eternity. He imagines the grossness of sensory experience to be the pure essence of feeling and perception. He fabricates his own standards of morality and behavior and calls them good, irrespective of their inharmony with eternal Divine Law. And he thinks that his ego, his mortal sense of being—with its inflated self-importance as the almighty doer—is the image of his soul as created by God....

"Ordinary man is dumbfounded by the enticing propositions of illusory sense experiences, and clings to delusive material forms as though they were the reality and the cause and security of his existence. The yogi, on the other hand, is ever conscious inwardly of the sole Reality, Spirit, and sees *maya* and *avidya*—universal and individual delusion— as merely a tenuous web holding together the atomic, magnetic, and spiritual forces that give him a body and mind with which to play a part in the cosmic drama of the Lord's creation" (*God Talks With Arjuna: The Bhagavad Gita,* commentary on 1:8).

man and influence him to turn of his own free will toward the Abode of Bliss. Satan counteracts in every instance with deceptive, charmingly pleasant contrivances of temporary satisfaction to dupe gullible man into seeking permanent happiness in impermanent materiality. People succumb to Satan's offerings because he puts honey in his evil pleasures; they taste nice in the beginning but end in dire consequences.

The Almighty could annihilate Satan in an instant. By divine fiat He could wholly subjugate the Satanic Force. Various world scriptures speak of partial dissolutions of the earth because of excessive evils. As described in Genesis, much of the earth during Noah's time was devastated by a flood. But God does not illogically use His omnipotence to arbitrarily destroy His self-perpetuating creation, for that would contradict His own laws and the independence of action given by Him to Satan, empowering that Force to use these principles of manifestation.

Since God gave independence to man as well as to Satan, He can free souls only with their permission and cooperation. Satan has created such a delusive attachment to the instrumentality of a physical body that even if God were at this moment to offer liberation to the masses, I daresay not many would be eager to depart this merry playground—to leave behind their accustomed bodily residence with its possessions and sensory opportunities. To most persons even the concept of an existence in heaven is of a familiarly similar, though far more glorious, sentient bodily form and habitation. The body-identified sense-oriented are rigidly unconvinced that it is worthwhile to forgo known pleasure for the arcane bliss of Spirit. So many learning experiences must be undergone before man is ready to use his free will to choose God above all else. Earth, in the meantime, is the schoolhouse in which he must pass examinations in how to discriminate and choose between the soul-binding delusive patterns of Satan and the liberating patterns of God.

Man rebelliously protests: If God knows that we are suffering, why does He, being almighty and eternally blessed, allow weak mortals to suffer from the temptations and scourge of evil? It should not be assumed that God is enjoying His eternal blessed state in selfish happiness; He is suffering the tragedies of man's existence, delayed evolution on earth, and belated return to Paradise through all-emancipating wisdom. His compassion is not elsewhere expressed more munificently than in His incarnate sons, divine saviors, through whom His silent Voice speaks audibly to man. Jesus, as a manifestation of God, came to speak for God of the eternal kingdom of Heaven, upon whose threshold no

151

sorrow can tread. His message of God's love is that permanent happiness can be found only in God: "Lay not up for yourselves treasures upon earth, where moth and rust doth corrupt" (Matthew 6:19).

Possessing Christ Consciousness, Jesus realized fully the tug-of-war between the perfect, universally intelligent Holy Ghost Vibration manifesting Divine Goodness and Satan's pull of imperfection toward the evil in finite creation. He exemplified the love of God the Father, and that Father's eagerness to alleviate man's suffering and ignorance, as God's power flowed through him to heal the maladies of body, mind, and spirit. He represented God's love for erring humanity in acts and sermons of forgiveness and compassion that showed how God is continuously trying to use the superior force of Divine Love expressed as parental, friendly, filial, and all-surrendering pure conjugal love to coax man to forsake his cooperation with Evil's forces of hate, anger, jealousy, lust, and selfishness. And he exhorted those he blessed to repent of their past wrong actions that had caused their suffering: "Go and sin no more."

Man cannot be held responsible for being tempted: Satan interjected into the perfect makeup of man's sentient being the potentials for terrible physical enticements that constantly urge him to transgress morally and spiritually. Satan thereby tries to keep human beings deluded by greed, anger, fear, desire, attachment, and ignorance; so God uses the psychological counterparts of self-control, calmness, courage, satisfaction, unattached divine love, and wisdom to bring man to His Divine Kingdom. Though temptation is Satan's doing, man is responsible for not using his reason and will power to conquer evil by knowing and following God's laws of happiness.

The gauntlet flung at the feet of Everyman is to face Evil, battle it with the armaments of wisdom, and win the victory.*

The duplexity of Satan as both subjective and objective accounts for the whole of evil manifestations. An objective Satan, as an independent adversarial force opposing Divinity, explains the origin of evil that cannot be relegated solely to the individual or collective subjective ignorance of man. Satan has to be acknowledged as conjointly

---

* "Finally, my brethren, be strong in the Lord, and in the power of His might. Put on the whole armour of God, that ye may be able to stand against the wiles of the devil. For we wrestle not against flesh and blood, but against principalities, against powers, against the rulers of the darkness of this world..." (Ephesians 6:10–12).

the objective evil in nature, and as a power that can also work as the wrong subjective consciousness in man.

Recognizing the existence of Satan does not negate the conception of one God who alone is the Alpha and Omega in the cosmos. In essence, in real-ity, there is nothing but Spirit, the only Substance: ever-existing, ever-conscious, ever-new Bliss. The evil of delusion exists only in form, not in the essence of

Perceiving the taint-less Spirit by tran-scending the dualities of delusion

the Spirit. As long as there is creation, a coalescence of finite phenomena in the Infinite Substance, formal delusion will produce the consciousness of a conception of imperfection apart from the Absolute Inimitability.

In St. John 1:10–11 it is written: "He was in the world, and the world was made by him, and the world knew him not. He came unto his own, and his own received him not."* Spirit, the Prime Cause and Substance of creation, pervades the creation It has made; but the world neither perceives nor understands this Divine Inherence. "Made" does not mean created as man builds a house. Rather, as water transforms itself into ice, so the Spirit, by the condensing power of will, material-ized Itself by cosmic delusion into a fabulous universe. "He came unto his own, and his own received him not." That is, having manifested It-self as Its own creation, that creation did not "receive," did not reflect, its true Spirit Essence. The illusory dichotomy falsely defined matter as a substance apart from Spirit, whereas nothing exists that is not Spirit, everlastingly indivisible.

Spirit is perceived as the only Reality, the sole Eternal Substance, when one's consciousness enters the deep *samadhi* experience of divine union with Spirit. After attaining this realization, one is then qualified to say assuredly that there is neither a subjective nor objective Satan, but only the blissful Spirit. However, while the incarnate soul views its existence as a part of the dualities of creation, there must needs be ac-knowledgment that God and Satan are facts, even if the latter exists only in a delusive, relative nonreality. If one is dreaming, he cannot deny the resultant dream pain of the collision of his dream head with a dream-conceived wall. While dreaming the delusion of the universe, one cannot say that Satan or evil, or pain, or disease, and matter do not exist. This transcendent overview sets apart one who awakens in Cosmic Consciousness. His soul rejoices in the repossession of its

---

* Commented on in Discourse 1.

memory of wisdom: "Ah, nothing exists but Pure Eternal Goodness—the one Immutable Spirit."

While Jesus was striving to reach the final state of complete absorption in Spirit—enacting the full drama of human consciousness to set a pattern for the world—Satan began to tempt him and try to dissuade him from God through the accumulated memory of subjective and objective evil born of delusive mortal habits of incarnations of short-lived pleasures from contact with finite sensory objects.

Jesus did not deny this Evil Force. His intuitive knowledge recognized this power as a conscious Satan who lured him with the patterns of evil arrayed side by side with the divine patterns of God. Addressing this objectified Force, Jesus destroyed its binding effect with the power of wisdom in his command: "Get thee behind me, Satan"—which is to say: "Let delusion be left behind my soul racing toward Spirit."

It is folly to deny subjective or objective evil while one is still grappling with delusion. The urgent need is to be watchful and protect oneself from the destructive patterns of evil everywhere, as temptations within and as imperfection and strife in Nature. One should never think it possible to best Satan at his own game. Just when one feels sure of invulnerability, the devil tricks his opponent with some ruse and the challenger loses. It is better not to enter into sport with his temptations. There are plenty of entertaining good games in God's playing fields in which to test one's mettle and prove oneself a worthy winner. One should rally the patterns of the Christ Consciousness–inspired goodness in one's conscience and reason, and in the presence of God as the harmony and beauty in all Nature. When the consciousness of goodness is strengthened, its light dispels the perilous darkness of Satan's evil influence.

Jesus' Temptation in the Wilderness

"Jesus was both human and divine....Jesus the man met with temptations, he wept, he suffered like any other human being; but he exerted his will supremely to overcome evil and the delusion of his material nature."

*T*hen was Jesus led up of the Spirit into the wilderness to be tempted of the devil. And when he had fasted forty days and forty nights, he was afterward an hungred. And when the tempter came to him, he said, "If thou be the Son of God, command that these stones be made bread."

But he answered and said, "It is written, 'Man shall not live by bread alone, but by every word that proceedeth out of the mouth of God.'"

Then the devil taketh him up into the holy city, and setteth him on a pinnacle of the temple, and saith unto him, "If thou be the Son of God, cast thyself down: for it is written, 'He shall give His angels charge concerning thee': and 'in their hands they shall bear thee up, lest at any time thou dash thy foot against a stone.'"

Jesus said unto him, "It is written again, 'Thou shalt not tempt the Lord thy God.'"

Again, the devil taketh him up into an exceeding high mountain, and sheweth him all the kingdoms of the world, and the glory of them; and saith unto him, "All these things will I give thee, if thou wilt fall down and worship me."

Then saith Jesus unto him, "Get thee hence, Satan: for it is written, 'Thou shalt worship the Lord thy God, and Him only shalt thou serve.'" Then the devil leaveth him, and, behold, angels came and ministered unto him.

—Matthew 4:1–11

Jesus' Temptation in the Wilderness

Then was Jesus led up of the Spirit into the wilderness to be tempted of the devil. And when he had fasted forty days and forty nights, he was afterward an hungred. And when the tempter came to him, he said, "If thou be the Son of God, command that these stones be made bread."

But he answered and said, "It is written, 'Man shall not live by bread alone, but by every word that proceedeth out of the mouth of God'" (Matthew 4:1–4). *

Jesus, in lifting himself from the Holy Ghost state of omnipresent Cosmic Vibration and its Christ Consciousness immanent in vibratory space into oneness with Cosmic Consciousness—the transcendental, vibrationless God the Father as well as the Father's reflection as the universal Christ Consciousness—experienced a matterward pull of cosmic delusion, a reminder of confining, limiting, human habits of incarnations. The Divine Spirit had led Jesus into the silence of the wilderness to be tested, to see if his Christ Consciousness could be retained despite the deluding influence of all mortal memories.

A superman, even though he is fixed in a high state of consciousness by deep meditation, is still subject to the temptations of

---

* Jesus is quoting Deuteronomy 8:3. Cf. parallel references in Mark 1:12–13 and Luke 4:1–4.

Cosmic Delusion so long as he dwells in the realm of *maya*. The demands of a bodily form will coerce him to recollect past-life and postnatal memories of dependence on sensory experiences and enjoyment of their offerings. While Jesus was engaged in the divine bliss contact of God, he was "tempted of Satan; and was with the wild beasts" (Mark 1:13). The cosmic delusion of metaphysical Satan instigated psychological temptations of beastly passions, of cunning allurements for power and possessions, and of fierce mortal desires issuing from physical pain and hunger to entice him away from his transcendent wisdom-perceptions. The apostles relate that for forty days and nights in the wilderness solitudes Jesus was "tempted of the devil." With God as his sole witness and ally, he fought off the Evil Force with fasting to conquer the delusions of body consciousness, prayer to strengthen the mind in faith and determinate will, and the ecstasy of meditation that reaffirmed the identity of his soul as an awakened son of God.

A Jesus who was a ready-made, imported-from-heaven son of God, already complete and perfect, would have no temptations to overcome. The machinations of Satan, and Jesus'

The human and divine nature of Jesus

victory, would then be nothing more than divine acting. How could that accomplishment be a human ideal? A God-manufactured spiritual being has no credit of being what one should become by self-effort, and is therefore no exemplar for struggling, temptation-riddled human beings.

The inspiriting truth is that Jesus was both human and divine: he was a liberated soul, one of the greatest that ever came on earth; and he was a human, who by spiritual labor of past incarnations of self-discipline, prayer, and meditation had reaped the plenteous spiritual harvest of God Consciousness. Through his accumulated development, he exteriorized the potential image of God Consciousness hidden within him; he became a Christ, one endowed with Christ Consciousness. It was during the Christ state, in which he could feel his consciousness in every atomic cell of his cosmic body of all matter, that he could act as a savior of mankind. Only a soul who attains this universality is able to feel perfect identity with God, qualified thereby to become an emissary of the Divine.

The Heavenly Father sent Jesus on earth to serve His misery-laden children as a spiritual example. Jesus the man met with temptations, he wept, he suffered like any other human being; but he exerted his will

"Get Thee Behind Me, Satan"

And Jesus being full of the Holy Ghost returned from Jordan, and was led by the Spirit into the wilderness, being forty days tempted of the devil....And Jesus answered and said unto him, "Get thee behind me, Satan."

—Luke 4:1–2, 8

Every time man is tempted to do wrong, he should remind himself that it is not his subjective mind alone that is tempting him, but also objective Satan. He should adamantly refuse to cooperate with the Evil One who would destroy him. That is why Jesus said, "Get thee behind me, Satan" when that Evil Force showed him kingdoms of temporal glory, which could be his if he worshiped delusion....By emerging victorious from temptation, he is a shining example for all souls struggling to regain their divine sonhood.

—Paramahansa Yogananda

Drawing by Heinrich Hofmann

supremely to overcome evil and the delusion of his material nature, and ultimately succeeded. Two quotations from Saint Paul bear on this point:

> *For verily he took not on him the nature of angels; but he took on him the seed of Abraham.*
>
> *Wherefore in all things it behoves him to be made like unto his brethren, that he might be a merciful and faithful high priest in things pertaining to God, to make reconciliation for the sins of the people. For in that he himself hath suffered being tempted, he is able to succor them that are tempted (Hebrews 2:16–18).*
>
> *For we have not an high priest which cannot be touched with the feeling of our infirmities; but was in all points tempted like as we are, yet without sin (Hebrews 4:15).*

All prophets of God during their earthly incarnations were tested and had to overcome the human frailties of mortal embodiment in order to attain the final state of mergence in Cosmic Consciousness. A master's striving to regain finality while on earth sets an ideal pattern for other advancing souls.

The ordinary man's encounter with "the Tempter" is primarily as subjective ideas subtly luring him through prenatal and postnatal bad habits and the come-hither attraction of his mate- *How Satan tempted* rial environment. To obstruct the highly advanced, *Jesus to forsake his* Satan may take objective form and use vibratory *unconditioned divine* voices in his desperate last attempt to dissuade the *state* Godward-fleeing master.

Great masters approaching final liberation can distinctly see Satan and his legions of evil spirits take personified forms to mount a decisive resistance against the masters' liberation in Spirit. Satan mysteriously tries great devotees of God with various temptations that come unpredictably into their lives as they advance spiritually. These alone are often sufficiently effective to achieve Satan's purposes. But when devotees are very near God, Satan then forsakes his subtleties and from his hiding place openly appears to defy the Lord's saints. Buddha was confronted by Mara who appeared to him in the shape of dancing-girls, tempting him to give up his divine bliss for sensual pleasure and comfort for his body emaciated by ascetic discipline. When Buddha remained unaffected, final liberation came to him. Similarly, when Satan saw a resurgence of spiritual power in Jesus, sundering the incarnating bonds of *maya*, he took an objective shape, talked to him, and promised him the temporal happiness which all his evil patterns of life could afford if Jesus would only forsake God.

During Jesus' forty days of fasting and self-denial, his consciousness remained on an exalted plane of spiritual duality: On the one side blessed by Spirit, and on the other cajoled by the Adversary. When he returned fully to incarnate consciousness, he was renewed in spirit, but felt the hunger of his mortal body deprived of its accustomed nourishment.

As souls, individualized sparks of unconditioned Spirit, children of God are immortal, free from any dependence on materiality. The cells of flowers, plants, animals, and human beings were intended by God to live recharged by Cosmic Energy and not by cruelly feeding on one another. It is only when the soul is identified with the Satan-desecrated human body that man feels the hunger of dependence on nature's store. The Cosmic Delusive Force has led body-conscious man to believe that without physical sustenance his existence would be terminated. In turning to earth-products for nourishment (breath and "bread"), man remains earthbound, forgetful of his true nature that lives solely by the Cosmic Energy and will of God.

Satan wanted Jesus to forget his divine state of unconditioned existence. He began to tempt the Christ Consciousness of Jesus by playing upon the primal need of the human body to satisfy its hunger. Satan worked through the mind of Jesus, expressing a tempting proposition: "Why don't you use your divine power to change stones into bread?"

Jesus—being one with the Divine Intelligence that has vibrated Itself into solids, liquids, and gases, and is holding them in balance by magnetic, electrical, and thermal laws—had the power to manipulate those principles to convert stones into bread by changing their rate of electronic vibration. But he recognized Satan's delusively plausible suggestion as a ruse to encourage the mortal habit of catering to the psychology of physical hunger, which in that instance would have been a betrayal of the realization that as an immortal, he lived by God's Infinite Energy. This does not mean that after this experience Jesus foreswore human sustenance. He partook of simple foods, and of feasts prepared by loving hosts; but he did it as a God-man, and not as a deluded human subject to the body's habit of physical hunger.

So Jesus answered the metaphysical Satan with a great vibratory force of thought within himself, refusing to misuse his divine powers: "Man shall not live by bread alone, but by every word that proceedeth out of the mouth of God." Jesus quoted the scriptural truth, not theoretically as do theologians, but from his own realization of the mystery and origin of life, experienced in his fast and intense meditation: "I have found the divine way of living by God the Father through the Holy Ghost as the fountainhead of all life," he signified, "and will not again acknowledge dependence on physical bread."

Man is not sustained only by "bread," the limited relative energies derived from the solids, liquids, and gases of the physical sources that nourish life, but primarily by "every word" (unit of unlimited Cosmic Energy vibrating from the Holy Ghost—the great *Aum* or Amen) descending into the human body through the "mouth of God" (medulla oblongata). To consciously experience this truth, as did Jesus, is to realize the eternal link between the human and divine, matter and consciousness—the irrevocable oneness of the Self with the Creator.

Metaphysical meaning of "mouth of God"

The medulla oblongata at the base of the brain is the seat of life, formed from the seed cell, the original nucleus, entered by the soul at the time of conception. Like radio waves, which are unseen but can be drawn out of the ether by a receiving apparatus, vibrating life energy from the omnipresent cosmic source is continuously received through the subtle astral center in the medulla. It is stored in the dynamo of astral power in the brain, whence it flows out through the medulla— it "proceedeth out of the mouth of God"—and is distributed throughout all the cells of the body. If that beam of energy were taken away, the body would drop dead immediately.

Man thinks he lives on "bread"—food, oxygen, and sunshine— but these are nothing but condensed Cosmic Energy. Radiant energy from the sun feeds plants; the plants are eaten by animals and humans; and in turn the plants eat them when they die. Directly or indirectly, solar energy is the primary physical source of life. When a person ingests food, life energy in the body begins to work on digesting and metabolizing it, ultimately drawing the stored solar energy out of that food to supply the body. So the scientists say that the cells of the body operate by energy radiated from the sun, released through the chemical reaction of oxidation. The very construction of protoplasm is made possible by this solar radiation, which gives off electric forces that enliven the cells. When man responds to the senses through perceptions and actions, he expends some of that energy; and when the body's supply is too depleted he feels weak. Then he decides to eat something or breathe deeply or go out into the sunlight to be replenished with energy-radiations.*

The ordinary man, identified with his animal body, thinks that his entire existence depends upon food, water, oxygen, and sunshine. But the time comes in the life of every individual when, regardless of what food he eats, or how many breathing exercises he does or sunbaths he takes, he is forced to admit: "No matter what I do, my health is failing." Likewise, oxygen inflated into the lungs of a dead man, and food stuffed into his stomach, and his body exposed to sunshine, will not bring back life. The material agencies that support the body are only indirect sources of vitality and are dependent upon Cosmic Energy, the direct source of life.

Man's body is like an automobile battery, which is able to generate some electricity from its components and the distilled water supplied it from outside. But the power available from these chemical reactions is only temporary; they have to be continually recharged with electric current from the car's generator, or else the battery "dies." Similarly, the life in man's body is not maintained solely by means of indirect sustenance (food, liquids, oxygen, and sunshine) but by the direct source of vibrating life current, the "word" of God.

Cosmic Energy: the inner source of life in man's body-battery

Electricity from the generator recharges the automobile battery and restores its power to generate more electricity from its chemicals and distilled water; likewise, Cosmic Energy coming into the body through the medulla enables the body to convert food and gross elements into life-giving energy. This same Cosmic Energy, in its universal creative role, made solids, liquids, and gases what they are; when

---

* "What we eat is radiation; our food is so much quanta of energy," Dr. George W. Crile of Cleveland told a gathering of medical men on May 17, 1933, in Memphis. "This all-important radiation, which releases electrical currents for the body's electrical circuit, the nervous system, is given to food by the sun's rays," he pointed out.

Someday scientists will discover how man can live directly on solar energy. "Chlorophyll is the only substance known in nature that somehow possesses the power to act as a 'sunlight trap,'" William L. Laurence writes in *The New York Times*. "It 'catches' the energy of sunlight and stores it in the plant....We obtain the energy we need for living from the solar energy stored in the plant-food we eat or in the flesh of the animals that eat the plants. The energy we obtain from coal or oil is solar energy trapped by the chlorophyll in plant life millions of years ago. We live by the sun through the agency of chlorophyll." —*Autobiography of a Yogi*

we ingest them, the intelligent life energy in the body must convert those solid, liquid, and gaseous forms of nourishment into energy that can be utilized by the body. The body's intelligent life energy is *prana*, lifetrons, deriving from the life-giving functions of the astral body. The difference between materially active forms of energy (electricity, light, heat, magnetism) and life energy (*prana*) is that the former are merely mechanical forces while the latter, being lifetronic, possesses an inherent divine intelligence.

In truth, the inner life energy is self-sufficient; it alone can support the body. But through evolutionary generations of bad habits, it has been conditioned to complete dependence upon food—becoming encapsulated, as it were, in gross vibrations—and refuses to function properly, or even to remain in the body, without material sustenance. Man, as a "food addict," has simply forgotten how to draw directly upon the bodily life force and its continuous supply of Cosmic Energy. When an opium addict is suddenly denied any access to the drug, he becomes sick or dies; similarly, when a person is addicted to Satan's delusive laws of the material conditions of life, which have become second nature to man, he must work off gradually such dependence by realizing his true spirit nature, or in ignorance he will die a mortal's death without those life supports.

To live by the evolutionary standard of eating food is not a sin; but to believe only in physical means as sustaining life is delusion. Through vibratory power and the various forces of nature, it is ultimately God alone who sustains life, His power that digests food and changes it into bodily nourishment, tissue, and blood. It is right to give tacit appreciation and obedience to Nature and her ways, but the consciousness should remain unfettered by these material limitations.

The seemingly solid body is itself a nonmaterial electromagnetic wave made up ultimately of underlying astral lifetrons, which in turn are made of Cosmic Consciousness. God has ingeniously condensed His consciousness into lifetrons, lifetrons into electrons and protons, these subatomic particles into atoms, and atoms into molecules and cells—all of which live by radiations from the Cosmic Source. An actor on the movie screen seems so real; but he is nothing but radiation divided into light and shadow issuing from the projection booth. Man should realize the ethereal nature of his being—made of light and consciousness, divine and indestructible, projected on the screen of time and space by the creative Cosmic Beam of God.

Man is a threefold being; his body is a battery within batteries. The body battery is contained in the mind and soul batteries. It is con-

Role of the mind and soul in health of the body

tinually recharged by Cosmic Energy from the mind-driven will, which in turn draws its power from Cosmic Consciousness flowing through the superconsciousness of the soul.

The body, mind, and soul batteries are interrelated. From the outside, the mind battery is charged by life energy generated by bodily metabolism; and inwardly it is charged by the superconsciousness of the soul. Likewise, the soul battery is charged with a good mind, good life energy, and good chemical energy of the body from the outside; and inwardly the soul is charged by Cosmic Consciousness.

A weak, dilapidated body weakens the mind; but a healthy body does not always mean a remarkable mind, unless it is charged with the superconsciousness of the soul. A diseased body discourages the mind and suppresses the expression of the soul, when the mind and soul are attached to the body. On the other hand, a strong soul, which reclaims its joy in meditation, makes the mind indomitably positive; such a powerful mentality in turn can influence a disease-stricken body to manifest healing and vitality.

The more one daily meditates deeply, and feels his joy increasing, the more his soul battery will be recharged with wisdom poured out from God. Meditation, the company of saints and intelligent, mentally powerful people, good books, introspection, creative work in art, science, literature, and business—all further the development of a strong mind, receptive to the wisdom of the soul.

Since the soul has descended into matter from Spirit and has made the imperfect body its playground, the perfection of Spirit and soul needs to be established in the mind in order to enable the erstwhile flesh-entangled soul to manifest within and through the body its Spirit nature. Its native immortality, diseaselessness, and immutable happiness must be evidenced in complete mastery of the mind over the body.

Man's intelligence, a reflection of Divine Intelligence, controls the very atoms of his body.* God's Cosmic Consciousness flowing through

---

* Man's intelligence, or mind, is not a simple single faculty. Yoga has minutely analyzed its physiological, psychological, and spiritual components, defining it as a conglomerate of the ego principle (*ahamkara*)—the agent or subjective doer and perceiver; the consciousness or feeling and awareness (*chitta*); the sense mind (*manas*) consisting of the enlivening power of the five senses of knowledge (smell, taste, sight, touch, hear-

the soul battery empowers the mind; and it is the power of will wielded by the mind that draws the conscious creative life force, or "Word," from the invisible dynamo of Cosmic Energy and causes it to flow into the body through the medulla oblongata, or "mouth of God."

Will is the operator of the switch that controls the flow of energy into the body. Every movement requires an act of will to empower it with energy. Merely to lift one's hand is to inject energy and consciousness into the entire system. When one is unwilling to do a task, he is tired from the beginning; but when he is willing, he is full of energy.

Will power draws Cosmic Energy into the body

One who does everything with willingness and interest finds that he is able to draw unceasingly from the reservoir of cosmic power. To remain apathetically passive and not use the will in a face-off with every duty and challenge in life—as some misguided dogmatists interpret Jesus' words: "Not my will, but Thine, be done" —is to shut off from the body the reinforcing free flow of divine currents. It is when the will to live becomes paralyzed, by overpowering disease or other difficulties, that the death of the body ensues.

By will power alone man can recharge his bodily cells, which are nothing but electrical globules. One who judiciously fasts for a long time will notice that he feels less and less need for food, that something else sustains the body. The currents of energy locked up in the brain and cells are drawn upon by the mind and will, which are capable of converting man's body from a "wet battery" to a "dry battery."

A wet battery is dependent on replenishment of its water supply to generate electricity.* A dry battery, however, is sustained by its own internal reservoir of energy recharged solely by electricity. By developing his will power, man can gradually lessen his dependence on chemical atomic energy from gross food, and instead learn to sustain

---

ing) and five senses of action (locomotion, exercise of manual skill, speech, elimination, and procreation); and discrimination (*buddhi*). From these principles evolve the five life energies, the fivefold function of *prana* responsible for empowering the performance of the crystallizing, assimilating, eliminating, metabolizing, and circulatory activities of the body. Man is thus a highly complex aggregate of intelligent energies and consciousness, all of which derive from the soul and its source in the Cosmic Consciousness of God.

* When Paramahansa Yogananda put forth this hypothetical metaphor, it was necessary to add water regularly to wet batteries to replace that which was lost in evaporation. The more recently developed sealed batteries, common to most users today, require no such water replacement. (*Publisher's Note*)

and revitalize his flesh and mental faculties from increasingly finer mediums of Cosmic Energy. He can draw more of his sustenance from oxygen, or from sunlight. Ultimately, saints have shown that it is possible to live by the Word of God alone.

Saints who live without eating

In a book entitled *Amanzil,* about Therese Neumann, the peasant girl of Konnersreuth, Bavaria, taken from an address of Right Reverend Joseph Schrembs, D.D., Bishop of Cleveland, delivered February 12, 1928, we find striking facts about Therese Neumann's life relative to living by divine energy.*

1. "She possesses the wounds of the crucified Savior. The wounds remain always the same. They neither fester nor heal."
2. "She goes through the Passion of our Lord each Friday."
3. "She repeats the Aramaic words spoken by Christ."
4. "She divines the innermost secrets of the heart."
5. "She takes neither food nor drink. Has eaten no solid food since 1923, except water or a little fruit juice."

"But on Christmas Day of the year 1926 she ceased entirely taking any food or any drink, so that almost for two years now, this girl has neither eaten nor drunk anything except to receive Holy Communion every morning....The verdict of all the doctors from the University of Berlin, from Prague, from Frankfurt, from Munich—doctors without any faith—is this: 'Deception and fraud are absolutely out of the question in the case of Therese Neumann.' She is not emaciated, despite lack of food since Christmas 1926, and is as healthy looking as anyone around you. On Fridays she loses about eight pounds. Six hours after the vision of the Passion is over, she is again back to her normal weight of one hundred and ten pounds."

When I saw Therese Neumann in Bavaria in 1935, she had lived without food for twelve years, but she looked as fresh as a flower.†

In the case of Therese Neumann we find one of God's many anomalies, a divine nudge to keep man's complacency humbly off center. She is moderately active, enjoys sunshine and tending her garden, her heart

---

* *Amanzil* was reprinted from the *Catholic Universe Bulletin,* Cleveland, Ohio (eleventh edition).

† In *Autobiography of a Yogi,* Chapter 39, "Therese Neumann, the Catholic Stigmatist," Paramahansa Yogananda relates in detail his meeting with this modern-day mystic and his personal experience of her ecstatic vision of Christ's Passion. Therese Neumann passed away in 1962. *(Publisher's Note)*

and circulatory system and breath work normally, but she does not live by edible solids nor liquids. Therese Neumann's life demonstrates in this age the teaching of Jesus that the body does not live by "bread alone." As she expressed it to me, "I live by God's light." The saintly stigmatist lives by her will drawing on Cosmic Energy from the ether, sun, and air; and by the Cosmic Consciousness of Christ.*

The Bengali woman saint Giri Bala had lived without eating for more than fifty-six years when I visited her in 1936. She told me that ever since her guru had initiated her into a technique that frees the body from dependence on physical food, she has been able to live entirely on Cosmic Energy. In all these years of noneating, she has never been sick or experienced any disease. Her nourishment is derived from the finer energies of the air and sunlight, and from the cosmic power that recharges the body through the medulla oblongata.

I asked her the purpose of her having been taught to live without eating. "To prove that man is Spirit," she replied. "To demonstrate that by divine advancement he can gradually learn to live by the Eternal Light and not by food."†

The atypical lives of saints such as Therese Neumann and Giri Bala are used by God to demonstrate man's essentially incorporeal nature. In higher evolutionary ages it will be the norm for food to consist primarily of oxygen, sunshine, and etheric energy. Extracting nutrients from gross foodstuffs is such a roundabout way of getting at the encased energy for repairing the decay of bodily tissues. Drawing energy from oxygen and sunshine is far more efficient. And to tap directly the unlimited supply of free Cosmic Energy is to restore the soul's natural power to sustain its bodily instrument by the Vibratory Word of God.

The yoga science of mastering the energies that sustain the body

Certain yogis of India, in the suspended state, have shown the sustaining power of Cosmic Energy, even in the absence of energy from oxygen and sunshine. Sadhu Haridas, under rigid observation of medical men, was buried several

---

* Among other Christian saints who lived without eating (they were also stigmatists) may be mentioned Saint Lidwina of Schiedam, Blessed Elizabeth of Rent, Saint Catherine of Siena, Dominica Lazzari, Blessed Angela of Foligno, and the nineteenth-century Louise Lateau. Saint Nicholas of Flüe (Bruder Klaus, the fifteenth-century hermit whose impassioned plea for union saved the Swiss Confederation) was an abstainer from food for twenty years.

† See *Autobiography of a Yogi,* Chapter 46.

feet beneath the surface of the earth in the courtyard of a well-guarded palace. His body survived without food, oxygen, or sunshine for forty days. When he was disinterred, he was pronounced dead; but to the amazement of his attendant English and French physicians, the suspended life in his body returned.*

When the yogi puts himself in a trance of suspended animation, he halts decay in the bodily cells. While he is buried, the cold earth acts like a refrigerator, preserving the body from the destructive work of heat. The inner life force additionally creates a sort of coolness in all the cells, which helps to preserve them. In this state, the cells temporarily forget their bad habit of addiction to food, and live by the vibration of Cosmic Energy.

Science postulates that each gram of flesh in the human body has enough energy in its electroprotonic constituents to run the electrical supply of the city of Chicago for two days. The life force in the ordinary human body is accustomed to deriving power from the chemical energy in food; nature's cumbersome procedures have blocked the process of living solely on the lifetronic energy stored in the electrons and protons of body cells. In the state of suspended animation, yogis know how to utilize this electroprotonic energy to keep the body cells electrified like trillions of dry batteries.

All consciousness, energy, and forms evolve from and exist in God's immanent and transcendent Cosmic Consciousness. We exist only because our Creator allots infinitesimal segments of His Being to masquerade as a multitude of beings. The ordinary man thinks of himself as a body whose faculties produce consciousness. Self-realized yogis, to the contrary, know that it is the consciousness and subconsciousness in the brain and spine that sustain and animate the body. They understand how to withdraw life and consciousness into the astral cerebrospinal centers and connect them with the source of all consciousness, God's Cosmic Consciousness.

Just as ships can be controlled by a distant radio, so God sustains all thought processes and cells in the body by continually sending Cosmic Consciousness and Cosmic Energy to them. Even if one is not conscious of this Sustaining Power, no one can live without the inner in-

---

* In *Thirty-five Years in the East* (London: H. Bailliere, 1852), Dr. John Martin Honigberger, physician to the Court of Lahore, India, writes of the feats of Sadhu Haridas, which he gathered from eyewitness accounts.

telligence of subconsciousness, charged with God's consciousness, utilizing the Cosmic Energy "radioed" into the body through the medulla and stored in the protonic center of all bodily cells.* During the suspended state of the body, unless the cell and thought radios are tuned in with the dynamo of Cosmic Consciousness, or with the subdynamo of the superconsciously charged subconscious, the cells and bodily functions will be destroyed because of the lack of a controlling intelligence. When consciousness departs from the spine and brain in the suspended body, death is instantaneous, and decay ensues.

The suspended animation accomplished by yogis such as Sadhu Haridas is useful primarily for the purpose of demonstrating advanced psychophysiological laws. A suspended state of unknowingness is not necessarily spiritually beneficial. Any kind of suspended animation when one is unconscious outside and unconscious inside is only a mental chloroform and should be discarded. Certain teachers produce a state of suspended animation in animals or themselves by pressing glands. This produces a state of inner and outer unconsciousness which should be strictly avoided as metaphysically useless. In the spiritual yoga of *samadhi* meditation, though the body may assume a trancelike suspension, the consciousness remains fully awake in oneness with God in the bliss of conscious divine communion.

In the state of divine ecstasy, the life force becomes concentrated in the spiritual cerebrospinal centers and electrifies all of the trillions of cells of the body, not only preventing their decay but rejuvenating them with a powerful elixir of Cosmic Energy. When the cells are electrified with this supercurrent, they cease their accustomed mutations of growth and decay. This is what is meant by ecstatic "suspended animation." The body, being a cluster of atomic, cellular, circulatory, muscular, and astral lifetronic motions, depends usually

Meditation: connecting one's limited energy and consciousness with the Infinite Life and Cosmic Consciousness

---

* Consciousness as a factor in human sustenance is demonstrable in the phenomenon of sleep. The human mechanism must periodically be recharged by retiring into the subconsciousness in the state of sleep, wherein the consciousness and body cells are revivified by contact with the superconsciousness of the soul. The rejuvenating effects of sleep are due to man's temporary unawareness of the body and breath. The sleeping man becomes a yogi; each night he unconsciously performs the yogic rite of releasing himself from bodily identification, and of merging the life force with healing currents in the main brain region and in the six subdynamos of his spinal centers. Unknowingly, the sleeper is thus recharged by the Cosmic Energy that sustains all life.

upon such motion for its existence. But the yogi in *samadhi* meditation consciously suspends the activity of change in the muscles, blood, nerve force, and all tissues, and supports the body by the changeless power of Cosmic Energy from Cosmic Consciousness. If one gently touches the spring of a fine watch, it will stop; and when the watch is shaken, it will run again. In the same way, when the body functions are stilled by quieting the restless activity of the mental processes, the life force and human consciousness cease their outward activity with the material world and temporarily suspend their slavery to oxygen, food, and sunshine; they learn to depend wholly upon the true body supporters, God's Cosmic Energy and Cosmic Consciousness.

To return to activity, the yogi stirs his will and consciousness in the spine and brain. When he turns on the switch of the will, the thoughts begin to stir. With the connecting of the mind to the sensory powers of perception and action, the life force restores complete animation to the body.

A Sadhu Haridas who can put the body into a subconscious trance state of suspended animation; a Therese Neumann or Giri Bala who can subsist on pure energy from the air, sunshine, and vibratory light of God; an avatar such as Mahavatar Babaji for whom breath, bodily atoms, life itself, are no more than manipulatable light and God-thoughts—all provide dramatic proof of man's potential to master the life forces of his erstwhile materially stubborn body.

Jesus showed his mastery over the body by the manifestation of Cosmic Consciousness during his forty days of fasting and meditation. After attaining such a state, it makes no difference whether a master eats normally to remain in touch with his human nature, or whether he eats sparingly or not at all.

Extreme examples are cited not as an objective toward which the average man or even the God-seeker should aspire, but to show that if such remarkable control of the physical being is possible, it is also possible for a person living a normal life to so spiritualize his body that he can experience the Divine Power as the real source of his life, and can consciously use that Power to help free himself from physical suffering and other grief-inflicting mortal limitations.

Meditation is the method of realizing the connection between one's body-circumscribed life energy and the infinite Cosmic Energy of God, the connection between the conscious and subconscious states and the Cosmic Consciousness of God. Through *Kriya Yoga* meditation, the consciousness is gradually transformed from identification with the inept and often treacherous physical body, with its love of breath and "bread," to awareness of the inner astral body of self-renewing vibrant life energy, and thence to one's ultimate nature as a soul image of God: ever-existing, ever-conscious, ever-new Bliss. Jesus, Elijah, Kabir, and other prophets were past masters in the use of *Kriya* or a similar technique, by which they could cause their bodies to materialize or dematerialize at will—even as Jesus resurrected his crucified body; and as he witnessed, in his former incarnation as Elisha, his guru Elijah dissolve his body into fiery energy and ascend into heaven.*

Deep *samadhi* meditation is possible only when all bodily functions are stilled. Proper diet and fasting are helpful in conditioning the body for this state of quiet and interiorization. Jesus acknowledged this principle by fasting to spiritualize his body and free his mind during his forty days in the wilderness.

Value of proper diet and periodic fasting

To meditate when the stomach is empty is a good practice because the energy that runs the nervous system is not then as busy with bodily functions. Meditation after heavy meals sets up a tug-of-war between the body consciousness and the soul's superconsciousness. With a full stomach, the heart, lungs, and digestive and nervous systems are all engaged in digesting food, burning carbon, and maintaining circulation to the lungs to rid the blood of carbon dioxide. This keeps the subconscious mind busy, which in turn injects its restlessness into the conscious mind. Such invasion of the consciousness precludes inner God-communion. But when the inner activities of the body are still, the heart is calm. When the heart is calm, the life current is switched off from the senses, and the mind is freed from restless thoughts to concentrate wholly on God.

People who habitually overeat and never fast harness the life force in their bodies to a relentless activity of burning carbon and cleansing venous blood, overworking the heart and keeping the five sense-telephones constantly active. Fasting in connection with meditation slows the activity in the muscles, heart, circulation, diaphragm, and lungs by denying carbon and chemicals to the blood, thus helping to

---

* See Discourse 2: "...there appeared a chariot of fire, and horses of fire...and Elijah went up by a whirlwind into heaven" (II Kings 2:11).

Kabir was a great sixteenth-century saint in India. See Discourse 75.

draw the attention away from the body and its functions. Metaphysically, fasting helps to open up the life-giving inner source of Cosmic Consciousness and Cosmic Energy.*

Long fasting should never be undertaken without the guidance and direction of a competent preceptor. Long fasting (that is, for more than one day a week, or three days once a month or every forty-five days — taking sufficient fluids) is not necessary in order to demonstrate the vital sustenance of Divine Power. Nourish the body and spirit with meditation.

The mind sets the tone for all the activities of the body. Thus, affirmations are helpful: "I live by the power of God and not by physical means only." A state of such freedom is nearly inconceivable to the typical body-bound individual, who cannot even begin his day without first paying homage to his need for morning toast and coffee. But Jesus demonstrated the truth that man lives by Divine Power, and that by the proper effort he can become aware of his inherent connection with God Consciousness and Cosmic Energy.

Meditation is the most effective way to spiritualize the body. Meditative effort to make the body live on this higher plane is aided by right eating at all times. Even a spiritual man eating food injudiciously would find the body obstructing the practices that lead to spiritual realization. Dietetics is not delusion so long as the body itself asserts its existence in the realm of manifestation. Healthful food, pure oxygen through proper breathing, and sunshine are Nature's requirements for the upkeep of this body battery.

---

* "Recent Indo-German studies have revealed that fasting can prolong life span," reports an article in *The Deccan Chronicle*, Hyderabad, India, January 23, 1995. "The experiments, carried out by the Hyderabad-based Centre for Cellular and Molecular Biology (CCMB) in collaboration with the Max Planck Institute for Experimental Endocrinology (Germany) noted that fasting conserved a lot of energy. This excess energy could be utilized for carrying out other functions of the human body or for keeping the body fit, thus increasing longevity.

"During the experiments, which subjected rats to fasting, it was found that the turnover or replacement of internal lining cells, which requires a lot of energy, was completely stopped. There also was no physiological cell death, and intestinal cells became more efficient in absorbing nutrients, Dr. P. D. Gupta, Deputy Director of the CCMB and leader of the study group, said.

"Dr. Gupta said there were instances of Jain *munis* fasting for more than 200 days. However, it was found that fasting up to three days stopped 'physiological cell death' completely. Fasting for one or two days intermittently over a period of one month was always beneficial, the study found." *(Publisher's Note)*

The proper diet should be chosen and care should be taken never to overeat. There is a lot of truth in the adage that man digs his own grave with his knife and fork! Most kinds of meat (especially beef and pork) and other vibrationally gross foods overtax the life force, making it difficult to disengage its preoccupation with the senses and overworked vital organs, and to reverse the current of life and consciousness toward God when one sits for devotional communion.

One should choose a healthful balanced diet of natural foods rich in life force that are easily processed by the body—fruits, vegetables, whole grains, legumes, nuts, some dairy products—and avoid foods in which the life force has been denatured or destroyed by improper processing or are otherwise unsuited for the human system.* Additionally, fanaticism is to be avoided. A food fanatic, constantly obsessed with fastidious observance of health and dietary laws, will find his attachment to the body a real hindrance to spiritual realization. Eat rightly, never admitting dependence on food. Know that it is God's Cosmic Energy and Cosmic Consciousness that changes the food into the energy of life.

The soul is above hunger and the desire for food. This does not mean that the spiritual aspirant should stop eating, but it does mean that he should eat properly and joyously to maintain the body-temple of God, and not just to satisfy sense craving. The sense of taste should not be debased with greed and indigestion from wrong eating and overeating; its purpose is to select and enjoy the right food to keep the body healthy and vibrant for the use of the soul. To eat only for the pleasure of taste produces greed, slavery, indigestion, disease, and premature death. To eat for the maintenance of the body-temple produces self-control, long life, health, and happiness.

Through fasting and meditation, Jesus realized fully that hunger is a delusion connected with the law of change in the body, and can be overcome—that one can live entirely by God's energy. By not accepting Satan's suggestion to turn stones into bread, Jesus performed a greater miracle of conquering his mortality by the divine memory of

---

* My guru, Swami Sri Yukteswar, concisely set forth principles of the ideal diet natural to man as being vegetarian, based on an analysis of "the formation of the organs that aid in digestion and nutrition, the teeth and digestive canal" and "observation of the natural tendency of the organs of sense—the guideposts for determining what is nutritious—by which all animals are directed to their food." (*The Holy Science*, Chapter 3; published by Self-Realization Fellowship.)

his self-sustaining unconditioned spiritual existence. From then on it was at his option to live with or without sustenance from food.

The spiritual lesson in Jesus' refusal to change stones into bread

For Jesus to have miraculously created food to satisfy the needs of his human body would have been a misuse of his divine powers. Great souls who attain the highest do not employ their powers for their own benefit. Their unspectacular demeanor in personal affairs embraces the difficulties common to all human beings, whose struggles they have come on earth to share. The only power they use for themselves is their exceptional love and devotion for God. It is this supreme miracle with which they also seek to attract others to the Divine Presence.

Miracles are held in esteem by earthbound mortals, who try to satisfy their own feelings of inadequacy by challenging God to prove Himself. But divine souls do not test the attention and love of God, because that is to doubt Him. If Jesus had invoked a miracle for the mere trifle of appeasing hunger, that would have been an assault on his faith in God and a denial of his reliance on God's all-protecting power. Jesus' triumph over this temptation was a severe defeat to Satan, whose strongest delusion holding man in bondage is attachment to the mortal body consciousness.

Satan saw in Jesus his nemesis that would snatch many souls from his domain, so he was not deterred in his efforts to prevent Jesus' ascendancy.

～

Then the devil taketh him up into the holy city, and setteth him on a pinnacle of the temple, and saith unto him, "If thou be the Son of God, cast thyself down: for it is written, 'He shall give His angels charge concerning thee': and 'in their hands they shall bear thee up, lest at any time thou dash thy foot against a stone.'"

Jesus said unto him, "It is written again, 'Thou shalt not tempt the Lord thy God.'"

Again, the devil taketh him up into an exceeding high mountain, and sheweth him all the kingdoms of the world, and the glory of them; and saith unto him, "All these things will I give thee, if thou wilt fall down and worship me."

Then saith Jesus unto him, "Get thee hence, Satan: for it is written, 'Thou shalt worship the Lord thy God, and Him only shalt thou serve.'" Then the devil leaveth him, and, behold, angels came and ministered unto him (Matthew 4:5–11).*

There is an esoteric meaning to the above two metaphorical passages.

The body and spirit of Jesus were tempted and taunted both subjectively and objectively by Satan. The Evil Force has many contrivances at his command. He does not always employ his easily recognized objectified manifestations. Often his best strategy is subtly to creep subjectively into the very thought processes and imagination of his would-be captive. In this psychological guise, Satan took *Symbolism of "the holy city" and "pinnacle of the temple"* hold of the mind of Jesus while he was on the very height of the temple of meditation situated in the "holy city" of his universal Christ Consciousness. The consciousness of Jesus was concentrated "on a pinnacle" of the cerebrospinal axis at the point between the eyebrows, in the heavenly center of Christ perception. Satanic delusion wanted him to fall down to the lower region of the spine—the lumbar, sacral, and coccygeal plexuses—the plane of the senses with their bodily attachments.

Although the consciousness of Jesus had reached the pinnacle of meditative intuitive experience of the Christ state, its residence in the body predisposed the mind of Jesus to be subject still to the temptation of delusion. Jesus' past delusive habit of identification with the body, finding constant defeat in his sacred consciousness, was roused by Satan to make a culminative effort to dislodge the habit of his divine thinking. His memory of delusive mortal habits cast a tempting thought into his mind: "Since I have regained in meditation my high state of divine Sonhood, it is safe for me to cast myself down into realms of bodily temptation. God will protect me through my guardian angels of spiritual conviction, intuitive experiences, and meditation-born wisdom. Even if I fall into delusion, the angels of spiritual thoughts will lift me up again to my high estate of consciousness, and will prevent my foot of strong will power from dashing against the stone of misery-making spiritual error."

---

* In his replies to the devil, Jesus is quoting Deuteronomy 6:16 and 6:13. Cf. parallel reference in Luke 4:5–13.

The preeminent spiritual habit conquered, and Jesus replied in his introspective thought: "The highest scriptural wisdom is that the attention must never stray from God. He is the Father and Creator of all forms of consciousness, cosmic and human. No expression of that divided Indivisibility should succumb to the temptation of delusive experience to feel itself separate from Him, and thus drag that manifestation of Divinity matterward. The consciousness must remain concentrated in the truth of its transcendental identification with God, untouched by satanic temptations."

All craving and desire in man should be transmuted and turned toward God, instead of being allowed to enshroud in delusion the God-image in man. Satanic temptation's delusive, compelling, conflicting, happiness-expecting thought leads to misery-producing error. Divine temptation summons man to pursue happiness-making truth. Knowing this, Jesus snubbed the devil's temptation, and scorned its audacity to tempt the God in him.

It is never wise to tempt the protecting grace of God merited by acquired virtues. Even advanced devotees have fallen into delusion by self-assured, presumptuous reliance on their righteous attainments as a safeguard against a lapse, even momentarily, in requisite right behavior and discriminative judgment. "Thou shalt not tempt the inner Divine Consciousness to prove Itself." It is for the devotee to remain always at one with the immutable Sheltering Presence.

Again, the psychological Satan followed Jesus to his very high, mountainlike state of Self-realization; and in an instantaneous mental vision arrayed before him all the temporal power and glory of material possessions and position; and thus lured him with the thought: "I will give you kingdoms of power and wealth." The psychological past delusive habit of pleasurable familiarity with the body, pressing its momentary opportunity to regain control of the wisdom-guided free choice and will of Jesus, made him feel that, having gained mastery over the laws of nature, it had the power to give him enjoyment of all glorified material things if only he would fall down to the plane of sensory gratifications from his high state of self-mastery and joy in Spirit.

Temptations of sensory and material gratifications versus self-mastery and spiritual joy

Jesus answered within his discriminative introspection: "O ye senses of smell, taste, sight, touch, and hearing, you were made to be devoted to Spirit, and constantly to act and serve the soul in its con-

176

tact with matter without interrupting its transcendent, conscious experience of the joy of Spirit."

The senses were given to serve man with perceptions of God incarnate in matter, not for man to cater to their insatiable cravings—an innovation of satanic delusion. As the servants of man, the God-created senses, guided with discrimination, produce self-control, long life, health, and happiness. Controlled by the temptations of Satan, the senses enslave man in the misery of body identification and soul forgetfulness.

The Cosmic Intelligent Force, which has turned away from God, throws its searchlight of vibratory luminosity upon matter to extol it and captivate man with its shimmering tinsel glory.

To use the soul's searchlight of attention for worshiping the speciousness of changing, temporary-pleasure-yielding matter is to become mesmerized by the charm of Satan's sensory kingdom of finitude.

To reverse the searchlight of attention and focus it upon the God-knowing soul in meditation is to behold and enjoy the changeless, everlasting, joy-giving Spirit.

The great drama of cosmic existence honors man's free choice and power of reason. Man, made in the image of God, has the same liberty of free choice in his sphere as has God the Father. God can redeem man only when in every way he chooses to act in accordance with divine laws of right living.

Man's free choice and power of reason are his redemption

God is coaxing man with a limitless exhibition of good happenings to influence him for his own highest welfare. Satan is tempting man with deceptive contrivances that are pleasant-looking and promise happiness, but after a little evanescent pleasure give evil consequences instead.

Man stands in the middle between God and Satan, each ready to pull him in whichever direction he wishes to go. Satan is on the left side with his kingdom of misery cloaked in ostentation, and God is on the right side with His kingdom of happiness bathed in eternal light. It is up to man to signal God or Satan as to which direction he wants to be pulled. Man is perfectly free to act, controlled neither by God nor Satan. Whenever he initiates good actions, or has a pure, ennobling thought, that is the signal to God; and he is automatically pulled toward God, toward a paradise of Bliss hidden in the womb of eternal futurity. But as soon as man thinks or acts in accord with evil, he is automatically pulled toward Satan, toward entanglement in the realm of misery-making dualities.

When man succumbs to temptation, or is angry, or jealous, or selfish, or greedy, or revengeful, or restless, he has accepted Satan's invitation to come to his side. When man is master of himself—moderate, calm, understanding, unselfish, forgiving, practicing meditation—he is inviting God to help him.

God is very anxious for all His children to get back to His kingdom, free from suffering and death and all other terrors and uncertainties of human life in which Satan keeps man constantly involved through bondage to the senses. Every time man is tempted to do wrong, he should remind himself that it is not his subjective mind alone that is tempting him, but also objective Satan. He should adamantly refuse to cooperate with the Evil One who would destroy him. That is why Jesus said, "Get thee behind me, Satan" (Luke 4:8) when that Evil Force showed him kingdoms of temporal glory, which could be his if he worshiped delusion.

The wisdom of Jesus could not be swayed. If someone offered a man a million dollars, and someone else held before him a thousand dollars as an alternative, only a fool would prefer the paltry offering. Jesus spoke from his soul-realization: "I have chosen imperishable Bliss; what care I for anything temporal?"

The deluded man muses how wonderful it would be if he were as rich as Henry Ford or Andrew Carnegie, but where are they now? Why desire things that must be abandoned at death? The great poet Saadi of Persia said: "If thou dost conquer the world and bend all the people to thy will, what then? You will one day have to leave it all."

As a result of the choice Jesus made, he has eternal life in God's Bliss. By emerging victorious from temptation, he is a shining example for all souls struggling to regain their divine sonhood. He showed the way: On the mountain peak of high meditation, Jesus lifted the veil of body consciousness, sense appearances, and matter, and identified himself with the "only begotten Son," Christ Consciousness. It is then that a soul knows its divine status as a son of God.

There was a time when I believed Satan was a symbolical force, a metaphysical delusion; but now I know and add my testimony to the testimony of Jesus Christ that Satan is responsible for all the creation of evil on earth and in the minds of men. I have consciously seen Satan many times obstructing me by mysterious misfortunes, and by consciously taking materialized forms while I was receiving the grace of God.

On one occasion I was beholding the face of Christ, and just as
he passed out of my vision I saw the evil force too as Satan. It was a
terrific vision: Those two forces passed through my
body, one of them the universal Christ-joy and   *In highest samadhi,*
peace, the other the great cosmic delusion. The Evil   *"the devil" of delusive*
Force didn't touch me, only tried to frighten me. As   *dualities departs from*
one goes into the Spirit he sees those two forces dis-   *man's consciousness*
tinctly; but when I reached the highest *samadhi* I
found there is nothing else there but God. But before that realization
is reached, that Cosmic Dichotomy will not yield its illusory reality as
two forces, the power of evil and the power of Christ, the power of
Satan and the power of God.

When the Psychological Satan had finished tempting Jesus, the
delusion of memories of mortal habit departed, for a time at least, giving rise to the feeling of victory for the permanent habit of spiritual
consciousness. The Gospel According to St. Luke notes: "And when
the devil had ended all the temptation, he departed from him for a season."* The departing of Satan "for a season" signifies the transcendental state of fixed self-mastery, when the devotee rises above duality and its compulsory struggle with evil.

Every master who has attained the realization of the state of
nirvikalpa samadhi feels the obsession of ignorance within him gone.
With the disappearance of the mindset of ignorance that sees everything in terms of mortal consciousness, sublime changes occur within
that advanced devotee. Under the influence of cosmic delusion, even
sincerely aspiring devotees behold matter as matter, and see the dualities of good and evil and the relativity of consciousness, which reveals
matter as different forms of solids, liquids, gaseous, and astral substances. But when the influence of Satan is completely terminated, the
liberated devotee finds only the presence of the omnipresent, ever-
existing, ever-conscious, ever-new blessed Spirit. All evil, all discrepancies of nature, disappear as forgotten shadows from the consciousness of the illumined devotee.

When Jesus in the wilderness was victorious in defeating the
temptations of Satan, the mortal delusive habit disappeared, and the
angels of Intuition, Calmness, Omniscience, and Self-realization appeared in the consciousness of Jesus to serve him with lasting Bliss.

---

* Luke 4:13.

Jesus Meets His First Disciples

Rabbi, "Master": As Guru, One Who Is Master of Himself

❖

True Gurus Draw Disciples by the Spiritual Magnetism
of Their God-realization

❖

Jesus' Disciples Recognize Him as the Messiah,
Incarnation of Christ Consciousness

❖

Finding a True Guru:
A God-Sent Guide on the Path to Self-realization

❖

Unconditional Love, Loyalty, and Obedience
Are Hallmarks of the Guru-Disciple Relationship

❖

Following the Wisdom-Guidance of the Guru
Bestows Freedom of Will and Liberation

"Jesus knew the secret law of emancipation inherent in the guru-disciple relationship, and its pact of mutual help, as God began to send to him those disciples destined to help him and to find liberation through his instrumentality."

*A*gain the next day after John stood, and two of his disciples; and looking upon Jesus as he walked, he saith, "Behold the Lamb of God!"* And the two disciples heard him speak, and they followed Jesus.

Then Jesus turned, and saw them following, and saith unto them, "What seek ye?"

They said unto him, "Rabbi," (which is to say, being interpreted, Master,) "where dwellest thou?"

He saith unto them, "Come and see." They came and saw where he dwelt, and abode with him that day: for it was about the tenth hour.

One of the two which heard John speak, and followed him, was Andrew, Simon Peter's brother. He first findeth his own brother Simon, and saith unto him, "We have found the Messiah," which is, being interpreted, the Christ.

And he brought him to Jesus. And when Jesus beheld him, he said, "Thou art Simon the son of Jona: thou shalt be called Cephas," which is by interpretation, a stone.

The day following Jesus would go forth into Galilee, and findeth Philip, and saith unto him, "Follow me."

—John 1:35–43

---

* "John" in this verse refers to John the Baptist. See Discourse 6 for discussion of "Lamb of God." *(Publisher's Note)*

DISCOURSE 9

Jesus Meets His First Disciples

When great masters come on earth, they bring with them select advanced disciples from past incarnations to help them in their mission and to further or culminate the preparations of those disciples for liberation. Through association with the master, receiving his guidance in the higher teachings of soul freedom, and having their spirituality tested in the applied science of life in this earth-school, while also assisting the guru in his God-ordained work, such disciples and their guru fulfill in the highest way the divine covenant of the guru-disciple relationship. Among the throng who followed Jesus were many disciples, of greater or lesser qualification, known to him from lives past. From among these disciples he chose and appointed twelve to serve as apostles—those who are "sent forth"—notwithstanding that one among them failed his test, and succumbing to delusion was the instrument of betrayal and the cause of his own lost opportunity of salvation for many, many lifetimes of sorrow.

The mission of a savior on earth may be primarily quantitative, to influence as many people as possible with his uplifting God-sent spiritual message, thus urging the world forward in a right trend. The receptivity of the ordinary person among the masses, however, has a limited capacity; he may be satisfied with merely one thought or a few precepts from the master's teachings as being all he feels he needs or wants to improve himself to an adequate degree in his settled stratum of life. Other masters concentrate primarily on qualitative good: to serve those souls—be they few or many—who are eager to know God, to help uplift them into Christ Consciousness and ultimate liberation. Still other saviors, such as Christ, serve the world both quantitatively and qualitatively. The qualitative task requires the endeavor of the disciple and the blessing and guidance of the master in a mutual relationship sanctified by God. Students are those who follow the master more or less superficially according to their pick-and-choose inclination. But the disciple is one who accepts wholly, with open heart and mind. He does not have to be coaxed, but follows through his own will and determination. He remains steadfast, dedicated, and devoted to the end, until he has found freedom in God. The Lord Christ and the Lord Krishna both had such disciples.

God-ordained gurus feel intuitively the spiritual vibrations of their disciples, whether near or far; and when a guru mentally calls his disciples, they come, drawn by their soul attunement with the teacher, the channel of divine grace appointed by God.

In his supportive role of assisting the mission of Jesus, John the Baptist turned many of his own followers toward Jesus—in particular, those who had been disciples of Jesus in past lives. The first of these was Andrew, brother of Simon Peter; and the other unnamed person of the "two" with John the Baptist has been logically proposed as being John the Apostle himself, since his is the only Gospel that relates this episode. These two devotees, on the commendation of John the Baptist, and responding to their own inner devotional attraction, followed Jesus to his residence, addressing him reverentially as Rabbi, or Master.

The word *rabbi* is a Jewish title of respect which means "my Master," a form of address recognizing one who is qualified to teach. Applied to one's guru, *Master* is synonymous with the proper form of addressing the guru with the respectful suffix of *ji* or *deva*: Guruji, Gurudeva, Master. The word *master* may be traced etymologically back through Latin, *magnus*, great; with *magnus* being akin to Sanskrit *mahat* (great; important, high, eminent: *maharishi*, a great knower of God). The widespread generic usage of *master* as a title (as also that of *guru*) to denote any ordinary teacher or mentor should not disrespectfully belie the proper usage: as an appellation for a God-knowing, divinely endowed guru.

Rabbi, "master": as guru, one who is master of himself

From the cradle to the grave to ascension in Spirit, the whole of civilization is based on the passing down of knowledge from the learned to the learning. The infant learns from his parents, the youth from his schoolteachers and professors, the worker from his trained supervisors, the artist or musician from his superiorly accomplished instructors. The level of attainment rises or falls with the aptitude of the "student" and the qualification of the "mentor." In no other field is this as true as in spirituality. In India, where religious doctrines are melted in the crucible of testing experience to separate truth from dogma, the verdict is that the only sure way of finding God is to learn about Him from one who knows Him. The Hindu scriptures say, "When a spiritually blind novitiate is led by a blind teacher, then both are misled"—an admonition voiced similarly by Jesus.*

God is *The* Master, ruler of the universe; and those who manifest their oneness with Him may also be honored as masters. A spiritual master is not a wielder of authority over others, but rather a master of himself, fully self-possessed and controlled in body, speech, and mind, with all his senses fully reined. He never allows himself to be compelled by temptation to do anything against his discrimination-guided will, unlike those who think that freedom, or free will, is to do whatever entices their minds. A master is he who knows in what lies the best interest of his true Self, the soul, and so never entertains evil in thought or deed.

Self-mastery is the citadel of wisdom. When the title of Master is used in addressing a personage of this stature, it signifies reverence for him who knows truth offered by one who desires to have that knowledge conferred on himself by the guru.

Andrew, after he and his companion had been with Jesus for a day, was so saturated with the spiritual magnetism emanating from Jesus that he understood who Jesus was, recognizing him as the Christ. The Christ Consciousness cannot be intellectually inferred, but has to come through intuitional awareness. God-ordained gurus do not have to convert their inner circle of disciples by soapbox preaching; they communicate primarily

True gurus draw disciples by the spiritual magnetism of their God-realization

by the silent emanation of the vibrations of their God-realization. My Master drew me that way when I first saw him, without introduction, in a busy market lane in Banaras. (I have written about my experiences with great masters and with my Guru in my memoirs, published un-

---

* "Fools dwelling in darkness, wise in their own conceit, and puffed up with vain knowledge, go round and round staggering to and fro, like blind men led by the blind" (Mundaka Upanishad I.ii.8, translated by Max Muller, *Sacred Books of the East,* Volume 15, 1884).

Jesus said: "Can the blind lead the blind? shall they not both fall into the ditch?" (Luke 6:39). See commentary in Discourse 33.

der the title of *Autobiography of a Yogi.**) The first contact between guru and disciple is usually sufficient to awaken memories of the everlasting bonding of that relationship. They feel a connection of oneness at first sight in their exchange of magnetism.

The sum total of a person is expressed in his magnetism. His very being, in fact, has its origin in magnetism—in the creative ideational powers of man's causal body, the God-ideas that form man's astral and physical bodies and sustain the soul's incarnation. Through the medulla oblongata, Cosmic Consciousness and Cosmic Energy enter into the subtle astral cerebrospinal centers of life and consciousness, and thence into the physical body, as positive and negative currents, forming a series of attracting magnets. Each individual is a bundle of these magnets, with attracting power according to their magnetic strength. Jesus was a Christ magnet empowering him to attract multitudes, as compared with the ordinary man who can attract very little.

All the parts of the body that come in pairs—eyes, ears, tongue and the little uvula tongue, hands, feet, and so on—have their positive and negative sides. They receive and radiate positive and negative lifetronic currents, each pair forming a magnet. The optical magnet can charm, enthrall, and strongly draw people; they will feel the magnetism of the soul of that person through his eyes. Some highly developed persons are able to spiritualize or heal others, even a whole audience, just by the magnetism of the eyes.

The spiritual practice of "laying on of hands" to send healing rays into the body of a patient electrocutes the germs and other agents of disease. There is tremendous power in the life force flowing through the hands, provided it is made strong by a pure, indomitable will. A will that refuses to be discouraged by anything, and that flows continually and energetically toward accomplishment of its object, becomes divinely empowered. The strong will of man guided by wisdom is Divine Will.

As each person carries with him a telltale silent evidence of his own vibrations, individuals residing in the same house, sharing the same rooms, soon come to know each other, even if they verbally communicate very little, because of an exchange of the magnetic vibrations of their consciousness, nature, vitality, and feelings. Each feels the silent emanation of the other's thoughts and life force, and the range and strength of his vital magnetism.

---

* Published by Self-Realization Fellowship.

Unbiased, spiritually sensitive souls can know people simply by looking into their eyes, or by merely coming in close proximity with them and feeling their radiating vibrations. Worried, calm, timid, brave, cruel, wise, or godly vibrations can be felt instantly even by people with little spiritual perception.

Persons with ordinary perception are usually sensitive to others only when within near range of their magnetism. Great minds, however, can feel another person from a distance, although receptivity is stronger if they have been closely associated for a while. Thus it was that Andrew's soul, after remaining for some hours with Jesus, felt unquestionably his Christ magnetism and could proclaim to his brother Simon: "We have found the Messiah."

In the words of Andrew we find the differentiation between the name Jesus and the title Christ (Messiah). Jesus ("Isa," Lord of Creation*) was his given family name, signifying a divine child. The title Christ was appended later when he began his ministry and was recognized as the one whose coming had been prophesied, in whom Divinity would be incarnate. Thus Christ signifies the Christ Consciousness, the reflection of God which became manifest in the consciousness of Jesus.

Jesus' disciples recognize him as the Messiah, incarnation of Christ Consciousness

The concept of Christ as a state of consciousness, as well as linguistic variants of the word itself, is very ancient, referring to the unchangeable Intelligence, the pure Reflected Consciousness of God, present in every atom of matter and every pore of finite creation—the Christ Consciousness, known from time immemorial by India's *rishis* as *Kutastha Chaitanya*.

Jesus the Christ signifies that the body of Jesus was the vehicle in which was manifested the Christ Consciousness. The title *Christ* is more anciently found in India in the word *Krishna*. Perhaps the Christ title was first bestowed on Jesus during his sojourn in India. Sometimes I purposely spell *Krishna* as *Christna* to show the correlation. Similarly, *Yadava* was the family name of the beloved Hindu avatar who lived in India centuries before Jesus,† and *Krishna* (*Christna*) was his spiritual epithet. Thus, the words *Christ* and *Krishna* are the spir-

---

*See Discourse 5.

†The date of Sri Krishna's incarnation is uncertain. Though archaeologically indefinite, a popular concept is that he lived sometime between 1500 and 900 B.C.

itual titles for these two illumined beings: Jesus Christ and Yadava Krishna.*

People throughout different ages have sought the Messiah, many believing he would be a temporal king who would reign in a golden age of opulence and well-being, free from travesties of suffering and oppression.† Few were to understand that the purpose of a Messiah, a Christ, would be to turn their soul's attention from the consciousness of attachment to little portions of the matter-world—country, society, family, possessions —to the omnipresence of Christ Consciousness. When souls, descending into form to experience the Lord's cosmic drama of *maya*-creation, lose their identification with the universality of Christ Consciousness, they are diminished into limited egos entangled in mortal relationships, circumscriptions, and national and social identities. Blind attachments lead to selfishness, quarrelsomeness, delusion of permanent possession, inharmony, worries; and on a national scale produce commercial greed, desire of wresting the possessions of others, and terrible wars.

After accumulating a bewildering collage of adventurous and often painful incarnations, the beleaguered soul cries, "Enough!" and a serious search for emancipation begins.

One has to wonder how our Creator must feel that most of His truant children turn to Him only when in desperation, after being impelled by the scourge of sorrow. Nevertheless, whether through suffering, or wonderment, or discriminative reasoning, when they do begin to long for God and deliverance, and pray deeply to Him, God is touched and responds with loving help. The Heavenly Father, who is ever watchful of the inclination of the human heart, favors the truth-

---

* There are many derivations given to the word *Krishna,* the most common of which is "dark," referring to the hue of Krishna's complexion. (He is often shown as dark blue to connote divinity. Blue is also the color of the Christ Consciousness when epitomized in the spiritual eye as a circle of opal-blue light surrounding the star-opening to Cosmic Consciousness.) According to M. V. Sridatta Sarma ("On the Advent of Sri Krishna"), of the various other meanings given to the word *Krishna,* several are found in the *Brahmavaivarta Purana.* He states that according to one of these derivations, "*Krsna* means the Universal Spirit. *Krsi* denotes a generic term, while *na* conveys the idea of the self, thus bringing forth the meaning 'Omniscient Spirit.'" In this we find a parallel to the Christ Consciousness as the Intelligence of God omnipresent in creation, the *Kutastha Chaitanya.* It is of interest that a colloquial Bengali rendering of *Krishna* is *Krista* (cf. Greek *Christos* and Spanish *Cristo*). *(Publisher's Note)*

† The word "Messiah" comes from the Hebrew *Mashiakh,* "Anointed," the expected King and deliverer of the Hebrews. Translated into Greek, "anointed" became *Christos,* "Christ."

seeking devotee with some form of assistance, commensurate with the
depth of the supplicant's desire and readiness. During the period of a
seeker's philosophical curiosity, God causes a seem-
ingly chance contact with the precepts of a good   *Finding a true guru: a*
book or the counsel of some spiritual teacher. But   *God-sent guide on the*
when the aspirant is not satisfied with meager pla-   *path to Self-realization*
cations from religious treatises or mediocre instruc-
tors, and his heart is corroding with eagerness to find God, then the
Father sends unto His child one who knows God and is empowered
to confer that realization on others. God does not reveal Himself in
the beginning to an undeveloped truth-seeker, emerging from haloed
clouds to proffer blessings and wisdom; He uses the transparent intuition, God-consciousness, and teachings of a master, an enlightened
soul, to bring the devotee unto Himself. The guru is therefore not an
ordinary teacher, but a preceptor-messenger celestial who guides the
devotee through wisdom and reason, and the discipline of spiritual
practices, *sadhana*, throughout one life, or as many lives as necessary,
until the soul is again free in Spirit.

The whims of fickleness and the mental excitement of love of the
new are real deterrents on the spiritual path. Sampling one church after another, one teacher after another, collecting an incompatible hash
of ideas, is a sure formula for developing theoretical indigestion. The
way to wisdom lies in assimilating truths into one's own personal realization, not in the amassing of concepts left untried and unproven. The
method of finding God is different from the methods of gathering
knowledge and storing it in the brain employed by universities to edu-
cate specialists in any field. Even so, a medical student, for example,
will never learn his speciality if he roams willy-nilly from subject to
subject, switching from one medical institution to another and listening to a few lectures at each, but not going through intensive training
in the necessary courses in an effectively integrated program to earn a
degree. The serious spiritual aspirant, also, needs to commit himself to
the time and lessons necessary for Self-realization, to the practice of
those proven methods that have produced God-knowing saints.

There are many worthy teachers who selflessly serve and help others; but there is also much scope for unscrupulous abuse by those who
would take advantage of the emotional vulnerability of persons who
in seeking support from religion become blindly attached, all hidebound, to a teacher's personality and self-conceived assertions. In my

early years of seeking God, not a few such pseudo-gurus tried to impress me with grandiose displays of piety and scriptural verbosity; but there was no godliness in their do-as-I-say-not-as-I-do facade and in the hollowness of holy words that they rolled out from rote rather than from the resonance of realization.

It is good to discriminate between the so-called teacher—who uses religion as a livelihood or to make money, or to gain fame and following—and the genuine teacher, who uses his religion (and principled business methods in religion) solely to serve his brethren with real spirituality. Discretion and caution are particularly necessary in accepting a guru, one to whom explicit loyalty and trust are given.

One may have many teachers in the beginning of his search, but when one's heart and soul are confidently settled in a guru-disciple relationship ordained and blessed by God, the disciple has only one guru, and no other teachers thereafter. The devotee remains loyal to such a guru, being spiritually fulfilled by the God-sent messenger. To forsake the guru and his ideals is to spurn the help sent by God, the One Guru of gurus: "the Lord God of the holy prophets";* He whom alone "seers great, and heaven's-path successful ones," do worship.†

Unconditional love, loyalty, and obedience are hallmarks of the guru-disciple relationship

The spiritual soul contact between guru and disciple is one of eternal, unconditional divine love and friendship, bearing no taint of any selfish consideration. Human love is conditional and based upon merit and inborn attachments. Unconditional divine love is the Christ-love with which God embraces all His children, high or low, naughty or good, under all circumstances. Only a master, one who has cast off his ego with its biases and selfish expectations, is capable of serving as a perfect channel through which God's divine love may flow without measure.

In the spiritually receptive, loyalty to the guru rises spontaneously when the disciple's heart is bathed in the aura of the guru's unconditional love. The soul knows that it has found at last a true friend, counselor, and guide. The disciple strives therefore to reciprocate the guru's unconditional love, especially when tested, even as the faith and loyalty of Jesus' disciples were often tried with nonunderstanding. Many were with Jesus at the feasts and sermons, but how few at the cross!

---

* Revelation 22:6.

† *God Talks With Arjuna: The Bhagavad Gita* XI:21.

190

The Boy Jesus With the Doctors in the Temple

And it came to pass, that after three days they found him in the temple, sitting in the midst of the doctors, both hearing them, and asking them questions. And all that heard him were astonished at his understanding and answers.

—Luke 2:46—47

We know of mental geniuses, whose brains absorb knowledge at astonishing speed. They are endowed with learning and learning abilities from past lives, which predisposes them to superefficient brain development. Spiritual geniuses have, in addition, the superconscious ability to tap the wisdom library of soul realization—the all-knowing intuitive faculty of the soul that manifests its oneness with the infinite Divine Intelligence.

Narratives about godly youthful savants abound in the spiritual lore of India. It is widely accepted that those who come on earth for a God-given purpose are graced with divine intervention that blesses them with wisdom transcending the natural growth of the intellect.

—Paramahansa Yogananda

Painting by Heinrich Hofmann

Yet from among loyal followers, advanced disciples greatly help the master in ways common and unique. Even a Christ could scarce fulfill his mission without those who are steadfast and in tune with him.

Jesus knew the secret law of emancipation inherent in the guru-disciple relationship, and its pact of mutual help, as God began to send to him those disciples destined to help him and to find liberation through his instrumentality.

In Andrew, Jesus found the receptivity to intuit the presence of the Christ Consciousness in the bodily vehicle of the Master. In John the beloved, Jesus saw the devotion that would hold this disciple steadfast and take him deep into the experience of the yogic science of God-union that he would later record in the Book of Revelation. In Simon Peter, Jesus discerned a divine strength on which to build the early foundation of his teachings, and predicted that the spiritual life of Simon would be as firm as a stone (Hebrew: *cephas;* Greek: Peter, "a rock").*

In meeting Philip, Jesus, remembering their previous guru-disciple relationship, said to him without hesitation, "Follow me." By this command, Jesus exercised his spiritual responsibility as preceptor to his disciple Philip. He indicated that Philip should tune his instinct-guided reason and will power with the higher wisdom-guided reason and will of Jesus, the way by which Philip could free himself from mortal delusion and overcome the common compelling temptations and attachments of the flesh.

Delusion and bad habits may completely overpower the judgment and will power of a disciple during crucial tests when the factitious dictates of his own reason seem to him to be valid, even virtuous. In this state, the disciple should not *Following the wisdom-* trust to his own decisions. Vice wears the cloak of *guidance of the guru* virtuous reason to lure the unwary one who finds it *bestows freedom of* pleasant to submit to conclusions that serve his *will and liberation* wishes. Determinations should be matched with the wisdom-guidance of the preceptor and followed obediently, even though the disciple's befogged reason may rebel. In the delusive state,

---

* "To the Jews of Palestine, this special sign of giving someone a new name—as in Genesis God had changed the name *Abram* to Abraham and *Jacob* to Israel—indicated that the person was chosen for a divine mission. Once again, Jesus harked back to Old Testament tradition even as he inaugurated his revolutionary movement of spiritual renewal."—from *Jesus and His Times,* Kaari Ward, ed. (Pleasantville, New York: Reader's Digest Association, 1987). *(Publisher's Note)*

the devotee may find that even the best-intentioned of undertakings may nevertheless end in a disaster; for Satan, the Universal Metaphysical Tempter, tries by every means to instigate faulty reason and unspiritual behavior in the virtuous devotee on the spiritual path.

My guru Sri Yukteswar said to me, when he accepted me for training: "Allow me to discipline you; for freedom of will does not consist in doing things according to the dictates of prenatal or postnatal habits or of mental whims, but in acting according to the suggestions of wisdom and free choice. If you tune in your will with mine, you will find freedom." In attunement with his God-guided, wisdom-guided will, I did find freedom.

Sri Krishna says in the Bhagavad Gita: "Comprehending that wisdom from a guru, thou wilt not again fall into delusion....Even if thou art the chief sinner among all sinners, yet by the sole raft of wisdom thou shalt safely cross the sea of sin" (IV:35–36). One who is spiritually ill-equipped to pilot the boat of his own will through rough seas will surely founder. But if he clings to the wisdom-raft of the guru's guidance, he will reach safe harbor.

He is not a guru who leads his followers into blind subjugation. Teachers who slavishly control their students after a dogmatic pattern destroy in them the power of free will. Such teachers want the student to see only as the teacher sees. Obedience to a true guru, however, does not produce any such spiritual blindness in the disciple. On the contrary, the guru wants the disciple to keep his eyes of reason open, and in addition he helps to develop in the disciple another eye: the "single eye" of wisdom and intuition whereby he may act wisely out of his own free choice. A guru disciplines the disciple only until the latter can guide himself through his own unfolding soul wisdom.

The God-sent guru has no selfish interest, only the highest interest of the disciple. Everyone needs a psychological mirror in order to see the blemishes that have become an accustomed and favored part of the acquired personality of one's second nature. The guru serves as this mirror. He holds up to the devotee a reflection of his perfect soul-image over which is superimposed the flaws of the ego that yet mar perfection. In ways both open and subtle the guru brings to the fore in the disciple lessons to be learned that perhaps for incarnations have lain shelved in the dusty corners of the consciousness. In an inevitable sooner-or-later choice the devotee accepts and learns or balks and avoids these admonitions. Wiser for the learning, he moves nearer to freedom; obstinate in ego comfort, delusion continues to hold him tightly.

Very few persons enjoy true freedom of will. To follow one's desires, compelled by the dictates of instincts and habits, or to be good and refrain from evil simply because one has become accustomed to that good behavior, is not freedom. When the will is guided by discriminative wisdom to choose good instead of evil in any and every instance, then indeed one is free. Harnessed to wisdom, no longer swayed by prejudice and error or by the influences of heredity, prenatal or postnatal habits, family, and social and world environment, the will becomes established in righteousness. Until then, the way to all righteousness lies in following the wisdom-guidance and *sadhana* of a master who is divinely empowered to bestow enlightenment on others. Such was the Master recognized by the disciples of Jesus, who began one by one to seek spiritual shelter in his grace and blessings.

DISCOURSE 10

"Hereafter Ye Shall See Heaven Open"

Jesus' Discourse to Nathanael

Sincerity: A Virtue of Virtues on the Spiritual Path

❖

"Fig Tree": The Cerebrospinal Tree of Life
With Its Astral Nerve Branches and Roots

❖

Man's Astral Body Ascends at Death and Descends at Rebirth

❖

What and Where Is Heaven?

❖

The Astral Heaven of Light and Beauty Described

❖

How to "See Heaven Open" Through the Spiritual Eye

❖

The Nature of Angels, and How to Commune With Them

"...a promise that man has a divine inheritance to reclaim the omni-science of spiritual perception, that heaven and its wonders can be re-alized in the here and now."

Now Philip was of Bethsaida, the city of Andrew and Peter. Philip findeth Nathanael, and saith unto him, "We have found him, of whom Moses in the law, and the prophets, did write, Jesus of Nazareth, the son of Joseph."

And Nathanael said unto him, "Can there any good thing come out of Nazareth?" Philip saith unto him, "Come and see."

Jesus saw Nathanael coming to him, and saith of him, "Behold an Israelite indeed, in whom is no guile!"

Nathanael saith unto him, "Whence knowest thou me?"

Jesus answered and said unto him, "Before that Philip called thee, when thou wast under the fig tree, I saw thee."

Nathanael answered and saith unto him, "Rabbi, thou art the Son of God; thou art the King of Israel."

Jesus answered and said unto him, "Because I said unto thee, I saw thee under the fig tree, believest thou? Thou shalt see greater things than these." And he saith unto him, "Verily, verily, I say unto you, hereafter ye shall see heaven open, and the angels of God ascending and descending upon the Son of man."

—John 1:44–51

"Hereafter Ye Shall See Heaven Open"

Jesus' Discourse to Nathanael

Now Philip was of Bethsaida, the city of Andrew and Peter. Philip findeth Nathanael, and saith unto him, "We have found him, of whom Moses in the law, and the prophets, did write, Jesus of Nazareth, the son of Joseph" (John 1:44–45).

Philip cites the intuitive revelations of Moses and the prophets about the coming of the Christ, when he announces to Nathanael that the long-awaited one had come in the form of Jesus of Nazareth.

Prophecy does not mean that all happenings on earth, including earthly human affairs, are predestined. It is not an art that can be practiced reliably by those who possess some small degree of psychic power. All events that have happened in the past leave vibratory impressions in the ether, which sensitive people may sometimes tune in as mental images or visions. Similarly, the karmic law of cause and effect projects into the ether vibratory *potentials* of future events that are a probable outcome, or effect, of previously initiated causes. Future events forming in the ether from causes originated by human actions are not always inevitable; they evolve and can change dramatically according to the transmuting power of man's free-will actions integrating into those karmic vibrations. One who has the ability to

197

link past and future may predict a certain outcome according to extant conditions; but if those conditions are altered, the outcome may negate the foretelling. Doomsday "prophets" find themselves embarrassingly duped by their imagination and misreading of heavenly and scriptural signs.

Only the rare true prophet who is in tune with the will of God can make sure and accurate predictions, such as the foreseeing of the coming of Jesus. Such God-given predictions are concerned little with temporal matters that blow in the winds of whimsical human actions and their effects. Their primary and loftier purpose is to influence the spiritual betterment of man with both encouraging and cautionary revelations.

Thus, Moses and Isaiah and other prophets of the Old Testament who foretold the advent of Jesus were able, by intuitive foresight, to trace the law of cause and effect which governs the drama of human existence. They knew also the law of God that sends self-emancipated, Christlike souls onto the earth at different ages, when the masses, burdened with the sin of ignorance, are in dire need of divine light.

∾

And Nathanael said unto him, "Can there any good thing come out of Nazareth?" Philip saith unto him, "Come and see."

Jesus saw Nathanael coming to him, and saith of him, "Behold an Israelite indeed, in whom is no guile!" (John 1:46–47).

Nathanael was a plainspoken, sincere man. He knew the backward, socially and politically insignificant status of Nazareth and expressed doubt that a savior would come forth from such an inconsequential place. Philip was practical, and without offering an argument sought instead to bring Nathanael into the transmuting personal magnetism of Jesus. Philip knew from the blessing he himself had received that Christ, by his very look and magnetic life force, could remove whatever stubborn impressions of skepticism had formed in the brain of Nathanael. The transforming power conveyed to one who comes reverently into the presence of a holy personage is referred to in the traditions of India as *darshan,* an experience that is a veritable purifying rite.

Sincerity: a virtue of virtues on the spiritual path

Jesus gave Nathanael a soul-penetrating look, the vibration of which dispersed ages of ignorance; and like a shaft of light on a sensitive film, took an intuitive photograph of his disciple's life. Pleased with the image, Jesus said: "Behold an Israelite indeed, in whom there is no guile." Behold a soul that is free from satanic insincerity.

Guilelessness means sincerity, the simplicity or natural state of one's true being, free from duplicity, dissembling, hypocrisy, and all other self-serving guises. It has no association with crudeness or rude hurtfulness in the name of being honest. Craftiness, the cunning to outwit others for selfish purposes or spite, is a demented use of intelligence. The quiet humility of guilelessness is the sapience that distinguishes a truly spiritual personality. What magnetism it has! Sincerity is a virtue of virtues in the realm of spirituality. All other qualities a disciple may offer as the sum of his being at the feet of the guru must borrow a great measure of their worth from sincerity. Words and deeds are a sham without it. But a heart that is pure in its intention is the way to touch the heart of God.

~

Nathanael saith unto him, "Whence knowest thou me?"

Jesus answered and said unto him, "Before that Philip called thee, when thou wast under the fig tree, I saw thee."

Nathanael answered and saith unto him, "Rabbi, thou art the Son of God; thou art the King of Israel" (John 1:48–49).

Nathanael was astonished to hear Jesus speak of him with the familiarity one would expect only from long association. How could a stranger thus analyze him so candidly? Jesus responded: "Before Philip called thee, I saw thee." This seeing was not by the superficial sensory eyes, it was the intuitive photography of Nathanael's soul imprinted on the omnipresent perception of Jesus by the art of divine telepathy.

"Fig tree": the cerebrospinal tree of life with its astral nerve branches and roots

Jesus explained: "I saw thee under the fig tree"; that is to say, "I saw through my spiritual eye thy soul resting beneath the astral nerve branches of the cerebrospinal tree of life." Man's body is figuratively an upturned tree with roots of cranial nerves feeding the spinal trunk and sending forth life and consciousness to the burgeoning branches of the nervous system. The Bhagavad Gita, similarly, likens the composite of man—consciousness, life force, and the nervous system—to the "*ashvattha* tree [pipal or holy fig, *Ficus religiosa*], with roots above and boughs beneath."* A spiritual adept with divine sight, looking deeply into another person, can see the soul garbed in its astral nervous system. Persons imbued with spiritual qualities have a refined astral nervous system, vibrantly luminous, while the astral nervous system of the materialist is bedimmed with life-sapping "figs" of sensory desires vibrating on its branches.

Now Jesus may have seen with his divine vision the actual physical form of Nathanael resting under a fig tree in a distantly placed scene. But it was the perception of Nathanael's soul and astral form that had attracted the consciousness of Jesus. With this penetrating insight, the Master recognized and drew to him yet another rediscovered disciple of lives past,† searching him out in the realm of astral manifestation—remote to myopic physical eyes, but proximate to the vision of the telescopic spiritual eye.

Every soul is garbed with its own unique individuality. When a soul changes its fleshly garment from one incarnation to the next, donning a newly inherited racial and familial appearance, it is no longer recognizable to those who look only to physical features. But masters can peer behind the purely physical facade and with intuitive perception recognize the soul's individuality, unchanged from one lifetime to another. There are even telltale indications in the eyes, facial features, and bodily characteristics that reveal certain similarities to the soul's garb in a former existence—signs that a master knows how to read. The eyes, especially, change very little, for they are the windows of the soul.

Nathanael could feel the astral body of Jesus permeating his own being, suffusing his consciousness with vibratory blessings. With the enlightenment bestowed by that *darshan,* in which the disciple partook of the omniscient consciousness of Jesus, Nathanael recognized in an instant: "Thou art the Son of God; thou art the King of Israel." In awe, Nathanael spoke of the Master as preeminent in heaven and on earth: son of the Owner of the Universe, entitled also to the ter-

---

* See *God Talks With Arjuna: The Bhagavad Gita* xv:1-2.

† Nathanael is commonly thought to be also known as Bartholomew, a disciple among the "inner circle" of Jesus' followers chosen as one of the twelve apostles.

restrial honorific of King of Israel—a diminutive kingdom situated on the little pill of earth embracing its place in the Infinite Kingdom of God.

~

*Jesus answered and said unto him, "Because I said unto thee, I saw thee under the fig tree, believest thou? Thou shalt see greater things than these." And he saith unto him, "Verily, verily, I say unto you, hereafter ye shall see heaven open, and the angels of God ascending and descending upon the Son of man" (John 1:50–51).**

J esus responded: "Because I said unto thee, I saw thee under the fig tree, believest thou? Thou shalt see greater things than these." Jesus was pleased with Nathanael's receptivity, in that his belief was the result of the incontrovertible vibratory experience he had received from Jesus.

Many people cling to their shadowy doubts even when an inner feeling urges belief in a truth; but when belief is transmuted into realization, mental wandering ceases. In the clear atmosphere of faith, realization continues to unfold. Jesus' words were said to encourage Nathanael: "As you believe in me receiving my astral and thought vibrations, greater things than this you will be able to perceive; you shall see heaven open and the angels of God ascending and descending upon the son of man."

Man's astral body ascends at death and descends at rebirth

"Son of God" refers to the soul, the individualized expression of the "only begotten" Christ Consciousness reflection of God omnipresent in creation. The "son of man" signifies the physical body with its faculties, which even in the divine man is at best a limited instrument for the material expression of the soul. The senses of the physical body are enamored with impressions of the world of matter, but they have no inkling of the marvels of God's overspreading creation unseen within and beyond the gross manifestations. In that hidden realm of cosmic beginnings, sustenance, and dissolution lie all the

---

* Unique to St. John's Gospel are numerous statements by Jesus emphatically and solemnly prefaced by "verily, verily"—"Amen, Amen" in the original Greek and Hebrew. Cf. Revelation 3:14: "These things saith the Amen, the faithful and true witness...."

mysterious wonder-workings of the macrocosmic universe and the microcosm of man.

Jesus said to Nathanael that as he had already been able to intuit that grand other world that supports the three-dimensional sensory world, he would be able thereafter to develop further his divine sight: "Through the opening of the spiritual eye you shall see the glories of the astral heaven, and the transmigration of luminous astral bodies ascending out of death's dark abyss of discarded physical bodies into the light of the astral kingdom. Also you shall behold astral beings descending from the celestial spheres into the to-be-formed physical bodies of newly conceived babies." Birth and death—creation's most tantalizing mystery revealed!

At the end of each earthly sojourn the soul emerges from its fleshly prison, garbed in its heavenly causal and astral coverings of consciousness and life energy—an "angelic" contrast to the corruptible physical form. Astral freedom is temporary for those whose karma compels eventual return to physical incarnation; but those who transcend the self-woven cause-effect nets of earthbound desire progress by continuing spiritual effort through ever higher spheres of the astral heaven and the even finer causal heaven, eventually earning enrollment in the Heavenly Host of perfected beings. Thus does each soul rise to its source in Spirit.

Genesis in the Bible tells us of the universal becomings. In brief: *"In the beginning God created the heaven and the earth. And the earth was without form, and void* (pure consciousness, the creative thoughts of God that are the ideational causes of all beginnings)....*And God said, 'Let there be light': and there was light* (the basic building block of manifested forms—the structural essence of God's triune creation: the vibratory light of thoughtrons, lifetrons, atoms)....*And God said, 'Let there be a firmament in the midst of the waters* (creative elements), *and let it divide the waters from the waters'* (the subtle causal and astral elements from the gross physical elements). *And God made the firmament* (fine vibratory etheric space providing a background for gross manifestation and serving as a curtain to divide the physical universe from the overlying astral realm), *and divided the waters which were under the firmament from the waters which were above the firmament....And God called the firmament Heaven* (the astral world secreted behind etheric space)....*And God said, 'Let the waters* (gross elements) *under the heaven be gathered together into one place, and let the dry land appear* (materialization of the gross elements into a physical universe)'" (Genesis 1:1–9).

Heaven may be said to consist, overall, of three regions: where the Heavenly Father lives in vibrationless Infinity; where Christ Intelligence reigns — omnipresent in but transcendentally untouched by vibratory creation — and in which the ───•─── angels and highest evolved saints reside; and the vi- *What and where is heaven?* bratory spheres of the ideational causal world and lifetronic astral world. These heavenly realms, vibratory and transcendent, are only figuratively "above" the gross vibrations of earth "below": They are in fact superimposed one on the other, with the finer screened from the denser manifestation through the medium and intervention of the "firmament," vibratory etheric space, hiding the astral from the physical manifestation, the causal from the astral, and the transcendent Christ and Cosmic Consciousness from the causal. Without this integration — producing a physical instrumentality empowered by astral life, guided by individualized intelligence, all arising from consciousness — there could be no meaningful manifestation.

So this earth and its beings seemingly floating in limitless space as the result of blind forces is not happenstance at all; it is highly organized.

The physical cosmos is diminutive in relation to the enormously larger and grander astral cosmos, as is the astral universe in relation to the causal — both the astral and causal heavens are permeated with the Christ Consciousness; and interlacing all is the Cosmic Consciousness of God, extending into the boundless infinity of blissful Spirit.

No one can measure Eternity. Man has yet to plumb the immensity of even this limited physical cosmos; there are untold billions of stars in the heavens that still have not been seen. The Lord has Infinitude as His space in which he dangles the intricately designed baubles of these physical, astral, and causal worlds, intriguingly reflecting as well as mysteriously hiding facets of His Immutable Being.

Different cultures and sects conceive of heaven according to their racial, social, and environmental habits of thought: a happy hunting ground; a glorious realm of endless pleasures; a kingdom with streets of gold and winged angels making celestial music on harps; a *nirvana* in which consciousness is extinguished in an everlasting peace.

Jesus said: "In my Father's house are many mansions" (John 14:2). These "many mansions" include comprehensively the Infinitude of Spirit, the Christ Consciousness sphere, and the diverse higher and lower planes of the causal and astral realms. In general, however, the designation of heaven is relegated to the astral world, the immediate heaven relevant to beings on the physical plane.

At death of the physical body, a soul garbed in its astral form ascends to the astral heavenly level merited by the balance of that person's good and evil actions on earth. It is not by virtue of death that one becomes an exalted angel in heaven. Only those persons who become angelic in spiritual behavior and God-communion on earth are able to ascend to the higher regions. While persons of wicked deeds are attracted to astral nether regions and may experience something akin to periodic dreadful nightmares, the majority of souls awaken in a luminous land of incredible beauty, joy, and freedom, in an atmosphere of love and well-being.*

The astral kingdom is a realm of rainbow-hued light. Astral land, seas, skies, gardens, beings, the manifestation of day and night—all

The astral heaven of light and beauty described

are made of variegated vibrations of light. Astral gardens of flowers, planted on the soil of the ether, surpass human description. The blossoms glow like Chinese star shells, ever-changing but never fading, adapting themselves to the fancy of the astral beings. They disappear when not wanted and reappear with new colors and fragrance when desired again.

Astral beings drink prismatic light from lifetronic fountains cascading from the bosom of ethereal mountains. Oceans heave with opalescent azure, green, silver, gold, red, yellow, and aquamarine. Diamond-bright waves dance in a perpetual rhythm of beauty.

Astral beings use all their subtle senses as physical man uses them in the dreamland. The difference is that inhabitants of the astral heaven consciously and at will control their surroundings. The earth is so full of decay and destruction; in the astral world, havoc caused by any clash of inharmonious vibrations could be remedied by mere willing.

The astral kingdom is many times older and longer-lived than this earth. Every physical object, form, and force has an astral counterpart. This astral heaven is veritably the factory of life, the world of life force

---

* A gloriously comprehensive description of the astral and causal worlds is given in *Autobiography of a Yogi*, Chapter 43. *(Publisher's Note)*

from which this atomic universe is being created. But the heavenly manifestations haven't the limitations of earth life. Everything is vibrating energy. Though beings and objects there have form and substance and therefore seem solid, one manifestation can pass through another without collision or harm: just as with photographic techniques so many physically impossible things can be done in the movies.

Colors on the earth-plane are crude imitations of their astral source. Lifetronic colors are beyond human conception, far more beautiful than any sunset or painting or rainbow or aurora borealis. The most exquisite colors in nature, if blended together in scenic portrayal, still would not depict the beauty of the astral world; the motley physical hues are such dense vibrations of their astral counterparts. In the delicacy of the astral land, neither dull skies nor blinding sun assaults the senses. The astral luminosity dims all physical light, yet is never harsh or glaring.

The boundary of the earth is the cosmic sky. The boundary of the astral heaven is a deep circumventing nimbus, rainbow-like in the seven colors of the spectrum—diaphanous, translucent rays blended with infinite taste and beauty of the Father. Within this astral firmament are the "pearly gates" referred to in Revelation 21:21. These "gates," of the luster of pearls, are the primary channels of ingress and egress between the vibratory spheres and the vibrationless realm of God, and for the movement of creative forces and souls between the astral and physical worlds. The pearly luster is the Lord's creative white light tinged with the blue of Christ Consciousness flowing into the vibratory sphere, where in the astral realm it is refracted into the multicolors of rainbow hues.

Birth and death in the astral world are merely a change in consciousness. When the physical body dies, a being loses the consciousness of flesh and becomes aware of his subtle astral form in the astral world. At a karmically predetermined time that astral being loses consciousness of his astral form to undergo rebirth in the physical world. When the astrally garbed soul leaves the astral world, at the end of its astral life, it is attracted to parents and an environment on earth (or to similar inhabited planets in other island universes) which are suited to the working-out of that individual's store of good and bad karma.

No one is born of a woman's body in the astral kingdom. There is only spiritual marriage in that realm, without cohabitation. If children are desired, they are created by inviting a soul—usually recently departed from earth—into an astral body imaged by the immaculate method of condensing the positive and negative thoughts, and will, and feeling tendencies of parents into the form of a male or female child. A predominantly positive-charged thought of lifetronic energy produces a male child, a predominantly negative-charged thought of lifetronic energy produces a female child. The form of the child, as with most astral beings, resembles that of their recently discarded earth body, but without its decrepitude.

The earth memories of astral beings gradually fade, but they meet and recognize many of their loved ones lost to them on earth—so many mothers, fathers, children, friends, spouses, of so many incarnations; it becomes difficult to isolate special feelings for one over another. The soul rejoices to embrace them all in its consciousness of universal love.

Astral beings have all the faculties of perception and cognition to which man is accustomed in his physical body, but as instruments of intuition independent of the limitations of the imperfect mortal senses and rationalizing intelligence. The astral land is thus conspicuous for the absence of books, a distinctly material omnium-gatherum for storing and transmitting man's ideas and knowledge. Astral beings can concentrate upon anything in the particular stratum to which they are assigned and know about its nature through the instantaneous knowledge-producing power of intuition. Though they need not depend on the tedious methods of book-learning, advanced beings who wish to record their special thought vibrations have only to visualize those concepts, which are then immediately transformed into a permanent record of astral light vibrations.

As there are both highly developed saints and also ordinary beings in the astral realms, they use their own degree of semi- or fully awakened intuition to complement their highly receptive astral intelligence. Only after a soul reunites with God is there no longer a need to read books or to concentrate upon anything in order to know it by intuition. The soul identified with Spirit already knows all and sees all.

Advanced astral beings can traverse any plane or region of the vast astral heaven, traveling faster than the speed of light in a vehicular mass of luminous lifetrons. Ascending to the causal heaven of ideational consciousness, the causal being transcends time and distance altogether in the instancy of thought—with every experience, consciously willed, an exquisite throb in the tranquil essence of consciousness.

When Jesus told Nathanael that he would "see heaven open, and angels ascending and descending on the Son of man," it was a promise that man has a divine inheritance to reclaim the omniscience of spiritual perception, that heaven and its wonders can be realized in the here and now.

How to "see heaven open" through the spiritual eye

This son of man, this human body and consciousness, has become dissociated from its heavenly essence because of its identity with the physical world. But Jesus intimated that all those who tune their physical self with their spiritual Self can perceive the astral world and transcend the consciousness of physical limitations. If a radio is not properly tuned in, it cannot catch the songs and voice-information passing through the ether. If a television set is dysfunctional, it cannot receive the vibrations of televised electronic images. Analogously, the human body is tuned in with matter. That is why it doesn't perceive the presence of divine beings and all finer forces just behind the astral etheric firmament separating heaven and earth, and one's finer constituent lifetronic form within the gross manifestation of the physical body.

Though paradise is not visible to the eyes of most mortals, nevertheless it is real. There was a time when people would have dismissed with utter skepticism the idea of radio and television vibrations in the ether, but now millions hear and see them daily. Likewise, any devotee can tune in the celestial sights and sounds of the angelic realms through the soul's powers of super-audition and super-vision, when by meditation the inner television and heart- and mind-radio are freed from the static of restlessness and mortal desires.*

---

* Since the divergence of science and religion in centuries past, scientists have typically greeted the idea of "higher dimensions" with skepticism. At the forefront of advanced physics today, however, is the theory of superstrings—a theory that not only allows for additional dimensions but *requires* them, writes Brian Greene, Ph.D., in *The Elegant Universe: Superstrings, Hidden Dimensions, and the Quest for the Ultimate Theory* (New York: Vintage Books, 2000).

Furthermore, reports *Los Angeles Times* science writer K. C. Cole, scientists acknowledge that cosmic forces as yet unnamed by physics may well exist in the other dimensions required by string theory. "If so," she writes in *The Hole in the Universe* (New York: Harcourt, 2001), "they could have far-reaching effects, and perhaps even explain some of physics' most difficult puzzles."

String theorists explain that we don't detect the additional dimensions in the universe because even though forces emerge from them, spatially they are tightly "curled up" to almost infinitesimal size. Other scientists, including William Tiller, Ph.D., pro-

To "see heaven open," as expressed by Jesus, is possible in two ways: (1) By removal of the vibrations of etheric space with its boundary walls of light through the command of the Ultimate Intelligence. (2) By overcoming the limitations of the physical eyes and penetrating the spiritual eye of omnipresent perception.

Now as to the first supposition, imagine the chaos if the Lord were to remove the dividing firmament between earth and heaven. If heaven were bombarded by all the noises and discord of the earth, even the angels couldn't stand it! Heaven is heavenly because the Lord has made it a place of respite from mortal mania. Conversely, the physically circumscribed instrumentality of the ordinary man could not cope with the intrusion of a dimension it could neither enter nor control. God keeps man focused on the learning tools and lessons he is to master in this earthly schoolhouse. At the same time, the Lord has guarded the astral universe so that the cacophony of human beings on earth cannot disturb with the gross vibrations of their troubles the rapturous pleasures and meditations of astral beings.

The door to heaven, through which one can enter the divine spheres consciously, and as a welcome visitor, is the spiritual eye in the Christ center in the forehead. The eye of mythological Cyclops is true in concept, but as a spiritual, not a malevolent, instrument of perception. The third eye of the gods is a more accurate depiction: The aspect of God as Lord Shiva—God's power of dissolution for the renewal of

---

fessor of materials science and engineering at Stanford University, maintain that higher dimensions remain invisible not because they are small but because they are "inaccessible to the physical sensory system, or to present-day instrumentation."

A proposal that is all the more remarkable in that it comes from a Nobel Prize–winning physicist has been put forth by Professor Brian Josephson of Cambridge University, renowned for key discoveries in subatomic quantum mechanics: "Mystical experience by self-development through meditation, etc., is not only the key to one's own development but also the key...to putting this attempt to synthesize science and religion on a solid foundation....If we follow this path of a synthesis of science with religion (using meditation as an observational tool), what we are doing is using our own nervous systems as instruments to observe the domains in which God works. Ordinary scientific instruments like telescopes, galvanometers, and particle detectors are not going to be good in this context because they are designed to function in the material domain. Our nervous systems, on the other hand, are designed to allow us to interact not only with the material level of existence but also with the spiritual levels....All the different levels are open to exploration if we develop our nervous systems so that they tune in. One can imagine that this would be a part of the scientific training of the future." —from *Nobel Prize Conversations With Sir John Eccles, Roger Sperry, Ilya Prigogine, Brian Josephson* (Dallas: Saybrook Publishing Company, 1985). *(Publisher's Note)*

created forms—for example, is shown with two physical eyes and one divine eye in the middle of the forehead. Similarly, in astral beings the two physical eyes are but faintly visible, their sight is through the single intuitive spiritual eye. Those who are advanced enough to peer into the physical cosmos from their heavenly home open the two eyes when they want to see the relativity of matter.* All saints, also, receive their communion with God and the supernal realms through the spiritual eye. The eyes of saints in ecstatic communion are always upturned, locked in that center of divine perception.

By the right method of meditation and devotion, with the eyes closed and concentrated on the spiritual eye, the devotee knocks at the gates of heaven.† When the eyes are focused and still, and the breath and mind are calm, a light begins to form in the forehead. Eventually, with deep concentration, the tricolored light of the spiritual eye becomes visible. Just seeing the single eye is not enough; it is more difficult for the devotee to go into that light. But by practice of the higher methods, such as *Kriya Yoga,* the consciousness is led inside the spiritual eye, into another world of vaster dimensions.

In the gold halo of the spiritual eye, all creation is perceived as the vibratory light of the Holy Ghost. The blue light of Christ Consciousness is where the angels and deity agents of God's individualized pow-

---

* Yoga explains that the two physical eyes are an externalization of the finer forces in the single spiritual eye of the astral body. From the seat of the spiritual eye in the subtle center in the medulla, a bifurcated current of life energy flows into the physical eyes, giving the dual or dimensional perception of matter. In deep meditation, when the gaze of the two eyes is concentrated at the point between the eyebrows, the dual positive and negative currents flowing from the medulla into the two eyes reunite, and the meditator beholds the "single" or spiritual eye.

Modern scientific evidence that our two eyes begin as a single structure is found in the research of molecular neurobiologist Yi Rao of the Washington University School of Medicine, reported in *Discover,* May 1997. Dr. Rao studied eye development in frog embryos and isolated the so-called "Cyclops" gene, which may control eye development. By the time the embryo is twenty-one hours old, the two dark spots that later form into the eyes are visible. Dr. Rao found that these two spots had originated as a single band. His experiments demonstrated that if the brain does not signal cells in this "single band" to shut down and allow two separate eyes to form (which happens in normal development), one-eyed tadpoles are the result. Furthermore, his research suggests that this process "is general to all vertebrate species." *(Publisher's Note)*

† "Ask, and it shall be given you; seek, and ye shall find; knock, and it shall be opened unto you: For every one that asketh receiveth; and he that seeketh findeth; and to him that knocketh it shall be opened" (Matthew 7:7–8).

ers of creation, preservation, and dissolution abide—as well as the most highly evolved saints. Through the white light of the spiritual eye, the devotee enters Cosmic Consciousness; he ascends unto God the Father.

Science itself confirms that with our limited senses we perceive only a certain range of vibrations of matter: We do not perceive it as its constituent dancing electrons, and the solid body as an electromagnetic wave. In the spiritual eye, the veritable darkness of physical light disappears and the electronic and astral lifetronic nature of substances is perceived through the sixth sense of intuition. The materially formidable firmament between heaven and earth becomes only a diaphanous veil revealing astral scenes and beings. When I enter the sanctuary of meditation and peer through the portals of the spiritual eye, in a trice the lights of the material creation around me vanish and I am in that other world. The ordinary astral phenomena hold no interest for me, but it is the greatest joy to be in the presence of the angelic saints and of the Mother of the Universe.

Angels are God-ordained heavenly beings who serve God's purposes throughout creation. They are either personified powers or qualities of God, or are fully liberated souls in whose beings the perfect spirit of God is encased. The latter, having overcome both material and heavenly desires and attachments, have merged in Spirit and then reemerged in bodies of pure energy—omnipotent, omniscient forces of the Divine Will.

God's angels and exalted saints in the immanent-transcendent sphere of omnipresent Christ Consciousness can move freely in any realm of Infinity. They can ascend to the region of the Father; there the Self is dissolved in the unfathomable Blissful Spirit. Yet the impression of their individuality remains and can be reclaimed at will or at God's command. In the Christ Consciousness sphere they have individuality, but are in an ecstatic state. They dissolve their astral bodies there. When they descend into the vibratory region, they can be seen with astral bodies, which look just like a physical body, except made of a glow of light. That body has substance as a manifested form, but not gross solidity—just as dream images seem so solid, and yet are composed of the subtlety of astral light. By changing the vibrations of their super-electric forms, angels can make themselves large or small, visible or invisible at will, not only in the astral but also in the physical ether—as when angels appeared to laud the birth of Jesus. At

The nature of angels, and how to commune with them

other times, also, angels and divine beings in their astral forms, seen or unseen, intersperse the blessings of their presence into the happenings on earth, as when in response to devotional supplication or good karma a person or condition merits divine intervention.

It is not insurmountably difficult to see and commune with angels. But it requires deep concentration long enough so that all the disturbances of the mind drop away and the heart becomes perfectly attuned to the fine, heavenly vibrations. When the physical body and mind are restless, the consciousness does not record the presence of angels and spiritual beings. One must know how to tune in with them in order to see the divine ones "ascending and descending upon the Son of man."

The heart, or center of feeling—the conscious awareness principle in man, described in Yoga as *chitta*—is the receiver of perceptions, as the radio or television set receives sounds and images passing through the ether. The spiritual eye of intuition broadcasts those perceptions from omnipresence into the consciousness. Therefore, in a state of deep concentration attained in the practice of the scientific methods of yoga meditation, the feeling (the aggregate mind-stuff of intelligent consciousness) and the spiritual eye work together to tune in the finer vibrations of spiritual manifestation by refining and uplifting the human consciousness, the son of man, to a receptive state. Neither the higher heavenly realms nor their exalted saints and angels can be contacted through such means as mediums or psychic demonstrations—which at utmost can reach only the ordinary or lower astral planes and their beings, or, more commonly, unreliable earthbound entities.*

In his words to Nathanael, Jesus spoke of this spiritualization of consciousness toward which the disciple was to aspire under the guidance of the Master; ultimately to see the highest heaven open and the physical body or son of man translated into a son of God. When the spiritual eye is opened and the consciousness embraces all creation in the Christ state, the devotee knows that his own true Self is an angelic being—an immortal immutable soul. He realizes that in the incarnate state it is the astral body that is the real body, the purveyor of life, sensory powers, consciousness—more tangible than the gross atomic form, and powerfully invulnerable to sickness, diseases, and troubles.

---

* See Discourse 24.

Satanic delusion transforms perfect soul-angels into mortal devils, or at the least into individuals forgetful of their divine status. But even an ocean of sins cannot spoil the soul. Sin means error. Renounce the sin of ignorance and its delusive enticements of evil doings. Keep the heart free from jealousy, anger, selfishness; love all persons unconditionally, in spite of their weaknesses—that is the way to become an angelic son of man, in tune with the angels and fully liberated sons of God. By following Jesus, Nathanael would be led into his own position among that holy heavenly host.

Water Into Wine:
"This Beginning of Miracles...."

Why and When God Permits His Emissaries
to Work Miracles

❖

Did Jesus Support the Drinking of Wine?

❖

Control Over Atomic Matter by the Power of Universal Mind

❖

Relationship of Matter, Energy, and Thought

❖

The Power to Effect Miraculous Changes
in the Material World

"Jesus performed his first public miracle not to sanction intoxication by the social use of wine, but to demonstrate to his disciples that behind every diversity of matter is the one Absolute Substance."

*A*nd the third day there was a marriage in Cana of Galilee; and the mother of Jesus was there: And both Jesus was called, and his disciples, to the marriage. And when they wanted wine, the mother of Jesus saith unto him, "They have no wine."

Jesus saith unto her, "Woman, what have I to do with thee? Mine hour is not yet come."

His mother saith unto the servants, "Whatsoever he saith unto you, do it." And there were set there six waterpots of stone, after the manner of the purifying of the Jews, containing two or three firkins apiece.*

Jesus saith unto them, "Fill the waterpots with water." And they filled them up to the brim. And he saith unto them, "Draw out now, and bear unto the governor of the feast." And they bare it.

When the ruler of the feast had tasted the water that was made wine, and knew not whence it was: (but the servants which drew the water knew;) the governor of the feast called the bridegroom, and saith unto him, "Every man at the beginning doth set forth good wine; and when men have well drunk, then that which is worse: but thou hast kept the good wine until now." This beginning of miracles did Jesus in Cana of Galilee, and manifested forth his glory; and his disciples believed on him.

—John 2:1–11

---

* Jewish tradition called for water to be available for ritualistic washing of hands and feet before eating, without which one was considered unclean. See, for example, Mark 7:2, in which the Pharisees criticized Jesus' disciples for eating bread before observing this ceremony. The capacity of each of these vessels, described in English as "two or three firkins" (Greek *metreta,* "measure") is uncertain.

Water Into Wine: "This Beginning of Miracles...."

Jesus addressed his mother impersonally as "woman" because he saw himself only as Spirit—not as a mortal son born of the flesh of earthly parents of one transient incarnation, but as a son of the Divine who was his everlasting Mother and Father. Similarly, Swami Shankara sang of the enlightenment of bodily transcendence: "No birth, no death, no caste have I. Father, mother, have I none. I am He, I am He; blessed Spirit, I am He."

All souls are "children of the most High" (Psalms 82:6). To forget this divine pedigree is to accept the limitations of a soul-humiliating identity with a "dust-thou-art" human body. One who knows God remembers at all times that the Heavenly Father-Mother-Creator is the true Parent of the souls and the bodies of all. It is the Divine Potter who has made the mortal clay and fashioned out of it temporary bodily dwelling-places for father and mother and offspring alike.

Jesus' divine attitude of nonattachment implied no disregard of the God-given command to "honor thy father and thy mother." His love was evident; at the time of his crucifixion, for example, when he asked his disciple John to take care of his mother.* The spirit of motherhood should be reverenced as an expression of the unconditional love of God, as also honor belongs to the father-figure as imaging the wisdom

---

* John 19:26–27. See also Matthew 15:4 (Discourse 44) in which Jesus chides the Pharisees for not upholding the divine command to honor one's parents.

guardianship of the Heavenly Father. Devotion to parents is thus a part of devotion to God, which first and foremost is filial love for the Parent behind the familial caregivers, the Divine Father-Mother who has delegated parents to nurture the child. When the heart is divinely attuned, close human relationships are opportunities to imbibe God's infinite love from the vessels of many hearts. Without this perceptive understanding, these God-given relationships easily degenerate through the influence of cosmic delusion into limiting, unfulfilling attachments, with their sad partings and their separations at death.

When the mother of Jesus made a request of him during the marriage feast at Cana, Jesus responded from his paramount loyalty to God: "Woman, I cannot accede to your request just because you entreat me as a loving mother. It is God only who can appoint the time and the means through which He will manifest His glory through me." Jesus meant no disrespect for his mother, and Mary understood. She told the servants, in an expression of faith in the Divine Will, to be attentive to whatever her son asked of them.

Having felt intuitively an inner divine guidance and permission, Jesus forthwith asked the servants to fill six large pots with water, which he instantaneously changed into fine wine. All this he did before the eyes of his disciples in order that they might know that the water became wine through divine power and not through some sleight-of-hand or other trickery.

The Gospel account distinctly implies that this first miracle of Jesus was not to accommodate his mother, or to display his supernatural abilities for the amazement of the wedding throng, none of whom were privy to what had occurred. The miracle was in obedience to God's direction, solely for the benefit of Jesus' earnest disciples, who had just begun to follow him—to enhance their faith in God's power and in His manifest presence in the one sent to them as savior.

Miracles attract curiosity seekers; the love of God draws highly developed souls. The Lord has already arrayed before man a bounty

Why and when God permits His emissaries to work miracles

of wonders to behold: What could be more miraculous than the evident presence in every speck of creation of a Divine Intelligence? How the mighty tree emerges from a tiny seed. How countless worlds roll in infinite space, held in a purposeful cosmic dance by the precise adjustment of universal forces. How the marvelously complex human body is created from a single microscopic cell, is endowed with self-conscious intelligence, and is sustained, healed, and enlivened by invisible power. In every atom of this astounding universe, God is ceaselessly working miracles; yet obtuse man takes them for granted.*

The all-knowing, ever-understanding Lord silently goes on regulating His vast family of the cosmos without compelling any recognition from man by an overt show of His power and excellence. Having hidden Himself humbly behind the universal veils of forms and forces, He nevertheless intimates His presence in myriad ways, and calls souls through inner whispers of His love. No miracle demonstrates more surely the presence of God than attunement with even one touch of His loving omnipresence. God's highest gift to man is free will—freedom to choose Him and His wisdom or the lures of *maya's* satanic

---

* "The rise of science served to extend the range of nature's marvels, so that today we have discovered order in the deepest recesses of the atom and among the grandest collection of galaxies," writes Paul Davies, Ph.D., well-known author and professor of mathematical physics, in *Evidence of Purpose: Scientists Discover the Creator* (New York: Continuum Publishing, 1994).

Systems theorist Ervin Laszlo reports in *The Whispering Pond: A Personal Guide to the Emerging Vision of Science* (Boston: Element Books, 1999): "The fine-tuning of the physical universe to the parameters of life constitutes a series of coincidences—if that is what they are....in which even the slightest departure from the given values would spell the end of life, or, more exactly, create conditions under which life could never have evolved in the first place. If the neutron did not outweigh the proton in the nucleus of the atoms, the active lifetime of the Sun and other stars would be reduced to a few hundred years; if the electric charge of electrons and protons did not balance precisely, all configurations of matter would be unstable and the universe would consist of nothing more than radiation and a relatively uniform mixture of gases....If the strong force that binds the particles of a nucleus were merely a fraction *weaker* than it is, deuteron could not exist and stars such as the Sun could not shine. And if that force were slightly *stronger* than it is, the Sun and other active stars would inflate and perhaps explode....The values of the four universal forces [electromagnetism, gravity, and the nuclear strong and weak forces] were precisely such that life could evolve in the cosmos."

Notes Professor Davies: "Quite a list of 'lucky accidents' and 'coincidences' has been compiled....For a recent review see *Cosmic Coincidences* by John Gribbin and Martin Rees (New York: Bantam, 1989)." Davies estimates that if—as some scientists maintain—there were no inherent guiding intelligence and cosmic evolution were governed only by the chance operation of strictly mechanical laws, "the time required to achieve the level of order we now meet in the universe purely by random processes is of the order of at least $10^{10^{80}}$ years"—inconceivably longer than the current age of the universe. Citing these calculations, Laszlo wryly observes: "Serendipity of this magnitude strains credibility," and concludes: "Must we then face the possibility that the universe we witness is the result of purposeful design by an omnipotent master builder?" *(Publisher's Note)*

delusion. As the Cosmic Lover of all souls, the Lord's one desire is that perchance man might use his free will to cast away the mercurial inducements of Satan and embrace the consummate fulfillment of Divine Love.

If God revealed Himself as the Eminent Creator or spoke to the world as Indisputable Authority, human beings would in that instant lose their free choice; they could not refrain from rushing to His manifest glory. If He displayed His omnipotence in grandiose miracles, the awestricken masses would be attracted to God compulsively by these phenomena instead of choosing Him by their soul's spontaneous love. So even through the instrumentality of His saints God does not draw souls to Himself by using spiritual power that abrogates free choice.

The *maya*-vitiated intellect of man seems nevertheless constrained to prefer some definite demonstrable proof of God's existence before turning to Him—in blind effrontery challenging his Creator again and again to prove Himself through "signs and wonders." But if man does not take a hint from the evidence that every so-called natural manifestation is itself a miracle expressing God's immanence, he is unlikely to get any other signs that he can better appreciate. It is easy to believe when the senses are presented with comprehensible spiritual phenomena; no efforts to bring out the faith latent in the soul are then necessary. Jesus expressed this in his words to Thomas: "Because thou hast seen me, thou hast believed: Blessed are they that have not seen, and yet have believed."

One who truly desires God has no inclination toward powers and miracles. It is the Lord's nature to reveal Himself silently and subtly —only rarely openly—unto devotees who crave naught else more than the Creator. At the proper time, before people who have the possibility of spiritual awakening, He permits His saints to exhibit the extraordinary; but never to satisfy idle curiosity. Though Jesus had a unique role as a world savior that began in a dark, unenlightened age requiring open demonstration of God's power to make a permanent impression in the annals of time, he nevertheless often refused to offer spectacular signs and miracles to prove his divinity and God's presence.* Jesus worked his miracles of healing, raising the dead, walking

---

* See, for example, John 2:18–22. Jesus declined to demonstrate his powers when challenged by onlookers after evicting the money changers from the temple, discussed in Discourse 12.

on the sea, for the sake of true believers, strictly under divine guidance and permission. He always emphasized that he was doing the will of God who sent him, awaiting first his Father's command.

A so-called convincing argument made in support of drinking wine is that Jesus himself drank wine and even produced it as one of his miracles. In that arid land, even the scant re-sources of water were often polluted, with no knowledge at that time of purification methods; the juice of fermented grapes provided supplemental

Did Jesus support the drinking of wine?

liquid for the body, and was even considered hygienic as well as sacramental. Notwithstanding the invalidity under different circumstances, people are quite opportunistic to imitate those actions of a master that justify their own inclinations, while they are wanting in equal fervor to emulate his spiritual example! First become like Jesus—drink the wine of his inspiration, the wine of God-consciousness, which placed him above worldly compulsions.

Great masters throughout the ages have talked against the use of intoxicants. Their effects are very bad; they dull man's most precious endowment, his fine instruments of consciousness. One who indulges in drink finds all awareness of God obliterated. The temptation of drink, which provides a temporary euphoria, was created by the satanic force to divert man from seeking true bliss in God. The soul's need for refreshment in transcendence, which becomes degenerated under the influence of delusion, has induced every culture to develop its spurious forms of escape in inebriation, producing instead a pernicious enslavement. God-consciousness is a thousand times more intoxicating than drunkenness, and elevates the spirit of man rather than degrading his potential. Jesus' disciples on the day of Pentecost were as if drunk; but with the wine of God-consciousness. One who is inebriated with God needs no other palliative to ease whatever woes befall him. So the great ones enjoin man to sit quietly and go deep into meditation. After the resisting restless thoughts have been stilled, the devotee finds his "cup runneth over" with an ecstatic divine elixir of joy.

Jesus performed his first public miracle not to sanction intoxication by the social use of wine, but to demonstrate to his disciples that behind every diversity of matter is the one Absolute Substance.

To Jesus wine was not wine. It was a specific vibration of electrical energy, manipulatable by knowledge of definite superphysical laws.

All of God's creation operates according to law. Events and processes governed by already discovered "natural" laws are no longer considered miraculous; but when the law of cause and ef-

Control over atomic fect operates too subtly for man to discern how
matter by the power something comes to pass, he calls it a miracle.
of Universal Mind By the ordinary mechanical process we know
how wine is made: through fermentation caused by microscopic organisms that change sugar into alcohol. But to convert a substance made of certain elements (such as water) into one made of different elements (such as wine) requires atomic control. Jesus knew that underlying and controlling all atomic matter is the one unifying and balancing power of Divine Intelligence and Will—that all matter can be followed back to its origin in consciousness if dissolved into its constituent parts. Jesus understood the metaphysical relation of matter to thought, and demonstrated that one form of matter could be changed into another form not only by chemical processes, but by the power of Universal Mind. By his oneness with the Divine Intelligence that permeates all creation, Jesus changed the arrangement of electrons and protons in the water and thus turned it into wine.

According to modern scientists, there are more than a hundred different elements of which material stuff is composed. Though possessing a multiplicity of properties and characteristics, all these elements can be resolved into electrons, protons, neutrons, and other subatomic building blocks; and subtle units of energy and light. Water and wine and all things else in material creation are made of the same particles, but in differing combinations and with different rates of vibration, thus constituting creation's endless variety of substances and forms.

The law of causation of all material manifestations can be traced to the activity of subatomic particles; but beyond that the operation of the law of cause and effect is lost sight of—scientists do not know why electrons and protons arrange themselves into different molecular forms to create diverse kinds of matter. Herein nature submissively makes room for a Divine Intelligence, says the scientist, inasmuch as there must be some Power that directs the subtle electronic-protonic bricks to arrange themselves in different combinations, creating innumerable substances in exceedingly complex configurations, including intelligent life-forms.

Spirit is the power that gives intelligence and life to matter. There is no fundamental difference between matter and Spirit. Thought and

220

matter both originate in the creative vibratory power of God.* Thought, energy, and matter differ only in terms of relativity of vibration, thought being the subtlest vibration, which condenses into the light of life energy (*prana*) and ultimately into the gross vibrations of matter. Thoughts when energized become visible im-   *Relationship of matter,* ages, as in dreams; matter is the crystallized thought   *energy, and thought* of God, the crystallized dreams of God.

The vibrations of the creative thoughts of God differ from the vibrations of matter in quality and quantity. Matter is a gross vibration evolved from the consciousness of God, and thought is the originating subtle vibration of Divine Consciousness—the active and activating vibratory power.

Matter consists of relatively fixed vibrations of consciousness; but thought—the basic unit of God's creative activity—is moving and progressive consciousness, capable of unending transformations. Watching a child advance through the various stages of maturation, we can see the progress of changing thought within him. The child's thoughts are transformed into those of the youth, which in turn mature into the thoughts of the adult; yet all these thoughts arise from the consciousness of the same person.

Thoughts are subjective vibrations of consciousness. They are sufficiently differentiated to be classified, yet not as rigidly differentiated as objectified matter. Thoughts of fear, of joy, of hunger, of ambition —all these are different; yet they are interrelated inasmuch as they are all manifestations of the same consciousness. Every phase of thought touches other thoughts in an interchange of communication.

Matter is vibration that gives the idea of the want of interrelation. Matter can be divided or classified in different ways without interrelation; that is, each object has its own distinct fixity. You can divide a piece of cake and place it in two rooms without interrelation, but our thoughts of today and tomorrow are interrelated and are conscious of each other. The objectified consciousness of matter cannot think of itself, or of its interrelation with other matter. It is fixed consciousness, instinct-bound. What is instinct-bound? Thought vibrations that generate only one kind of consciousness.

A glass before me, whenever I look at it, gives me the fixed consciousness of a glass only. Though material things were created to pro-

---

* See Discourse 1.

duce fixed consciousness within us, still, human consciousness can modify them to some extent. A natural stone producing the fixed consciousness of a stone can be modified, as when the stone is made into a cup. But human consciousness has its limitations; it understands the stone from which that cup is made to remain always stone.

A person under hypnosis may be induced to dive onto the floor and make the motions of swimming if the hypnotist has suggested that he see a pond spread out before him. Similarly, a process of cosmic hypnosis impinges on man the ordinary consciousness of matter, making him perceive water as fluid, solid things as impenetrable, air as an invisible current, fire as light and heat.

It is cosmic delusion that gives the idea of fixed, differentiated finite substances and objects with definite unchanging properties. The universal creative force, or *maya,* conjures apparent limitations in the Unlimited; it makes the vibrationless Infinite Substance appear as finite things through vibration, motion, the process of change. In the ultimate sense nothing in this universe is finite, except the various phases of change that materiality undergoes.

Waves on the ocean are finite because they appear temporarily and then dissipate—again temporarily, until they rise again. When the ocean is thrown into waves, and the waves disappear on the bosom of the ocean, would anyone say that the water in the waves has been lost? No. It resolved into its source. Only the particular surging form that the water assumed has disappeared.

When water passes into steam, the collected steam can be condensed into water again. Though its form and characteristics change as the water passes through various physical processes, in its elemental composition it remains the same.

Thus with all matter: Whirling particles, metamorphosing energies, come together and part in an unending vibratory dance of change, producing for a span of time objects and substances that have the appearance of being finite, of being separate from other things, of having a beginning and end. Yet all matter in its underlying essence is unlimited and unchangeable: Its changing phases are impermanent, but the Power that vibrates into change is permanent. Deluded by *maya* or metaphysical Satan, the human thought-process cognizes only changing phenomena, not the underlying divine Noumena.*

---

* Similar views are now espoused by visionaries of modern science. The renowned

Thought is human consciousness in vibration. Human consciousness is delimited God-consciousness in vibration. In the process of thought man's consciousness vibrates. One whose consciousness vibrates under the control of Maya, the Cosmic Hypnotist, remains fixated upon finitude. Through psychophysical techniques of yoga one can regain mastery of his mind, stilling the restless thought vibrations of human consciousness and entering the ecstasy of God-consciousness.*

By spiritual development, one rises to a state wherein the fixed consciousness generated from contact with matter vanishes. Finite ob-

---

work of Dr. David Bohm, late professor of physics at the University of London, has provided "an entirely new way of understanding the fundamental nature of the physical universe, as glimpsed through the data and laws of physics," writes Will Keepin, Ph.D., in "Lifework of David Bohm: River of Truth" (*ReVision* magazine, Summer 1993). "Prior to Bohm, science had generally regarded the universe as a vast multitude of separate interacting particles. Bohm offers an altogether new view of reality....'unbroken wholeness in flowing movement.' What is remarkable about Bohm's hypothesis is that it is also consistent with spiritual wisdom down through the ages."

In quantum physics, the notion of matter being composed of definite particles has now been superseded by the discovery of an all-pervading "field" of powerful invisible forces. This discovery, writes K. C. Cole in *The Hole in the Universe: How Scientists Peered Over the Edge of Emptiness and Found Everything* (New York: Harcourt, 2001), showed that "particles of matter were in themselves rather irrelevant; they were only the spigots through which various forces flowed. A solid object, if you like, was something like a fountain composed of intersecting cascades of water, all flowing from tiny pointlike orifices. The 'real' stuff of matter was the flowing water, or forces."

"The concept of field," Cole explains, "was a huge revolution in thought that remains completely unknown to most laypeople....[But] Einstein called the 'change in conception of reality' from particles and empty space to fields 'the most profound and fruitful one that has come to physics since Newton.'...Matter, in this view, is simply a place where some of the field happens to be concentrated. Matter condenses out of field like water droplets condense out of water vapor in a steamy bathroom. Particles of matter are concentrations of field that travel through the field like ripples in a rope or a wave in water. The essential 'stuff'—that is to say, the rope or the water—does not travel from place to place. Only the kink travels...."

"This view of matter explains, among other things, why every electron in the universe is exactly the same as every other electron, every top quark the same as every other top quark. A particle doesn't really exist in its own right. It is only a particular manifestation of a field. And globally speaking, the field is everywhere the same."

Professor N. C. Panda, Ph.D., sums up the implications in *Maya in Physics* (Delhi: Motilal Banarsidass, 1991): "Science has discarded the concept of pluralism and has accepted field or space as one and a single continuous entity as the basis of the appearance of the multifarious world. This basic entity is one and continuous; it is the source of the heterogenous manifestation of the universe. The one gives rise to many; the invisible gives rise to multifarious invisible-cum-visible ones; the formless gives rise to pluralities of forms. Thus monism is established in science." *(Publisher's Note)*

* "Be still, and know that I am God" (Psalms 46:10).

jects are seen as naught but imprisoned consciousness; and the formerly rigid differentiations of matter are experienced as relativities of

The power to effect
miraculous changes in
the material world

thought, all interrelated in the preeminent, unifying Divine Intelligence from which they flow. In his oneness with that imperial Christ Intelligence, Jesus had wakened from the grand mayic dream; he had transcended the fixed consciousness under the control of the Cosmic Hypnotist. Thus he could at will convert the materialized thoughts of stones into bread or those of water into wine.

Ordinary human beings have to go through material processes to effect changes in the physical world because they are limited by the law of duality and the relative difference between vibrations of matter, energy, and thought. But one who by the higher consciousness of Unity realizes the true nature of creation can perform any metamorphosis, just as a movie director can make any miracle appear on the screen by manipulating projected beams of light. Jesus was sitting in the booth chamber of Eternity, from which he saw all creation as projected thoughts of God, actual thought particles of the consciousness of the Supreme Creator, made visible through vibratory light of life energy. As Jesus was one with the Divine Mind, it was nothing for him to direct one informing vibration to change into another.

Driving the Money Changers Out of the Temple

When Forceful Behavior Is a Righteous Response to Wrongdoing

❖

Meekness Does Not Mean to Become a Doormat

❖

Driving Restless Thoughts From the Temple
of Concentrated Prayer

❖

Jesus' Refusal to Perform a Miracle to Satisfy the Skeptics

❖

How Masters Read Character
Through the Soul's Faculty of Intuition

"The Lord's liberated sons act purposefully and effectively in this world of relativity, adopting any characteristic necessary to accomplish the Divine Will, without deviation from inner attunement with the unruffled calmness, love, and bliss of Spirit."

*A*fter this he went down to Capernaum, he, and his mother, and his brethren, and his disciples: and they continued there not many days. And the Jews' Passover was at hand, and Jesus went up to Jerusalem. And found in the temple those that sold oxen and sheep and doves, and the changers of money sitting: And when he had made a scourge of small cords, he drove them all out of the temple, and the sheep, and the oxen; and poured out the changers' money, and overthrew the tables; and said unto them that sold doves, "Take these things hence; make not my Father's house an house of merchandise."

And his disciples remembered that it was written, "The zeal of Thine house hath eaten me up."

Then answered the Jews and said unto him, "What sign shewest thou unto us, seeing that thou doest these things?"

Jesus answered and said unto them, "Destroy this temple, and in three days I will raise it up."

Then said the Jews, "Forty and six years was this temple in building, and wilt thou rear it up in three days?" But he spake of the temple of his body. When therefore he was risen from the dead, his disciples remembered that he had said this unto them; and they believed the scripture, and the word which Jesus had said.

Now when he was in Jerusalem at the Passover, in the feast day, many believed in his name, when they saw the miracles which he did. But Jesus did not commit himself unto them, because he knew all men, and needed not that any should testify of man: for he knew what was in man.

—John 2:12—25

Driving the Money Changers Out of the Temple

🌿

After this he went down to Capernaum, he, and his mother, and his brethren, and his disciples: and they continued there not many days. And the Jews' Passover was at hand, and Jesus went up to Jerusalem. And found in the temple those that sold oxen and sheep and doves, and the changers of money sitting: And when he had made a scourge of small cords, he drove them all out of the temple, and the sheep, and the oxen; and poured out the changers' money, and overthrew the tables; and said unto them that sold doves, "Take these things hence; make not my Father's house an house of merchandise."

And his disciples remembered that it was written, "The zeal of Thine house hath eaten me up" (John 2:12–17).

Parallel reference:

And Jesus went into the temple of God, and cast out all them that sold and bought in the temple, and overthrew the tables of the moneychangers, and the seats of them that sold doves, and said unto them, "It is written, 'My house shall be called the house of prayer; but ye have made it a den of thieves'" (Matthew 21:12–13).*

---

* Cf. additional parallel references in Mark 11:15–17 and Luke 19:45–46. St. John's Gospel places this incident at the beginning of Jesus' public ministry; the other three

Meekness is not weakness. A true exemplar of peace is centered in his divine Self. All actions arising therefrom are imbued with the soul's nonpareil vibratory power—whether issuing forth as a calm command or a strong volition. Nonunderstanding minds might critique

--------•-•--------

When forceful behav-
ior is a righteous re-
sponse to wrongdoing

Jesus' confronting the temple mercenaries with a scourge as contradicting his teaching: "Resist not evil: but whosoever shall smite thee on thy right cheek, turn to him the other also."* The forceful use of a whip to drive the merchants and money chang-

ers out of the house of worship may not seem wholly in keeping with the propagated lamblike image of Jesus, who taught forbearance and love. The actions of divine personalities, however, are sometimes willfully startling to shake complacent minds out of their vacuous acceptance of the commonplace. An accurate sense of spiritual propriety in a world of relativity requires a ready wit and a steady wisdom. The proper course of behavior is not always discerned by scripture-quoting dogmatists whose literal dependence on inflexible dictums may pay homage to the letter rather than the spirit of spirituality in action.†

Jesus responded to an untenable situation, not from an emotional compulsion to wrath, but from a divine, righteous indignation in reverence for the immanence of God in His holy place of worship. Inwardly, Jesus did not succumb to anger. Great sons of God possess the qualities and attributes of the ever tranquil Spirit. By their perfected self-control and divine union, they have mastered every nuance of spiritual discipline. Such masters participate fully and empathetically in the events of man, yet maintain a transcendental soul freedom from the delusions of anger, greed, or any other form of slavery to the senses. Spirit manifests Itself in creation through a multiplicity of elevating, activating, and darkening forces, yet remains simultaneously in Uncreated Bliss beyond the teeming vibrations of the cosmos. Similarly, the Lord's liberated sons act purposefully and effectively in this world of relativity, adopting any charac-

---

Gospels relate it near the end of Jesus' life, during his last visit to Jerusalem (see Discourse 64). Though no definitive explanation for this can be given, some scholars believe that these were two separate incidents, occurring three years apart. *(Publisher's Note)*

* Matthew 5:39. See Discourse 27.

† "Many disciples have a preconceived image of a guru, by which they judge his words and actions. Such persons often complained that they did not understand [my guru] Sri Yukteswar. 'Neither do you understand God!' I retorted on one occasion. 'If a saint were clear to you, you would be one!'"—*Autobiography of a Yogi*

teristic necessary to accomplish the Divine Will, without deviation from inner attunement with the unruffled calmness, love, and bliss of Spirit.

The meekness of divine personalities is very strong in the infinite power behind their gentleness. They may use this power in a forceful dramatization to admonish those who are stubbornly irresponsive to gentler vibrations. Even as a loving father may resort to firm discipline to deter his child from harmful actions, so Jesus put on a show of spiritual ire to dissuade these grown-up children of God from ignorant acts of desecration, the effects of which would surely be spiritually harmful to themselves as well as to the sanctity of the temple of God.

Divinely guided actions may command extraordinary means to right a wrong; but they are never activated by wanton rage. The Bhagavad Gita, the revered Hindu Bible, teaches that anger is an evil enveloping one in a delusion that obscures discriminative intelligence, with consequent annihilation of proper behavior.*

If Jesus had been motivated by a real spate of anger, he might have used his divine powers to destroy utterly these desecrators. With his little bundle of cords he could not have seriously hurt anyone. In fact, it was not the whip but the vibration of colossal spiritual force expressing through his personality that routed the merchants and money changers. The spirit of God was with him, a power that was irresistible, causing a throng of able-bodied men to flee before the intensely persuasive vibration of a single paragon of meekness.

Spirituality abhors spinelessness. One should always have the moral courage and backbone to show strength when the occasion calls for it. This is well illustrated by an old Hindu story.

Once upon a time, a vicious cobra lived on a rocky hill on the outskirts of a village. This serpent extremely resented any noise around his dwelling, and did not hesitate to attack any of the village children who disturbed him by playing *Meekness does not mean* thereabout. Numerous fatalities resulted. The vil- *to become a doormat* lagers tried their utmost to kill the venomous reptile, but met with no success. Finally, they went in a body to a holy hermit who lived nearby, and asked him to use his spiritual powers to stop the death-dealing work of the serpent.

---

* "Anger breeds delusion; delusion breeds loss of memory (of the Self). Loss of right memory causes decay of the discriminating faculty. From decay of discrimination, annihilation (of spiritual life) follows" (*God Talks With Arjuna: The Bhagavad Gita* II:63).

Touched by the earnest prayers of the villagers, the hermit proceeded to the dwelling place of the cobra, and by the magnetic vibration of his love coaxed the creature to come forth. The master told the snake it was wrong to kill innocent children, and instructed him never to bite again, but to practice loving his enemies. Under the saint's uplifting influence, the serpent humbly promised to reform and practice nonviolence.

Soon thereafter, the hermit left the village for a year-long pilgrimage. Upon his return, as he was passing the hill he thought: "Let me see how my friend the serpent is behaving." Approaching the hole where the serpent dwelt, he was startled to find the hapless reptile lying outside, half dead with several festering wounds on his back.

The hermit said: "Hello, Mr. Serpent, what is all this?" The serpent dolefully whispered: "Master, this is the result of practicing your teachings! When I came out of my hole in quest of food, minding my own business, at first the children fled at the sight of me. But before long the boys noticed my docility, and began to throw stones at me. When they found that I would run away rather than attack them, they made a sport of trying to stone me to death each time I came out in search of sustenance to appease my hunger. Master, I dodged many times, but also got badly hurt many times, and now I am lying here with these terrible wounds in my back because I have been trying to love my enemies."

The saint gently caressed the cobra, instantly healing his hurts. Then he lovingly corrected him, saying: "Little fool, I told you not to bite, but why didn't you hiss!"

Although meekness is a virtue to be cultivated, one should not abandon common sense nor become a doormat for others to tread over with their misconduct. When provoked or unfairly attacked, one should show noninjurious strength in support of one's just convictions. But even a pseudodisplay of anger should not be attempted by anyone who has the tendency to lose his temper and self-control in violent behavior.

Jesus "hissed" at the merchants and money changers because he was not willing that the house of God be demeaned by worldly vibrations of selling and individual profit. His words and actions signified to the people: "Remove this crass commerciality from God's temple, for materialistic vibrations quite obscure the subtle presence of the Lord. In the temple of God the singular thought should be to possess, not worldly profit, but the imperishable treasure of the Infinite."

The subtle law of magnetism is that each object or person or action radiates a characteristic vibration that engenders specific thoughts in the consciousness of one who enters its sphere of influence. The vibration of a candle or oil lamp in the temple induces thoughts of unruffled peace or of the illumination of wisdom—light being the first manifestation of Spirit—whereas any form of commerciality involving worldly goods stirs restlessness and sensory desires. There may be no negative vibration attached to the unobtrusive selling of scripture or other God-reminding books in the temple when offered as a service to devotees, provided the proceeds are used to support the house of worship and its spiritual good works. The selling of other merchandise in the house of God, and marketing goods for individual profit, set up derogatory vibrations contrary to the purpose and spiritual consciousness of the holy place.

"The zeal of Thine house hath eaten me up." The disciples corroborated the words of Jesus with this scriptural saying. The fervor to worship God inspired by a sanctuary dedicated to the Supreme Being should be all-consuming, uncontested by material zeal or vibrations that would swallow up the spiritual vibration of God's presence.*

The subjective admonition to be drawn from this action of Jesus in the temple is that the sincere worshiper of God must reverentially observe the law of devoted concentration. To give superficial attention to one's prayers, while entertaining in the background of the mind thoughts of one's life enterprises—getting and having, planning and doing—is to take the name of God in vain. The manifesting power of concentration comes from centering the mind upon one thing at a time. "Buying and selling"— the unending "busy-ness" of material life—should be carried on in the marketplace of one's duties; whereas it is distractingly intrusive in the temple of prayer—just as an altar and preaching in a shop would be an unwelcome imposition on the legitimate conduct of commerce. Halfhearted, unconcentrated mental rambling during the time of prayer brings neither a response from God nor the focused power of attention necessary for material success.

Driving restless thoughts from the temple of concentrated prayer

Though God tries to respond to the earnest prayers of His children, His voice resonating in intuition-felt peace is wholly distorted by restlessness-producing transactions between the senses and the outer world, and by the aroused attention-demanding associated thoughts.

---

* The disciples were quoting Psalms 69:9.

231

The Lord recedes humbly into a remote silence when the temple of His devotee's concentration becomes a noisy marketplace desecrated by these mercenaries of material consciousness. Soul intuition—the inner Christlike preceptor and guide of man's sublime thoughts and feelings —must come and wield with will power the whip of spiritual discipline and self-control to drive out the intruders. Repeated practice of scientific techniques of meditation fully concentrates the attention within, blessing the temple of inner communion with a tranquil surcease of sensory commerce. The devotee's consciousness is thereby restored to a sanctuary of silence, wherein alone is possible true worship of God.*

~

> *Then answered the Jews and said unto him, "What sign shewest thou unto us, seeing that thou doest these things?"*
>
> *Jesus answered and said unto them, "Destroy this temple, and in three days I will raise it up."*
>
> *Then said the Jews, "Forty and six years was this temple in building, and wilt thou rear it up in three days?" But he spake of the temple of his body. When therefore he was risen from the dead, his disciples remembered that he had said this unto them; and they believed the scripture, and the word which Jesus had said (John 2:18–22).*

The bystanders in the temple protested the assault on the merchants and money changers, unwilling to cede Jesus the right to interfere with their customary ways. If he were a prophet with authority over their human affairs, he ought to prove it by some miraculous sign from God.

In a distinctively beautiful way Jesus accepted their challenge. He did not respond with a miracle. He felt no compulsion to convince naysayers of his divine commission. He simply told them what would happen as a result of his actions in fulfilling the wish and work of

---

* Meditation—concentration upon God—is the portal through which every seeker of every faith must pass in order to contact God. Withdrawal of the consciousness from the world and the senses for the purpose of communing with God was taught by Christ in these words: "But thou, when thou prayest, enter into thy closet (draw the mind within), and when thou hast shut thy door (the door of the body and senses), pray to thy Father which is in secret (within you)" (Matthew 6:6; see Discourse 28).

God. He knew that the greatest proof of his divinity would be the future event of his crucifixion, precipitated by the law of cause and effect, as a result of which God would perform the miracle of miracles: the resurrection and ascension of his body after his crucifixion, and the Father permitted him to reveal this to the masses.

———•—•—

Jesus' refusal to perform a miracle to satisfy the skeptics

Jesus' obscure saying about raising the temple in three days was naturally misinterpreted. How could Jesus reconstruct the temple of Jerusalem in three days if it were destroyed, when forty-six years were required to build it the first time? His words, however, registered with his disciples, who were to realize later that he spoke of resurrecting the temple of his body after death, as had been spoken of in scripture.* To remake the bodily atoms into a living form after death has extracted its grim toll far surpasses in wonder any reassembling of a broken stone building, no matter how instantly accomplished.

Great masters cannot be coerced to flaunt miracles just for effect, even when seemingly expedient, and regardless of consequences. An astonishing story is found in chronicles of the life of Tegh Bahadur, a great master in medieval India and revered ninth successive guru of the Sikh lineage.

The saint was renowned for the numerous miraculous healings he had performed. Word of these wonders reached the emperor—a tyrannical ruler who brooked no opposition. He had the guru forcibly brought to court with the purpose of converting him to Islam; or otherwise to show his miraculous powers. Even when threatened to perform or die, Tegh Bahadur remained immovable.

Finally, after being forced to witness the barbaric torture and death of several of his disciples, the guru sent word to the emperor that he would comply with the royal demand for a miracle. With a string he tied around his neck a slip of paper, declaring that this "charm" would protect him by miraculously deflecting the executioner's sword. The emperor's swordsman was invited to put this claim to the test then and there. Before the horrified eyes of the onlookers, the saint's severed head fell to the floor, the "charmed" paper falling loose on the marble. When it was retrieved and read aloud, Tegh Bahadur's real "miracle" was revealed; the note was inscribed with the

---

*For example, Hosea 6:1–2.

words: *"Sir diya, sar na diya"*—"I have given my head, but not the secret of my religion."*

Saints feel no need to satisfy the challenges of unbelievers. Devotees who with humility seek from the guru the disclosure of his God-realization will see things much more wonderful than a display of phenomenal powers—as Jesus' disciples saw, and as I saw in my Master.

~

Now when he was in Jerusalem at the Passover, in the feast day, many believed in his name, when they saw the miracles which he did. But Jesus did not commit himself unto them, because he knew all men, and needed not that any should testify of man: for he knew what was in man (John 2:23–25).

Jesus was little impressed by the growing popular acclaim accorded him as a result of his miracles. He knew that in the fickle emotionalism of the masses there was scant durable response capable of upholding his teachings or adding one whit to his divine credentials. He therefore did not count on man's testimony as a criterion of success. The preaching of his gospel was impelled solely by God's infinite force.

Fame is at best a fair-weather friend whose loyalty easily chills at an unfavorable change in the winds of public opinion. The best of one's intentions, if lacking in the stability of wisdom, is woefully subject to the mutating distortions of erroneous judgment.

A master well knows, without prejudice, the nature of man. He can instantly ascertain the salient features of any person's consciousness just by looking at him. Jesus did not rely on people's reputation in the com-

---

* "Tegh Bahadur (b. 1621?, Amritsar, India—d. Nov. 11, 1675, Delhi), ninth Sikh Guru....ran afoul of the Mughal authorities by giving aid and shelter to some Hindu holy men from Kashmir who had been ordered by the emperor Aurangzeb to accept Islam. The Hindus sent word to the Emperor that they would accept Islam if the Guru became a Muslim. Tegh Bahadur was arrested and confined to the fortress in Delhi. Rivals at court, wishing to harm him further, accused him of having worldly desires because he gazed constantly at the emperor's harem, which lay to the west of the prison. When confronted with this charge, the Guru allegedly replied: 'Emperor, I was not gazing at your queen's apartments. I was looking in the direction of the Europeans who are coming from beyond the western seas to destroy your empire.' Aurangzeb, his patience at an end, ordered the Guru to embrace Islam or perform a miracle. Tegh Bahadur refused to do either and, after the Guru recited the *Japji* (the most important Sikh scripture), the executioner decapitated him." —*Encyclopaedia Britannica*

munity, or on the image presented by their appearance or demeanor, in order to know their character and innermost thoughts; he "knew all men" through the soul's wisdom faculty of intuition.

Knowledge of a person's character may be sought through various means. The different schools of psychology are able to identify specific personality types and their prominent traits. Other methods of appraising character have been advanced at various

How masters read character through the soul's faculty of intuition

times—such as phrenology (study of the structure of the head), physiognomy (deducing a person's nature through analysis of facial and bodily features), and pathognomy (the study of man's feelings and emotions through the outward signs of his facial expressions and bodily movements, and through study of his emotional reactions to diverse incidents in his life). But these various methods are liable to bring about wrong conclusions. Socrates' physical unattractiveness caused some people to think him evil, yet he was an advanced soul. Conversely, sometimes an appealingly beautiful and fair-spoken man or woman is at heart a treacherous human being. It is not the appearance or outer demeanor or renown that is the true index of a person's nature, but what he is within.

A master responds not to the words of people but to their thoughts, not to any psychological inference but to actual perception of their inner self. Intellectual analysis or the deductions of reason are dependent upon data furnished by the fallible sensory instruments. Intuition is direct knowledge of truth, independent of unreliable sensory data and the intellections of the lower mind. Intuitive perception is deeper than telepathy: Even with telepathic awareness of another person's thoughts and feelings, it is possible to misjudge them. A master, however, knows people through apperception of their consciousness, by being one with their life.

Perceiving the limited spiritual capacity of the newly converted throngs in Jerusalem, Jesus did not entrust himself to them, nor speak the full measure of his realization to their nonunderstanding minds.* His unconditional love and blessings embraced all equally, even while he sought from among the masses genuinely sincere seekers, such as Nicodemus in the verses that follow.

---

* "And great multitudes were gathered together unto him....And he spake many things unto them in parables....And the disciples came, and said unto him, 'Why speakest thou unto them in parables?' He answered and said unto them, 'Because it is given unto you to know the mysteries of the kingdom of heaven, but to them it is not given'" (Matthew 13:2–3, 10–11; see Discourse 37).

The Second Birth of Man—
In Spirit

Dialogue With Nicodemus, Part I

True Religion Is Founded Upon Intuitional Perception
of the Transcendental Reality

❖

Jesus' Esoteric Teachings Reveal the Universality of Religion

❖

To "See the Kingdom of God"

❖

Matter and Consciousness:
The Perpetual Duality of Manifest Creation

❖

"The Wind Bloweth Where It Listeth...."

❖

Spiritual Birth—to Be Born Again in Spirit—
Is Bestowed by a True Guru

"The term 'born again' means much more than merely joining a church and receiving ceremonial baptism....The twenty-one verses describing Nicodemus' visit present, in condensed epigrammatic sayings so typical of Oriental scripture, Jesus' comprehensive esoteric teachings relating to the practical attainment of the infinite kingdom of blissful divine consciousness."

*T*here was a man of the Pharisees, named Nicodemus, a ruler of the Jews: The same came to Jesus by night, and said unto him, "Rabbi, we know that thou art a teacher come from God: for no man can do these miracles that thou doest, except God be with him."

Jesus answered and said unto him, "Verily, verily, I say unto thee, except a man be born again, he cannot see the kingdom of God."

Nicodemus saith unto him, "How can a man be born when he is old? Can he enter the second time into his mother's womb, and be born?"

Jesus answered, "Verily, verily, I say unto thee, except a man be born of water and of the Spirit, he cannot enter into the kingdom of God. That which is born of the flesh is flesh; and that which is born of the Spirit is spirit. Marvel not that I said unto thee, 'Ye must be born again.' The wind bloweth where it listeth, and thou hearest the sound thereof, but canst not tell whence it cometh, and whither it goeth: so is every one that is born of the Spirit."

—John 3:1–8

The Second Birth of Man— In Spirit

Dialogue With Nicodemus, Part I

There was a man of the Pharisees, named Nicodemus, a ruler of the Jews: The same came to Jesus by night, and said unto him, "Rabbi, we know that thou art a teacher come from God: for no man can do these miracles that thou doest, except God be with him."

Jesus answered and said unto him, "Verily, verily, I say unto thee, except a man be born again, he cannot see the kingdom of God" (John 3:1–3).

Nicodemus visited Jesus secretly in the night, for he feared social criticism. It was an act of courage for one of his position to approach the controversial teacher and to declare his faith in Jesus' divine stature. He reverently affirmed his conviction that only a master who had actual God-communion could work the superlaws that govern the inner life of all beings and all things. In reply, Christ forthrightly directed Nicodemus' attention to the heavenly Source of all phenomena in creation—mundane as well as "miraculous"—pointing out succinctly that anyone can contact that Source and know the wonders that proceed therefrom, even as Jesus himself did, by undergoing the spiritual "second birth" of intuitional soul-awakening.

The superficially curious crowds attracted by displays of phenomenal powers received only scantily from the wisdom trove of

Jesus, but the manifest sincerity of Nicodemus elicited from the Master determinate guidance that emphasized the Supreme Power and Goal on which man should concentrate.* Miracles of wisdom to enlighten the mind are superior to miracles of physical healing and the subjugation of nature; and the even greater miracle is the healing of the root-cause of every form of suffering: delusive ignorance that obscures the unity of man's soul and God. That primordial forgetfulness is vanquished only by Self-realization, through the intuitive power by which the soul directly apprehends its own nature as individualized Spirit and perceives Spirit as the essence of everything.

All bona fide revealed religions of the world are based on intuitive knowledge. Each has an exoteric or outer particularity, and an esoteric or inner core. The exoteric aspect is the public image, and includes moral precepts and a body of doctrines, dogmas, dissertations, rules, and customs to guide the general populace of its followers. The esoteric aspect includes methods that focus on actual communion of the soul with God. The exoteric aspect is for the many; the esoteric is for the ardent few. It is the esoteric aspect of religion that leads to intuition, the firsthand knowledge of Reality.

True religion is founded upon intuitional perception of the Transcendental Reality

The lofty *Sanatana Dharma* of the Vedic philosophy of ancient India—summarized in the Upanishads and in the six classical systems of metaphysical knowledge, and peerlessly encapsulated in the Bhagavad Gita—is based on intuitional perception of the Transcendental Reality. Buddhism, with its various methods of controlling the mind and gaining depth in meditation, advocates intuitive knowledge to realize the transcendence of *nirvana*. Sufism in Islam anchors on the intuitive mystical experience of the soul.† Within the Jewish religion are

---

* In the Buddhist scrolls discovered in a Tibetan lamasery and published by Nicholas Notovitch (see Discourse 5), Jesus is quoted as saying:

"Put not your faith in miracles performed by the hands of men, for He who rules nature is alone capable of doing supernatural things, while man is impotent to arrest the wrath of the winds or cause the rain to fall.

"One miracle, however, is within the power of man to accomplish. It is, when his heart is filled with sincere faith, he resolves to root out from his mind all evil promptings and desires, and when, in order to attain this end, he ceases to walk the path of iniquity."

† See Paramahansa Yogananda's *Wine of the Mystic: The Rubaiyat of Omar Khayyam — A Spiritual Interpretation* (published by Self-Realization Fellowship).

esoteric teachings based on inner experience of the Divine, evidenced abundantly in the legacy of the God-illumined Biblical prophets. Christ's teachings are fully expressive of that realization. The apostle John's Revelation is a remarkable disclosure of the soul's intuitional perception of deepest truths garbed in metaphor.

The elite traditions of Western philosophy and metaphysics laud the intuitional knowing power of the soul. The Greek mystic, philosopher, and mathematician Pythagoras (born c. 580 B.C.) emphasized inner experience of intuitive knowledge. Plato (born c. 428 B.C.), whose works have come down to us as a primary foundation of Western civilization, likewise taught the necessity for supersensory knowledge to apprehend eternal truths. The Neoplatonist sage Plotinus (A.D. 204–270) practiced Plato's ideal of intuitional knowing of Reality: "Often I have woken to myself out of the body, become detached from all else and entered into myself," he wrote, "and I have seen beauty of surpassing greatness, and have felt assured that then especially I belonged to the higher reality, engaged in the noblest life and identified with the Divine."* He died exhorting his disciples "Strive to bring back the god in yourselves to the God in the All."†

The Gnostics (first three centuries A.D.); the early Church fathers such as Origen and Augustine; great Christian luminaries such as Johannes Scotus Erigena (810–877) and Saint Anselm (1033); the monastic orders founded by Saint Bernard of Clairvaux (1091–1153) and Hugh, Richard, and Walter of Saint Victor (twelfth century)—all practiced intuitive contemplation of God.

Illumined Christian mystics of medieval times—Saint Thomas Aquinas (1224–1275); Saint Bonaventure (1217–1274); Jan van Ruysbroeck (1293–1381); Meister Eckhart (1260–1327); Henry Suso (1295–1366); Johannes Tauler (1300–1361); Gerhard Groote (1367–1398); Thomas à Kempis (1380–1471), author of *The Imitation of Christ;* Jacob Boehme (1575–1624)—sought and received ultimate knowledge through the light of intuition.‡ Christian saints through the centuries—

---

* *Enneads,* iv. 8.

† Porphyry, *Life of Plotinus* 2.

‡ "Let no one suppose," says the *Theologia Germanica,* "that we may attain to this true light and perfect knowledge...by hearsay, or by reading and study, nor yet by high skill and great learning." "It is not enough," says Gerlac Petersen, "to know by estimation merely: but we must know by experience." So Mechthild of Magdeburg says of her revelations, "The writing of this book was seen, heard, and experienced in every

Juliana of Norwich, Hildegard of Bingen, Catherine of Siena, Teresa of Avila, and many more known and unknown—partook of soul intuition in their attainment of divine realization and mystical union with God.

British poets such as Wordsworth, Coleridge, Blake, Traherne, and Pope aspired to intuit and write about the all-pervading Spirit. Emerson (1803–1882) and other American Transcendentalists sought personal experience of immanent spiritual reality through intuition. The German Idealist philosophers Hamann (1730–1788), Herder (1744–1803), Jacobi (1743–1819), Schiller (1775–1854), and Schopenhauer (1788–1860) emphasized it; and the great modern French philosopher Bergson calls intuition the only faculty capable of knowing the ultimate nature of things.*

The "second birth," the necessity of which Jesus speaks, admits us to the land of intuitional perception of truth. The New Testament may

Jesus' esoteric teachings reveal the universality of religion

not have been scribed with the word "intuition," but it is replete with references to intuitive knowledge. Indeed, the twenty-one verses describing Nicodemus' visit present, in condensed epigrammatic sayings so typical of Oriental scripture, Jesus' comprehensive esoteric teachings relating to the practical attainment of the infinite kingdom of blissful divine consciousness. These verses have been largely interpreted in support of such doctrines as baptism of the body by water as a prerequisite for entering God's kingdom after death (John 3:5); that Jesus is the only "son of God" (John 3:16); that mere "belief" in Jesus is sufficient for salvation, and that all are condemned who do not so believe (John 3:17–18). Such exoteric reading of scripture engulfs in dogma the universality of religion. A panorama of unity unfolds in an understanding of esoteric truth.

Truth is one: exact correspondence with Reality. Divine incarnations do not come to bring a new or exclusive religion, but to restore the One Religion of God-realization. The great ones, like waves, all bathe in the same Eternal Sea and become One with It. The outwardly varying messages of the prophets are part of the necessary relativity

---

limb....I see it with the eyes of my soul, and hear it with the ears of my eternal spirit." —quoted in *Mysticism*, by Evelyn Underhill, Part I, Chapter 4.

* An overview of exponents of intuitional experience in Christianity may be found in *The Presence of God: A History of Western Christian Mysticism*, three volumes, by Bernard McGinn (New York: Crossroad, 1991). *(Publisher's Note)*

that accommodates human diversity. It is narrow-mindedness that creates religious bigotry and divisive denominationalism, constricting truth to ritualistic worship and sectarian dogma; the form is mistaken for the spirit. The essential message of actual contact between man and Maker is diluted with ignorance. Humanity drinks of the polluted waters, understanding not at all why its spiritual thirst remains. Only pure waters can quench a vexing thirst.

The undreamed-of technical advances in civilization made possible by the splitting of the atom and the harnessing of subatomic energies will ultimately bring all peoples into such close proximity in travel and communication that humanity will have to reevaluate its attitudes. Either persistence in ignorant intolerance will spawn mass suffering, or an openness to the common spiritual link of souls will presage a global well-being of peace and amity. This is a clarion call that the time has come to separate truth from spurious convictions, knowledge from ignorance. The teachings of Jesus as understood in harmony with the revelations of the Great Ones of India will revive the practical methods of the intuitive knowing of truth through Self-realization. Realized truth and scientific knowledge are the sure means to combat the shadowy doubts and superstitions hedging humanity. Only a mighty flood of the light of truth through actual communion with God can dispel the gathered darkness of the ages.

⁓

Jesus answered and said unto him, "Verily, verily, I say unto thee, except a man be born again, he cannot see the kingdom of God."

Nicodemus saith unto him, "How can a man be born when he is old? Can he enter the second time into his mother's womb, and be born?"(John 3:3–4).

This choice of words by Jesus is an allusion to his familiarity with the Eastern spiritual doctrine of reincarnation. One meaning to be drawn from this precept is that the soul has to be born repeatedly in various bodies until it reawakens to realization of its native perfection. It is a false hope to believe that at bodily death the soul automatically enters into an everlasting angelic existence in heaven. Unless and until one attains perfection by removing the debris of karma (effects of one's

To "see the kingdom of God"

actions) from the individualized God-image of his soul, he cannot enter God's kingdom.* The ordinary person, constantly creating new karmic bondage by his wrong actions and material desires, adding to the accumulated effects of numerous previous incarnations, cannot free his soul in one lifetime. It takes many lifetimes of physical, mental, and spiritual evolution to work out all karmic entanglements that block soul intuition, the pure knowing without which one cannot "see the kingdom of God."

The principal import of Jesus' words to Nicodemus goes beyond an implied reference to reincarnation. This is clear from Nicodemus' request for further explanation of how an *adult* could reach God's kingdom: Must he reenter his mother's womb and be reborn?† Jesus elaborates in the succeeding verses as to how a person can be "born again" in his present incarnation—how a soul identified with the flesh and sense limitations can acquire by meditation a new birth in Cosmic Consciousness.

---

* "Be ye therefore perfect, even as your Father in heaven is perfect" (Matthew 5:48; see Discourse 27).

† Nicodemus, as mentioned in the Bible verses above, was a Pharisee. The first-century Jewish historian Josephus records the following about the Pharisees' beliefs: "They say that all souls are incorruptible, but that the souls of good men only are removed into other bodies, but that the souls of bad men are subject to eternal punishment" (*Wars of the Jews*, ii, 8, 14). Some religious scholars hold that this is a reference to reincarnation; others claim it is merely a statement of the Pharisees' doctrine of the ultimate resurrection of the virtuous. Regardless, there is ample evidence that many Jews believed in reincarnation.

The German encyclopedia *Meyers Konversationslexikon* states: "At the time of Christ most of the Jews believed in the transmigration of the soul. Talmudists thought that God had created a limited number of Jewish souls that would come back as long as there were Jews....However, on the day of resurrection they would all be purified and rise in the bodies of the righteous in the Promised Land."

"The fact that reincarnation is part of Jewish tradition comes as a surprise to many people," writes Yaakov Astor in *Soul Searching: Seeking Scientific Foundation for the Jewish Tradition of an Afterlife* (Southfield, Michigan: Targum Press, 2003). "Nevertheless, it's mentioned in numerous places throughout the classical texts of Jewish mysticism....The *Zohar* and related literature are filled with references to reincarnation.... The *Bahir*, attributed to the first-century sage, Nechuniah ben Hakanah, used reincarnation to address the classic question of theodicy—why bad things happen to good people and vice versa:...'This is because the [latter] righteous person did bad in a previous [life], and is now experiencing the consequences.'"

That the concept of reincarnation was known to the Jews is evidenced in several New Testament passages, as when the "priests and Levites" ask John the Baptist, "Art thou Elijah?" (John 1:21, Discourse 6); and when Jesus' disciples tell him, "Some say that thou art John the Baptist: some, Elijah; and others, Jeremiah, or one of the prophets" (Matthew 16:14; see Discourse 45). (*Publisher's Note*)

～

*"Except a man be born of water and of the Spirit, he cannot en-
ter into the kingdom of God" (John 3:5).*

To be "born of water" is usually interpreted as a mandate for the
outer ritual of baptism by water—a symbolic rebirth—in order
to be eligible for God's kingdom after death. But Jesus did not mention a *re*birth involving water.* "Water" here means protoplasm; the
body is made up mostly of water and begins its earthly existence in
the amniotic fluid of the mother's womb. Though the soul has to go
through the natural process of birth that God has established through
His biological laws, physical birth is not enough for man to be fit to
see or enter into the kingdom of God.

The ordinary consciousness is tied to the flesh, and through the
two physical eyes man can see only into the diminutive playhouse of
this earth and its encircling starry sky. Through the small outer windows of the five senses, body-bound souls perceive nothing of the wonders beyond limited matter.

When a person is high aloft in an airplane he sees no boundaries,
only the limitlessness of space and free skies. But if he is caged in a
room, surrounded by windowless walls, he loses the vision of vastness.
Similarly, when man's soul is sent out of the infinity of Spirit into a
sensory-circumscribed mortal body, his outer experiences are confined
to the limitations of matter. So Jesus alluded to the fact, as expressed
by modern scientists, that we can see and know only as much as the
limited instrumentality of the senses and reason allow. Just as by a two-
inch telescope the details of the distant stars cannot be seen, so Jesus
was saying that man cannot see or know anything about the heavenly
kingdom of God through the unaugmented power of his mind and
senses. However, a 200-inch telescope enables man to peer into the vast

---

* Nowhere in the four Gospels is it specifically stated that Jesus instructed his disciples
to practice the ritual of water baptism. However, the Gospel According to St. Matthew
quotes Jesus as issuing to his followers, after his resurrection, what Christian theologians call the "Great Commission": "Go ye therefore, and teach all nations, baptizing
them in the name of the Father, and of the Son, and of the Holy Ghost: teaching them
to observe all things whatsoever I have commanded you" (Matthew 28:19–20).

The nature of the baptism intended by Jesus is apparent in John the Baptist's declaration that though John baptized with water, Jesus "shall baptize you with the Holy
Ghost, and with fire." (See Discourse 6.)

reaches of star-peopled space; and similarly, by developing the intuitional sense through meditation he can behold and enter the causal and astral kingdom of God—birthplace of thoughts, stars, and souls.

Jesus points out that after man's soul becomes incarnate—born of water, or protoplasm—he should transcend the mortal impositions of the body by self-development. Through awakening the "sixth sense," intuition, and opening the spiritual eye, his illumined consciousness can enter into the kingdom of God. In this second birth the body remains the same; but the soul's consciousness, instead of being tied to the material plane, is free to roam in the boundless, eternally joyous empire of Spirit.

God intended His human children to live on earth with an awakened perception of the Spirit informing all creation, and thus to enjoy His dream-drama as a cosmic entertainment. Alone among living creatures, the human body was equipped, as a special creation of God, with the instruments and capacities necessary to express fully the soul's divine potentials.* But through the delusion of Satan, man ignores his higher endowments and remains attached to the limited fleshly form and its mortality.

As individualized souls, Spirit progressively unfolds Its power of knowing through the successive stages of evolution: as unconscious response in minerals, as feeling in plant life, as instinctive sentient knowledge in animals, as intellect, reason, and undeveloped introspective intuition in man, and as pure intuition in the superman.

It is said that after eight million lives traveling the successive steps of upward evolution like a prodigal son through the cycles of incarnations, at last the soul arrives in a human birth. Originally, human beings were pure sons of God. Nobody knows the divine consciousness enjoyed by Adam and Eve except the saints. Ever since the Fall, man's misuse of his independence, he has lost that consciousness by associative equivalence of himself with the fleshly ego and its mortal desires. Not altogether uncommon are persons more like instinct-motivated animals than intellectually responsive human beings. They are so materially minded that when you talk about food or sex or money they understand and reflexively respond, like Pavlov's famous salivating dog. But try to engage them in a meaningful philosophical exchange about God or the mystery of life, and their uncomprehending reaction is as though their conversationalist were crazy.

---

* See Discourse 7, pages 144–45.

The spiritual man is trying to free himself from the materiality that is the cause of his prodigal wandering in the maze of incarnations, but the ordinary man does not want more than a betterment of his earthly existence. As instinct confines the animal within prescribed limits, so also does reason circumscribe the human being who does not try to be a superman by developing intuition. The person who worships reason only and is not conscious of the availability of his power of intuition—by which alone he can know himself as soul—remains little more than a rational animal, out of touch with the spiritual heritage that is his birthright.

~

"That which is born of the flesh is flesh; and that which is born of the Spirit is spirit" (John 3:6).

These words of Jesus rest upon the truth that both consciousness and matter are perpetual and self-perpetuating—they continue to propagate as long as Spirit maintains Its creation.

The Transcendental Absolute has a dual manifestation: subjective and objective, Spirit and Nature, noumena and phenomena. Objectively, vibrating Spirit manifests as conscious Cosmic Light, which through progressive condensation produces *Matter and consciousness: the perpetual duality of manifest creation* the triune causal, astral, and material creation as well as the causal, astral, and physical bodies of man. Subjectively, Spirit is immanent in the cosmic creative Light as Consciousness, the ultimate Source and Sustainer of all: Christ Consciousness in the causal-astral-physical macrocosm, and the soul in the causal-astral-physical microcosm of man.*

The consciousness of God is self-perpetuating in the consciousness of man. Man bequeaths salient characteristics of his consciousness to children or disciples, and his physical characteristics are passed down in the flesh of descendents. Both the consciousness and the body

---

* "O Arjuna, by the knowers of truth, this body is called *kshetra* ('the field' where good and evil karma is sown and reaped); likewise, that which cognizes the field they call *kshetrajna* (the soul). Also know Me to be the *Kshetrajna* (Perceiver) in all *kshetras* (the bodies evolved out of the cosmic creative principle and Nature). The understanding of *kshetra* and *kshetrajna*—that is deemed by Me as constituting true wisdom" (*God Talks With Arjuna: The Bhagavad Gita* XIII:1–2).

are vibrations of eternal Spirit, and there is no essential difference between them; but each perpetuates its own nature according to the characteristic duality of manifest creation.

Man apprehends the phenomena of objective nature (more or less, according to their subtlety) with his senses and reasoning intellect. The noumenon behind the phenomenon—consciousness as the causal essence of man and creation—is beyond the grasp of human intelligence. Human intelligence can give knowledge only of phenomena; noumena must be known through intuition, the power by which consciousness apprehends itself. The ordinary man therefore cognizes the natural universe around him but not the immanent Spirit, and cognizes himself as so many pounds of flesh rather than as pure consciousness indwelling as the soul.

Thus man is born of both flesh and consciousness, and flesh has become predominant. The body born of flesh has the limitations of the flesh, whereas the soul, born of the Spirit, has potentially limitless powers. By meditation, man's consciousness is transferred from the body to the soul, and through the soul's power of intuition he experiences himself not as a mortal body (a phenomenon of objective nature), but as immortal indwelling consciousness, one with the noumenal Divine Essence.*

─────────────

* Man's angelic astral body of light and life energy, which possesses an invisible counterpart for all the physical organs and which interfaces with the fleshly body through the brain and the intricate physical and astral pathways of life energy, helps to explain the so-called "phantom limb phenomenon," known to persons who lose a limb through accident or surgery. Though physically missing, that limb may remain intact in the astral body, causing amputees to feel sensations and movements in the missing limb exactly as if it were still part of the body. "For nearly 70 percent of them their missing arms, hands, legs, or feet continue to experience all-too-real feelings of pressure, pain, warmth, cold, tingling, or other sensations," according to *The Mind and the Brain* by Jeffrey M. Schwartz, M.D., and Sharon Begley (New York: HarperCollins, 2002).

In *Phantoms in the Brain: Probing the Mysteries of the Human Mind* (New York: HarperCollins, 1998), Professor V. S. Ramachandran, M.D., Ph.D., Director of the Center for Brain and Cognition at the University of California at San Diego, describes the complex neurological mechanism behind this phenomenon. His research has revealed how amazingly lifelike are the sensations and kinesthetic reality maintained by the brains of those with phantom body parts. These experiments, he says, "have helped us understand what is going on in the brains of patients with phantoms....But there's a deeper message here: *Your own body* is a phantom, one that your brain has temporarily constructed purely for convenience....

"For your entire life, you've been walking around assuming that your 'self' is anchored to a single body that remains stable and permanent at least until death. Indeed, the 'loyalty' of your self to your own body is so axiomatic that you never even pause

~

*"Marvel not that I said unto thee, 'Ye must be born again.' The
wind bloweth where it listeth, and thou hearest the sound thereof,
but canst not tell whence it cometh, and whither it goeth: so is
every one that is born of the Spirit" (John 3:7–8).*

Jesus was describing a metaphysical law of noumena (substance, or
cause) and phenomena (the appearances of substances, or effect)
when he compared the Spirit, and the souls emerg-
ing from It, with the invisible wind, and its presence   *"The wind bloweth
declared by its sound. Just as the source of the wind   where it listeth...."*
is hidden but the wind is made known by its sound,
so the Spirit-substance is invisible, hidden beyond the reach of human
senses; and the incarnate souls born of the Spirit are the visible phenomena. By the sound, the invisible wind is known. By the presence
of intelligent souls, the invisible Spirit is declared.

Jesus was stating that, as it is difficult to find the source of the wind,
so it is difficult to find the Spirit-Source from which all things come.
There is a parallel quotation in the Hindu scripture, the Bhagavad Gita
(II:28): "The beginning of all creatures is veiled, the middle is manifested, and the end again is imperceptible." All beings come from the
ocean of Spirit and dissolve again in the ocean of Spirit. Everything
emerges from the Invisible, to play upon this earth for a little while, and
then enters the invisible state again at the end of life. Only the middle
of life we behold; the beginning and end are hidden from sight in the
subtler spiritual realms. To illustrate: Think of a huge chain out in the
ocean. If you lift the middle of the chain above the surface of the water,
you can see a few of its links, but the ends are still unseen in the depths.
So the outer manifestations of life are perceptible to man's sensory mind,
but their origin and ultimate destiny are unknown to man in ordinary

_____

to think about it, let alone question it. Yet these experiments suggest the exact opposite—that your body image, despite all its appearance of durability, is an entirely transitory internal construct....merely a shell that you've temporarily created."

In summing up the implications, Dr. Ramachandran quotes the *Vivekachudamani*
("Crest Jewel of Wisdom") of Swami Shankara: "You never identify your self with the
shadow cast by your body, or with its reflection, or with the body you see in a dream
or in your imagination. Therefore you should not identify yourself with this living
body, either." *(Publisher's Note)*

consciousness. He perceives only the middle of the chain of eternal existence and consciousness, that which is visible between birth and death.

Man remains firmly convinced that he is essentially a body, even though he daily receives proof to the contrary. Every night in sleep, "the little death," he discards his identification with the physical form and is reborn as invisible consciousness. Why is it that man is compelled to sleep? Because sleep is a reminder of what is beyond the state of sleep— the state of the soul.* Mortal existence could not be borne without at least subconscious contact with the soul, which is provided by sleep. At nighttime man dumps the body into the subconscious and becomes an angel; in the daytime he becomes once more a devil, divorced from Spirit by the desires and sensations of the body. By *Kriya Yoga* meditation he can be a god in the daytime, like Christ and the Great Ones. He goes beyond the subconscious to the superconscious, and dissolves the consciousness of the body in the ecstasy of God. One who can do this is born again. He knows his soul as a waft of the invisible wind of Spirit—soaring free in the unbounded heavens, entrapped no longer in a whirling dust devil traipsing heedlessly over the toilsome tracks of matter.

This earth is a habitat of trouble and suffering, but the kingdom of God that is behind this material plane is an abode of freedom and bliss. The soul of the awakening man has followed a hard-earned way —many incarnations of upward evolution—in order to arrive at the human state and the possibility to reclaim his lost divinity. Yet how many human births have been wasted in preoccupation with food and money and gratification of the body and egoistic emotions! Each person should ask himself how he is using the precious moments of this present birth. Eventually the bodies of all human beings fall painfully apart; isn't it better to separate the soul from the body consciousness —to keep the body as the temple of the Spirit? O Soul, you are not the body; why not remember always that you are the Spirit of God?†

Jesus said that we must reestablish our connection with Eternity; we must be born again. Man has either to follow the circuitous route

---

* All human beings experience three states: waking, dream-broken slumber, and dreamless sleep. The latter, even when brief, is revivifying; man is then unconsciously resting in his soul nature. Hindu scriptures also speak of *turiya,* literally, in Sanskrit, the "fourth" or superconscious state. Persistent yogis and all other great devotees of God enter the *turiya* state: conscious, unforgettable realizations of soul as one with Spirit.

† "Know ye not that ye are the temple of God, and that the Spirit of God dwelleth in you?" (I Corinthians 3:16).

of reincarnations to work out his karma, or—by a technique such as *Kriya Yoga* and the help of a true guru—to awaken the divine faculty of intuition and know himself as a soul, that is, be born again in Spirit. By the latter method he can see and enter the kingdom of God in this lifetime.

Spiritual birth—to be born again in Spirit— is bestowed by a true guru

Sooner or later, after a few or many painful incarnations, the soul in every human being will cry out to remind him that his home is not here, and he will begin in earnest to retrace his steps to his rightful heavenly kingdom. When one is very desirous to know Truth, God sends a master through whose devotion and realization He plants His love in that person's heart.

Human birth is given by one's parents; but the spiritual birth is given by the God-ordained guru. In the Vedic tradition of ancient India, the newly born child is called *kayastha,* which means "body identified." The two physical eyes, which look into alluring matter, are bequeathed by the physical parents; but at the time of initiation, spiritual baptism, the spiritual eye is opened by the guru. Through the help of the guru, the initiate learns to use this telescopic eye to see Spirit, and then becomes *dwija,* "twice-born"—the same metaphysical terminology used by Jesus—and begins his progress toward the state of becoming a *Brahmin,* one who knows Brahman or Spirit.*

The matter-bound soul, lifted into the Spirit by God-contact, is born a second time, in Spirit. Alas, even in India this initiation from body consciousness to spiritual consciousness has become just a formality, a caste ceremony performed on young Brahmin boys by ordinary priests—tantamount to the symbolic ritual of baptism with water. But Jesus, like great Hindu masters of ancient and modern times, conferred the actual baptism of Spirit—"with the Holy Ghost, and with fire." A true guru is one who can change the disciple's brain cells by the spiritual current flowing from God through his enlightened consciousness. All will feel that change who are in tune—who meditate sincerely and deeply and, as in the practice of *Kriya Yoga,* learn to send the divine current into the brain cells. The soul is bound to the body by cords of karma, woven by lifetimes of material desires, behavior, and habits. Only the life current can change one's life, destroying those millions of karmic records. Then one is born again; the

---

* Cf. *God Talks With Arjuna: The Bhagavad Gita,* commentary on III:24.

251

soul opens the inner window of oneness with the Spirit and enters into the perception of the wondrous omnipresence of God.*

So the term "born again" means much more than merely joining a church and receiving ceremonial baptism. Belief alone will not give the soul a permanent place in heaven after death; it is necessary to have communion with God now. Human beings are made angels on earth, not in heaven. At death, wherever one leaves off in his progress, he will have to start in again in a new incarnation. After sleep one is the same as before sleep; after death one is the same as before death. That is why Christ and the Masters say it is necessary to become saintly before the sleep of death. It cannot be done by filling the mind with mortal attachments and useless diversions. One who is engrossed in storing up treasure on earth is not busy with God; one who is intent on God does not want many fillers in his life. It is by freeing oneself from earthly desires that one gains entry into the kingdom of God. The Lord patiently waits for one hundred percent of man's devotion; for those who diligently seek Him every day, and who fulfill His commandments through godly behavior, He opens the door to the kingdom of His presence.

A multitude of lectures about sunshine and scenic beauties will not enable me to see them if my eyes are closed. So it is that people do not see God who is omnipresent in everything unless and until they open their spiritual eye of intuitive perception. When one can perceive

---

* True meditation (*dhyana*, the seventh step of the Eightfold Path of Yoga as delineated by Sage Patanjali) is spoken of as giving "conception of the magnitude of *Aum*," the Biblical Holy Ghost or Word. In *The Holy Science*, Swami Sri Yukteswar writes:

"What is needed is a Guru, a Savior, who will awaken us to *Bhakti* (devotion) and to perceptions of Truth....Any advanced sincere seeker may be fortunate in having the Godlike company of some one of such personages, who may kindly stand to him as his Spiritual Preceptor, *Sat-Guru*, the Savior. Following affectionately the holy precepts of these divine personages, man becomes able to direct all his organs of sense inward to their common center—the sensorium, *Trikuti* or *Sushumnadwara*, the door of the interior world—where he comprehends the Voice...[the Cosmic Vibration that is] the Word, Amen, *Aum*....From the peculiar nature of this sound, issuing as it does like a stream from a higher unknown region and losing itself in the gross material creation, it is figuratively designated by various sects of people by the names of different rivers that they consider as sacred; for example, Ganga by the Hindus, Yamuna by the Vaishnavas, and Jordan by the Christians. Through his luminous body, man, believing in the existence of the true Light—the Life of this universe—becomes baptized or absorbed in the holy stream of the sound. The baptism is, so to speak, the second birth of man and is called *Bhakti Yoga*, without which man can never comprehend the real internal world, the kingdom of God."

that he is not the mortal body but a spark of the Infinite Spirit cloaked in a concentration of life energy, then he will be able to see the kingdom of God. He will realize that the composition of his body and the universe is not soul-imprisoning matter, but expansive, indestructible energy and consciousness. Science has proved this truth; and each individual can experience it. Through *Kriya Yoga,* he can have the unshakable realization that he is that great Light and Consciousness of Spirit.

O man, how long will you remain a rational animal? How long will you fruitlessly try to look into the endless tracts of creation with only your myopic eyes of senses and reason? How long will you remain bound to satisfying the demands of animal man? Shed all constraining fetters; know yourself as something immortal, having limitless powers and faculties. No more this age-old dream of rational animal! Wake up! you are the intuitional child of immortality!

DISCOURSE 14

The Ascension of Man— Lifting Up the Serpent in the Wilderness

Dialogue With Nicodemus, Part II

Heavenly Truths Can Be Fully Known Only Through Intuition

❖

The Potential to Remain in Heavenly Consciousness
Regardless of Outer Circumstances

❖

"Lifting Up the Serpent":
Kundalini Force at the Base of the Spine

❖

Yoga: Science of Switching Off the Senses
and Entering Superconsciousness

❖

Common Fallacies About Kundalini Awakening

"Whosoever believes in the doctrine of lifting the bodily consciousness (Son of man) from the physical to the astral by reversing the life force through the coiled passage at the base of the spine...will gradually acquire the immutable state — Christ Consciousness."

Nicodemus **answered** and said unto him, "How can these things be?"

Jesus answered and said unto him, "Art thou a master of Israel, and knowest not these things? Verily, verily, I say unto thee, we speak that we do know, and testify that we have seen; and ye receive not our witness. If I have told you earthly things, and ye believe not, how shall ye believe, if I tell you of heavenly things?

"And no man hath ascended up to heaven, but he that came down from heaven, even the Son of man which is in heaven. And as Moses lifted up the serpent in the wilderness, even so must the Son of man be lifted up: that whosoever believeth in him should not perish, but have eternal life."

—John 3:9–15

DISCOURSE 14

The Ascension of Man—Lifting Up the Serpent in the Wilderness

Dialogue With Nicodemus, Part II

Nicodemus answered and said unto him, "How can these things be?"

Jesus answered and said unto him, "Art thou a master of Israel, and knowest not these things? Verily, verily, I say unto thee, we speak that we do know, and testify that we have seen; and ye receive not our witness. If I have told you earthly things, and ye believe not, how shall ye believe, if I tell you of heavenly things? (John 3:9–12).

Jesus, in addressing Nicodemus, observed that merely holding the ceremonial office of a master of the house of Israel did not guarantee an understanding of the mysteries of life. Often persons are accorded religious titles by virtue of intellectual knowledge of the scriptures; but a full comprehension of the esoteric depths of truth can be known only by intuitive experience.

"We speak that we do know" is knowledge deeper than the information derived through sensory-dependent intellect and reason. Since the senses are limited, so is intellectual understanding. The senses and mind are the outer doors through which knowledge percolates

into the consciousness. Human knowledge filters in through the senses
and is interpreted by the mind. If the senses err in perception, the conclusion drawn by the understanding of that data is

Heavenly truths can
be fully known only
through intuition

also incorrect. A white gossamer cloth fluttering in
the distance may look like a ghost, and a supersti-
tious person believes that it is a ghost; but closer
observation reveals the error of that conclusion.
The senses and understanding are easily deluded because they cannot
grasp the real nature, the essential character and substance, of created
things. Jesus, with his intuition, had full realization of the noumena
supporting the workings of the cosmos and its diversity of life, so he
said authoritatively: *"We do know."*

Jesus was attuned to the grand scheme of manifestation behind all
space, behind earthly vision. To belligerent minds he could not speak
openly of his omnipresent perceptions—even the truths he did tell
brought crucifixion! He said to Nicodemus: "If I tell you about matters pertaining to human souls who are visibly present on earth, and
how they can enter into the kingdom of God, and you believe not, then
how can you believe me if I tell you about happenings in the heavenly
realms, which are completely hidden from the ordinary human gaze?"

Though Jesus regretted, with accommodating patience, that
Nicodemus doubted the intuitional revelations of the Christ state, he
went on to tell his visitor the way in which he—and any other seeker
of truth—could experience these truths for himself.

So many doubt heaven because they do not see it. Yet they do not
doubt the breeze simply because it is unseen. It is known by its sound
and sensation on the skin and the motion in the leaves and other objects. The whole universe lives, moves, breathes because of the invisible presence of God in the heavenly forces behind matter.

Once a man gave some olives to another who had never seen
olives, and said, "These have a lot of oil in them." The person cut the
fruit but could see no oil—until his friend showed him how to squeeze
the olives in order to extract the oil from the pulp. So it is with God.
Everything in the universe is saturated with His presence—the twinkling stars, the rose, the song of the bird, our minds. His Being permeates everything, everywhere. But one has metaphorically to "squeeze"
God out of His material concealment.

Inner concentration is the way to realize the subtle, prolific
heaven behind this gross universe. Seclusion is the price of greatness

and God-contact. All who are willing to snatch time from the greedy material world to devote it instead to the divine search can learn to behold the wondrous factory of creation out of which all things are born. From the heavenly causal and astral spheres every physically incarnate soul has descended, and every soul can reascend by retreating to the "wilderness" of interior silence and practicing the scientific method of lifting up the life force and consciousness from body identification to union with God.

~

"And no man hath ascended up to heaven, but he that came down from heaven, even the Son of man which is in heaven. And as Moses lifted up the serpent in the wilderness, even so must the Son of man be lifted up: that whosoever believeth in him should not perish, but have eternal life" (John 3:13–15).

This passage is very important, and little understood. Taken literally, the words "lifted up the serpent" are at best a classic scriptural ambiguity. Every symbol has a hidden meaning that must be rightly interpreted.

The word "serpent" here refers metaphorically to man's consciousness and life force in the subtle coiled passageway at the base of the spine, the matterward flow of which is to be reversed for man to reascend from body attachment to superconscious freedom.*

As souls we were all originally in God's bosom. Spirit projects the desire to create an individualized expression of Itself. The soul becomes manifest and projects the idea of the body in causal form. The idea becomes energy, or the lifetronic astral body. The astral body becomes condensed into the physical body. Through the integrated spinal passageway of these three instrumental media, the soul descends into identification with the material body and gross matter.

Man's supernal nature as an angelic being garbed in thought and light

"He that came down from heaven" means the physical body. (Jesus refers to the human body as "man"; throughout the Gospels he spoke of his own physical body as "the Son of man," as distinguished from his Christ Consciousness,

---

* See Discourse 6 regarding the subtle anatomy of the spine.

"the Son of God.") Man descends from the heavenly planes of God's creation when his soul, garbed in its causal body of God-congealed ideas and its astral body of light, takes on an outer covering of material tissue. So not only Jesus but all of God's children have "come down from heaven."

Just as the little threads of flame percolating through the holes of a gas burner are part of the one flame under the burner plate, so also the one flame of Spirit underlying all creation appears as a separate soul-flame in every individual being. When the burner is turned off, the many individual jets retire into the one central flame. The separate threads of fire had first to come out of the primary flame before they could go back into it. This illustrates what Jesus said about souls ascending to heaven, having descended from heaven.

No human body has ascended into heaven, the etheric essence of which does not accommodate corporeal forms; but all souls can and will enter the supernal realms when, through death or through spiritual transcendence, they cast off physical consciousness and know themselves as angelic beings garbed in thought and light.

We are all made in the image of God, beings of immortal consciousness cloaked in diaphanous heavenly light—a heritage buried beneath the cloddish flesh. That heritage we can only acknowledge by meditation. There is no other way—not by reading books, not by philosophical study, but by devotion and continuous prayer and scientific meditation that uplifts the consciousness to God.

Jesus spoke of an extraordinary truth when he mentioned "the Son of man which is in heaven." Ordinary souls behold their bodies ("Son of man") roaming only on the earth, but free souls such as Jesus dwell simultaneously in the physical and in the astral and in the astral and causal heavenly kingdoms.

Highest ecstasy: being united with God while simultaneously active in the world

A motion picture can portray human beings, animals, trees, mountains, oceans, on the screen; all of which have descended from the projection booth, projected through a beam of light. Similarly, every figure in this world has emerged from the booth of eternity. The physical body or "Son of man" is a projection of the cosmic beam of God's light. So Jesus' words are very simple and very wonderful: Even while dwelling in a body in the physical world, he was beholding himself as a ray of God descending from heaven. He demonstrated this conclusively after his death, re-creating his physical body from rays of cosmic creative light, and later dematerializing it in the presence of his disciples when he ascended back to heaven.*

Some masters in their oneness with God may preserve the projection of their bodily form indefinitely. Other masters in their God-union dissolve the bodily image in Spirit when they depart from the earth; but they can reappear at will in response to the earnest soul-entreaty of a yearning devotee—either in vision or actually rematerializing their physical form, as Jesus did for Saint Francis and as my own Master, after his passing, did for me. Or, at the behest of the Divine Father, they may voluntarily return to earth in a new incarnation to usher souls from the realm of delusion into the kingdom of God.

While Jesus, in his God-ordained incarnation, was effectually engaged in his Heavenly Father's work in the world, he could in truth proclaim: "I am in heaven." This is the highest ecstasy of God-consciousness, defined by yogis as *nirvikalpa samadhi,* an ecstatic state "without difference" between external consciousness and interior God-union. In *savikalpa samadhi,* "with difference," a less exalted state, one is not conscious of the outer world; the body enters an inert trance while the awareness is immersed in interior conscious oneness with God. The most advanced masters can be fully conscious of God and not show any signs of the body being transfixed; the devotee drinks God and simultaneously is conscious and fully active in his external environment—if he so chooses.

This declaration of Jesus offers great encouragement to every soul: Although man is beset with the perplexities that accompany residence in a physical body, God has provided him with the potential to remain in heavenly consciousness regardless of outer circumstances. An inebriate takes his *The potential to remain in heavenly consciousness regardless of outer circumstances* drunkenness with him no matter where he goes. One who is sick is all the time preoccupied with his sickness. One who is happy is ever bub-

---

* By the same power, a master who realizes that the body is a manipulatable mass of light and energy can replicate his material form in order to appear simultaneously in two or more places in identical bodies. This phenomenon, known as bilocation, has been demonstrated by numerous Christian saints down the ages. In *The Story of Therese Neumann* (Bruce Pub. Co.), A. P. Schimberg describes several occasions on which this Christian saint has appeared before, and conversed with, distant persons needing her help. In *Autobiography of a Yogi* I have recounted several instances in the lives of Hindu masters I have known.

bling with good cheer. And the one who is conscious of God enjoys that supreme Bliss whether he is active in the outer world or absorbed in inner communion.

When one is engrossed in watching a convincingly played scene of tragedy in a motion picture, it may so impinge itself on the consciousness and emotions that it begins to feel real. But when one is troubled by a particular scene of cruelty, such as the catastrophic destruction of human life in a burning city, if the viewer looks up from the picture to the beam of light from the projector and analyzes its relation to the figures and events on the screen, the seemingly real material nature of everything being shown—buildings, landscapes, the misery of human beings—is seen as nothing but light.

Likewise, the materially engrossed individual beholds his ever-changing surroundings, birth, death, marriage, acquisition and loss, as material facts. But the individual who awakens into the consciousness of God through constant ecstasy, or union with God, begins to see a light trembling in all creation. He perceives that the different forms of matter—solids, liquids, gaseous substances—as well as human life and thought, are nothing but the diverse vibrations of that all-pervading, quivering light of God. By further development one can actually perceive God as the Almighty Creator dreaming this Cosmic Dream.

While watching a movie, one person might concentrate on the pictures, while another might keep his attention on the projection beam that causes their "materialization" on the screen. The moviegoing experience of these two individuals would be quite different—one becoming immersed in the story, forgetful of the beam; and the other seeing only rays of light without any pictures. But there is a third possibility: a person sitting in the motion-picture house enjoying the pictures on the screen, while remembering their source by keeping a part of his attention on the pictureless beam.

A person concentrating on matter will see only material objects, and a person absorbed in God's light in the initial state of ecstasy (*savikalpa samadhi*) beholds only God. But one who has advanced to the highest state of consciousness, *nirvikalpa samadhi,* sees the great pictureless light of Cosmic Energy coming from God, and simultaneously beholds on the vast screen of space the motion picture of the universe produced by God's Creative Light.

Jesus' words in this passage make clear that all souls who are promoted back to heaven had originally descended from heaven and become entrapped in earthbound desires by the spurious realism of the cosmic drama, but were able to reascend by conquering every delusive attachment to material allurements. Again and again in the Gospels, Jesus emphasizes that what he attained, all may attain. His next re-mark to Nicodemus shows how.

Jesus said that each son of man, each bodily consciousness, must be lifted from the plane of the senses to the astral kingdom by reversing the matter-bent outflowing of the life force to ascension through the serpent-like coiled passage at the base of the spine—the son of man is lifted up when this serpen-tine force is uplifted, "as Moses lifted up the serpent in the wilderness." *

"Lifting up the ser-pent": kundalini force at the base of the spine

We must reascend, just as Moses, in the spiritual wilderness of silence in which all his desires were no more, lifted his soul from body con-

---

* Reference is to Exodus 4:2–4. When in the wilderness God spoke to Moses out of the burning bush, Moses asked of God some sign of spiritual authority by which he could be recognized as sent by God to accomplish the tasks to which God had ap-pointed him. "And the Lord said unto him, 'What is that in thine hand?' And he said, 'A rod.' And He said, 'Cast it on the ground.' And he cast it on the ground, and it be-came a serpent....And the Lord said unto Moses, 'Put forth thine hand, and take it by the tail.' And he put forth his hand, and caught it, and it became a rod in his hand."

The "rod" is the spine, in which reside the subtle astral centers of life and con-sciousness that are the dynamos not only of all physical vitalities, but of all divine pow-ers and spiritual perceptions when awakened by the lifting of the fiery serpent of life force at the base, "tail," of the spine. The metaphors of the "serpent" and "rod" are variously repeated in the story of Moses, in keeping with scriptural tradition of linking historical events with esoteric symbology. The rod, or staff, of Moses was the medium through which he demonstrated miraculous powers according to the will of God in carrying out his special dispensation to free the Israelites from thralldom in Egypt—such as the oft-cited parting of the Red Sea; and the saving of the people, in the wilderness, from death by fiery serpents created by their misdeeds, to counteract which the Lord directed Moses: "Make thee a fiery serpent, and set it upon a pole: and...every one that is bitten, when he looketh upon it, shall live" (Numbers 21:6–8). Spiritual death results from the mis-use of the animating fiery life force; spiritual life is the blessing bestowed when the life force and consciousness are uplifted to the highest center of divine consciousness in the body at the top of the spinal "pole" in the cerebrum, where God dwells as the soul.

A similar analogy exists in the scriptures of India, citing the serpentine life force at the base of the spine, as described in this Discourse, and the spine itself referred to as *meru-danda.* Mt. Meru is the loftiest of mythological mountains; and *danda,* "a rod, a staff," is representative of the spine with its spiritual centers, the crest of which is re-ferred to as the holy Meru, the highest center of divine consciousness. Many yogis honor this symbology by keeping among their sparse ascetic accoutrements a *danda,* staff, in recognition of the spine as the symbolic scepter of the soul's sovereign power over the kingdom of the body.

sciousness into God-consciousness through the same path by which it had descended.

As explained earlier, man's physical, astral, and causal bodies are tied together and work as one by a knotting of life force and consciousness in the seven cerebrospinal centers. In descending order, the final tie is a coiled knot at the base of the spine, preventing the ascension of consciousness into the heavenly astral kingdom. Unless one knows how to open this knot of astral and physical power, the life and consciousness remain attracted to the mortal realm, emanating outward into the body and sensory consciousness.

Most energy moves through space in a spiral form—a ubiquitous motif in the macrocosmic and microscopic architecture of the universe. Beginning with galactic nebulae—the cosmic birth-cradle of all matter—energy flows in coiled or circular or vortex-like patterns. The theme is repeated in the orbital dance of electrons around their atomic nucleus, and (as cited in Hindu scriptures of ancient origin) of planets and suns and stellar systems spinning through space around a grand center of the universe. Many galaxies are spiral-shaped; and countless other phenomena in nature—plants, animals, the winds and storms— similarly evidence the invisible whorls of energy underlying their shape and structure.* Such is the "serpent force" (*kundalini*) in the micro-

---

* In 1953, scientists discovered that DNA, the basic molecule of life, is also constructed in a helical shape. The deep-seeing Italian mathematician Leonardo Fibonacci (1170– 1250) perceived that countless patterns in nature conform to a spiral shape mathematically expressed as a logarithm deriving from the so-called Fibonacci numbers (1, 1, 2, 3, 5, 8, 13, 21, 34, 55, etc.), where each number is the sum of the two preceding in the series. This exact spiral appears in such seemingly disparate manifestations as the pattern of petals in sunflower blossoms and of leaves in pineapples, artichokes, and many trees; the progressive volume of chambers in a nautilus seashell; the light-years-wide sweep of spiral galaxies.

Philosophers down the centuries have inferred the intelligence of a Divine Architect from the fact that the further one progresses in the Fibonacci series, the closer the terms come to expressing "the golden mean" or "golden ratio" (1:1.618033989) and its derivative "golden rectangle" and "golden spiral"—a "sacred geometry" observable throughout nature. In *Atomic Vortex Theorem of Energy Motion,* quantum physicist Derek Bond discusses the theory that all energy expresses in a vortex pattern: "This is evidenced to us constantly from the largest things, such as our spiral galaxies and the very curve of space-time itself, to the very smallest as evidenced by the miniature atomic vortices created by atomic particles. The vortical flow in particles' atomic path vortices, as imaged by the CERN 3.7 meter bubble chamber, when measured, is in accordance with ratio of 1:1.618033989. This ratio is a never-ending decimal and is a perfect pattern for infinite flows in time/space. This ratio will repeat the same propor-

cosm of the human body: the coiled current at the base of the spine, a tremendous dynamo of life that when directed outward sustains the physical body and its sensory consciousness; and when consciously directed upward, opens the wonders of the astral cerebrospinal centers.

When the soul, in its subtle sheaths of causal and astral bodies, enters physical incarnation at the time of conception, the entire body grows from the seed cell formed from the united sperm and ovum, beginning with the first vestiges of the medulla oblongata, brain, and spinal cord.

From its original seat in the medulla, the intelligent life energy of the astral body flows downward—activating the specialized powers in the astral cerebrospinal *chakras* that create and give life to the physical spine, nervous system, and all other bodily organs. When the work of the primal life force in creating the body is complete, it comes to rest in a coiled passage in the lowest, or coccygeal, center. The coiled configuration in this astral center gives to the life energy therein the terminology of *kundalini* or serpent force (from Sanskrit *kundala*, "coiled"). Its creative work completed, the concentration of life force in this center is said to be "sleeping" *kundalini,* for as it emanates outward into the body, continuously enlivening the physical region of the senses—of sight, hearing, smell, taste, and touch, and of the earthbound physical creative force of sex—it causes the consciousness to become strongly identified with the delusive dreams of the senses and their domain of activity and desires.

Moses, Jesus, the Hindu yogis, all knew the secret of scientific spiritual life. They unanimously demonstrated that every person who is yet physically minded must master the art of lifting up the serpent force from sensory body consciousness in order to accomplish the first retracing of the inward steps toward Spirit.

Any saint of any religion who has attained God-consciousness has, in effect, withdrawn his consciousness and life force from the sense regions up through the spinal passage and plexuses to the cen-

---

tion infinitely. Many spiral galaxies' arms and these atomic particle paths make a perfect match with the 'golden ratio' and prove that these particles are traveling in infinite flows."

The golden ratio is considered to be the basis of harmony and beauty of form in classical art, architecture, and design—identified as such by (among many others) Pythagoras, Plato, Leonardo da Vinci, and the builders of the Great Pyramids at Giza. *(Publisher's Note)*

ter of God-consciousness in the brain, and thence into omnipresent Spirit.

When one is sitting quietly and calmly, he has partially stilled the life force flowing out into the nerves, releasing it from the muscles; for the moment his body is relaxed. But his peace is easily disturbed by any noise or other sensation that reaches him, because the life energy that continues to flow outward through the coiled path keeps the senses operative.

Yoga: science of switching off the senses and entering superconsciousness

In sleep, the astral life forces are withdrawn not only from the muscles but also from the sensory instruments. Every night each man accomplishes a physical withdrawal of the life force, albeit in an unconscious way; the energy and consciousness in the body retire to the region of the heart, spine, and brain, giving man the rejuvenating peace of subconscious contact with the divine dynamo of all his powers, the soul. Why does man feel joy in sleep? Because when he is in the stage of deep, dreamless sleep, unconscious of the body, physical limitations are forgotten and the mind momentarily taps a higher consciousness.

The yogi knows the scientific art of withdrawing consciously from his sensory nerves, so that no outer disturbance of sight, sound, touch, taste, or smell can gain entry into the inner sanctum of his peace-saturated meditation. Soldiers posted for days on the front lines are able to fall asleep despite the constant roar of battle, because of the body's mechanism of unconsciously withdrawing the energy from the ears and other sensory organs. The yogi reasons that this can be done consciously. By knowledge and practice of the definite laws and scientific techniques of concentration, yogis switch off the senses at will—going beyond subconscious slumber into blissful superconscious interiorization.

Though the soul is given periods of freedom from body consciousness at regular intervals in its existence—for a few hours each night, and for a longer respite between physical incarnations during the sleep of death—the unenlightened man inevitably finds that his unfulfilled earthly yearnings stir him once again to the consciousness of the body. When he has sufficiently recovered from his sensory fatigue, the sleeping man's wants cause him to return to wakefulness, just as unfulfilled urges for earthly experiences impel man's reembodiment after a temporary rest in the astral realm between physical incarnations.

The state of subconsciousness, experienced in sleep, thus affords man only partial transcendence. So long as the life force and consciousness remain tied to the body by the activities of heart, lungs, and other vital organs, man cannot enter superconsciousness. The yogi, in the ecstasy of deep meditation, completely switches off the life force and consciousness from the physical body, refocusing on superconscious perception of the soul's invisible heavenly nature of Bliss. Repeated and prolonged sojourns into the sublimity of ecstasy satisfies the devotee's every desire and frees him from earth-binding compulsions with their cycles of reincarnation.

Whoever cynically thinks that seeking spiritual progress in meditation is a waste of time should reflect on the consummate benefits of being able to lift the consciousness into the elevated states of superconsciousness. In sleep all the dualities and miseries of physical existence are forgotten; indeed, the whole world vanishes into the invisible vastness of subconscious peace. If one learns to produce that mental freedom consciously and at will in *samadhi,* then when afflicted by suffering or confronted by death he is able to transfer his consciousness to the boundless inner kingdom of bliss, which is secreted behind the wakeful and subconscious minds even as the misery-quelling subconsciousness of sleep is hidden behind the conscious mind.

Every human being has learned to enter subconsciousness in sleep; and everyone can likewise master the art of superconscious ecstasy, with its infinitely more enjoyable and restorative experience than can be gleaned from sleep. That higher state bestows the constant awareness that matter is the frozen imaginings of God, as in sleep our dreams and nightmares are our own ephemeral thought-creations, condensed or "frozen" into visual experiences through the objectifying power of our imagination. A dreaming person does not know that a nightmare is unreal until he wakes up. So also, only by awakening in Spirit—oneness with God in *samadhi*—can man disperse the cosmic dream from the screen of his individualized consciousness.

Ascension in Spirit is not easy, because when one is conscious of the body he is in the grip of his second nature of insistent moods and habits. Without timidity, one must vanquish the desires of the body. A body-bound "son of man" cannot ascend to heavenly freedom just by talking about it; he has to know how to open the coiled knot of *kundalini* force at the base of the spine in order to transcend the confinement of the fleshly prison.

Every time one meditates deeply, he automatically helps to reverse the life force and consciousness from matter to God. If the current in the astral knot at the base of the spine is not lifted up by good living, good thoughts, meditation, then materialistic thoughts, worldly thoughts, base thoughts, are emphasized in one's life. With every good act man performs he is "ascending to heaven"—his mind becoming more focused at the Christ Center of heavenly perception; with every evil act he is descending into matter, his attention captivated by the phantoms of delusion.

The true meaning of *kundalini* awakening is little understood. Ignorant teachers often associate *kundalini* with sex force and enshroud

Common fallacies about kundalini awakening

it in mystery to frighten neophytes about the danger of awakening this sacred serpentine power. To confuse the awakening of *kundalini* with the arousal of sex consciousness is an extremely ridiculous and wholly corrupt conception. On the contrary, in *kundalini* awakening the yogi's life force is withdrawn from the sensory nerves, particularly those associated with sex, giving him absolute mastery over sensory and sexual temptations.*

To think that this *kundalini* force can be easily awakened or roused by accident is another fallacy. Awakening the *kundalini* force is exceedingly difficult and cannot be done accidentally. It takes years of concerted meditation under the guidance of a competent guru before one can dream of releasing the heavenly astral body from its bondage to physical confinement by awakening the *kundalini*. One who is able to awaken the *kundalini* fast approaches the state of Christhood. Ascension through that coiled pathway opens the spiritual eye of spherical vision, revealing the whole universe surrounding the body, supported by the vibratory light of heavenly powers.

The senses of sight, hearing, taste, touch, and smell are like five searchlights revealing matter. As the life energy pours outward through those sensory beams, man is attracted by beautiful faces or captivating sounds or enticing scents, flavors, and tactual sensations. It is natural; but what is natural to the body-bound consciousness is unnatural to the soul. But when that divine life energy is withdrawn from the autocratic senses, through the spinal path into the spiritual center of infinite perception in the brain, then the searchlight of astral energy is cast

---

* See also Discourse 41.

onto the boundlessness of eternity to reveal the universal Spirit. The devotee is then attracted by the Supernal Supernatural, the Beauty of all beauties, the Music of all music, the Joy of all joys. He can touch Spirit all over the universe and can hear the voice of God reverberating throughout the spheres. The form dissolves in the Formless. The consciousness of the body, confined to a temporal, little form, illimitably expands into the formless, ever-existing Spirit.

Jesus explains that whosoever believes in the doctrine of lifting the bodily consciousness (son of man) from the physical to the astral by reversing the life force through the coiled passage at the base of the spine, will not perish, that is, be subject to mortal changes of life and death, but will gradually acquire the immutable state—Christ Consciousness, the Son of God.

God's Love Gave to the World His Only Begotten Son

Dialogue With Nicodemus, Part III (Conclusion)

Jesus Never Meant That He Was the Only Savior for All Time

❖

Those Who Disavow Their Divine Source "Condemn" Themselves
to the Jailhouse of Finitude

❖

Expanding One's Consciousness of the Infinite Christ Intelligence

❖

Salvation Comes Not Through Blind Belief,
but Through Direct Experience of God

❖

To "Love Darkness Rather Than Light":
The Soul-Obscuring Power of Bad Habits

❖

The Inner Voice That Leads One to Follow Truth

---

*"The all-pervading light of God, imbued with the universal Christ In-
telligence, silently emanates divine love and wisdom to guide all beings back to the Infinite Consciousness."*

"**F**or God so loved the world, that He gave His only begotten Son, that whosoever believeth in him should not perish, but have everlasting life. For God sent not His Son into the world to condemn the world; but that the world through him might be saved. He that believeth on him is not condemned: but he that believeth not is condemned already, because he hath not believed in the name of the only begotten Son of God.

"And this is the condemnation, that light is come into the world, and men loved darkness rather than light, because their deeds were evil. For every one that doeth evil hateth the light, neither cometh to the light, lest his deeds should be reproved. But he that doeth truth cometh to the light, that his deeds may be made manifest, that they are wrought in God."

—John 3:16—21

God's Love Gave to the World
His Only Begotten Son

Dialogue With Nicodemus, Part III (Conclusion)

"For God so loved the world, that He gave His only begotten Son, that whosoever believeth in him should not perish, but have everlasting life. For God sent not His Son into the world to condemn the world; but that the world through him might be saved. He that believeth on him is not condemned: but he that believeth not is condemned already, because he hath not believed in the name of the only begotten Son of God" (John 3:16–18).

The confusion between "Son of man" and "only begotten Son of God" has created much bigotry in the community of churchianity, which does not understand or acknowledge the human element in Jesus—that he was a man, born in a mortal body, who had evolved his consciousness to become one with God Himself. Not the body of Jesus but the consciousness within it was one with the only begotten Son, the Christ Consciousness, the only reflection of God the Father in creation. In urging people to believe in the only begotten Son, Jesus was referring to this Christ Consciousness, which was fully manifest within himself and all God-realized masters throughout the ages, and is latent within every soul.* Jesus said that all souls who lift their phys-

---

* The writings of many gnostic Christians from the first two centuries A.D., including

273

ical consciousness (Son of man consciousness) to the astral heaven, and then become one with the only begotten Christ Intelligence in all creation, will know eternal life.

Jesus never meant that he was the only savior for all time

Does this Bible passage mean that all who do not accept or believe in Jesus as their Savior will be condemned? This is a dogmatic concept of condemnation. What Jesus meant was that whoever does not realize himself as one with the universal Christ Consciousness is condemned to live and think as a struggling mortal, delimited by sensory boundaries, because he has essentially disunited himself from the Eternal Principle of life.

Jesus never referred to his Son-of-man consciousness, or to his body, as the only savior throughout all time. Abraham and many others were saved even before Jesus was born. It is a metaphysical error to speak of the historical person of Jesus as the only savior. It is the Christ Intelligence that is the universal redeemer. As the sole reflection

---

Basilides, Theodotus, Valentinus, and Ptolemaeus, similarly express an understanding of the "only begotten Son" as a cosmic principle in creation—the divine *Nous* (Greek for intelligence, mind, or thought)—rather than as the person of Jesus. The celebrated church father Origen quotes from the writings of Theodotus that "the only begotten Son is *Nous*" (*Excerpta ex Theodoto* 6.3). In *Gnosis: A Selection of Gnostic Texts* (Oxford, England: Clarendon Press, 1972), German scholar Werner Foerster quotes Irenaeus as saying: "Basilides presents *Nous* originating first from the unoriginate Father." Valentinus, a teacher greatly respected by the Christian congregation in Rome around A.D. 140, held similar views, according to Foerster, believing that "in the Prologue to the Gospel of John, the 'Only-begotten' takes the place of *Nous*."

At the Council of Nicaea (A.D. 325), however, and at the later Council of Constantinople (A.D. 381) the church proclaimed as official doctrine that Jesus himself was, in the words of the Nicene Creed, "the only begotten Son of God, begotten from the Father before all ages, light from light, true God from true God, begotten not made, *homoousios* ['of one substance'] with the Father." After the Council of Constantinople, writes Timothy D. Barnes in *Athanasius and Constantius: Theology and Politics in the Constantinian Empire* (Harvard University Press, 1993), "the emperor enshrined its decisions in law, and he subjected Christians who did not accept the creed of Nicaea and its watchword *homoousios* to legal disabilities. As has long been recognized, these events marked the transition from one distinctive epoch in the history of the Christian church and the Roman Empire to another." From that point on, explains Richard E. Rubenstein in *When Jesus Became God: The Struggle to Define Christianity During the Last Days of Rome* (New York: Harcourt, 1999), the official teaching of the church was that to not accept Jesus as God was to reject God Himself. Through the centuries, this view had enormous and often tragic implications for the relationship between Christians and Jews (and later, Muslims, who regarded Jesus as a divine prophet but not as part of the Godhead), as well as for the non-Christian peoples in the lands later conquered and colonized by European nations. *(Publisher's Note)*

of the Absolute Spirit (the Father) ubiquitous in the world of relativity, the Infinite Christ is the one mediator or link between God and matter, through which all matter-formed individuals—irrespective of different castes and creeds—must pass in order to reach God.* All souls can free their matter-confined consciousness and plunge it into the vastness of Omnipresence by tuning in with Christ Consciousness.

Jesus said: "When ye have lifted up the Son of man, then shall ye know that I am he."† He realized that his physical body was to remain on the earth plane for only a little while, so he made clear to those for whom he was the savior that when his body (son of man) was gone from the earth, people would still be able to find God and salvation by believing in and knowing the omnipresent only begotten Son of God. Jesus emphasized that whosoever would believe in his spirit as the Infinite Christ incarnate in him would discover the path to eternal life through the meditative science of interiorized ascension of the consciousness.

"That whosoever believeth in him should not perish." The forms of nature change, but the Infinite Intelligence immanent in nature is ever unchanged by the mutations of delusion. A child who is temperamentally attached to a snowman will cry when the sun rises high in the heavens and melts that form. Likewise do the children of God suffer who are attached to the mutable human body, which passes through infancy, youth, old age, and death. But those who interiorize their life force and consciousness and concentrate on the inner soul-spark of immortality perceive heaven even while on earth; and, realizing the transcendent essence of life, they are not subject to the pain and suffering inherent in the incessant cycles of life and death.‡

Jesus' majestic words in this passage were meant to convey a divinely encouraging promise of redemption to all humanity. Instead, centuries of misinterpretation have instigated wars of intolerant hatred, torturous inquisitions, and divisive condemnations.

---

* See Discourse 70: "I am the way, the truth, and the life; no man cometh unto the Father except by me" (John 14:6).

† John 8:28 (see Discourse 51).

‡ "The heavens shall be rolled back, and the earth unfurled before your eyes. The one who has life from the Living One sees neither death nor fear."—Gospel of Thomas, verse 111. (*Publisher's Note*)

Lord Krishna in the Bhagavad Gita (II:40) speaks thus about the yoga science: "Even a tiny bit of this real religion protects one from great fear (the colossal sufferings inherent in the repeated cycles of birth and death)."

"For God sent not His Son into the world to condemn the world; but that the world through him might be saved." "The world" in this verse means the whole of God's creation. The Lord's purpose in reflecting His Intelligence in creation, making a structured cosmos possible, was not to devise a jailhouse of finitude where souls are confined as willy-nilly participants in the *danse macabre* of suffering and destruction, but to make Himself accessible as an impelling Force to urge the world from ignorance-darkened material manifestation to an illumined spiritual manifestation. It is true that the vibratory creative manifestation of the Universal Intelligence has originated the myriad attractions of the cosmic playhouse through which man is constantly bemused to move away from the Spirit to material life, to turn away from the Universal Love to the infatuations of human life. Still, perception of the Absolute beyond creation is intimately close through the intermediary of Its reflected Intelligence in creation. Through this contact, the devotee realizes that God sent the Christ Intelligence (His only begotten Son) to produce not a torture chamber but a colossal cosmic motion picture, whose scenes and actors would entertain for a time and ultimately return to the Bliss of Spirit. In the light of that understanding, regardless of one's circumstances in this relative world, one feels his connection with the Universal Spirit and apprehends the vast Intelligence of the Absolute working in all the relativities of Nature. Anyone who believes in and concentrates on that Intelligence—Christ—instead of Its products—the external creation—finds redemption.

Those who disavow their Divine Source "condemn" themselves to the jailhouse of finitude

To think that the Lord condemns nonbelievers as sinners is incongruous. Since the Lord Himself dwells in all beings, condemnation would be utterly self-defeating. God never punishes man for not believing in Him; man punishes himself. If one does not believe in the dynamo and cuts the wires that connect his home to that source, he forfeits the advantages of that electrical power. Likewise, to disavow the Intelligence that is omnipresent in all creation is to deny the consciousness its link with the Source of divine wisdom and love that empowers the process of ascension in Spirit.

Recognition of the immanence of God can begin as simply as expanding one's love in an ever-widening circle. Man condemns himself to limitation whenever he thinks solely of his own little self, his own family, his own nation. Inherent in the evolution of nature and man back to

God is the process of expansion. The exclusivity of family consciousness —"us four and no more"—is wrong. To shut out the larger family of humanity is to shut out the Infinite Christ. One who disconnects himself from the happiness and welfare of others has already condemned himself by isolation from the Spirit that pervades all souls, for he who does not extend himself in love and service to God in others disregards the redeeming power of connection with the universality of Christ. Each human being has been given the power to do good; if he fails to utilize that attribute, his level of spiritual evolution is little better than the instinctive self-interest of the animal.*

Expanding one's consciousness of the infinite Christ Intelligence

Pure love in human hearts radiates the universal Christ-love. To expand continuously the circle of one's love is to attune human consciousness with the only begotten Son. Loving family members is the first step in expanding self-love to those nearby; loving all human beings of whatever race and nationality is to know Christ-love. It is God alone as the Omnipresent Christ who is responsible for all expressions of life. The Lord is painting glorious scenery in the ever-changing clouds and sky. He is creating altars of His fragrant loveliness in the flowers. In everything and everyone—friends and enemies; mountains, forests, ocean, air, the wheeling galactic canopy overarching all—the Christ-devotee sees the one blended light of God. He finds that the myriad expressions of the one Light, often seemingly chaotic in conflict and contradictions, were created by God's intelligence not to delude human beings or to afflict them, but to coax them to seek the Infinite whence they have emerged. One who looks not to the parts but to the whole discerns the purpose of creation: that without exception we are moving inexorably toward universal salvation. All rivers are moving toward the ocean; the rivers of our lives are moving toward God.

The waves on the surface of the ocean constantly change as they sport with the wind and tidal elements, but their oceanic essence remains constant. He who concentrates on one isolated wave of life will

---

* "A human being is part of a whole, called by us the 'Universe,' a part limited in time and space. He experiences himself, his thoughts and feelings, as something separated from the rest—a kind of optical delusion of his consciousness. This delusion is a kind of prison for us, restricting us to our personal desires and to affection for a few persons nearest us. Our task must be to free ourselves from this prison by widening our circles of compassion to embrace all living creatures and the whole of nature in its beauty."—*Albert Einstein*

suffer, because that wave is unstable and will not last. This is what Jesus meant by "condemned": Body-bound man creates his own condemnation by isolating himself from God. To be saved he must reestablish his realization of inseparable unity with the Divine Immanence.

> "In waking, eating, working, dreaming, sleeping,
> Serving, meditating, chanting, divinely loving,
> My soul constantly hums, unheard by any:
> God! God! God!"*

In this way one remains continually aware of his connection with the changeless Divine Intelligence—the Absolute Goodness underlying the provocative riddles of creation.†

"He that believeth on him is not condemned; but he that believeth not is condemned already." This highlights also the role of "belief" in

Salvation comes not through blind belief, but through direct experience of God

the condemnation or noncondemnation of man. Persons who do not understand the immanence of the Absolute in the relative world tend to become either skeptical or dogmatic, because in both cases religion is a matter of blind beliefs. Unable to reconcile the idea of a good God with the seeming evils in creation, the skeptic rejects religious belief as stubbornly as the dogmatist clings to it.

The truths taught by Jesus went far beyond blind belief, which waxes and wanes under the influence of the paradoxical pronouncements of priest and cynic. Belief is an initial stage of spiritual progress necessary to receive the concept of God. But that concept has to be transposed into conviction, into experience. Belief is the precursor of conviction; one has to believe a thing in order to investigate equitably about it. But if one is satisfied only with belief, it becomes dogma—

---

* From *Songs of the Soul* by Paramahansa Yogananda (published by Self-Realization Fellowship).

† "Seemingly eclipsed by My own Yoga-Maya (the delusion born of the triple qualities in Nature), I am unseen by men. The bewildered world knows not Me, the Unborn, the Deathless" (*God Talks With Arjuna: The Bhagavad Gita* VII:25).

"He sees truly who perceives the Supreme Lord present equally in all creatures, the Imperishable amidst the perishing....When a man beholds all separate beings as existent in the One that has expanded Itself into the many, he then merges with Brahman" (*God Talks With Arjuna: The Bhagavad Gita* XIII:27, 30).

narrow-mindedness, a preclusion of truth and spiritual progress. What is necessary is to grow, in the soil of belief, the harvest of direct experience and contact of God. That indisputable realization, not mere belief, is what saves people.

If someone says to me, "I believe in God," I will ask him, "Why do you believe? How do you know there is a God?" If the reply is based on supposition or secondhand knowledge, I will say that he does not truly believe. To hold a conviction one must have some data to support it; otherwise it is mere dogma, and is easy prey for skepticism. If I were to point to a piano and proclaim that it is an elephant, the reason of an intelligent person would revolt against this absurdity. Likewise when dogmas about God are propagated without the validation of experience or realization, sooner or later when tested with a contrary experience reason will assail with speculation the truth about those ideas. As the scorching rays of the sun of analytical inquiry get hotter and hotter, frail unsubstantiated beliefs wilt and wither away, leaving a wasteland of doubt, agnosticism, or atheism. Transcending mere philosophy, scientific meditation attunes the consciousness to the highest mighty truth; with every step the devotee moves toward actual realization and avoids bewildered wandering. To persevere in efforts to verify and experience beliefs through intuitional realization, which can be attained by yoga methods, is to build a real spiritual life that is proof against doubt.

Belief is a powerful force if it leads to the desire and determination to experience Christ. This is what Jesus meant when he urged people to "believe in the name of the only begotten Son of God": Through meditation, withdraw the consciousness and life energy from the senses and matter to intuit the *Aum,* the Word or all-pervading Cosmic Vibratory Energy that is the "name" or active manifestation of the immanent Christ Consciousness.* One can assert incessantly an intellectual belief in Jesus Christ; but if he never actually experiences the Cosmic Christ, as both omnipresent and incarnate in Jesus, the spiritual practicality of his belief is insufficient to save him.

No one can be saved just by repeatedly uttering the Lord's name or praising Him in crescendos of hallelujahs. Not in blind belief in the name of Jesus or the adoration of his personality can the liberating power of his teachings be received. The real worship of Christ is the

---

* See Discourse 1, commentary on John 1:12: "As many as received him, to them gave he power to become the sons of God, even to them that believe on his name."

divine communion of Christ-perception in the wall-less temple of expanded consciousness.

God would not reflect His "only begotten Son" in the world to act like an implacable detective to track down unbelievers for punishment. The redeeming Christ Intelligence, abiding in the bosom of every soul regardless of its bodily accumulation of sins or virtues, waits with infinite patience for each one to awaken in meditation from delusion-drugged sleep to receive the grace of salvation. The person who believes in this Christ Intelligence, and who cultivates with spiritual action the desire to seek salvation through ascension in this reflected consciousness of God, no longer has to wander blindly along the delusive path of error. By measured steps he moves surely toward the redeeming Infinite Grace. But the unbeliever who scorns the thought of this Savior, the only way of salvation, condemns himself to body-bound ignorance and its consequences, until he awakens spiritually.

~

"And this is the condemnation, that light is come into the world, and men loved darkness rather than light, because their deeds were evil. For every one that doeth evil hateth the light, neither cometh to the light, lest his deeds should be reproved. But he that doeth truth cometh to the light, that his deeds may be made manifest, that they are wrought in God" (John 3:19–21).

The all-pervading light of God, imbued with the universal Christ Intelligence, silently emanates divine love and wisdom to guide all beings back to the Infinite Consciousness. The soul, being a microcosm of Spirit, is an ever present light in man to lead him through discriminative intelligence and the intuitive voice of conscience; but all too often the rationalization of desireful habits and whims refuses to follow. Tempted by the Satan of cosmic delusion, man chooses actions that obliterate the light of discriminative inner guidance.

The origin of sin and its resultant physical, mental, and spiritual suffering therefore lies in the fact that the soul's divine intelligence and discrimination are suppressed by man's misuse of his God-given free choice. Though nonunderstanding people ascribe to God their own vengeful propensities, the "condemnation" of which Jesus spoke is not punishment meted out by a tyrannical Creator, but the results man brings on himself by his own actions, according to the law of cause and effect (karma) and the law of habit. Succumbing to desires that keep their consciousness concentrated on and confined in the material world—the "dark- ness" or gross portion of cosmic creation in which the illumining Divine Presence is heavily obscured by the shadows of *maya*-delusion—benighted souls, humanly identified with mortal egos, repeatedly indulge their erroneous ways of living, which then become firmly entrenched in the brain as bad habits of mortal behavior.

To "love darkness rather than light": the soul-obscuring power of bad habits

When Jesus said that men love darkness rather than light, he was referring to the fact that material habits keep millions away from God. He did not mean that all men love darkness—only those who make no effort to resist the temptations of Satan, taking instead the easy way of rolling down the hill of bad habits and thus becoming inured to the darkness of worldly consciousness. Because they shut out the voice of Christ Consciousness whispering in their personal conscience, they shun the infinitely more tempting experience of joy to be had through the good habits urged by the guiding wisdom-light in their souls.

Material temptation promises happiness from gratification of a desire, but giving in to temptation will bring misery, the annihilation of happiness. People who succumb to the allurement of evil often do not realize this until the habit of yielding is established. Those who form bad habits before being exposed to the superior joy of good habits prefer—instead of the slightest effort at self-improvement—to endure the consequences of wrong indulgence because of the prospect of even a little temporary satisfaction. Eventually they become so adapted to surrendering automatically to the instigations of bad habits, despite the inevitable repercussions, that the very thought of forsaking such traitorous pleasure is rejected outright. They balk at the mere suggestion that a little self-control of lust and greed might be beneficial—erroneously believing that they would be unhappy, even tormented, if denied their indulgences.

Restless worldly people, habituated to continuous activity, feel suffocated at the thought of the deliberate stillness of meditation. They disregard the soul-comfort offered in God-communion, convinced that they are far more at ease in catering to their second-nature tendencies —no matter how potentially destructive—of worry, nervousness, useless talk, and material desires, rather than endeavoring to experience an as-yet-unfamiliar joy of God-contact. The first priority of most persons, after awakening each morning, is a hasty breakfast followed by a headlong rush into their routine of busyness. To precede the day's activities by allocating time to cultivating God-centered inner peace and happiness through the spiritual habit of meditation is altogether foreign to them. Accustomed to the darkness of worldly ignorance, they abhor the Christ light eternally present in their souls. Their perverse habit of worldly attachment can be overcome only by a stronger attachment to divine peace and bliss resulting from nurturing the opposite good habit of daily meditation.

Thus Jesus' emphasis that by the light of soul awakening, the mortal habit of preferring the delusive darkness of materiality can be dispelled from man's consciousness. With repeated acts of will power to meditate regularly and deeply, one attains the supremely satisfying Bliss-contact of God and can recall that joy to his consciousness anytime, anywhere.

In contrasting men of darkness and men of light, Jesus cited the universal psychological error committed by the habit-enslaved: They avoid all thoughts of the greater fulfillments of mind and body awaiting them in the practice of good habits, because they fear that in giving up their imagined pleasures of the flesh they will suffer the pangs of deprivation. Just as the owl loves the nighttime and hides away during the day, so persons governed by dark habits shun the light of self-improvement.

Persons who by meditation have formed the habit of peacefulness gravitate naturally toward the company of high-minded and saintly souls, just as materially restless individuals prefer worldly associates. People of bad habits seek bad company and avoid those who are virtuous; but this is foolish, because if they mix openheartedly with those who have good habits they will find an automatic mechanism at work that causes their evil compulsion to leave them. The right company provides the essential impetus for improving oneself. To imitate the good is to engage in good actions; good actions form good habits; and good habits will dislodge bad habits.

But somehow evil people feel rebuked in the company of the good, though the really good never scold persons for their past bad behavior if they are seriously trying to reform themselves. One should never heap scornful judgment on the sinner, for he is all too familiar with the self-tortures resulting from his sin. He ought not to be further punished by condemnation or hatred; but if he does not heed a loving, helping hand, he should be given a chance to learn his own lessons in the school of hard knocks. In time he will be ready and willing to benefit from constructive advice.

As long as a person is intoxicated with evil thoughts and ways, his dark mentality will hate the light of truth. The one good thing about bad habits, however, is that they seldom keep their promises. They are eventually found out to be inveterate liars. That is why souls cannot forever be deceived or enslaved. Though people of bad habits initially recoil from the thought of better living, after they have had enough of evil ways and reach the point of satiety, and have suffered enough from the consequences, they turn for relief toward the wisdom-light of God, despite any entrenched bad habits that must yet be vanquished. If they continually practice ways of living in harmony with Truth, then in that light they come to realize the joy and inner peace brought by self-control and good habits.

"But he that doeth truth cometh to the light, that his deeds may be made manifest, that they are wrought in God." Truth is a very slippery term; Christ himself refused to define it when interrogated by Pilate.* Absolute standards cannot always be applied in this relative world. To adhere to truth in everyday living, man must be guided by intuitive wisdom; that alone illumines unerringly what

The inner voice that leads one to follow truth

is right and virtuous in any circumstance. The voice of conscience is the voice of God. Everyone has it, but not everyone listens to it. Those who have a trained sensitivity can detect wrong by the inner disturbance of uneasiness it engenders. Virtue is known by the vibration of harmony it creates within. Always the light of God is there, guiding through discriminative wisdom and through calm feeling. If one does not disturb feeling by emotion, or discriminative intelligence by rationalized wrong behavior, he will be aided by that inner voice. To follow the light of inner wisdom-guidance is the way to true happiness, the way to be always of God, the way to disengage oneself from the coercive influence of bad habits that usurp man's decision-making power.

Enslaved by bad habits, so many people become psychological antiques—never changing, year after year committing the same faults,

---

* John 18:38.

deteriorating in their fixations. But the divine seeker, trying every day to change something that is not good in his nature, gradually transcends his old habit-bound material ways. His deeds and his very life are re-created, "wrought in God"; he is in truth born anew. Adhering to the good habit of daily scientific meditation, he sees and is baptized in the light of Christ-wisdom, the divine energy of the Holy Ghost, which actually erases the electrical pathways in the brain formed by bad habits of thought and action. His spiritual eye of intuitive perception is opened, bestowing not only unerring guidance on the path of life, but the vision of and entry into God's heavenly kingdom—and ultimately, oneness with His omnipresent consciousness.

DISCOURSE 16

Rejoicing in the Voice
of the Bridegroom

"He Must Increase, but I Must Decrease":
What John the Baptist Meant

❖

Symbolic Meaning of the Divine "Bridegroom"

❖

"Voice of the Bridegroom": Cosmic Sound of Aum

❖

True Meaning of "the Wrath of God"

"In the womb of Mother Nature, Spirit gives birth to creation....Jesus was one with the omnipresent positive consciousness of Spirit....He was a complete manifestation of God — the Bridegroom, universal Spirit wedded to universal Nature."

After these things came Jesus and his disciples into the land of Judea; and there he tarried with them, and baptized. And John also was baptizing in Aenon near to Salim, because there was much water there: and they came, and were baptized. For John was not yet cast into prison.

Then there arose a question between some of John's disciples and the Jews about purifying. And they came unto John, and said unto him, "Rabbi, he that was with thee beyond Jordan, to whom thou barest witness, behold, the same baptizeth, and all men come to him."

John answered and said, "A man can receive nothing, except it be given him from heaven. Ye yourselves bear me witness, that I said, I am not the Christ, but that I am sent before him.

"He that hath the bride is the bridegroom: but the friend of the bridegroom, which standeth and heareth him, rejoiceth greatly because of the bridegroom's voice: this my joy therefore is fulfilled. He must increase, but I must decrease.

"He that cometh from above is above all: he that is of the earth is earthly, and speaketh of the earth: he that cometh from heaven is above all. And what he hath seen and heard, that he testifieth; and no man receiveth his testimony. He that hath received his testimony hath set to his seal that God is true.

"For he whom God hath sent speaketh the words of God: for God giveth not the Spirit by measure unto him. The Father loveth the Son, and hath given all things into his hand.

"He that believeth on the Son hath everlasting life: and he that believeth not the Son shall not see life; but the wrath of God abideth on him."

When therefore the Lord knew how the Pharisees had heard that Jesus made and baptized more disciples than John, (though Jesus himself baptized not, but his disciples,) he left Judea, and departed again into Galilee. And he must needs go through Samaria.

—John 3:22—4:4

The Childhood of Jesus

And the child grew, and waxed strong in spirit, filled with wisdom: and the grace of God was upon him.

—Luke 2:40

It is related in the Infancy Gospels that father Joseph found the extraordinary talent of his son of incredible assistance in his carpentry trade—not as an artisan with hammer and chisel, but when by error "Joseph had any thing to make longer or shorter, or wider or narrower, the Lord Jesus would stretch forth his hand towards it. And presently it would become as Joseph would have it."...This was as elementary for Jesus as later it would be for him to change water into wine, or to multiply the loaves and fishes.

—Paramahansa Yogananda

Drawing by Heinrich Hofmann

Rejoicing in the Voice of the Bridegroom

❧

The opening verses of this Discourse again call attention to the difference between symbolic baptism with water and the true baptism of Spirit. John observed the outer purificatory rite of physical immersion in water to highlight the superior spiritual initiation of baptism with the Holy Ghost that Jesus as the long-awaited Christ had come to bestow. As a God-ordained savior, Jesus had begun to attract masses of souls with the magnetism of his divine love and power.

The fact that Jesus was drawing larger crowds than the theretofore acclaimed John the Baptist became part of a dispute between some of John's disciples and the Jews about purification. When they brought to John the report of Jesus' fame, John reminded them of his previous commendation of Jesus, who had come with a greater role to play than himself in manifesting God on earth.* It was thus the will of God that the renown of Jesus would increase while his own role would now decrease. He pointed out to them that man could have no powers except those received from the Heavenly Spirit. This does not mean that souls are specially created with individual advantages and limitations predestined by Heaven. Spirit is the fountain, and all created things—stars, souls, thoughts, universes—are Its spray. In the case of each evolving soul a person

> *"He must increase, but I must decrease":* what John the Baptist meant

_____

* See Discourse 6.

manifests God more or less completely according to the right use or misuse of his innate divine power. But as applicable to liberated souls who return to earth at God's behest, John's words mean that each is individually invested by God with those powers and characteristics that would best serve his divine commission and support the delusive realism of the cosmic drama by making real, in the relative sense, the experiences they undergo in their incarnate portrayals. So here John is referring specifically to the will of God that designated significant differences between himself, who came in this incarnation as an ordinary saint, and Jesus, who incarnated as a world savior.

Advanced souls, those who are able partially or fully to manifest the Divine as a result of promoting their own spiritual evolution through incarnations of endeavor, are sent by God to help in the accomplishment of His divine plan on earth. Saints and prophets who come to earth to aid in the upliftment of souls, but who are not fully liberated or have no world mission to perform, may be called partial incarnations (*khanda avatars*). Those liberated masters in whom God openly manifests as a world savior, or who have a divine dispensation to facilitate the redemption of the masses, may be called full incarnations of God (*purna avatars*). Jesus Christ, Bhagavan Krishna, Mahavatar Babaji, Lahiri Mahasaya, Swami Sri Yukteswar, and many others down the ages have been full manifestations of God. John the Baptist, though liberated in his previous incarnation as Elijah, was sent on earth as John in a more humble but distinctive role: to bear witness of a world savior; to declare the special divine dispensation of the coming of Jesus.

It is providential that masters who come on earth with a public mission be declared, or properly introduced, so that people may recognize their importance and attentively receive their spiritual services. As it takes an expert gemologist to rightly declare the value of a gem, so preeminent incarnations, divinely humble and never trumpeting their own greatness, can be identified only by qualified souls. Thus was John sent to testify to the God-given credentials of Jesus, so that people might readily know him and embrace his wisdom.

John's analogy of Jesus as the divine Bridegroom is a symbolism that appears in several passages in the New Testament.* Similarly, one of the epithets applied to Bhagavan Krishna, the Christ of India, is

---

* E.g., Matthew 9:15; 25:1.

Madhava: *Ma,* Prakriti, or Primordial Mother Nature; *dhava,* husband. Both Jesus and Krishna, as perfect embodiments of the omnipresent Krishna-Christ Consciousness, were con-
sorts of the Divine Spirit as Prakriti, or Primordial   *Symbolic meaning of the*
Mother Nature, which has created and become all   *divine "Bridegroom"*
matter and space.

To manifest creation, Spirit causes a vibration of duality, dividing
Its One Being into the transcendent inactive Creator and His active
Creative Power: God the Father and Cosmic Mother Nature. Spirit
and Nature, subject and object, positive and negative, attraction and
repulsion—it is duality that makes possible the birth of the many out
of the One. In His active objectifying Creative Vibration (Holy Ghost
or Maha-Prakriti), God Himself is subjectively present in an unchanged, unaffected reflection, the Universal Spirit in creation: *Ku-*
tastha Chaitanya, Krishna or Christ Consciousness. That immanent
guiding Intelligence—the subjective consciousness or soul of the universe—empowers the structuring of the omnipotent Vibratory Force
into myriad objective manifestations; in the womb of Mother Nature,
Spirit thus gives birth to creation.*

Jesus was called the Bridegroom because his consciousness was one
with the omnipresent positive consciousness of Spirit united with the
negative vibration of Cosmic Nature, the Bride, that engenders the vast
universe. The positive universal consciousness flows toward Spirit,
counterbalancing the outward flow of negative matter-projecting Cosmic Energy or Nature. It is by becoming one with the Christ Intelligence
that a man of realization can see Spirit and Nature together—beholding the Imperishable amidst the perishing, and realizing the endless permutations of life, change, and death as the ecstatic dance of Spirit and
Nature on the stage of infinite space and time. "Whatever exists—every
being, every object; the animate, the inanimate—understand that to be
born from the union of *Kshetra* and *Kshetrajna* (Nature and Spirit). He
sees truly who perceives the Supreme Lord present equally in all crea-

---

* In the noncanonical Gospel of the Hebrews, which scholars date to the early second
century, Jesus is quoted as referring to the Holy Ghost as "my mother." The great
church father Origen (c. 185–254) wrote in his *Commentary on John 2:12:* "And if
any accept the Gospel of the Hebrews, here the Savior says: 'Even so did my mother,
the Holy Spirit, take me by one of my hairs, and carry me to the great Mount Tabor'"
(quoted in *Gospel Parallels,* by Burton H. Throckmorton, Jr.; Nashville: Thomas Nel-
son, 1992). *(Publisher's Note)*

tures, the Imperishable amidst the perishing."* Ordinary persons see only Nature because their consciousness is focused externally on the screen of material vibration; but when the consciousness is reversed into the Cosmic Booth from which all pictures of creation are projected, then it is possible to perceive the singularity of the Christ Consciousness present in all space—to realize that in truth it is Spirit that has become creation, that all things are naught else but a glorious diversification of God. Jesus had reached this state; he was a complete manifestation of God—the Bridegroom, universal Spirit wedded to universal Nature.

When John spoke of his rejoicing in the Bridegroom's voice, he was referring to the Cosmic Sound of *Aum* (Amen), the active vibration that

"Voice of the Bridegroom": cosmic sound of Aum

is the voice or "witness" of the inherent Christ Intelligence.† That voice of Cosmic Vibration can be heard through practice of a specific Self-Realization Fellowship method of yoga meditation.‡ John had heard the Cosmic Sound and perceived the Christ Intelligence in it, but it was on Jesus that he focused attention as the one who had penetrated beyond the Cosmic Sound and Nature vibration into the pure realm of Christ Intelligence contained within them. John contrasted himself as having had glimpses of the omnipresent wisdom of Christ, whereas the infinite consciousness of Jesus actually felt itself as the Christ in every unit of vibrating space in all creation.

The advancing yogi first *listens* to the Cosmic Sound within his body, and then becomes able to hear it in any part of creation. Next, he *feels* the Christ Intelligence in the sound in his own body, and then he feels the Christ Intelligence throughout creation. John refers to himself as "the friend of the bridegroom, which standeth and heareth him...this my joy therefore is fulfilled." He had heard the Cosmic Sound and indirectly felt the presence of Christ Intelligence in it. He rejoiced at being in the company of Jesus who as the divine Bridegroom, one with the Spirit as the positive reflection of omnipresent Christ Consciousness, had won as his Bride the Universal Spirit manifesting as Universal Nature. He who perceives Spirit as both transcendental and immanent is one with Spirit as the Bride, God's consciousness omnipresent in and as

---

* *God Talks With Arjuna: The Bhagavad Gita* XIII:26–27.

† "These things saith the Amen, the faithful and true witness, the beginning of the creation of God" (Revelation 3:14).

‡ See page 1575.

Cosmic Mother Nature (Maha-Prakriti), as well as one with Spirit as transcendent consciousness in creation as Christ Consciousness and beyond manifestation as Cosmic Consciousness, the Absolute.

In his reference to Jesus, John extols Christ-illumined souls, those whose consciousness is not actuated by downward-pulling earthly desires but by the uplifting Cosmic Consciousness from above: "He that cometh from above." Body-bound souls, being identified with earthly things, focus their attention exclusively matterward: "He that is of the earth is earthly." Spiritually awakened souls, attuned with and guided by Cosmic Consciousness, are thus said to "come from heaven" and are "above" all others; they have ascended higher on the ladder of evolution and enjoy the transcendent awareness of the supernal heavenly kingdom within.

John further points out that divine souls do not speak from book knowledge or from intellectual imagination that fancies its own realisms and absolutes; they speak only the truth that they hear, perceive, and see through the all-knowing power of soul intuition. No mortal man, who depends on the testimony of his limited senses, can grasp the depth and magnitude of truth perceived by persons of Self-realization; but uplifted souls who develop their intuition by meditation can not only comprehend the truth declared by prophets, but prove it to themselves. Through their own experience, they authenticate with the unchallengeable "seal" of intuitional conviction the seer's ecstatic proclamation that God is the only true Eternal Substance, and that all phenomena of Nature are but waves of Spirit playing on the Infinite Bosom.

The words of guidance of a true messenger of God come forth only according to what God speaks through him. On such souls God bestows His wisdom not in proportion to the caliber of their acquired intellectual powers, but with the outpouring of measureless grace that characterizes an all-loving Father. Those that are one with God are God themselves.

As the only reflected Intelligence of transcendental God the Father in vibratory creation, the Son or Christ Intelligence has control over all matter—God "hath given all things into his hand." Christ Consciousness is God's Divine Love—"the Father loveth the Son"—reflected in creation and in liberated saints in all its purity, coaxing created beings with its magnetic attraction back to blissful unity in Spirit. Any devotee who believes in, and gradually becomes one with, this immutable Immanent Intelligence—by merging with the Cosmic Sound of *Aum* heard in meditation—shall receive the everlasting life of Christ.

The only way to Cosmic Consciousness consists in penetrating through the encrusting shell of material vibrations to the living essence

True meaning of "the wrath of God"

of immanent Christ Intelligence. Persons whose eyes are shut to the light of Cosmic Vibration and the Christ Intelligence hidden in matter fail to reach God. "He that believeth not the Son...the wrath of God abideth on him." God is both angry and sorry for such souls, as a mother would be angry and sorry for a son who hurts himself by misuse of his free choice. The "wrath of God" is the Biblical terminology for the Lord's just law of karma, which metes out the consequential effects of a man's self-initiated actions. God need not intervene to impose a decree apart from His relentless and exacting karmic law; but His compassion that mitigates karmic effects may be withheld, blocked by man's sheer ignorance and oftentimes willful stupidity.

After God announced the coming of Jesus through John, and showed to the Pharisees the magnetic drawing power of Jesus—attracting crowds of soul-bees by the Divine Fragrance manifested in him—Jesus left Judea and departed for Galilee to preach there the Gospel (revelations of truth, which God spells* or speaks through man's intuition). He had a special mission to redeem a fallen disciple of former incarnations, the woman of Samaria. That is why it was written: "And he must needs go through Samaria."

---

* *Spell* derives from the Old English word *spel,* "talk." See "gospels" in glossary.

DISCOURSE 17

The Woman of Samaria

The Redemption of a Fallen Past-Life Disciple

❖

Jesus Shunned the Evils of Racial Prejudice
and Caste Consciousness

❖

The "Living Water" of Divine Bliss in the Soul

❖

Sincere Cooperation With One's Guru Can Save
Even the Worst Sinner

❖

How a Master Perceives the Innermost Thoughts of a Disciple

*"The meeting of Jesus with the woman of Samaria was not a chance
encounter, but a divinely devised guru-disciple reunion."*

$\mathcal{T}$**hen cometh he to a city** of Samaria, which is called Sychar, near to the parcel of ground that Jacob gave to his son Joseph. Now Jacob's well was there. Jesus therefore, being wearied with his journey, sat thus on the well: and it was about the sixth hour.

There cometh a woman of Samaria to draw water: Jesus saith unto her, "Give me to drink." (For his disciples were gone away unto the city to buy meat.)

Then saith the woman of Samaria unto him, "How is it that thou, being a Jew, askest drink of me, which am a woman of Samaria?" for the Jews have no dealings with the Samaritans.

Jesus answered and said unto her, "If thou knewest the gift of God, and who it is that saith to thee, 'Give me to drink'; thou wouldest have asked of him, and he would have given thee living water."

The woman saith unto him, "Sir, thou hast nothing to draw with, and the well is deep: from whence then hast thou that living water? Art thou greater than our father Jacob, which gave us the well, and drank thereof himself, and his children, and his cattle?"

Jesus answered and said unto her, "Whosoever drinketh of this water shall thirst again: But whosoever drinketh of the water that I shall give him shall never thirst; but the water that I shall give him shall be in him a well of water springing up into everlasting life."

The woman saith unto him, "Sir, give me this water, that I thirst not, neither come hither to draw."

Jesus saith unto her, "Go, call thy husband, and come hither."

The woman answered and said, "I have no husband."

Jesus said unto her, "Thou hast well said, 'I have no husband': for thou hast had five husbands; and he whom thou now hast is not thy husband: in that saidst thou truly."

The woman saith unto him, "Sir, I perceive that thou art a prophet."

—John 4:5–19

294

The Woman of Samaria

Then cometh he to a city of Samaria, which is called Sychar, near to the parcel of ground that Jacob gave to his son Joseph. Now Jacob's well was there. Jesus therefore, being wearied with his journey, sat thus on the well: and it was about the sixth hour.

There cometh a woman of Samaria to draw water: Jesus saith unto her, "Give me to drink." (For his disciples were gone away unto the city to buy meat.)

Then saith the woman of Samaria unto him, "How is it that thou, being a Jew, askest drink of me, which am a woman of Samaria?" for the Jews have no dealings with the Samaritans.

Jesus answered and said unto her, "If thou knewest the gift of God, and who it is that saith to thee, 'Give me to drink'; thou wouldest have asked of him, and he would have given thee living water" (John 4:5–10).

The meeting of Jesus with the woman of Samaria was not a chance encounter, but a divinely devised guru-disciple reunion. The Samaritan woman was a morally lost disciple of a previous incarnation whom Jesus wanted to redeem.

As with many great masters, Jesus had among his following a number of disciples from past lives. The guru-disciple covenant they had established in previous lifetimes drew them together again by the unseen magnetism of divine law. These were not only the twelve who had qualified themselves in past incarnations to be among the inner circle of Jesus' disciples; others there were as well. Jesus recognized those disciples who were continuing the relationship they had begun with him in a former life as distinguished from those who were coming to him for the first time for enlightenment. However, even a close associate or past-life disciple of

The redemption of a fallen past-life disciple

a great master may not be a perfected devotee, as was demonstrated in the ignominious betrayal of Jesus by his disciple Judas. It is for the sake of the unredeemed that the guru must come back to earth: By taking human incarnation or by appearing in vision to guide and bless those who are in tune—or sometimes even by using the instrumentality of another qualified master—the God-ordained savior continues to help his disciples when their own efforts permit him to do so, until all are finally liberated. No matter what their degree of advancement, disciples once accepted by a true guru hold a secure place in that relationship as they gradually progress, and ofttimes falter, incarnation after incarnation.

The woman of Samaria was one such disciple. It appears that during his trip from Judea to Galilee Jesus purposely planned this meeting, waiting alone at Jacob's well where the woman would be likely to encounter him while the disciples went into the city to obtain food.

Contrary to the prevailing attitude at that time, that Samaritans were shunned by the Jews as "low-caste," Jesus engaged the woman

Jesus shunned the evils of racial prejudice and caste consciousness

in conversation and asked her to draw water for him. The Samaritan's astonishment at Jesus' request to her highlights the differentiation observed by the people in the time of Jesus between the Jews and the Samaritans; the Jews being considered of a higher religion and race as compared to the Samaritans,* even as the Brahmins in India are held by an artificial standard to be high-caste and spiritually superior to the lower castes of society.

Christ did not see people in terms of their race, creed, or social position. He saw the Divine in all. It is ego consciousness that prejudicially discriminates among God's children, creating boundaries of exclusivity. Thus the ordinary human being relates to and identifies with his family first; then his neighbors, or persons of his own caste

---

* Sychar (or Shechem), where Jesus' encounter with the woman of Samaria took place, was located about twenty-five miles north of Jerusalem, at the foot of Mt. Gerizim. Samaria, the district between Judea and Galilee, was home to a people of mixed ancestry. Centuries earlier, when Palestine was conquered by the Assyrians, the Jewish population of that area intermarried with foreigners who were sent to colonize the land, and who adopted some of the Jewish religious beliefs. The Samaritans were the descendants of this cultural medley. Being of mixed race, they were viewed with contempt by most full-blooded Jews.

or social position, or members of his own religion; then his race; and finally his nation. There his consciousness stops—his ego imprisoned in concentric barriers, cribbed in an isolated corner of its insular world, cut off from the universality that Jesus and the great ones lived by: "God hath made of one blood all nations."*

In India, rigidified caste consciousness has been productive of many evils.† In America and other lands, bigotry based on color and national origin has created injustice, hatred, and racial conflict. And throughout the world, blind assertion of the superiority of one religion over all others has perpetuated misunderstanding, fear, and hostility. The Christian missionary calls the Hindus heathen; with equal disdain the Brahmin priests of India permit no Westerners to defile with their presence the holy temples of Hinduism—though all love the same one God.

So long as any form of arrogant, intolerant consciousness will remain, war and great miseries will continue to visit the earth. The most powerful ammunition for the guns of war, and the cause of so many other forms of mass destruction and suffering, are selfishness and the limiting race consciousness of egoistic human beings. The Heavenly Father is the progenitor of every race; His children are duty-bound to love their whole family of nations. Any country that goes against that principle of love for humankind will not long prosper, for lack of international harmony and mutual cooperation puts a nation in conflict not only with its neighbors but with Divine Law, the Organizing Principle of the cosmos. Through evolutionary coaxings of the Christ Intelligence, with Its cosmic heartbeat of coalescent love, God is trying to bring unity in the universe. Those who are in tune with this cosmic beneficence, as was Jesus, have love and understanding that embraces the totality of humanity, setting the standard for all of God's children to follow.

---

* Acts 17:26.

† Caste demarcations developed in India in a higher age of Vedic wisdom as a natural form of social organization that honored and gave place to each individual according to qualifications and the capacity to serve society as a whole. Those whose innate qualities made them fit to be spiritual teachers or clergy were called Brahmins; others, whose nature suited the duties of soldiers and rulers, were called Kshatriyas; those inclined to business were known as Vaishyas; and persons whose chief contribution to society lay in manual labor belonged to the fourth caste, that of Sudras. As the spiritual understanding of humanity declined, caste divisions began to be based not on individual merit but on heredity. Thus evolved the manifold injustices and evil divisiveness that Mahatma Gandhi and other saints of India down the centuries worked tirelessly to abolish. [See *God Talks With Arjuna: The Bhagavad Gita,* commentary on 11:31.—*Publisher's Note*]

To Jesus no one was a stranger; he loved unconditionally, and gauged individuals solely by their inner qualifications: their spiritual sincerity and receptivity to Truth.

Thus, despite the woman of Samaria's expectation that Jesus would shun her as a racial outcast, he asked her to share with him the water she drew from the well, a gesture of friendliness through which she could become acquainted with him. Having perceived that as a fallen disciple of past lives she had the potential to be resurrected spiritually, Jesus had created this opportunity, during the absence of his other disciples, so that without disturbance he could give to her the everlasting elixir of divine awakening. When he said, "If thou knewest the gift of God, and who it is that saith to thee," Jesus was hinting to the woman that God had blessed her in previous incarnations with the greatest of all gifts, a divine savior (guru) who had followed her to this life to redeem her. Jesus sought to stir her dormant memory of the past; thus he intimated that if she but knew that it was her God-given guru who was asking for the drink, she would hasten to ask him for the living water of God's contact, without which no human being can quench his spiritual thirst.*

⁓

The woman saith unto him, "Sir, thou hast nothing to draw with, and the well is deep: from whence then hast thou that living water? Art thou greater than our father Jacob, which gave us the well, and drank thereof himself, and his children, and his cattle?"

Jesus answered and said unto her, "Whosoever drinketh of this water shall thirst again: But whosoever drinketh of the water that I shall give him shall never thirst; but the water that I shall give him shall be in him a well of water springing up into everlasting life" (John 4:11–15).

The woman of Samaria, steeped in ignorance, could not yet understand the oblique reference of Jesus to "living water," hence her foolish question: "[Since] thou hast nothing to draw with...from whence then hast thou that living water?"

---

* "O Lord, the hope of Israel, all that forsake Thee shall be ashamed, and they that depart from me shall be written in the earth, because they have forsaken the Lord, the fountain of living waters" (Jeremiah 17:13). See also Discourse 50, "out of his belly shall flow rivers of living water."

Jesus spoke of the inner experience, the uncovering, with the help of one's guru, of the wellspring of divinity within the soul. He said, in effect, that whosoever depends solely upon physical sustenance remains bound by mortal body con- *The "living water" of* sciousness, with its never-ending thirst for sensory *divine bliss in the* experiences and the fulfillment of material desires. *soul* Oblivious of the all-sustaining, all-desire-quenching Divine Life and Bliss within his soul, the material man will die unfulfilled. His yearnings will remain with him even after death, a latent thirst that will impel him to reincarnate again and yet again in search of satisfaction.

But whosoever drinks of the fountain of eternal bliss in God will find the thirst of every desire of all his incarnations quenched forever. Souls who discover the everlasting Well of Bliss within themselves are never thirsty for the evanescent satisfactions of a mortal existence and its material desires.

The worldly man, on the other hand, having lost his soul contact with God-Bliss, tries to satisfy himself with pleasures of the senses—a foolish expectation. Millions of people die of broken hearts, having tried vainly to "lay up for themselves upon earth" a treasure of lasting happiness garnered from material things, when joy inexhaustible in God awaits the seeker in the temple of meditation. Thus did the Lord speak to Prophet Jeremiah: "For My people have committed two evils; they have forsaken Me the fountain of living waters, and hewed them out cisterns, broken cisterns, that can hold no water." *

Gratifying the body and ego with material experiences and possessions can never compensate man for his lost infinite soul-happiness. Indeed, the materialist's quest achieves the opposite of what he intended, making him susceptible instead to every form of sorrow and suffering inherent in the cosmic scheme of dualities.

Mortal desires promise happiness, but give sorrow instead. "Because sense pleasures spring from outward contacts, and have beginning and end (are ephemeral), they are begetters only of misery. No sage seeks happiness from them." †

The soul of even the most worldly person is inwardly conscious of its supernal Bliss, lost only in its outward identification with the

---

* Jeremiah 2:13.

† *God Talks With Arjuna: The Bhagavad Gita* v:22.

299

flesh. That is why it can never remain contented for long with the temporary pleasures of the senses. If one has lost a diamond, he will not satisfy himself by replacing it with bits of broken glass that he finds shining in the sunlight. The glitter of sense pleasures, no matter how alluring, soon yields disappointment, satiety, and disgust.

"The thirst of incarnations is slaked by whosoever will drink the effervescent waters of the well of Divine Bliss in the soul, springing up into everlasting life"—this is the wisdom Jesus sought to convey to the woman at the well.

~

> *The woman saith unto him, "Sir, give me this water, that I thirst not, neither come hither to draw."*
>
> *Jesus saith unto her, "Go, call thy husband, and come hither."*
>
> *The woman answered and said, "I have no husband."*
>
> *Jesus said unto her, "Thou hast well said, 'I have no husband': for thou hast had five husbands; and he whom thou now hast is not thy husband: in that saidst thou truly."*
>
> *The woman saith unto him, "Sir, I perceive that thou art a prophet" (John 4:15–19).*

A flicker of receptivity stirred in the woman. So Jesus tested the character of this fallen disciple, the degree of her degradation. He asked her to call her husband; and when she said that she had no husband, he was pleased with her truthfulness in tacitly admitting that the man with whom she was presently coupled was not a lawful spouse. Jesus then revealed that he knew of her promiscuous behavior in having had five such illicit relationships. Rather than lying to defend herself, she recognized Jesus as a divine prophet who alone could have known her secret. In this moment of spiritual submission, Jesus saw the genuine quality of her sincerity. Her immorality lay like a clay crust over her pure, truth-loving soul, hiding it only temporarily.

Sincere cooperation with one's guru can save even the worst sinner

Insincerity, prevarication, and treachery toward a guru-preceptor are devastating sins, for these are deliberate, willful transgressions and, as such, are worse evils than flesh transgressions, which are to a considerable extent due to instinctive compulsion.

300

Some persons, owing to immoral behavior in a past life, are born with a compelling inclination that overrules almost all sense of shame, church threats, conscience, social discomfiture, or efforts toward self-control. Sincerity in recognizing and acknowledging their faults, and in following the advice of their spiritual doctor, will give these individuals mental and moral strength that will remedy the malady.

The disciple who is insincere toward his guru in attempting to hide or rationalize his moral disease shuts out the healing help of the master. Hypocritical evasion causes the moral transgression in the error-stricken disciple to spread tenaciously within him. To hide moral disease from the spiritual doctor is dangerous to spiritual health, just as concealing physical symptoms of disease from a medical doctor imperils bodily health.

In any case, the guru is not deceived, no matter how cunning the evasive disciple. The master can perceive the inmost character of a disciple exactly and immediately. Masters rarely, if ever, make errors in discerning the qualities of those who come to them. Even when a guru accepts a disciple who later exhibits evil or treacherous tendencies, it is not because the master was unknowing. Jesus had his Judas; why did he accept such a follower? There was a karmic connection, in that Judas had been his disciple in a previous life. When a guru sees the soul of a disciple fallen in ignorance, his God-given duty and heartfelt concern leave no choice but to help. Every soul can be rescued, no matter how entangled in error, if the mind makes a genuine commitment to cooperate spiritually. The guru provides repeated opportunities for the disciple to make this breakthrough from ignorance. Though one's sins be as deep as the ocean, still he can be saved if he is sincere and loyal to his master, linking himself with the channel that draws him to God.

How did Jesus know the intimate details of the life history of the woman of Samaria? Did Jesus read her thoughts from her subconscious, conscious, or superconscious mind? If a person holds his mind absolutely still, free from the oscillations of restless thoughts, he can reflect within him the thoughts that pass through the consciousness of another person. This is only possible when one is versed in the art of subduing his own thinking for any desired length of time; then, on the virgin unexposed film of his mind, he can "photograph" any thought that is present in the conscious mind of another individual.

How a master perceives the innermost thoughts of a disciple

It entails greater mental power to know the buried subconscious thought-experiences of others. Subconscious thoughts are those that remain below the conscious mind, hidden behind its closed doors. By consciously projecting one's subconscious mind into the subconscious mind of another person, one can know the tabloid thought-experiences closeted there. This is possible when by the right method of concentration one can delve into his own subconscious mind and feel the experiences stored there without being intruded upon or influenced by the thoughts of the conscious mind.

In the third and more advanced way, a master whose mind has plumbed the depths of meditation and who has gained control of his all-seeing eye of intuition can transfer his consciousness to the region of soul bliss of the superconscious mind. The superconsciousness hides behind the restlessness of conscious life and the fanciful dream state and memories of subconscious life, and knows everything, not by reason or sense perception, but by God-given intuition, the direct all-knowing power of the soul. This intuitive power can be developed by learning the step-by-step methods of scientific deepest meditation that lead to Self-realization.

With fully developed superconscious intuition, one can instantly feel all that is going on in the consciousness of another individual, all that is hidden in his subconscious mind, and all the prenatal experiences of former incarnations that are stored permanently in his superconsciousness. Jesus had this usable, controlled power of intuition; he knew at once everything that lay in the conscious, subconscious, and superconscious minds of the woman of Samaria.

Jesus openly manifested his omniscience by revealing to his fallen former disciple his knowledge of her moral indiscretions. A master very seldom tries to attract new followers by a mental miracle other than by the expression of the love of God, but everything is right in its own place. This display of a miracle was not performed by Jesus in order to satisfy the mental curiosity of a stranger, but to lift a fallen disciple. The woman of Samaria witnessed this omniscient power of Jesus because she confessed to a master; and the master, out of compassion, let her know that her privacy was in safe hands. With her veracity, she had passed his test of true discipleship. And the salutary effect of the miracle was that the woman of Samaria was spiritually awakened to the realization that she was in the presence of a prophet of God.

Worship God "in Spirit and in Truth"

The Woman of Samaria, Part II

Ceremonial Worship Versus Actual Communion With God

❖

Where Is the Best Temple for Worshiping God?

❖

Salvation Comes to All Who Have Made Sufficient Spiritual Effort

❖

Definitions of "God" and "Spirit"

❖

Worshiping "in Spirit and in Truth"

❖

Personal Attributes and Manifestations of God

❖

The Higher State of God-realization:
Oneness of the Soul With Spirit

"To truly worship God is to worship Him as transcendent Spirit in Nature and beyond Nature....It is then that the devotee finds emancipation by becoming one with the Spirit."

"**O**ur fathers worshipped in this mountain; and ye say, that in Jerusalem is the place where men ought to worship."

Jesus saith unto her, "Woman, believe me, the hour cometh, when ye shall neither in this mountain, nor yet at Jerusalem, worship the Father. Ye worship ye know not what: we know what we worship: for salvation is of the Jews. But the hour cometh, and now is, when the true worshippers shall worship the Father in spirit and in truth: for the Father seeketh such to worship Him. God is a Spirit: and they that worship Him must worship Him in spirit and in truth."

—John 4:20–24

Worship God "in Spirit and in Truth"

The Woman of Samaria, Part II

H aving recognized Jesus as a prophet of God, the woman of Samaria sought from him spiritual guidance on the disputed question as to which was the right place to worship: Jerusalem, as the Jews believed; or the mountain nearby, which was sacred to her forefathers.*

In reply, Jesus set aside both the mountain and Jerusalem and spoke of Self-realization, the inner Jerusalem,† where true devotees of God, having ascended the sacred mountain of meditation, worship Him in the temple of actual Spirit-to-soul communion.

---

* The woman was referring to Mount Gerizim, adjacent to the well at Sychar (Shechem) where she met Jesus. Abraham (Genesis 12:7) and Jacob (Genesis 33:20) set up altars at Shechem. Joshua 8:33 recounts how on Gerizim God's blessings were proclaimed on the Israelites, as promised by Moses in Deuteronomy 28:1–68. The Samaritans held that Abraham offered up Isaac on Gerizim. Later, the mountain became especially significant to the Samaritans, for when the Jews who returned to their homeland after the Babylonian Exile would not accept the help of the mixed-race Samaritans in the building of the Second Temple of Jerusalem, the Samaritans built their own temple on Mount Gerizim, which—until its destruction in 129 B.C.—was the center of their worship even as Jerusalem was for the Jews.

† "Him that overcometh will I make a pillar in the temple of my God, and he shall go no more out: and I will write upon him the name of my God, and the name of the city of my God, which is new Jerusalem, which cometh down out of heaven from my God" (Revelation 3:12).

305

Jesus declared that the mass of religious believers take part in ceremonies or rituals but never know the Object of their worship. It is those

*Ceremonial worship
versus actual com-
munion with God*

who have God-consciousness, who commune with
God, that can truly speak of worshiping God. Ceremonial worship—whether it be of diverse images
venerated by different cultures down the ages, or cus-
tomized prayers, chants, or hymns, or symbolic rites
—without inner communion rarely uplifts the consciousness of the worshiper beyond vague concepts of Divinity to actual perception of God.
This is why Jesus said, "You know not what you worship."

If a person is deeply sincere and devout, no matter what words
are used to address God or what concept of the Divine informs those
words, God will answer. But most people do not worship with the
conviction, born of experience, that God is real and that He is listening to their prayers; that He is just behind their thoughts, just behind
the words of their prayers, just behind the love with which they love
Him. If they would pray with heart and mind indivisibly concentrated
on that indwelling Presence, they would know the One they worship.

The reason that God remains unknown to millions who worship
Him in temples and churches, and in holy cities and places of pilgrimage,
is that the physical instruments of knowledge can apprehend only the
products of the Creator; Divinity Itself is perceived by the supramental
faculty of intuition, the soul's God-given power of knowing truth. When
mental restlessness is stilled and the consciousness is interiorized, in touch
with the soul, the God-revealing intuitive faculty is awakened.

The tabernacle of deep meditation, the temple of soul intuition, is
where the devotee is first introduced to God. To one who finds Him
within, God is no longer an unknown mystery concealed by His various
material manifestations. Thus in answer to the woman's inquiry as to the
best outer place for worship, Jesus spoke instead of the difference between
the theological priestly conditions of worship and the saintly way of worshiping God in actual communion with Him "in spirit and in truth."

*Where is the best
temple for worshiping
God?*

A magnificent, multimillion-dollar temple might
draw an aristocratic congregation of worshipers, impressed with the comfort of cushioned velvet seats,
ornamental architecture, and elaborate services. But
the omnipresent God, who lives in the temple of the
cosmos, with the star-decked dome of Eternity, illumined by suns and
moons, is not lured by a display of pomp and wealth into pride-created

man-made edifices. He is easily coaxed, however, onto the altar of meditation by those who establish the temple of God within themselves.

"The most High dwelleth not in temples made with hands; as
saith the prophet, 'Heaven is My throne, and earth is My footstool:
what house will ye build Me?' saith the Lord: or 'What is the place of
My rest? Hath not My hand made all these things?'"*

In my early years of traveling and lecturing throughout the West,
I was often struck by the contrast between the practice of religion as
I learned it from God-knowing sages in India and the customary West-
ern approach. God once showed me an illustrative vision:

In one place, there stood an immense temple, resplendent with
marble decorations and a skyscraper golden dome, comfortably seat-
ing a congregation of ten thousand. Its walls echoed with organ music and a glorious choir chanting hymns to God. It was all impressive
and enjoyable, and I appreciated and admired it.

Then God showed me sitting in meditation under a tree, beneath
a canopy of free skies, with only a few true souls; His light was passing through all of us. God asked me which I would prefer, the magnificent church without Him or the tree-temple with Him. Without question, I chose to be under the tree enwrapped in God. He laughed,
however, when I countered that some big buildings would be necessary
for His work and that He could be in them as well as under the tree.

God is in the temple, and He is under the tree. But He is perceived
only in interiorized meditation when the inner sanctuary door of silence opens. Neither pomp nor penury opens that door. It swings open
wide, as if on magical hinges, when the high vibration of the worshiper's soul turns the key.

Quiet mountaintops and holy places sanctified by the presence of
masters are fit places of worship, yet in themselves are of marginal benefit to restless materially minded people. Worldly people have built temples on hilltops and lived in places of pilgrimage, only to find that their
inner environment is still a den of matter worship of sense-bound
thoughts. That is why Jesus emphasized that true worship of God is not
conditioned by location or found in the imaginary communion of mere
outer silence, but takes place in the inner contact of spiritual perception.

Devotees who by meditation interiorize the outgoing consciousness, withdrawing their attention from identification with the mortal

---

* Acts 7:48–50 (quoting Isaiah 66:1–2).

body and material Nature, discover through direct experience what God is. They alone know what it means truly to worship Him; they alone have found the way to attain salvation.

When Jesus said that "salvation is of the Jews," he was not referring to the Jews as a nation, but to the exalted class or caste of spiritually developed souls. In India the highest caste, the *Salvation comes to all* Brahmins, originally designated those who knew *who have made suffi-* God (Brahma). Hereditary membership in that caste *cient spiritual effort* is not a guarantee of such realization; only those who have made sufficient spiritual effort and have become knowers of God can rightfully lay claim to the title of Brahmin; and for them liberation is assured. So Jesus' statement that salvation is of the Jews did not exclude the rest of mankind. He meant that salvation is for the spiritually exalted—the position, socially speaking, generally accorded to the Jews, who were held to represent the highest standard of spirituality in that place and time.*

Jesus said: "God is a Spirit: and they that worship Him must worship Him in spirit and in truth."

The terms *God* and *Spirit,* theosophically speaking, are mutually exclusive, but are semantically interchangeable in common usage where no distinction is required.

Definitions of "God" *Spirit* signifies the unmanifested Absolute. In *and "Spirit"* the darkless dark and lightless light of eternal infinity—void of even the slightest ripple of thought or vibratory activity to manifest creation; where even the categories of space, time, and dimension are nonexistent— there abides only ever-existing, ever-conscious, ever-new Bliss that is Spirit. "Where no sun or moon or fire shines, that is My Supreme Abode."†

God implies the transcendental Creator, beyond creation but existing in relation to the manifestation that evolves from Him. When relative creation is dissolved again into its Creator, then God becomes Spirit, the unmanifested Absolute.‡

---

* In the verses cited in the next Discourse, Jesus showed his willingness to remain with the Samaritans for two days, during which his presence and teaching so uplifted them that they acknowledged him as "Savior of the world"—not just for one race or religion.

† *God Talks With Arjuna: The Bhagavad Gita* xv:6.

‡ See Discourse 1.

God remains transcendental as both the source of cosmic becomings and immanent as their sum and substance. In manifesting creation, when Spirit becomes God the Creator, His transcendence is reflected in creation as the guiding Universal Intelligence. Thus, God is Divine Intelligence manifesting creation. Spirit is Divine Intelligence with creation dissolved in It. So, in truth, God is Spirit become the Father of creation. He is all things in creation; but the manifestations of creation are not God. His Spirit nature never changes, though a portion of that Consciousness is garbed in a delusive medley of diversification.

Since the waves of creation distort their oceanic Source in appearance, but not in essence, the true vision of God lies in the perception of the Spirit Ocean without the waves of creation—the realization of God as unmanifested *Worshiping "in spirit* Spirit: the only existing substance, Truth, without *and in truth"* the delusion of matter or phenomena.

Jesus said that so long as a devotee's consciousness is limited to manifested creation and its inherent delusion of separate things, he has not yet attained the ultimate enlightenment. He remains in delusion, his consciousness absorbed in ever-changing phenomena. Though God is manifest everywhere, His essence is secreted behind the veil of Nature's phenomena. The devotee has to lift that illusory veil and see God first as transcendent *in* His creation. After that realization, the devotee can realize God as transcendent *beyond* manifestation.

Unless the devotee is able to perceive the Father of Creation as the unmanifested Absolute Spirit—pure, ever-conscious Bliss, without delusion's shadows of imperfect creation—he does not know Truth, the noumenal Substance of all phenomena.

As Absolute Spirit is reflected as God's guiding Intelligence in macrocosmic creation, so is Spirit reflected in the microcosm of the body as the soul, the individualized image of Spirit in man. The true worshiper, he who actually communes with God, who experiences His presence in meditative realization, knows the truth that his soul and God the Creator are reflections of Spirit.

This knowing involves another theosophical nuance. God, the Father of manifestation, can be known by the soul either by perception of or oneness with any of His manifested attributes. Spirit, the Unmanifested Absolute, can be known only by oneness with Spirit.

God, in relation to the soul, presumes a duality—the Object to be perceived, God; and the perceiver or experiencer, the soul. The spiritually awakening man seeks some familiarity, some tangibility, in his relationship with his Creator. He begins by personalizing God's Pres-

Personal attributes and manifestations of God

ence. In the Bhagavad Gita, the Lord promises: "In whatever way people are devoted to Me, in that measure I manifest Myself to them. All men, in every manner (of seeking Me), pursue a path to Me" (IV:11).

The unmanifested Spirit as God makes His presence known to the devotee by manifesting some attribute of Divinity commensurate with the devotee's expectation. Jesus taught his followers to think of God as Father. In India it is more common to speak of God as Divine Mother. Saints of various persuasions have successfully communed with God by similarly idealizing other human relations—such as Friend or Beloved. It makes no difference. When I feel the gravity of wisdom, I speak of God as the Father. When I feel unbounded, unconditional love I call God Divine Mother. When I feel God as the nearest of the near, supporter and confidant, I call Him Friend.

Thus, it is a misnomer to refer to God always as "He." It is equally appropriate to call God "She." But in the ultimate, God is Spirit, neither masculine nor feminine. Spirit is above any human correlation. Similarly, the soul is neither male nor female, though karmic inclinations cause it to incarnate either with the body of a man or a woman.

Any personalized communion with God or worship of a conceptualized aspect or attribute of Divinity maintains the duality of wor-

The higher state of God-realization: oneness of the soul with Spirit

shiper and Worshiped, the ecstatic relationship sometimes preferred by saints. But the even higher state referred to by Jesus, beyond dualistic devotion, is Oneness with the Object of worship, and specifically, the ultimate union: oneness of the soul with Spirit. God as Spirit, the Absolute, beyond form, qualities, manifestations, cannot be perceived, but only experienced by the supreme realization of Spirit and soul union. This ecstasy, a supernal Bliss that no human tongue can tell or rational thought conceive, is described simply by India's *rishis:* "He who knows, he knows; naught else knows."

God, being in truth the unmanifested Absolute, wants all His true devotees to know that they are emanations of that Spirit, and as such, to reunite with their immortal, ever conscious, pure Bliss-Essence. That is why Jesus said: "But the hour cometh, and now is, when the true worshippers shall worship the Father in spirit and in truth: for the Father seeketh such to worship Him."

All devotees who worship God as the manifested Intelligence of creation—the guiding power within the universal laws and forces and forms of the cosmos—are gradually taught by Him, through awakening of the soul's intuition, to worship Him as the unmanifested Absolute, or Spirit. The link between the manifest and the Unmanifest is the Holy Ghost, the Holy Vibration of *Aum;* and the way to cross this bridge is by communion with that Holy Ghost Vibration.

In spiritual ecstasy the meditator perceives the individual vibration of his life and all lives as informed from the cosmic Holy Ghost, inherent in which is God's reflected Christ Intelligence, which in turn uplifts the consciousness into the transcendental Spirit.

Therefore, to truly worship God is to worship Him as transcendent Spirit in Nature and beyond Nature, to worship the Substance and Its presence in the delusive phenomena evolved from It, to worship the ocean of God with its delusive waves of creation* —and then to realize God solely as Spirit, the only existing substance, Truth, Bliss, without any delusive manifestation.

The persevering devotee advances in the realization that God is Spirit, the Unmanifested Absolute, and understands the truth about Him as being the ever-existent, ever-conscious, ever-new Bliss without the delusion of a material cosmos. It is then that the devotee finds emancipation by becoming one with the Spirit. It is only by worshiping God and His presence in Nature, and then by worshiping God as unmanifested Spirit, by Spirit-and-soul union, that the devotee reaches the final state of emancipation, from which there is no fall.

In the brilliance of sunlight, one may close one's eyes and thereby create a darkness in which to live and move. But when the eyes are open, darkness is no more. So the consciousness of matter as the perdurable reality of existence is due to man's having closed his God-perceiving eye of wisdom. When the wisdom eye is opened, the con-

---

* "The way to acknowledge and know Him, as taught in the highest Yoga philosophy, is by constantly keeping the attention absorbed in His holy vibration, *Aum*. If the yogi hears that vibration—through the medium of intuition—and merges his attention in it, and worships it continuously, then he will see beyond doubt that there is a God....All may know Him through the right method of meditation on *Aum*. Through *Aum* only can the manifested Spirit be realized" (*God Talks With Arjuna: The Bhagavad Gita,* commentary on VII:1).

sciousness of relativity of the pairs of opposites—birth and death, sorrow and pleasure, good and evil—disappear, and the Spirit, as everexisting, ever-conscious ever-new Joy, is realized as the sole existent Substance.* Then all creation, with its attendant evils, is found to be a manifestation of cosmic delusion; its darkness and fears created by closing the eyes in spiritual ignorance, and not by any absence of God's light, which is omnipresent and thus ever-present.

Learn to worship God in the temple of super-communion, or *samadhi*. In divine communion, the cosmos, like a shadow of darkness, dissolves as a non-existent illusion with the opening of the eye of wisdom to the light of the only existing Truth, Spirit, the ever blissful Absolute.

---

* "At birth all creatures are immersed in delusive ignorance (*moha*) by the delusion of the pairs of opposites springing from longing and aversion. But righteous men, their sins obliterated, and subject no longer to the oppositional delusions, worship Me steadfastly. Those who seek deliverance from decay and death by clinging to Me know Brahman (the Absolute)" (*God Talks With Arjuna: The Bhagavad Gita* VII:27–29).

DISCOURSE 19

"My Meat Is to Do the Will of Him That Sent Me"

The Woman of Samaria, Part III (Conclusion)

Overcoming the Delusion That Man Is Essentially a Physical Being

❖

Become Attuned to God's Will: In the World but Not of the World

❖

Discovering God's Will for One's Destined Role
According to the Divine Plan

❖

The Soul Needs Nothing but to Remember
the Divine Wealth It Already Possesses

❖

Human Life Is Affected by Mass Karma as Well as Individual Karma

❖

Should a Spiritual Teacher Use Advertising and Publicity?

"Cheerful cooperation with God's will is the secret of a dynamic existence, charging body and mind with divine life....That is why Jesus wished to show the disciples that the consciousness of man should not be predominantly on a material diet, but on the nourishment of divine wisdom."

*T*he woman saith unto him, "*I know that Messiah cometh, which is called Christ: when he is come, he will tell us all things.*"

Jesus saith unto her, "*I that speak unto thee am he.*"

And upon this came his disciples, and marvelled that he talked with the woman: yet no man said, "*What seekest thou?*" or, "*Why talkest thou with her?*"

The woman then left her waterpot, and went her way into the city, and saith to the men, "*Come, see a man, which told me all things that ever I did: is not this the Christ?*" Then they went out of the city, and came unto him.

In the mean while his disciples prayed him, saying, "*Master, eat.*"

But he said unto them, "*I have meat to eat that ye know not of.*"

Therefore said the disciples one to another, "*Hath any man brought him ought to eat?*"

Jesus saith unto them, "*My meat is to do the will of Him that sent me, and to finish His work. Say not ye, 'There are yet four months, and then cometh harvest'? Behold, I say unto you, lift up your eyes, and look on the fields; for they are white already to harvest. And he that reapeth receiveth wages, and gathereth fruit unto life eternal: that both he that soweth and he that reapeth may rejoice together. And herein is that saying true, 'One soweth, and another reapeth.' I sent you to reap that whereon ye bestowed no labour: other men laboured, and ye are entered into their labours.*"

And many of the Samaritans of that city believed on him for the saying of the woman, which testified, "*He told me all that ever I did.*"

So when the Samaritans were come unto him, they besought him that he would tarry with them: and he abode there two days. And many more believed because of his own word; and said unto the woman, "*Now we believe, not because of thy saying: for we have heard him ourselves, and know that this is indeed the Christ, the Saviour of the world.*"

—John 4:25–42

314

"My Meat Is to Do the Will of Him That Sent Me"

The Woman of Samaria, Part III (Conclusion)

꧁

The woman saith unto him, "I know that Messiah cometh, which is called Christ: when he is come, he will tell us all things."

Jesus saith unto her, "I that speak unto thee am he."

And upon this came his disciples, and marvelled that he talked with the woman: yet no man said, "What seekest thou?" or, "Why talkest thou with her?"

The woman then left her waterpot, and went her way into the city, and saith to the men, "Come, see a man, which told me all things that ever I did: is not this the Christ?" Then they went out of the city, and came unto him (John 4:25–30).

Having unconsciously received the telepathic message of the presence of God and Christ Consciousness emanating from Jesus as to his spiritual identity, the woman of Samaria said: "I know that the Messiah cometh." Diffidently, she was seeking some response from Jesus in confirmation of her inner feeling that he indeed might be the long-awaited Messiah.

Great saints, free of even the subtlest wish for celebrity, often keep their godliness intentionally hidden most of the time, revealing their eminence only as prompted by the Divine Will to accomplish some specific purpose related to their mission. Their full spiritual stature may not be recognized even by those mixing intimately with them. God wanted to declare the glory of Jesus through the woman of Samaria, who, having been spiritually healed by him of her entrenched immoral tendencies, was to serve as a "test case" demonstrating to others the miracle of soul healing. To remove the ignorance that eclipses man's divine nature is the most important of all forms of healing; that is the blessing Jesus would impart to all who attuned themselves with the Christ in him.

Jesus reinforced the glimmer of understanding in the woman by declaring the truth about himself. His purpose was to deepen her receptivity to the all-healing Christ Consciousness in him. Jesus saw her alone because, considerate as he was, he wanted to avoid causing embarrassment to the woman by revealing before his other disciples his prophetic knowledge of her moral indiscretions.

God has given to each human being the privacy of thought in which to fight his inner battles in secret instead of before others' curiosity and prying, prompting their sarcasm and condemnation. If there were not invisible walls between our mental processes and those of others, we would have no peace; and we would lose, to a large degree, our independence of thought and determination and thus the right to receive our own knocks and score our own victories.

One may get inklings of the thoughts of others from the expressions of their faces and eyes. This makes the mystery of life all the more challenging and interesting; for many times their thoughts are read correctly. Yet people frequently jump to conclusions about the feelings and motives of others and make horrible blunders. One's mistakes in such psychological reading should teach a prudent caution and prevent overconfidence in the sufficiency of one's "intuitions"; that misguided surety often arises prematurely from one or two correct hunches about the thoughts of others.

Even a master does not intrude with his intuitive perception into the mind of another if his help is unwelcome. He leaves the touch-me-not temperament to its own devices of conscience and karma. But Jesus found no such exclusion from the consciousness of his Samaritan disciple.

The disciples traveling with Jesus, lacking his ability to discern the inner quality of souls, were surprised to see him flouting convention by his warm demeanor toward a common woman of Samaria. Yet the pure vibrations of their newfound Master quelled any expression of criticism. That is why nobody asked: "Why talkest thou with her?"

Perhaps to the modern mind of a world society this instance seems un-worthy of remark, but to those cultures of the past, persisting in some closed regions even today, such rigid social structure was considered of great consequence, the material and psychological backbone of both nations and provinces. "Caste," in whatever form, is a divisive evil that deeply embeds itself in the ego of man; but it cedes its power to the wisdom and soul magnanimity of one such as Christ.

The woman of Samaria was so overwhelmed by the power of her meeting with Jesus that, returning to the city in a state of divine joy, she spoke freely of her past moral blemishes and of the wonderful soul-healing she had received from Jesus, exhorting the townspeople to come with her to meet him. She thus became the first among the gen-eral populace to act as a public messenger to declare Jesus the Christ.

～

In the mean while his disciples prayed him, saying, "Master, eat."

But he said unto them, "I have meat to eat that ye know not of."

Therefore said the disciples one to another, "Hath any man brought him ought to eat?"

Jesus saith unto them, "My meat is to do the will of Him that sent me, and to finish His work" (John 4:31–34).

When the Samaritan woman left to bring the townspeople to Jesus, his disciples offered him food they had brought from the city. But Jesus demurred: "I have meat to eat that ye know not of."* The dis-ciples incorrectly presumed that Jesus had already been given food by

---

* "Meat" is the term used in the King James Bible, the edition used by Paramahansa Yogananda for his New Testament commentary. The word in the original Greek is *broma*, which literally means "that which is eaten"; some other versions of the Bible in English translate it simply as "food."

Regarding the customary diet among Jewish families of Jesus' time, the book *Jesus and His Times* (Kaari Ward, ed.; Pleasantville, New York: Reader's Digest Association, 1987) states: "Most families ate two meals. Breakfasts were likely to be light and were carried to the fields or other places of work and eaten at mid-morning or midday. Sup-pers, by contrast, were substantial. Vegetables, eggs, cheese, bread, butter, wine, nuts, and fruit might all be served, and perhaps chicken or wild fowl. Fish was a common food, but red meat was a rarity, except on special occasions, when the fatted calf and the sacrificial lamb were presented with fanfare and ritual." *(Publisher's Note)*

someone else; but he explained: "My meat is to do the will of Him that sent me and to finish His work." The mind of Jesus was in an exalted state, attuned with the divine power of Christ Consciousness that had filled and nourished his own body when he healed the woman of Samaria. At such times, the Divine Satiety in a master laughs at the delusive "necessity" of supplying the body with the insipid grossness of material sustenance. Jesus felt his life coming directly from God—as he had said before: "Man shall not live by bread alone, but by every word that proceedeth out of the mouth of God."* Every moment he was conscious of that connection. He knew himself as a soul; the only "meat" it needed for nourishment was the blessedness and eternal wisdom of God.

Jesus was also trying to heal the spiritual ignorance of his disciples: the delusion that man is essentially a physical being. When a master is

Overcoming the delusion that man is essentially a physical being

with his disciples, he makes use of every opportunity, no matter how significant or insignificant, to help them spiritualize their consciousness. No lapse into identification with accustomed mortal habits is too trite to warrant correction. The untangling of delusion's net is achieved one knot at a time. Jesus wanted the disciples, first and foremost, to think of the body as an instrument for doing the will of God, even as he was demonstrating by his example that the sole purpose for his life on earth was to finish whatever work God wished him to do. The secondary concern is to care for the body only as necessary to maintain it as a fit instrument.

Ordinary food temporarily nourishes the perishable body and gives it a passing pleasure arising from the sense of taste. But even if a person were to sate himself with any and all food he desired, still his hunger would burn; man cannot appease the hunger of the soul by satisfying the desires of the body. Jesus was telling his disciples that although they had brought food for his human body—the token need for which he did not deny—his real Self tasted the ever-satisfying, eternally nourishing manna of Divine Wisdom and celestial ever-new Bliss.

The disciples had been drawn to Jesus that they might learn how to nourish their souls. So Jesus spoke to them of the supremely sustaining "meat" of wisdom. When man is not guided by wisdom, material food does not even sustain the body: By wrong dietary choices or overeating people may forfeit their physical health and comfort.

---

* Matthew 4:4 (see Discourse 8).

Jesus and the Woman of Samaria

There cometh a woman of Samaria to draw water: Jesus saith unto her, "Give me to drink."...

Then saith the woman of Samaria unto him, "How is it that thou, being a Jew, askest drink of me, which am a woman of Samaria?" for the Jews have no dealings with the Samaritans.

Jesus answered and said unto her, "If thou knewest the gift of God, and who it is that saith to thee, 'Give me to drink'; thou wouldest have asked of him, and he would have given thee living water."

—John 4:7, 9–10

The meeting of Jesus with the woman of Samaria was not a chance encounter, but a divinely devised guru-disciple reunion. The Samaritan woman was a morally lost disciple of a previous incarnation whom Jesus wanted to redeem....

Jesus spoke of the inner experience, the uncovering, with the help of one's guru, of the wellspring of divinity within the soul....

"The thirst of incarnations is slaked by whosoever will drink the effervescent waters of the well of Divine Bliss in the soul, springing up into everlasting life"—this is the wisdom Jesus sought to convey to the woman at the well.

—*Paramahansa Yogananda*

Drawing by Heinrich Hofmann

In the homes of most materially minded persons in the West, the occupants wake up in the morning with the consciousness of a cup of coffee, toast, and ham and eggs, and go to sleep at night with their minds on the heavy beefsteak dinner they have eaten. In spiritual homes in India, the first thought in the morning is of drinking the nectar of peace from the bowl of deep contemplation; and at night, before retiring, they sit quietly in meditation to hear the voice of Divine Peace singing softly, inviting them to rest on the bosom of Divine Peace.

As long as one is identified with the body, he is tempted to seek happiness in fulfilling its desires and appetites. He dreams of being a millionaire, of having a luxurious home, expensive cars, and the best meals money can buy. However, even a cursory observation of those who have these things dispels their illusory sufficiency. Material surfeit attracts swarming pests of worry, restlessness, boredom, psychological and spiritual dissatisfaction. Upon wakening in the morning, and at night before going to sleep, and at mealtime, people should rid their consciousness of the material pestilence with the thought of God.

Seeking in deep meditation to become attuned to God's will enables one to be in the world but not of the world. To remain unattached, like the dewdrop on the lotus leaf, is to be really happy, ready to slip the consciousness into God. As a dewdrop cannot slide on blotting paper, so the mind of the *Become attuned to* average person cannot readily slide into thoughts of *God's will: in the* God if it is absorbed in an inner environment of *world but not of the* earthly desires or an outer environment of materi- *world* ally minded companions.

The way to remain spiritually free and nonattached is to realize that this earth belongs solely to God. All of man's so-called possessions are loaned to him only that he may play a role in this colossal drama of life. None of the props belongs to man, not even his body, which is but a temporary costume that must be surrendered when his particular part in the drama is over and God calls him behind the curtain of death. Until man's histrionics are finished, happiness lies in perfecting his performance, without personal attachment, according to the promptings of the Divine Director. The will of God is to plan for every actor the best finale; in that lies the true joy of living.

Thus Jesus said that as food is the pleasurable sustenance that man depends on for life, so the relish that supported the vitality of his life consisted in doing the will of God—cheerfully, willingly, not like a puppet. Cheerful cooperation with God's will is the secret of a dynamic existence, charging body and mind with divine life. Man is made of the blissful consciousness of God, and lives by that Consciousness. The more cheerful a person is, the more his positive thoughts draw vitality into his body cells from the abundance of Divine Consciousness. One who allows the episodes of life to make his mind habitually cross and moody finds his bodily energies depressed accordingly, no matter how much or what type of food he eats. That is why Jesus emphasized to his disciples that the consciousness of man should not be predominantly on a material diet, but on the nourishment of divine wisdom. That wisdom which feeds man's body with vitality, his mind with invulnerability, and his soul with celestial bliss is to do the will of God.

As prophets are sent on earth to fill a world need according to the Lord's cosmic plan, Jesus knew the stupendous mission he had to perform, and the possible consequences that could come to him as a result of his actions. Yet he was sustained in the peace and joy of his commitment "to do the will of Him that sent me." "To finish His work" signifies finishing, in the short span that was left to him, the God-given task that was his part to carry out during his incarnation as Jesus—not the completion of the work of redemption, which God and His avatars have to carry on throughout eternity.

Every human being has a unique part in the drama of life, destined according to that individual's self-created karmic pattern. God has so choreographed the divine plan that each part is important, whether one appears on the earth stage as sovereign or servant. All roles are needed for the show to go on. No one should feel unworthy if one's present incarnation is not a starring role. It should be played with wisdom, nonattachment, and inner freedom, remembering that Reality lies not in but beyond the tragicomic scenes of life and death.

Discovering God's will for one's destined role according to the divine plan

If one is disgruntled with his designated role and rejects the scenes that are karmically necessary to him, attempting instead a part more appealing to his desires, he disrupts the cosmic harmony and spoils the better drama God's love and laws had scripted for him. That is the fate of most human players on the stage of life. They follow not the wisdom will of the Divine Director but their own blind will. Thus they turn their scenes into tiresome tragedies. They have to reappear on stage incarnation after incarnation until they become perfected thespians in the Lord's cosmic entertainment. Heeding Divine Direction, they ennoble the drama and earn liberation.

It is easy to do what one wants to do, but difficult to do what one should do. How may one even know the will of God as to what one should do? So many have told me that they are divinely guided; but I know they are not, because I see they have not even communed with God. So how could they be guided by Him? I try to warn them; but when they are immovably fixed in the delusion that they know God's will, I have then to remain silent and watch the ego make a mess of their determinations. It is often a sad spectacle.

Of course, through prayer and meditation and faith one does get some inner spiritual sense of direction. No one should be without this attunement. But to be consciously guided by God, rather than by the manipulative rationalizations of one's desires or whims or habits, is another matter, of deeper realization. For most people, the will of God is best understood through a God-sent guru. Guru is one who knows God, and who shows the way to Him. To follow a divine manifestation is the sure way to God-realization. One who knows God becomes the speaking voice of the silent God. Attunement with the wisdom-guided will of a true guru teaches one how to guide his will according to God's will. Those who follow the voice of their own ego, ascribing to it a halo of divine guidance, find out too late that no amount of deluded rationalization will relieve one of the karmic responsibility of wrong actions. To be led by an ego-bound will is to stumble into painful delusive entanglements. Do not remain entangled! Be free!

The will of God is to free every soul. Man's part is to cooperate with that purpose by living in harmony with God's laws as defined by a God-realized guru. Man thereby learns his destined purpose and understands what God wants him to do with his life. Acting accordingly, he "finishes God's work" that is his unique assignment on the stage of incarnation. With Christ, he ingests the "meat" of wisdom and becomes an instrument in fulfilling the Divine Will.

～

"Say not ye, 'There are yet four months, and then cometh harvest'? Behold, I say unto you, lift up your eyes, and look on the fields; for they are white already to harvest. And he that reapeth

*receiveth wages, and gathereth fruit unto life eternal: that both
he that soweth and he that reapeth may rejoice together. And
herein is that saying true, 'One soweth, and another reapeth.' I
sent you to reap that whereon ye bestowed no labour: other men
laboured, and ye are entered into their labours" (John 4:35–38).*

Mortal life is governed by the law of karma: "As you sow, so
shall you reap." In this passage, however, Jesus used the parable of the sower, the laborer, the harvesting time, and the harvest to illustrate that the immortal soul of man, a reflection of transcendent
Spirit, is above creation's cause-and-effect subjugation. To one who is
identified with his assumed mortal nature, the karmic law metes out
wisdom and happiness only according to one's earned merit. One who
is identified with Spirit reaps without measure the infinite wealth of
Divinity.

Thus did Jesus elucidate the superior law of the Divine Harvest: In
ordinary farming there is a great deal of labor, and the harvest comes in
about four months after planting; but Jesus said that
reaping divine abundance is not a matter of laboring,
waiting, and finally acquiring the spiritual harvest.
The soul need acquire nothing. As a child of God, it
needs only to remember what it already possesses in
latent form: its infinite wisdom-inheritance from the
Divine Father. The moment man's consciousness transcends body identification into Self-realization, the soul's contact with God becomes
manifest, its God-essence revealed from beneath the wisdom-seared veil
of ignorance.*

*The soul needs noth-
ing but to remember
the divine wealth it al-
ready possesses*

Human wisdom has to be cultivated gradually through the instrumentality of the senses and rational intelligence; but the measureless
harvest of divine wisdom can be reaped instantaneously through the
medium of intuition, developed by meditation. Jesus exhorted his followers, "Lift up your eyes, and look on the fields," for all one has to
do is to lift the consciousness from the plain of material vibrations to
the ever-ready harvest of wisdom, glistening on the pure white fields of
Cosmic Consciousness. The two physical eyes see only material Nature.

---

* "As enkindled flame converts firewood into ashes, so does the fire of wisdom consume to ashes all karma. Verily, nothing else in this world is as sanctifying as wisdom"
(*God Talks With Arjuna: The Bhagavad Gita* IV:37–38).

Raising the gaze and consciousness in deep meditation to the third eye of spiritual perception, the aspirant beholds in the starry white light of soul realization the wisdom- and bliss-abundance that is his divine birthright—long forgotten, never lost, and instantly reclaimable.

As the darkness of closed eyes is dispelled immediately when one opens his eyes, so the instant one opens his eye of wisdom, the gloom of ignorance is banished and he beholds himself as a perfect soul in the light of God. This is a great consolation, for to reach perfection through the karmic consequential process of trial and error seems a near impossibility, requiring countless incarnations. Man must labor to acquire prosperity, wisdom, and happiness; a Self-realized child of God, reclaiming his divine inheritance, already possesses everything.

So much effort is required to reap a harvest of material worth— a relative waste of time when one must inevitably lose, sooner or later, all that has been acquired. Jesus points out that it is far better to make the effort to know what one already possesses as a divine child. The soul that has cast off its mortality claims its birthright and enjoys throughout eternity the harvest of Bliss in God.

Material habits and indolence cause many otherwise spiritually inclined persons to say: "Well, it takes prodigious effort to be spiritual." I say: "No." The only effort we have to make is to forget our unspiritual mortal consciousness; as soon as that is done, we know we are gods. "He that reapeth receiveth wages, and gathereth fruit unto life eternal." He who reaps soul knowledge through meditation receives the wages of Divine Wisdom, and gathers the resultant fruits of immortal, ever new Bliss.

"That both he that soweth and he that reapeth may rejoice together" signifies that God, as the Sower of Wisdom in souls, is pleased when He finds that His true children reap the harvest grown by Him, and not the harvest of evil sown and reaped by mortal ignorance.

"One soweth and another reapeth" can be interpreted on two levels of meaning: first, as relating to the harvest in man's soul; and second, as relating to man's influence on his fellow beings in the world.

Primarily, Jesus' words signify that God is the Sower, the sole Source, of wisdom, and that His children have only to reap what He has already grown for them in their souls. God sent human beings on earth to reap the soul harvest of wisdom and bliss, for which no human effort was made. In the world, just forgetting that one lives in poverty does not make one rich; one has to work to acquire material wealth. But as God's children, the moment in deep meditation that they forget their self-created mortal consciousness, they immediately become divine, spiritually enriched with their endowment from God.

"Other men laboured and ye are entered into their labours" means that worldly persons labor for perishable material acquisitions and for unfulfilling and unrealistic goals; God's devotees should not foolishly imitate them. For all people to become in this lifetime as rich as a Henry Ford would be impossible, because of the limitations of earthly existence. But every human being has the potential to become Christlike in one life by proper meditation, because all are already sons of God, made in His image. By meditation and calmness, man opens his agelong closed eyes of wisdom. The light of awakening actualizes his latent potentials, and he finds himself one with the Owner of the entire cosmos.

The fruits of one's spiritual awakening are a blessing not only on one's own life, but on the world at large. This is the second meaning of "one soweth and another reapeth": a reference to

Human life is affected by mass karma as well as individual karma

mass karma. Every person sows good or bad actions in the soil of his life, and not only does he himself reap the karmic harvest of those actions, but he makes others reap them as well. If a person writes a degrading novel, all who read it reap the evil effects of the author's thoughts. The law of cause and effect operates in even subtler ways as well. The actions of each individual leave electromagnetic etchings in his brain, influencing his future actions; and they also leave vibrational traces in the ether, which register in and influence the minds of others.

In Mysore I visited a sandalwood factory; each piece and shaving of sandalwood contributes to the atmosphere of the whole place, and anyone who enters enjoys the wonderful fragrance. Similarly, when I come to our Self-Realization Fellowship temples, there are so many good souls earnestly seeking God that I feel the spiritual vibration emanating from their collective goodness. Conversely, a gathering of persons given to drinking and rowdyism would produce a strong negative atmosphere.

The overall quality and character of any community, any civilization, is produced by mass karma, the accumulated effects of actions left in the ether by the populace in general. Each individual is responsible for contributing to the mass karma, which in turn influences every individual.

324

The person who keeps himself cleansed of all wrong vibrations produces a powerful uplifting effect on his contemporaries. One moon gives more luster than all the stars; so a moonèd soul—one who purely reflects the light of God—can influence the masses much more than the masses influence each other. Thus, individual effort can be even more important than mass karma. One who in every way tries to uplift himself, harmonizing body, mind, and soul with the Divine, creates positive karma not only in his own life, but in his family, neighborhood, country, and world. Hence it is not justified to say, "Thousands of people are misbehaving, so what does it matter if I am, too?" No! The goodness of one soul may effectively neutralize the mass karma of millions.

Such was the accomplishment of Mahatma Gandhi: he brought freedom to 400 million people by his spiritual influence. He was scoffed at and spent many years in prison, but still he went on. Ultimately, his spirit of righteousness triumphed, and he became instrumental in freeing India by peaceful means. His life stands as a monumental example of the practical application of Christ's doctrines. Because one individual sowed goodness, millions reaped that goodness and freedom.

Each drop of water contributes to the existence of the ocean. So even if one's life seems no more than a droplet in the sea of humanity, that life can have a significant influence. One who makes himself godlike automatically uplifts countless others on the divine path. One who makes himself evil demotes others from the spiritual plane by a negative effect on their potential weaknesses. He who has reformed himself has reformed thousands; for what one sows in the ether, by the vibrations of his thoughts and character, others will surely reap.

~

And many of the Samaritans of that city believed on him for the saying of the woman, which testified, "He told me all that ever I did."

So when the Samaritans were come unto him, they besought him that he would tarry with them: and he abode there two days. And many more believed because of his own word; and said unto the woman, "Now we believe, not because of thy saying: for we have heard him ourselves, and know that this is indeed the Christ, the Saviour of the world" (John 4:39–42).

Many Samaritans were roused to belief in Jesus because of the testimony of the woman he had spiritually healed. True testimonials from benefited students as to their master's qualities enable him to become known to others so that he can serve them through the power of his wisdom.

Advertising and publicity of spiritual teachings is deplorable when tainted with commerciality or selfish motive by teachers who feign an

Should a spiritual teacher use advertising and publicity?

ability to impart wisdom to others but never practice the lofty principles they preach. To wantonly promote spiritual quackery is despicable. But to use whatever media are available to draw the attention of people to a usable, beneficial spiritual teaching or teacher is admirable. Word-of-mouth was the primary medium of "publicity" in the time of Jesus. Even flowers advertise by their fragrance, calling people to come near and bathe in the fountain of sweetness. Similarly, by the perfume of their holiness, real spiritual teachers draw eager souls to divine teachings. They convey the value of their services principally through personal example, not merely through eloquent promises or easily dispensed advice.

Jesus attracted multitudes by demonstrating his divine power, not as a matter of ostentatious display, but in the cause of helping the spiritually, mentally, and physically sick. He also attracted people by the fragrance of divine love and magnetism that saturated his lotus soul. That is the best kind of advertisement.

When the fragrance of a flower is experienced by a few and then described to those who have not yet discovered its sweetness, the latter are able to seek out that beauty and savor it themselves. A spiritual man who remained unknown, enjoying God in solitude, would be like a fragrant blossom "born to blush and die unseen." Truly advanced souls, no matter how much they love seclusion, never selfishly fail to serve others with the solace of their acquired wisdom. Great saints who experience the intoxicating joy of God-contact love to share that joy and to exercise their spiritual healing powers for the sake of worthy seekers.* This serves a double purpose: Those in need

---

* "Solitude is necessary to become established in the Self, but masters then return to the world to serve it. Even saints who engage in no outward work bestow, through their thoughts and holy vibrations, more precious benefits on the world than can be given by the most strenuous humanitarian activities of unenlightened men. The great ones, each in his own way and often against bitter opposition, strive selflessly to in-

receive healing; and when they feel better they broadcast, with the sincerity born of personal experience, their teacher's ability to serve and to heal, so that others may likewise receive.

Jesus, actuated by Divine Will in healing the woman of Samaria, thereby drew many souls to God through the instrumentality of her convincing encomium: "Many of the Samaritans of that city believed on him for the saying of the woman....When the Samaritans were come unto him, they besought him that he would tarry with them: and he abode there two days."

Many persons are initially attracted to a teacher through the testimonials of benefited followers, but others have the keen perception to recognize and believe in him by tuning in with his emanating spiritual vibrations. In Samaria some were convinced not by the woman's enthusiasm, but by going to Jesus themselves and feeling his divinity: "Now we believe...for we have heard him ourselves, and know that this is indeed the Christ, the Saviour of the world." Having been introduced to a teacher or a path, earnest seekers should then fully satisfy their hearts by attunement with the teacher and application of his teaching. Convictions become firmly based, not on the uncertain foundation of hearsay, but on the indestructible rock of personally experienced wisdom.

---

spire and uplift their fellows. No Hindu religious or social ideal is merely negative. *Ahimsa*, 'non-injury,' called 'virtue entire' (*sakalo dharma*) in the *Mahabharata*, is a positive injunction by reason of its conception that one who is not helping others in some way is injuring them." —*Autobiography of a Yogi*

"Thy Son Liveth": The Healing Power of Thought Transformation

A Master Can Heal the Body
by Restructuring Its Underlying Energy Matrix

❖

How Concentration of Human Thought and Will
Acts on the Cells of the Body

❖

Healing by Affirmations:
The Dynamic Vibratory Power of the Spoken Word

❖

Vibrations of Healing and Prayers for Others
Are Effective at Any Distance

❖

Harnessing Mind Power to Heal
by Positive Thinking, Affirmation, or Prayer

"A divinely strong mind, implanting a thought of health and perfection in another person, can dissolve a stubborn thought of illness and cause a surge of restorative healing energy."

*T*hen when he was come into Galilee, the Galileans received him, having seen all the things that he did at Jerusalem at the feast: for they also went unto the feast.

So Jesus came again into Cana of Galilee, where he made the water wine. And there was a certain nobleman, whose son was sick at Capernaum. When he heard that Jesus was come out of Judea into Galilee, he went unto him, and besought him that he would come down, and heal his son: for he was at the point of death.

Then said Jesus unto him, "Except ye see signs and wonders, ye will not believe."

The nobleman saith unto him, "Sir, come down ere my child die."

Jesus saith unto him, "Go thy way; thy son liveth." And the man believed the word that Jesus had spoken unto him, and he went his way.

And as he was now going down, his servants met him, and told him, saying, "Thy son liveth."

Then enquired he of them the hour when he began to amend. And they said unto him, "Yesterday at the seventh hour the fever left him."

So the father knew that it was at the same hour, in the which Jesus said unto him, "Thy son liveth": and himself believed, and his whole house.

This is again the second miracle that Jesus did, when he was come out of Judea into Galilee.

—John 4:45—54

DISCOURSE 20

"Thy Son Liveth": The Healing Power of Thought Transformation

❧

Then when he was come into Galilee, the Galileans received him, having seen all the things that he did at Jerusalem at the feast: for they also went unto the feast.

So Jesus came again into Cana of Galilee, where he made the water wine. And there was a certain nobleman, whose son was sick at Capernaum. When he heard that Jesus was come out of Judea into Galilee, he went unto him, and besought him that he would come down, and heal his son: for he was at the point of death.

Then said Jesus unto him, "Except ye see signs and wonders, ye will not believe."

The nobleman saith unto him, "Sir, come down ere my child die."

Jesus saith unto him, "Go thy way; thy son liveth." And the man believed the word that Jesus had spoken unto him, and he went his way (John 4:45–50).

Part of Jesus' mission was to make visible God's healing mercy. Through his public miracles, Jesus demonstrated that even "incurable" diseases and "insoluble" problems can be surmounted, sometimes instantly, by attunement with Divine Will. The purpose of these miraculous healings was not to glorify the perishable body, but to rouse faith in the omnipresence of God and in man's innate ability to contact and personally know his Heavenly Father. Jesus knew that worldly mentalities have difficulty accepting their personal access to the Merciful Omnipotence. Thus, when asked by the nobleman to heal his son who was dying at Capernaum, Jesus observed wryly: "Except ye see signs and wonders, ye will not believe." It was a gentle rebuke: "You are loath to believe in God's message of salvation sent through me unless He first demonstrates His presence in me by a display of miracles that benefits primarily your temporal needs." God should not have to prove Himself through miracles to earn the love and trust of His children. Each one, through his own free will and perfect accord, should make a voluntary choice of the heart to love God and to seek to know Him. In the wisdom of a master, one should recognize the Divine Presence and be inspired toward God-realization without the impetus of supernatural demonstrations. Nevertheless, seeing that the nobleman's faith was sincere, Jesus sympathetically told him: "Go thy way; thy son liveth."

These few words, supported neither by persuasive eloquence nor obvious evidence, were yet sufficient to satisfy the nobleman; he could sense the divine vibration of healing power in Jesus. Thus, "he believed the word that Jesus had spoken unto him, and he went his way."

～

And as he was now going down, his servants met him, and told him, saying, "Thy son liveth."

Then enquired he of them the hour when he began to amend. And they said unto him, "Yesterday at the seventh hour the fever left him."

So the father knew that it was at the same hour, in the which Jesus said unto him, "Thy son liveth": and himself believed, and his whole house.

This is again the second miracle that Jesus did, when he was come out of Judea into Galilee (John 4:51–54).

The many instantaneous physical healings wrought by Jesus were accomplished through his knowledge of the same scientific law by which he had earlier changed water into wine: the relationship of thought, life energy, and matter. [See Discourse 11.]

The universe, being a product of Divine Mind, can be changed by Divine Mind at any time. God's will created all things through condensation of His invisible ideations into the light of life energy and thence into atomic matter. God-realized souls who are in tune with the Divine Will can instantaneously produce any desired changes in matter, including the human body, by concentrated thought, which acts on and restructures the subtle energy matrix underlying each material form. As the energy in man's body can be directed by his will to initiate or influence the movement of any bodily part or function, so also, by omnipresent Divine Will, any vibratory movement effecting atomic changes can be initiated in any body, in any thing, and at any place, no matter how far distant.*

A master can heal the body by restructuring its underlying energy matrix

The creative vibratory thought of sickness was firmly fixed in the consciousness of the nobleman and his son, but Jesus thought differently,

---

* Scientific exploration of the body's underlying energy template is described on page 119 n. "Scientists in the Soviet Union have been researching the electromagnetic radiation (called 'bioplasma') given off by the human body," reports Marilyn Ferguson in *The Brain Revolution* (New York: Bantam, 1973). "They have charted the effects of different stimuli on that radiation. They found that chemicals, such as adrenaline, had the weakest effect. Massage of acupuncture points had the next strongest effect, followed by electrical stimulation and exposure to mild laser light. Most powerful of all, as observed by changes in the bioplasma, is human volition. If the subject quietly directs his thought toward a specific part of the body, the bioplasma shows corresponding changes."

In *Healing Words: The Power of Prayer and the Practice of Medicine* (HarperSanFrancisco, 1993), Larry Dossey, M.D., noted author of many books on the relationship of spirituality and medicine, writes of the scientific research that has been done on healing through prayer: "I found an enormous body of evidence: over one hundred experiments exhibiting the criteria of 'good science,' many conducted under stringent laboratory conditions, over half of which showed that prayer brings about significant changes in a variety of living beings."

Researchers Marilyn Schlitz, Ph.D., and William Braud, Ph.D., describe experiments that have proved the efficacy of different forms of "mental intentionality" (including prayer) to affect the growth rate of plants and cell cultures, the healing of wounds and cancerous tumors in animals, and a variety of other living systems. Using these non-human subjects, explain Schlitz and Braud, the distant healing hypothesis has been put to the test by measuring biological changes in a range of target systems "while ruling out suggestion or self-regulation as counter-explanations" ("Distant Intentionality and Healing: Assessing the Evidence," in *Alternative Therapies*, Vol. 3., No. 6, November 1997).

"Experiments with people showed that prayer positively affected high blood pressure, wounds, heart attacks, headaches, and anxiety," Dr. Dossey reports. "Remarkably the effects of prayer did not depend on whether the praying person was in the presence of the organism being prayed for, or whether he or she was far away; healing could take place either on site or at a distance." *(Publisher's Note)*

and so the son recovered. Jesus was able to displace the dream of sickness in the son by a dream of health. A divinely strong mind, implanting a thought of health and perfection in another person, can dissolve a stubborn thought of illness and cause a surge of restorative healing energy.

Ultimately, all disease can be found to have psychological roots, with every thought, in turn, being an ideation of consciousness. Thought is thus the brain, the architect, of the cells and units of life force in every particle of bodily tissue, influencing the functions of the underlying intelligent lifetrons. Hence, disease thoughts can upset the entire government of the life force in the cells; if strong enough or chronic enough, such thoughts manifest as bodily disease. Conversely, a strong thought of health can correct any disorder in the cellular system.

Concentrated human thought touches Divine Thought; it is that which can heal, not unfocused fanciful thought or imagination. To ef-

How concentration of human thought and will acts on the cells of the body

fectively move Divine Thought, one must be conscious of the relation of thought, life force, and the physical body. Rather than merely asserting the delusive, unreal nature of the body and its diseases, it is better to say: "The body is not what it appears to be." It does exist, though only as the frozen thought and energy of God. Instead of intellectualizing the delusive nature of the body, one should make the effort to realize how thought condenses into energy, and energy into flesh and blood and tissue. Neither fanatic fancy nor dogmatic belief bestows this realization; it comes by tuning in with God through some technique of awakening His consciousness in the soul. In this state of enlightenment, one fully realizes that the physical body and the entire cosmos are but frozen dreams of the Creator; and that our consciousness, an individualization of His consciousness, is the perceiver of and participator in His creative activity. Flowing water directed over an iceberg sculpts the berg into a new shape, either melting it partially or adding to its substance by becoming frozen itself. Likewise, a powerful mind and will can make consciousness interact with frozen consciousness to manipulate it for good or for ill.

The life force in the body has the absolute power to construct or destroy the body. But the life force can only perform according to the will of the bodily owner. Most persons do not know that their will can be trained to command the body to bring about miraculous changes in it; hence the wonder-working life energy remains disobedient most of the time to their conscious directives. Neither can the life force be mobilized by a will that has become paralyzed by persistent physical or mental infirmity. When one's will is debilitated by disease, it can be stimulated by the strong will of a mighty healer; the will of the healer and the renewed will of the patient awaken the life force to perform the desired healing.

Most persons who are ineffectual in trying to heal themselves have allowed their thoughts of health to be weakened by the mental habit of chronic thoughts of sickness. If for fifty years a person has enjoyed health, he thinks he can never be sick. If he suddenly finds himself physically ill, he thinks at first he will get well; but if the disease persists for six months, he becomes convinced that he will never get well. It is a regrettable psychological error to allow oneself to be manipulated by negative thoughts. One should visualize the conviction of one's healthful experiences to strengthen one's health consciousness and thereby dislodge any die-hard conviction of disease. If the strong mind of a healer can revive the will of the patient who has become paralyzed with the consciousness of sickness, then the patient can change his thought and energy, and thus heal himself. No one can heal us except through the cooperation of the hidden power of our own thoughts. A God-realized master can produce healing in an unresponsive person, but it is much more difficult; and only a master would be aware of the karmic circumstances that would make such a healing possible.

The power of thought in the healing of disease sets into motion a whole metaphysical process cooperative with the laws of creation that bring matter into manifestation. A dynamic thought of healing begins with modulation of the consciousness, of the thoughtrons of the superconscious mind, activating the lifetronic energy, the *prana* or life force in the body, to make changes in the subatomic electrons, and in the atoms, molecules, and cells. Any wave of consciousness thus sent forth to accomplish a purpose in the manifested realm traverses the whole spectrum of natural laws requisite to fulfilling its goal. Not in the least confounding to the orderly working of the intelligent principles of creation, the entire complex healing process can be effected instantaneously when so willed by divine fiat of a master in tune with God's mind; or, according to the wisdom of karmic conditions or other purposes, a healing may take place over a circumstantial period of time. The slower progression of the physical healing is simply catching up with the spiritual healing that has already taken place.

Physical healing, no matter what method initiates it, depends in the final analysis on the action of the life energy in the body to correct the diseased or otherwise inharmonious condition. A master such as Jesus, through his attunement with divine will, can administer vibrations of life energy directly to effect cures in cases where all other attempts have failed.

Healing by affirmations: the dynamic vibratory power of the spoken word

In various instances cited in the Gospels, Jesus employed the divine healing power of life energy in diverse ways, depending on the circumstances. In many cases, he transmitted the healing life force by direct touch. Others he cured by rousing their faith in the power of God emanating through him, thereby stimulating and reinforcing the dormant life energy within them. In the case of the nobleman's son in Capernaum, he utilized the dynamic vibratory power of the spoken word.

Vibratory healing consists in creating and consciously directing vibrations of life energy to individuals afflicted with disease or other maladies. This may be done internally by mentally projecting energy charged with will power, or externally by the vibrations of chants, intonations of the human voice, and enlivening words, phrases, and affirmations impregnated with superconsciousness.

As all creation consists of varying rates of vibration, sound has very great power. When one says softly, "Oh," a little vibration goes through the speaker and into the ether surrounding him. But if a big cannon is fired, its sound will pass through those in proximity and their whole body will be shaken and windows will be shattered. Intelligently spoken words are not merely sounds of communication, but vibrations of consciousness and energy. Their potency is determined not only by the physical force with which they are uttered, but even more by the magnitude of the thought- and energy-vibrations behind them.

A spoken word is composed of three vibrations—mental vibration, astral or energy vibration, and flesh vibration. Thus the vibratory sound of an utterance such as "Thou art peace" has behind it: (1) the vibration of thought that initiates the act of will, the original cause of vibrations of energy and flesh that result in the word "peace" being uttered; (2) the vibration of life energy sent by the will from the brain through the nerves to the vocal cords and tongue to allow the word "peace" to be spoken; and (3) the physical movement of the vocal cords that produce the sound, and the vibratory effect on the physical body and its environs created when the word "peace" is voiced.

Vibration means motion, which keeps all manifestations—material, mental, or spiritual—in an elastic state, subject to change. All phenomena—solids, liquids, gases; sound, X-rays, visible light; life energy, emotions, intelligence—are grosser or finer vibrating variations of the one Cosmic Vibration of the Creator. The grosser vibrations of matter are relatively fixed, within a circumscribed range. The mind of a matter-bound individual, attuned to the crimped vibrations of the material sphere, also remains relatively fixed. It vibrates with limited power. But potentially the mind has infinite elastic power; no matter how much you stretch it, it will not break. By spiritual techniques that develop concentration and will power and expand the consciousness, the matter-habituated mind is released from those constraints to vibrate at a finer rate, in tune with the astral and causal vibrations of God's creative activity and ultimately with the Creator Himself. One who knows how to use mind power can do anything.

The words of ordinary persons have limited effectiveness to create changes in vibratory matter because of the enfeebled mind power that projects them. But any imaginable transformation is possible to one who connects his utterances with the omnipotent vibration of God —He whose Word made the light, stars, stones, trees, human beings; He who is sustaining the incredible activity of the innumerable worlds moving in a purposeful order through space.*

When behind the spoken word is the word of God, the vibration of God (when one not only says the word *God,* but feels God as that word), the vibration of the voice goes forth with infinite power. When Jesus said, "Thy son liveth," it was a divine command. Behind his words were the consciousness and perception of God, impregnating his utterance with God's almighty healing power.

God's omnipotence omnipresent in creation is insulated in space. The vibratory etheric firmament separates the material realms of creation from the subtler realms, where the divine creative forces are not obscured by gross matter. The mind of a spiritually advanced person pierces the etheric insulation and contacts the higher vibratory forces emanating from God in the astral and causal worlds of all becomings.

In the presence of God-realized saints, when they are acting as conduits of the Divine Power, God is not insulated. Even a little men-

---

* "The infinite potencies of sound derive from the Creative Word, *Aum,* the cosmic vibratory power behind all atomic energies. Any word spoken with clear realization and deep concentration has a materializing value. Loud or silent repetition of inspiring words has been found effective in Couéism and similar systems of psychotherapy; the secret lies in the stepping-up of the mind's vibratory rate."—*Autobiography of a Yogi*

tal tuning-in with a master who is in divine consciousness will engender a change in an individual. This is why so many crowds were magnetically drawn to Jesus and were healed by that contact.

The healing of the nobleman's son did not even require direct contact with Jesus. In absent healing, there is a transcendence of time and

Vibrations of healing and prayers for others are effective at any distance

space, mocking their illusory persistence. As songs can be broadcast to float through the ether, ready to be caught by a radio, so it is that broadcast healing vibrations can be picked up by sensitive soul radios. When Jesus spoke the healing command, his voice set in motion his will-charged soul force, broadcasting into the ether the God-given healing vibrations, which were received by the faith of the nobleman, and thence relayed to his son, who became well immediately. Songs broadcast at any given moment from Los Angeles reach New York with no perceptible delay, because the sound is carried by electromagnetic radio waves moving at the speed of light. If radioed sound waves can be carried with such speed, then sound vibrations impregnated with healing soul force and transmitted through the Divine Omnipresence in the ether can reach their goal with perfect instancy.

All vibrations of sound let loose in the ether produce some momentary mental effect upon the hearer; but the vibrations of words saturated with soul force remain long in the ether, ever ready to work for the benefit of the recipient. This principle is operative in the effectiveness of prayers offered on behalf of others. The moment the healing vibrations reach the superconsciousness of the person to be healed, his soul sends a surge of energy from the brain down through the spine

Harnessing mind power to heal by positive thinking, affirmation, or prayer

into the body. It is that divine life energy, reinforced by the vibrations of God's healing power broadcast through the ether, that effects a cure.

Man does not realize the power of God that has been implanted by Him in the mind. It controls all the bodily functions, and when its power is properly exercised it can promote any condition in the body.* In divine healing, first the mind receives the suggestion of healing through positive thoughts, affirmation, or prayer. Then, through the superconscious con-

---

* An immense and continuously growing body of scientific research conducted over the past few decades has conclusively corroborated this ancient yogic teaching of "mind over matter." A whole new field of study and medical treatment has emerged, called

viction of the soul, the latent power of God in the mind becomes manifest. Finally the brain releases the divinely recharged life energy to heal.

In praying to God, the supplicant must churn the ether with his prayers; God will listen, even as He listened through the instrumen-

---

psychoneuroimmunology—harnessing the power of mind to enhance the functioning of the body's immune system to prevent and cure disease—as a few minutes spent in the "health and healing" section of any library or bookstore today will show.

A fascinating and comprehensive survey of scientific and historical material documenting the incredible power of the human mind is presented in *The Future of the Body: Explorations Into the Further Evolution of Human Nature* by Michael Murphy (Los Angeles: Jeremy P. Tarcher, 1992). "By showing that the central nervous system interacts with and can directly affect the immune system," writes Murphy, "such demonstrations have confirmed the long-standing belief of many doctors, philosophers, and spiritual teachers that mental images, attitudes, and emotions help determine sickness and well-being."

In one seven-year study, Dr. Suki Rappaport analyzed twenty-five individuals who had accomplished extraordinary physical transformations—overcoming birth defects, recovering from "incurable" illnesses, regaining function after severely crippling accidents, etc. "All these people told me the same thing," she reported. "They all had an image in their minds of who and what they wanted to be. And they literally grew their physical bodies into that imagined form."

O. Carl Simonton, M.D., noted pioneer in cancer treatment, has stated: "When we look at spontaneous remission [of cancer] or at unexpectedly good responses and try to figure out what happens in common, we find the same spontaneous occurrence of visualizing oneself being well....I have not found any case of spontaneous remission in which the patient did not go through a similar visualizing process."

In *The Holographic Universe* (New York: HarperCollins, 1991), Michael Talbot describes psychiatric studies of Multiple Personality Disorder (MPD), a condition "that graphically illustrates the mind's power to affect the body....Biological changes take place in a multiple's body when they switch personalities. Frequently a medical condition possessed by one personality will mysteriously vanish when another personality takes over....By changing personalities, a multiple who is drunk can instantly become sober. Different personalities also respond differently to different drugs. Dr. Bennett Braun records a case where 5 milligrams of diazepam, a tranquilizer, sedated one personality, while 100 milligrams had little or no effect on another....Speech pathologist Christy Ludlow has found that the voice pattern for each of a multiple's personalities is different, a feat that requires such a deep physiological change that even the most accomplished actor cannot alter his voice enough to disguise his voice pattern. One multiple, admitted to a hospital for diabetes, baffled her doctors by showing no symptoms while one of her nondiabetic personalities was in control. There are accounts of epilepsy coming and going with changes in personality....

"The systems of control that must be in place to account for such capacities is mind-boggling....What unknown pathways of influence enable the mind of a multiple...to suspend the effects of alcohol and other drugs in the blood, or turn diabetes on and off? At the moment we don't know and must console ourselves with one simple fact. Once a multiple has undergone therapy and in some way becomes whole again, he or she can still make these switches at will. This suggests that somewhere in our psyches we all have the ability to control these things." *(Publisher's Note)*

tality of Jesus to the urgent entreaties of the nobleman. As was the case in Capernaum, there is no limit to the response and the love of God, if one has faith and loves Him truly. Jesus, in that Love, said, "Thy son liveth." Immediately his thought vibration pierced the ether, and powerful life-force currents and light began to play in the nobleman's son, changing the constitution of the ailing body. By divine fiat Jesus performed this miracle, demonstrating that his thought was connected with the omnipresent cosmic creative energy of God that is the source of all life. The light in a lamp can be switched off and on again if it is connected to the current from the dynamo. God created the body lamp and is also the Dynamo that lights it with His cosmic energy. Even if the lamp is broken, its Creator can repair and light it again.

Jesus showed what it is to be in touch with the Cosmic Dynamo. When one feels God's presence, His vibratory energy, the strength of His infinite power, any thought he declares will materialize.

DISCOURSE 21

"What Things the Father Doeth, These Also Doeth the Son Likewise"

Jesus' Discourse on Judgment and Resurrection
After the Healing at the Pool of Bethesda

———————

Effect of Past Wrong Actions on Present Human Suffering

❖

Metaphysical Meaning of "Death":
Liberating the Soul From All Three Bodies

❖

Communing With Cosmic Vibration in Meditation
Brings Imperishable Life

❖

Did Jesus Teach Bodily Resurrection of the Dead?

❖

True Meaning of "Gabriel's Trumpet"

———————

"The Son is thus God's love in creation—a magnetic power of harmony and intelligence working to evolve all manifestations to ever higher levels....Neither God nor Jesus as the Christ Intelligence is a despotic disciplinarian passing judgment on the actions of man."

*A*fter this there was a feast of the Jews; and Jesus went up to Jerusalem. *

Now there is at Jerusalem by the sheep market a pool, which is called in the Hebrew tongue Bethesda, having five porches. In these lay a great multitude of impotent folk, of blind, halt, withered, waiting for the moving of the water. For an angel went down at a certain season into the pool, and troubled the water: whosoever then first after the troubling of the water stepped in was made whole of whatsoever disease he had.

And a certain man was there, which had an infirmity thirty and eight years. When Jesus saw him lie, and knew that he had been now a long time in that case, he saith unto him, "Wilt thou be made whole?"

The impotent man answered him, "Sir, I have no man, when the water is troubled, to put me into the pool: but while I am coming, another steppeth down before me."

Jesus saith unto him, "Rise, take up thy bed, and walk."

And immediately the man was made whole, and took up his bed, and walked: and on the same day was the Sabbath.

The Jews therefore said unto him that was cured, "It is the Sabbath day: it is not lawful for thee to carry thy bed."

He answered them, "He that made me whole, the same said unto me, 'Take up thy bed, and walk.'"

Then asked they him, "What man is that which said unto thee, 'Take up thy bed, and walk'?" And he that was healed wist not who it was: for Jesus had conveyed himself away, a multitude being in that place.

---

* It is not known precisely where this story of the healing at the pool of Bethesda fits into the sequence of events recounted in the other three Gospels, which are silent about the period from Jesus' forty days in the wilderness until the beginning of his preaching the Gospel in Galilee (related in Discourse 22). St. John's Gospel, the only one in which the Bethesda story is related, merely says that it occurred after the healing of the nobleman's son (Discourse 20) and before the feeding of five thousand with five loaves and two fish (Discourse 42). *(Publisher's Note)*

Afterward Jesus findeth him in the temple, and said unto him, "Behold, thou art made whole: sin no more, lest a worse thing come unto thee."

The man departed, and told the Jews that it was Jesus, which had made him whole. And therefore did the Jews persecute Jesus, and sought to slay him, because he had done these things on the Sabbath day.

But Jesus answered them, "My Father worketh hitherto, and I work."

Therefore the Jews sought the more to kill him, because he not only had broken the Sabbath, but said also that God was his Father, making himself equal with God.

Then answered Jesus and said unto them, "Verily, verily, I say unto you, the Son can do nothing of himself, but what he seeth the Father do: for what things soever He doeth, these also doeth the Son likewise. For the Father loveth the Son, and sheweth him all things that Himself doeth: and He will shew him greater works than these, that ye may marvel. For as the Father raiseth up the dead, and quickeneth them; even so the Son quickeneth whom he will. For the Father judgeth no man, but hath committed all judgment unto the Son: That all men should honour the Son, even as they honour the Father. He that honoureth not the Son honoureth not the Father which hath sent him.

"Verily, verily, I say unto you, he that heareth my word, and believeth on Him that sent me, hath everlasting life, and shall not come into condemnation; but is passed from death unto life. Verily, verily, I say unto you, the hour is coming, and now is, when the dead shall hear the voice of the Son of God: and they that hear shall live. For as the Father hath life in Himself; so hath He given to the Son to have life in himself; And hath given him authority to execute judgment also, because he is the Son of man. Marvel not at this: for the hour is coming, in the which all that are in the graves shall hear his voice, and shall come forth; they that have done good, unto the resurrection of life; and they that have done evil, unto the resurrection of damnation.

"I can of mine own self do nothing: as I hear, I judge: and my judgment is just; because I seek not mine own will, but the will of the Father which hath sent me. If I bear witness of myself, my witness is not true. There is another that beareth witness of me; and I know that the witness which he witnesseth of me is true. Ye sent unto John, and he bare witness unto the truth. But I receive not testimony from man: but these things I say, that ye might be saved. He was a burning and a shining light: and ye were willing for a season to rejoice in his light.

"But I have greater witness than that of John: for the works which the Father hath given me to finish, the same works that I do, bear witness of me, that the Father hath sent me. And the Father Himself, which hath sent me, hath borne witness of me. Ye have neither heard His voice at any time, nor seen His shape. And ye have not His word abiding in you: for whom He hath sent, him ye believe not. Search the scriptures; for in them ye think ye have eternal life: and they are they which testify of me. And ye will not come to me, that ye might have life. I receive not honour from men. But I know you, that ye have not the love of God in you.

"I am come in my Father's name, and ye receive me not: if another shall come in his own name, him ye will receive. How can ye believe, which receive honour one of another, and seek not the honour that cometh from God only? Do not think that I will accuse you to the Father: there is one that accuseth you, even Moses, in whom ye trust. For had ye believed Moses, ye would have believed me: for he wrote of me. But if ye believe not his writings, how shall ye believe my words?"

—John 5:1–47

"What Things the Father Doeth, These Also Doeth the Son Likewise"

Jesus' Discourse on Judgment and Resurrection After the Healing at the Pool of Bethesda

After this there was a feast of the Jews; and Jesus went up to Jerusalem.

Now there is at Jerusalem by the sheep market a pool, which is called in the Hebrew tongue Bethesda, having five porches. In these lay a great multitude of impotent folk, of blind, halt, withered, waiting for the moving of the water. For an angel went down at a certain season into the pool, and troubled the water: whosoever then first after the troubling of the water stepped in was made whole of whatsoever disease he had.

And a certain man was there, which had an infirmity thirty and eight years. When Jesus saw him lie, and knew that he had been now a long time in that case, he saith unto him, "Wilt thou be made whole?" (John 5:1–6).

During a feast time, Jesus went to Jerusalem and came to the pool of Bethesda. He went among a crowd of stricken people who were waiting to immerse themselves when, at certain periods, the waters were moved by an inner healing force that was believed to be an angel. The pool vibrated and emanated healing earth currents (electromagnetic), and many who bathed in the pool at those times were healed.*

Belief in the healing power of the water was also a factor, causing a mental reaction that roused the natural healing power within the body. When sickness weakens the mind and paralyzes the will, one cannot throw off the troubling illness. Faith revives one's all-healing, all-powerful will to release the nascent life energy in the brain to effect the healing of any diseased part of the body.

Jesus felt compassion for the man who had been afflicted for thirty-eight years, and who was unable to get into the pool by himself. He asked the suffering man, *"Wilt thou be made whole?"*

~

The impotent man answered him, "Sir, I have no man, when the water is troubled, to put me into the pool: but while I am coming, another steppeth down before me."

Jesus saith unto him, "Rise, take up thy bed, and walk."

And immediately the man was made whole, and took up his bed, and walked: and on the same day was the Sabbath (John 5:7–9).

The divine law of healing requires the proper soil of faith on the part of the patient, and the proper seed of mental healing power on the part of the healer, in order for the roots and branches of the plant of healing to reach deep and broad enough into the consciousness of the person to be healed. Jesus prepared the

Both the seed of healing power and the soil of faith are necessary

soil of faith by creating in the stricken man the desire to be healed by the immediacy of divine law, which does not depend on external factors. When Jesus found that the sick man was receptive, he said, "Rise, take up thy bed, and walk." He showed the stricken man that he need not wait to be made whole by the waters of the pool, but

---

* The site of the pool of Bethesda was discovered by archaeologists in the nineteenth century. However, historians and Biblical scholars have not been able to ascertain the nature of its healing benefits, since the only extant records are in this passage in the Gospel According to St. John. *(Publisher's Note)*

that he could be healed at once by the unlimited power of God hidden within the human will and mind.

The man was instantaneously made whole by (1) the uninterrupted flow of the infinite all-healing energy of God through the mental transparency of the consciousness of Jesus; and (2) by his own awakened faith and the revival of his paralyzed will, which served as the antenna to attune himself to the vibrant cosmic energy from Jesus that combined with and recharged the latent life energy of his own brain.

&

> *The Jews therefore said unto him that was cured, "It is the Sabbath day: it is not lawful for thee to carry thy bed."*
>
> *He answered them, "He that made me whole, the same said unto me, 'Take up thy bed, and walk.'"*
>
> *Then asked they him, "What man is that which said unto thee, 'Take up thy bed, and walk'?" And he that was healed wist not who it was: for Jesus had conveyed himself away, a multitude being in that place (John 5:10–13).*

Not wishing to express amazement at the healing performed by Jesus, for that would be an acknowledgment of his superiority, skeptical observers displayed instead a sham zeal for the laws of the Sabbath day.

&

> *Afterward Jesus findeth him in the temple, and said unto him, "Behold, thou art made whole: sin no more, lest a worse thing come unto thee" (John 5:14).*

Jesus was warning the healed man that his sickness had been the result of his own prenatal actions from past incarnations as well as postnatal evil behavior of his present life; and lest he succumb again, he should not persist in his sinful ways. Jesus was pointing out the importance of freeing one's power of independent action from the influence of the tendencies of past wrong actions. If the man's transgressions continued, the cumulative evil of the past and the evil accruing from new actions would result in a condign punishment of an even worse disaster.

Traces of past evils lie hidden within the consciousness in the brain, potentially ready to be roused by a stimulus of fresh misdeeds. Those

-----•-•-----

Effect of past wrong actions on present human suffering

malevolent tendencies can instead be eradicated with the electrifying force of newly acquired wisdom.

Jesus clearly signified that the consequences of sin, as also the rewards of virtue, do not come from unknown causes or from a decree of God, but are the result of human wrong or good actions, the law of cause and effect, which governs the life of man. Persons who do not lead scientifically discriminative lives ascribe good fortune or misfortune to an inscrutable, whimsical destiny. This irrational quirk in some strange way seems to offer comfort in its false sense of irresponsibility. This misconception should be courageously renounced and replaced by wisdom. Instead of moaning over one's fate and blaming destiny, one should adopt discriminative good behavior, which will mitigate and counteract the effect of past evil doings.

In this healing incident, Jesus pronouncedly makes every man responsible for his own suffering. It further points out that not only is man's life governed by the law of action, but that reincarnation alone can explain the inequalities and seeming injustices that visit human beings from their birth. The remedy is that a chronic physical, moral, or mental sickness can be healed in one of two ways: either by direct divine intervention of one of God's intermediaries, and cooperation with his advice; or by adopting the counteracting good actions that will destroy, or at least minimize, the effects of past wrong actions.

≈

The man departed, and told the Jews that it was Jesus, which had made him whole. And therefore did the Jews persecute Jesus, and sought to slay him, because he had done these things on the Sabbath day. *

-----

* All four Gospels record that throughout his public ministry Jesus encountered opposition from some elements of the Jewish community. Especially singled out in various passages are persons among "the chief priests," "the Pharisees," "the Sadducees," and "scribes" or "doctors of the law" ("lawyers"). It is only in the Gospel According to St. John that Jesus' antagonists are referred to collectively as "the Jews." Many historians, pointing out that Jesus and his disciples were themselves born into the Jewish tradition, maintain that pejorative references to "the Jews" entered the accounts of Jesus' life decades after the fact,

But Jesus answered them, "My Father worketh hitherto, and I work."

Therefore the Jews sought the more to kill him, because he not only had broken the Sabbath, but said also that God was his Father, making himself equal with God (John 5:15–18).

The critics of Jesus mechanically followed the letter of the rules in observing the Sabbath and their other ethics of living, whereas Jesus followed the spirituality of rules, often ignoring superficiality and man-made formality. The spirit of the Sabbath consists in setting aside material and social engagements and remaining in an inner worshipful state of devotion with the consciousness focused on God. In cessation of material activity without spiritual communion, it is possible to be conscious, not of God, but of little more than the idleness of the body. In the name of God, Jesus could perform a material act on the Sabbath day without its being in the least material. To him every day was a Sabbath, lived in wisdom and God-consciousness.

That is why Jesus said: "My Father worketh hitherto, and I work."* Whatever work Jesus did on earth was actuated by his consciousness of the Father and guided by the intuitional direction he received from God; it therefore could contain no taint of evil nor violate any spiritually legitimate law.

Actions guided by God automatically accord with spiritual laws

No matter what a God-attuned devotee does, his actions, will, and reason are of his own free choice, but he feels them guided by the

---

reflecting the growing dissension faced by Christian communities at the time the Gospels were put into writing. As is clear from Paramahansa Yogananda's commentaries, the real import of such passages refers to ignorant and malevolent opposers of the spiritual truths preached by Jesus, irrespective of their social or religious status. *(Publisher's Note)*

* Speaking through Sri Krishna of the ceaseless work of divine activity, the Lord says: "If I did not perform actions, these universes would be annihilated" (*God Talks With Arjuna: The Bhagavad Gita* III:24). From the commentary: "God, as the Creator of universes, works immanently as the Universal Intelligence in matter and in human consciousness for the purpose of maintaining order while working out His cosmic plan. He says, 'If I, the Father of all, did not act in creation, all universes would explode and vanish. My cosmic consciousness keeps the floating islands of planets swimming rhythmically in the cosmic sea. It is My intelligence as *Kutastha Chaitanya* that consciously holds all atoms together and keeps them working in coordination.'...

"If God removed His cohesive Intelligence, all universes and beings would disappear from objectivity, just as the scenes and actors vanish from a screen when the light running through a film is shut off."

wisdom of the Heavenly Father. Such devotees are not slaves of God; rather, in acting wisely of their own volition, they find that the wisdom in man's soul is the wisdom that comes from God. The Lord never constrains His devotees to do anything; but those who feel the presence of God know the wisdom of His will and prefer His guidance rather than their own egoistic determinations.

"Thy will be done" does not involve enslavement of man's will; but as demonstrated by Jesus, a man's wisdom-guided will is identical with God's wisdom-guided will, since all wisdom is His alone.

~

> *"Verily, verily, I say unto you, the Son can do nothing of himself, but what he seeth the Father do" (John 5:19).*

In these words, Jesus told exactly how he worked. He showed his great love for God and reverential deference. With such love and wisdom, he saw God and God's actions as the Father of creation. As he saw how the Heavenly Father acted, and felt the effects of those actions as governed by love as well as by law, Jesus acted likewise out of his own free choice.

What the Son "seeth the Father do" suggests an intimacy possible only in manifestation. As omnipresent Jesus appeared in bodily form after his resurrection, so also the infinite formless God can appear in a Deity-form materialized out of the ether, or as a manifested Light or Voice as experienced by Jesus on the mountaintop.* It is this personalization of God that Jesus addressed in reverent familiarity as Father.†

---

* See Discourse 45.

† The Hindu scriptures resolve the apparent contradiction in the transcendent-immanently active aspects of God in the concept of the Deity as Ishvara (from Sanskrit root *ish*, to rule):

"The Absolute united to Its Creative Intelligence, Maha-Prakriti (Holy Ghost), becomes Ishvara, the Cosmic Ruler, God the Father of Creation, the Causal Universal Dreamer by whose divine will universes evolve and dissolve in orderly cycles. Ishvara is thus both transcendent and immanent—beyond vibratory manifestation and active through Maha-Prakriti in bringing forth the primordial causal forms of all becomings" (*God Talks With Arjuna: The Bhagavad Gita*, commentary on IV:25).

The transcendence of Ishvara beyond vibratory manifestation obtains also in its immaculate reflection as the *Kutastha Chaitanya*/Universal Christ-Krishna Intelligence that is omnipresent in creation yet is perdurably immutable midst Maha-Prakriti's vibratory mutations of *maya*. (See also Discourse 5.)

In the phrase, "he seeth," Jesus spoke of divine sons who could see by their intuitional eye what the Omnipresent Father or Spirit is working in all creation. The physical body of Jesus saw through its physical eyes, as do other human beings, but the inner Jesus could see everything with his spiritual eye of intuition. The inner spirit of Jesus the Son, with the countless eyes of omnipresence, saw or intuitively perceived the Omnipresent Father secretly residing and working in the heart of atoms, of electrons and protons contained in everything materially created. The Cosmic Consciousness of the Father, inactive beyond all creation, works only indirectly in His reflected intelligence as the Son, the Christ Intelligence in all vibratory creation, and is directly active as the creative Holy Ghost vibration bringing God's cosmic dreamings into manifestation. No physical eyes can see the Omnipresent, Invisible Father and know of His awesome secret work in His cosmic kingdom.

∾

"What things soever He doeth, these also doeth the Son likewise" (John 5:19).

Any incarnate son of God feels himself tuned with the Universal Christ Intelligence and knows that that Consciousness is the reflection of God the Father's Intelligence. The sun reflected in a crystal ball is divided into two, the light of the sun beyond the crystal ball and the light of the sun in the crystal ball. The light in the crystal ball, though limited, is the same as the sunshine beyond the crystal ball. Likewise, the Christ Consciousness shining within creation, though limited, is the same as God the Father's Cosmic Consciousness shining beyond vibratory creation. Therefore, Jesus says that he, as a son of God, one with the reflected Christ Presence of God in all creation, could only do as His Father's Consciousness actuated him to perform.

∾

"For the Father loveth the Son and sheweth him all things that Himself doeth: and He will shew him greater works than these, that ye may marvel" (John 5:20).

351

God the Father differentiated Himself into the Holy Ghost or Cosmic Vibratory Creation. In the womb of the Holy Ghost, with its myriad manifestations, was born the Christ Intelligence of God the Father. Since God differentiated Himself into God the Father beyond creation and God the Son in all creation, He respected all the differences that He created through the Christ-imbued Holy Ghost Cosmic Vibration. So, God the Father beyond creation, being ever new Bliss and Love, caused the same ever new Bliss and Love to be reflected in the Son or Christ Intelligence present in all vibratory creation. This is what is meant by the "Father loveth the Son." The Son is thus God's love in creation—a magnetic power of harmony and intelligence working to evolve all manifestations to ever higher levels of perfection.

The Father showing all things to the Son denotes that God the Father's Intelligence beyond creation reveals all His qualities in His reflection as the Christ Intelligence in creation. Hence as Omnipresent God knows everything, so also a true son who can feel the omnipresence of God likewise participates in His omniscience.

Revelation of greater works to the Son signifies that all things have their origin in God the Father of creation and proceed toward manifestation through the Son, or Christ Intelligence. As a Self-realized master advances toward complete liberation and mergence in God, he perceives more and more of the endless manifestations of God's power in eternally progressive creation, in which there will always be greater works throughout eternity—more wonderful than all those revealed up to any given time. The progress of creation in God is endlessly new, for God the Creator is eternal and eternally new in His expression.

∼

"For as the Father raiseth up the dead, and quickeneth them; even so the Son quickeneth whom he will" (John 5:21).

As the Father has the power to reanimate a dead body by charging it with life force, so a master, if he is commanded by God, can similarly restore life, as was demonstrated by Jesus. Metaphysically speaking, however, real death means not only extinction of life in the physical body of sixteen elements, but also the dissolution of the two other bodies in which the soul is encased—the astral body of

nineteen elements and the causal body of thirty-five elemental ideas.*
Death is a condition applicable only to these three bodies. It is the immortal soul that "the Father raiseth up" from the
delusive death-dealing tentacles and attachments of   *Metaphysical meaning*
its three bodies, provided it has regained realization   *of "death": liberating*
of its unity with the consciousness of the Omni-   *the soul from all three*
present Father. Advanced souls by meditation tech-   *bodies*
niques and God's grace free themselves from imprisonment in the three bodies. Such souls, their bodily encasements
being metaphysically dead, are forthwith spirited away from the limitations of mortal consciousness to the perception of the kingdom of
infinite life—transferred from the bodily death-state of their forgotten omnipresence to experience the resurrection of their true universal
Self.

In the Bible, we find Christ defined as "the first begotten of the
dead, and the prince of the kings of the earth."† This definition is very
deep and subtle. The soul wave, individualized out of the ocean of
Spirit by encasement in the physical, astral, and ideational bodies, is
corked therein by ignorance (delusion) and material desires and is unable to mingle with the ocean of Spirit surrounding it. With the change
of the physical body called "death," the soul still remains encased in
its astral and ideational bodies, unable to loosen its oceanic essence to
join the ocean of Spirit. By a liberating technique of highest meditation, the soul frees itself completely and merges itself in Christ Consciousness, the "first-begotten" state of the soul raised from the death
of mortal confinement.

In human consciousness, the soul experiences itself as ego, identified with the physical body, name, titles, possessions, nationality, and
all the other factors of I, me, and mine. In the subconscious state, the
soul cognizes itself as the restless power of dreams, or as the dreamless peace of deep sleep. In the superconscious state, the soul feels itself as undiluted, formless, ever new joy. In the state of Christ Consciousness, the soul, emerging from its three metaphysically dead
bodies, feels itself commingled with the Christ Intelligence in all creation, the ever-conscious, supreme princely Intelligence guiding all
other kingly intelligent forces that govern the earth and all matter.

---

* See "astral body" and "causal body" in glossary.

† Revelation 1:5.

Jesus, the man, could feel his consciousness, not only as residing in and governing his mortal body, but also as the Christ Intelligence pervading all the space cells of his vast cosmic body.

As God helps to resurrect souls from entombment within the delusive sepulchre of the three bodies, so also, a true son—a master or God-realized guru—can raise any devoted, aspiring disciple into the omnipresent Spirit. The guru who is one with the Father can help the deeply meditating disciple to expand his consciousness and life from the limited sensations of the body out into unlimited space to feel all life in omnipresence. That is the meaning of the "Son quickeneth" or the "Father quickeneth."

~

"For the Father judgeth no man, but hath committed all judgment unto the Son: That all men should honour the Son, even as they honour the Father. He that honoureth not the Son honoureth not the Father which hath sent him" (John 5:22–23).

The transcendental God the Father beyond all creation reflected Himself as the Christ Intelligence in creation, to be the underlying guiding Intelligence of all manifestations. The intelligent creative forces of Cosmic Nature all emerge from the supreme Christ Intelligence as accessories of the Holy Ghost Cosmic Vibration. Thus Christ Intelligence is directly responsible for the creation of man and for giving to each man his power of free choice to do good or evil. Hence, all human beings are in turn directly responsible to the Christ Intelligence for the use or misuse of their free will.

"The Father hath committed all judgment unto the Son" does not mean that the Christ Intelligence punishes or rewards each person, but that each individual must suffer the consequences

The all-loving Christ never renders vengeful judgment or punishment on man

of his own actions when he makes wrong determinations. Man, whose soul is made in the image of the Infinite Christ, should naturally live as a Christ; but when he resists and acts against the Christ conscience in him, he puts himself in disharmony with the ever-flowing judgment or wisdom or harmony or love or peace of Christ. A river follows its natural course to make a land fertile; but if an embankment is put up which impedes that flow, the river indirectly, with no subjective intent, passes judgment of punishment by denying its theretofore freely given water. So also, when man erects a wall of ignorance and non-receptivity and matter-identified living, he finds that the divine waters of Christ-wisdom have passed judgment not to flow in his life, in respect of his free will. It would be wrong to ascribe to Christ (who suffered on the cross, saying: "Father, forgive them for they know not what they do"), and to God or Godlike souls, any revengeful judgment or action.

The Father, hidden in all space, manifests Himself through His true incarnate sons who receive and reflect His wisdom. Those who respect the Father and are desirous of knowing Him, but cannot hear His guiding voice, should honor and follow these true sons of God— God-sent enlightened gurus—through whose voices God speaks to truth-seeking devotees. It is so easy for devotees to hear the voice of God in the definite guidance of God-known masters. Ignorant people do not know God because they do not purify their minds to receive Him. Jesus and Christlike souls manifest God; and therefore persons who do not honor or offer respectful attention to these pure channels similarly deny respectful attention to the Father who is responsible for His emissaries' missions of redemption on earth.

~

"Verily, verily, I say unto you, he that heareth my word, and believeth on Him that sent me, hath everlasting life, and shall not come into condemnation; but is passed from death unto life. Verily, verily, I say unto you, the hour is coming, and now is, when the dead shall hear the voice of the Son of God: and they that hear shall live. For as the Father hath life in Himself; so hath He given to the Son to have life in himself; and hath given him authority to execute judgment also, because he is the Son of man" (John 5:24–27).

"Verily, verily, through the certitude I feel through my intuitive oneness with the universal Christ Consciousness, I say unto you and all mankind that devotees who listen to the Cosmic Vibration, the Word or comforting Holy Ghost and my guided wisdom of Christ Intelligence felt in it, believe and know that my wisdom comes from God the Father."

355

Devotees who by constant meditation and spiritual ecstasy feel Christ in all creation are the real Christ-ians. Through direct experience they

Communing with Cosmic Vibration in meditation brings imperishable life

know and believe in Christ Intelligence and the Father who reflected that Intelligence in all creation, and they know Christ as manifested in the Cosmic Vibration. That is why it is emphasized "he that heareth my word...hath everlasting life"; that is, he who listens to the Cosmic Vibration and intuitively feels Christ-wisdom flowing into him not only knows and believes in God and Christ, but becomes one with the imperishable life emanating from Them.

Such souls who are one with Cosmic Vibration and the Christ Intelligence in it, and with God's Intelligence beyond creation, are free from condemnation; that is, from the law of action and its inscrutable judgment that governs man's life.

The devotee seeking everlasting life needs to practice the consciousness-expanding technique of listening to the Cosmic Vibration and feeling Christ Consciousness within it. When he is consciously able to do that and to lift his soul from perceiving the sensations of the physical body, the power and energy of the astral body, and lastly, the thought confinement of the causal body, he raises himself from the tomb of the metaphysically dead three bodies to pass on into the perception of perpetual freedom in Spirit.

Ordinary persons who have no direct knowledge or experience of the Cosmic Vibration—the comforting Holy Ghost, which Jesus promised to send and which devotees can feel by practicing Self-Realization methods—actually have relatively little conscious awareness after death during their deep peaceful rest between incarnations. But the time will come to such persons, and verily the time has arrived now for advanced disciples, when by the guru's help and by meditation they shall hear the cosmic sound of the Holy Ghost Vibration and feel their expanding wisdom as emanating from the Son of God, the Christ Consciousness. Those devotees who commune with the all-comforting Holy Ghost Vibration (as taught in Lahiri Mahasaya's technique and in which Christ instructed his close disciples) shall not experience the ordinary oblivion of death, but shall live in a continuity of consciousness in the everlastingness of life that flows from God the Father, linking their life with the omnipresent life in all creation.

An ordinary person appears to live only once, in his present lifetime, because he cannot remember his identity during the process of

transition from one life to another, as his soul passes through many incarnations. In that sense, man does not live forever, even though his immortal soul never dies. But a fairly advanced master passing through a
few last incarnations required to finish up his latent ties to earth
bondage can preserve in his memory the continuity of the identity of
his soul. Gradually such souls learn to live forever in God without their
consciousness being interrupted by death.

As the Father is the Source of Cosmic Life, so has He bequeathed
that power to His reflected presence as the Christ Intelligence in all vibratory creation. In the Christ Intelligence God has also placed the universal laws that govern all aspects of creation. Through these righteous
principles that uphold the universe, the Son executes judgment.* That
is, whensoever any of these divine codes are transgressed, a consequential judgment is automatically imposed by the Universal Intelligence. As
the Christ Intelligence can be manifest also in a human form, "the son
of man," as it was in Jesus and other true sons of God who received
God-consciousness through the transparency of their consciousness,
such a one speaks with the authority of God's wisdom in guiding souls
to live in harmony with God's divine principles and on occasion mitigating the judgmental effects of those laws at God's behest.

---

* The scriptures of India refer to these universal governing principles as *dharma*: duty,
eternal laws of righteousness. In his commentary on the Bhagavad Gita, *God Talks
With Arjuna*, Paramahansa Yogananda wrote:

"*Dharma*, from the Sanskrit root *dhri*, 'to uphold or support'—often translated
simply as religion or righteousness—is a comprehensive term for the natural laws and
eternal verities that uphold the divine order of the universe and of man, a miniature
universe. Sankhya philosophy thus defines true religion as 'those immutable principles
that protect man permanently from the threefold suffering of disease, unhappiness, and
ignorance.' India's vast body of Vedic teachings are amassed under the umbrella-term
Sanatana Dharma, 'Eternal Religion.'"

"The universe exists because it is held together by the will of God manifesting as
the immutable cosmic principles of creation. Therefore He is the real *Dharma*. Without God no creature can exist. The highest *dharma* or duty of every human being is to
find out, by realization, that he is sustained by God.

"*Dharma*, therefore, is the cosmic law that runs the mechanism of the universe;
and after accomplishing the primary God-uniting *yoga-dharma* (religious duties), man
should perform secondarily his duties to the cosmic laws of nature....

"Man should perform virtuous *dharma*, for by obedience to righteous duty he can
free himself from the law of cause and effect governing all actions. He should avoid irreli-
gion (*adharma*) which takes him away from God, and follow religion (*Sanatana Dharma*),
by which he finds Him. Man should observe the religious duties (*yoga-dharma*) enjoined
in the true scriptures of the world. Codes for all aspects of human conduct, as given in the
laws of Manu, are also considered *dharmas* or duties for the guidance of man."

～

"Marvel not at this: for the hour is coming, in the which all that
are in the graves shall hear his voice, and shall come forth; they that
have done good, unto the resurrection of life; and they that have
done evil, unto the resurrection of damnation" (John 5:28–29).

This age of logic, having struggled out of a long dark night of superstition, belies belief in a literal interpretation of Christ's words
in this verse. The word "graves" used by Jesus gave Biblical interpreters
of little or no direct intuitional perception the thought that after death
man's soul waits with its cold corpse entombed, able to rise only on
Resurrection Day when archangel Gabriel blows his
trumpet. It appears that for twenty centuries Gabriel
has not sounded his trumpet, because the skeletons
of millions can be found still in their graves.*

Did Jesus teach bodily
resurrection of the
dead?

This misconception of resurrection, that God
would keep living souls refrigerated for years beneath the cold sod,
and then suddenly warm them up to be sent to Hades or Heaven, is
baseless, revolting, injurious, and unreasonable.

If that is the plan, what injustice it is that sinners and the virtuous alike, without discrimination, have been kept waiting for centuries. Surely the just law of cause and effect has something better to
offer those who strived sincerely to live a righteous life. Are we to believe that an autocratic God, without rhyme or reason, dumps all souls
after death under a clod of earth and keeps them sleeping peacefully
or dreaming in nightmares for centuries until His mood suddenly
chooses to command Gabriel to blow the trumpet and wake the dead?
And what of those highly spiritual souls whose bodies are not buried
but were cremated and the ashes scattered in the winds and seas?

---

* The traditional Christian belief that the Resurrection on the last day will be heralded
by the angel Gabriel blowing his trumpet is not specifically mentioned in the Bible. In
various New Testament passages, the Resurrection is said to be heralded by an (unnamed) angel sounding a celestial trumpet or by the voice of Christ (as in the verses
explained in this Discourse), or both. For example, in Matthew 24:30–31, speaking
of "the end of the world," Jesus says: "He shall send His angels with a great sound of
a trumpet...." Saint Paul wrote that at the time of the Resurrection "the trumpet shall
sound" (1 Corinthians 15:52), and also of the Lord's coming "with the voice of the
archangel, and with the trump of God..." (1 Thessalonians 4:16–17). See also footnote on page 364.

If Gabriel sounds the trumpet tomorrow, souls who died today would wake up after only a few hours, along with the souls who have been dead for centuries before the time of Christ. To drug immortal souls with the sleep of death for centuries, to gag their expression in the gloom of the tomb for aeons, to chloroform their intelligence for millenniums, and then suddenly wake them up and sort them out for Heaven and Hades, is an untenable conception to ascribe to a just and loving God.

How would God select from the various grades of dead sinners and the various degrees of virtuous people, and the babies who have had no time to be either virtuous or evil, which ones are to go eternally to Heaven and which eternally to Hades? From such a medley of imperfect, half-perfect, and neutral souls no divine justice could perform any reasonable selections. If God arbitrarily makes persons of reasonable or unreasonable mentality, souls predisposed to be either good or bad, nudged by a favorable or unfavorable earthly inheritance, and endows babies with reason and then lets them die before they can express their potentials, just for the sake of variety, then this earth is a hopeless mess, and its creatures hapless puppets dancing on strings of chance. Our common sense tells us that there must be a wiser purpose from a Creator who is wisdom itself. The reason and free choice of every human being must have time and equal opportunity to evolve and express the full God-given divinity of the soul.

The true meaning of these verses becomes clear when understood in the light of the law of karma and reincarnation, according to which the Christ Intelligence immanent in the Holy Ghost Vibration ("his voice") judges the fate of each human being after death. This "voice," or Gabriel's trumpet, signals the transition, governed by cosmic law, from one vibratory state of existence to another.*

---

* As explained on page 356, man need not wait for death to be uplifted by the "voice" of Cosmic Vibration of *Aum* or Amen (Holy Ghost): Through scientific techniques of meditation he may commune with the Holy Ghost vibration of *Aum* or Amen, experiencing the celestial consciousness spoken of by Saint John in the Book of Revelation:

"I was in the Spirit (spiritual consciousness) on the Lord's day (the day of contacting the divine realms of truth) and heard behind me (in the subtle center of spiritual consciousness in the medulla oblongata, 'behind' or in the back of the head) a great voice, as of a trumpet (the great, blissful sound of *Aum*)....

"After this I looked, and, behold, a door was opened in heaven: and the first voice which I heard was as it were of a trumpet talking with me; which said, 'Come up hither, and I will shew thee things which must be hereafter'" (Revelation 1:10; 4:1).

The slipping of the lifetronic astral body from the atomic physical body at death causes the hum of released lifetronic energy. This

True meaning of "Gabriel's trumpet"

sound, resonating with the uplifting Cosmic Sound, every person, virtuous or sinful, automatically hears with his subtle astral senses during the transition from the physical to the astral world.

"All that are in the graves shall hear his voice, and shall come forth" refers to another transition of consciousness effected by "Gabriel's trumpet" or the divine voice of Cosmic Vibration. "Graves" signifies a temporary after-death state of mental stupor or unconscious sleep which most souls, except those who are advanced, undergo when they depart from the physical body. A comparison may be made with the state of sleep. The wakeful consciousness of man nightly rests in the subconsciousness of sleep, during which man is not aware of the body and his sleep state. The astral body and the causal body semiretire from the muscles and sense organs and rest in the internal organs and the spine and subconscious mind. At the moment of awakening, the life force vibrates outward with many sounds and resurrects the sleeping astral body and mind of man into the state of conscious wakefulness.

Similarly, in the after-death state there is a period of unconscious rejuvenating sleep, referred to metaphorically by Jesus as a grave, in which souls are "entombed" within their resting astral and causal bodies. The time of this death sleep is different for various people, according to their individual qualities and good or bad karma—even as people of various habits sleep for long or short periods.

Just as the vibrating life force resurrects the consciousness of the sleeper into the wakeful state, so the energy voice of the Holy Cosmic Vibration, the great Amen or *Aum* sound, lifts souls of good or bad karma, with their astral and causal bodies, from the "tomb" of after-death oblivion to awareness of the spiritual environment of the astral heaven, or to reincarnation in a karmically attracted good or bad environment of earthly life.

"For the hour is coming," that is, it is imminent with the physical death of each man that he shall hear the sound of Cosmic Vibration (the trumpet of Gabriel) and shall forsake the unconscious sleep of the after-death state. Those who have stored up effects of good actions will be resurrected into conscious awareness of life in the glorious astral realm—for a karmically predetermined time—and then be reincarnated into a spiritual earth life. Those who have stored up evil in their past lives may experience in their astral bodies the dark astral realms of distressing or nightmarish dreams; eventually, by the damnation of the karmic law of reaping what one has sown, they will be led by the Cosmic Vibration to reincarnate in new physical bodies with their same evil tendencies impinged on the brain, and the effects of their past wrong actions.

Explanation of the real after-death resurrection

In sleep the first thing that is forgotten is the body. In death, likewise, the first thing that is forgotten is the physical body. In sleep, however, there is still a link between the body and the soul, so in wakefulness the person becomes conscious again of the same forgotten body. In death the soul's connection with the physical form is permanently severed: After the sleep of death is finished, a soul awakens not in the same body but in a different body. In the exceptional case of Jesus Christ, though death separated his soul from his physical body, he rebuilt his same broken body by an act of divine will with the Holy Ghost cosmic energy and housed his soul therein again.

Thus the word resurrection, "to rise again" after death, means reincarnation, which may occur from the physical to the astral, or from the astral to the physical; or for supremely advanced souls, from the physical to the spiritual, from which place souls are never forced to leave again. "Him that overcometh will I make a pillar in the temple of my God, and he shall go no more out."*

In the astral, souls have luminous bodies of lifetronic energy. In the physical world, souls condense the lifetronic energy of their astral bodies into the grosser atomic structure of the physical body. In the spiritual realm, souls dissolve their delusive bodily forms and dreams of a little body into the consciousness of the Infinite, either as tenuously individualized souls in the causal realm or in complete mergence in Spirit. Ordinary souls have to reincarnate repeatedly from the physical to the astral, then back to the physical, until they become developed enough to resurrect from the physical to the astral and then to the all-liberating spiritual realm.

No matter where the soul is, it receives a chance to use its reason consciously, or subconsciously, or superconsciously (if its actions are very good), in the causal, astral, or physical world. God-given reason and free choice can never be withdrawn, even if temporarily con-

---

* Revelation 3:12.

strained by karmic effects of one's evil actions. Souls must be reborn countless times until they have full opportunity to use their free choice to disengage themselves from the woesome bondage to matter, and thereby return to God.

As a saint once said to God, "Thou hast made us for Thyself, and our hearts are restless until they rest in Thee."* To this I will add: "until they *deserve*—by our free-will efforts to rise above all restless desires that divert us matterward—to rest in Thee."

Only during nocturnal sleep or during the big sleep of death may a soul rest for a while from external stimuli and the ceaseless activating force of desire; but though its bodily instruments sleep, the ever conscious soul keeps stirring all the time. If one sleeps peacefully or fretfully, then, on waking, one feels peaceful or worried, as the case may be. So, in deathly sleep, man's deep consciousness keeps stirring—the life and intelligence is continuously invigorating itself. After he has had sufficient respite from external stimuli, his unfulfilled desires begin to revive, increasing in strength until they cause him to reawaken—either in an astral environment or in a new physical incarnation, depending on his karma and the inclination of his desires.

Any stir of intelligence during life or death is vibratory change, the motion of which creates sound—as all vibration is manifested from the Holy Cosmic Vibration and all sound from its sound of Amen or *Aum.* The great uplifting vibratory change instilled by Cosmic Law at the karmically appointed time of death to release physically captive souls into the freedom of the diseaseless, accidentless, painless astral sphere is one meaning of the "resurrection after Gabriel blows his trumpet." Gabriel's trumpet sounds again after a soul's preallotted time in the astral world: The Cosmic Intelligent Vibration, "his voice," leads that soul—encased in an astral body wherein its past good and bad karmic tendencies are stored—to enter into a newly built protoplasmic home of a united sperm and ovum cell, which then develops into the embryo and a new physical body.† This

---

* *The Confessions of Saint Augustine,* Book One.

†Though current scientific theory does not include the idea of past-life tendencies being conveyed via a soul's astral body into a new physical body at the time of reincarnation, scientists admit that they do not fully comprehend the mechanism by which specific physical, psychological, and emotional traits are inborn in each unique human being. The current understanding is that the DNA molecule, discovered in 1953, encodes in every cell of every living creature the entire genetic material for the creation of a physical body, as well

Cosmic Vibration serves like dancing waves in the sea of ether to float the astral-causal–body-encased soul from the astral world to the shores of a good or evil environment in earth life, commensurate with that individual's good and bad karma accrued from the good and evil actions performed by the use of free will.

Like attracts like. One's karmic pattern draws him to incarnate in an advantaged or disadvantaged, good or evil, body and mentality,

_____

as blending the characteristic genetic traits of both parents into a new combination when they conceive a child. "This, however, is not free from difficulties," writes systems theorist Ervin Laszlo in *The Whispering Pond: A Personal Guide to the Emerging Vision of Science* (Boston: Element Books, 1999). He reports that Nobel-winning biologist François Jacob says that the development of embryos is in fact very little understood, and that much of it is, in Jacob's words, "a complete mystery."

Lynne McTaggart elaborates in *The Field: The Quest for the Secret Force of the Universe* (New York: HarperCollins, 2002): "The modern scientific view is that DNA somehow manages to build the body and spearhead all its dynamic activities just by selectively turning off and on certain segments, or genes, whose nucleotides, or genetic instructions, select certain RNA molecules, which in turn select from a large alphabet of amino acids the genetic 'words' which create specific proteins. These proteins supposedly are able to both build the body and to switch on and off all the chemical processes inside the cell which ultimately control the running of the body." Where this explanation leaves a gap, McTaggart reports, "is in explaining exactly how DNA knows when to orchestrate this...."

"When a fertilized egg starts to multiply and produce daughter cells, each begins adopting a structure and function according to its eventual role in the body. Although every daughter contains the same chromosomes with the same genetic information, certain types of cells immediately 'know' to use different genetic information to behave differently from others....Furthermore, somehow these genes know how many of each type of cell must be produced in the right place....At the moment, scientists shrug their shoulders as to how this might all be accomplished, particularly at such a rapid pace."

Laszlo continues: "For example, while the molecular anatomy of a human hand is understood in some detail, almost nothing is known about how the human organism instructs itself to build a hand. It appears that the organism can both build, and to some extent rebuild, its damaged parts with great precision. For example, when a finger of the human hand is amputated above the first joint and the wound is not sealed surgically with skin, the tip of the finger can be regenerated. Astonishingly enough, the regrown fingertip is complete down to the finest detail, reproducing even the individual's unique fingerprints."

Fingerprints, known to biologists and criminologists alike as mathematically unique to one individual, are apparently not produced by genetic instructions from DNA, since it has been thoroughly documented that even identical twins—who share the exact same DNA—have different fingerprints. What this suggests, according to scientists like Harold S. Burr, is that the growth and maintenance of the body depends on some organizing template of subtle intelligent energy that possesses characteristics unique to each individual and that guides the development and functioning of each physical body. (See page 119 n.) *(Publisher's Note)*

family, and environment that not only reflect the effects of one's past actions, but provide the necessary challenges for learning from past errors. Thus they who have done good come forth resurrected into a higher life of better circumstances; and they who have done evil come forth on earth "unto the resurrection of damnation," to face and work out the consequences of their misdeeds, in a new life and opportunity to learn and change their ways. The Cosmic Law and Cosmic Holy Ghost Vibration are only guides to help both good and bad to their respective new-life destinations, Nature's secretive way of working to carry out God's creative plan in a wondrous, mysterious dignity.

The law of resurrection, or reincarnation, thus teaches man that he must never give up, even if old, discouraged, or at death's door. He should try every minute of his existence to improve himself, knowing that life continues after death into the better land of the astral plane, and thence into new encouraging surroundings on the physical plane. At last he will wake up to Gabriel's trumpet call of ultimate wisdom in the spiritual kingdom, from which there is no forced return to earth. Even as Jesus by overcoming mortal consciousness attained supreme power over life and death, so every man, by the right method of deep meditation, can learn consciously to lift the soul from body consciousness into the presence of God. When the last trumpet sounds for that soul, death will hold no mystery. The prodigal soul is taken back from its wanderings in matter to its ever-blessed spiritual home in God.*

---

* "Now this I say, brethren, that flesh and blood cannot inherit the kingdom of God; neither doth corruption inherit incorruption. Behold, I shew you a mystery; we shall not all sleep, but we shall all be changed, in a moment, in the twinkling of an eye, at the last trump: for the trumpet shall sound, and the dead shall be raised incorruptible, and we shall be changed. For this corruptible must put on incorruption, and this mortal must put on immortality. So when this corruptible shall have put on incorruption, and this mortal shall have put on immortality, then shall be brought to pass the saying that is written, 'Death is swallowed up in victory. O death, where is thy sting? O grave, where is thy victory?' The sting of death is sin; and the strength of sin is the law. But thanks be to God, which giveth us the victory through our Lord Jesus Christ" (I Corinthians 15:50–57).

Saint Paul thus describes the "trumpet" of Cosmic Vibration, which resurrects man's consciousness at the end of each earthly incarnation from mortal confinement to the greater freedom after death. Ultimately, "at the last trumpet," the soul is raised to liberation in God through the Christ Consciousness inherent in the Holy Ghost Vibration, "the victory through our Lord Jesus Christ," after repeated incarnations of spiritual advancement have destroyed all "corruption," mortal consciousness and desires, and their resultant karma. Then "death is swallowed up in victory," the karma-compelled cycles of birth and death are over for that soul.

~

"I can of mine own self do nothing: as I hear, I judge: and my judgment is just: because I seek not mine own will, but the will of the Father which hath sent me" (John 5:30).

Jesus speaks from his universal Christ Consciousness: "I, the Christ Consciousness present in all creation and all souls, seek not to materialize my wishes on earth, but to obey the just cosmic law of creation as guided by the will and wisdom of the Cosmic Consciousness, the Father who is present beyond creation as the Transcendental Absolute, and in creation as myself, the Christ Intelligence."*

Neither God nor Jesus as the Christ Intelligence is a despotic disciplinarian passing judgment on the actions of man. The Christ Intelligence in all matter never punishes anybody; instead, according to the self-created vibrations of good or evil present in man, the cosmic law in the Christ Intelligence, reflecting the divine will, or wisdom, of the Father, automatically pronounces a judgment of a good or evil effect equal to its cause. This judgment is just, based on the equity of the law of cause and effect.

Karmic law judges justly, reflecting the Father's divine wisdom

The divine law of harmony metes out just conditions for all persons. When anyone acts against this law, he hurts himself. For example, the human flesh in the hand is sensitive—if it is dipped in cool water it receives a soothing effect. If it is plunged in fire, it burns. The fire does not willingly burn an individual, nor does the cool water produce from choice the coolness in anyone's hand. The one who touches the fire or dips his hand in the water is solely responsible for the ensuing effect.

The karmic law is just, because its judgment is never an eternal imposition. A few evil actions cannot condemn a soul made in the image of God to suffer perpetually. A few good actions could not qualify a soul to enjoy everlasting happiness. The amount of good and evil

---

* Cf. John 12:48–50 (Discourse 66): "He that rejecteth me, and receiveth not my words, hath one that judgeth him: the word that I have spoken, the same shall judge him in the last day. For I have not spoken of myself; but the Father which sent me, He gave me a commandment, what I should say, and what I should speak. And I know that His commandment is life everlasting: whatsoever I speak therefore, even as the Father said unto me, so I speak."

in man merely brings him nearer to God or sends him farther away from God. Man is thus inherently law-bound to be happy when he is harmonious with God and Christ Consciousness. And he is equally law-bound to suffer when he acts against the harmony of God. But no matter how much sin man has acquired, though he be the greatest of sinners, sinning for many incarnations, still he cannot be judged and damned forever. A finite cause cannot have an infinite effect. Nor should a good man rest on the laurels of past good actions; they must be dutifully and continually compounded.

That is why Jesus clearly says, "I can of mine own self do nothing: as I hear, I judge." That is, the Christ Intelligence acts according to the vibrations of the cosmic law of God that governs our lives.

The words of Jesus are a strong exhortation to put one's life in order, in accord with the cosmic law, the divine will of God, lest by wrong living one create a physical and mental hell of suffering even greater than the imaginary judgment of an after-death hellfire. Far better that by good living man create within himself the sweetness of a portable heaven.

Only when man attains the final good, or God, does he escape the inescapable judgment of the mortal law of action into the immortal Divine Transcendence.

∾

"If I bear witness of myself, my witness is not true. There is another that beareth witness of me; and I know that the witness which He witnesseth of me is true" (John 5:31–32).

66 It is not true, right or proper, if I give testimony about my own being. There is another, the transcendental Cosmic Consciousness beyond creation (God the Father) whose reflected Christ Consciousness in all matter bears witness of my being; that is, declares my wisdom as derived from Him. And I, one with Christ Consciousness, intuitively know that the testimony of God the Father is true, whatever He declares through my voice and teachings about me and my characteristics and about my being the prophesied savior come to aid in the redemption of all beings."

∾

"Ye sent unto John, and he bare witness unto the truth.* But I receive not testimony from man: but these things I say, that ye might be saved. He was a burning and a shining light: and ye were willing for a season to rejoice in his light" (John 5:33–35).

6 6 Y ou believed in John, who declared the truth that he witnessed within himself. You thus received the truth of God indirectly through the testimony of John's human consciousness. But I, Jesus Christ, whose consciousness is one with the Intelligence in all creation, do not speak from the borrowed knowledge of another man; these truths which I declare and which will save you from the suffering entailed in identity with physical consciousness, I receive through God the Father. John was aflame with divine love and shining with God's wisdom, and you all were willing for a little while to rejoice by watching the glory of God in him, but without sincerely following him."

~

"But I have greater witness than that of John: for the works which the Father hath given me to finish, the same works that I do, bear witness of me, that the Father hath sent me. And the Father Himself, which hath sent me, hath borne witness of me. Ye have neither heard His voice at any time, nor seen His shape. And ye have not His word abiding in you: for whom He hath sent, him ye believe not" (John 5:36–38).

6 6 B ut, I, Christ Consciousness, in my universal perception, witness and behold greater wisdom even than that of John. John inspired you in God, but my work of resurrecting souls again unto God, as manifest in the changed lives of the disciples who follow me, and the miracles that I have to work according to the wishes of the Father, and the divine reformations that God has given me to finish during my earth life, bear sufficient testimony that God's absolute consciousness is vibrating in me. My various demonstrations of divine power prove His manifestation in me, and that my works, my consciousness, my teachings are witnessed and upheld by the Cosmic Consciousness of the Heavenly Father.

---

* Reference to John 1:19, when the priests sent a delegation to John the Baptist to find out if he were the Messiah. (See Discourse 6.)

"O ye who are body-identified, you have never at any period of your life heard the Cosmic Intelligent Sound emanating from all vibratory creation in the cosmos, nor have you seen the Cosmic Light emanating from that Vibration as spread within everything in the realm of the cosmos. If any of you had been blessed with such experience, you would have known that God can be seen as this Cosmic Light and His voice heard as this Cosmic Sound omnipresent in creation, as intuitively perceived by intelligently guided devotees through their ecstatic communion. If you knew God as the all-creative Cosmic Vibration of light and sound, you would have understood that He can take the shape of any saint and appear before your eyes and talk to you.

"Because you believe not in the Christ Intelligence manifest in my consciousness, that shows that you have not felt the Cosmic Vibration of God within you. All devotees who have heard the uplifting Cosmic Sound know that it is not an ordinary vibration, but that within it is the intelligence and inspiration of Christ Consciousness."

~

"Search the scriptures; for in them ye think ye have eternal life: and they are they which testify of me. And ye will not come to me, that ye might have life. I receive not honour from men. But I know you, that ye have not the love of God in you.

"I am come in my Father's name, and ye receive me not: if another shall come in his own name, him ye will receive. How can ye believe, which receive honour one of another, and seek not the honour that cometh from God only?" (John 5:39–44).

66 Search the words of wise men in the timeless wisdom of scriptures in which you have belief in the promise of eternal life, for those very scriptures spoke of my coming. And yet, you do not accept me, I who am the very embodiment of eternal life. I have come to show you how your isolated little lives floating away from God can unite with Cosmic Life. By connecting with the Life Eternal, you will find freedom from the cyclic wheel of life and death created by your material desires, which will have found complete fulfillment in God, who is the Most Desirable.

"I seek no personal honor from men, for I have received the consummate recognition and love of God. I ask only that you listen to me that I may deliver unto you the message of Him who sent me. I know that your hearts are forgetful of God, diverted from Him by your love for the manifestations of the material world. Those who attract your attention by their eloquence, exaggeration, and emotional appeal, cast over you the false glamor of their own egoistic personality. I have come to declare not myself, but my Heavenly Father.

"You refuse to receive in your consciousness my all-redeeming wisdom about the Father. How can you believe that His certification and assurance is the highest security, honored by all creation, when you crave instead for the futile, short-lived, hollow praise of man? The acclaim of people is fickle; the honor of God's loving attention is lasting and insures ever certain security and guidance. Do not waste time seeking the praise of man; utilize every moment in doing those works that will draw the attention and favor of God."

⌇

> *"Do not think that I will accuse you to the Father: there is one that accuseth you, even Moses, in whom ye trust. For had ye believed Moses, ye would have believed me: for he wrote of me. But if ye believe not his writings, how shall ye believe my words?" (John 5:45–47).*

"Do not think that because you do not heed my words I will accuse you and hold you blameworthy before the Father. But the prophet Moses will justly accuse you because you trust in him; and if you truly believed Moses, you would also have to believe me, for Moses wrote about my coming in the scriptures. If you do not believe the visible prophetic writings of Moses, how indeed could you believe my words?"*

A comparison is also made here in Jesus' forgiving the people for their ignorance and his reference to Moses as accusing them for their

---

* "For he wrote of me": Among the passages from the Biblical books ascribed to Moses taken by some commentators as prophesying the coming of Christ are: Genesis 22:18 (the seed of Abraham in whom all the nations of the earth would be blessed); Genesis 49:10 ("the sceptre shall not depart from Judah, nor a lawgiver from between his feet, until Shiloh ['the Peaceful'] come; and unto him shall the gathering of the people be"); Deuteronomy 18:15 (the coming prophet who would be like Moses himself, and to whom the people of Israel should hearken).

nonbelief. Moses was a prophet of God's law. He thus expressed the "fatherly" aspects of God's love as conditioned by law. If a son is good, the father (in whom the masculine quality of reason predominates) shows his love for the son; if the son is bad, the father punishes him. Moses treated his disciples and followers with that conditional fatherly love. The love that Jesus gave was from the "motherly" aspect of God; a mother's love (when it comes predominantly from the feminine quality of feeling) is unconditional toward the son, no matter whether he is good or bad.

The way of Jesus, in his humbleness, was to try to persuade his ignorance-bewildered brethren through reason and the manifest love of God, rather than by theological threats and the fear of providential punishment. If Almighty God used force to make His prodigal children come back to Him, they would be mechanical, not soulful, creations.

Jesus, with all miraculous powers at his command, used only his love and persuasive reason to plead with the ignorant crowds in trying to awaken their wisdom, through which they would use their free will to forsake the evils of the world and seek the lasting ever new bliss of God.

DISCOURSE 22

"Repent Ye,
and Believe the Gospel"

How Prophets Foretell the Future Unfolding of God's Plan

❖

Dispelling the Darkness of Ignorance by the Light
of Christ-Wisdom

❖

The Kingdom of Heaven Is to Be Found
Within the Consciousness of Man

❖

Inner Meaning of Jesus' Counsel to "Repent"

❖

What Did Jesus Ask People to "Believe"?

❖

The Science of Yoga Unifies the Diverse Paths of Religious Belief

---

*"Withdraw your outflowing consciousness and turn it inward toward
Spirit. In intuitional communion, align your actions, thoughts, life, and
will with God's Word of salvation-bestowing truth."*

*A*nd Jesus returned in the power *of the Spirit into Galilee: and there went out a fame of him through all the region round about. And he taught in their synagogues, being glorified of all.**

—Luke 4:14–15

Now when Jesus had heard that John was cast into prison, he departed into Galilee; and leaving Nazareth, he came and dwelt in Capernaum, which is upon the sea coast, in the borders of Zabulon and Nephthalim: that it might be fulfilled which was spoken by Isaiah the prophet, saying:

"The land of Zabulon, and the land of Nephthalim, by the way of the sea, beyond Jordan, Galilee of the Gentiles; the people which sat in darkness saw great light; and to them which sat in the region and shadow of death light is sprung up."

From that time Jesus began to preach, and to say, "Repent: for the kingdom of heaven is at hand."

—Matthew 4:12–17

...Jesus came into Galilee, preaching the gospel of the kingdom of God, and saying, "The time is fulfilled, and the kingdom of God is at hand: repent ye, and believe the gospel."

—Mark 1:14–15

---

* Jesus had been in Jerusalem for the Passover (Discourse 12), after which he taught Nicodemus in Jerusalem (Discourses 13–15) and then spent time in the Judean countryside where many persons were baptized by his disciples (Discourse 16). When John the Baptist was imprisoned by Herod Antipas in Machaerus, a fortress on the shore of the Dead Sea east of Judea, Jesus departed Judea for Galilee, passing through Samaria (Discourses 17–19). Reaching Galilee, he healed the son of the nobleman of Capernaum (Discourse 20). The verses in this Discourse 22 continue the narrative of events after Jesus' return to Galilee. *(Publisher's Note)*

DISCOURSE 22

"Repent Ye, and Believe the Gospel"

Here the New Testament chronology of Jesus' life and teachings shifts from the Gospel of St. John, whose early chapters provide a background of the esoteric core of the teachings of Jesus, to the so-called synoptic narrative Gospels of Matthew, Mark, and Luke. Jesus begins to preach openly, in divinely simple terms for the masses, his panacea for all human woes: "Repent ye, and believe the gospel.... the kingdom of heaven is at hand." The underlying message: "Forsake your slavish worship of matter; withdraw your outflowing consciousness and turn it inward toward Spirit. In intuitional communion, align your actions, thoughts, life, and will with God's Word of salvation-bestowing truth; and you will know, with the conviction of personal experience, that the kingdom of Heavenly Bliss can be found here and now."

Returning from Judea, Jesus went to dwell in Capernaum, which is on the Sea of Galilee at the border between the lands of Zabulon and Nephthalim, in fulfillment of the prophecy of Isaiah.* God used

---

* Cf. Isaiah 9:1–7, one of the oft-cited Old Testament prophecies about the coming of Christ:

"The land of Zebulun and the land of Naphtali...by the way of the sea, beyond Jordan, in Galilee of the nations.

"The people that walked in darkness have seen a great light: they that dwell in the land of the shadow of death, upon them hath the light shined. Thou hast multiplied the nation, and not increased the joy: they joy before Thee according to the joy in harthe prophet Isaiah as His mouthpiece to declare the coming of Jesus, as in different climes and ages He has used other prophets to make

How prophets foretell the future unfolding of God's plan

known, sometimes centuries ahead, some fortuitous divine plan. When prophecies of enlightened seers come true, it is definitive testimony, which should convince even unbelievers, of the consciously initiated plan of God in the world. Though it is usually a mystery as to what may be forthcoming in life's events and strange happenings, once in a while definite prophecies, veiled in complex language, are given to humankind to awaken realization of the subtle presence of God's hand in creation.*

Just as a motion-picture director plans the filming of various scenes to project at the proper time, so also, God and His angel assistants plan the timing for the materialization and projection of certain great events in the cosmos. There is a time for everything, the universe being mathematically adjusted by God and His angels so that it runs like a clock. At certain periods when ignorance like an inky mist encircles the minds of mundane people, God sends His saints to redeem

---

vest, and as men rejoice when they divide the spoil. For Thou hast broken the yoke of his burden, and the staff of his shoulder, the rod of his oppressor....

"For unto us a child is born, unto us a son is given: and the government shall be upon his shoulder: and his name shall be called Wonderful, Counsellor, The mighty God, The everlasting Father, The Prince of Peace.

"Of the increase of his government and peace there shall be no end, upon the throne of David, and upon his kingdom, to order it, and to establish it with judgment and with justice from henceforth even for ever."

Zabulon and Nephthalim were sons of Jacob after whom two of the twelve tribes of Israel were named. The city of Capernaum, where Jesus dwelt during most of his ministry, was between the lands anciently belonging to these two tribes, on the northwest shore of the Sea of Galilee.

* Various passages in the Gospels cite the "fulfillment of the scriptures" by events in the life of Jesus. Among these are divine predictions made through the prophets' intuitive foreknowledge about the coming Messiah, such as are discussed here and in other Discourses. However, the Greek word used for "fulfill" in the original text (*pleroo*) has a range of connotations. Thus scholars propose that the Gospel writers cited some Old Testament passages as being "fulfilled" not as prophecy, but simply that the principle, truth, or figure of speech it voiced is a parallel—or otherwise also applicable—to present circumstances. Historians point out that early Christians saw Jesus' entire life as a "fulfillment of the scriptures"—the consummation of the Law and historical destiny revealed in the sacred writings; thus it was important to the Gospel authors to provide the community of believers with links between events that actually occurred in the life of Jesus and familiar passages from the holy texts. *(Publisher's Note)*

souls submerged in darkness. "The time is fulfilled" signifies that the moment had arrived for enactment of the divine plan presaged by Isaiah long before: Jesus' mission to bring God's light to the world. When Jesus reached Galilee he felt the divine vibrations of the cosmic cycle prepared for his coming, and he put the love of his heart and the dynamism of his soul into giving God to all. At this auspicious time, Jesus was filled with the Holy Ghost, having been baptized in Spirit by John the Baptist; thus when he began his mission in Galilee it was "in the power of the Spirit."

Jesus knew about the declaration of the prophet Isaiah, and that he had been thus divinely guided to follow his foretold dispensation into Galilee to preach the gospel.* As prophesied by Isaiah, the people who abode in the darkness of ignorance in that land beheld in the advent of Jesus the all-revealing light of Christ-wisdom. Just as aeons of darkness lodged in a mountain cave are dislodged by a single lighted match, so the vibrations of a people's gathered ignorance of ages can be dispelled by a saint who bears the illumining torch of God's wisdom.

Dispelling the darkness of ignorance by the light of Christ-wisdom

Among those persons who sit in the darkness of ignorance, many love it and do not wish to be displaced from its complacent familiarity. But others there are who become conscious of the stolid gloom of unknowing and earnestly long for freedom from its torpidity. Through the gathering of knowledge and arousal of subconscious memories in the soul, seekers of wisdom receive glimpses of their lost experience of God's light and increasingly abhor their fallen state. So, in Galilee, those people who realized their abject darkness, those who were inwardly clamoring for light, were receptive to the wisdom vibrations of Jesus.

Lord Krishna, in the Bhagavad Gita, speaks of this earth as the aggregate of delusive mysteries and as the ocean of affliction.† Isaiah speaks of worldly people as sitting "in the region and shadow of death," the constantly changing temporal events of this earth. For people steeped in spiritual ignorance, life is a series of mysterious

---

* Later, when preaching in the synagogue at Nazareth, Jesus read aloud from the Book of Isaiah other prophecies that were fulfilled in the unfolding of his divine dispensation. (See Discourse 39.)

† See commentaries on Bhagavad Gita XII:6–7 and XIII:5–6 in *God Talks With Arjuna*.

375

changes; nothing remains the same or retains any permanency. The influence of this cosmic dream is such that persons behold with frenetic attachment life and shadowy death and all concomitant dualities; but when they awaken in wisdom, they behold all seeming contradictions harmonized in the Oneness of God's Light. The very presence of Jesus and his luminous wisdom relieved many of their delusive inner gloom.

Again, the Hindu scriptures cite an apt metaphor: Saints, in their nonattachment, are considered by ordinary men to reside in a darkness of material poverty, while actually they live in the light of opulent Eternal Wisdom; whereas most persons bask in an imagined light of prosperity in material possessions, while they are in truth enveloped in a thick darkness of spiritual ignorance.*

Jesus knew he was empowered by heaven to give spiritual light to man. In that power of Spirit, he preached the gospel: the "good message" or enlightening revelation of God's pronouncements — commandments and laws for attaining the kingdom of heaven and its happiness. He preached truth as he perceived it through his own God-realization: "The kingdom of God is at hand."

Many people look for heaven at some point in space beyond the clouds, far away from the noxious, sinful vapors of the earth. Jesus'

The kingdom of heaven is to be found within the consciousness of man

words "at hand" signify the nearness of heaven, which lies just behind the darkness of closed eyes, within the consciousness of man; and that with ease, people could find God through the mediation Jesus was offering to them. In deep meditation, when one shuts out the land of finitude and matter, the realm of Eternity, the vast heavenly kingdom of God's omniscience, is found to lie tier upon tier in endless vistas before the inner vision.

Therefore, the first commandment Jesus gave to the people was "Repent ye," signifying the withdrawal of the principal attention from

---

* The Bhagavad Gita says: "That which is night to all creatures is (luminous) wakefulness to the man of self-mastery. And what is wakefulness to ordinary men, that is night to the divinely perceptive sage." The meaning is: "While creatures slumber in delusion's gloom, the X-ray eyes of the seer are open to wisdom's light. The power of *maya* that keeps all beings engrossed in the wakefulness of attachment to material objects induces in saints only the slumber of nonattachment" (*God Talks With Arjuna: The Bhagavad Gita* II:69).

matter to God. Every soul, upon spiritually awakening, should repent of its folly of expecting permanent happiness from fleeting sense pleasures. The poor taste for sorrow-producing evil should be displaced by the superior inclinations for joy-producing good.

People are foolish to look for Paradise in earthly things. How could changeless, perfect happiness be wrung out of imperfect earth surroundings, a motley perplexity of events of sorrow and joy, disease and health? Earth conditions, being born of delusion, will always be more or less defective. Heaven on earth is found only within by the contact of the illuminating Immutable Wisdom perceived in meditation. Jesus' spiritual persuasion made people open their closed eyes of soul wisdom to dispel their self-created darkness: The Fountain of Light springs forth from the cleft soil of dark delusion.

If man repents of his excessive attention given to the finite cosmos, and regularly devotes time to deep meditation, he will find the heavenly land of infinity within him. The wise man repents because he sees the frivolity of worldly life and knows the miseries resulting from the contact of matter, not only in himself but in empathetic feeling for all beings.

In *The Holy Science,* my guru, Swami Sri Yukteswar, elaborated on the deep spiritual meaning of Jesus' oft-repeated exhortation to "repent."* The turning of one's mind from matter to God necessitates a reversal of man's life energy *Inner meaning of Jesus'* and consciousness from absorption in the dark ig- *counsel to "repent"* norance of materiality to communion with the Holy Ghost, the Word or Cosmic Vibration of *Aum* or Amen through which man is uplifted to Christ the Son, and God the Father:

"When man directs all his organs of sense toward their common center, the sensorium or *Sushumnadwara,* the door of the internal world, he perceives...*Pranava Sabda,* the Word of God. Thus perceiving, man naturally believes in the existence of the true Spiritual Light, and, withdrawing his self from the outer world, concentrates himself on the sensorium....By this *Samyama* or concentration of self on the

---

* The English verb "repent" derives from the Latin *paenitere,* "to be sorry." The deeper meaning of Jesus' usage as the reversal of mind from matter to Spirit may be found in the fact that in the New Testament, *repent* is used to translate the original Greek *metanoein,* meaning "to turn one's mind in the opposite direction; to change one's mind (by adopting an opposite view)": from *meta,* "to change, or to be in opposition to"; and *nous,* "mind."

377

sensorium [through yoga techniques of meditation], man becomes baptized or absorbed in the holy stream of the Divine Sound....

"[He] begins to repent and return toward his Divinity, the Eternal Father, whence he had fallen. See Revelation 2:5: 'Remember therefore from whence thou art fallen, and repent.'"

Along with repentance,* it is necessary also to believe in the Gospel, God's Word of truth to man. First, one must believe in God's message as sent through His saints and avatars, as in the gospel preached by Jesus, and repent of the folly of matter attachment. When one's repentance turns his mind toward truth and he believes in the kingdom of God within, then, by constant meditation, he will in time perceive, through the intuitive knowing of his soul, that Kingdom of Eternity lying close at hand in the inner realization of his uplifted consciousness.

What did Jesus ask people to "believe"?

Jesus' exhortation to "believe the gospel" does not refer to study of or belief in scriptural writings per se.† In the original Greek in which the New Testament was written, the word used for gospel is *euangelion,* "good news" or "good message." As used by Jesus it expressed the "good message," the revelations of truth, he was bringing to man from God.

When Jesus said to "believe the gospel," he meant more than a casual mental acceptance of his message. Belief in general is that conditional receptive attitude of mind that must precede an experience in order to cognize it. One must have sufficient belief in a concept in order to put it to the test, without which one cannot possibly verify its

---

* Further commentary on Jesus' teaching of repentance will be found in Discourse 31.

† "While two of the New Testament gospels use the word 'gospel' (it is missing in Luke and John), they use it to indicate not the written works themselves, but rather the message preached either by Jesus (in Matthew) or about him (in Mark). Not until the middle of the second century are documents about the words and deeds of Jesus called gospels." —Robert J. Miller, ed., *The Complete Gospels: Annotated Scholars Version* (HarperSanFrancisco, 1994).

"The English word *gospel* is a descendant of the Anglo-Saxon word *godspel* or *good news. Godspel* was an accurate equivalent of the original Greek word *euangelion,* literally a *good message* or *good tidings.* And the oldest surviving Greek manuscript copies of the four canonical gospels bear only the headings According to Matthew, Mark, Luke, or John (the four books together comprise the whole of the single *gospel;* and the word *canonical* derives from the Greek *kanon* or *measuring rod* and indicates, in this case, those few gospels that were approved as holy scripture by the orthodox church of the late second century)." —Reynolds Price, *Three Gospels* (New York: Simon and Schuster, 1997). *(Publisher's Note)*

validity. If a man is thirsty and is advised to quench his thirst with the water from a nearby good well, he must believe in that advice sufficiently to make the effort to go to the well and drink from it.

Similarly, Jesus emphasizes that truth-seeking souls must not only repent of the foolishness of following unsatisfying material ways of living, and believe in the truths experienced by him through God; they must also act accordingly that they might realize those truths for themselves.

To be an orthodox unquestioning believer in any spiritual doctrine, without the scrutiny of experimentation to prove it to oneself, is to be ossified with dogmatism. Jesus did not ask the people merely to believe in his message, but to keep faith in his divine revelations with the assurance that by believing in, and hence concentrating upon, the gospel, they would surely and ultimately experience within themselves the truths in those revelations. Belief is wasted on false doctrines; but truth poured out to man through the authority of God-realized saints is worthy of belief and sure to produce divine realization.

Even on the authority of the fame of scriptural text, one cannot judge what it teaches, for various are the meanings and consequent distortions drawn from holy writ, some of which defy the laws of both reason and wisdom. Also, who can deny what errors might have come down through the centuries in the form of mistranslations or mistakes made by scribes? The Bible and the Vedas may well be inspired texts that came from heaven, but the ultimate test of truth is one's own realization, direct experience received through the medium of the soul's omniscient intuition.

Belief, faith, in themselves are only bypaths. Yoga, "divine union," is the consummate path; it is both the way to attain God-realization and the universal experience of that attainment.

Travelers to New York from different parts of the *The science of yoga* country, for example, will journey along different *unifies the diverse* routes. But when they reach New York, they will all *paths of religious belief* see the same things. Every true religion leads to God, but some paths take a longer time while others are shorter. No matter what God-ordained religion one follows, its beliefs will merge in one and the same common experience of God. Yoga is the unifying path that is followed by all religionists as they make the final approach to God. Before one can reach God, there has to be the "repentance" that turns the consciousness from delusive matter to the kingdom of

God within. This withdrawal retires the life force and mind inward to rise through the spiritualizing centers of the spine to the supreme states of divine realization. The final union with God and the stages involved in this union are universal. That is yoga, the science of religion. Divergent bypaths will meet on the highway of God; and that highway is through the spine—the way to transcend body consciousness and enter the infinite divine kingdom.*

Religionists may argue, "My faith is better than yours." They are like the blind men who fought about descriptions of the elephant they had been washing. One had been washing the trunk, so he said that the elephant was like a snake. One said the elephant was like a pillar; he had been washing the leg. Another said the elephant was like a wall; he had been washing the massive sides. The man washing the tusks proclaimed confidently that the beast was no more than two pieces of bone. The man washing the tail was sure all were wrong, for the elephant was a rope leading high up toward heaven! Then the driver said, "Friends, you are all right and you are all wrong." Because each blind man had been washing a part of the elephant, they were all partly right; but they were also wrong because the part was not the whole.

The purpose of religion, of life itself, is to find God. Man will not be able to rest until he reaches that Goal, because all the forces of the universe will seem to conspire to entrap him in his karma until he heeds the gospel of repentance and realizes that "the kingdom of God is at hand"—within himself in the here and now.

---

* See *yoga* in glossary. Among the world's spiritual teachings, yoga offers the most precise and scientific descriptions and psychophysiological techniques pertaining to the ascent of the soul to God. However, the same basic experiences of ascension, presented in less specific terminology or cloaked in metaphor, are to be found in the experiences and writings of God-realized saints of every religion.

Evelyn Underhill, in *Mysticism* (Part 1, Chapter 4), wrote: "It is one of the many indirect testimonies to the objective reality of mysticism that the stages of this road, the psychology of the spiritual ascent, as described to us by different schools of contemplatives, always present practically the same sequence of states. The 'school for saints' has never found it necessary to bring its curriculum up to date.

"The psychologist finds little difficulty, for instance, in reconciling the 'Degrees of Orison' described by St. Teresa—Recollection, Quiet, Union, Ecstasy, Rapt, the 'Pain of God,' and the Spiritual Marriage of the soul—with the four forms of contemplation enumerated by Hugh of St. Victor, or the Sufi's 'Seven Stages' of the soul's ascent to God, which begin in adoration and end in spiritual marriage. Though each wayfarer may choose different landmarks, it is clear from their comparison that the road is one."

DISCOURSE 23

Fishers of Men

Fishing for Souls in the Ocean of Delusion

❖

To Acquire Soul Wisdom and Impart It to Others
Is the Highest Service

❖

Teaching the Truth About Virtue and Evil in an Effective Way

❖

Soul Magnetism More Important Than Oratorical Ability

❖

Qualifications and Requirements for Spiritual Teachers

❖

Preaching With the God-Saturated Conviction of the Soul

"Wise men consider this world an ocean of delusion in which human fish are constantly chased by the sharks of the senses....That is why Jesus began to call qualified disciples from their natural labors to assist him in drawing souls from the waters of delusion into the ever-living wisdom of God's oceanic presence."

*A*nd it came to pass, that, as the people pressed upon him to hear the word of God, he stood by the lake of Gennesaret,* and saw two ships standing by the lake: but the fishermen were gone out of them, and were washing their nets. And he entered into one of the ships, which was Simon's, and prayed him that he would thrust out a little from the land. And he sat down, and taught the people out of the ship.

Now when he had left speaking, he said unto Simon, "Launch out into the deep, and let down your nets for a draught."

And Simon answering said unto him, "Master, we have toiled all the night, and have taken nothing: nevertheless at thy word I will let down the net."

And when they had this done, they inclosed a great multitude of fishes: and their net brake. And they beckoned unto their partners, which were in the other ship, that they should come and help them. And they came, and filled both the ships, so that they began to sink.

When Simon Peter saw it, he fell down at Jesus' knees, saying, "Depart from me; for I am a sinful man, O Lord." For he was astonished, and all that were with him, at the draught of the fishes which they had taken: And so was also James, and John, the sons of Zebedee, which were partners with Simon.

And Jesus said unto Simon, "Fear not; from henceforth thou shalt catch men." And when they had brought their ships to land, they forsook all, and followed him.

—*Luke 5:1-11*

---

* Another name for the Sea of Galilee.

[Variant telling recorded in the Gospel According to St. Mark:*]

Now as he walked by the sea of Galilee, he saw Simon and Andrew his brother casting a net into the sea: for they were fishers.

And Jesus said unto them, "Come ye after me, and I will make you to become fishers of men." And straightway they forsook their nets, and followed him.

And when he had gone a little farther thence, he saw James the son of Zebedee, and John his brother, who also were in the ship mending their nets. And straightway he called them: and they left their father Zebedee in the ship with the hired servants, and went after him.

And they went into Capernaum; and straightway on the Sabbath day he entered into the synagogue, and taught. And they were astonished at his doctrine: for he taught them as one that had authority, and not as the scribes.

—Mark 1:16–22

---

* See also parallel reference in Matthew 4:18–22.

Fishers of Men

As the fame of Jesus spread with his ministry, the time had come for him to call those select disciples into service who would not just be among his followers, but would give their all to help fulfill his work on earth. The opportune occasion came at the Sea of Galilee. As he stood at the water's edge, throngs pressed upon Jesus to hear his gospel and receive his blessing. He boarded a fishing boat, moored on land belonging to Simon (Peter) and his brother Andrew, and asked Simon to move the vessel a little offshore, from which vantage place he taught the people.

Afterward, he instructed Simon: "Launch out into the deep, and let down your nets for a draught." Simon obeyed, even while he protested the futility in that no fishes had been hauled aboard though they had labored all night. With Jesus' silent intervention, however, so many fishes filled Simon's net that it broke. The partners of Simon and Andrew, the brothers James and John, were called to launch their boat from shore to help with the catch. Both ships became so laden they began to sink—an abundant contradiction to Simon's assertion that there were no fish to be had.

Jesus wanted to demonstrate to Simon the bountifulness of God to those who trust in Him, and to show that even the fish obeyed the

Fishing for souls in the ocean of delusion

Divine Command. Andrew, James, and John were astonished at the surfeit of fishes. And at this sign from God, Simon Peter bowed down in humble contrition before Jesus, repenting of his sins and lack of faith. Jesus now voiced the purpose of the miracle: "Fear not; from henceforth thou shalt catch men....Follow me, and I will make you fishers of men." This was Jesus' first intimation to these disciples that their role would be to serve as an extension of his own self in the spread of his teachings.*

Masters often teach in parables and metaphors to test the depth of their disciples' intuitive perception. Jesus thought as a Hindu master would think, when in calling his disciples to become fishers of men he sought to instill in their minds the imagery: "O Beloved God, as I pass by the sea of my consciousness, I behold my ego catching the small bony fishes of material objects—name, fame, coins of good fortune. Bless me so that I may see, instead, in the sea of my unruffled desire-free consciousness, the way to make a far more worthy catch with the net of devotional God-given wisdom—the large fishes of divine truth-seeking souls. May I learn how to cast the net of truth over soul-fishes roaming in the fetid waters of delusion, to release them in the immortalizing sea of God-wisdom."

Wise men consider this world an ocean of delusion in which human fish are constantly chased by the sharks of the senses. Satan then casts upon these piscine mortals his colossal dragnet of entangling desires, and is pulling his catch to the shores of destruction. God wants true fishers of men to learn the art of casting the net of personal spiritual magnetism to catch error-bound souls and bring them to Him. Those who are brought with wisdom into God's presence are ever protected in the clear waters of immortality.

When, through the help of wise men, souls are transferred from the brine of material desires to the sweet waters of Bliss, they bring rejoicing to the august Giver of Life. God loves to see His sons consciously seek Him, and He is extremely pleased when one influences others to come unto Him. When a reformed Spirit-bound soul inspires another spiritual fugitive to return to God, that service to a fellow being is considered the highest human duty.† Blessed are those who fish for souls in fulfillment of this noblest spiritual activity on earth. The achievement of catching truth-

To acquire soul wisdom and impart it to others is the highest service

---

* Simon, Andrew, and John had met Jesus earlier and recognized him as the Messiah. (See Discourse 9.)

† "Whosoever shall impart to My devotees the supreme secret knowledge, with utmost devotion to Me, shall without doubt come unto Me. Not any among men performs more priceless service to Me than he; in all the world there shall be none dearer to Me" (*God Talks With Arjuna: The Bhagavad Gita* XVIII:68–69).

seeking souls in the net of one's own truth conviction and heavenly devotion to draw them to God brings the blessing of the Divine to the soul-fisherman, and also eventually liberates him.

To furnish food to the hungry is good, to give inner strength to the mentally weak so that they can fend for themselves is even more important, and to impart all-freeing wisdom to the soul-bewildered is of supreme consequence. Material or mental help is only transitory consolation for human embroilments; Heaven is the permanent panacea for all human afflictions.

The givers of food and mental power enrich themselves temporarily by the goodwill of those benefited; but the givers of soul nourishment benefit themselves throughout eternity, as also the receivers of the divine manna. The effect of food and mental power more or less wears off in time unless constantly replenished, but the marks of soul wisdom impinged upon the inner being can seldom be erased. That is why Jesus began to call qualified disciples from their natural labors to assist him in drawing souls from the waters of delusion into the ever-living wisdom of God's oceanic presence.

To be a good fisherman, one must learn the tools and skills of the trade. In order to become a spiritual fisherman, one must become adept in the art of spiritual fishing. To give salvation to others without having it oneself is impossible. No matter how well-meaning, a person can give only what he has, nothing else. In order to give spiritual power, one must first acquire that power himself. Just as a gift of food presupposes its possession by the giver, so also, wisdom can only be conferred upon others by those who possess it. Enlightenment can be imparted only by one who himself reflects that inner light.

Jesus knew this requisite, that anyone willing to be a fisher of souls must intensely spiritualize himself first. He voiced this quite plainly in the Sermon on the Mount: "Thou hypocrite, cast out first the beam out of thine own eye, and then shalt thou see clearly to pull out the mote that is in thy brother's eye."

A fisher of men must save himself from the ocean of ignorance by sincerely offering himself unto God with constant effort and vigilance. The Heavenly Father wants to see His fishers of men escape from Satan's nets of delusion and destruction so that they can help other entrapped souls. To seek one's own salvation and then not use it to benefit others is extreme selfishness. But to seek salvation for oneself so that ultimate freedom may be shared with others is divine.

In the first stage of spiritual progress, a clear line of demarcation must be established between good and evil in order that the latter may be superseded by the former. A great tug-of-war is going on between the divine forces and the forces of depravity over the possession of the human soul. Peace, joy, divine bliss, forgiveness, self-control, un- selfishness, and so forth, stimulate good habits to produce lasting happiness and pull man toward emancipation. On the other side, disquietude, sorrow, sense pleasure, revengefulness, temp- tation, selfishness, inflame bad habits that lead to bondage and trou- ble. It is nature's quixotic teasing of man that strenuous self-control produces ultimate happiness, and the effortlessness of momentarily pleasurable indulgence brings eventual unhappiness.

Teaching the truth about virtue and evil in an effective way

Evil, once established within man, is made so attractive that he easily inclines toward evil actions, evil habits, and evil tendencies. Dis- criminating souls who have compared the results of evil experiences with the outcome of righteous behavior have inevitably concluded that evil, though ever so appealing in the beginning, is really a loathsome harbinger of acute suffering, while virtue, though initially difficult to pursue, is the ambassador of invariable ultimate good.

Hysterical moralists decry evil as an ugly, vile abomination to be summarily discarded. But when some of their followers taste the in- toxicating comfort of temptation, it seems neither ugly nor vile; they dismiss the fear of evil consequences and embrace the freely given mo- mentary pleasure. Long afterward—or sometimes in the resounding crash of instancy—the mask of attractiveness falls off, and the satanic nature of evil appears with its consequential ravages.

It is not enough to preach against evil, for its deceptive cunning will counteract every argument. Man needs to be convinced of the eventual, everlasting blessings of virtue. It is better for teachers to tell the truth—that evil is very attractive and enjoyable in the beginning, like poisoned honey, sweet to taste; but it is deathly bitter once swal- lowed. Good may be troublesome and therefore unpalatable for a time, but only until its subtle effects stir the soul to exude the incred- ible sweetness it draws from the nectarine sea of the inner Elysium. It is far better to abhor the trouble-producing instant gratification of evil for the lasting happiness earned through the urge and labor of virtu- ous actions. This is the ultimate realization the clear thinker comes to as to why good is preferable to evil.

Indulging in evil is a cultivated habit. The first time a person smokes, it burns his nose, throat, and lungs; but after some time the habit takes over and he enjoys a smoke and becomes very uncomfortable without it. If the inveterate smoker later accurately analyzes the effect of smoking on his health and mind and tries to forsake the habit, he is hard put and often unsuccessful in doing so. Evil has a gripping affect. But so have virtuous ways.

When evil arrives first and firmly establishes itself in a person's life, it takes advantage of its priority and deludes its host with the consciousness of its supreme attractiveness. This blinds that person to the superior offerings of goodness and virtue. Many people are thus so steeped in error that they enter the grave without ever realizing their deluded state. Their evolution is delayed as they carry their progression in evil into the next life, or several lives, until through the inevitable effects of their wrongdoings they come to a rude awakening.

So, before evil mesmerizes one's mind with false expectations, the power of goodness should be cultured to become the in-charge of one's life. God is the goal of man's existence. To find Him and share Him with others is the tremendous work He has placed before every man. As Jesus called his disciples to be fishers of souls by becoming teachers of his gospel, so God has charged everyone to perfect themselves in His love and wisdom and help bring others back to Him through unspoken sermons of their spiritual example. When one's whole being is with God, others will be drawn to Him by the silent eloquence of that divine magnetism.

The question arises: Why did Jesus call Simon (as also several of his other unlettered disciples) to be a teacher when he had not undergone even rudimentary instruction in spiritual teachings? Those who became apostles were certainly not chosen on the basis of academic credentials. Jesus had taught Simon in the principles of discipleship and God-knowledge in their relationship in a previous incarnation, not immediately remembered by Simon. Jesus could see Simon's spiritual attainments in the astral marking in his brain, so on that certification he recognized and chose Simon to be foremost among his missionaries.

Soul magnetism more important than oratorical ability

In the early years of my work in the West I used to hold seminars to create teachers to spread the message of the Masters. But I soon abandoned that practice. Too often, those who were the least qualified spiritually were the most eager to emote and aggrandize themselves as leaders. I did not want to add to the world's surfeited roster of orators who are silver-tongued and lead-minded. Spiritual eloquence is less a matter of articulation than of soul magnetism born of virtuous living and meditative inner communion with God. Spreading the word of God should not be used as a medium for glorifying one's ego and indulging its penchant for recognition.

Until I feel a disciple is true from the past, I would not ask him to teach. If a devotee has good karma and sincere willingness to listen, it does not take much to train him. Attunement is the most important requisite. All great masters have chosen their disciples according to that, notwithstanding the Judases in whom latent egotistical tendencies awake to snatch away their spirituality. Humility, love for God and doing everything with the thought of God, forgetting self, are the fundamental criteria characterizing a true servant of God's word. Additionally, I would include the following requirements and practices, principles that Jesus also, in one form or another, instilled in his apostles during the time they spent in his company absorbing his spirit and ideals:

Qualifications and requirements for spiritual teachers

A spiritual teacher should have Self-realization, or at least be sincerely striving for that God-attunement and subversion of the ego.

He should have an appreciative, respectful, comparative knowledge of religions, while being grounded in truth, free from hidebound dogma. He should know the difference between true religion and custom, discriminating between universal spirituality and denominational observances.

In order to transmit truth effectively, one must be inspired by the inner perception of truth. The highest type of spiritual teacher spends much time in the divine communion of prayer and meditation — preferably, every morning, noon, and night. This is the way to be able to arrive at the truth in any given situation.

He should believe in and be well versed in the truths he wants to teach, and then strive to realize those truths in himself. The intuitional teacher is the most qualified. The intuitive power of the soul, once awakened by meditation, does not have to depend on reason; it knows.

A teacher should always meditate before instructing others, a practice more valuable than gleaning ideas from books or dialogues with other people.

He must keep his mind on God that he might in the highest way be able to convey thoughts of God to others.

He must have complete faith in God, believing that His help will come when needed. The divine law works!

The best sermon a teacher can give is through the voice of his character and actions; he should be one with God in exemplary qualities. He should be morally upright, balanced and evenminded, honest, and agreeable. He should wear a soulful smile; cheerfulness that comes from the soul.

Proper decorum and knowing the rules of etiquette are highly desirable, but even more important than manners is sincerity. He should always keep his word with people; one's word is one's bond.

He should be natural and loyal to his ideals. He should always stand firm for the truth, but never be angry with or entertain revengeful thoughts against people who criticize him. He should never spread gossip or speak unkind words about others.

One cannot transmit truth if he is not sympathetic. A spiritual teacher should be free from racial and class prejudices and preferences, and give spiritual help to those seeking relief from their troubles as well as to those seeking spiritual development.

Spirituality should never be used for commercial or personal gain. It is preferable that a spiritual teacher not receive a salary. Once he begins to take money for his service to God's work, it becomes merely a job; his mind will be on making a living and wanting more money, not upon the Christlike ideal of serving without thought of remuneration. That is why I have never allowed paying teachers of Self-Realization Fellowship. I am concentrating on monastic teachers who renounce all for God's work. They must be free to give unselfishly of themselves. That is the way I was trained, and that is what I believe. God's work and those who serve it will be supported by God through the goodwill offerings of those who are benefited, as well as through the proceeds from spiritual goods and services that spread the work.

A spiritual teacher should never try to compete with others; he should stick to his goal and teach loyalty to that purpose.

He should never allow himself to be controlled by those who would compromise his ideals for financial or organizational favors given.

Only a true disciple who has undergone the purifying discipline of the *sadhana*, spiritual practices, of a master will make a good teacher. The disciple cleanses his delusion-infected ego by obeying the word of his guru implicitly, because he recognizes the master as a channel of wisdom and purity. Those who themselves become true gurus by divine commission remain also, at all times, true disciples.

~

And they went into Capernaum; and straightway on the Sabbath day he entered into the synagogue, and taught. And they were astonished at his doctrine: for he taught them as one that had authority, and not as the scribes (Mark 1:21–22). *

J esus spoke with God-saturated conviction of the truth in his work. Words are dynamically effective if they are charged with superconscious realization. To try to sell an object, or an idea, or a belief in which the promoter does not himself wholly believe is to mouth words that, no matter how clever, will lack the luster and vibratory seal of conviction. Jesus was absorbed in his realization of God; his authority was demonstrably indisputable.

Preaching with the God-saturated conviction of the soul

Speaking about God from one's own imagination without knowing God is ignorance. But the devotee who knows Him, who feels Him in every fiber of his being, who can perceive His manifested presence, who talks to Him just as he talks to those who are his nearest and dearest and receives His answer—when that devotee speaks about God, true souls listen.

---

* Cf. parallel references in Matthew 7:28–29 and Luke 4:31–32.

A first-century synagogue that most scholars believe to be "almost certainly" the one in which Jesus preached, as described in this verse, was discovered by archaeological excavation in Capernaum in the 1960s, according to Jeffrey L. Sheler in *Is the Bible True?* (New York: HarperCollins, 1999). This synagogue was the scene of at least one divine healing by Jesus, as told in Luke 4:33–37 (see Discourse 24). Sheler also reports that additional excavation in Capernaum, at the site of a Byzantine church dating from about A.D. 400, uncovered a deeper stratum of evidence that indicated the building had originally been a house built about sixty years before Jesus' birth and renovated a few decades after his passing. Some researchers believe this to have been the family residence of the Apostle Peter—where Jesus was known to have spent time during the early part of his ministry—since the walls of the ancient structure found under the Byzantine church had extensive early Christian graffiti, "including at least two references to Peter," and since reports from pilgrims visiting Capernaum in the fourth century mention visiting Peter's house, "which they said had been turned into a church." *(Publisher's Note)*

Teachers who know nothing about God offer to their audiences secondhand ideas gleaned from hours spent poring over books and scriptures. It is a sham to represent oneself as an authority on jewels if one knows nothing about gemology. Similarly, it is unprincipled to present oneself as spiritually qualified if no endeavor is made to commune with God. If one is sincerely making a deep spiritual effort, it is all right. But those who espouse God only from the pulpit, having little or nothing to do with Him otherwise, are of the ilk characterized by Jesus as "hypocrites." They hardly ever pray; they read, and they preach what they have read. People in their congregation, for the most part, let their unlived sermons pass through one ear and out the other.

That is the great import of this verse depicting Jesus in the synagogue. He did not preach like the scribes, with empty words. When he spoke, his words were filled with the Word, the Cosmic Energy, of God. His doctrine was replete with the conviction of realization, born of his Christ stature and Cosmic Consciousness, vibrating with the authority of God's wisdom. His sermons bore the seal of God's assurance.

Is this not a hint to all ministers of the gospel? It is not enough to commit to memory the words of the scriptures, or to receive a Doctor of Divinity degree. One must digest truth and then preach with the power and conviction of the soul. When God speaks through a soul, mountains of delusion are removed from the minds of listeners.

Face-to-face realization of truth gives one intuitive experience, true vision and understanding. Such wisdom gives power; it is the energy that moves the Cosmic Factory, producing control over all things. That power declares the absolute authority of infallible truth. Jesus spoke not with the fanaticism or rote of the scribes, but with the authority of Self-realization of God and a knowledge of all His mysteries.

When one has been a devotee for years, living virtuously and meditating upon God, and thereby succeeds in pleasing Him, then He chooses that soul to bring others back to His kingdom. These advanced souls are saturated with the spirit, intelligence, and power of God; anyone physically, mentally, or spiritually sick, coming in contact with them, receives God's healing blessing.

Holy sermons create a vague devotion in the minds of people. The power of a true emissary of God heals man of his most pernicious affliction, the spiritual sickness of ignorance.

DISCOURSE 24

Casting Out Devils

Difference Between Psychological Obsession
and Possession by Disembodied Spirits

❖

Demystifying the Truth About Disembodied Evil Spirits

❖

Characteristics of Souls in the After~Death Realm

❖

Explanation of the Phenomenon of Possession by "Tramp Souls"

❖

How Jesus Exorcised an Unclean Spirit
Through Will Power and Cosmic Energy

❖

Spiritual Forces of Good and Evil
That Vie for Influence Over Man's Consciousness

❖

Satan's Evil Intelligence at Work in Creation

❖

How Satanic Tendencies Become Obsessions in the Human Mind

❖

Freeing the Consciousness From the Influence of Satan's Devils

*"One should have a working knowledge of and healthy respect for the
ever present delusive satanic power and thereby keep oneself wholly
immune to evil influences."*

*A*nd in the synagogue there was a man, which had a spirit of an unclean devil, and cried out with a loud voice, saying, "Let us alone; what have we to do with thee, thou Jesus of Nazareth? art thou come to destroy us? I know thee who thou art; the Holy One of God."

And Jesus rebuked him, saying, "Hold thy peace, and come out of him." And when the devil had thrown him in the midst, he came out of him, and hurt him not.

And they were all amazed, and spake among themselves, saying, "What a word is this! for with authority and power he commandeth the unclean spirits, and they come out." And the fame of him went out into every place of the country round about.

And he arose out of the synagogue, and entered into Simon's house. And Simon's wife's mother was taken with a great fever; and they besought him for her. And he stood over her, and rebuked the fever; and it left her: and immediately she arose and ministered unto them.

—Luke 4:33–39

DISCOURSE 24

Casting Out Devils

And in the synagogue there was a man, which had a spirit of an unclean devil, and cried out with a loud voice, saying, "Let us alone; what have we to do with thee, thou Jesus of Nazareth? art thou come to destroy us? I know thee who thou art; the Holy One of God."

And Jesus rebuked him, saying, "Hold thy peace, and come out of him." And when the devil had thrown him in the midst, he came out of him, and hurt him not.

And they were all amazed, and spake among themselves, saying, "What a word is this! for with authority and power he commandeth the unclean spirits, and they come out." And the fame of him went out into every place of the country round about (Luke 4:33–37). **

Casting out devils is not an antiquated superstition. The art of casting out devils and healing the spiritually sick of evil obsessions has been largely forgotten due to the lack in all religions of God-tuned apostles who know the subtle workings of the good and evil forces in the world.

On many occasions Jesus drove evil spirits from the afflicted, as in this present verse, and as once he commanded the entities to take leave of a tormented man and enter into the bodies of pigs, who then perished

---

* Cf. parallel reference in Mark 1:23–28.

395

in the sea.* And also in the case of the woman of Canaan and her daughter, who was "grievously vexed with a devil," and whom Jesus healed through the mother's great faith in him.† No amount of so-called progressive "liberal" thinking can accurately explain away these works of Jesus. Each time, he distinctly called forth the evil spirit and the victim was then made whole. Jesus, with his perfect integrity and divine knowledge, would not have referred to such cases as possession by evil spirits if they had instead been psychological, as in hysteria or lunacy.

In modern times many people scoff at the idea of anybody being possessed by an unclean devil. They dismiss such assertions as a myth or superstition—and no doubt there are many quasi-superstitious outgrowths in beliefs and practices. In the olden days of superstition and candle light, devils seemed to be plentiful; but now, in the electrical age, the evil spirits appear to be scared away. However, psychiatrists can tell of the many cases of mental obsessions by fixed ideas, little knowing that some patients may indeed be suffering from actual possession by unclean spirits. Real cases of possession may be misdiagnosed as brain-derangement, or as a state of hallucination, or as spells of hysteria. On the other hand, many psychological cases have been erroneously described as spirit possession by credulous spiritualists. Actual cases of spirit possession, while true, are relatively rare; more common is mental obsession caused by the evil forces of delusion.‡ Whatever the cause, physical and mental and spir-

Difference between psychological obsession and possession by disembodied spirits

---

* Luke 8:26–33 (see Discourse 38).

† Matthew 15:21–24 (see Discourse 44).

‡ One of the fathers of modern psychology, Professor William James of Harvard, wrote: "The refusal of modern 'enlightenment' to treat 'possession' as an hypothesis to be spoken of as even possible, in spite of the massive human tradition based on concrete evidence in its favor, has always seemed to me a curious example of the power of fashion in things scientific. That the demon-theory will again have its innings is to my mind absolutely certain. One has to be 'scientific' indeed to be blind and ignorant enough to suspect no such possibility."

The respected Benedictine monk and author Father Bede Griffiths of Shantivanam Ashram in south India compared the *asuras* mentioned in Hindu scriptures to the demons and evil spirits mentioned in the Christian Bible. He wrote in *The Marriage of East and West* (London: Collins, 1982): "It cannot be too strongly affirmed that these are real powers which act on the unconscious...that is, on the lower levels of consciousness, bringing man into subjection to the powers of nature. The fact that modern man does not recognize them is one of the many signs that he is under their power; only when they are recognized can they be overcome." *(Publisher's Note)*

itual healing are possible when one, like Jesus, can employ divine power to cast out devils and the forces of evil from the threefold nature of man.

The human body and mind, being products of Nature, individualized from Spirit by cosmic delusion, are subject to various kinds of mortal diseases. Jesus, as a true minister of Self-realization, the perfection of the real Self or soul, not only knew how to win people away from satanic ignorance and bring them into divine vibrations by his words of wisdom, but he knew also how to heal them of their diverse kinds of maladies. While preaching in the synagogue (a place where people usually go for their souls to be healed by the salve of inspiring sermons), Jesus encountered a man possessed by an unclean devil. Forthwith Jesus healed this stricken victim.

There is nothing mysterious about devils or disembodied evil spirits except in the ignorance of people who have not studied their characteristics. Many scientific secrets that formerly lay hidden in nature are now commonplace matters. Someday, when people will be more spiritually advanced they will *Demystifying the truth* understand the mysteries of life and death and the *about disembodied* nature of disincarnate souls that have gone into the *evil spirits* unknown.

By long successful practice of meditation, a devotee can transfer his will and attention beyond the portals of the conscious and the subconscious minds into the superconscious. When he can go deeper and project his concentration consciously from superconsciousness felt within his body into the light of Christ Intelligence hidden beyond the state of wakefulness, dreams, subconsciousness, and superconsciousness, he can then behold the vast astral universe of luminous vibratory planets and vibratory spheres peopled with millions of disincarnate souls.

The inhabitants of the astral world are garbed in forms made of energy and light, and are confined to higher or lower astral spheres according to their karma. There are, however, a few astral beings known as "tramp souls." They are earthbound because of strong material urges and attachments. They roam in the ether, desirous of reentering a physical form to satisfy their need for sense enjoyments. Such beings are usually harmless, invisible "ghosts," and have no power to affect the ordinary person. However, tramp souls do occasionally take possession of someone's body and mind, but only such vulnerable persons who are mentally unstable or have weakened their mind by keeping it often blank or unthinking. Owing to their mental emptiness, and karmic attraction, they unwittingly invite the advent of vagrant spirits within their bodies. If one leaves his car unlocked with the key in the ignition, any uncouth character may get in and drive off. Tramp souls, having lost their own physical-body vehicle to which they were inordinately attached, are on the watch for such unattended conveyances.

Unclean devils, cited in the cases of possession that Jesus exorcised, are those astral beings among tramp souls who on earth were murderers, robbers, and other criminals, drunkards and licentious persons, and especially vicious and treacherous beings, who did not cleanse themselves of their evil propensities before death. Even the greatest sinner, if he cleans his subconscious mind and memory by contacting the superconsciousness in meditation before death, does not carry his unpurged wickedness into a sphere beyond death. But those persons who leave their physical bodies in a state of sin, as also those who ruthlessly and foolishly commit suicide, are considered unclean souls in the astral world. They roam in the lower astral spheres, imprisoned in their astral and causal bodies, finding no rest, and either hating to be reborn on the earth or grieving for the loss of their physical incarnation. These forlorn souls have to wander about in the ether until some of the karmic effects of their bad actions are worn out through the operation of the divine law. The devilish spirits among them are very unscrupulous, even as they were during earth life.

Satan, the Cosmic Evil Intelligence, has his satellites in disreputable persons who have lost in the moral and spiritual battle, working through these decadent beings not only on earth while they are living but also in their afterlife astral existence. As evil-possessed persons do mischief on earth, so these Satan-obsessed astral beings continue their mischief in the astral world as well as in the physical world as tramp souls. They seek out persons with similar karmic potentials, attracted by their negative vibrations. They intelligently possess and punish such earthly human beings during the term of their own astral punishment determined by their specific transgressions in worldly life.

Characteristics of souls in the after-death realm

Why should it be considered amazing that such disembodied evil spirits reside on the other side of life when devils and devilish persons exist right on this side of life? If souls are immortal, then, according to the law of cause and effect, it is logical to expect that when a devilish person sheds the mortal coil and passes through the door of the mortal change called "death," into the afterlife, he does not become an angel, but continues to be a devil. Only a soul who has been angelic on earth can continue to be so after crossing the gulf of death, entering not the dark astral spheres but the finer atmosphere of Heaven.

As a good boy turned to evil ways can be called a devil, so the disincarnate astral consciousness of a person gone wrong becomes devilish in its behavior. Such wicked beings pass through many strange experiences in the afterlife. As people of calm disposition usually have deep soothing sleep, so good souls, when they sleep the sleep of death, experience a wondrously refreshing peace and uplifting dream visions before reincarnating to continue working out their earthly karma. But as restless and excitable persons often experience nightmares during sleep, so also when people of evil-disturbed disposition die, they experience during the great death sleep, according to the law of cause and effect, only horrible astral nightmares, reflections of their own accumulated evil.

As a man may sleep a few hours or three hours or twelve hours or may have sleeping sickness, so some souls after death remain in the state of unconscious sleep for a little while or a long time, according to their karma in earthly life. Souls with good karma are able to be awake in the astral land after their sleep of death. Those who have practiced many virtues enjoy the results of their good karma on heavenly astral planets where the limitations of earth life are non-existent. Most souls, neither categorically virtuous nor evil, after sleeping the sleep of peaceful unconscious death, with occasional experiences of astral wakefulness, wake up in the womb of their new earthly mother.

Only souls who by meditation can control the life-force functions of heart and breath and remain engrossed in the constant ecstasy of God-consciousness during their earth life can remain conscious unbrokenly during the transition of death and also in the astral world. It is the testimony of these devotees who can retain their consciousness in the after-death state that declares the mystery of the astral experience.

As worms live in the earth, fish live in the water, humans live on earth, birds live in the air, and angels live in the fine airless vibratory realms, so also there are various atmospheres and vibratory regions in the astral universe where souls of varying degrees of advancement reside, according to the merits and demerits of their pre-astral existence in earth life.*

---

* "In my Father's house are many mansions" (John 14:2).

Fish cannot live for long out of their watery habitat; similarly, tramp souls, unclean spirits, must remain in gross vibratory astral plan-

———•—•———

Explanation of the phenomenon of possession by "tramp souls"

ets, whereas finer souls reside in the subtly vibrating luminous planets. If tramp souls dared to approach these finer regions, they would be shocked or "astralocuted" by the high voltage of astral energy.

As people walk in sleep or cry out during a bad dream, so, during the sleep after death, unclean spirits move about in the ether crying out for relief. Often they try to get hold of some passive bodily vehicle through which to express their agony and pent-up wickedness. As a sleepwalker does many strange things, so these ghostly sleepwalkers engage in many strange antics. But they can never infest brains occupied with intelligent thinking, or people with strong will power or vibrations of spiritual perception. That is why one should never make the mind negative, or blank, in order to open oneself to messages from disincarnate spirits. This presents an ideal opportunity for possession by low-type tramp souls seeking human vehicles for expression and experience.*

The minds of spiritually advanced persons cannot be occupied by devilish souls; but these devotees can invoke the presence of and communion with saintly souls by use of the proper technique of astral intuition. One must learn the right technique from one's guru. Divine saints do not appear through mediums and séances; they respond only when they are invited by the urge of the devotion of advanced devotees. Such devotees can see or talk to saints in vision. When they develop even further, they can see with open eyes the materialized form of saints and can talk to them or touch them, even as the advanced disciples of Jesus were able by their devotion to see and touch Jesus Christ in flesh after his resurrection.

So the idea of devils possessing weak-brained, thought-unoccupied persons cannot be discarded as superstition. But a strong personality fully occupies his brain, thereby shutting out the invasion of tramp souls. Devotees who are sincerely seeking God, and who practice scientific methods of prayer and meditation, need never fear such beings; for no harm from negative spirits can come to one whose thoughts are on God. While one meditates on God, one can be absolutely convinced that his body is so charged with a high voltage of cosmic energy emanating

---

* Cf. commentary on Bhagavad Gita xvii:4, *God Talks With Arjuna.*

from the thought of God that he is protected from the lower-astral intruders. If any such spirits would even try to possess the bodies of God-tuned souls, those entities would be shocked and driven back to the dark spheres of the astral world.

There is a distinct difference between the condition of a person acting under the influence of possession by a tramp soul or unclean devil, and that of one acting under a hypnotic spell or the obsession of a subconscious idea, or autosuggestion. Men and women under the influence of hypnosis or strong obsession of the subconscious mind can be made to act in either a noble or a devilish way. Real possession consists of the actual presence in one's body of a soul that has cast off its own physical garment and in its astral form is partially, completely, or spasmodically incapacitating the rational faculties of the possessed. One human body ordinarily cannot house another being along with its own self (except in the case of a mother carrying a child). But spiritual experts are able to distinguish true cases of spirit possession, because by their psychic powers they are able to behold, within the person possessed, the astral body of the invisible visitor side by side with the astral body of the host. The only way a layman is able to deduce a case of spirit possession is by analyzing the different states of paroxysm and wild behavior to which a possessed person is subject. The evil-spirit-possessed person usually displays unusual physical strength, bloodshot eyes, uncanny expression, and general lack of normal behavior. This bestial irrationality is variously displayed and described in the instances of spirit possession exorcised by Jesus.

Like attracts like, so the possessed man in the synagogue, by the attraction of his own sinful vibration, drew unto himself an unclean spirit. Jesus, possessing the universal Christ Consciousness, could feel exactly what was going on within the body of the bedeviled man. And the unclean spirit, through the intuition of its astral body, could feel the power of Jesus. (Astral-bodied souls perceive through the sixth sense of intuition; but they can use it to perform the functions of vision, audition, smell, taste, touch, and so forth.) The unclean, wicked spirit kept the mind of the possessed man in a state of suspension, neutrality, and sub-hypnosis of obsession, so that its victim's instruments of consciousness—senses, brain, and body—could be used without interference. A possessed individual may or may not be unconscious within his spirit-controlled

How Jesus exorcised an unclean spirit through will power and cosmic energy

401

body, just as a person under hypnosis may manifest the unconsciousness of sleep or the superficially normal state of the obsessed conscious mind. The unclean spirit saw Jesus through the eyes of the possessed man, and used his voice to cry loudly: "Let us alone; do not deny us our freedom of expression, be it good or evil."

The possessive spirit, itself obsessed with satanic evil, recognized in Jesus the opposing force of godly good: "I know thee...the Holy One of God." The spirit rightly feared that Jesus, with his Christ Consciousness having control over all life, would put an end to the unauthorized, forced occupation of the possessed man's mind. It knew that the omnipresent Christ Consciousness in Jesus was the Lord of creation. Astral beings, whether clean or unclean, know that it is the Christ Intelligence and not Satan's *maya* that has ultimate power over the inner world, even though Satan tries to exert his influence in the astral world to the same degree he succeeds on earth. But heaven is not a comfortable place for a fallen archangel.

Jesus did not want the unclean devil, in its irritated state, to do harm to the brain of the obsessed man. If possession by unclean devils or disembodied souls continues for long, great mischief is done to the brain, mind, and sense organs of the possessed individual, posing a threat of the advent of permanent insanity. By his life-controlling will power, Jesus spoke: *"Hold thy peace and come out of him."* That is, stop the devilish work of wrecking possessed brains; hold on to the inner peace of the soul, hidden behind the dark barrier of self-created past evil propensities, and restore again your right behavior by coming out of the body you have forcibly and unethically occupied.

It requires strong concentration and divine will power to dislodge an evil spirit. If one has dynamic spiritual force, the entity can be thrown out by constantly looking into the eyes of a stricken individual, using steady, silent will power continuously, inwardly commanding the evil spirit to leave. The entity will depart provided the will of the healer to drive the evil force out is stronger than the latter's will to remain.

By the repeated whisper of "*Aum*" in the right ear of a possessed individual, the evil spirit is bound to leave. Tramp souls, having wandered out of the dark lower astral regions, cannot stand the high vibration of spiritual thoughts and consciousness. The utterance of holy names and words, especially *Aum, Aum, Aum,* into the ear of possessed individuals usually brings forth a quick, frightened reply from the individual like: "I am going; don't utter that holy word," which indicates spirit possession.

Jesus, drawing power from the Cosmic *Aum* Vibration, commanded, with his *Aum*-impregnated voice, the devil to come out of the body of the afflicted individual. The devil, unwilling to obey Jesus, fought against the powerful vibration. This created convulsions in the body of the bedeviled man as the powerful Cosmic Current vibrating within him tried to dislodge and shake out the intruding spirit. At last the evil entity came out of the body violently, leaving the man limp and shaken but not hurt, unable to harm him due to the intervention of the divine Christ Jesus. The people who beheld this casting out of an unclean spirit were in awe of the sovereign authority in the word of Jesus, which even demonic entities were constrained to obey — adding far and wide to the renown of Jesus.

Why be concerned about the harassment of ghostly tramp-souls? Such threat is negligible. Normal, healthy minded persons are impervious to their mischief. A far greater danger to one's well-being exists right within and around every human being. Good and evil are fighting for supremacy — the one force is trying to save us, and the other to harm us. We are caught in the middle of this cosmic war between God and His "fallen archangel" Satan. One cannot dismiss this problematic conflict by rationalizing that Satan is a mere delusion. Jesus himself acknowledged the actuality of the adversary when he said: "Get thee behind me, Satan" and "Deliver us from evil." It would hardly be necessary to pray to God at all if there were no devil and works of the devil from which man requires divine intervention to be delivered.

Spiritual forces of good and evil that vie for influence over man's consciousness

Satan, with his power of *maya,* exists in order to provide the dichotomy of Spirit necessary to bring into manifestation and perpetuate the universal cosmic drama. But though God allows the shadows of troubles to play amidst His light, He also tries to help us out of delusion's turmoils. God and His angels and countless good spirits, spiritual forces, are trying to establish divine harmony in man and his cosmic environment. Every beneficial quality is created by a divine agent of God. These personified spiritual forces are constantly implanting noble thoughts in man's mind. At the same time, Satan, with his evil spirits, is fomenting chaos in the world and restive temptations to distress man's consciousness.

As all good is organized by God and His angels, and as He sends His spiritually advanced children on earth from time to time to eradicate evil, similarly, the mighty evil force, Satan, with a vast horde of evil spirits, personified evil forces, is carrying on a campaign of organized wickedness throughout the universe.

Millions of harmful bacteria and a mélange of evil diseases, evil thoughts, evil passions, are all potentially implanted by the evil force into the mind and body of man. Though man is essentially made in the image of God, when his mortal vulnerability succumbs to obsession by the latent satanic forces in him of greed, selfishness, anger, or any of the evil tendencies, these overcloud the purity of the human soul.

God's light is present in every being as the soul with its godly reflections of divine forces and qualities; Satan is also present in every being as ignorance with distinct reflections of himself as evil forces or spirits. Thus, each individual is influenced both by the soul and its good qualities and by Satan and his evil qualities.

So the truth is that the direct creator of evil—as concerns the relative existence and experience of man—is this Satanic Force, the archangel that turned away from God and misused his God-given power in order to create evil as a counterpart of all the good that God has created. Thus we find in each man opposite qualities—good created by God, evil created by Satan; love created by God, hate created by Satan; kindness created by God, selfishness created by Satan; intoxication of divine ecstasy created by God, and intoxication of evil gratifications created by Satan.*

When a person is beset with an evil obsession, physically, mentally, or spiritually—such as chronic disease; insidious emotions, habits, or desires; spiritual ignorance—it is the manifestation of a spirit reflection of Satan, a devil, that needs to be cast out as decidedly

---

* In yogic terms, the Bhagavad Gita explains the good and evil forces in man as a war between two contending armies, one led by the powers of the divine discrimination of the soul and the other by the materialistic mind and its baser instincts of the delusion-influenced senses. These contending powers in man are energized either by the spiritualized Godward forces in the astral centers of life and consciousness in the spine, brain, and spiritual eye; or contrarily in matterward energies drawn toward expression in the debased inclinations of the senses and their allied cohorts of evil behavior in egotism, fear, desires, anger, greed, attachment, pride, habits, temptations. The full yoga science of the battle endemic in man's consciousness between good and evil (God and Satan)— and how practice of that science bestows soul-liberating victory over these universal psychological enemies—is described in Paramahansa Yogananda's detailed commentary on Chapter 1, verses 1-18 in *God Talks With Arjuna: The Bhagavad Gita. (Publisher's Note)*

as the exorcism of a tramp soul, or unclean devil, in a case of spirit possession. Such, indeed, were among the many healings effected by Jesus, as in the following incident.

∾

And he arose out of the synagogue, and entered into Simon's house. And Simon's wife's mother was taken with a great fever; and they besought him for her. And he stood over her, and rebuked the fever; and it left her: and immediately she arose and ministered unto them (Luke 4:38–39). *

Diseases are due to the lack of proper operation of the conscious beneficial forces that govern the body, and are also due to the evil forces which consciously allow the bane of disease to spread in the body. Some diseases are brought about by physical transgressions against the laws of health, but the disease germs themselves are engendered and intelligently controlled by the evil force of Satan, which tries to destroy the beautiful creation of God—the human body. Whenever a person transgresses physically, mentally, or spiritually, a portal is opened for a specific disease or malady to enter the body, according to the nature of the transgression. Vibrations are generated that attract the agencies of evil in the form of disease germs.

Disease germs have a dormant intelligence that at an opportune time is roused and directed by Satan. Jesus could see the evil force that was responsible for the introduction of fever into the body of Simon's wife's mother, and thus he rebuked it away and restored the harmony of health. Jesus commanded the predominating evil force to

Satan's evil intelligence at work in creation

depart from the body of the stricken woman, thus reinstating the conscious astral forces that govern normal health. He knew all the intelligent evil forces that create havoc in people and was able, through his all-powerful Christ Consciousness, to talk in the vibratory language of the fever and command it to depart from the ailing body of the woman. That is what is meant by Jesus "rebuking the fever."

All evil has some intelligence by which it works its mischief. Note how cleverly it insinuates itself into the mind of a person through false

---

* Cf. parallel references in Matthew 8:14–15 and Mark 1:29–31.

405

reasoning. Vice takes the cloak of virtue and fools the gatekeeper of reason, and thus enters the forbidden sanctum of virtue. Each soul is independent and free to act according to the good influences of God and soulful qualities, or to act under the influence of Satan's evil qualities and Satan's reflections, the devils which obsess the being of man. While good and evil actions can be freely chosen, after one has acted he has no free choice as to consequences. If he acts in a good way he must receive a good result and if he acts in an evil way he must receive an evil result. The cohort reflections of Satan in each man constantly urge him to do wrong through the lure of temptations that appeal to his prenatal karmic tendencies and present habits. God tries to influence a being through conscience and soul peace found in meditation. As a free agent, man must choose either to act under the influence of God's direction or Satan's evil incitements.

When one acts according to the influence of conscience or good qualities, he creates good tendencies and good habits which automatically draw him toward God. Whenever an individual acts evilly under the influence of evil habits or evil qualities, then automatically he is drawn toward Satan, ignorance, and satanic ways.

This explanation of good and evil is to point out that man is not responsible for being *tempted* to do evil under the influence of anger, greed, or fear, or other evils, implanted in him by Satan, but he is re-

How satanic tendencies become obsessions in the human mind

sponsible if he chooses to *act* according to the temptations of the evil forces. Such temptations appear in man as evil impulses and inner promptings to do wrong. When the evil forces are successful, obsessed man feels compelled to act out those urges.

Human beings thus succumb to evil not only through the influence of their prenatal or postnatal tendencies and bad habits, but also because they are consciously pushed by the satanic entities residing in the brain. When the evil entity of an obsession is dislodged from the brain by higher meditations, self-controlled right actions, and the help of one's guru, then a soul really becomes free. Jesus healed Mary Magdalene from seven devils, visitations of the evil forces.* Great masters, like Jesus, can transmit their light of spirituality into the mind of a person obsessed with an evil intent and thereby dislodge the specific evil force causing the affliction.

---

* Luke 8:2 and Mark 16:9.

If a man sits in a room full of light, beholding beautiful objects, to him light exists. If another man sits in the same room with eyes closed, to him darkness exists—albeit self-created. Similarly, there are two kinds of people in this world. One kind have their spiritual eyes of wisdom open; they see God and His goodness existing everywhere, in everything. The second kind have their spiritual eyes closed; they experience creation as rife with Satan and his evils.

Man is responsible for harboring the darkness of evil if he does not cultivate the true perception of wisdom. Devotees are those souls who obey the wishes of God to keep their eyes of wisdom open and focused only on good; and deluded persons are those who heed the voice of evil and keep their eyes of spirituality closed, thus courting the darkness of misery, sickness, and the whole host of Satan's evils.

God is alluring His devotees by all good things to come unto Him; and Satan, by the allurement of false promises of happiness, is coaxing people deeper into his pit of ignorance and misery. Man should consider the whisperings of his conscience and good tendencies as the call of God within him. Conversely, he should recognize and resist the promptings of evil thoughts and urges as the lure of Satan.

If man continuously listens responsively to the whisperings of his conscience and nascent virtues and gets used to better ways of living, he ultimately discovers the eternal good within the God-image of his soul, and through this Self-realization becomes liberated. Because Satan breaks his promises to give lasting happiness to his followers, they will all finally turn away from him to God.

Satan's devils, the originators and pioneers of evil working through evil tendencies in man, should therefore be cast out from ignorance-haunted souls. Spiritualizing one's life through righteous behavior and especially through God-communion in deep regular meditation is the way to expel the evil entities and open up the latent perceptions of heaven within. To rid the conscious- *Freeing the conscious-ness from the influ-ence of Satan's devils* ness of obsessing evil forces is the real metaphysical way of freeing a soul forever from the influences of Satan's devils that have carried on their misery-dealing work through incarnations in one who chose to misuse his power of reason.

Jesus, being omniscient, had full knowledge of how Satan and his evil forces worked in torturing human beings. Thus, he knew the metaphysical art of casting out those devils, as did his specially ordained apostles. The art is known to all masters, who then teach other souls how to be free forever from the innate influences of evil entities, by consciously establishing within themselves the preeminence of God.

Great masters can heal the ignorance in truth-seeking devotees by contact with the Christ Consciousness and transmitting to them that spiritual power. I have seen how my guru, Swami Sri Yukteswarji, cast out devils from obsessed beings and healed so-called incurable sicknesses and preached through his exemplary living. Masters who are entirely free from evil show others thereby how to be likewise free.

By the contact of God through advanced concentration and meditation, as with the Self-Realization techniques, and by spiritually developing oneself with the help of the guru, devotees can actually dislodge the originator of evil, Satan and his obsessing entities, from within the sacred sanctum of their body temple.

Illumined saints have declared how the spirit entity of evil takes shape and leaves the body permanently, after highest spiritual attainment. When the evil entity departs, the cleansed consciousness of the devotee becomes not only absolutely impervious to evil but cannot see evil in anything anymore. He sees God alone everywhere.*

In summary, the lesson to be drawn from the dramatic demonstrations of Jesus in casting out devils is not that one should concentrate on and fear possession by tramp souls (a rare actuality) or obsessions by Satan's evil entities (innate in the human psyche). Rather, one should have a working knowledge of and healthy respect for the ever-present delusive satanic power and thereby keep oneself wholly immune to evil influences.

Listen to the voice of God echoing in your good thoughts. These are strong intimations from God and His angelic spirits to guide and help you. Satan also is exerting his influence with his own kind of contrary mental instigations. Every time a bad thought or impulse comes, cast out that devilish entity; then Satan cannot do anything to you. Why remain a mortal captive, oscillating between good and evil? Escape into the heart of Spirit where Satan and his horde will be unable to reach you.

---

* See Discourse 8, page 179.

"One who knows his soul knows how to work miracles through the life force....Jesus used various outward means of transmitting the cosmic energy."

*A*nd at even, when the sun did set, they brought unto him all that were diseased, and them that were possessed with devils. And all the city was gathered together at the door. And he healed many that were sick of divers diseases, and cast out many devils; and suffered not the devils to speak, because they knew him.

And in the morning, rising up a great while before day, he went out, and departed into a solitary place, and there prayed. And Simon and they that were with him followed after him. And when they had found him, they said unto him, "All men seek for thee."

And he said unto them, "Let us go into the next towns, that I may preach there also: for therefore came I forth."

And he preached in their synagogues throughout all Galilee, and cast out devils.

—Mark 1:32—39

Healing the Sick

✿

And at even, when the sun did set, they brought unto him all that were diseased, and them that were possessed with devils. And all the city was gathered together at the door. And he healed many that were sick of divers diseases, and cast out many devils; and suffered not the devils to speak, because they knew him (Mark 1:32–34).

Parallel references:

When the even was come, they brought unto him many that were possessed with devils: and he cast out the spirits with his word, and healed all that were sick: that it might be fulfilled which was spoken by Isaiah the prophet, saying, "Himself took our infirmities, and bare our sicknesses" (Matthew 8:16–17).

* * *

Now when the sun was setting, all they that had any sick with divers diseases brought them unto him; and he laid his hands on every one of them, and healed them. And devils also came out of many, crying out, and saying, "Thou art Christ the Son of God." And he rebuking them suffered them not to speak: for they knew that he was Christ (Luke 4:40–41).

An understanding of the general science of the nature of disease and its cure will give an increased comprehension and appreciation of the divine law of healing as employed by Jesus. A disease consists of an inharmonious condition producing pain or unhappiness

———◆·◆———

The three types of af-
flictions to which
man is subject

immediately or remotely in a living creature. Human beings are subject to three kinds of diseases, those that affect the body, the mind, and the soul.

The body is affected by bacteria, viruses, toxins, wounds, and organic troubles, which cause physical suffering. To free man from bodily ailments constitutes physical healing.

The mind is susceptible to infection by mental bacteria of fear, worries, melancholia, psychological nervousness, anger, greed, insatiable sensual temptations, selfishness, jealousy, and morbid tendencies, all of which produce mental discomforts and agonies. The healing of psychological diseases is called mental healing.

The soul is haunted by the disease of ignorance born of cosmic delusion, which causes man to forget his perfect divine nature and concentrate on his imperfect human nature. Ignorance creates inharmony between mind and body, soul and mind; and in addition engenders every other form of trouble.

Physical pain does not bring mental suffering if the mind is strong; martyrs whose minds are firmly fixed in devotion to God have maintained their inner serenity even while being burned at the stake. But mental suffering usually brings with it its companion of physical suffering; and when the soul cedes the expression of its powers to ignorance, body and mind are automatically subject to physical and mental ailments, for it is the disease of ignorance that produces in man the consciousness of the body and the body-identified mind.

Realized souls, who have healed themselves of ignorance, behold the body as a dream of God, frozen mind of Divinity. When the eye of wisdom is opened by meditation, the gloom of mortal ignorance and physical and mental agonies is dispelled by God's light reflected in the soul. Jesus knew the causal relation between mind and body, and between soul and God. That is how he was able to control the atomic structure of cells and harmonize psychological agitations, and thus restore any ailing body or mind.

Body and mind, being evolutes of the immortal soul-image of God, can reflect the soul's perpetual beauty, youth, everlasting peace, and immortality. The world lauds itself for its material advancements, but has yet to discover the science and art of the highest human achievement, that celestial blessedness which Jesus and the conclave of great saints and masters have been enjoying ever since they freed themselves from mortal ignorance, and will continue to enjoy to the end of endlessness.

There are various ways of healing oneself of the above three kinds of diseases. Delusion is dispelled by deeper and deeper meditation until one has ecstatic contact of the ever new bliss of God. Meditative efforts are supported and en- *Methods of healing* hanced by reading true scriptures with intuitional *the soul of ignorance* understanding and by discriminative introspection on religious truths; by association with God-contacting saints; by attunement in thought and action with the ideals and guidance of one's guru; by devotion; by good actions of helping oneself and others to be free from physical, mental, and spiritual suffering; and by moral living. Attending religious services and keeping good company only shows that a person is interested in spirituality. Liberation from delusion must be preceded by an actual commitment to following and practicing the precepts of one who contacts God and who can teach the technique of God-contact. One should never be satisfied with dogmatic beliefs or the mere assurance of salvation promised by others. Unless one *knows* God, he must keep seeking Him until delusion is sundered and he becomes settled in that unquestionable realization.

Psychological diseases receive the healing support needed from self-analysis, attentive introspection, and association with and emulation of mentally healthy people. Concentration on spiritualized thoughts in meditation actually eradi- *Cure of psychological* cates the causes of mental diseases and corroding *diseases and bad* bad mental habits. In meditation the mind becomes *habits* interiorized and withdraws the externally activating life force from the muscles and nerves and concentrates it in the brain cells where the evil tendencies are recorded. This concentrated life energy in meditation burns out the "grooves" or patterns of mental habits that are lodged in the brain.*

---

* "Through meditation...you can set the stage for important mind- and habit-altering brain change," concluded Herbert Benson, M.D., Professor of Medicine at Harvard Medical School, after extensive research reported in his book, *Your Maximum Mind* (New York: Random House, 1987). "Over the years," he writes, "you develop 'circuits' and 'channels' of thought in your brain. These are physical pathways which control the way you think, the way you act, and often, the way you feel. Many times, these

All habits are mental. They are automatic mental machines that make the performance of psychological or physical tasks easier. Attention is the needle that etches the grooves of mental good or bad habits, recording repeated experiences or actions in the brain. Whenever attention is given to these recordings, they automatically manifest themselves in mental and muscular activity. The bad patterns need to be deprived of their controlling power by the destruction of their ability to haplessly repeat themselves.

Will power and autosuggestion initiated by others can be useful in destroying mental bad habits. Will power can concentrate energy in the brain patterns with healing results. Autosuggestion, implanting in the subconscious mind a positive thought or imagery by concentrated repetition, is useful when one's will is paralyzed by the experience of continued mental disease. When the person to be healed receives a

---

pathways or habits become so fixed that they turn into what I call 'wiring.' In other words, the circuits or channels become so deeply ingrained that it seems almost impossible to transform them."

However, advances in medical technology have enabled scientists for the first time to measure the profound effects of meditation on *neuroplasticity*—the mind's ability to alter the electrical patterns by which habits and deeply rooted behavioral tendencies are stored in the brain. An article in *The Wall Street Journal* (January 10, 2003) by its science writer Sharon Begley discussed new evidence that "alterations in brain wiring... could be induced by meditation." She reported research conducted by neuroscientist Dr. Richard Davidson at the University of Wisconsin, which focused on various forms of Buddhist meditation: "After eight weeks, and again 16 weeks later, EEG measurements showed that activity in the frontal cortices of the meditators had shifted: There were now more neuronal firings in left than right regions nestled just behind the forehead. That pattern is associated with positive feelings such as joy, happiness and low levels of anxiety, Professor Davidson and others had found in earlier studies."

Dr. Davidson is quoted in the article as saying: "The idea that our brains are the result of the unfolding of a fixed genetic program is just shattered by the data on neuroplasticity."

"Scientific research has shown that electrical activity between the left and right sides of the brain becomes coordinated during certain kinds of meditation or prayer," Dr. Benson writes. "Through these processes, the mind definitely becomes more capable of being altered and having its capacities maximized....When you are in this state of enhanced left-right hemispheric communication...'plasticity of cognition' occurs....If you focus or concentrate on some sort of written passage which represents the direction in which you wish your life to be heading, [this] more directed thought process will help you to rewire the circuits in your brain in more positive directions....When we change our patterns of thinking and acting, the brain cells begin to establish additional connections, or new 'wirings.' These new connections then communicate in fresh ways with other cells, and before long, the pathways or wirings that kept the phobia or other habit alive are replaced or altered....Changed actions and a changed life will follow. The implications are exciting and even staggering." *(Publisher's Note)*

Healing the Sick

Now when the sun was setting, all they that had any sick with divers diseases brought them unto him; and he laid his hands on every one of them, and healed them.

—Luke 4:40

Healing by sending energy through the hands is based on the healer's ability to connect with and consciously direct the cosmic energy of God. The body lives in an omnipresent sea of this vibratory power....One who knows his soul knows how to work miracles through the life force, the master of life and death, by sending it through the hands in healing rays to burn out disease in any stricken person.

* * *

Wondrous was the love and compassion of Jesus as he journeyed through the busy cities and villages teaching in the synagogues the gospel, God's vibratory truth, and giving forth of his divine power to heal all manner of suffering. His universal heart felt for the multitude....

—Paramahansa Yogananda

Drawing by Heinrich Hofmann

firm thought of healing from one trying to help him, and then makes that suggestion his own by concentration on its manifesting power, he can reinforce his own will power by the suggestion of another's strong will that he be healed. Autosuggestion, which is used in most forms of psychological healing, can revive the disease-paralyzed will—which then sends energy into the brain, effecting the removal of the destructive pattern lodged in the brain cells.

Mental bad habits will also yield their hold by association with persons who have good mental habits. The timid should associate with the brave, the sensual with those possessing self-control, the restless with those who have meditative habits. Exercise of will power translated into won't power, and staying away from the bad company and environment that feed a specific bad mental habit, can starve the life out of compulsions to behave wrongly.

Because the ailments of the body have psychological roots, and because the body itself is condensed thought, bodily afflictions can be treated in two ways: by physical methods and by mental methods. The different processes of physical *Physical and mental* healing stimulate to a greater or lesser degree the life *methods of healing* force, which effects the cure. Medical procedures, *the body* medicinal drugs, herbal treatment, the various techniques of mental and spiritual therapy—all are valid methods of healing, effective to the degree that they harmonize and restore the proper flow of life energy in the body, which is the direct cause of healing.

One physical means of treating disease consists of judicious fasting to purify the body of toxins and to rejuvenate the life force. In fasting, the will reverts to dependence on Spirit and draws energy from the cosmic source, reinforcing and stimulating the healing energy in the body. In fasting one should be guided by expert advice as to the method and length of the fast. Most persons, in the absence of prohibitive medical problems, can benefit from fasting on orange juice, or other unsweetened fruit juice, one day a week or three consecutive days once a month.

The chemical properties and nutrients in fresh herbs have been shown since ancient times to be beneficial in healing by eliminating poisons and destroying bacteria in the blood. Medicines are synthesized from extracts from herbs and other sources in nature. Therefore, medicines also have healing power. Those who decry medicine and its beneficial effects on the human system should be as readily able to abandon food as well, for whoever eats food uses the medicinal or health-giving properties of those nature-made products.

But while I speak of the power of medicine derived from the God-created elements of nature, I must add that medicine in itself has not that power of healing possessed by the mind if one knows how to use that mental power. Those who put all their confidence in medicine weaken their minds and find that they have to live by dependence on medicine, just as some people I have known seem absolutely depend-ent on periodic operations (though in certain cases operations are nec-essary to remove diseased tissue to prevent it from affecting healthy tissue). But whatever mode of treatment one adopts, the mind in large measure may still determine the outcome, positive or negative. Doubt, depression, pessimistic thoughts, lack of will, weaken the flow of heal-ing life energies; the conscious direction of the mind's powers by pos-itive thoughts, prayers, affirmations, visualization, will, cheerfulness, stimulates the natural healing processes of the body with the vital life force necessary to aid in restoring health. People should learn to draw more on the all-healing power of the mind, along with observance of healthful habits: proper eating, exercise, fresh air and sunshine, hy-giene, physical and mental relaxation, and conscious recharging of the life force.

The primary medicine of the future will be rays, the vibratory na-ture of which is more compatible with the molecular atomic nature of the human body. Healing rays can reach into the atomic disorder of cells in chronic diseases. There is also much healing energy in the sun's rays, though the harmful effects of overexposure must be avoided.*

---

* The biological potency of specific wave-patterns of vibratory energy on bodily cells was "decisively demonstrated" by Jacques Benveniste, M.D., research director of France's National Institute for Health and Medical Research, according to journalist Lynne McTaggart in *The Field: The Quest for the Secret Force of the Universe* (New York: HarperCollins, 2002).

"Both specific molecules and intermolecular bonds emit certain specific frequen-cies which can be detected billions of light-years away, through the most sensitive of modern telescopes," McTaggart reports. "These frequencies have long been accepted by physicists....Benveniste's contribution was to show that molecules and atoms had their own unique frequencies by using modern technology both to record this fre-quency and to use the recording itself for cellular communication....

"Over thousands of experiments, Benveniste and Guillonet recorded the activity of the molecule on a computer and replayed it to a biological system ordinarily sensi-tive to that substance. In every instance, the biological system has been fooled into thinking it has been interacting with the substance itself and acted accordingly, initi-

Spinal adjustments and massage are effective promoters of healing, for they release obstructed life force to carry out its function as the sure healer of physical diseases.

Yoga exercises, the postures or *asanas* of Hatha Yoga, are an excellent means of adjusting the spinal vertebrae to release the pressure on the spinal nerves and bring about the normal flow of life force in the nervous system, promoting healing of many diseases. The Energization Exercises in *Self-Realization Fellowship Lessons* are a method of exercise that directly awakens the all-healing life force for the maintenance of health and the direct healing of disease.*

The mental way of healing physical disease is made possible by stimulating the will, imagination, emotion, or reason in the ailing patient. The healer must be a person of great concentration who can exercise his own will, imagination, emotion, or reason on his patients. He must be an adept at reading character so that he can detect the true nature of his patients and treat *Power of the mind to* them accordingly, stimulating will in the strong- *rouse curative life* willed patients, imagination in imaginative ones, *energy* and so forth.

An incident of healing by the power of intense emotion is recorded in the case of a person who had lost his power of speech. Seeing a sudden fire in the building he was in, he began to shout "Fire! Fire!" The subconscious disease-habit of his disability was healed in that instant by the strong emotions of shock and excitement roused by imminent danger.

Will, emotion, imagination, and reason have no healing power of themselves. They only stimulate the partially inactive life force in the

---

ating the biological chain reaction, just as it would if in the actual presence of the genuine molecule....

"In perhaps the most dramatic of his experiments, Benveniste showed that the signal could be sent across the world by email or mailed on a floppy disk. Colleagues of his at Northwestern University in Chicago recorded signals from ovalbumin (Ova), acetylcholine (Ach), dextran, and water" and sent them on computer disk or by email to Benveniste's laboratory in Paris. There, the researchers "exposed ordinary water to the signals of this digital Ova or Ach or ordinary water and infused either the exposed water or the ordinary water to isolated guinea pig hearts. All the digitized water produced highly significant changes in coronary flow....The effects from the digitized water were identical to effects produced on the heart by the actual substances themselves." *(Publisher's Note)*

* The Energization Exercises, which are fully explained in the *Lessons,* utilize a method I discovered in 1916 of drawing cosmic energy into the body and directing it, by conscious will, to recharge the various parts of the body.

physically sick individual. Most mental healers use methods of auto-suggestion and reason to stimulate the imagination and will in their patients. The roused will and imagination in turn awaken the patient's torpid life force, which then cauterizes disease-making bacteria and other such physical causes, and brings about healing.

Most persons have no idea of the tremendous power of the mind; and concomitantly, that nothing can heal one if his life energy fails him. From a microscopic cell this body was made; everything in its physical structure has been created by this energy and mind. Those supreme companionate forces of healing are right within every being, empowered by the soul.

One should never ignore any mode of healing that operates any measure of divine law. But one should remember that the exercise of mental power is more effective than physical methods of healing alone; and it is best by faith and meditation to call into operation the un-failing, unlimited power of God for healing not only the body and mind but for awakening the potential omnipotence of the soul.

We are told that on the occasion at Capernaum cited in the above Bible verses, Jesus exercised that power to heal the many who came to him. This was possible because they came with recipiency and faith.

How a master trans-mits the unlimited healing power of God

The spirit of Jesus had control over cosmic en-ergy. The faith of the sick allowed Jesus to send the all-healing energy out of his body to reinforce their weakened life force. The energy in the body of Jesus and the energy in the bodies of the persons healed both came from the cosmic energy of God. Jesus commanded his will to connect the cosmic energy with the energy in his brain and send it down through his hands in ever-flowing, potent rays to the body of the afflicted person.

Healing by sending energy through the hands, "He laid his hands on every one of them, and healed them," is based on the healer's abil-ity to connect with and consciously direct the cosmic energy of God. The body lives in an omnipresent sea of this vibratory power. This en-ergy sustains life and recharges the vitality of the body as it becomes depleted by physical and mental activity. The life of the body depends primarily upon the cosmic energy that flows in automatically through the mouth of the medulla, or is consciously drawn in by the tuning power of the human will. The energy derived directly from the cosmic ether, and energy derived indirectly from food and oxygen, becomes concentrated in the main cerebral dynamo of power in the head, whence it is poured into the entire body through the six sub-dynamos of the subtle centers in the spine. The supreme center in the brain and the six centers in the cerebrospinal axis send energy through the nerves to all the vital and sensory and motor parts of the body. So, from each body part—as the eyes, hands, feet, heart, navel, nose, mouth, and every projection from the body—there emanates current.

The nerve current radiating from the eyes, hands, and feet is stronger than from other parts. The right side of the body is a positive pole and the left side is a negative pole. The positive right side is stronger than the negative left. Though the power of these poles can sometimes be transposed in the physical sense, as is indicated in cases of left-handed people, the conformation of the "physiology" in the astral body remains the same.

The power of the life force transmitted outwardly for healing others is proportionate to the power of the will of the healer. Masters, such as Jesus, who have infinite control of their will, can radiate the all-creative healing ray of life through any organ, but especially through the hands, feet, or eyes. Simply laying the positive and negative poles of one's hands on another person produces some exchange of magnetism from the energy therein, but does not convey the potency necessary to heal. It is the consciously generated and directed power of the life force flowing through the hands that causes healing by employing the life-force activity, which creates, integrates, disintegrates, crystallizes, metabolizes, and produces and sustains the complex body of differentiated cells. This life force is intelligent but diminished and out of one's control in bodies governed by weak, ego-identified minds. In persons who have identified themselves with their souls, the intelligent creative life force in its full potential is controlled by the wisdom of the soul.

One who knows his soul knows how to work miracles through the life force, the master of life and death, by sending it through the hands in healing rays to burn out disease in any stricken person.

The various means used by Jesus to heal by cosmic energy

The verses cited above, as well as other accounts in the Gospels, relate that Jesus used various outward means of transmitting the cosmic energy: laying on of hands, divinely charged words of healing, transmission of energy by will through the ether, powerful thoughts broadcast to the one in need.

419

Absent healing typically involves the principle of autosuggestion. A powerful thought accompanied by vibratory energy is sent by the healer's will to the person to be healed, whose response to that vibration rouses his own latent imagination and will to release the healing life force within him. Instantaneous mental healings are caused when the healer and the person to be healed are perfectly tuned to each other. If the healer has a strong will and imaging power and the person to be healed has faith in the healer's ability to awaken his will and imagination, then the patient will be quickly healed through his own reanimated life force. The time element in healing arises when either the healer is deficient in his healing power or the person to be healed is not properly receptive to the healer's healing vibrations, because of lack of faith, karmic restrictions, or persistence in bad habits of thought and action whose negative vibrations counteract the positive healing vibrations.

The cosmic energy, and its individualized expression as life force in the body, is finer even than X-rays, and thus has the power to destroy not only physical germs but mental bacteria of evil tendencies and the bacteria of delusion's ignorance that obfuscates the perfection of the soul.

Jesus and great savants healed others in spite of their karma or bad mental habit patterns by sending the cosmic energy into the brain of the diseased patient, where all physical, mental, and spiritual ailments have their roots. The divine energy sent by a master unites with the partially inactive brain energy of the patient, and their combination burns away physical-disease bacteria, or diseased habits, or constraints of ignorance—all of which are lodged in the conscious, subconscious, or superconscious patterns in the brain.*

This divine way of healing was used by Jesus the Christ to heal possessed souls or the lame or the blind. Only masters have sufficient divine will force to use the cosmic energy, if they have God's permis-

---

* A method of healing through a yoga technique that employs the principles of thought and energy transmission through the ether is practiced daily by members of the Self-Realization Fellowship Prayer Council originated by Paramahansa Yogananda. The Council is composed of monks and nuns at SRF ashram centers who pray for all who request help and for world peace. This method, which can be used effectively by any sincere devotee to invoke God's healing help in alleviating the physical, mental, or spiritual afflictions of others, is also regularly practiced by the thousands of members of the Self-Realization Fellowship Worldwide Prayer Circle. A booklet describing the Worldwide Prayer Circle and the healing technique is available from Self-Realization Fellowship. Requests for prayers are always welcome.

sion, to materialize renewed body parts in the affected individual, thereby curing disabled limbs or restoring sight instantaneously. The powerful energy transmitted by a Christlike soul into the brain of a psychologically diseased individual has a similarly direct effect in burning out bad karma and entrenched harmful mental tendencies. God-realized gurus thereby free their receptive disciples from habits of ignorance that have hounded them for many incarnations.

When Jesus healed a person who was possessed, he did it by two ways. First, his consciousness being in tune with the Christ Intelligence in all creation, he used the Christ Will, which governs the astral forces and entities, to compel the unclean spirit to leave the body of the diseased individual. Second, he used his will power to send the cosmic energy into the brain of the possessed individual and destroy there the obsessions caused by the unclean spirit, as well as the karmic and habit patterns that made the person prone to possession.

In the present verses under consideration, it is related that when Jesus exorcised the devils from many, they came out crying, "'Thou art Christ, the Son of God.' And he rebuking them suffered them not to speak." Since all things of the astral world are hidden according to the will of God, concealing the dynamics of the mysterious workings of material creation, Jesus did not want himself to be revealed except in the natural human way by the declaration of his works in fulfillment of the words of the prophets.

In even a cursory review of the science of various forms of healing, it is evident that the basis of every formula is the vibratory power of the life force supported by the receptivity of the person to be healed. Positive-minded confidence in the effectiveness of the remedy stimulates the healing life force. Therefore, methods of mental or physical healing should be administered to people according to their mental inclinations and mental habits. Jesus said, "Render unto Caesar the things which are Caesar's" —that is, in adaptation, those who believe in medical healing, let them go to the medical doctors; those who believe in healing by the methods of osteopaths or homeopaths or other "natural" remedies, let them use such methods; those who believe in mental healers, let them go to the mental healers. But above all, no matter what one's health practices, the most important belief must be in the unlimited healing power of God and the intercession of masters who are one with God.

Choosing the appropriate mode of healing for individual circumstances

Jesus, being in touch with God and His all-healing, all-creative Cosmic Energy, could change the atomic structure of any diseased part of the body into a healthy atomic configuration. Ordinary healers who have no such command over the creative forces would be wise not to take onto themselves the full responsibility of handling cases of severe illness that would prudently benefit from the expertise of the material science of medical doctors. Such medical intervention should not be thought of as a negation, but rather an enhancement, of the effectiveness of continually applied mental and spiritual methods of promoting healing. Those more malleable conditions that have a psychological basis—such as nervous or emotional disorders, mild obsessions, bad habits—as well as common physical ailments that merely require an arousal or reinforcement of weakened life force, most readily respond to the healer's and patient's use of suggestion, divine will force, and invocation of God's power. God created the physical laws of science as well as the underlying subtler divine laws. Belief in and application of one does not necessarily contradict the other so long as one's faith inheres in the Creator Himself.

Only God has unlimited power of healing. Man's power may fail, but God's power can never fail. Yet even though our Father does not want to see us suffer from disease, He cannot heal us until we open the gates of our willingness to be healed: By misusing our God-given free choice, we shut God out of our lives; by using it properly, we allow Him to become manifest within us. To be sure of God's healing power, one must know Him, one must feel Him deeply, in meditation daily. He is not some unfeeling Cosmic Power that one can switch on and off at one's convenience or need—with expectation of instant blessings in times of dark distress, but to which one can remain blithely oblivious in the bright contentment of good fortune. One who does not feel the need for God in the most trifling as well as significant happenings in one's life has yet to realize the indispensable connection between man and his Maker. To misuse free choice in actions that cause forgetfulness of Him is the uttermost woeful affliction of ignorance.

So, if one by deep devotion and meditation constantly tunes himself with God and with unflinching faith goes on asking the Father's help in spite of the invasion of undesirable doubts or contrary evidence, he will certainly find the desired result. But often one who lacks the concentration to tune in with the seeming intangibility of God can find quicker healing by tuning in with those saints and masters who are already united to God. As they give all their devotion to God, so also God gives to them His unlimited power for healing of body, mind, and soul. Devotees who seek to be healed of ignorance, the root cause of all maladies, should adhere steadfastly to faith in their true God-sent guru and his guidance and intercession on their behalf.

Jesus used only the divine power of healing; and he gave to God all the credit for those miraculous cures, for he did not feel within himself the "I" or ego-consciousness born of the identifica-tion of the soul with the physical body. Even when Jesus said, "I say unto you, arise"—become healed —he spoke not of the "I" of the ego, but of the un-limited God-consciousness with which his soul was

Egotism: a pitfall to be avoided in practice of spiritual healing

united. Unless the soul divests itself of the "I am" ego-consciousness, by the divine intuitional consciousness of interiorized meditation, one re-mains ineptly disunited from Spirit. When an ordinary person says, "I will do this," the "I" refers to his body-identified ego-consciousness. He cannot differentiate himself from his physical form, and hardly feels the deeper consciousness of his soul. But when Jesus referred to the "I" within him, he always meant his soul-consciousness united with God-consciousness.

No matter how effective one's powers of healing, they are limited as compared to the infinite healing power of God. Hence, instead of merely commanding one's own healing powers, one should set himself apart from the ego and invoke the unlimited divine power of God to flow through himself as a clear channel. In the practice of healing one-self or others, one should be sure of divine communion, and then com-pletely absorb oneself in God preceding the attempted performance of every healing. A divine healing can take place only when the healer serves as a perfect medium through which God's omnipotence can flow without obstruction. Egotism and loud declaration, and self-laudation, such as, "I healed her," or "God is working through me," should be strictly avoided both in speech and mind. Let the all-knowing God de-clare His power in the self-evident healing.

Even a sincere devotee, if not truly one with God by Self-realization, can have traces of ego hiding in him undetected when he puts himself for-ward as a healing instrument and says to the sick, "Be healed by God's power." But the superman, having transcended all separating egotism in actual God-union, speaks from perfect humility even when he declares,

"I say unto thee, arise and be healed." Here "I" signifies the "God alone" which the realized saint feels within himself.

The words of Isaiah's prophecy about Jesus cite an important expression of grace in divine healing: "Himself took our infirmities, and bare our sicknesses." Powerful healers, such as Jesus, can only wipe away the effects of evil karma in an individual according to the principles involved in the workings of the law of cause and effect. If anyone, through wrong eating, for example, is carrying a load of poison in his body, he can take a counteracting medicine to create a new cause with an effect that can destroy the virulence in the system. So Jesus, with his powerful consciousness, could by various means counteract the adverse effects of past wrongs acquired by and accumulated in erring persons. But no one, not even a Jesus, can break the law of cause and effect created by God. Nature's judgments must be compensated in kind or by a fair exchange. Certain mechanics of the law of karma can be manipulated by the wisdom of a master, and also by corrective or palliative measures taken by the afflicted—such as prayer, intense love for God, faith, yoga meditation, conscious direction of the life force by will power—to minimize or nullify adverse effects of past wrong actions. In extreme cases of deep-seated karma; or in response to the devotional faith and receptivity of a supplicant; or to hasten the spiritual evolution of a disciple, a master can take onto himself a karmic condition of a devotee, or a portion of it, and work out the effects on his own body.

How masters take on the bad karma of suffering individuals

Thus Jesus could stop the impending result of an evil action by astrally taking the consequences of that action upon himself, thereby sparing the person guilty of the transgression. To illustrate the principle in simple terms, suppose a frail man named John angered a more robust acquaintance, who then raised his hand to beat John; but I suddenly came between John and the well-directed blow, sparing John the hurt. I, being stronger, might be affected to a far lesser degree, or not at all, by the fistic display.

So, also, when wrong actions have condemned a person to suffer, according to the law of cause and effect, a powerful soul such as Jesus could deflect the havoc and work it out by spending its force within himself. Some saints have been known to take into their own bodies the actual diseases of afflicted persons, and thus cause the sufferers to be relieved. This does not mean that one has to suffer in order to cure by spiritual law. Only extraordinary Christlike healers and masters know the sacred method by which they can take on the physical, mental, or spiritual sufferings of others and work them out in their own bodies. The purpose of a world savior or guru is to heal humanity of its threefold ills. Their bodily instrument having already fulfilled its purpose of expressing God-realization is then used for the sake of redeeming others by whatever means are most advantageous for the devotee.

This is why it is said of Jesus that he gave himself as a ransom for many. He took upon himself the sins of his disciples, and many other souls, and let his body be crucified. He had the power to save himself by prayer to God: "...and He shall presently give me more than twelve legions of angels. But how then shall the scriptures be fulfilled, that thus it must be?"* Especially by his taking on the consequences of his disciples' karma through his sacrifice, they were highly spiritualized to be able to receive the Holy Ghost that later descended on them, baptizing them with the divine consciousness and attunement to carry on and spread the mission of Jesus. Whether in the body or in omnipresent Spirit, the redeeming grace of a world savior or God-realized guru remains the same, obliging every humble entreaty of a receptive heart.

No matter what one's ailment or blessing of cure, the only way all undesirable karma can be permanently destroyed is by God-contact. The body is impermanent; even though it be granted a pardon from sickness, it must in its full season perish. The mind is pliant and can by a strong will be inured to many of the assaults of its environment; yet it too remains susceptible to the fallibilities of delusion. The ultimate healing that must be sought is freedom from the contagious disease of spiritual ignorance, the enervation of soul-expression, which is at the root of all other ills. If one removes by meditation and God-contact the disease of ignorance constraining the soul, then automatically mental and physical karmic compulsions lose their hold as well. In the kingdom of God-consciousness, the authoritative power of karmic law— which operates only as a corrective guiding force in the presence of delusion—serves no further purpose and is dissolved in Wisdom. Thus did Jesus admonish: "Seek ye first the kingdom of God (destroy delusion) and all else (the consummation of all man's prayers, including for healing of the body, mind, and soul) will be added unto you (as your divine birthright as a child of God)."

---

* Matthew 26:53–54.

∼

*And in the morning, rising up a great while before day, he went out, and departed into a solitary place, and there prayed. And Simon and they that were with him followed after him. And when they had found him, they said unto him, "All men seek for thee" (Mark 1:35–37).**

E ven great masters seek times of solitude to renew themselves in Spirit. Though the omnipotence of the soul cannot be diminished, the bodily instrument of Jesus was heavily taxed by the multitudes— just as an electrical machine shows fatigue if run nonstop though its power from the dynamo is not lessened. The crowds drew from Jesus healing energy and spiritual strength; and as he moved among them he was in a sea of the vibrations of their worries and human emotions. He became one with them in their pains and sorrows as he uplifted them. So we see from the Gospels it was his wont to withdraw periodically into solitude and prayer—to leave behind for the moment the troublesome realm of transgressions and consequences and enter the transcendent inner blissful kingdom of God-communion.

In this present account, Jesus arose before the morning brought upon him the press of his responsibilities, and sought out a solitary place for prayer. This is the way people in general should learn to outwit the demands that would steal all of one's attention from prayer and meditation. There is a time to be given to everything needful. People regularly eat their meals at certain hours each day to nourish the perishable body. They work many hours daily to make money to maintain themselves and others who are dependent upon them. In childhood, the "working" hours are spent in schooling to nourish the mind and prepare it for assuming life's responsibilities. Six to eight hours are passed in the restorative oblivion of sleep. What precious moments of the day survive unclaimed should be wisely apportioned. The right mental education should give each individual at least the common sense to know what methods to adopt in order to perform uniformly all the physical, mental, and spiritual duties calculated to bring real happiness. That mind-set is fruitless which makes an indi-

Making time for God in silence and solitude

---

* Cf. parallel reference in Luke 4:42.

426

vidual one-sided, either materially, intellectually, or spiritually. The performance of one duty should not starve out other important duties. One-sidedness is a sure formula for unhappiness. It will create a painful paucity in other aspects of one's threefold nature.

God is often the last to receive attention on one's daily agenda: "As soon as I get time, I will meditate." Where does that time go? Yet anyone who performs the highest duty of knowing God is automatically guided in accordance with God's will in the performance of the roster of other lesser duties. It is disastrous to seek prosperity at the cost of health or to seek health while entirely neglecting to strive to be successful and prosperous. But since God is the source of all power, it is right to seek Him first, for, with God, health and prosperity are added; but with the acquirement of health and prosperity alone, God is not attained. So the commitment of ardent renunciants to seek God first by forsaking material goals is the consummate life; for God, once attained, enriches one with imperishable life and eternal opulence.

Whatever be one's vocation in life, one needs to feel his connection with God. The cultivation of a spiritual life requires solitary places for divine communion. God can be felt easily in inspiring scenic surroundings free from noise. Man's mind is usually busy with the sensations of sight, sound, touch, smell, and taste. Sound is the most distracting sensation. The sight of material objects or material activities also snares man's attention. But by closing the eyes, one can quickly get rid of the sight sensation, whereas freedom from sound sensations can best be attained by being in a quiet place. The novice devotee who attempts to meditate in noisy surroundings finds his time of "silence" entirely taken up in battling the restless thoughts the noises arouse. In a quiet atmosphere, one can go deep into the silence without any preliminary skirmish with the sensations of sounds. However, if a person makes a super effort of will, he can concentrate in spite of such distraction.

In noisy places there are also people to interrupt one's meditative endeavors. The vibrations of their restless thoughts and activities pass through the body of the meditating individual and keep his energy rushing toward the senses instead of being released to flow toward God. While it is very helpful to the beginner to meditate on quiet occasions and in solitary places, this does not mean that one should not meditate unless one has a chance to travel to a place of solitude. A room in one's home where nobody will disturb the meditation period is all that is really necessary. One should repair to that room and create his own inner quietness by deep meditation on the Infinite. Once God is contacted, no outward disturbance can bother the soul.

There is a proper time and proper place for performing one's different duties. Just as sleep takes place at night in a quiet bedroom, as business is carried on during working hours in an atmosphere of business, and as intellectual studies are carried on in scheduled times in the halls of learning or in a quiet library, so, there should be a proper time and place for meditation, or God-communion. Whatever be one's sanctuary of solitude, he will find it especially beneficial to pray and meditate any time during the following periods: from the earliest hour of dawn, from 5 to 8 a.m.; noontime from 10 a.m. to 1 p.m.; evening from 5 to 8 p.m.; and nighttime from 10 p.m. to 1 a.m. The masters of India have taught that the hours surrounding the transitional times of dawn, noon, sunset, and midnight of each solar day are conducive to the cultivation of spiritual development. The magnetic cosmic laws of attraction and repulsion that affect the body are more harmoniously equilibrated during the above four periods. This helps a meditating individual to interiorize himself in divine communion. To meditate in the quietness of the early mornings and at night is to meditate in a solitary place. During those times, most people are asleep, and the city, or one's surroundings, are quiet. The results of peace realized from meditation are easily obtained due to less noise and wrong vibrations of restless people.

On holidays and in leisure moments, instead of wasting time with senseless diversions and worldly people, the devotee-seeker enjoys time with God—taking a refreshing walk to a quiet lonely place to meditate, for example. Jesus lived in a temperate climate, conducive to his choice of outdoor solitude in nature during the early morning hours.

When the disciples found Jesus in his solitude, they called him forth: "All men seek for thee." Just as the fragrance of flowers draws the bees, so souls such as Jesus who are fragrant with God automatically draw spiritually thirsty souls unto themselves.

~

And he said unto them, "Let us go into the next towns, that I may preach there also: for therefore came I forth."

And he preached in their synagogues throughout all Galilee, and cast out devils (Mark 1:38–39).

Parallel reference:

> *And Jesus went about all Galilee, teaching in their synagogues, and preaching the gospel of the kingdom, and healing all manner of sickness and all manner of disease among the people.*
>
> *And his fame went throughout all Syria: and they brought unto him all sick people that were taken with divers diseases and torments, and those which were possessed with devils, and those which were lunatick, and those that had the palsy; and he healed them.*
>
> *And there followed him great multitudes of people from Galilee, and from Decapolis, and from Jerusalem, and from Judea, and from beyond Jordan (Matthew 4:23–25).* *

Jesus could not confine his preaching to one locale only. In the short span of his mission on earth, he went from place to place within the domain of the Israelites, so designated by God as the birth center of his special dispensation†—to draw true souls from the crowds. His precious time could not be given to the superficial appeasing of the multitudes only. Real souls are rare and hard to find, and it was in them he could plant the seeds of his future continuing harvest. His message was universal; his teachings were destined to spread among all spiritually needy peoples, irrespective of caste, creed, or race. He came from the Spirit to give his message to all children of the Spirit. That is what he meant by: "Therefore came I forth."

---

* Cf. additional parallel reference in Luke 4:43–44.

† See explanation of Matthew 15:21–24 (Mark 7:24–26), Discourse 44.

DISCOURSE 26

The Beatitudes

The Sermon on the Mount, Part I

❖❖❖

The Bliss Known to Those Who Are Free
From Material Attachment

❖

Satisfying One's Inner Hunger for Truth

❖

Jesus the Merciful Expressed the True Nature of God

❖

Yoga: Purifying the Inner Being for God-Perception

❖

The Real "Peacemaker":
One Who Meditates and Follows the Christ-Method of Living

❖

The Kingdom of Joy Earned by Those
Who Live and Die in Right Behavior

❖

Spiritual Persons Are "the Salt of the Earth"
and "Light of the World"

❖❖❖

"Beatitude signifies the blessedness, the bliss, of heaven. Jesus here sets forth with power and simplicity...tenets by which man's life becomes blessed, filled with heavenly bliss."

*A*nd seeing the multitudes, he went up into a mountain: and when he was set, his disciples came unto him: And he opened his mouth, and taught them, saying,

"Blessed are the poor in spirit: for theirs is the kingdom of heaven.

"Blessed are they that mourn: for they shall be comforted.

"Blessed are the meek: for they shall inherit the earth.

"Blessed are they which do hunger and thirst after righteousness: for they shall be filled.

"Blessed are the merciful: for they shall obtain mercy.

"Blessed are the pure in heart: for they shall see God.

"Blessed are the peacemakers: for they shall be called the children of God.

"Blessed are they which are persecuted for righteousness' sake: for theirs is the kingdom of heaven.

"Blessed are ye, when men shall revile you, and persecute you, and shall say all manner of evil against you falsely, for my sake.

"Rejoice, and be exceeding glad: for great is your reward in heaven: for so persecuted they the prophets which were before you.

"Ye are the salt of the earth: but if the salt have lost his savour, wherewith shall it be salted? It is thenceforth good for nothing, but to be cast out, and to be trodden under foot of men.

"Ye are the light of the world. A city that is set on an hill cannot be hid.

"Neither do men light a candle, and put it under a bushel, but on a candlestick; and it giveth light unto all that are in the house.

"Let your light so shine before men, that they may see your good works, and glorify your Father which is in heaven."

—Matthew 5:1–16

The Beatitudes

The Sermon on the Mount, Part I
(With References From the Sermon on the Plain)*

꙳

And seeing the multitudes, he went up into a mountain: and when he was set, his disciples came unto him (Matthew 5:1).

In a vast unmanageable throng, there is very little opportunity for a personal exchange of spiritual magnetism between a master and his disciples. Therefore, on many occasions Jesus avoided the multitudes to give his full attention to receptive disciples to whom he could impart his spirituality. He preferred the company of even one sincerely seeking soul to soul-indifferent crowds of the merely curious.

∼

And he opened his mouth, and taught them, saying, "Blessed are the poor in spirit: for theirs is the kingdom of heaven" (Matthew 5:2–3).

---

* Discourses 26–30 cover the teachings Jesus gave to his disciples in the "Sermon on the Mount" recorded in the Gospel According to St. Matthew, chapters 5–7. Much of this counsel is also presented in the Gospel of St. Luke—either in the "Sermon on the Plain" (Luke 6:17–49, which contains about a quarter of the material cited by Matthew in the Sermon on the Mount), or in other contexts. Because Matthew and Luke record these teachings in identical or nearly identical words, the Sermon on the Mount and parallel passages from the Sermon on the Plain are treated together in the commentary in this series of Discourses. (*Publisher's Note*)

Parallel reference:

> *And he lifted up his eyes on his disciples, and said, "Blessed be ye poor: for yours is the kingdom of God" (Luke 6:20, Sermon on the Plain).*

During his teaching, Jesus let loose, through his voice as well as through his eyes, his divine life force and godly vibration to spread over the disciples, making them calmly attuned and magnetized, able to receive through their intuitional understanding of the full measure of his wisdom.

The lyric verses of Jesus that begin "Blessed are..." have become known as The Beatitudes. To beatify is to make supremely happy; beatitude signifies the blessedness, the bliss, of heaven.* Jesus here sets forth with power and simplicity a doctrine of moral and spiritual principles that has echoed undiminished down the ages—tenets by which man's life becomes blessed, filled with heavenly bliss.

The word "poor" as used in the first Beatitude signifies wanting in any outer superficial elegance of spiritual wealth. Those who possess true spirituality never make an ostentatious display of it; they rather express quite naturally a humble paucity of ego and its vainglorious trappings. To be "poor in spirit" is to have divested one's inner being, his spirit, of desire for and attachment to material objects, earthly possessions, materially minded friends, selfish human love. Through this purification of inward renunciation, the soul finds that it has ever possessed all riches of the Eternal Kingdom of Wisdom and Bliss, and thenceforth dwells therein in constant communion with God and His saints.

The bliss known to those who are free from material attachment

Poverty "in spirit" does not imply that one should necessarily be a pauper, lest deprivation of basic bodily necessities distract one's mind from God. But it certainly means that one should not settle for material acquisitions instead of spiritual opulence. Persons who are materially rich may be poor in inner spiritual development if wealth gorges their senses; while those who are materially "poor" by choice—who

---

* "Beatify" is derived from Latin *beatus*, happy + *facere*, to make. The word used for "blessed are..." in the original Greek of the Gospels is *makarios*, which in Latin is *beati*, from which comes the English *beatitude*, state of blessedness or utmost bliss.

have simplified the outer conditions of their life to make time for God —will garner spiritual riches and fulfillment that no treasury of gold could ever buy.

Thus Jesus commended those souls who are poor in spirit, wholly nonattached to personal worldly goals and fortune in deference to seeking God and serving others: "Ye are blessed for your poverty. It will open the gates to the kingdom of all-sufficient God, who will relieve you from material as well as spiritual want throughout eternity. Blessed are you who are in want and seek Him who alone can relieve your deficiencies forever!"

When the spirit of man mentally renounces desire for objects of this world, knowing them to be illusory, perishable, misleading, and unbecoming to the soul, he begins to find true joy in acquiring permanently satisfying soul qualities. In humbly leading a life of outer simplicity and inner renunciation, steeped in the soul's heavenly bliss and wisdom, the devotee ultimately inherits the lost kingdom of immortal blessedness.

~

"Blessed are they that mourn: for they shall be comforted" *(Matthew 5:4).*

Parallel reference:

"Blessed are ye that weep now: for ye shall laugh" (Luke 6:21, Sermon on the Plain).

The pangs of sorrow suffered by the ordinary person arise from mourning the loss of human love or material possessions, or the nonfulfillment of earthly hopes. Jesus was not extolling this negative state of mind, which eclipses *The blessing brought* psychological happiness and is utterly detrimental *by insatiable yearning* to the retention of spiritual bliss obtained by arduous efforts in meditation. He was speaking of that *for the Divine* divine melancholy resulting from the awakening consciousness of separation from God, which creates in the soul an insatiable yearning to be reunited with the Eternal Beloved. Those who really mourn for God, who wail incessantly for Him with ever-increasing zeal in medi-

435

tation, shall find comfort in the revelation of Wisdom-Bliss sent to them by God.*

The spiritually negligent children of God endure life's painful traumas with resentful, defeatist resignation instead of effectively soliciting Divine Aid. It is the adorably naughty baby, crying continuously for spiritual knowledge, who at last attracts the response of the Divine Mother. To Her persistent child, the Merciful Mother comes with Her solace of wisdom and love, revealed through intuition or by a glimpse of Her own Presence. No surrogate consolation can assuage instantaneously the bereavement of unnumbered incarnations.

Those whose spiritual mourning is appeased by material fulfillments will find themselves grieving again when those fragile securities are snatched away by the exigencies of life or by death. But those who weep for Truth and God, refusing to be quieted by any lesser offering, will be forever comforted in the arms of Blissful Divinity.

"Blessed are you who cry for God-realization now, for by that single-minded yearning you shall attain. With the entertainment of ever new joy found in divine communion, you shall laugh and rejoice throughout eternity!"

~

"Blessed are the meek: for they shall inherit the earth" (Matthew 5:5).

Humbleness and meekness create in man a bottomless receptacle of recipiency to hold Truth. A proud irascible individual, like the proverbial rolling stone, rolls down the hill of ignorance and gathers no moss of wisdom, while meek souls at peace in the valley of eager mental readiness gather waters of wisdom, flowing from sources human and divine, to nourish their flowering vale of soul qualities.

The imperious egotist is easily riled, defensive, and resentfully offensive, repelling emissaries of wisdom who seek entry into the castle of his life; but the meek and humbly receptive attract the unseen assistance of beneficent angels of cosmic forces proffering material, mental,

---

* "But the Comforter, which is the Holy Ghost, whom the Father will send in my name, he shall teach you all things, and bring all things to your remembrance..." (John 14:26; see Discourse 70).

and spiritual well-being. Thus do the meek of spirit inherit not only all wisdom, but the earth, that is, earthly happiness, along with it.*

~

"Blessed are they which do hunger and thirst after righteousness: for they shall be filled" (Matthew 5:6).

Parallel reference:

"Blessed are ye that hunger now: for ye shall be filled" (Luke 6:21, Sermon on the Plain).

The words "thirst" and "hunger" provide an apt metaphor for man's spiritual quest. One must first have thirst for the theoretical knowledge of how to attain salvation. After he quenches this thirst by learning the practical technique of actually contacting God, he can then satisfy his inner hunger for   *Satisfying one's inner*
Truth by feasting daily on the divine manna of spir-   *hunger for Truth*
itual perception resulting from meditation.

Those who seek appeasement in material things find that their thirst of desires is never slaked, nor is their hunger ever satisfied in the acquirement of possessions. The urge in every man to fill an inner emptiness is the soul's desire for God. It can only be alleviated by realizing one's immortality and imperishable state of divinity in God-union. When man foolishly tries to quench his soul thirst with the substitutes of sense happiness, he gropes from one evanescent pleasure to another, ultimately rejecting them all as inadequate.

Sense pleasures are of the body and lower mind; they bring no nourishment to man's inmost being. Spiritual starvation, suffered by all who would subsist on sense offerings, is allayed only by righteousness—the actions, attitudes, and attributes that are right for the soul: virtue, spiritual behavior, bliss, immortality.

Righteousness means acting rightly in the physical, mental, and spiritual departments of life. Persons who feel a great thirst and hunger for fulfilling the supreme duties of life receive the ever new

---

* "But the meek shall inherit the earth; and shall delight themselves in the abundance of peace" (Psalms 37:11).

bliss of God: "Blessed are you who thirst for wisdom and who esteem virtue and righteousness as the real food to appease your inner hunger, for you shall have that lasting happiness brought only by adhering to divine ideals—unparalleled satisfaction of heart and soul."

~

"Blessed are the merciful: for they shall obtain mercy" (Matthew 5:7).

Mercy is a sort of fatherly heartache for the deficiency in an erring child. It is an intrinsic quality of the Divine Nature. The life story of Jesus is replete with accounts of mercy sublimely manifest in his actions and personality. In perfected divine sons of God, we see revealed the hidden transcendent Father as He is. The God of Moses is depicted as a God of wrath (though I do not believe Moses, who spoke to God "face to face, as a man speaketh unto his friend,"* ever thought of God as the vengeful tyrant portrayed in the Old Testament). But the God of Jesus was so gentle. It was that gentleness and mercy of the Father that Jesus expressed when, instead of judging and destroying the enemies who would crucify him, he asked of the Father to forgive them, "for they know not what they do." With the patient heart of God, Jesus looked upon humanity as little children who did not understand. If a wee child picks up a knife and strikes you, you do not want to kill that child in retaliation. It does not realize what it has done. When one looks upon humanity as a loving father looks after his children, and is ready to suffer for them that they might receive a little of the sunshine and power of his spirit, then one becomes Christlike: God in action.

Jesus the merciful expressed the true nature of God

The wise alone can be really merciful, for with divine insight they perceive even wrongdoers as souls—God's children who deserve sympathy, forgiveness, help, and guidance when they go astray. Mercy implies the capacity for being helpful; only developed or qualified souls are capable of being practically and mercifully useful. Mercy expresses itself in usefulness when the fatherly heartache tempers the rigidity of exacting judgment and offers not only forgiveness but actual spiritual help in eliminating the error in an individual.

* Exodus 33:11.

The morally weak but willing-to-be-good, the sinner (he who transgresses against his own happiness by flouting divine laws), the physically decrepit, the mentally impaired, the spiritually ignorant—all need merciful help from souls whose inner development qualifies them to render understanding aid. Jesus' words exhort the devotee: "To receive divine mercy, be merciful to yourself by making yourself spiritually qualified, and be merciful also to other deluded children of God. Persons who continuously develop themselves in every way, and who mercifully feel and alleviate the lack of all-round development in others, surely will melt the heart of God and obtain for themselves His unending and matchlessly helpful mercy."

~

"Blessed are the pure in heart: for they shall see God" (Matthew 5:8).

The consummate religious experience is direct perception of God, for which the purification of the heart is requisite. On this, all scriptures agree. The Bhagavad Gita, India's immortal scripture of yoga, the science of religion and God-union, speaks of the blessedness and divine perception of one who has attained this inner purification:

> The yogi who has completely calmed the mind and controlled the passions and freed them from all impurities, and who is one with Spirit—verily, he has attained supreme blessedness.
>
> With the soul united to Spirit by yoga, with a vision of equality for all things, the yogi beholds his Self (Spirit-united) in all creatures and all creatures in the Spirit.
>
> He who perceives Me everywhere and beholds everything in Me never loses sight of Me, nor do I ever lose sight of him.*

Since ancient times, the *rishis* of India have scrutinized the very core of truth and detailed its practical relevance to man. Patanjali, the renowned sage of the yoga science, begins his *Yoga Sutras* by declaring: *Yoga chitta vritti nirodha*—"*Yoga* (scientific union with God) is the neutralization of the modifications of *chitta* (the inner 'heart' or power of feeling; a comprehensive term for the aggregate of

Yoga: purifying the inner being for God-perception

---

* *God Talks With Arjuna: The Bhagavad Gita* VI:27, 29–30.

439

mind-stuff that produces intelligent consciousness)." Both reason and feeling are derived from this inner faculty of intelligent consciousness.

My revered guru, Swami Sri Yukteswar, one of the first in modern times to reveal the unity of Christ's teachings with India's *Sanatana Dharma,* wrote profoundly about how man's spiritual evolution consists of the purification of the heart. From the state in which consciousness is completely deluded by *maya* ("the dark heart"), man progresses through the successive states of the propelled heart, the steady heart, the devoted heart, and ultimately attains the clean heart, in which, Sri Yukteswarji writes, he "becomes able to comprehend the Spiritual Light, Brahma [Spirit], the Real Substance in the universe."*

God is perceived with the sight of the soul. Every soul in its native state is omniscient, beholding God or Truth directly through intuition. Pure reason and pure feeling are both intuitive; but when reason is circumscribed by the intellectuality of the sense-bound mind, and feeling devolves into egoistic emotion, these instrumentalities of the soul produce distorted perceptions.

Restoration of the lost clarity of divine sight is the purport of this Beatitude. The blessedness known to the perfectly pure of heart is none other than that referred to in St. John's Gospel: "But as many as received him, to them gave he power to become the sons of God." To every devotee who receives and reflects the omnipresent Light Divine, or Christ Consciousness, through a purified transparency of heart and mind, God gives power to reclaim the bliss of divine sonhood, even as did Jesus.

Transparency to Truth is cultivated by freeing the consciousness, the heart's feeling and the mind's reason, from the dualistic influences of attraction and aversion. Reality cannot be accurately reflected in a consciousness ruffled by likes and dislikes, with their restless passions and desires, and the roiling emotions they engender—anger, jealousy, greed, moody sensitivity. But when *chitta*—human knowing and feeling—is calmed by meditation, the ordinarily agitated ego gives way to the blessed calmness of soul perception.†

---

* See Chapter 3, Sutras 23–32 in *The Holy Science* by Swami Sri Yukteswar (published by Self-Realization Fellowship).

† "The man of self-control, roaming among material objects with subjugated senses, and devoid of attraction and repulsion, attains an unshakable inner calmness" (*God Talks With Arjuna: The Bhagavad Gita* II:64).

Purity of the intellect gives one the power of correct reasoning, but purity of the heart gives one the contact of God. Intellectuality is a quality of the power of reason, and wisdom is the liberating quality of the soul. When reason is purified by calm discrimination it metamorphoses into wisdom. Pure wisdom and the divine understanding of a pure heart are the two sides of the same faculty. Indeed, the purity of heart, or feeling, referred to by Jesus depends on the guidance of all action by discriminative wisdom—the adjusting of human attitudes and behavior by the sacred soul qualities of love, mercy, service, self-control, self-discipline, conscience, and intuition. The pure-eyed vision of wisdom must be combined with the untainted feeling of the heart. Wisdom reveals the righteous path, and the cleansed heart desires and loves to follow that path. All wisdom-revealed soul qualities must be followed wholeheartedly (not merely intellectually or theoretically).

Ordinary man's occluded vision cognizes the gross shells of matter but is blind to the all-pervading Spirit. By the perfect blending of pure discrimination and pure feeling, the penetrating eye of all-revealing intuition is opened, and the devotee gains the true perception of God as present in one's soul and omnipresent in all beings—the Divine Indweller whose nature is a harmonic blend of infinite wisdom and infinite love.

"Blessed are the peacemakers: for they shall be called the children of God" (Matthew 5:9).

They are the real peacemakers who generate peace from their devotional practice of daily meditation. Peace is the first manifestation of God's response in meditation. Those who know God as Peace in the inner temple of silence, and who worship that Peace-God therein, are by this relationship of divine communion His true children.

The real "peacemaker": one who meditates and follows the Christ-method of living

Having felt the nature of God as inner peace, devotees want the Peace-God to be always manifest in their home, in the neighborhood, in the nation, among all nationalities and races. Anyone who brings peace to an inharmonious family has established God there. Anyone who removes the misunderstanding between souls has united them in God's peace. Anyone who,

441

forsaking national greed and selfishness, works to create peace amidst warring nations, is establishing God in the heart of those nations. The initiators and facilitators of peace manifest the unifying Christ-love that identifies a soul as a child of God.

"Son of God" consciousness makes one feel love for all beings. Those who are God's true children cannot feel any difference between an Indian, American, or any other nationality or race. For a little while immortal souls are garbed in white, black, brown, red, or olive-colored bodies. Are people looked upon as variously foreign when they wear different colored clothes? No matter what one's nationality or the color of his body, all of God's children are souls. The Father recognizes no man-made designations; He loves all, and His children must learn to live in that same consciousness. When man confines his identity to his clannish human nature, it gives rise to unending evils and the specter of war.

Human beings have been given potentially limitless power, to prove that they are indeed the children of God. In such technologies as the atomic bomb we see that unless man uses his powers rightly, he will destroy himself. The Lord could incinerate this earth in a second if He lost patience with His erring children, but He doesn't. And as He would never misuse His omnipotence, so we, being made in His image, must also behave like gods and conquer hearts with the power of love, or humanity as we know it will surely perish. Man's power to make war is increasing; so must his ability to make peace. The best deterrent against the threat of war is brotherhood, the realization that as God's children we are one family.

Anyone who stirs up strife among brother nations under the guise of patriotism is a traitor to his divine family—a faithless child of God. Anyone who keeps family members, neighbors, or friends fighting through fostering falsehoods and gossip, or who is in any way a maker of disturbance, is a desecrator of God's temple of harmony.

Christ and the great ones have given the recipe for peace within and among individuals and nations. How long man has lived in the darkness of misunderstanding and ignorance of those ideals. The true Christ-method of living can banish human conflicts and the horror of war and bring about peace and understanding on earth; all prejudices and enmities must fall away. That is the challenge placed before those who would be the peacemakers of God.

～

*"Blessed are they which are persecuted for righteousness' sake:
for theirs is the kingdom of heaven" (Matthew 5:10).*

The bliss of God will visit those souls who endure with equanimity the torture of the unjust criticism of so-called friends, as well as enemies, for doing what is right, and who remain uninfluenced by wrong customs or society's harmful habits. A devotee of righteousness will not bend to social pressure to drink just because he happens to be at a gathering where cocktails are served, even when others mock him for nonparticipation in their *The kingdom of joy earned by those who live and die in right behavior* pleasure. Moral rectitude brings short-term ridicule but long-term rejoicing, for persistence in self-control yields bliss and perfection. An eternal kingdom of heavenly joy, to enjoy in this life and the beyond, is earned by those who live and die in right behavior.

Worldly people who prefer sensory indulgences to God-contact are truly the foolish ones, because by ignoring what is right, and therefore good for them, they will have to reap the consequences. The righteous devotee pursues that which is beneficial for him in the highest sense. One who relinquishes the desultory ways of the world and cheerfully stands the scorn of shortsighted friends for his idealism demonstrates that he is fit for the unending bliss of God.

The above verse also offers encouragement to those who are persecuted and tortured by sensory temptations and bad habits when they have resolved to cling to moral ideals and spiritual practices. They are righteous indeed, following the right way of self-control and meditation, which will in time defeat temptations and win the kingdom of eternal joy for the victorious.

No matter how powerful temptations are, or how strong bad habits, they can be resisted with the wisdom-guided power of self-control and by holding to the conviction that no matter what pleasure is promised by temptation, it will always give sorrow in the end. The irresolute inevitably become hypocrites, justifying wrong behavior while succumbing to the wiles of temptation. The honey of God, though sealed in mystery, is what the soul truly craves. Those who meditate with undaunted patience and persistence break the mystery seal, and uninhibitedly imbibe the heavenly nectar of immortality.

Heaven is that state of transcendental, omnipresent joy where no sorrows ever dare to tread. By steadfast righteousness, the devotee will ultimately reach that beatific bliss from which there is no fall. Vacillating devotees, not fixed in meditation, can slip from this supernal happiness; but those who are resolute gain that blessedness permanently. The kingdom of Cosmic Consciousness is owned by the King of Heavenly Bliss, and by the elevated souls who are merged in Him. Hence it is said of devotees who unite their ego with God, becoming one with the King of the Universe: "Theirs is the kingdom of heaven."

~

> "Blessed are ye, when men shall revile you, and persecute you, and shall say all manner of evil against you falsely, for my sake.
>
> "Rejoice, and be exceeding glad: for great is your reward in heaven: for so persecuted they the prophets which were before you" (Matthew 5:11–12).

Parallel reference:

> "Blessed are ye, when men shall hate you, and when they shall separate you from their company, and shall reproach you, and cast out your name as evil, for the Son of man's sake.
>
> "Rejoice ye in that day, and leap for joy: for, behold, your reward is great in heaven: for in the like manner did their fathers unto the prophets" (Luke 6:22–23, Sermon on the Plain).

The foregoing verses do not require one to conscript a band of revilers to make one fit for the kingdom of heaven. In spite of one's best efforts for good in the world and in oneself, the barbs of persecutors will never be absent, as Jesus well knew. The ornery nature of the ego makes the undisciplined man uncomfortable and mean-spirited toward those who are morally or spiritually different from himself. The goadings of satanic divisive delusion keep the self-appointed critic ever scanning for reasons to malign others. Jesus encouraged his followers not to be dismayed or intimidated if in trying to live spiritually they find that materially minded persons do not understand. Those who can pass through the test of scorn cheerfully, and without yielding to wrong ways in order to "fit in," will gain the happiness that results from clinging to virtuous bliss-yielding habits.

Be steadfast and even-minded in the face of worldly misunderstanding

It should be considered no great loss when the reproachers and haters and defamers "shall separate you from their company." Actually, persons who are thus shunned are blessed that by such ostracism their souls are kept away from the bad influence of the company of nonunderstanding, misbehaving persons.

The spiritually dedicated should never become despondent, no matter how people speak evil against them or vilify their good name in declarations of wrongdoing. Blessed are those whose name is denigrated for not cooperating with worldly or evil ways, for their names shall be engraved in the silently admiring heart of God.

The Bhagavad Gita similarly expresses the Lord's regard for such devotees: "He who is tranquil before friend and foe alike, and in encountering adoration and insult, and during the experiences of warmth and chill and of pleasure and suffering; who has relinquished attachment, regarding blame and praise in the same light; who is quiet and easily contented, not attached to domesticity, and of calm disposition and devotional—that person is dear to Me."*

One must follow what one knows to be right, in spite of criticism. Everyone should honestly, without egotistical bias, analyze himself; and if he is right, he should hold to his joy-producing righteous actions uninfluenced by either praise or blame. But if one is wrong, he should be glad of the opportunity to correct himself and thus remove one more obstacle to lasting happiness. Even unjust criticism will make the disciple purer than ever and enthuse him all the more to follow the ways of inner peace instead of yielding to temptations urged by bad company.

It is in the company of God that one remains blessed. One has to find time for Him in the peace of meditation. Why waste all of one's leisure hours in frequenting the movies or watching television, or in other idle pastimes? In cultivating and adhering to divine habits, the devotee finds true impetus to rejoice in his inner contentment and in knowing he will ultimately inherit the kingdom of eternal fulfillment.

The devotee who is denounced for holding to spiritual ways should not flatter himself that being persecuted for God's sake means he is doing the Lord some great favor. "To be persecuted for my sake" or "for the Son of man's sake," signifies being chastised for holding to those practices the devotee has undertaken at the behest of his Christlike guru for the sake of acquiring attunement with God.

---

* *God Talks With Arjuna: The Bhagavad Gita* XII:18–19.

445

Jesus spoke to his disciples and followers as their God-sent guru or savior: "Blessed are you when for following the Son of man (the Christlike guru-preceptor, the representative of God) you are criticized and belittled for preferring to walk in the light of his God-tuned wisdom instead of stumbling with the masses along worldly paths of darkness and ignorance."

To be hated, ostracized, reproached, or cast out is in itself no cause for blessing if one is morally or spiritually degenerate; but when despite persecution the devotee clings to truth as manifested in the life and teachings of a Christlike guru, then he will be free in everlasting blessedness. "Rejoice ye in that day, and feel the uplifting holy vibration of ever new joy; for behold, those who will toil and labor and accept pain to follow the divine way will be rewarded in heaven with eternal bliss.

"Those who persecute you are a continuity of the successive generations of those who persecuted the prophets. Think to what great evil those forefathers came, and consider what reward in heaven the prophets received from God for bearing the persecution from ignorant persons for His name's sake. Holding on to spiritual principles, even if one has to lose his body as did the martyrs of yore, brings the reward of divine inheritance of God's kingdom of Everlasting Exultation."

"Great is your reward in heaven" signifies the state of eternal bliss felt in stabilizing the divine contact of God experienced in meditation:

Finding the "reward" of heaven even while on earth
One who performs elevating good actions on earth will, according to the law of karma, reap the fruits of those deeds either in the inner heaven on earth while living, or in the supernal heavenly realms after death.

One's store of good karma and spiritual tenacity determines one's heavenly reward in life or in the afterlife. Advanced souls, those who by meditation are able to experience the ever-newly joyous state of Self-realization, and who can remain constantly in that inner heavenly bliss where God dwells, carry with them a portable heaven wherever they go. The astral sun of the spiritual eye begins to reveal to their consciousness the astral heaven wherein reside, in graduated spheres, virtuous souls and saints, liberated beings and angels. Gradually, the light of the spiritual eye opens its portals, drawing the consciousness into progressively higher spheres of heaven: the omnipresent golden aura of the Holy Ghost Cosmic Vibration in which are enfolded the mysteries of the finer forces that inform all regions of vibratory exis-

The Sermon on the Mount

And seeing the multitudes, he went up into a mountain: and when he was set, his disciples came unto him: And he opened his mouth, and taught them....

"After this manner therefore pray ye: Our Father which art in heaven, hallowed be Thy name...."

—Matthew 5:1—2; 6:9

Jesus came on earth to remind man that the Lord is the Heavenly Father of all, and to show His children the way back to Him. The way of effective prayer, he taught, is to banish diffidence and speak to God with joyous expectancy as to a devoted father or mother. For every human being, the Lord feels a love unconditional and eternal, surpassing even the sweetest human parental solicitude. This is implicit in Jesus' instruction to pray to "Our Father"— a Father who cares personally for each of His children.

—Paramahansa Yogananda

Painting by Carl Bloch

tence (wherein is found the "pearly gate" or entryway into the astral heaven through its pearl-like rainbow-hued firmament, or boundary wall*); the Christ Heaven of God's reflected Consciousness shining His intelligence on the vibratory realm of creation; and the ultimate heaven of Cosmic Consciousness, the everlasting, immutably blissful transcendental Kingdom of God.

Only those souls who can keep their consciousness fixed in the spiritual eye during earthly existence, even during trials and persecutions, will in this life or the afterlife enter the blissful states of the higher regions of heaven where the most extraordinary advanced souls dwell in the delightful proximity of God's all-freeing presence.

Though Jesus cites especially the great reward accruing to advanced souls, even a lesser measure of blissful God-communion will bring a commensurate heavenly reward. Those who make some progress and then compromise their spiritual ideals or give up meditating, because they feel inwardly persecuted by the effort required or are outwardly discouraged by worldly influences or by the criticism of relatives, neighbors, or so-called friends, lose the contact of heavenly bliss. But those who are divinely stalwart not only retain the bliss they acquire by meditation but are doubly rewarded, finding their stability giving rise to ever greater fulfillment. This is the psychological heavenly reward resulting from applying the law of habit: Anyone who becomes fixed in inner bliss by meditation will be rewarded with ever-increasing joy that will remain with him even when he leaves this earthly plane.

The heavenly state of meditative bliss felt in this life is a foretaste of the ever new joy felt in the immortalized soul in the after-death state. The soul carries that joy into the sublime astral regions of celestial beauty, where lifetronic *Celestial bliss and* blossoms unfold their rainbow petals in the garden *beauty of the astral* of ether, and where the climate, atmosphere, food, *realm* and inhabitants are made of different vibrations of multihued light—a kingdom of refined manifestations more in harmony with the essence of the soul than are the crudities of the earth.

Righteous people who resist temptation on earth, but who do not totally free themselves from delusion, are rewarded after death with a rejuvenating rest in this astral heaven among the many half-angels and half-redeemed souls who carry on a life that is exceedingly superior to

---

* See Discourse 10.

that on earth. There they enjoy the results of their good astral karma for a karmically predetermined span; after which time, their remaining earthly karma pulls them back into reincarnation in a physical body. Their "great reward" in the astral heaven enables them to manifest desired conditions at will, dealing entirely with vibrations and energy, not with the fixed properties of solids, liquids, and gaseous substances encountered during the earthly sojourn. In the astral heaven, all furnishings, properties, climatic conditions, and transportation are subject to the astral beings' will power, which can materialize, manipulate, and dematerialize the lifetronic substance of that finer world according to preference.

Completely redeemed souls harbor no mortal desires in their hearts when they leave the shores of the earth. These souls become permanently fixed as pillars in the mansion of Cosmic Consciousness, and never again reincarnate on the earth plane,* unless they do so willingly in order to bring earthbound souls back to God.

Such are God's prophets: souls who are anchored in Truth and return to earth at the command of God to lead others to spiritual ways

The godly traits extolled by Jesus as the way to beatitude

by their exemplary conduct and message of salvation. The spiritual state of a prophet or savior is one of complete union with God, which qualifies him to declare God in the mysterious spiritual way. They are usually extraordinary reformers who show to mankind extraordinary spiritual examples. They demonstrate the power and superior influence of love over hate, wisdom over ignorance, even if it means martyrdom. They refuse to give up their truths no matter the degree of physical or mental persecution, dishonor, or false accusations; and just as steadfastly, they refuse to hate their persecutors or to use the expediency of revenge to quell their enemies. They demonstrate and retain the restraint and forbearance of God's all-forgiving love, being themselves sheltered in that Infinite Grace.

In all the great ones—those who come on earth to show to humanity the way to everlasting blessedness or bliss consciousness—are found the godly traits extolled by Jesus as the way to beatitude. In the Bhagavad Gita, Sri Krishna enumerates comprehensively these requisite soul qualities that distinguish the divine man:

---

* "Him that overcometh will I make a pillar in the temple of my God, and he shall go no more out" (Revelation 3:12).

448

(The sage is marked by) humility, lack of hypocrisy, harmlessness, forgivingness, uprightness, service to the guru, purity of mind and body, steadfastness, self-control;

Indifference to sense objects, absence of egotism, understanding of the pain and evils (inherent in mortal life): birth, illness, old age, and death;

Nonattachment, nonidentification of the Self with such as one's children, wife, and home; constant equal-mindedness in desirable and undesirable circumstances;

Unswerving devotion to Me by the yoga of nonseparativeness, resort to solitary places, avoidance of the company of worldly men;

Perseverance in Self-knowledge; and meditative perception of the object of all learning—the true essence or meaning therein. All these qualities constitute wisdom; qualities opposed to them constitute ignorance.*

By cultivation of the above virtues, then even in this material world man can live in the beatific consciousness of the soul, a true child of God. He makes his own life, and many of those he contacts, radiant with the infinite light, joy, and love of the Eternal Father.

≈

"Ye are the salt of the earth: but if the salt have lost his savour, wherewith shall it be salted? It is thenceforth good for nothing, but to be cast out, and to be trodden under foot of men.

"Ye are the light of the world" (Matthew 5:13–14).

Jesus' metaphorical comparison of his disciples to the salt of the earth was particularly appropriate in his time when salt was considered a valuable item. Oriental people who had to travel in the extreme heat of the desert used to carry large pieces of rock salt, which they licked in order to lessen their thirst due to dehydration. If anyone shared that life-giving salt with another, it was said that the latter had "eaten his salt," or shared his highest confidence. It was to acquire this all-important commodity that the first trading routes were established in ancient civilizations. In

Spiritual persons are "the salt of the earth" and "light of the world"

---

* Bhagavad Gita XIII:7–11. See *God Talks With Arjuna* for extensive commentary.

some areas a measure of salt was valued as fair trade for an equal weight of gold. Roman legionnaires were allotted a *salarium,* or disbursement of salt—from which comes the modern term "salary."

In addition to its life-saving qualities, salt gives pleasurable flavor to food; without it, meals would be tasteless to most human beings. So, just as salt is an important commodity worldwide, similarly, man himself is the "salt of the earth," for among all creatures the human being has the highest capacity for doing good to others.

Jesus says that if salt loses its savor, it is useless for seasoning, nor can its quality be revived; it must therefore be thrown away. Similarly, if human beings, who are made in the image of God, desecrate that image through ignorant living, they lose the essential soul qualities and thus cease to be the most serviceable beings on earth. Persons who live unspiritual lives allow themselves to be trodden under foot by uselessness and death.

"Ye are the light of the world" signifies that human beings make this earth luminously meaningful by their presence. If the stars and the moon shone on this earth and the bleak mountains kept themselves decorated with silver peaks, they would nevertheless be in perpetual oblivion if no man lived to appreciate them. If blossoms with their alluring fragrance tarried and then faded without the gaze of souls ever entering their petal-doors, who would know the mystic beauty of flowers? Not the hard-hearted mountains nor the brainless skies nor burgeoning flora, but only souls, by the light of their consciousness, reveal the wondrous presence of Nature and God. Without the light of human consciousness, the star- and moon-decked night, and the ocean, the scenery, and the sun-decked day, would live in the womb of dark aeons.

Hence, man is the light of the world. No other living creature, only human consciousness, is endowed with the all-revealing lamp of a potentially limitless intelligence.

~

"A city that is set on an hill cannot be hid. Neither do men light a candle, and put it under a bushel, but on a candlestick; and it giveth light unto all that are in the house. *

---

* Cf. parallel reference in Luke 11:33 (Discourse 28).

"Let your light so shine before men, that they may see your good works, and glorify your Father which is in heaven" (Matthew 5:14–16).

Just as lighted candles are not meant to be covered by bushel baskets but put on candlesticks to shed their light, so also, souls are lighted with the inherent presence of God, not to be enshrouded by ignorance, uselessness, materiality, and death, but that they may, with the illumination of wisdom and goodness, enlighten spiritually darkened lives. Evil eclipses the light of the soul. As the flame of a candle is extinguished by lack of oxygen, so a soul loses its outer radiance without the vitality of goodness. Good persons should not hide their enlivened soul qualities, as expressed in Gray's "Elegy": "Full many a flower is born to blush unseen, and waste its sweetness on the desert air." They ought to engage in good actions among men, so that human darkness may be illumined.

No saint likes to perform miracles or display his divine powers to prove himself to disbelievers; no true devotee likes flattery or acclaim for his goodness. But when the candle of wisdom has been lighted within the devotee, he doesn't secret it in the back of his mind nor hide it under the bushel of indifference. He sets it on the candlestick of open and sincere living, that truth-seekers may see and profit by that light.

Awakened souls shine with the light of God; they make the invisible light of His goodness visible in their hearts and actions. Their enlightenment declares the presence of God and serves as a spiritual beacon to guide others out of the paths of darkness.

The transcendent Father, hidden behind the etheric walls of heaven, cloistered in Cosmic Consciousness, comes out of His secret place only to grace the altars of devotion templed in illumined souls. In their words, demeanor, and actions, the light within these advanced souls makes manifest the glory of the hidden Father, Creator of all goodness, man's sole Originator and supreme Benefactor.

To Fulfill the Law

The Sermon on the Mount, Part II

The Eternal Laws of Spirit Governing Human Life
and the Cosmic Order

❖

The Fulfillment of Righteousness
by Which Man Attains Cosmic Consciousness

❖

The Spiritual Dangers of Violence and Anger

❖

Understanding the Spiritual Laws of Sexual Morality

❖

Applying the Principle of Nonviolence (Ahimsa)

❖

The Soul Qualities of Openhearted Generosity
and Sympathy for All

❖

Christlike Ideal of Love and Forgiveness
Toward Enemies as Well as Friends

"Far more than just a noble ideal, the principle of love is verily the manifestation of God in His creation....Mortals express their innate divinity when from the pure magnanimity of their soul they give love for hate, and goodness for evil."

"**T**hink not that I am come to destroy the law, or the prophets: I am not come to destroy, but to fulfill. For verily I say unto you, till heaven and earth pass, one jot or one tittle shall in no wise pass from the law, till all be fulfilled.

"Whosoever therefore shall break one of these least commandments, and shall teach men so, he shall be called the least in the kingdom of heaven: but whosoever shall do and teach them, the same shall be called great in the kingdom of heaven.

"For I say unto you, that except your righteousness shall exceed the righteousness of the scribes and Pharisees, ye shall in no case enter into the kingdom of heaven.

"Ye have heard that it was said by them of old time, 'Thou shalt not kill; and whosoever shall kill shall be in danger of the judgment': But I say unto you, that whosoever is angry with his brother without a cause shall be in danger of the judgment: and whosoever shall say to his brother, 'Raca,' shall be in danger of the council: but whosoever shall say, 'Thou fool,' shall be in danger of hell fire.

"Therefore if thou bring thy gift to the altar, and there rememberest that thy brother hath ought against thee; leave there thy gift before the altar, and go thy way; first be reconciled to thy brother, and then come and offer thy gift.

"Agree with thine adversary quickly, whiles thou art in the way with him; lest at any time the adversary deliver thee to the judge, and the judge deliver thee to the officer, and thou be cast into prison. Verily I say unto thee, thou shalt by no means come out thence, till thou hast paid the uttermost farthing.

"Ye have heard that it was said by them of old time, 'Thou shalt not commit adultery': But I say unto you, that whosoever looketh on a woman to lust after her hath committed adultery with her already in his heart.

"And if thy right eye offend thee, pluck it out, and cast it from thee: for it is profitable for thee that one of thy members should perish, and not that thy whole body should be cast into hell. And if thy right hand offend thee, cut it off, and cast it from thee: for it is profitable for thee that one of thy members should perish, and not that thy whole body should be cast into hell.

"It hath been said, 'Whosoever shall put away his wife, let him give her a writing of divorcement': But I say unto you, that whosoever shall put away his wife, saving for the cause of fornication, causeth her to commit adultery: and whosoever shall marry her that is divorced committeth adultery.

"Again, ye have heard that it hath been said by them of old time, 'Thou shalt not forswear thyself, but shalt perform unto the Lord thine oaths': But I say unto you, swear not at all; neither by heaven; for it is God's throne: nor by the earth; for it is His footstool: neither by Jerusalem; for it is the city of the great King. Neither shalt thou swear by thy head, because thou canst not make one hair white or black. But let your communication be, 'Yea, yea'; 'Nay, nay': for whatsoever is more than these cometh of evil.

"Ye have heard that it hath been said, 'An eye for an eye, and a tooth for a tooth': But I say unto you, that ye resist not evil: but whosoever shall smite thee on thy right cheek, turn to him the other also.

"And if any man will sue thee at the law, and take away thy coat, let him have thy cloak also. And whosoever shall compel thee to go a mile, go with him twain.

"Give to him that asketh thee, and from him that would borrow of thee turn not thou away.

"Ye have heard that it hath been said, 'Thou shalt love thy neighbour, and hate thine enemy.' But I say unto you, love your enemies, bless them that curse you, do good to them that hate you, and pray for them which despitefully use you, and persecute you; that ye may be the children of your Father which is in heaven: for He maketh His sun to rise on the evil and on the good, and sendeth rain on the just and on the unjust.

"For if ye love them which love you, what reward have ye? Do not even the publicans the same? And if ye salute your brethren only, what do ye more than others? Do not even the publicans so?

"Be ye therefore perfect, even as your Father which is in heaven is perfect."

—Matthew 5:17–48

To Fulfill the Law

The Sermon on the Mount, Part II
(With References From the Sermon on the Plain)

*"Think not that I am come to destroy the law, or the prophets:
I am not come to destroy, but to fulfill. For verily I say unto you,
till heaven and earth pass, one jot or one tittle shall in no wise
pass from the law, till all be fulfilled" (Matthew 5:17–18).**

Parallel reference:

*"And it is easier for heaven and earth to pass, than one tittle of
the law to fail" (Luke 16:17).*

Jesus speaks firmly and clearly of the essentiality of upholding the
eternal laws of righteousness. These divine codes are expressed to
man from the Ruler of Creation through the medium of His true
prophets, and made evident in the wondrous fabric of the universe.
The cosmic order of universal laws that weaves the patterns of heaven
and earth expresses itself in no less exactitude as the moral order governing the lives of human beings. He who would ensure his present

---

* "Jot" in the original Greek is *iota*, the ninth and smallest letter in the Greek alphabet. "Tittle" is used to translate the Greek *kerea*, indicating the serif (a short extended
line) on Hebrew letters.

happiness and well-being and his ultimate arrival in the kingdom of
supreme beatitude must be neither a manipulator nor a scofflaw of

———•—•———   those righteous ways.

The eternal laws of   "The Law" for the Jewish people among
Spirit governing hu-   whom Jesus was teaching was the Law of Moses—
man life and the cos-   the Ten Commandments and other moral and reli-
mic order   gious precepts set forth in the Torah. From the
                              voices of the prophets issue proclamations of the
eternal truths, which are changeless, creedless, and universally applicable in all epochs; and also codes of conduct needed in a particular
age or set of circumstances, an adaptation of the eternal verities to the
specifics of human need. But the passage of time, the expediency of interpretation, and worldly ignorance in general causes a degeneration
of holy truths. Their priceless gold is amalgamated into an alloy of
partially observed religious principles tempered with the rationalizations of human weakness. Throughout history there have been times
when the priesthood has sunk to virtual merchandising of religion on
the one hand, and enshrouding it in autocratic theological mystery on
the other hand, in order to secure a hierarchical authority over the arbitrary trends of the masses.

Great prophets expose those pseudoreligious distortions, often
with the effect of arousing acrimonious response from the entrenched
priestly classes, who condemn the actions of true reformers as irreli-
gious, unscriptural, even blasphemous. To forestall such resistance
from the temple hierarchy, and to warn his followers not to be swayed
by false accusations, Jesus clearly emphasized: "I have not come to destroy the universal laws of righteousness, nor the ever true teachings
of the prophets, but to revive and fulfill them."

As the Christ Intelligence is the Eternal Principle governing all created manifestations, timeless, too, are the precepts of spiritual living
declared by the Christ in Jesus, extending from the Biblical generations
into the unseen future: "Heaven and earth shall pass away," he proclaimed, "but my words shall not pass away."* The eternal principles
behind their adaptations should never be dragged down or compromised in order that society might feel more comfortable with them.
Man should honestly acknowledge his present inability or even outright unwillingness to follow the godly ideals rather than pretending

———————

* Matthew 24:35 (see Discourse 67).

that their sanctity is subject to a "liberal" interpretation by those who deem spiritual standards unattainable or simply passé.

Moses fulfilled his special mission in the enunciation of the universal commandments of God; Jesus came to reveal the Christ Consciousness that maintains those laws in all creation, the goodness and truth that manifests as harmony, joy, and perfection whenever those dictums are fulfilled.*

All phenomena, whether of earth or heaven, are the inconceivably numerous manifestations of one Noumena, or divine Substance. That underlying Essence, which links all things in a cosmic unity, is Truth, Reality, God reflected in creation as the Christ Intelligence. The Truth of creation, its essential divinity or goodness, erstwhile hidden by *maya's* macabre masquerade, is revealed by those who, like Jesus, manifest the Christ Consciousness and Its righteousness.

The universal laws (*dharma*) that uphold the objective manifestation of creation emanate from that all-governing Divine Intelligence. Thus Jesus declared: "I tell you that it would be easier for the inconceivably vast causal, astral, and physical universes, 'heaven and earth,' to dissolve into nothingness than for even the tiniest portion of the divine law to fail to prove its reality."

"Till heaven and earth pass, one jot or one tittle shall in no wise pass from the law, till all be fulfilled." Earth and heaven alike are cosmic motion pictures, projected by the beam of God's intelligent vibratory energy. The earth is a grosser movie of material life played on the screen of human consciousness, and heaven is a subtler picture of astral existence played on the screen of soul consciousness. Jesus knew that all heavenly and earthly manifestations have one purpose: to make visible the Invisible Perfection through the active expression of the divine laws of righteousness. Jesus emphasized that until the laws of righteousness in all their details are fulfilled, as intended by God in His cosmic plan and declared by His true devotees, heaven and earth, with their congested limitations, will go on existing. The gross and subtle spheres of creation are battlegrounds where the perfect laws of God war with the patterns of imperfection introduced by Satan. When divine righteousness in its entirety becomes manifest on earth (the material cosmos) and in heaven, the delusive power of *maya* can no

---

* "For the law was given by Moses, but grace and truth came by Jesus Christ" (John 1:17; see Discourse 1).

longer obtain; finite creation, having served its purpose, will be reabsorbed into the bosom of God. When the law of ideal living with its auxiliary proscriptions and prescriptions is fulfilled in the lives of all human and astral beings, as active expressions of the all-pervading Christ, these truly righteous become, as Emerson expressed it, "not virtuous, but Virtue; then is the end of the creation answered, and God is well pleased."* Till then, worlds will come and go and the persistently unrighteous among men will sojourn through the seeming endlessness of the cosmic movie.

~

> "Whosoever therefore shall break one of these least commandments, and shall teach men so, he shall be called the least in the kingdom of heaven: but whosoever shall do and teach them, the same shall be called great in the kingdom of heaven.
>
> "For I say unto you, that except your righteousness shall exceed the righteousness of the scribes and Pharisees, ye shall in no case enter into the kingdom of heaven" (Matthew 5:19–20).

The kingdom of heaven referred to in this context is the state of Cosmic Consciousness, in which all dualities are abolished and the One Loving King, God the Father, reigns on the throne of Infinity. Though there is no essential difference among souls who have completely attained the state of Cosmic Consciousness,

The fulfillment of righteousness by which man attains Cosmic Consciousness

there are various grades of saints among those who have contacted God but are not yet irrevocably established in the final union—the "least" and the "great" in God's kingdom. The first contact of God may bring to a devotee great blessing and understanding, but that does not obliterate all of the effects of past actions. With continuous experience of God's contact, incarnations of stored-up effects of actions are gradually roasted out. The degree of completion of that purifying process is a measure of the greatness of a saint—that is, how near he is to absolute liberation in Cosmic Consciousness.

Divine laws are the patterns of God's presence in the matrix of creation. Man weaves a life in harmony with God to the extent that

---

* Address to Harvard Divinity School, 1838.

he abides by the code of righteousness. The foremost in the kingdom of God automatically obey the greatest and the least laws of the life divine; because they are one with Cosmic Consciousness, their actions are in effortless accord with truth. But whosoever does not live the life of righteousness in all its details, acting from less-than-perfect attunement with truth as commanded from within by the voice of conscience and intuition, shall not be as highly regarded, according to the standards of God-known souls.

Saints who observe the highest and the least laws of truth—who teach them vocally and especially by the example of their lives—are considered of high degree by those who live in the supreme Spirit-domain of Cosmic Consciousness. Those who do not completely practice spiritual doctrines, yet try to teach others the path of salvation, are accordingly deemed inferior to those saints who show people the Godward path through their daily lives in which the minutest laws of truth are flawlessly demonstrated. Even if saintly persons have contacted God, but disregard the less mandatory truths, they are called the least when viewed from the highest standards of righteousness. Whether intentional or unwitting, the breaking of any divine law by an otherwise good person teaches the weak-minded that dereliction of righteous duty is acceptable behavior.

Jesus emphasized the difference between the superficial righteousness of the scribes and Pharisees who practiced religion by rote, and the true righteousness of a God-tuned life. Jesus saw that even good religious men of the temple who thought and spoke a great deal about holy scripture, and who were punctilious in performing their duties and prescribed sacerdotal ceremonies, nevertheless lacked inner realization of the underlying truths of their vocational practices; their righteousness was only skin-deep, touching little on the consciousness within.

Thinking about truth is good if it increases the desire to follow the laws of truth. Thinking or talking about truth but neglecting to apply its laws in one's actions and behavior is productive not of righteousness but of hypocrisy—a double life of thinking or speaking one way, but acting another. Unless one harnesses his good thoughts to the corresponding noble activities, his lofty philosophizing tends to develop an ineffectual, even vainglorious, familiarity with ideas about truth, which breeds neglect of their actual application—a know-it-all, do-nothing attitude. Superficial righteousness, akin to that of the scholars and Pharisees cited as an example in this verse, may make one loyal to a theoretical philosophy or dedicated to a set of religious practices and beliefs, but it is an extreme dilution of the spiritual panacea of lived truth, and consequently does not produce much soul development. Jesus therefore spoke of the necessity of developing the consciousness of doing right and living truth, shorn of superficiality.

The absolute of righteousness is complete identification with all truth. Harmony with all truth, and not just its part, is only possible through meditation and *samadhi,* or ecstasy, in which the devotee, the act of meditation, and God as the object of contemplation become one.

Millions of people do not even think about religion; and of those who do, the majority are satisfied with religious worship one hour a week or reading a few spiritual books or practicing a few religious ceremonies. They never go deeper; they never attempt by scientific meditation to commune with the infinitely loving Father about whom they hear or read. This is the palpable reason so few attain Christhood and entry into God's Kingdom of Cosmic Consciousness, the domain of the humbly reigning Royal Spirit.

Desire-propelled human beings are like uncontrolled barges rushing down the floodstream of worldly life, headed over the rocky falls of crushing experiences into the oblivion of death. The boats of wisdom-guided lives steer out of the powerful current of social convention and customs and reach the shores of all-redeeming contentment in God.

This was a great truth that Jesus urged all to heed: "If you want to enter the kingdom of God, your righteousness must exceed the ordinariness of theoretical religious beliefs and living; it must transform your consciousness and whole being. Unless you follow the real way of actual God-communion in interiorized worship in deep meditation, your righteousness shall in no wise qualify you to enter the highest state of Cosmic Consciousness, the heavenly bliss from which you can never fall again."

~

"Ye have heard that it was said by them of old time, 'Thou shalt not kill; and whosoever shall kill shall be in danger of the judgment': But I say unto you, that whosoever is angry with his brother without a cause shall be in danger of the judgment: and whosoever shall say to his brother, 'Raca,' shall be in danger of

the council: but whosoever shall say, 'Thou fool,' shall be in dan-
ger of hell fire" (Matthew 5:21–22).

Having spoken in general of the eternal laws governing God's
creation, and of how their observance is necessary for attaining the kingdom of heaven, Jesus illustrates (in verses 21–48) specific
adaptations of those laws—ways of fulfilling their spirit of natural
righteousness.

He speaks first of the ancient commandment: "Thou shalt not
kill; and whosoever shall kill shall be in danger of the judgment."*
Those who destroy heaven-created human beings
misuse their reason and God-given independence   *The spiritual dangers*
and will be judged accordingly by the inscrutable   *of violence and anger*
karmic law of cause-and-effect justice. Murderers
not only counter the universal law of divine creation, but they deprive
their victims of the lawful opportunity to work out independently their
own karma—a preclusion of that individual's progress in his present
lifetime. God creates mortal life; to kill is to obstruct the highest divine wish of emancipating immortal souls through purification in the
self-created karmic fires of mortal trials, whence they emerge transformed by freewill initiated acts of wisdom.

Jesus pointed out that in the light of natural righteousness, evil
lies not only in murderous actions, but in angry thoughts and emotions that give rise to such actions. Jesus, who taught love even for
one's enemies, warned against being angry "without cause"—and
then went on to say that man should not indulge in hostility and scorn
toward his brothers under any circumstances, lest he place himself in
"danger of the judgment" of "the council"; and of "hell fire." Wrath
obliterates discrimination and prevents the mind from discerning the
right course during a momentous issue. Anyone who is angry with his
brother through the misunderstanding of facts or an emotionally perceived personal grievance is one who is angry without reason.

Anger, arising either from an actual cause or from an imaginary
perception, may create sufficient provocation in a person to impel him
to violence. In cases of extreme anger, people may mentally wish their
enemies dead. Sometimes they voice their ire: "I could shoot that
man!" Though it may not be meant literally, it is still very bad. The

---

* See Exodus 20:13.

thought and talk of death to another are mental chemicals that can potentially explode into violent activity. The thought of killing precedes the physical act in a preconditioned response awaiting provocation. No willful killing is possible without being triggered by thought. So, to fulfill the law "Thou shalt not kill," Jesus said, not only the act but all thoughts, speech, and actions relative to killing must be strictly avoided. He spoke in consonance with the sages of India who honor the scriptural injunction of *ahimsa,* inner and outer nonviolence.

Once my guru, Swami Sri Yukteswarji, watched me raise my hand to kill a mosquito that was siphoning my blood. But I suddenly changed my mind, remembering the decree of nonviolence. Master said: "Why don't you finish the job?" In astonishment, I replied: "Why, Master? Do you advocate killing?" To that he responded: "No, but you have killed the mosquito in your mind and thus have already committed the sin."

My Guru did not mean that whenever anybody has an impulse to kill, he should do so; he was making the point that one should not feel the desire to kill at all. Of course, it is better to suppress the desire to kill than to commit the actual act; but the greater achievement is to remain free from evil thoughts, which are the basic cause of evil actions.*

Thought, the forerunner of outer action, is itself action on a subtler plane. In that sense, according to the law of karma or action, righteousness and sin lie in one's thoughts and motives as well as in his external behavior. One man commits murder and is hanged for it;

---

* In *Autobiography of a Yogi* I recorded the following discussion I had with my Guru about Patanjali's *Yoga Sutras* II:35: "In the presence of a man perfected in *ahimsa* (nonviolence), enmity [in any creature] does not arise." Sri Yukteswar said:

"By *ahimsa* Patanjali meant removal of the *desire* to kill....This world is inconveniently arranged for a literal practice of *ahimsa.* Man may be compelled to exterminate harmful creatures. He is not under a similar compulsion to feel anger or animosity. All forms of life have an equal right to the air of *maya.* The saint who uncovers the secret of creation will be in harmony with Nature's countless bewildering expressions. All men may understand this truth by overcoming the passion for destruction."

I then asked: "Guruji, should one offer himself a sacrifice rather than kill a wild beast?"

"No, man's body is precious. It has the highest evolutionary value because of unique brain and spinal centers. These enable the advanced devotee fully to grasp and express the loftiest aspects of divinity. No lower form is so equipped. It is true that a man incurs the debt of a minor sin if he is forced to kill an animal or any other living thing. But the holy *shastras* teach that wanton loss of a human body is a serious transgression against the karmic law."

another man kills many human beings on the battlefield in defense of his country and is given a medal. It is the inner motive that differentiates the two. Human moralists judge outer appearances, believing in absolute rules; but Divine Law, the true arbiter of virtue and vice in this world of relativity, judges man's inner being. However, one's motives must be wisdom-pure. I remember the opportunistic students in my classes who found this opening in the door of right behavior a convenient exit: "My motive justified my actions." My response, with gratitude to the author for a succinct rebuttal, was to quote: "The road to Hades is paved with good intentions."

The law of cause and effect bestows good or bad fruits of actions according to a person's good or bad activities. Every action—mental or physical—produces a result in the form of a tendency, which is lodged in the mind as a karmic seed. This mental-tendency seed germinates into action when the conditions of environment provide the necessary "watering." A good mental seed produces good action and a bad seed results in evil performance. One should be very careful how he acts, for the power of leftover corresponding tendencies makes actions repeat themselves—becoming more deeply integrated into one's nature with each repetition. It is all right when good actions are repeated, but disastrous when evil actions insinuate themselves against the will of the performer. Every wrong action brings calamity from "the judgment"—from the result proceeding from the law of cause and effect.

One can measure one's emotional self-control by testing it on those nearest and dearest to him. If he can neutralize his impulses to become angry (or to vent any other acrid emotion) in response to provocations, then he is developing himself in the spirit of the law as admonished by Jesus. To control the external expression of anger while seething within creates an inner vibratory heat that cooks one's brain like a slowly baked potato. Lahiri Mahasaya gave those methods of meditation by which one can instead roast the seeds of wrong impulses. Scientific meditation harmonizes the whole being, creating an inner calmness of self-mastery.

Jesus makes another point in these verses: Words are very potent vibratory actions, affecting favorably or adversely the one who utters them and also the one to whom they are directed. To express contempt to any individual ("say to his brother, 'Raca'"*) is spiritually libelous

---

* *Raca:* a derogatory term in Aramaic (literally, "I spit on you") conveying extreme contempt.

against that individual's soul, which is ever perfect regardless of how loathsome his egoistic expression. By scorning a fellow being, one demeans his own soul's forbearing nature and subjects himself to the scrutiny of the tribunal of his conscience and its records of his many regrettable failings. It would be a humbling, if not horrific, experience if one had to face an archival reading of the shames in all of his past incarnations. The merciful God has forgiven so much in every man who is consciously struggling toward the light of wisdom; it is the awakening nobility of the soul that likewise feels patience rather than contempt for others whose actions show no such awakening.

Further, anyone who calls another a "fool"* shall himself suffer from the fire of ignorance. Ignorance is hell, as it engenders all manner of evils and burns away wisdom. True knowledge and wisdom are the source of salvation from the miseries of the human condition. To inhibit the potential unfoldment of anyone's soul wisdom by a strong suggestion of ineptness is to do them a great wrong. Negating anyone's will and branding the subconscious mind with defeatist thoughts of inferior abilities is reprehensible. To foster in anyone an attitude of surrender to ignorance sets in motion the lawful principle that to pull down another human being is a sin that puts oneself "in danger of hell fire"—the fire of ignorance that consumes one's own spiritual merit in the act of willfully demoralizing, humiliating, or denigrating another person.

It is plain that Jesus spoke figuratively in his reference to hellfire.† He did not mean that the omnipresent God of love has created leap-

---

* Original Greek *moros,* "moron"; English "idiot" or "fool."

† See also Discourses 48 and 68. The concept of eternal damnation in hellfire, as in orthodox interpretations, is not supported in this verse or elsewhere in the New Testament. The word used for "hell" in the original Greek of the Gospel is *Gehenna,* from Hebrew *Ge Hinnom,* the valley of Hinnom southwest of Jerusalem, where children were formerly burned as living sacrifices to the Ammonite god Moloch (II Chronicles 28:3; Jeremiah 7:31–32). In Jesus' time, according to Biblical historians, the valley was used as a dump for the filth of the city, where continual fires were kept to consume it —"a place," according to commentator John Gill, "whose fire was never quenched; and in which they burned the bones of any thing that was unclean, and dead carcasses, and other pollutions." The name was thus commonly used by the Jews to denote the after-death realm of punishment. *Encyclopaedia Britannica* states about *Gehenna:* "Mentioned several times in the New Testament (e.g., Matthew, Mark, Luke, and James) as a place in which fire will destroy the wicked, it also is noted in the Talmud, a compendium of Jewish law, lore, and commentary, as a place of purification, after which one is released from further torture."

ing tongues of fire in a hell at some point of space to burn the disembodied souls of sinners, rife with bad karma. The Heavenly Spirit who is the Father of all human children could not possibly roast them alive forever because they made some temporary mistakes during their sojourn on earth.

~

"Therefore if thou bring thy gift to the altar, and there rememberest that thy brother hath ought against thee; leave there thy gift before the altar, and go thy way; first be reconciled to thy brother, and then come and offer thy gift.*

"Agree with thine adversary quickly, whiles thou art in the way with him; lest at any time the adversary deliver thee to the judge, and the judge deliver thee to the officer, and thou be cast into prison. Verily I say unto thee, thou shalt by no means come out thence, till thou hast paid the uttermost farthing" (Matthew 5:23–26).†

Though God does not take up into Himself from the temple altar the material objects that are presented to Him, He does receive the devotion of the heart that actuates those offerings. No one can really present to God a gift from the bounty of His creation, because all things belong to Him; but to give unto God the gifts that are given by Him shows an appreciative heart. Most of all, God loves the gifts of love, peace, and devotion offered in the temple of one's own heart or through the temples of the hearts of others.

Therefore, Jesus stressed that one's heart must be made pure if one's gift to God is to be a worthy offering. Ill will toward an estranged brother is a defilement of the inner temple of harmony. To "agree with thine adversary" does not mean to condone or cooperate with his evil, but to cleanse oneself of malice and rancor. To seek reconciliation in forgiveness of wrongs is to please God in the forgiver and the forgiven.

Inharmony, resulting from enmity, is the judge and the officer which casts one into the prison of inner disturbance. Verily, no one

---

* Cf. Mark 11:25–26, Discourse 35.

†The latter part of the above verses is paralleled in Luke 12:58–59, and is commented on in that context in Discourse 56.

can come out of the prison of inharmony unless he loses the last farthing of anger, resentment, and vengefulness from within himself. To
behold anyone as an enemy is to eclipse the presence of God residing
in that person's soul. A wise man does not lose the consciousness of
the omnipresence of God by being unable to see Him in everyone, even
when He is hidden behind the smoke screen of hatred with which an
enemy brother surrounds his heart.

~

> *"Ye have heard that it was said by them of old time, 'Thou shalt
> not commit adultery': But I say unto you, that whosoever
> looketh on a woman to lust after her hath committed adultery
> with her already in his heart.*
>
> *"And if thy right eye offend thee, pluck it out, and cast it
> from thee: for it is profitable for thee that one of thy members
> should perish, and not that thy whole body should be cast into
> hell. And if thy right hand offend thee, cut it off, and cast it from
> thee: for it is profitable for thee that one of thy members should
> perish, and not that thy whole body should be cast into hell"*
> *(Matthew 5:27–30).* *

Jesus said that not only is the physical act of adultery sinful, but
that, according to spiritual law, a lustful gaze involves the committing of adultery in the mind. It is a common occurrence, especially
in modern permissive societies, for men and women to leer at each
other with sensuous thoughts and yearning. This
attraction seems to flatter the recipients, some of
whom even attire themselves or adopt other ruses
in order to draw that kind of admiration. It is not
only sinful to bestow lustful glances, but it is
equally wrong willfully to awaken sex thoughts in the opposite sex,
and also to feel flattered by such attentions.

*Understanding the
spiritual laws of sex-
ual morality*

According to human law, unless there is physical adultery, there is
no cause for condemnation. Human law passes no judgment on lascivi-

---

* Jesus repeats this guidance in much the same words in Matthew 18:8–9. His counsel in that context, as well as in Mark 9:45–48 (where he again uses this metaphor),
is commented on in Discourse 48.

ous mental behavior. But the Divine Law condemns mental adultery also, because without its advent, physical adultery would not be enacted.

The Hindu scriptures speak of the following ways of committing adultery (equally applicable to women as well as men):

1. To think lustfully of a woman, without the woman being present before the physical eyes.
2. To talk about a woman with lustful desire.
3. To touch a woman with lustful desire.
4. To gaze upon a woman with lustful desire.
5. To hold private intimate talks with a woman with the ultimate hope of physical union.
6. The act of physical union without the consecration of marriage.

"Sin" requires a complex definition. It is not a transgression against an arbitrary code of behavior decreed by a whimsical God. The Creator made man a spiritual being, a soul endowed with an individualization of His own divine nature. He gave to the soul, evolved from its own Self, the instruments of a body and a mind with which to perceive and interact with the objects of a *maya*-manifested universe. The soul's mental and physical instruments come into being and are held in existence by specific lawful processes of God's creative power. If man lives in perfect harmony with the machinations of these principles, he remains a spiritual being in charge of his body and mind. Sin is that which compromises that perfect self-mastery. It has its automatic negative effect to the degree of the influence of delusion within it—involving no condemnation of an irate God. Man's free-will actions simply harmonize and strengthen the expressed essence of his soul perfection, or weaken and degrade it into mortal enslavement.

Thus, how many ways there are to sin against natural law no living mortal knows. The category of sex is a particularly puzzling one. Unless the sex urge were given to man from within, by the process of evolution after the fall from Eden,* he would not feel the desire. Since physical union is the law of propagation of the species, it should be treated with that regard.

Animals cannot commit adultery, even though they are indiscriminate from the human standpoint, because their sexual engagements merely obey the nature-impelled instinct to procreate their species. They do not indulge in self-created sex thoughts.

---

* See Discourse 7.

Man, being endowed with reason and free will, commits sin by adding his lascivious, insatiable, lustful thoughts to the instinct of procreation. According to spiritual law, therefore, to use the sexual instinct solely to gratify sensual desire is considered sinful, detrimental to man's godly image. A married man also commits sin, as pointed out by Jesus, if he thinks lustfully of his wife, whose feminine nature should be respectfully loved and regarded as God's motherly aspect.

Healthful hunger can be appeased by using the sense of taste to select the right foods, but greed for food can never be satisfied and compounds its ill effects by choosing an unhealthful diet. Similarly, physical union for procreation is as nature intends, but indulgence is never appeased, and is destructive to health and the nervous system, disturbing the entire mental, neural, and spiritual faculties.

The mind is single-tracked when it becomes fixated on an impulse. Once it gets used to sex habits, it is very difficult to make it move in the elevating channels of meditation. Sex-addicted persons are very nervous and restless; their minds wander constantly on the plane of the senses, making it difficult to concentrate upon the inner peace that leads the consciousness to the all-intoxicating, ever new bliss of God-communion.

The vital essence lost in physical union contains untold atomic units of lifetronic intelligence and energy; the loss of this power, due to indiscriminate excesses, is extremely harmful to spiritual development. It exacerbates the outflow of life force through the lowest subtle center at the base of the spine, concentrating the consciousness on identification with the body and external sensory perceptions. When one is habituated to this state, no ascension of consciousness to the higher centers of spiritual realization and God-communion is possible. People who live on the sex plane with its momentary allurement and physical excitation cannot even imagine, much less desire to achieve, the incomparable bliss of Spirit in interiorized meditation. Yogis enhance their great spiritual power and realization by a natural, not suppressed, conservation of the vital essence, transmuting it into divine vibrations in meditation that awaken the higher centers in the spine with their exalted states of consciousness.

Speaking figuratively of how even looking at the opposite sex with impure thoughts arouses lust, Jesus said that it is better to lose an eye than that the whole bodily instrument be desecrated by evil— it is better to forgo illicit sensory indulgence than to lose the infinite unending joys of the soul's communion with Spirit.

Christ used a dramatic metaphor to emphasize that if the mind becomes enslaved by desires arising from any sensory perception ("eye") or sensory action ("hand") it profanes the divine soul-image within man, leaving him oblivious of God. Nothing in life, no matter how pleasurable, is of any value or lasting happiness if one remains ignorant of God. Without knowing Him, life becomes a "hell" of insecurity with unforeseen disasters and grievous troubles. It is better that man's misuse of the senses and his wrong actions "should perish" than to allow his passions to annihilate his entire happiness in Spirit.

How thoughtlessly people give up the kingdom of immortal bliss for their material desires for name, fame, lustful gratification, possession, money. Christ decried that shortsighted investment of one's life; it is more "profitable for thee" to cast off whatsoever casts the happiness of one's true being into a "hell" of delusive soul-oblivion.

∼

"It hath been said, 'Whosoever shall put away his wife, let him give her a writing of divorcement': But I say unto you, that whosoever shall put away his wife, saving for the cause of fornication, causeth her to commit adultery: and whosoever shall marry her that is divorced committeth adultery" (Matthew 5:31–32).

This seems to be a very drastic law to people who part from each other due to incompatibility of temper, and then decide to marry someone else.

The sin lies in marrying the wrong person, actuated by social custom or physical instinct. One should get married only when one finds soul unity with a proper mate. And the two thus united in holy vows should remain together, steadfastly loyal to one another. Proper marriage nurtures real love, union on a higher plane, and sublimates the uncontrolled lusts of living on the sex plane.

People who marry and divorce time and again never give the seeds of divine love a chance to grow on the soil of faithful commitment. The minds of such persons, being concentrated upon sex and physical attraction, remain spiritually fallow. Hence, divorce for flimsy reasons is adulterous behavior as it focuses primarily on sexual gratification as an end in itself. Marriage should be honored by husband and wife as an opportunity for nurturing growth and understanding through

471

mutual exchange of their finest qualities. And conjugal union should be respected as a means of procreation on the physical plane (inviting the birth of souls into a proper family environment). Sublimation of a marital relationship culminates in the procreation of "children" of unconditional love and ultimate emancipation on the spiritual plane.*

~

"Again, ye have heard that it hath been said by them of old time, 'Thou shalt not forswear thyself, but shalt perform unto the Lord thine oaths': But I say unto you, swear not at all; neither by heaven; for it is God's throne: nor by the earth; for it is His footstool: neither by Jerusalem; for it is the city of the great King. Neither shalt thou swear by thy head, because thou canst not make one hair white or black. But let your communication be, 'Yea, yea'; 'Nay, nay': for whatsoever is more than these cometh of evil" (Matthew 5:33–37).

A solemn oath sworn to God or in His name was in olden times, as in the here and now, considered morally and spiritually (and in a court of law, legally) binding. In making a sacred promise to God one may not resort to evasive or outright falsehoods, or thereafter break that oath, without consequence. It had thus become a custom among the Jewish population that in mundane or trivial matters swearing was done in reference to specific creations of God rather than in direct appeal to God Himself, presuming thereby no absolute obligation.

Jesus was a bold voice on behalf of the spirit of the laws that govern man's behavior. Hypocritical skirting of those principles may avoid present consequences, but the evil effects engendered in the consciousness will inevitably have their day of retribution. So Jesus was not advising against oaths taken in the proper circumstance for the proper reason, and the solemnity that should be accorded them, but rather against the flippant avowal of an insincere intent. He points out the impossibility of performing actions outside

Why Jesus spoke against the swearing of oaths

---

* Cf. Matthew 19:9 and Luke 16:18, Discourse 62, for further commentary on Jesus' teaching about marriage and divorce.

472

of God's presence. A person is, in principle, no less beholden if he swears in the name of heaven or earth, for heaven is God's transcendental realm of blissful retirement where He rests on His throne of Infinity, hidden behind the walls of space and light rays. The earth is the footstool of God; that is, it is a place where God as the Creator works with His "feet" of motion and activity. Neither should one swear by Jerusalem or any holy city or place which has had the sacred manifestation of the Royal God through the presence, worship, and realization of His saints. Neither should one swear by the head because it is the holy sanctuary of the soul.

From the practice of swearing frivolously to enhance one's self-perceived eminence, there has devolved the crude commonality of swearing merely to punctuate one's statements. Such swearing is the result of overworked emotion. During the mental obliteration of clear thinking caused by emotion, as in a heated argument, or anger, or a strong impulse to stress a point, one is apt to speak untruth or to make a violent false assertion. To add to impulsive untruthful statements, or even self-serving factual assertions, the sacred name of God, or by implication anything in which He is manifested, is to drag down that which is holy to support something that is wrong or egocentric or trifling.

Coarse swearing reveals weakness of character, absence of fineness, and lack of reverence. It makes one cheap and also cheapens the atmosphere around him, undermining respect for things sacred and affecting the sanctity and seriousness of good souls in his company. Swearing exposes one's mental deficiency in having to resort to emotional exclamations instead of using the clarity of reason to prove a point. A true statement firmly asserted does not need to be supported or emphasized by swearing, which rather desecrates and denigrates and may fasten upon one the habit of prevarication, exaggeration, and misrepresentation. Swearing fosters profane language, an impulsive and overbearing nature, and hasty and impatient assertions. In conversation and argument, it is best to use "yea, yea," or "nay, nay," calmly or emphatically administered, as the occasion demands; that is, to be restrained, concise, and truthful. A person of devious temperament is unreliable, feeling no constraints regardless of any avowal; an upright person is always sincere and honest with or without the commandment of a sworn oath.

∼

> *"Ye have heard that it hath been said, 'An eye for an eye, and a tooth for a tooth': But I say unto you, that ye resist not evil: but whosoever shall smite thee on thy right cheek, turn to him the other also.*
>
> *"And if any man will sue thee at the law, and take away thy coat, let him have thy cloak also. And whosoever shall compel thee to go a mile, go with him twain.*
>
> *"Give to him that asketh thee, and from him that would borrow of thee turn not thou away" (Matthew 5:38–42).*

Parallel reference:

> *"And unto him that smiteth thee on the one cheek offer also the other; and him that taketh away thy cloak forbid not to take thy coat also.*
>
> *"Give to every man that asketh of thee; and of him that taketh away thy goods ask them not again" (Luke 6:29–30, Sermon on the Plain).*

The Mosaic law of "an eye for an eye and a tooth for a tooth" was to serve not only as a punishment, but also as a deterrent to other would-be criminals by making the punishment match the crime.* A literal reading may have been justified in the time when people, in the words of Moses, "have corrupted themselves...they are a perverse and crooked generation....neither is there any understanding in them. O that they were wise, that they understood this, that they would consider their latter end!"† Spiritual laws are eternally true, but their application as inscribed in judgments governing a society may in different climes and ages require more or less modification according to the nature of the environment in which they are enacted. Though no social system can survive without an orderly code of justice to restrain wrongdoers and uphold a standard of human dignity, laws best fulfill their purpose when they protect the innocent and encourage reformation of the guilty.

The "eye for an eye" law serves only the purpose of punishment for the sake of revenge. It does not teach right actions to the wrongdoer, but may well make him more hateful. To wreak vengeance does

---

* Exodus 21:24, Leviticus 24:19, Deuteronomy 19:21.

† Deuteronomy 32:5, 28–29.

not stop the recurrence of an evil act; rather, it is more likely to foster evil thoughts and further acts of retaliation.

Therefore, Jesus again, as in the principle of nonkilling, speaks of the ideal of noninjury (*ahimsa*) to any human being—in word, thought, speech, or action. It enjoins freedom from the desire for revenge and not resisting evil with evil methods. Jesus advises man to conquer evil by the infinitely powerful virtue of forgiveness and love. He speaks figuratively of turning the other cheek to illustrate

Applying the principle of nonviolence (ahimsa)

the influence of goodness over inimical behavior. If anybody vents his anger with a slap and receives a slap in return, it only increases his anger and desire to deliver stronger blows—and maybe a kick or a bullet! A calm response, on the other hand, is quite disconcerting and disarming. With a resentful second blow his physical wrath is quite likely to be spent. Wrath is increased by wrath as fire increases by fire, but as fire is extinguished by water, so also, wrath is subdued by kindliness.*

One whose immunity of calmness and love can resist the hatred from an angry brother thereby prevents that virus of disquieting emotion from entering within himself.

The ideal of nonretaliation does not justify supine surrender to wrongdoing or tacit approval of evil. To turn the other cheek is not calculated to make a person into a mental or moral weakling, or to suggest enduring an abusive or violent personal relationship, but to instill the strength of self-control gained by overcoming the impulse to act under the influence of revenge. It is an easy reflex to retaliate, but it requires great mental strength not to strike back. It takes a highly principled person of strong spiritual character to resist evil with virtue. Otherwise, it would seem ridiculous to allow a second blow after receiving one hard knock. Even if the aggressor does not admit it, he will be inwardly overpowered by the person of noble behavior and will know in his heart that that person was in the right.

While it is better to have courage to fight an enemy than to "forgive" him and run away through fear, if one can courageously face down an erring brother with love, that is to possess a mighty spiritual power—the transforming, healing power of divine love. A person perfected in nonviolence lets no one steal his inner peace. When by spiritual example and adamant determination he can maintain his ideal

---

* "A soft answer turneth away wrath: but grievous words stir up anger" (Proverbs 15:1).

personality in spite of any robbers of disquietude, he becomes a towering example of truth in the eyes of others.

When assailed by someone, it is hard to give love. The best way, while taking commonsense steps to remedy the situation, is to pray to God to change the heart of that person. Never ask God to punish anyone. It is surprising how sincere prayer will change the attitude of an antagonist. If that person becomes penitent, the giver of love has won that heart.

The early Christians were considered fools for their nonviolent resistance against Roman tyranny, but the kingdom of Jesus' teachings endured and flourished while the Roman empire deteriorated into oblivion.

A spiritual man of high order feels no grievous loss when he is parted from any of his material possessions, for whatever reason — be it from court judgments or for someone in need.

The soul qualities of openhearted generosity and sympathy for all

His heartfelt generosity of spirit gives with an open hand. The spiritual man sees God not only in his own body but in the bodies of others. In oneness with God, he sees himself as the Self of all, and finds equal enjoyment whether he himself dons his "cloak" or takes it off from his one body and puts it on another one of his bodies. Whatever the divine person does for another, he feels by such action that he has in a nonattached way done this for himself, only in another body — just as one transfers a ring from one finger to another.

Giving away one's "cloak" as well as one's "coat" may seem like very unpractical advice in the modern world. No doubt, one must use discrimination. Abnegation of one's own material needs can best be completely practiced only by saints or by people living under ideal conditions. One is under no spiritual compulsion to give his home away to an unscrupulous defrauder; instead, he is compelled to demand lawful justice from those who are unjust to him.

It would be ludicrous to offer a thief or a blackmailer more than was demanded, or for a victim to suggest to a kidnapper who has taken him forty miles away from his home, he would be willing to go forty miles further! The spiritual ideal in these words of Jesus is to be selflessly generous and openhearted, and willing to go that extra mile in helping others.

One should practice the virtue of giving to deserving people what one can afford to give without causing himself or those dependent upon him for their needs an enforced hardship. One should not "rob

Peter to pay Paul." It is not spiritual to starve one's family in order to be a philanthropist. Mahatma Gandhi convinced his family of the virtue of sacrifice and then gave away all of his possessions without saving even any bonds or stocks for the security of his wife and children. Such action is admirable if the sacrifice is performed with the willing agreement of the other persons concerned. Gandhi had a mission to fulfill, which would be best accomplished by identifying himself materially as well as spiritually with the downtrodden masses.

Practical sympathy toward those in need dispels the darkness of separation between souls and is the light by which one can see all hearts tied together with the singular golden cord of divine love. God throbs in all hearts, suffering in the afflicted, rejoicing in those that are whole.

The same spirit of nonattachment should accompany the sharing of one's goods with would-be borrowers. It shows compassion to lend to needy people, but let not that virtue be negated by anger if the money is not returned. It is better not to lend at all than to become upset or ugly because the debtor is unable to pay back what he owes. Practical advice would be to lend only what one can afford to give away and forget all about it. Conscientious persons will make good on what they owe when and as they are able, and unscrupulous persons will not honor their debt even if they can afford to.

To lend money with the assurance of a returned favor, or the gain of a favorable interest, is ordinary business. But to lend to the needy who may or may not be able to repay—to help others without the desire for material reward; to give something without the hope of getting something better in return—is divine. Those who give of their material goods with the presumption of compensation receive temporary material things or advantages only; those who give with an open heart, just for the pleasure of giving pleasure to others, receive their repayment with a dividend of divine love.

There is nothing wrong in expecting the return of what one lends to others, not only for tending to one's own needs but for further sharing with others. But those things that one can spare, and that have been given to others to use, should not be demanded back simply to assert one's right of ownership. Possessiveness shows meanness of heart. It is delusion for one to think that his material possessions belong to him exclusively and in perpetuity. Man owns nothing on this earth; he is only given the use of things from its cosmic store. At death, everything has to be forsaken. Rockefeller and Henry Ford were not able to take with them into heaven a single dollar of their vast fortunes. If through some good actions a person has been fortunate enough to qualify for a generous loan from God of money, property, and possessions, that person should adopt the noble ideal of helping other children of God by openhanded assistance.

Thus the spirit of Jesus' admonition: "Give something, within your power, to whomever asks of you. By always exercising the soul quality of sympathy, your heart will expand to become as the heart of God, who does everything for all. Cultivate the consciousness that whatsoever you possess belongs to God, and as such is common property to be used in serving all His children. When God sees that you are unselfish with what He has given to you, He gives you more, that your liberal capacity to share might be enlarged as an extension of His own beneficent Hand."

~

> *"Ye have heard that it hath been said, 'Thou shalt love thy neighbour, and hate thine enemy.' But I say unto you, love your enemies, bless them that curse you, do good to them that hate you, and pray for them which despitefully use you, and persecute you; that ye may be the children of your Father which is in heaven: for He maketh His sun to rise on the evil and on the good, and sendeth rain on the just and on the unjust"* (Matthew 5:43–45).

Parallel reference:

> *"But I say unto you which hear, love your enemies, do good to them which hate you, bless them that curse you, and pray for them which despitefully use you....*
>
> *"But love ye your enemies, and do good, and lend, hoping for nothing again; and your reward shall be great, and ye shall be the children of the Highest: for He is kind unto the unthankful and to the evil"* (Luke 6:27–28, 35, Sermon on the Plain).

Love and forgiveness form the nucleus of the Christ teachings. Far more than just a noble ideal, the principle of love is verily the manifestation of God in His creation. The universe endures by a play between good and evil. The effect of evil, delusion, is to divide and obscure and cause inharmony. Love is the attracting power of Spirit that unites and harmonizes. The vibratory force of God's love, consciously directed by man, neutralizes the power of evil. Hate, anger, revenge, are offspring of the evil force and thus serve to reinforce the evil vibration.

Christlike ideal of love and forgiveness toward enemies as well as friends

The millenniums of resistance of evil by retaliation in kind have never succeeded in eradicating the scourge of enmity from man's heart. God could instantly destroy evildoers; but instead, He uses love to coax created beings back to Him. In the simple words, "Love your enemies," Jesus urged man to cooperate with God in this divine plan of redemption: to love one's neighbors, and to have a place in one's love for enemies as well. A wise man beholds in the circumference of his cosmic love a galaxy of friends and also those who consider themselves to be his enemies. Naughty or good, all people are equally God's children.

Those who, under the influence of passion, think antagonistically toward others, forget that all human beings are made in the image of God and are brothers. Hatred and anger becloud the divine image in vengeful persons, and delusion makes them lose the consciousness of their inner divinity. Why give hate for hate and thus imitate the vileness of ignorance? One must cultivate the consciousness of justice and love by knowing how to separate the God-image in the soul of a person from the evil in his ego expression. Just as the subtle vibratory ether is present in dark places and in the sunlight also, so one learns to recognize God in those who love him and also in those who hate him. To see God equally in friend and enemy is a testimony to one's spiritual realization.

One who extends his love to friends and enemies alike ultimately beholds the presence of the One Love everywhere—in flowers, animals, and especially in the souls of God's human children. In order to see this omnipresence of God, the devotee must behold Him not only through the open portal of friendship, but must tear away the dark screen of hate and behold His erstwhile hidden presence even in the heart of enemies.

It is not necessary to mix with one's enemies. It is often better to love them from a distance, unless by acts of kindly association one's love can affect a change in those persons. If one does happen to come in contact with enemies, he should remember that it is his spiritual duty to do so in love, because God is in them trying to straighten out the crookedness in their hearts.

If one talks love as a matter of diplomacy to win over an enemy, but harbors enmity in his heart, that insincerity will not work for very long. The human heart is intuitive; it is not easy to deceive its intuitive perception. The heart must absolutely give up all manner of hatred because ill will, no matter how expertly controlled outwardly, travels through the ether into the heart of the person on which it is focused. Thinking love while talking love will surely mollify and change one's enemies, even if they do not immediately recognize or admit it. Love is a divine cleanser and a lastingly effective way of winning one's enemies. Hatred may temporarily suppress and put down an enemy, but he will still remain an enemy. The poison of hate increases by hatred and can be counteracted and neutralized only by the chemical of love.

Inimical persons burn themselves with hatred and anger, consuming their inner peace. One who returns their enmity likewise burns up his own inner equanimity, his peace which offers to his entire life absolute protection from the devastation wrought by human miseries. So to hate anyone is against one's own interest.

Without any expression or feeling of malice or sarcasm, a wronged person should just say within himself: "I forgive you." It is such a healing, elevating experience. That mental expression of love also travels through the ether into the heart of a wrongdoer. It is one of the most effective ways to change an enemy. To hate an enemy is to make him stronger, whereas his enmity is weakened by kindness until he may finally realize his fault.

Thus, Jesus says: "Bless them that curse you"—that is, wish good for those who wish evil for you. If, as often as anyone wishes evil on a person, that person responds by wishing good in return, the assailant cannot long retain his evil attitude against that well-wisher. It is ordinary to think that by retaliation hateful curses can be stopped; but even if the enemy is weak and outwardly cowed down, his hatred will grow all the more, just waiting for the next opportunity to ignite it. A curse for a curse cannot stop an enemy's hatred, but to love and bless a malicious scorner is to place before him a good example that may serve to change his attitude.

Action speaks louder than words. Thus Jesus says, "Do good to them that hate you." Not only should one mentally love a detractor, but actually do good to him. With no trace of a "holier-than-thou" attitude, sincere gestures of goodwill are reminders of the relation of divine brotherhood that is the unifying principle among all human beings.

God is ever merciful, solely because He considers all souls as His children, placing no conditional demands on them in return. So should

God's children try to act divinely toward one another without ulterior motives. That is what Jesus urged: "Help all, and you will feel the pleasure of heartening others; help all, because God is your Father and everyone is your kin. Love and help even your enemies in that spirit of divine brotherhood. And your wisdom shall be great, for God's divine love shall grow within you; and by that you shall know you are not delimited mortals, but the children of the Highest."

Even if one can in no way approach those who hate him in order to do good to them in some tangible expression, it is always possible to follow Jesus' counsel to "pray for them that despitefully use you, and persecute you." Pray to the omnipresent God that He bless them with freedom from their hatred. If one cannot take away the hatred from his enemies by example and loving-kindness, God can do so, for His omnipresence is in their heart and mind. By praying for one's antagonists, one not only uses his own loving attitude but reinforces that with God's power to heal the error-stricken. If prayer is sincere and strong, God will be moved to help change an enemy if the intervention of His grace is the best course for all concerned.

If one's prayer to change his enemy's attitude is not fulfilled, then the supplicant must know that God wants him to pass the test of unconditional love, even in the throes of persecution from his enemy's lies, hateful talk, and evil actions. In His own time God can and will remedy all inharmonious conditions. One should continue to pray to God that one's enemies may be forgiven and spared from suffering the otherwise inevitable results arising from their evil actions. That is the divine way to pray. God recognizes the spiritual nobility in trying to rescue brothers fallen into the pit of malicious behavior, and rewards with divine wisdom and love those souls who respond to them with Christlike understanding and actions.

Anyone who wants to know God must learn to love, as He does, His virtuous and sinful children alike. The Heavenly Father knocks with His love at the heart-doors of the vicious as well as the virtuous. The virtuous man, with his ears of wisdom, hears God's summons and opens eagerly the doors of devotion that God might enter; vicious persons, their consciousness raucous with error, are insensible to the Divine Visitation. God's infinite love, undeterred, keeps knocking just the same until that wondrous moment in the soul's evolution when at last the closed mental doors will open. Ordinarily, with time, a person forgets anyone who has turned indifferent or hostile to him; but God, with "unhurrying chase, and unperturbèd pace," never stops pursuing His estranged children who forget Him.*

Those who love their enemies are surely loved by the Heavenly Father and become like Him, for God "maketh His sun to rise on the evil and on the good, and sendeth rain on the just and on the unjust." Bhagavan Krishna similarly said: "He is a supreme yogi (one united to God) who regards with equal-mindedness...friends, enemies...the virtuous and the ungodly."†

As God loves all of His children, regardless of merit, so also "that ye may be the children of your Father which is in heaven," the true children of God open their hearts to all their human brethren. Though God's light of mercy shines equally on the good and the evil, and the rain of His helpful powers is showered on the just and the unjust alike, this is not to be understood that the good and bad are able to reflect in equal measure God's infinite grace. Charcoal cannot reflect the same amount of sunlight that the diamond does. Similarly, dark mentalities do not reflect God as do virtuous mentalities. But God does not deprive His unjust child because of his evil ways, but rather gives to His naughty child the same measure of love and opportunity so that he may have a chance to recover his forgotten divine image. The naughty child needs access to the light of God since he lives in self-created darkness. God is worried and anxious for His wicked child, but the evil son can-

---

* "I fled Him, down the nights and down the days;
  I fled Him, down the arches of the years;
  I fled Him, down the labyrinthine ways
  Of my own mind; and in the mist of tears
  I hid from Him, and under running laughter.
  Up vistaed hopes I sped;
  And shot, precipitated,
  Adown Titanic glooms of chasmèd fears,
  From those strong Feet that followed, followed after.
  But with unhurrying chase,
  And unperturbèd pace,
  Deliberate speed, majestic instancy,
  They beat—and a Voice beat
  More instant than the Feet
  'All things betray thee, who betrayest Me....'"
           —from "The Hound of Heaven," by Francis Thompson

Paramahansa Yogananda often quoted from this well-loved poem; a recording of his reading of it is available from Self-Realization Fellowship. (Publisher's Note)

† God Talks With Arjuna: The Bhagavad Gita VI:9.

not utilize his Father's spiritual gifts unless he changes his froward ways. The prodigal son has to redeem himself by penitently making his way back to God; the good son who walks in God's light is already there.

~

"For if ye love them which love you, what reward have ye? Do not even the publicans the same? And if ye salute your brethren only, what do ye more than others? Do not even the publicans so?

"Be ye therefore perfect, even as your Father which is in heaven is perfect" (Matthew 5:46–48).

Parallel reference:

"For if ye love them which love you, what thank have ye? for sinners also love those that love them. And if ye do good to them which do good to you, what thank have ye? for sinners also do even the same. And if ye lend to them of whom ye hope to receive, what thank have ye? for sinners also lend to sinners, to receive as much again....

"Be ye therefore merciful, as your Father also is merciful" (Luke 6:32–34, 36, Sermon on the Plain).

Even the ordinary man returns love for love as a natural response, and salute for salute as a common courtesy. But more is expected of the children of God—to express in every nuance of behavior the soul's qualities of perfection endowed to them by their Perfect Father. As God is kind and helpful to all, even to His evil children, so in order to know and feel what God is, it is expected of His good children that they be merciful and sympathetic like their Father.

Mortals behave like mortals by giving in the same measure what they receive, but they express their innate divinity when from the pure magnanimity of their soul they give love for hate, and goodness for evil. By the silent giving of love to man, and lovingly talking to him through the whispers of his conscience, God is helping man's slow but sure emancipation. The more the self-deluded mortal responds to this freely given grace, the more he demonstrates Christ's command: "Be ye therefore perfect, even as your Father which is in heaven is perfect."

The Lord's Prayer:
Jesus Teaches His Followers
How to Pray

The Sermon on the Mount, Part III

"Enter Into Thy Closet": Practice Techniques for Attaining
Inner Silence of Mental Interiorization

❖

Acquiring the Concentrated Attention and Devotion
That Make Prayer Effective

❖

The Lord's Prayer: A Spiritual Interpretation

❖

Suffering and Penance: A Perverted Notion of Spirituality

❖

The Single Eye, Through Which Man's Body and the Cosmos
Are Seen as Filled With God's Light

"The Lord's Prayer embodies a universal understanding of how the needs of body, mind, and soul may be fulfilled through man's relationship with God."

"*Take heed that ye* do not your alms before men, to be seen of them: otherwise ye have no reward of *your Father which is in heaven.*

"*Therefore when thou doest thine alms, do not sound a trumpet before thee, as the hypocrites do in the synagogues and in the streets, that they may have glory of men. Verily I say unto you, they have their reward.*

"*But when thou doest alms, let not thy left hand know what thy right hand doeth: that thine alms may be in secret: and thy Father which seeth in secret Himself shall reward thee openly.*

"*And when thou prayest, thou shalt not be as the hypocrites are: for they love to pray standing in the synagogues and in the corners of the streets, that they may be seen of men. Verily I say unto you, they have their reward.*

"*But thou, when thou prayest, enter into thy closet, and when thou hast shut thy door, pray to thy Father which is in secret; and thy Father which seeth in secret shall reward thee openly.*

"*But when ye pray, use not vain repetitions, as the heathen do: for they think that they shall be heard for their much speaking. Be not ye therefore like unto them: for your Father knoweth what things ye have need of, before ye ask Him.*

"*After this manner therefore pray ye:*

"*Our Father which art in heaven, hallowed be Thy name. Thy kingdom come, Thy will be done in earth, as it is in heaven.*

"*Give us this day our daily bread. And forgive us our debts, as we forgive our debtors.*

"*And lead us not into temptation, but deliver us from evil: For Thine is the kingdom, and the power, and the glory, for ever. Amen.*

"*For if ye forgive men their trespasses, your heavenly Father will also forgive you: But if ye forgive not men their trespasses, neither will your Father forgive your trespasses.*

"*Moreover when ye fast, be not, as the hypocrites, of a sad countenance: for they disfigure their faces, that they may ap-*

pear unto men to fast. Verily I say unto you, they have their reward.

"But thou, when thou fastest, anoint thine head, and wash thy face; that thou appear not unto men to fast, but unto thy Father which is in secret: and thy Father, which seeth in secret, shall reward thee openly.

"Lay not up for yourselves treasures upon earth, where moth and rust doth corrupt, and where thieves break through and steal: But lay up for yourselves treasures in heaven, where neither moth nor rust doth corrupt, and where thieves do not break through nor steal: For where your treasure is, there will your heart be also.

"The light of the body is the eye: if therefore thine eye be single, thy whole body shall be full of light.

"But if thine eye be evil, thy whole body shall be full of darkness. If therefore the light that is in thee be darkness, how great is that darkness!"

—*Matthew 6:1–23*

The Lord's Prayer: Jesus Teaches His Followers How to Pray

The Sermon on the Mount, Part III

❧

"Take heed that ye do not your alms before men, to be seen of them: otherwise ye have no reward of your Father which is in heaven.

"Therefore when thou doest thine alms, do not sound a trumpet before thee, as the hypocrites do in the synagogues and in the streets, that they may have glory of men. Verily I say unto you, they have their reward.

"But when thou doest alms, let not thy left hand know what thy right hand doeth: that thine alms may be in secret: and thy Father which seeth in secret Himself shall reward thee openly" *(Matthew 6:1–4).*

Even as God humbly shrouds Himself in utmost secrecy and anonymity while bestowing ceaseless munificence—sunlight, air, food, life, love, wisdom—so should His children learn from Him the gracious art of selfless, silent giving. Human beings, bound in body-confining egotism, need to expand their "I-me-mine" consciousness into divinely inclusive love for all—it is a primary lesson to be mastered in this school of mortal life.

Almsgiving is a material expression of the extension of one's feelings to others. But giving should be with a pure motive. In this series of verses, Jesus decries the use of charity—or any other religious act—to bolster one's pride. The Bhagavad Gita instructs man in the art of giving by differentiating those gifts that expand the consciousness of the giver from those that merely feed his sense of self-importance.* It is the spiritually

Charity that expands one's consciousness versus that which feeds one's pride

degenerate individual, bereft of humility, who performs religious rites pretentiously in order to impress others. Hypocrites, who feign religiosity to gain honor and human attention, form the bad habit of using spiritual rites to acquire mundane praise instead of divine recognition. Praise received for the performance of praiseworthy deeds should serve as an impetus to perform greater spiritual deeds. Love of praise as an end in itself deviates the mind from God and centers it on the self-satisfaction of the ego.

Ostentatious givers of alms delude themselves with a false sense of superiority arising from ignorance, the conceit of personal ownership. But no human being owns anything. For the brief interlude in which man is a guest on God's earth, he is allowed the use of things—more or less according to the measure of his past karma, but always dependent upon Heaven's bounty. His own freewill-initiated actions, in this and past incarnations, earn his place in life; yet he could not get anything had God not anticipated man's needs and structured creation accordingly. It is by using the God-given gifts of intelligence, creative ability, and will power that man achieves his self-proclaimed wonders. In the final reckoning, all things are gifts of God, even though He makes man work for them that through the struggle of right endeavor he might hasten his evolution.

The evolution of even the most materially dynamic man is inconsiderable so long as he remains hidebound in self-centered concerns. Selfishness is a clamshell existence, tightly enclosing a soul in one body

---

* "The good or sattvic gift is one made for the sake of righteousness, without expectation of anything in return, and is bestowed in proper time and place on a deserving person. That gift is deemed rajasic [fostering worldly consciousness] which is offered with reluctance or in the thought of receiving a return or of gaining merit. A tamasic [degrading] gift is one bestowed at a wrong time and place, on an unworthy person, contemptuously or without goodwill" (*God Talks With Arjuna: The Bhagavad Gita* XVII:20–22).

and one personality. Some people are so limited to their physical form and its sensations that they are little, if ever, aware of the feelings of others. Unselfishness and generosity make a person cognizant of the souls of others and the tremors of their consciousness. To serve others —by identifying their necessities as one's own and providing whatever one can in the way of material needs, psychological succor, or spiritual enlightenment—is wondrously expansive, uniting one's consciousness with the lives and hearts of others.

During the bestowal of gifts, the devotee should feel that he is serving the Indwelling Lord in the body-temples of others. Whatever God-gifted bounty he has received should be shared with God's needy children as an offering to the Father of all. Thus is God served as the extended Self in the selves of others.

It is the silent giver, presenting gifts to his brethren in secret, who receives the heavenly reward of feeling God's omnipresence in other hearts. Anyone who gives alms or words of wisdom to another and brags about it destroys the sanctity of his charitable act. To boast, "I gave..." or "I helped to redeem..." is not sanctity but sanctimony. A person who broadcasts his "piety" may receive material reward by gaining some indiscriminate admirers and some followers, but glorifying oneself will keep away wise friends and the all-wise God. The Heavenly Law does not give the reward of revelation to braggarts; the prating ego hears nothing of truth.

The braggadocio, with his desire for publicity, reaps some beneficial results from the good done to others by his bestowal of gifts; he is at least better than the miser. But the prideful giver remains limited in egotism, satisfied with its evanescent reward of the insincere applause of man. He thus denies himself the reward of Heaven, blessed expansion of self in the hearts of others. But gifts given in quiet humility joyously unite the heart of the giver with the hearts of the benefited, and with the omnipresence of the spirit of God.

The Lord is the supreme philanthropist, Bestower of all things on His mortal children—and to His good children He has even given Himself. Those liberated sons of God, one with the Infinite Giver, likewise offer whatever is available to make Him happy in the bodies of others. Everyone should embrace that example, sharing each day their kindness and at least something of their earthly good fortune with worthy, needy persons; and, on a broader scale, supporting the needs of worthy, divine causes, which benefit many.

Most people are willing to offer advice and sympathy; but when it comes to sharing their hard-earned money with others, they feel compelled to be "tightwads" with closed purse strings, believing only in family happiness—"us four and no more." A person of means who is worried about losing a hundred thousand dollars on the stock market may not stop to think of the many people who possess little or nothing at all. Some people never hesitate when it comes to buying a yacht or a new luxury car, but are miserly when it comes to giving to a legitimate needy cause. There they economize and feel righteous when donating a token sum.

As one lovingly, naturally, joyously, remorselessly gives the best gifts to himself, without seeking publicity, so should one give to others without ostentation. Giving freely and quietly to others, one finds the divine law of supply secretly working in his life: When attachment to God is more than to God-given possessions, automatically a channel is opened through which His abundance flows.

When giving to others with the right hand, or the right spirit, let not the left hand, or egotism, be conscious of it. Those who think of themselves as generous givers are not equal to those who give so openhandedly that they are hardly aware of their benevolence. If one has concern for others as he regards himself, the Spirit will reward him with the perception of Omnipresence—God's all-pervasive love and bliss sent openly into his heart.

~

> "And when thou prayest, thou shalt not be as the hypocrites are: for they love to pray standing in the synagogues and in the corners of the streets, that they may be seen of men. Verily I say unto you, they have their reward.
>
> "But thou, when thou prayest, enter into thy closet, and when thou hast shut thy door, pray to thy Father which is in secret; and thy Father which seeth in secret shall reward thee openly" (Matthew 6:5-6).

True prayer is an expression of the soul, an urge from the soul. It is a hunger for God that arises from within, expressing itself to Him ardently, silently. Vocalized prayers are wonderful only if the attention is on God, and if the words are a call to God out of the abundance of the soul's desire for Him. But if an invocation becomes merely a part of an ecclesiastical ceremony, performed mechanically—con-

Prayer that touches the heart of God

centration on the form of religion rather than its spirit—God does not much like that kind of prayer. One who prays loudly is liable to become hypocritical if his attention is focused on the practiced intonation of his voice falling on his auditory nerves—words spoken for effect, to attract and impress others. This is the tendency of many otherwise sincere spiritual people—to show off their love for God, rather than strive to touch the heart of God alone. Unless there is simultaneously an increasing intensity of zeal and love for God, praying aloud to be heard by others can be spiritually corruptive. No matter how wonderful it is within, spiritual realization loses something of its intensity when it is expressed outwardly.

When a devotee's prayer comes from deep within, so that the words are tipsy with love for God, then others around him consciously enjoy his contact with God and drink of the contagion of love for Him. But if the devotee is not very strong, those in his presence may steal away that love from him. They begin to praise him who seems so devout; and if he feels flattered that because he has inspired others, therefore he must be great, then he becomes weakened—his love is stolen from his heart, and pride takes its place.

Sometimes, no loud or even whispered words can I pray; for when deep feeling for God possesses you, you cannot utter any words. That love is secret within, an inner communion, silently giving its oblations into the Spirit. Like a sacred fire, that love burns the darkness from around the soul, and in that light one beholds the mightiness of Spirit.

Jesus admonished those who pray not as a sincere heart-offering to God, but as a public display of devotion to manufacture a reputation of holiness. They are hypocrites, for their egotistical motives are not synchronized with their pious actions. It is reprehensibly sinful to use God and prayer to secure the devotion of people under false pretenses. By inspiring simple, trusting people in the thought of goodness, such individuals may reap a reward of earthly power and the devotion of blind followers; but God, who sees the heart and never responds to false prayers, keeps Himself remote. Hypocrites who make a show of spirituality to garner temporary prestige are foolish, for they forfeit the eternal, all-redeeming blessing of God won by a true heart's private romance with the Divine.

Most houses of worship practice demonstrative prayer. It provides some inspiration and devotion; but insofar as it keeps the attention externalized, it is, in itself, ineffective in producing actual God-communion. Public or congregational prayer should be supplemented by deep, secret, soul-loving prayers in the quietness of seclusion.

As the parlor awakens social consciousness, the library fosters reading consciousness, and the bedroom suggests sleeping, so everyone should have a room or a screened-off corner, or a well-ventilated closet, used exclusively for the purpose of silent meditation. Traditional homes in India always have such a shrine for daily worship. A sanctuary in one's home is very effective in fostering spirituality, because unlike a place of public worship it becomes personalized, and also because it is accessible for spontaneous devotional expressions throughout the day. The children in India are not forced to frequent the shrine, but are inspired to do so by the parents' example. In these home temples, families learn to find the soul peace hidden behind the veil of silence. Here they introspect, and in prayer and meditation recharge themselves with the inner power of the soul, and in divine communion attune themselves to discriminative wisdom by which they may govern their lives according to the dictates of conscience and right judgment. Interiorized prayer brings forth the realization that peace and service to divine ideals are the goal of life, without which no amount of material acquisition can assure happiness.

Modern religion needs to rediscover and emphasize the individual search for God, the method of divine romanticism in seclusion. Important to this practice is knowledge of scientific spiritual techniques for actually communing with the Lord in the inner silence of mental interiorization. Usually, even persons who physically sequester themselves for prayer and devotions are so hounded by their restless thoughts that they fail to enter the soul sanctuary of concentrated communion, where real worship becomes possible.

"Enter into thy closet": Practice techniques for attaining inner silence of mental interiorization

Those who pray without knowing the scientific art of interiorization often complain that God does not respond to their entreaties. Such devotees may be compared to the person who retires to his study and requests a friend to call him on the telephone, but then keeps the line ceaselessly occupied with other incoming and outgoing calls. Try as he may to respond, the friend is continually thwarted by a "busy" signal!

The mind of the ordinary person is uncontrollably active with incoming messages from the five senses of sight, hearing, smell, taste, and touch; and with directing outgoing messages to the motor nerves in response. True concentration, whether on prayer or God or anything else, is impossible so long as the mind is thus outwardly distracted. Most persons experience surcease from the sensory tumult only in the state of sleep, when the mind automatically stills the flow of the life energy that activates the sensory and motor nerves. The science of yoga meditation teaches techniques of controlling the life energy consciously, enabling one to disconnect the mind at will from the intrusion of the senses. This produces not an unconscious oblivion, but a blissful transference of identity from the false reality of the body and sensory world to the truth of one's being: the supernal soul, made in God's image. In that interiorized silence wherein the soul's divine sonship is no longer squandered in the prodigal outward consciousness, true prayer and divine communion with the Heavenly Father are not only possible, but dynamically effective.*

God hears all prayers; but His children do not always hear His response. In every age, those who succeeded in their efforts to commune with God were those who found entry into the inner silence.† That is

---

* The science of *Kriya Yoga* includes these techniques, which are taught in the *Self-Realization Fellowship Lessons.*

† Lord Krishna referred to the requisite interiorization of consciousness in these words: "When the yogi, like a tortoise withdrawing its limbs, can fully retire his senses from the objects of perception, his wisdom manifests steadiness" (*God Talks With Arjuna: The Bhagavad Gita* II:58).

Those who find the way to actual perception of the Divine know its universality—whether they call it yoga or use some other terminology. The illumined Saint Teresa of Avila used the identical metaphor to teach her nuns the way to enter the "interior castle" to commune with Christ: "When we are seeking God within ourselves (where He is found more effectively and more profitably than in the creatures, to quote Saint Augustine, who after having sought Him in many places, found Him within) it is a great help if God grants us this favour [conscious interiorization]. Do not suppose that the understanding can attain to Him, merely by trying to think of Him as within the soul, or the imagination, by picturing Him as there. This is a good habit and an excellent kind of meditation, for it is founded upon a truth—namely, that God is within us. But it is not the kind of prayer that I have in mind....What I am describing is quite different. These people are sometimes in the castle before they have begun to think about God at all.... They become markedly conscious that they are gradually retiring within themselves; anyone who experiences this will discover what I mean: I cannot explain it better. I think I have read that they are like a hedgehog or a tortoise withdrawing into itself; and whoever wrote that must have understood it well."—Saint Teresa of Avila, *The Interior Castle,* trans. E. Allison Peers (Garden City, New York: Image Books, 1961), Chapter 3.

why Jesus taught: "But thou, when thou prayest, enter into thy closet (withdraw the mind into the silence within), and when thou hast shut thy door (the door of the senses), pray to thy Father which is in secret (in the inner transcendent divine consciousness); and thy Father which seeth in secret shall reward thee openly (shall bless you with the ever new Bliss of His Being)."

In all of man's pursuits he is seeking the fulfillment of love and joy. The motive behind the evil ways of even the utmost sinner is that he expects to attain therefrom something that will lead to happiness. God is that happiness. But the urge to seek Him is drowned in the urge to indulge in sense pleasures. When that sensory compulsion disappears, then the craving for God automatically appears.

Sensations pouring in through the sensory nerves keep the mind filled with myriad noisy thoughts, so that the whole attention is toward the senses. But God's voice is silence. Only when restless thoughts cease can one hear the voice of God communicating through the silence of intuition. That is God's means of expression. In the devotee's silence God's silence ceases. For the devotee whose consciousness is inwardly united with God, an audible response from Him is unnecessary—intuitive thoughts and true visions constitute God's voice. These are not the result of the stimuli of the senses, but the combination of the devotee's silence and God's voice of silence.

God has been with His children on earth all the time, talking to them; but His voice of silence has been drowned out by the noisiness of their thoughts: "Thou didst love me always, but I heard Thee not." He has always been near; it is the consciousness of man that has been wandering away from Him.

In spite of man's indifference and pursuit of sense pleasures, still God's love abides, and always will. To know this, one must withdraw one's thoughts from sensations and be silent within. Silencing the thoughts means tuning them in to God. That is when true prayer begins.

When the devotee is in tune with God, he will hear the divine Voice: "I have loved thee through the ages; I love thee now; and I shall love thee until thou comest Home. Whether thou knowest it or not, I shall always love thee."

He speaks to us in silence, telling us to come Home.

$\sim$

"But when ye pray, use not vain repetitions, as the heathen do: for they think that they shall be heard for their much speaking. Be not ye therefore like unto them: for your Father knoweth what things ye have need of, before ye ask Him" (Matthew 6:7–8).

To repeat "My Lord, I love You," countless times, sincerely, feelingly, so that with each utterance the devotee's love and understanding of God grow deeper, is a sure method of contacting God through prayer. "Vain repetition" signifies praying aloud or mentally,

Acquiring the concentrated attention and devotion that make prayer effective

"God, God, God," while the background of the mind is occupied with something else—a vacation trip, a sumptuous dinner, how to make more money. This is using the name of God fruitlessly,* for He will never manifest Himself so long as He knows that other desires have precedence in the devotee's heart and mind.

"Heathen" refers to persons who are engrossed in their bodies, their consciousness externalized in communion with the "gods" of sensory distractions rather than internalized in devoted worship of God "in spirit and in truth." Their prayers are a mere physical practice of parroting or chanting the name of God with no iota of real thought about Him. Such prayers are little better than the automatic vocalizations of a parrot taught to repeat the name of God. If a young man carried a recording that played "I love you" and used it to express his love to his beloved, she would certainly say, "My dear friend, if you are trying to convince me of your love, it is in vain; you don't mean it at all!"

An aunt of mine used beads to aid her constant repetition of prayers; no matter where she went, her fingers worked those beads. But after forty years of this practice, one day she confided to me that the Lord had never responded. Though her "prayers" may have numbered in the millions, her attention was everywhere but on God. I was glad for the opportunity to initiate her in *Kriya Yoga* and the true art of divine communion.

The Lord who knows each devotee's innermost thoughts cannot be deceived by mechanically parroted prayers, no matter how polished their composition. It is better to offer a single, simple prayer from the heart—deeply, understandingly, and intensely—than a profusion of prayers consisting of thoughtless repetitions. Formulaic invocations with the mind absent creates hypocrisy, gratifying the ego with a sense

---

* "Thou shalt not take the name of the Lord thy God in vain" (Exodus 20:7).

496

of piety that in fact has little spiritualizing effect. To expect divine intervention "on demand" in answer to unthinking, unfeeling prayers is unscientific superstition.

Though God does not respond in the manner hoped for when offered such talkative, blindly repeated prayers, yet He cannot remain aloof or deny the true devotee who prays with sincerity, faith, and the determination never to give up. Elsewhere the New Testament conveys Jesus' teaching to "pray without ceasing."* Unceasing prayer involves repetition—not vain or mechanical, but spiritualized with ever-increasing, thoughtful, heartfelt devotion. That devotee is sure to find divine contact who continuously keeps the mind on God, intensifying the thoughts of his prayer, unceasingly reining in the attention regardless of how many times it wanders away. The Gita similarly teaches: "On Me fix thy mind, be thou My devotee, with ceaseless worship bow reverently before Me. Having thus united thyself to Me as thy Highest Goal, thou shalt be Mine own."†

Prayers sent out soulfully once or many times, mentally or orally, bring a demonstrative response from God. To utter "God" with devotion, and increase the concentration and devotion with each repetition of His name, is to plunge the mind deeper and deeper in the ocean of His presence until one reaches fathomless depths of divine peace and ecstatic joy, the sure proof that one's prayers have touched God.

Prayer with devotion is a wonderful means of opening oneself to the freely flowing blessings of God, a necessary link of man's life to the Infinite Source of all benefaction. But it takes a long time for prayer to be effective when the mind is outwardly roaming. That is why one hour of *Kriya Yoga* meditation can bestow more effect than twenty-four hours of ordinary prayer. Those who practice the technique of *Kriya* deeply for even a little while, and sit long in meditation in the resultant stillness, find that the force of their prayer is doubled, trebled, a hundred times more powerful. If one enters the inner temple of silence and worships before the altar of God with prayer and invocation of His presence, He comes quickly. When the consciousness is withdrawn from the sensory surface of the body and its surroundings and centralized in the cerebrospinal shrines of soul perception, that is the most effective time to pray.

---

* I Thessalonians 5:17.

† *God Talks With Arjuna: The Bhagavad Gita* IX:34.

Jesus described as "vain" the supplications of body-bound "heathens" with their disunion from God's indwelling Essence. Ordinary man has so entangled himself in the finite law of cause and effect that it is not simple to break his consequential karmic bonds. God does not arbitrarily contravene the orderly workings of His universe. Man must work to harmonize his life and actions with God's laws, and thereby initiate favorable new effects to neutralize past errors. However, the devotee who by pure love, faith, and divine knowing born of meditation reestablishes his consciousness of oneness with the Infinite Father transcends finitude and its laws, instantly receiving God's grace, His mitigating unconditional love. To reclaim one's soul status as a child of God is thus the sovereign way to fulfillment of prayers. Approaching the Lord not as a mortal beggar but as a loving divine son, the devotee knows that whatever the Father possesses, that also is his own.

Devotees who love God deeply, knowing He is their loving Father, never feel they have to beg Him for their daily necessities, for He will give to them what is needful without their even having to ask. God does not want His children to approach Him as beggars. Beggary prayers express doubt as to one's divine birthright as an heir to His infinite kingdom. A beggar gets a beggar's share, but a son has the right to a son's share. That is the consciousness in which to approach the Heavenly Father: He is ever ready to provide, if only His children would make themselves able to receive by fully realizing their immortal kinship with Him.

~

> *"After this manner therefore pray ye:*
> *"Our Father which art in heaven, hallowed be Thy name. Thy kingdom come, Thy will be done in earth, as it is in heaven.*
> *"Give us this day our daily bread. And forgive us our debts, as we forgive our debtors.*
> *"And lead us not into temptation, but deliver us from evil: For Thine is the kingdom, and the power, and the glory, for ever. Amen" (Matthew 6:9–13).*

Parallel reference:

> *And it came to pass, that, as he was praying in a certain place, when he ceased, one of his disciples said unto him, "Lord, teach*

us to pray, as John also taught his disciples."

And he said unto them, "When ye pray, say,

*"Our Father which art in heaven, hallowed be Thy name.
Thy kingdom come. Thy will be done, as in heaven, so in earth.*

*"Give us day by day our daily bread. And forgive us our sins;
for we also forgive every one that is indebted to us.*

"And lead us not into temptation; but deliver us from evil"
(Luke 11:1–4). *

Jesus came on earth to remind man that the Lord is the Heavenly Father of all, and to show His children the way back to Him. The way of effective prayer, he taught, is to banish diffidence and speak to God with joyous expectancy as to a devoted father or mother. For every human being, the Lord feels a love unconditional and eternal, surpassing even the sweetest human parental solicitude. This is implicit in Jesus' instruction to pray to "Our Father"—a Father who cares personally for each of His children.

Jesus gave a model prayer for both worldly people and spiritual people: The highly devout individual wants nothing from God but His love, and spiritual development; the materially minded person seeks God's help for all-round success and well-being in earthly life, including a modicum of spiritual achievement. "The Lord's Prayer" embodies a universal understanding of how the needs of body, mind, and soul may be fulfilled through man's relationship with God. The simple eloquence and spiritual depth of Jesus' words inspired in me the following interpretive perception:†

The Lord's Prayer: a spiritual interpretation

"When you pray, address God from your heart with the full attention of your mind; and in the manner I have shown to you, say:

"Our Father Cosmic Consciousness, Fountain of the consciousness of all, present in the vibrationless region of Heavenly Bliss and hidden in the depths of Heavenly Intuition, may Thy Name be glori-

---

* The Lord's Prayer as given in the Gospel According to St. Luke (and its parallel in Matthew) is commented on in Discourse 54. Paramahansa Yogananda there offers a further insightful commentary in which he plumbs the esoteric depths of this universal prayer for the realization of the soul's relationship with God. *(Publisher's Note)*

† Paramahansaji wrote, additionally, a variant rendering for his book of answered prayers and inspirations, *Whispers from Eternity,* published by Self-Realization Fellowship.

fied on earth. May Thy hallowed Name, the cosmic vibrations emanating from Thee in earthly manifestations, be consecrated for cultivating Thy consciousness and not material consciousness. Let Thine absolute royal consciousness come forth and appear in human consciousness. May Thy spiritual kingdom come and be substituted for the material kingdom of earthly consciousness. Let Thy wisdom-guided will be the guiding force of deluded human beings on earth, even as Thy will is followed by angels and liberated souls in the heavenly astral realms.

"Give us our daily bread, the physical, mental, and spiritual manna that nourishes our bodies, minds, and souls: food, health, and prosperity for the body; efficiency and power for the mind; love, wisdom, and bliss for the soul.

"Forgive, Thou, our faults, O Lord, and teach us likewise to forgive the faults of others. As we forgive a brother who is indebted to us and forget his obligation, forgive us, Thy children, for our sins of not remembering our indebtedness to Thee—that we owe our health, our life, our soul, everything to Thee.

"Lead us not into temptation, even by way of testing our limited spiritual power. And leave us not in the pit of temptation wherein we fell through the misuse of Thy given reason. But if it is Thy will to test us when we are stronger, then, Father, make Thyself more tempting than temptation. Help us that by our own effort, through Thy spiritual force within us, we may be free from all misery-making, physical, mental, and spiritual evils.

"Teach us to behold the earth as ruled not by material forces, but by Thy Kingdom's power and glory which abide forever. We bow to Thee through our contact with Thee as the Holy Cosmic Vibration of *Aum,* Amen."

In Jesus' words, "Hallowed be Thy name," is the recognition that though this earth came from God's divine vibration, it is yet to be consecrated by His name, or pure holy vibrations, because of the wickedness of the people who reject that sacred presence among them. As God's bliss and wisdom are the only kingly powers that exist in the transcendence of Cosmic Consciousness, so in the words "Thy kingdom come" Jesus prays that those absolute powers of God may manifest in human consciousness, which is erstwhile steeped in delusion. Jesus also prays, "Thy will be done in earth, as it is in heaven": As the angels and divine souls in the heavenly realms are in tune with the wisdom of God's will, so also might earthly people willingly be guided by God's wisdom, rather than by the rationale of their delusion-encapsulated ego.

"Give us this day our daily bread": It might seem trifling to include a plea for bread when praying to the Almighty; yet in those days there was much poverty among the masses; they often had little to eat. Jesus knew he could not very well expect the people to hearken to a spiritual message that did not address their mundane concerns as well —a person with a hungry stomach has little incentive to strive for spiritual realization.

In any case, Jesus was referring to an all-inclusive sustenance for body, mind, and soul, not merely physical bread. He had said, "Man shall not live by bread alone, but by every word that proceedeth out of the mouth of God."* Man cannot live solely by material means. Every moment of his existence he is dependent on the life force flowing from God's creative Cosmic Vibration, His "word," and on the inherent wisdom and bliss of the omnipresent Christ Consciousness that supports his own consciousness. The more attuned one is to this divine vitality and wisdom, the more he is able to draw unto himself the fulfillment of his physical, emotional, mental, and spiritual needs. So man's first prayer should be for the spiritual bread of contact with God's Bliss, Wisdom, and Love, which alone feeds the soul; then efficiency for the mind in order to accomplish one's worthwhile goals; and lastly, material prosperity adequate to meet one's physical needs.

"Lead us not into temptation, but deliver us from evil": In these words, Jesus almost seems to make God responsible when man finds himself in the throes of temptation, having been purposively led into that predicament by his Heavenly Father. In a way it is true. God is the maker of delusion, so in that sense He is a tempter. But it would be wrong to think that God, with His wisdom, would lead mortals, who are poorly equipped with wisdom, into temptation just to test their response. That would not be fair. God is not a friendly prankster tempting man with a world of relentless enticements that may harm him. Good and evil are the light and shadows that create the contrasts necessary to produce God's cosmic motion picture. The white purity of goodness demonstrates its

A prayer for self-control, mastery of temptation, and overcoming delusion

---

* See Discourse 8.

virtue on the dark background of evil. God's children are tested by this duality of *maya*-delusion to develop the wisdom to distinguish between good and evil, and the will to overcome all tests and thereby be free from Satan's cat-and-mouse game of temptation.

The Lord could easily countermand the influence of satanic temptation, but to do so would negate man's free will and make him a puppet. The intrigue of God's drama of creation is to see if perchance His children will choose Him over the allurements of His cosmic show — not from any compulsion on His part, but solely of their own freely chosen response to His love. He wants His mortal reflections to enjoy the grand drama in this cosmic movie house with an unchanging remembrance of their innate divinity. To prove that divine nature is to pass successfully through trials and temptations that teach wayward man to bring out and manifest in every condition of his life the hidden God-identity of his soul. The Lord knows that His children will ultimately assert the power of Spirit within them to vanquish the power of temptation.

So when Jesus prayed "lead us not into temptation," he intended no indictment of the Lord as having any part in man's miseries. Rather, he expressed man's need to supplicate God for help in overcoming life's unavoidable delusions: "Leave us not in the pit of temptation wherein we fell through the misuse of Thy given reason." Man falls headlong into the abyss of evil when he does not use properly the faculties of God-given free choice. Satan snares the unwary with cosmic delusion, subverting reason and will with ignorance. That is how he so successfully obstructs God. Thus Jesus prayed that the Heavenly Father deliver every soul from the evil enthrallment of cosmic delusion.

The Bible says, "God made man in His own image";* but when one looks in the mirror he sees anything but God! Every night man becomes a god when he dumps his body consciousness in sleep; and every day he chooses to be a devil. What can the Father do? When man puts on mortal garb he should remember his divinity and not in any way ascribe mortal weakness to his soul. That is what the scriptures of India say. In the morning upon awakening, impress on the consciousness: "I am just coming out of Spirit. I am Spirit now; and I shall be Spirit evermore." But when one has a headache, he quickly

---

* Genesis 1:27.

forgets his sublimity and feels very mortal indeed. If man remembers at all times his true Self, he becomes free again. Simple but true. By continuous affirmation, associating with the wise, studying the scriptures, and above all by meditation in which the conscious dream of mortal limitation is completely dissolved in the superconscious perception of the soul, the persevering devotee will know he is a god. Divine communion restores man to his original Self. He realizes complete satisfaction in all goodness in his soul, and that to crave any tempting offerings of the senses would, to his heartbreak, eclipse the incomparable divine joy.

Self-control is the master of temptation. It does not speak highly of the human race when man acts like less evolved creatures. Even beasts behave more wisely, being guided by instinct. Only in the company of human beings do they learn to live unnaturally. There is no evil in them, because their actions have no discriminative freewill motivations. Man is spiritually bound to make choices between right and wrong—beneficial or harmful. Unless he develops self-control, he will act unwisely when tempted, even against his better judgment.

Many learn self-control only after getting burned in the enticing flames of harmful indulgences. It is better to avoid painful lessons by observation of consequences inflicted on others, by obedience to spiritual teachings, and by wise discrimination. Without discriminative self-control the refined beauty of virtue is overshadowed by the gaudy tinsel of the senses.

He who says temptation is not charming lies. By temptation man is blithely led into trouble because of the hypnotic allure of evil. No one would indulge in vices if they did not give pleasure. The drug addict, the alcoholic, the sex addict, the indiscriminate overeater, had a good time indulging their habit, but at the cost of slowly killing their happiness and themselves.

Temptation is the undue influence on the senses of something alluring that one thinks is harmless, but isn't. It is the desire to have a moment's pleasure, disregarding its future ill effects.

As counterfeit coins have no value but may be hard to differentiate from the genuine article, likewise it takes discrimination to know the difference between pleasure derived from attractive but worthless vices and real happiness, which is the valuable worth of virtue. Sincere prayer to God for help in the right use of reason and will weakens the confounding effect of delusion and prevents wrong choices between good and evil. The saints define as evil anything, no matter how nice it seems, that is subversive to God-contact and the expression of the soul's qualities, which produce true happiness.

The joy of God-communion, once tasted, is more tempting than all mundane temptations. If man tempts himself with that true pleasure, the temptation of the senses will wane. I have always prayed, "Lord, why don't You reveal Yourself in the very beginning and then there will be no suffering from seeking pleasure in harmful actions?" Because God is the supremely charming experience, it is only when man does not have that comparison that evil temptation has power. Would anyone eat rotten cheese if he had good cheese? Would anyone prefer suffering to joy? No. Man yields to temptation because of the delusion that it will bring happiness. Criminals think they will get happiness from money they steal; but they find that crime does not pay. Neither does succumbing to the temptations of the senses.

Sense perceptions are natural and necessary to man's conscious physical existence; the relentless predators of his happiness and well-being are the sensuous actions that arise from perceptions and that are ungoverned by discrimination. The senses of hearing, smell, and sight can usually be overtaxed with little ill effect. Few people are foolish enough to strain their eyes to the point of blindness. No one smells flowers or perfumes long enough to cause death. Unless the volume of sound is excessive, people do not make themselves deaf by continuously listening to good music. However, the sense of sight may be baited by attractions that result in wrong judgments and misery. The sense of hearing may mislead the weak-willed by receptivity to dulcet tones of flattery, or harsh vibrations that arouse anger. The sense of smell can stand much abuse without retaliation, but it is a powerful means of stimulating memory and habit impulses and sexual arousal.

Dreadful consequences follow when the sense of taste or touch is overtaxed. How easy it is, when catering to the palate, to overeat or to make unhealthful choices in food, which causes disease and hastens death. How easy it is, when enslaved by desires of the flesh, to succumb to physical temptations and indiscretions that bring ill health, satiety, social ostracism, matrimonial disaster—all manner of baneful consequences. God created infinite Bliss to attract man back to his true soul-nature; Satan created the sexual pleasure of the flesh, the strongest urge in man, along with self-preservation, to keep him infatuated with his mortal existence.

The misuse of Nature's law of procreation can be overcome, not by hypocritical suppression, but only by moderation in marriage and by self-control and abstinence by the unmarried, and by joyous contact with God in meditation. When the joy of God, felt in meditation with stillness of thoughts and breath, remains continuously in the soul, physical temptation is subdued in a natural way through contrast with this higher consciousness of divine Bliss.

So it is right for the devotee to pray to God, "Do not put before my weak impulses the temptations of Your cosmic *maya*." Delusive sensory temptations are like seeds, and weak mental impulses are their favorite soil. When the seeds of temptation are in a fertile mind, they begin to grow. But if they are dried up by wisdom and the realization of God as the only reality, latent material desires will lose their compelling power.

Man is surrounded by fascinations that lure his interest and cloud his reason. No one is safe from giving in to wrong influences in a weak moment until all desires and habits of the past that are grooved in the brain cells are cauterized. The influence of those habits and impulses is very strong. When man submits to them he renounces his free will and good judgment. He should refuse subjugation.

Until man is free from compulsions, he cannot trust himself. He acts like an automaton, moving to the remote-control influence of his immediate environment and the company he keeps as they arouse his own innate latent tendencies. Of course, a person may become good or bad due to his own free choice, but in most cases his behavior and habits can be ascribed to prenatal causes or hidden postnatal effects of actions.

The Hindu scriptures teach that it is difficult to get away from the effects arising from physical, mental, moral, or spiritual errors made in this life or in past lives. The results of good and bad actions are stored in the superconscious and subconscious minds as seed tendencies, *samskaras*, ready to germinate and grow when the specific suitable opportunity arrives.

That is why man should ask the Maker of cosmic delusion to protect him from temptation: "Lead us not into places and conditions where our karmic impulses coincide with the temptations of the evils of the world. Lead us into the joyous experience of Thy contact." Candlelight becomes lost in the light of the sun; the flicker of sense pleasures disappears in the conflagration of ecstasy. "O Lord, let us not be blinded by the proximity of the light of sense temptation so that we fail to see Thy divine effulgence spread silently over the universe."

Though God allows the relativities of *maya* as necessary to the existence of creation, it is up to man to decide whether to side with the temptations of evil or the better temptation of God's presence. Each person has to fight his personal battles in the war between his reason and sense impulses, to see which will win. To foolishly yield to the forces of temptation is to lose sovereignty over the kingdom of one's life. Saints are sinners who never gave up. They never gave up rejecting the temptations of the world while continuing to tempt themselves with the greater joy of God. "I weighed Thee and temptation and found Thee more tempting than temptation." One must be convinced in his heart and know he loves God more than temptation; then he will find God.

The ordinary person does not see, except in an objective way, the fierce resistance of Satan against the magnetic attraction of goodness and God. The devil has been known to manifest in form to tempt great saints who near liberation, but this conscious force knows it requires no such theatrics to catch the average man or the striving devotee — little subtle temptations usually suffice. The person who is trying to avoid temptation will find it suddenly "coincidental" that persons and opportunities seem to appear out of nowhere to conspire to take him from his determined path of self-control.

For every goodness and virtue, Satan has an equal storehouse of counteracting agents. God created forgiveness; Satan created revenge. God created calmness, fearlessness, unselfishness, spirit of brotherhood, peace, love, understanding, wisdom, and happiness, and for each of these Satan created its psychological opposite of restlessness, fear, greed, individual and material selfishness, war, hate; anger, revenge, and jealousy instead of understanding; ignorance in place of wisdom; and sorrow to destroy happiness. Conscience, the voice of God, always beckons man to do right. Temptation, the voice of Satan, coaxes him to do wrong.

The existence of this host of evils is the reason Jesus prayed: "Thy kingdom come," that man might use his independence to act rightly and thereby substitute the kingdom of God for the anarchy of evil. By perfected living, man helps to make God's heaven from Satan's earthly imperfections, effecting God's patterns to nullify the evil designs of Satan. The power of Satan is transient; the reign of God—His kingdom and power and glory—is forever.

~

"For if ye forgive men their trespasses, your heavenly Father will also forgive you: But if ye forgive not men their trespasses, neither will your Father forgive your trespasses" (Matthew 6:14–15). *

The Divine Father patiently forgives all the bad actors in His cosmic drama; and ultimately, through their better behavior, He receives them into His blessedness. When man expresses his higher Self and likewise forgives others their wrong actions against him, he cleanses his heart of harmful caustic feelings—without which no healing from hurt can take place. Even when possessed with power to retaliate, man should refrain from vindictive feelings, notwithstanding an obligation to resist or noncooperate with evil in a proper way and time. To do what one can to prevent or halt evil is necessary, but it should not be motivated by revenge. It is the function of the Divine Law to mete out just punishment of evildoers and enemies.†

When one receives praise and kindness from someone, it is easy for him to smile and respond warmly; it is when one is hurt that his spiritual character is tested. That is the time to practice forgiveness. It will not do to say, "Oh, no, I don't mind your slapping me," but inside seethe with vengeful thoughts. It is what one feels that matters; while one should not be a doormat, it is inner control that counts. To know that God is in all, and to forgive the deluded wrongdoers through whom God is trying, albeit as yet unsuccessfully, to express Himself, is to be a master.

"One should forgive, under any injury," says the *Mahabharata.* "It hath been said that the continuation of the species is due to man's being forgiving. Forgiveness is holiness; by forgiveness the universe is held together. Forgiveness is the might of the mighty; forgiveness is sacrifice; forgiveness is quiet of mind. Forgiveness and gentleness are the qualities of the Self-possessed. They represent eternal virtue."

~

---

* See also parallel verses in Mark 11:25–26 in Discourse 35.

† "Dearly beloved, avenge not yourselves...for it is written, 'Vengeance is Mine; I will repay,' saith the Lord" (Romans 12:19).

"Moreover when ye fast, be not, as the hypocrites, of a sad coun-
tenance: for they disfigure their faces, that they may appear unto
men to fast. Verily I say unto you, they have their reward.

"But thou, when thou fastest, anoint thine head, and wash
thy face; that thou appear not unto men to fast, but unto thy Fa-
ther which is in secret: and thy Father, which seeth in secret, shall
reward thee openly" (Matthew 6:16–18).

Fasting has been practiced by devotees of every religion since ancient times as an effective means of approaching God, a form of
austerity to help bring the willful body and mind under control to receive the spirit of God.*

Jesus, however, pointed out the hypocrisy of those who fast or
practice other austerities not to draw closer to God, but to impress oth-

ers by the privations they are capable of enduring.

Suffering and pen-
ance: a perverted no-
tion of spirituality

Imagining suffering to be a prerequisite of transcendence, and self-inflicted penance to be evidence of
exaltation, they attempt to hasten their ascent—if
not in actuality, at least in the eyes of their public.

Such perverted notions of spirituality are one reason many persons hesitate to embrace a serious search for God, believing it will require a life of "sackcloth and ashes." Nothing could be further from
the truth! To know God is to know Joy itself. True devotees are never
gloomy or morose; they know that to be cheerful is to please God. The
greater one's happiness, the greater his divine attunement. "Their
thoughts fully on Me, their beings surrendered to Me, enlightening
one another, proclaiming Me always, My devotees are contented and
joyful."†

My gurudeva, Swami Sri Yukteswar, did not hesitate to chastise
disciples who appeared in the hermitage "sad of countenance," as
though attending a funeral ceremony. "To seek the Lord, men need not
'disfigure their faces,'" he would say, quoting Lord Jesus. "Remember
that finding God will mean the funeral of all sorrows."

≈

---

* See Discourse 8.

† *God Talks With Arjuna: The Bhagavad Gita* x:9.

"Lay not up for yourselves treasures upon earth, where moth and rust doth corrupt, and where thieves break through and steal: But lay up for yourselves treasures in heaven, where neither moth nor rust doth corrupt, and where thieves do not break through nor steal: For where your treasure is, there will your heart be also" (Matthew 6:19–21). *

Foolish is man when he focuses all his efforts and attention on accumulating perishable material prosperity or physical health, devoting no time to win the Eternal Treasure. Money, prestige, sense pleasures, material luxuries—these will be wrested from him, either by the corruptions of nature and ill fortunes of karma, or by the unstoppable thief of death. And when, passing the portals of the grave, he loses all that he has most valued, what grief will possess him when he will not even be able to remain in the glory of heaven, but will be drawn back to this mortal plane to begin again his pursuit of unfinished desires.

"Lay up for yourselves treasure in heaven"

What little time man has on this earth, he spends thinking and planning to get the things he wants; when one desire is satisfied he begins to chase after something else. Like a dog hitched to a cart with a sausage hanging out in front on a pole, he pulls an ever-increasingly burdensome life as a slave to his cravings, always thinking, "I will be happy when I get this thing, or that thing." When will that day come? Be happy now, this minute! As soon as the thought of God comes in the mind, grasp it with devotion, strengthen and enliven it by making all other desires subservient. Jesus renounced everything because he had that immortal prosperity in God which no earthly condition could corrupt nor thief could steal.

It is perfecting oneself in spirituality that brings real happiness here and in the life hereafter. What else did Jesus have in mind when he exhorted people to lay up for themselves treasures in heaven by being virtuous on earth?

One might gain ownership of the whole world in this life, but if he has not God, he has not happiness or peace or anything of real value. When he leaves the shores of the earth, he will have nothing he can carry into the life hereafter. But one who by utmost effort in med-

---

* See commentary on Saint Luke's version of these verses (Luke 12:32–34), Discourse 56.

itation has found God, even if he has sacrificed all things material and is poor in the eyes of the world, is rich in eternal treasure. When his brief stay on earth is over, he will depart with an imperishable God-treasure of unending bliss, which will be his to enjoy unto eternity.

~

"The light of the body is the eye: if therefore thine eye be single, thy whole body shall be full of light.

"But if thine eye be evil, thy whole body shall be full of dark-ness. If therefore the light that is in thee be darkness, how great is that darkness!" (Matthew 6:22–23).

Parallel reference:

"No man, when he hath lighted a candle, putteth it in a secret place, neither under a bushel, but on a candlestick, that they which come in may see the light.*

"The light of the body is the eye: therefore when thine eye is single, thy whole body also is full of light; but when thine eye is evil, thy body also is full of darkness. Take heed therefore, that the light which is in thee be not darkness.

"If thy whole body therefore be full of light, having no part dark, the whole shall be full of light, as when the bright shining of a candle doth give thee light" (Luke 11:33–36).

The God-revealing light in the body is the single eye in the middle of the forehead, seen in deep meditation—the doorway into the presence of God. When the devotee can perceive through this spiritual eye, he beholds his whole body as well as his cosmic body filled with God's light emanating from cosmic vibration.

By fixing the vision of the two eyes at the point between the eye-brows in the interiorized concentration of meditation, one can focus the positive-negative optical energies of the right and left eyes and unite their currents in the single eye of divine light.† The ignorant, ma-terial man knows nothing of this light. But anyone who has practiced

---

* This verse parallels Matthew 5:15 and is commented on in Discourse 26.

† See Discourses 3, 6, and 10.

even a little meditation may occasionally see it. When the devotee is further advanced, he sees this light at will, with closed or open eyes, in the daylight or in darkness. The highly developed devotee can behold this light as long as he so desires; and when his consciousness can penetrate into that light, he enters the highest states of transcendent realization.

The single eye, through which man's body and the cosmos are seen as filled with God's light

But when one's gaze and mind are turned away from God and concentrated on evil motives and material actions, his life is filled with the darkness of delusion's ignorance, spiritual indifference, and misery-making habits. The inner cosmic light and wisdom remain hidden. "How great is that darkness" of the material man that he knows little or not at all of divine reality, accepting with glee or resentment whatever offerings of delusion come his way. To live in such dank ignorance is no valid life for the incarnate soul consciousness.

The spiritualized man—his body and mind inwardly illumined with astral light and wisdom, the shadows of physical and mental darkness gone, and the whole cosmos seen as filled with God's light, wisdom, and joy—he in whom the light of Self-realization is fully manifest, receives indescribable joy and the unending guidance of divine wisdom.

"Seek Ye First the Kingdom of God, and His Righteousness"

The Sermon on the Mount, Part IV

Jesus' Cardinal Message to Individuals and Nations of the World

❖

Is Renunciation of Possessions Necessary
in Order to Find God's Kingdom?

❖

Applying Christ's Doctrine to the Conditions of Modern Life

❖

Spiritual Attitude Toward the Material Needs of the Body

❖

Right Way of Seeking God's Kingdom: Yoga Science of Meditation

❖

Christ's Way to Happiness:
Seeking God Within and Keeping Material Life Simple

❖

Putting God First in One's Daily Life

"Seek God first; for to find Him is to open the door to all His gifts of health, power, financial sufficiency, wisdom. God is no miser....Man has but to learn how to receive."

"**No man can serve two masters:** *for either he will hate the one, and love the other; or else he will hold to the one, and despise the other. Ye cannot serve God and mammon.*

"Therefore I say unto you, take no thought for your life, what ye shall eat, or what ye shall drink; nor yet for your body, what ye shall put on. Is not the life more than meat, and the body than raiment?

"Behold the fowls of the air: for they sow not, neither do they reap, nor gather into barns; yet your heavenly Father feedeth them. Are ye not much better than they?

"Which of you by taking thought can add one cubit unto his stature? And why take ye thought for raiment? Consider the lilies of the field, how they grow; they toil not, neither do they spin: And yet I say unto you, that even Solomon in all his glory was not arrayed like one of these.

"Wherefore, if God so clothe the grass of the field, which today is, and tomorrow is cast into the oven, shall he not much more clothe you, O ye of little faith?

"Therefore take no thought, saying, 'What shall we eat?' or, 'What shall we drink?' or, 'Wherewithal shall we be clothed?' (For after all these things do the Gentiles seek:) for your heavenly Father knoweth that ye have need of all these things.* But seek ye first the kingdom of God, and His righteousness; and all these things shall be added unto you.

"Take therefore no thought for the morrow: for the morrow shall take thought for the things of itself. Sufficient unto the day is the evil thereof."

—Matthew 6:24–34†

---

* "Gentiles": in this context, heathens, pagans, worldly persons. Cf. Luke 12:30: "For all these things do the nations of the world seek after: and your Father knoweth that ye have need of these things."

† These words of Jesus are also recorded in the Gospel According to St. Luke 12:22–31 and are commented on in that context in Discourse 56.

"Seek Ye First the Kingdom of God, and His Righteousness"

The Sermon on the Mount, Part IV

No one can serve two contradictory ideals with equal devotion. A full-fledged matter- and pleasure-worshiper will forget God; one who is engrossed in the bliss of God will lose the craving for material gratifications. Reality and delusion — God and mammon* — are the two contradictory ideals. Those who "hold to the one" — who are attached to the wealth of material offerings — "will despise the other" — will abhor the requisites for seeking God, fearing deprival from loss of their best-loved pleasures.

Jesus in no wise told people to neglect acquiring material necessities; he spoke against giving to the body the soul's entire attention, as though that were the aggregate of the purpose of existence. He averred that the Giver of Life deserves man's principal thought, not the indifference that gives precedence to material needs and desires in utter oblivion of God. It is He who is the Creator and Owner of all commodities of nature from which man derives food, clothing, money, property, health, and vitality; it is He who gives all these things to man by which he can maintain his life on earth.

---

* *Mammon* is an Aramaic word meaning "wealth."

Seeking the kingdom of God first is the cardinal message of Jesus to individuals and nations of the world, because it is the surest way to

Jesus' cardinal message to individuals and nations of the world

lasting individual, social, and national happiness. Perishable material possessions do not contain the immortality and everlasting bliss of the kingdom of God, but His imperishable kingdom contains in it all the goodness of the world. To possess God is to own the universe. If the ear is pulled, the head comes with it. When by devotion one pulls God into his life, then automatically eternal prosperity of immortality, wisdom, and ever new blessings are added unto him.

In the Bhagavad Gita, the Lord similarly proclaims: "To men who meditate on Me as their Very Own, ever united to Me by incessant worship, I supply their deficiencies and make permanent their gains."*

Man should not seek possessions first, and then God, for he is apt to lose God. The mind is like blotting paper; when it soaks up impure material desires, it becomes saturated and cannot absorb the pure Divine Essence. The foolish materialist becomes wholly accustomed to working for pleasurable perishables; owing to the enslaving habit of his mind, he is unable to concentrate any attention on seeking God. The wise do not waste their effort in acquiring what they will perforce have to give up at the time of death. Those who are successful in attaining the kingdom of God, and in manifesting His righteousness, will have ever new bliss and the realization of their immortality, not only in this life but throughout eternity; and in addition, the fulfillment of all material needs. No sensible businessman could turn down such an offer!

In the words: "Take no thought for your life," Jesus did not excuse reckless disregard for the principles of healthful, successful living. He elaborated that it takes eternal life, the Word of God, to sustain human life and not the physical nourishment of "meat" alone; and that the body was made to express soul wisdom, and not merely to be adorned with clothing and comfort. Then why concentrate all one's energy in worrying about satisfying material wants, when life itself comes from God, is sustained by Him, and begs to express His innate glory?

Jesus stirs spiritual awakening with simple appealing analogies: "Behold the fowls of the air...." Their lives are not complicated by un-

---

* *God Talks With Arjuna: The Bhagavad Gita* IX:22.

necessary desires or yearnings; though they have no storehouse nor riches in the bank, God feeds them from nature's bounty. A child of God—who is more important than the sparrows and ravens—will also be looked after by the Heavenly Father, provided that child develops absolute faith in God as the Life behind his life, and the Divine Source of all bounty.

Man's arrogance of self-sufficiency belies his desire to be more powerful than his mortal limitations. By a mere thought or wish he cannot "add one cubit unto his stature." God's laws can be made to work for the benefit of man, but those laws cannot be transcended except by God Himself and devotees who are one with Him.

Man is directly sustained by God and the abundance of nature, and indirectly by his earning capacity and physical efforts. Not by all human care can man maintain himself without the help from God, He who is the Maker of Life and the Creator of sunlight, grain, water, and air, which support human life. But because man does his share to acquire the use of God-given things, he soon forgets the direct Divine Hand in human existence. Man cannot *make* grain, though he wields God's laws to propagate it; nor can he make the power of digestion to assimilate food, nor the life force that transforms the grain chemicals into his cellular tissues. Yet man is so solicitous of the wants of his body that he ornaments it and seeks to grant its every whim, seldom if ever considering that without the inherent Divinity, all he embellishes is a clod of earth.

"Consider the lilies of the field," how they are attired by God with ethereal fragrance and beauty, even though they make no conscious effort to spin their petaled clothing, nor feverishly toil to maintain and enhance themselves. "Even Solomon in all his glory," with his earthly powers and elegant royal robes, could not look so graceful and divine as the naive lilies clothed by God. The Creator, who has power over all things big and small, will certainly clothe with the power of divine magnetism to attract at will what is needed when man, made in His image, corrects his deficiency of faith in the immortal powers within him as a direct descendant of God. It is delusion that causes man to doubt that God will remember to care for him.

"O ye of little faith," see how God clothes the grasses with green attire for their short span of life, so soon to be withered by the fiery sun or burnt as fuel in ovens. All things of this earth are evanescent and meant to serve well their purpose. Man, clothed by God in a

517

unique psychophysical form, is too important to waste his life in nothing more than temporal concerns and be cast into the fires of ignorance and misery.

As for meeting the conditions imperative to life, "your heavenly Father knoweth that ye have need of all these things." He expects the God-seeking man to perform useful dutiful actions, but not as the materialist who has his eye and energies focused on selfish gain and sensuous pleasure. To "seek ye first the kingdom of God, and His righteousness" is to concentrate on the Eternal Life, the source of all lives, and to express the glory of that immortality in all interactions with the world.

Great scientists and literary savants also take care of the necessities of life, but their minds remain mostly engrossed in the subjects in which they have specialized. Similarly, as Jesus himself demonstrated, the divine man maintains his body as the temporary home of the immortal soul and fulfills all of his God-given responsibilities, but his consciousness is firmly centered in God. The ordinary man thinks only of food, possessions, and pleasure—that is all he pursues. Under the smoke screen of materiality he has totally hidden God from his perception, cutting himself off from life's invigorating Source, depleting his happiness and draining dry the truly satisfying divine joys that inhere in his soul. To acquire everything needful with the mind resting principally on God is the sure way to happiness. To go after inflated "necessities" in a state of God-forgetfulness will certainly lead to misery.

No matter how much the worldly man acquires, he never fully enjoys his situation; for he is never satisfied, is always looking for something more, or is afraid of losing what he has. The Western nations, at the height of industrial civilization, gorged with materiality, have not succeeded in producing a society free of depression and discontentment. Houses, money, automobiles may be necessary to modern existence; but if man does not also give some time to God and meditation, the formula of his life will be missing the catalyst necessary to produce true happiness. Unless one seeks the kingdom of God and establishes within himself its righteousness, peace, joy, and wisdom, the contrasts of pleasure and sorrow in his life will foment inner discontentment, unbalance, and physical and spiritual deficiencies.

India's civilization, in contrast to the West, became wholly absorbed in religion and God-seeking to the neglect of its material life;

and so in spite of its spirituality it suffered from poverty, famine, sickness, and centuries of foreign domination. The old doctrine of complete renunciation is extreme; if the masses let go their duties, then communities, cities, and whole societies would be dens of disease and poverty.

Is renunciation of possessions necessary in order to find God's kingdom?

Ideal renunciation does not require the total nonpossession of a wandering *sadhu,* or retreat into a mountain cave. It means giving up small delusive pleasures for the highest joys of the Spirit. By renouncing the world and its temptations and living in remote seclusion, one still might not find God, because incarnations of desires, trailing down the ages, will still be with the recluse. Few there are who can remain continuously in communion with God. When one is not meditating, it is better to keep the mind busy with wholesome work than to be idle.

It is possible with practice to hold the major portion of one's mind on God while one's hands and external attention are performing serviceful material duties and enjoying those many material things that express the goodness of God in creation, and with which He intended His children be entertained. Certainly for the masses, that is a better way of living, the happy medium of a yogi's life—to live in the world for God, rather than becoming a monk (the high, consecrate path for which only the minority are well-suited), or at the other extreme engaging in the abandon of a sybarite.*

In the context of these verses, Jesus was especially addressing his disciples to exhort them to set for mankind an example of living for God and not for the body and its worldly kingdom. This lofty standard of renunciation, complete nonattachment with faith in God as the Sole Provider, is the ideal that throughout the ages many devotees have embraced as a natural response to their single-hearted spiritual yearning. Though Jesus counseled his disciples in a literal sense of renunciation, he meant the spirit of his words to apply to the lives of all believers: Seek ye God first. God's emissaries necessarily speak in absolutes, knowing the penchant of human nature to pick and choose and adapt to one's own purposes and receptivity from the tomes of scriptural guidance. If there be men who cannot aspire to the summital applications of truth, then at least, as the prophets intend, those

---

* Jesus' ideals of inner and outer renunciation are discussed in Discourse 49.

absolutes serve as a proper guide for man's lesser adaptations. There is nothing to keep any person from the highest benefit of Christ's words, regardless of one's station or vocation in life: deeply seeking God, caring for the bodily instrumentality of the soul that it might be used to express God's righteousness and contribute some good to others, knowing all the while that it is God who is the beneficent Divine Giver.

The Bhagavad Gita teaches: "Actionlessness [oneness with transcendent Spirit] is not attained simply by avoiding actions. By forsaking work no one reaches perfection." "He is the true renunciant and also the true yogi who performs dutiful and spiritual actions without desiring their fruits....He who has not renounced selfish motive cannot be a yogi."* A man of God works diligently, performing dutiful actions to please God and to share the fruits of those actions with God's children; his efforts are not motivated by selfish desires or any influence of delusive evil.

The souls of human beings are sent on earth by God to work for Him in worthy ways that serve His cosmic drama. Hence, those who instead work for their ego and its desires become entangled in delusion's desire-filled net, entrapped for incarnations. The wise man fulfills his mortal obligations as a divine duty, because God has given him a body to look after with its related responsibilities. Such a man is free. The man who neglects his body and its environmental needs to the detriment of well-being sins against God's laws of creation; and the person who solicitously serves his body to please his vanity and mortal desires also divorces himself from God.

Though the floral beauties of nature's garden are elegantly clothed by God and have not to toil for a wage to purchase the sunshine, air,

Applying Christ's doctrine to the conditions of modern life

and soil chemicals they require, in the modern civilization man has to pay for his food, clothing, shelter—even the water he drinks. Though God has provided the basic essentials of life, man could not avail himself of these without intelligent thought and striving to acquire and adapt them for his purposes. In the Orient, when Jesus taught, people lived much more simply and so had fewer basic requirements to worry about; a spiritual man of renunciation could be fed and clothed without much effort through charity or

---

* *God Talks With Arjuna: The Bhagavad Gita* III:4, VI:1–2.

family help. Nowadays, conditions of life are changed; civilization is more individualistic and selfish; the businessman and the renunciant both have to struggle for their existence and give considerable thought to their maintenance.

Is it then impossible to apply the above Christ doctrine in modern life? No. In all eras, those who think that prosperity depends only upon man's effort and craftiness are mightily deluded. History shows that in every clime and age, the smartest, wealthiest individuals, with all their thought and effort and wit to acquire material success, have from time to time been made to wallow in the mire of poverty through the naive decree of fate. Wars, depression, failed ventures, political anarchy, natural disasters, can instantly alter the fortune of the fortunate. But the man who keeps his mind principally concentrated upon the Almighty Giver of all things will never be left destitute (unless it is a temporary test brought about by his personal karma) even in the worst of conditions that might come along.

It is all right to struggle to gain financial and material advantages, provided God is remembered as the Giver and that accrued good fortune becomes a means of rendering service and upliftment to others as well as to oneself. Those who have wealth by inheritance and need not labor for sustenance could well use that free time in cultivating their spiritual life—through meditation to achieve God-communion, good works that aid individuals and mankind as a whole, and in general elevating one's own consciousness to express God's righteousness. Alas, the rich who give only a token genuflection to God do not realize their spiritual poverty. Those who luxuriate in wantonness foolishly spend their unique opportunity in the most insecure happiness. It is a poor investment of the favorable fruits of good karma that those who have the necessities of life, as do the majority of persons in materially advanced Western nations, think first of breakfast, lunch, and dinner, and how much money to make in order to better clothe and house themselves and have a good time—relegating God to an occasional Sunday morning church service. To be always intent on the gifts of God, rather than on the Giver, is extremely wrong.

Spiritual attitude toward the material needs of the body

If one's whole life is based on the comfort of the flesh, coddling the little body, how can one know divine happiness? Why give so much attention to something that has to be cast away at a moment's notice? To be busy day and night with the body is a bad habit. It is a delusion by which one becomes more and more attached to his physical existence.

The worst habit of man is that he thinks of himself as a mortal body; that thought, being uppermost in his mind, keeps him away from God more than anything else. Many saints think of the body as merely a useful animal under their care—Saint Francis of Assisi used to refer to his body as Brother Donkey. It must be cared for, but not so much worried about. When a disciple in the ashram would bother too much about the body, my guru Sri Yukteswarji would say cryptically, "Throw the dog a bone." If the body eats a little, all right. If it sleeps a little, all right. The more one fusses about it, the more demands it will make. One should do his duties to the body and forget it. Remember, we are sons of God; we are not the body.

Weeks and months at a time the saints are hardly conscious of their bodies, but conscious of God always. In the nectared sustenance of ecstasy with God is life and health. Jesus had not all the hygienic conveniences of modern life. He kept his consciousness free from such imperatives.

Without being senselessly rash, one should learn to depend more on mind. It does not mean fanaticism, but more exercise of that marvelous God-given power. Mind power makes it possible for God to provide directly one's needs. Mind power and faith go hand in hand. One who possesses a firm conviction that God's power can heal can more readily avail himself of mental and spiritual healing. A person who feels dependent on the care of a doctor should have faith in the power of God working through medical science. Persons who believe only in material methods of health and sustenance find after a while that their will is paralyzed. But those who depend more on the mind discover that therein lies the infinite power of God. That power is pure and strong and limitless and instant.

As long as the mind accepts the sensation of hunger and other physiological functions, one cannot say that all is delusion and ignore physical needs. Is it not better then to eat the things that are good for the body instead of those that are harmful? If one could live solely on cosmic energy, then it would not matter. But as long as the body changes according to its nourishment, why shouldn't man save God the trouble of healing him by obeying His laws that lessen the chance of his getting sick? There is no sin in that. A person simply should not be so conscious of food and comforts that he cannot be God-conscious.

Until one is no longer bound by any of the effects of the law of duality, *maya*, matter does exist as more than an illusion in the mind. That is the practicality of yoga. It provides the means for actually realizing that the body and mind are a dream of God, and that He alone is caring and providing for this manifestation of His consciousness.

Ordinary man is obsessed with the limitations of his physical body and its afflictions of disease, suffering, pain, heartaches. But on the inner side of the body are the subtle centers of spiritual consciousness, with their untold powers and realization of the divine Self. When in meditation the mind follows the stream of inner consciousness, the devotee enters the supernal "kingdom of God" that exists behind physical manifestations. That is why Jesus said, "Behold, the kingdom of God is within you."* In devotional interiorization, the meditator experiences true communion with God in the actual perception of His presence as light, wisdom, love, bliss.

The constant desire for health and prosperity, the fulfillment of which is the focus of so many modern religious movements, is the way to slavery. First seek God, and then find health and prosperity through Him. When a soul, instead of seeking material things and becoming a mortal beggar who receives only a beggar's pittance, seeks first to return to the kingdom of God-consciousness and once again becomes a true child of God, he receives, without asking, the heavenly share of his divine birthright.

Of course, just blind belief in the kingdom of God will not suffice; nor will halfhearted prayers or a few good works. Neither will a lifetime of seeking the divine kingdom without receiving it bring the bounty of blessings promised by Jesus. The right way of seeking is through the God-given yoga science of entering the kingdom of God within, the technique of God-contact in which the sages of India have specialized. When ecstatic communion with God is an established fact, then the devotee will know that with the acquirement of the Celestial Kingdom, all things are within his reach. Jesus had that ultimate realization and could say: "I and my Father are One." That is how he could feed five thousand people with two fishes and five loaves of bread, and could re-create his body after death—achievements that no scientist has yet duplicated. Jesus had

Right way of seeking God's kingdom: yoga science of meditation

---

* Luke 17:21 (see Discourse 61).

God first, so he had power over life and death, destiny, and all conditions.

Man's mortal efforts are bound by the laws of cause and effect; he cannot get more than he deserves. All his life he may make the effort to become a millionaire; but he may never get there, because the attainment of earthly goals is fraught with limitations and obstructions —karmic and environmental. But for the devotee who approaches God first, limitations are surmounted. By the method of mortal begging from Providence, no human being can ever fulfill all his proliferous desires; but by first realizing his oneness with God, man can receive everything he needs, with a sense of complete satisfaction. He will not even need to pray, to supplicate or beg, for as a Self-realized son of God he will have everything his Father has. So is it not best to know by visualization and affirmation, and above all by realization born of divine contact in meditation, that one is already perfect in health and wisdom and abundance, rather than try to succeed by begging for these necessities of life?

The wonder of man's relationship with his Heavenly Father is that he does not even have to acquire God. He has Him already. As soon as the veil of *maya* is pulled away, he knows instantly that God is with him.

Each mortal being has in his heart a terrible hunger for happiness, love, peace, joy, the mastery of life, immortality. When one sees the

Christ's way to happiness: seeking God within and keeping material life simple

will-o'-the-wisp nature of these longings in delusive matter, and the troubles in life encountered in pursuing them, how can anyone desire anything but God? That desire by which one is first brought to the spiritual path is the desire that should be fulfilled. The Self in every being is of God, and so long as man does not express that inner divinity, becoming like Him in whose image he is made, his existence is going to be fraught with unending pains and disappointments. Why not remember the counsel of Jesus to seek the kingdom of supreme happiness first? One will then no longer have to suffer rude surprises throughout life. The masters of India similarly say: "To become one with the Supreme Being is to have destroyed all the roots of suffering." That is real freedom.

As long as God gives man life, he has an obligation to give some of that time to God. The hour will come when one's time is up; let it not have to be viewed with sadness at having been wasted. Be with

God; claim that real perennial happiness. Waste not golden spiritual opportunities on the fool's gold of material glitter. Where is the time for God if it is spent in constant fussing to satisfy the body's wants for what I have termed "unnecessary necessities"? Rather simplify life and use that saved time in meditation for God-communion and real progress in attaining life's necessary necessities of peace and happiness.

Real Christ-living should consist in seeking the comfort of meditation first and in also keeping material life simple while attending to one's dutiful activities. A complex material life is only pleasing to the eyes and the status consciousness of the ego, but few realize "what price material comforts." Economic slavery, nervousness, business worries, unfair competition, dissensions, lack of freedom, disease, misery, old age, and death are the harvest of a materially compacted existence. So much is missed when there is no time left for the appreciation of beauty, Nature, and God's many expressions in life.

If anybody remonstrates to me that material happiness is better than godly happiness, or that attention given to God can come later, it is revolting to me. Such rationalization is of delusion. One needs to get his mind settled in knowing God as the highest priority, and to master his life accordingly. When he is able through meditation and communion with God to carry a portable heaven within, he will know how to guide his life correctly. Once he has a mind that does not waver from God, whatever he does will be all right, not before. Jesus knew that when one is committed to the obligations of a material life, God flies out the back door of that person's consciousness. Thus his counsel to first strengthen one's spiritual consciousness so that no engagement in the world can take the mind away from God.

The spiritual path may be difficult until the devotee reaches the final goal; but so is the way hewed by the material man. In fact, the latter is much more difficult. Unless one has God-realization, he is still in delusion, in between two factors. On one side, love of the material pleasures of one's life, and on the other side, love of God. Love of life is annexed to miseries and death. In youth, one does not realize this, being wholly engaged in the abandon of discovering new experiences. But as the aging process of the bodily machine begins to exert a toll, the eyes begin to grow dim, the voice does not register resonant vibrations, the joints begin to creak, and the corrosive effects of disease require constant repair; one then says, "Well, life isn't the free ride I thought it was."

Relatively speaking, there is very little happiness in this world, only snatches of transient pleasure for the most part. I do not mean to paint a dark picture, but to urge those who want more from life to make themselves so spiritually strong within that it will serve as a divine bulwark against assaults of sorrow and suffering.

As long as the mind wanders haphazardly between spiritual incentives and worldly temptations, that course will be futile in producing spiritual happiness. Those who want the world, and place their faith in things that do not last, are like puppets, dancing on strings of their impulses and karma, any time to be taken away by death. Divine happiness is easier to get for it does not depend on life's fickle doles; and it is everlasting. No comparison with any rich man will be able to make the spiritually wealthy feel poor; for they know they are the richest of the rich in the kingdom of God and His righteousness within.

A master is one who understands in what lies his highest interest; he lives the words of Christ that we came on earth not for this material life, but for God. Delusive offerings are only the test of God, a learning experience to bring out the divinity of the soul. Man is not meant to remain in delusion, mesmerized by its chiaroscuro into thinking it is impractical to seek God, or that there is no time to do so because of the urgent impositions of other pursuits. Suppose God says, "I won't beat in your heart; I have more important things to do!" Where would man be then? Why waste time, when in a moment's notice one will be dragged out of the body? While others sleep, be awake in God-communion in meditation; and work for Him in the daytime, performing all duties with the thought of Him. If the desire is there, one can make time to spend with God.

The body and mind are the soul's precious instruments; they should be kept well and strong to aid one's efforts to find God. But it should be remembered all the while that there is a superior joy hidden behind the sensory experiences of the body. The awakening man should use his life to realize this truth. It is the guiding principle that has produced saints in every religion.

Man did not come into this world of himself, by himself, or for himself; that is why when he works for his own material desires and selfish ends they will always lead him to disappointment. One person wants a luxury home, and then gets sick and cannot enjoy it. Another, weary of nervous stress, seeks the quiet and solitude of a desert residence, and then gets lonely there, nagged by desires that only city life can grant. It is best to give all one's desires to God; and as Jesus adjured, "Seek ye God first...." Be content with what God brings, and be busy every minute doing good and becoming good.

This is the solution for every truly fulfilled existence, not only for spiritually minded people; because God alone, and "His righteousness," is the sole Source of all tantalizing glimmers of real happiness. It is the foundation of the many commandments given by Jesus: "Ye who are wise, ye who are thinkers, seek God first; for to find Him is to open the door to all His gifts of health, power, financial sufficiency, wisdom. God is no miser willfully withholding His everythingness from His children. Man has but to learn how to receive."

It pleases God when His children seek Him. He is hurt when they run away from Him to play with earth's baubles, like spoiled children forgetful of the Giver. The virtuous child conscientiously seeks out the Giver to offer Him a loving, appreciative heart. No matter the difficulties, the devotee persists sincerely, alive to the fact that he must know God, and must hear from Him—without throttling his own discriminative reason—the purpose of life. When that constancy characterizes the devotee's consciousness, then God will reveal Himself; but not until then.

God is suffering in so many souls because of their disunion from Him. Though every mortal will have salvation—no one will be lost—one person may be near liberation while others will yet inflict on themselves countless more incarnations. For whosoever wishes it delayed, it will be delayed; for those who wish to be redeemed, there is no obstacle that cannot be overcome. Desires have to be sublimated by proving to oneself that the supreme happiness is God. The devotee must absolutely convince himself of this. To take the long way to God by seeking satisfaction of desires first is a foolish way of thinking. But the devotee who meditates deeply every day, plunging his consciousness in devotion and yearning for God, who spends time with God at night if his day is too busy, who puts his whole heart and soul into seeking God, will surely find Him.

During the busy-ness of the day, the true God-seeker spiritualizes all actions with the thought of Him. He learns to keep the mind most of the time at the Christ center, the *Kutastha* center of the yogi, and finds the Infinite Christ pouring over his consciousness wave after wave of quiet heavenly joy. "He who watcheth Me always, him do

Putting God first in one's daily life

527

I watch. He never loses sight of Me, nor do I lose sight of him. He looks at Me through the niches of space, and I behold him through the pores of the sky."* When the devotee puts his mind on God, he will see that out of the invisible, out of the unseen skies, a perceptible Presence will speak to him. It is possible to talk to God. His voice can be heard in words, as well as through intuitive feeling, if the devotee loves Him deeply enough and refuses to give up. The desire for His response must be with all one's heart.

Whenever there is trouble or unhappiness, the highest recourse is to think of God steadily; just as the needle of a compass points northward, no matter which way the compass is turned, so must the mind be on God no matter what conditions prevail from moment to moment. There is a God of love and compassion who steals silently into the consciousness, seen only through the ever increasing light of devotion. Have faith in Him; He is ever present. None of the wonders of creation could happen without His omnipresent intelligence. This divine intelligence is the evidence, the trademark, of God—in the tree, in the flower, in the skies, in the moon, in the routine of the seasons, in one's life-supporting bodily system. How can one observe the workings of the intelligent universe and doubt the existence of God?

But no one can find God without continuous love for Him in the heart. To feel that love for God, one must practice it. It is unproductive to analyze and magnify one's defects and troubles. It is enough just to tell God, "Lord, You are the Divine Healer of all maladies; I give myself into Your charge. You are not only my doctor, but my compassionate mother, my wise father, my Creator-God. You cannot forsake me because You made me Your child. Naughty or good, I am Your loving child. Be with me." There is nothing greater than the love of God. If a devotee has found that, his work in the school of life is finished. Until then, precious time should not be wasted. Meditate daily, deeply; and work for God, performing all duties as offerings to Him.

Never give up. To the testimony of Lord Jesus, I humbly add my own: In all my life, I have never found God not to satisfy my needs or to grant my wishes. He sometimes makes me think He will not respond, but suddenly I find there is fulfillment—even more than I

---

* "He who perceives Me everywhere and beholds everything in Me never loses sight of Me, nor do I ever lose sight of him" (*God Talks With Arjuna: The Bhagavad Gita* VI:30).

could have hoped for. This is not to say that God gives what we pray for if we just sit idly and wait for Him to manifest for us whatever we have requested of Him. He expects us to do our part; He makes us work—sometimes with great difficulty—to create the right conditions and opportunities for fulfillment. Then through Divine Grace, His answer to our legitimate prayers comes to pass. It isn't that I want "things" from God, but just to know He is with me. I have said to Him: "I do not ask for things from You, but when I see what You give to me, knowing my heart and my needs, I rejoice in that gift because of Your own hand behind the giving of it."

I used to ask God for things for the work He has given me to do, but I see I don't need to ask now. I have merely to think and His hand is there. I only ask for His grace: "Give Yourself to me." In the beginning, the devotee will find it is then that God becomes silent. That is the hardest prayer for God to satisfy: "If I give Myself, I have nothing left." When God gives Himself to the devotee, He has given everything—His ever-existing, ever-conscious, ever-new Bliss, Love, Wisdom—oneness with Spirit in which the mystery of life is no more. Vanished is the duality of the multiplicity in the Indivisible Unity in the devotee's awakening from the Cosmic Dream. With the realization that all things are of God—all things are His dreaming consciousness—comes the consummate fulfillment of the words of Jesus that having Him, whatsoever shall be needful for one's role in the cosmic drama "shall be added unto you."

That state of oneness with God is granted by Him only when He is convinced the devotee does not want anything else. As long as there will be a single desire in the heart for other than God, then even though He will be near the devotee, He will not be fully manifest to him. While waiting patiently for there to be room in the devotee's heart for the giving of Himself, He continues lovingly to grant the devotee's simple, legitimate prayers: "Lord, although I have to satisfy a few material desires to get along as a mortal being, still in my heart there is only You. As Your child, O Lord, I have no desire, because I already have You; and as You have everything, so have You bequeathed that divine inheritance to me." When the devotee with that devotion seeks Him and lives righteously, he cannot fail in his God-seeking.

Jesus then summarized: "Take therefore no thought for the morrow: for the morrow shall take thought for the things of itself. Sufficient unto the day is the evil thereof." If the devotee lives with God each day, He who guides the destiny of the world, including the lives of His children, will plan the morrow for the divine seeker according to his acts of today. It is hard to get rid of the evil of material delusion, and thus cease accumulating seeds of desires and attachments for the mercurial promises of tomorrow, but it must be done sometime. Why not now?

DISCOURSE 30

To Build the House of Life Upon the Rock of Wisdom

The Sermon on the Mount, Part V

The Ideal of Being Nonjudgmental Versus One's Duty to Truth

❖

The Spiritual and Psychological Dangers of Gossip

❖

Be Not Inwardly Critical of Others; Practice Healthy Self-Criticism

❖

The Surety of God's Response to Sincere and Persevering Devotees

❖

Spiritual Truth in "The Golden Rule"

❖

A Warning to Gullible Victims of Unqualified Spiritual Teachers

❖

Anchoring One's Life in the Unshakable Security of God-Contact

"Real Christ followers are those who embrace in their own consciousness through meditation and ecstasy the omnipresent cosmic wisdom and bliss of Jesus Christ."

"**Judge not, that ye be not judged.** For with what judgment ye judge, ye shall be judged: and with what measure ye mete, it shall be measured to you again.

"And why beholdest thou the mote that is in thy brother's eye, but considerest not the beam that is in thine own eye? Or how wilt thou say to thy brother, 'Let me pull out the mote out of thine eye'; and, behold, a beam is in thine own eye? Thou hypocrite, first cast out the beam out of thine own eye; and then shalt thou see clearly to cast out the mote out of thy brother's eye.

"Give not that which is holy unto the dogs, neither cast ye your pearls before swine, lest they trample them under their feet, and turn again and rend you.

"Ask, and it shall be given you; seek, and ye shall find; knock, and it shall be opened unto you: For every one that asketh receiveth; and he that seeketh findeth; and to him that knocketh it shall be opened.

"Or what man is there of you, whom if his son ask bread, will he give him a stone? Or if he ask a fish, will he give him a serpent?

"If ye then, being evil, know how to give good gifts unto your children, how much more shall your Father which is in heaven give good things to them that ask Him?

"Therefore all things whatsoever ye would that men should do to you, do ye even so to them: for this is the law and the prophets.

"Enter ye in at the strait gate: for wide is the gate, and broad is the way, that leadeth to destruction, and many there be which go in thereat: Because strait is the gate, and narrow is the way, which leadeth unto life, and few there be that find it.

"Beware of false prophets, which come to you in sheep's clothing, but inwardly they are ravening wolves. Ye shall know them by their fruits. Do men gather grapes of thorns, or figs of thistles? Even so every good tree bringeth forth good fruit; but a corrupt tree bringeth forth evil fruit. A good tree cannot bring forth evil fruit, neither can a corrupt tree bring forth good fruit. Every tree that bringeth not forth good fruit is hewn down, and cast into the fire. Wherefore by their fruits ye shall know them.

"Not every one that saith unto me, 'Lord, Lord,' shall enter into the kingdom of heaven; but he that doeth the will of my Father which is in heaven.

"Many will say to me in that day, 'Lord, Lord, have we not prophesied in thy name? and in thy name have cast out devils? and in thy name done many wonderful works?' And then will I profess unto them, 'I never knew you: depart from me, ye that work iniquity.'

"Therefore whosoever heareth these sayings of mine, and doeth them, I will liken him unto a wise man, which built his house upon a rock: And the rain descended, and the floods came, and the winds blew, and beat upon that house; and it fell not: for it was founded upon a rock.

"And every one that heareth these sayings of mine, and doeth them not, shall be likened unto a foolish man, which built his house upon the sand: And the rain descended, and the floods came, and the winds blew, and beat upon that house; and it fell: and great was the fall of it."

And it came to pass, when Jesus had ended these sayings, the people were astonished at his doctrine: For he taught them as one having authority, and not as the scribes. When he was come down from the mountain, great multitudes followed him.

—Matthew 7:1—8:1

To Build the House of Life Upon the Rock of Wisdom

The Sermon on the Mount, Part V, Conclusion (With References From the Sermon on the Plain)

꧁

"Judge not, that ye be not judged. For with what judgment ye judge, ye shall be judged: and with what measure ye mete, it shall be measured to you again.

"And why beholdest thou the mote that is in thy brother's eye, but considerest not the beam that is in thine own eye? Or how wilt thou say to thy brother, 'Let me pull out the mote out of thine eye'; and, behold, a beam is in thine own eye? Thou hypocrite, first cast out the beam out of thine own eye; and then shalt thou see clearly to cast out the mote out of thy brother's eye" (Matthew 7:1–5). *

Parallel reference:

"Judge not, and ye shall not be judged: condemn not, and ye shall not be condemned: forgive, and ye shall be forgiven: Give, and it shall be given unto you; good measure, pressed down, and shaken together, and running over, shall men give into your bosom. For

---

* Verses 3–5 also appear in Luke 6:41–42 in a slightly different context; they are discussed in that context in Discourse 33.

*with the same measure that ye mete withal it shall be measured
to you again" (Luke 6:37–38, Sermon on the Plain).*

Whatever judgment one gives out, the same will he attract. In this passage Jesus enunciates that cause-and-effect mechanism of the karmic law as a sort of moral threat to those who mercilessly expose the faults of others, that their own faults similarly will be brought into the light of harsh scrutiny. In the same spirit in which one judges others, the divine law judges the censurer—motivation, as well as the action itself, is an integral part of the cause-effect equation.

Karmic consequences of being unkindly judgmental

Punishment or reward is not imparted by God either as an act of vengeance or of special favoritism; good and evil results are the reflex outcome of good and evil actions. Since even God does not judge anyone's actions, having delegated that function to the impartial law of karma, by what right do small-minded humans presume to do so? Those who are already judged and automatically sentenced by the karmic law for their misguided actions do not need to be criticized or condemned by anybody else. A person who misuses his free choice and opens himself to evil karmic effects needs sympathy instead of criticism. It pleases God when He beholds a spiritually fortunate individual trying to rescue an unfortunate brother who is being torn by the talons of the effects of bad actions. When He sees a soul helping another soul out of the entanglements of misery-making karma, He extends mercy and all-forgiving blessings by which the sympathetic soul finds himself free from many of the effects of his own direful karma.

By the operation of the same cosmic law, to judge others cruelly is to attract malicious criticism upon oneself. If one peddles the weaknesses of others, the divine law will mysteriously bring about the publicity of his own private faults. One who is tempted to cast aspersion on anyone else should first ask himself: "Am I without error?" Judge ye not others; judge and change yourself first.

Cruel speech and behavior have their origin in cruel thoughts. If one is constantly unkind, it means his mind is a harbor for unkind thoughts. According to the psychological law of habit, the more one gives mental space to mean thoughts the more he will accustom himself to being mean-spirited, exciting and angering others by his unconscionable behavior, and thereby attracting unkindness to himself.

Hence, it is insidiously undesirable to entertain judgmental thoughts about others under any circumstances, lest such inward ugliness become an intransigent habit of meanness. He is foolish who makes himself a chronic critic of others, for he draws to himself nothing but inharmony from all sides. He is truly wise who knows when it is right to speak and when it is better to remain silent.

There is a great deal of misconception about the ideal of being nonjudgmental versus one's duty to speak the truth. Discrimination is

The ideal of being nonjudgmental versus one's duty to truth

necessary. Once when I was lecturing in Trinity Auditorium in Los Angeles, someone came up to me afterward and told me that while I was speaking my assistant had left the book table to go and get a soda. I scolded the gossiper for petty tattling.

On the other hand, suppose someone confides to a friend: "I am going to let loose in John's room a rattlesnake. Now don't you tell him!" Is it not the duty of the friend to inform John of the danger? Those who abide the evil of human snakes become like them.

"Judge not, that ye be not judged" does not mean that if one overlooks the crimes of other people, his own illegal activities will be excused. It is contrary to human law for one to conceal knowledge of the felonies of others, such as robbing or murdering. One who does is held liable for helping criminals to evade punishment.

Likewise, "condemn not, and ye shall not be condemned" is not meant as a promise that obliviousness to others' faults somehow frees one from the karmic sentence of one's own. What Jesus meant is that one who is sympathetic to his fellows will attract the sympathy of others and God. If John tries to help Judas extricate himself from the miseries resulting from past evil actions, by giving him succor and guiding him to the path of righteousness, then according to the law of karma John will attract some advanced soul or souls who would help him escape having to endure the full burden of his own karmic recompense.

"For with what judgment ye judge, ye shall be judged." "What judgment" signifies that judging is of different kinds: kind or cruel, altruistic or self-serving, wise or ill-advised. The law of cause and effect, as articulated by Jesus in these verses, dictates that if one is used to judging others with kindness, and with the selfless motivation of being helpful, he receives in return the same treatment from Truth, which secretly and judiciously governs the eventual outcome of all potentialities. The divine law is thus seemingly kind or cruel in judging a person's faults to the degree that he has been kind or cruel in estimating the discrepancies of others.

Jesus' words do not signify that it is wrong through constructive criticism to warn an innocent person or a slightly immoral individual of the habit-forming dangers of continuing bad actions. It is all right to help a brother avoid a painful tumble into the same ditch of error into which one has fallen. To warn others about the hazards of evil, based on one's own bitter experience, is good if it is done in private with the sole desire of saving them from impending misery. To criticize others is hard enough on the recipients without hurting them — to no good purpose — by exposure, gossip, or malicious taunting. Self-appointed critics and informers have no right to expose others' faults publicly; it is a sin against God who dwells in the temple of the error-stricken as well as in the righteous. The stricken individual should be offered help in the form of wise counsel if such is requested, or in the form of the better example of one who is victorious over himself, or if totally belligerent he should be left alone to find his own spiritual remedy. In any case, one should never tell other people their faults in public — or even in private if they are unreceptive to being helped, unless it is positively one's duty.

In a family, it is the responsibility of the parents to guide and correct the children's behavior, but there is no need to criticize in front of the whole household. Similarly, to those who approach a guru-preceptor for help in improving themselves, the teacher generally speaks candidly but privately; and those in his spiritual family take such correction in the spirit of love and respect in which it is given. Just as a human mother wants her children to be clean and upright in demeanor before others, so is the Divine Mother wanting Her devotees to be spiritually decorous and cleansed of unbecoming traits. If jealousy, touchiness, unkindness, selfishness, are not excised from one's nature, they fester like boils and attract the flies of biting criticism from others. It is better that the psychological operation be done at home, or by the guru in the ashram, with kindness, love, and the highest interest of the "patient" uppermost in mind.

Right way to give correction and help others reform themselves

Even when punishment is justifiable, it should be administered to wrongdoers quietly and in a way that encourages them to try to reform themselves. The court judge punishes criminals for the sake of all society, as well as for miscreants' own good, so that they will not perpetrate further or greater crimes. The purpose of judgment should be curative only and not the revengeful retaliation of anger. To punish wrongdoers just to satisfy wrath, or in order audaciously to hurt them or bring them to ridicule, or for any other wrong purpose, is evil.

Cruel condemnation makes one forget that the sinner is but an error-stricken child of God whose divinity is eclipsed temporarily by ignorance. No one should be called a sinner; nor should anyone think of himself as a sinner. Hate the sin but not the sinner. The critic should treat the errant as he would hope to be treated for his own sinful mistakes. Those who are wrong do not need scornful kicks; they need a firm but loving hand extended to them. It is purposeless to rub the salt of acerbic criticism into others' character wounds. Give unto the erring the healing salve of proper sympathetic advice and appropriate support for any effort toward reformation. Give love to all, the only panacea that can redeem the world; that is the clarion call of Christ.

When one does not condemn others but tries to help them with love, then God's laws, being conscious forces, will treat that caring person likewise. "With the same measure that ye mete, it shall be measured to you again." One who forgives others who have wronged him will attract forgiveness unto himself. One who gives mental and material help to others with a heart overflowing with kindness will find the same coming back to him. This is the law of action applied to human hearts: that whatever one feels for others remains vibrating in the ether, attracting a return, measure for measure, of sympathies and kindnesses. The giver of negligible love receives negligible love; the greathearted giver will find the fullness of love coming back to him, now or in the future—despite any appearances to the contrary. Even if one's noble actions are unrecognized by one's contemporaries, the law of action unerringly insures that they will be recognized by God in this life or the life beyond. Good actions, like good treasures, once stored in the mind may remain unused, but are never lost. The karmic reward is there for the soul to use when the necessity or opportunity arises.

In telling man to forego uncharitable faultfinding, Jesus spoke primarily against sanctimonious judgment of human frailties—in particular, sexual immorality, which often grips otherwise virtuous persons despite their willingness and intention to follow the injunctions of moral rectitude. The physically compelling sex force is the result not only of metaphysical inheritance from fallen Adam and Eve, but also of bad prenatal past-life habits, which tend to influence heredity in forming the postnatal habits of an individual. That is why children are sometimes helplessly born with overstimulated appetites. The degenerating influence of bad company and environment—especially in this permissive era of prurient novels, entertainment, and advertising—is also to blame.

Some normally healthy persons habitually have little or no sex desire due to past-life moral habits; but that does not necessarily make them saints, for they may in other respects have a very wicked, insincere heart. Conversely, some otherwise very good individuals struggle day and night against the sex compulsion due to bad karma of past lives, or to inflammation or irritation of the nerves in the sex region, which may be caused by congestion of toxins in the system. Such sufferers should consult a physician, follow a healthful diet, and practice the technique of life-force control given by a true guru who has mastered every passion within himself and can teach the art of control by sublimation.

· A man who can match his will power against sex compulsion and win, and who can convince the mind that the peace and moral virility of the transmuting power of self-control is greater than sex indulgence, is a heroic conqueror of his lower self. A man who is innocent simply because of lack of exposure to temptation may harbor weakness and succumb when a sudden enticement arouses his dormant sexual instincts. Once stimulated by thought or action, sex is the most enslaving mortal habit and the most difficult sense desire to be controlled, regulated, and subjugated.

Jesus knew that some immoral persons, though mentally desirous of ridding themselves of their carnality, are extremely weak in resisting temptations of the flesh. He helped such persons by wisdom and love, and taught against increasing their troubles by unkind criticism and condemnation.

Persecution, gossip, commands, and taboos cannot remedy moral errors. There would be much less hypocrisy in the world if instead of tongue persecutions, persons were taught from childhood moral remedies, such as methods of self-control, right living, and proper hygiene, before they become the victims of evil through bad company and worldly influences.

Gossiping about the moral weaknesses of others is a wicked spiritual crime. It breeds hypocrisy in social and individual life. How incisively Jesus made his point when he said: "He that is without sin

————•-•-————   among you, let him first cast a stone."* One who

The spiritual and psy- occupies his mind with an unholy interest in the
chological dangers of moral weaknesses of others actually rouses and
gossip stimulates his own sleeping prenatal baser instincts.

Gossip, even among well-meaning friends, never has a favorable effect on the person talked about; it ruffles him, makes him mad, steeped in despair, ashamed, and strengthens his intractable behavior. There is a proverb that says: "The person who has lost one ear goes through the village at the side, showing the villagers his one good ear and hiding the lost ear. But he who has lost both ears goes through the center of the village, because he cannot hide his disfigurement from anyone." Any person whose moral errors are unduly exposed becomes desperate and shameless, like the man who lost both ears; he flaunts a devil-may-care attitude and makes no effort to be better. When persons lose face as a result of gossip about their faults, they also lose the desire and incentive to change. (Of course, in rare cases, just the fear of exposure and publicity keeps some people good.)

A small weakness in a person, once publicized, tends to grow in notoriety—if not in fact—proportionate to the attention given to it. Worldly minds are morbid; they thrive on sensationalism and often distort the facts or exaggerate the words of others, or repeat them out of context with no charitable consideration of pertinent circumstances. A psychological defect common to most human beings is to repeat negative reports about the faults of another without having first given the accused person a chance to disprove the allegations.

Never be drawn into psychological muddles. My Master used to say, when anyone would approach him confidentially with some supposedly scandalous disclosure: "If it is not something I can repeat to everyone, I don't wish to hear it." If someone has a grievance about another, or thinks he knows a secret about him, he should confront that person directly, or keep silent, rather than maligning the alleged wrongdoer for the love of gossip or impelled by an uncontrolled habit of indiscriminate talkativeness.

————————————

* John 8:7 (see Discourse 35).

Gossip seems to act like a stimulating tonic. Those who crave this titillation should satisfy that lust by loudly publicizing all the private sins they themselves have committed. They would find such disclosure unendurable even for one minute! A person who himself cannot stand such scrutiny should not in any way rejoice in exposing others. To reveal the moral weaknesses of others and bring to them senseless discomfiture is not the way of the wise.

Unscrupulous sensationalism is typical of many Western newspapers; they are uncharitable in their attitude because they are not healers of immorality, but rather scandalmongers. A spiritual crime is committed by journalists and publications that love to pickle gossip or to spice up reporting in order to sell more papers by catering to the degraded taste of gossip-loving readers.

Internal criticism is the malignant twin of verbal criticism. To seethe silently with critical thoughts is very foolish, creating disturbing vibrations that affect one's inner peace and are a subtly unpleasant effluence affecting persons around him. It is best to clean the mind of such negation. To be constantly judgmental is a sad misuse of man's God-given capacities of intelligence and discrimination. The wise person observes neutrally, allowing no acrimonious feelings to distort his perceptions of truth.

Be not inwardly critical of others; practice healthy self-criticism

To critique one's fellow beings in a spirit of intolerance or gloating over their faults is to call forth God's judgment: "In the light of My wisdom, I find no mortal perfect; and if I were to judge according to human standards of criticism, everyone who breathes My air of *maya* would be found wanting."

"Why beholdest thou the mote that is in thy brother's eye," said Jesus, "but considerest not the beam that is in thine own eye?" Man's task on earth is to keep busy expunging from his own consciousness the original temptation inherited from Adam and Eve. It is a psychological and metaphysical error to spend time in pointing out the mental dirt in others instead of cleaning out the dirt in the mansion of one's own soul. The would-be reformer of others' behavior must live wisely himself before he can accurately discern how to plant wisdom in the lives of those persons prone to misdeeds.

Critical people lack humility and therefore cannot themselves take criticism. Self-elected judges of others quite conveniently forget to scrutinize their own inner weaknesses. They think that they are all right because they magnify the faults of others to lessen the magnitude of their own. It is insidious to hide behind such a misconceived mental smoke screen. Insincerity and hypocrisy mar the character of one who does not care to overcome his weakness, yet professes hatred for such weakness. If he delights in tearing apart persons who suffer from the same personality flaws he possesses, he is a sadist and a coward, hiding his own defects behind sneers of criticism.

The irony is that unscrupulous people who love to castigate others about their faults usually possess the same faults themselves. Whatever annoys a person most in someone else may often be found festering within himself. Because such persons cannot look honestly at themselves without devastating feelings of guilt, they find satisfaction in scathing others to vent their frustration and snidely hide, sometimes even from themselves, their own reprehensibility. There are short-tempered people who themselves cannot stand anger in anyone else; those who are greedy, but cannot abide greed in others. Some people have bad social manners, yet disdain lack of decorum in boorish persons. One renounces the moral right to chastise others about the self-same faults that haunt oneself. There is little effect in a liar admonishing a liar; or in a confirmed immoralist passing judgment on immoral persons.

One who presumes to correct manifestations of ignorance in others should with equal zeal excise all ignorance from within himself. When one has acquired wisdom he will better perceive how to remove ignorance from the lives of those he wishes to help. Action and example will speak louder than his words. That is why Jesus said: "First cast out the beam out of thine own eye; and then shalt thou see clearly to cast out the mote out of thy brother's eye."

The example set forth by Jesus is to change oneself. As one saint of India said: "Wanted: Reformers—not of others, but of themselves."* As one changes himself, others around him are also changed. The salutary effects of this law can be seen in the transformed and transforming lives of all great masters.

To make a habit of analyzing people is spiritually profitless; and it also makes the critic unpleasant company. It is better, as Jesus

---

* Swami Ram Tirtha (1873–1906), well-known lecturer and poet. A musical arrangement of his poem "Marching Light" was included by Paramahansa Yogananda in his *Cosmic Chants* (published by Self-Realization Fellowship).

taught, to become like little children: guileless, calm, humbly sincere.* One who mentally dissects and analyzes the botanical properties of a flower misses a full appreciation of its beauty. But one who focuses on how beautiful that flower is, allowing one's intuitive feeling to respond to its pure essence, enjoys fully its loveliness.

There are times, of course, when it is prudent, even necessary, to use discrimination to find out the character of a person before entering into a close relationship or exchange—either personal or in business, and certainly before giving one's trust to one who purports to be a guru or spiritual teacher.† Otherwise, one should simply appreciate the gardens of flowering good qualities in human souls, leaving the tending of unlovely egoistic weeds and withered plants to those responsible for those fields—unless one is a qualified and duly commissioned spiritual gardener.

Effective analysis of one's associates requires clear-sightedness with some intuitive perception. Persons of emotional nature, without a ballast of wisdom, are likely to be prejudiced by undependable feelings, precluding objective appraisal. Intellectual types are equally susceptible to misunderstanding; owing to the activity of their hypersensitive imaginative rationalization of every nuance of behavior, they often impute wrong meanings to others' motives and actions. Such persons should balance reason with empathy, understanding that every individual life is difficult, complex, and as deserving of sympathy as their own. It is human nature to make broad allowances for one's own mistakes and shortcomings; certainly similar tolerance and understanding should be extended to others.

One should not open himself up to just anybody or everybody to critique his behavior or character. The opinions of those who are not qualified to criticize, especially those who carp and condemn in order to create disharmony or simply for the perverse pleasure it affords them, should be little noted or ignored altogether. There are two ways to disarm undeserving critics: to be abjectly indifferent to them, or to be lovingly indifferent to them. The latter is better. If one has the fault of which he is accused, no matter the source of accusation, he need not blatantly announce or confirm the disclosure of his fault, but qui-

---

* "Verily I say unto you, except ye be converted, and become as little children, ye shall not enter into the kingdom of heaven" (Matthew 18:3). See Discourse 47.

† See pages 550 ff.: "Beware of false prophets...."

etly and positively remove it from within himself. If the accusation is false, he should vehemently deny it, without argumentation and without being wrathful or disturbed. It is not necessary to let anyone know about one's private faults or past failings, except if someone is qualified to give help in cases where outside intervention is needed. Psychological privacy of one's thoughts is a God-given privilege; why supply "ammunition" that might fall into the hands of unconscionable persons who enjoy misusing such information?

To conceal one's faults that harm no one but oneself is not hypocrisy so long as one tries sincerely and mightily to rectify those flaws and thus save himself from the crucifixion of condemnation and spiritual impotency. How many young people would have matured into better adults if society had not forced hypocrisy on them as a way of getting ahead. Hypocrites take pleasure in their gains acquired by posing as virtuous when they are not. Such people feel no repentance and never try to reform. They love the accolades they receive by deceiving others about themselves.

Only the sincere, kind, wise, and perfectly balanced individual is fit to assess the virtues and vices of others. But Truth and God only, the Faultless Omniscience, can judge with absolute fairness. Man's judgment is conditional. God, who shares no base passions with man, is the Sole Impartiality in judging what is right. In His compassion, He never criticizes anyone openly — only silently, through one's conscience. The voice of an unstifled conscience is louder than words, more penetrating than sermons of human reformers. God criticizes His erring children through their reason, through their sense of moral judgment, which is instinctive, and confirms it through their conscience.

Introspection is a wonderful mirror in which to judge oneself. And even more accurate than that mirror is one's reflection in the mirror of a wise man's mind, or that of one's guru. In India, the masters undertake the guidance of a disciple only if that person is willing to undergo the discipline required for spiritual transformation. It is of utmost benefit to see oneself in the light of the wisdom of a master, to strive to measure up to the standards of his precepts and ideals. One who corrects himself according to that clear-sighted appraisal will find himself magnetically attractive and widely influential; and, most importantly, pleasing in the sight of God. It was this flawless mirror Jesus held up to his disciples. His words of wisdom expressed the perfection of soul qualities as the criteria to gauge their reflection; his divine example inspired their aspirations to become that perfect soul-image.

To be able to stand criticism is a mark of spiritual strength. It is weakness to allow resentment to conquer one's feelings when criticized. To be able humbly to stand the barbs of criticism, just or unjust, and to make continuous effort to improve one's attitudes and behavior when criticism is justified, will make one a saint.

~

"Give not that which is holy unto the dogs, neither cast ye your pearls before swine, lest they trample them under their feet, and turn again and rend you" (Matthew 7:6).

Spiritual advice is of no avail to unappreciative persons who snap at their would-be helper with cynicism and derision. Just as swine would doltishly trample on pearls cast before them, so people who are deeply wallowing in worldly muck are insensitive to the wisdom gems of saints who speak of the priceless happiness of a self-controlled existence. Attempts to reform with helpful sermons low-minded, confirmed evil persons, or those with an intransigent mind-set, will likely be met with sneers and even attempted injurious antagonism. Jesus' advice means that wisdom should be accorded the esteem due to something spiritually precious; it should neither be flaunted nor used as coercion. Similarly in the Bhagavad Gita the Lord mandates: "Never voice these truths to one who is without self-control or devotion, nor to one who performs no service or does not care to hear, nor to one who speaks ill of Me."* Persons caught up in evil or nonunderstanding have no wish or intention to change and only laugh at lofty principles and ridicule those who propound them.

Better it is to stay away from evil persons, and to remain reserved around the unreceptive. When an outstretched helping hand is slapped, it should be withdrawn for a time until the recipient is ready to accept it. One who gives sincerity that is not appreciated or is abused is casting away "pearls" uselessly; the wise reserve their spiritual treasure to benefit those who are receptive.

---

* *God Talks With Arjuna: The Bhagavad Gita* xviii:67.

~

"Ask, and it shall be given you; seek, and ye shall find; knock, and it shall be opened unto you: For every one that asketh receiveth; and he that seeketh findeth; and to him that knocketh it shall be opened.

"Or what man is there of you, whom if his son ask bread, will he give him a stone? Or if he ask a fish, will he give him a serpent?

"If ye then, being evil, know how to give good gifts unto your children, how much more shall your Father which is in heaven give good things to them that ask Him?" (Matthew 7:7–11).

Parallel reference:

And he said unto them, "Which of you shall have a friend, and shall go unto him at midnight, and say unto him, 'Friend, lend me three loaves; for a friend of mine in his journey is come to me, and I have nothing to set before him?'

"And he from within shall answer and say, 'Trouble me not: the door is now shut, and my children are with me in bed; I cannot rise and give thee.' I say unto you, though he will not rise and give him, because he is his friend, yet because of his importunity he will rise and give him as many as he needeth.

"And I say unto you, ask, and it shall be given you; seek, and ye shall find; knock, and it shall be opened unto you. For every one that asketh receiveth; and he that seeketh findeth; and to him that knocketh it shall be opened.

"If a son shall ask bread of any of you that is a father, will he give him a stone? Or if he ask a fish, will he for a fish give him a serpent? Or if he shall ask an egg, will he offer him a scorpion? If ye then, being evil, know how to give good gifts unto your children: how much more shall your heavenly Father give the Holy Spirit to them that ask Him?" (Luke 11:5–13).

The devotee who persistently asks the divine truth from God will receive it from his Omniscient Father. If he seeks God perseveringly behind the darkness of closed eyes in meditation, he will find Him. By the devotee's continuous knocking with prayerful urgency at the gate of silence leading to God, it shall be opened unto him, and his consciousness will enter into the heavenly region of blissful God-communion. Every devotee who with unrelenting zeal asks for God-realization receives that enlight-enment without fail.

The surety of God's re-sponse to sincere and persevering devotees

All prodigal sons of God, having run away from the bliss of God-contact into the slums of material distraction, will someday come back towards God through the interior gate of meditative peace to reenter their blissful inner home. Every child of God lost in the forest of material desires, but unflaggingly seeking a way out, will find his way back to God's Heavenly Mansion. He who knocks continuously at the door to God's presence with the throbs of his heartful devotion will certainly find that God will receive him. Unceasing devotion is the force that can open the gates of God's heart for the devotee to enter in.

If any human son of God asks the Heavenly Father for the bread of eternal life, He will not give him the stone of material ignorance. If the devotee asks of God the food of wisdom, God will not give him the serpent of delusion. If the devotee asks God for divine manna and all-around divine bliss, He will not give him the scorpion of restlessness and mental misery.

If even deluded human beings know how to give "good gifts" to their children, and friends willingly give of their store to needy friends, how much more will the Heavenly Father, who is the receptacle of all goodness, give to His human children the supreme gift of knowledge of communion with His creative Cosmic Vibration, the "Holy Spirit," manifester of all God's powers and infinite intelligence? God gives not only this highest wisdom and vibratory power to those children who demand it, but He also surrenders Himself unto the devotee whose desire for Him is unplacated by any lesser offering.

People do not get many of the things they pray for because they do not know how to ask God for them. One who *first* contacts God by the practice of meditation and then asks for legitimate material needs or for spiritual grace will receive consummation of his prayers. One's seeking must be wholehearted, minding not reverses, until he obtains his heart's desire. To the seeker of God Himself who offers continuous mental knocks of demand at the doors of inner silence—who waits patiently in the darkness of closed eyes in meditation, knocking persistently with the unabated ardor and devotion of his soul—God perforce will open those portals to admit that devotee into His infinite Kingdom of Fulfillment.

In these verses Jesus speaks of the surety of God's loving response. No true heart will be denied that "asketh" of Him, that "seeketh" Him and His wisdom trove, or that "knocketh" at the door to His Presence behind the pearly ramparts of heaven entered through the inner silence of deep meditation.

~

> *"Therefore all things whatsoever ye would that men should do to you, do ye even so to them: for this is the law and the prophets" (Matthew 7:12).*

Parallel reference:

> *"And as ye would that men should do to you, do ye also to them likewise" (Luke 6:31, Sermon on the Plain).*

That which one wants to see in others should first be manifested in oneself; for whatsoever goes forth from one's consciousness and in one's actions returns in kind. The goodness one hopes to receive from others should begin with goodness given to others. One should never behave in a way that he would abhor were he the recipient.* Persons who want people to speak kindly and understandingly to them, to behave toward them sincerely, honorably, and lovingly, must initiate such response by their own demeanor in relationships

---

* This "Golden Rule" is basic to the spiritual teachings of the world's religions:

From the Hindu scripture *Mahabharata* (Anusasana Parva 113.8): "One should not behave towards others in a way which is disagreeable to oneself. This is the essence of morality. All other activities are due to selfish desire."

From the *Analects of Confucius* (15.23): "Tsekung asked, 'Is there one word that can serve as a principle of conduct for life?' Confucius replied, 'It is the word *shu*— reciprocity. Do not impose on others what you yourself do not desire.'"

From the Jewish Talmud (Shabbat 31a): "What is hateful to you, do not to your fellow men. That is the entire Law; all the rest is commentary."

From the Buddhist text *Tripitaka Udana-varga* 5:18: "Hurt not others in ways that you would find hurtful."

And from the sayings of Prophet Mohammed (*Forty Hadith of an-Nawawi*): "Not one of you is a believer until he desires for his brother what he desires for himself." (*Publisher's Note*)

with others. The Divine Law and the prophets deal with people in the noblest way, that people in turn will learn to act always nobly. God is never cranky, mean, or spiteful even toward those of troublesome temperaments; people who feel *Spiritual truth in "The* punished by Him have rather disturbed themselves *Golden Rule"* due to their own rancorous thoughts and wrong actions. The infinite voice of God is silent, yet He is always whispering gently and lovingly through one's conscience: "Child, wake up, forsake the evil way." So even in the relationship between man and his Maker, God gives His great love to His children that they may forsake their misbehavior and learn to return love to Him from the abundance of their own hearts.

~

"Enter ye in at the strait gate: for wide is the gate, and broad is the way, that leadeth to destruction, and many there be which go in thereat: Because strait is the gate, and narrow is the way, which leadeth unto life, and few there be that find it" (Matthew 7:13–14). *

The gateway of delusion is wide, opening onto the broad pathway of evil. Many fools blithely go through the gate of ignorant impulses and find themselves on the path of evil actions. It is easy to perform evil, just as it requires no effort to roll down a hill; but every evil action repeated leads one further along the wide path of evil trod by the unthinking masses. *Outer and inner interpretation of "strait*

The "broadness" of the evil path signifies the *pretation of "strait* unlimited potentialities for committing evil deeds. *gate" and "narrow* The reckless throng, lured by temptations and com- *way"* pelled by iniquitous impulses, enters the easy gate of evil and follows the broad path of evil actions, arm-in-arm with their false promises of quick gratification. But as the evildoers jostle madly along, the path of evil suddenly ends in a precipitous fall into the valley of misery.

The strait gate of goodness in its restrictive singularity is less easy to pass through; and its path narrow and difficult, like climbing up-

---

* Cf. parallel reference in Luke 13:24, Discourse 57.

hill; fewer are those who choose this more arduous path of virtuous inclinations (gate) and righteous actions (way), which leads to everlasting life. Virtue arising from spiritual aspiration, though seemingly difficult and unattractive in the beginning and shunned by the worldly minded, yet leads those who persist in pursuing the singular way of goodness into a kingdom of undreamed-of splendor and unending bliss.

Jesus enjoined on man unswerving adherence to the path of virtue and morality, a course that all human beings must follow to evolve spiritually. He reiterated this in these verses, but also addressed his close disciples in a veiled metaphor. The "strait gate" and "narrow way" refer also to the gateway in the subtle astral center at the base of the spine, which opens into the astral spine's narrow, extremely fine pathway through which the life and consciousness ascend to the higher cerebrospinal centers of spiritual perception—the sole path to realization of God and union with Him.*

Conversely, when life and consciousness flow downward through this spinal channel and are dispersed outwardly through delusion's wide gate of sensory perceptions, into body consciousness and its broad range of material actions and attachments, that is the way that "leadeth to destruction"—forgetfulness of man's inherent divine nature.†

~

"Beware of false prophets, which come to you in sheep's clothing, but inwardly they are ravening wolves. Ye shall know them by their fruits. Do men gather grapes of thorns, or figs of thistles? Even so every good tree bringeth forth good fruit; but a corrupt tree bringeth forth evil fruit. A good tree cannot bring forth

---

* See Discourse 6.

† "Thou hast been in Eden, the garden of God (inner paradise of divine perception)....Thou wast upon the holy mountain of God (the pinnacle of transcendent consciousness, in the highest spiritual center in the brain); thou hast walked up and down in the midst of the stones of fire (the spinal chakras or astral dynamos of life force). Thou wast perfect in thy ways from the day that thou wast created, till iniquity was found in thee.

"By the multitude of thy merchandise (the commerce of the senses with the material world) they have filled the midst of thee with violence, and thou hast sinned: therefore I will cast thee as profane out of the mountain of God: and I will destroy thee from the midst of the stones of fire" (Ezekiel 28:13-16).

evil fruit, neither can a corrupt tree bring forth good fruit. Every tree that bringeth not forth good fruit is hewn down, and cast into the fire. Wherefore by their fruits ye shall know them" (Matthew 7:15–20).

With trenchant imagery, Jesus warns people who are gullible, eager to believe anything touted as advantageous to them, to beware of so-called teachers who exploit religion as a means of gaining a profitable sheep-like following. Spiritual pretenders commit the highest sin against God, using the Master of the Universe for personal or monetary gain. Jesus describes such teachers as "ravening wolves" of evil, dressed "in sheep's clothing" of feigned humbleness and spirituality. The qualifications of a teacher cannot be accurately judged by his outer appearance of superficial behavior. Any man in religious garb may look holy, but he cannot hide a wicked heart; it must eventually come out in his practical dealings as wicked actions. As grapes cannot be gathered from a thorn bush or figs from thistles, so goodness cannot be reaped from a dissimulating evil individual, no matter how clever his guise of piety. Undiscerning persons may be duped; but God is not deceived, nor is the karmic law.

A warning to gullible victims of unqualified spiritual teachers

One may argue that a beautiful lotus may be plucked from a murky pond, or that one may savor sweetmeats prepared by a person who himself subsists poorly on bowls of rice; or that one may even glean some profit by reading a good book written by an evil man. But it is an ineluctable truth that in spiritual matters, for ultimate realization and God-union, the shepherding of a "false prophet" will not do. The devotee needs to follow the path of a God-knowing person, chosen for him by God. A false prophet can never be a God-ordained guru, no matter how artfully he presumes such title. A false prophet is one who knows at heart his hypocrisy and moral weakness and yet professes goodness to attract and hold people who will follow him blindly for his own ends—financial and for gratification of his ego.

A true guru will not bring any such evil or misguidance to his followers. He can be known by his humility, uprightness, and God-attunement evidenced by his ability to enter the elevated states of God-communion in superconsciousness, Christ consciousness, and cosmic consciousness. The signs of a true guru who can enter these states at will are as follows: his eyes are still and unwinking whenever he wants them to be so; by the practice of yoga his heart and breath are quiet without his forcibly holding his breath in his lungs; his mind is calm without effort. If a man has eyelids that blink continually, lungs acting like bellows all the time, and a mind always restless like a butterfly, and he claims to be in cosmic consciousness, his assertion is laughable. Just as a man who is running about cannot effectively pretend to be sleeping, so one with restless eyes, breath, and mind cannot convince one who knows better that he is in cosmic consciousness. Just as sleep manifests in the body by certain physiological changes, so the muscles, eyes, heart, breath, all become still during the elevated states of God-communion—and even in the highest, non-trance *nirvikalpa samadhi* state these conditions of total interiorization can be produced at will. The true guru is a master, not of others, but of himself.

Every false prophet in time is exposed and cut down by the axe of wise and just criticism and is cast into the fire of oblivion. By the fruits of a teacher's actions, which emanate from the tree of his inner thoughts, the discriminating devotee will know the difference between a good prophet or guru and a false one. The true guru may instruct a few persons or a great many, but his whole intention is to raise his disciples to Christlike, Krishnalike, stature.

A great prophet, or savior, is one who comes on earth as a special messenger to answer a specific need of mankind, and accordingly aspires to reform a portion of mankind or to influence the entire populace. Anyone who knows himself as only wicked, and yet outwardly makes a colossal claim to be a prophet or protégé of God, is a stupendous hypocrite and a sinner against God. In condemning false prophets and the evil they do, Jesus was not castigating the sincere, humble person still struggling against a few inner weaknesses while trying to help others spiritually. His stern warning was directed at those who make false spiritual claims about themselves and preach a false, self-serving doctrine.

≈

"Not every one that saith unto me, 'Lord, Lord,' shall enter into the kingdom of heaven; but he that doeth the will of my Father which is in heaven.

"Many will say to me in that day, 'Lord, Lord, have we not prophesied in thy name? and in thy name have cast out devils?

*And in thy name done many wonderful works?' And then will I
profess unto them, I never knew you: depart from me, ye that
work iniquity" (Matthew 7:21–23).*

Hearken, ye would-be followers of Christ: It is not enough just to
laud the name of Jesus as "Lord, Lord" in conversation and
preaching. Professing belief in the divinity of Jesus
will not of itself assure entry into the Kingdom of   *Outer worship and*
God. Christians whose dedication consists merely   *mere belief in Jesus is*
of attending church services and absentmindedly   *insufficient for*
listening to Sunday sermons and hymns reach that   *salvation*
kind of inner heaven that bestows a degree of
peace, faith, some answered prayers, and a little spiritual satisfaction
— only that much and nothing more. Real Christ followers are those
who embrace in their own consciousness through meditation and ecstasy the omnipresent cosmic wisdom and bliss of Jesus Christ. This
is the meaning of "he that doeth the will of my Father which is in
heaven" — the region of Heavenly Bliss.

The true devotee, in daily intense meditation, retraces his wayward footsteps from the land of delusive sense pleasures and material
attachments back to his home of Cosmic Bliss in God. He who experiences oneness with God in the ecstasy of meditation retains that divine attunement and thus knows how to behave correctly during his
earthly sojourn, how to act according to God's will here.

At death, there is an instant review of one's life. The consciousness in the soul recalls one's attempts at virtue and tries thereby to gain
the recognition of the liberating Christ Consciousness; but if one's sins
and mental desires prevail, he is turned away and cast again onto the
rotating wheel of earthly incarnations. Jesus cites especially, by way of
example, the reprehensible actions of the "false prophets." Whatever
presumed good works one does in the holy name of God or His divine
emissaries are instead iniquitous if manipulated by impulses of self-
serving motives, fraudulent claims, or the hypocrisy of pretending to
be what one is not. Those who have acquired fortunes by selling the
name of God, or who have cast out the devils of evil from people only
momentarily in a spate of emotional imagination, or have similarly
performed spiritual "miracles" according to their own deluded estimation only, will not be recognized by the Infinite Christ and granted
entry into the Eternal Kingdom.

Sincere persons who have allowed themselves to become satisfied with mechanical spirituality and worship—emotional or theological —should not take for granted their salvation. Verbal praise to the Lord without actual perception of His corresponding response, and theological study without gaining Self-realization, are of little value in the eyes of God. The principles governing divine life are as exact as those of any other branch of science in God's creation. Devotees who want to be real Christ-ians, rather than just members of Christian churchianity, must know and truly feel the presence of Omnipresent Christ all the time, must commune with Him in ecstasy, and be guided by His Infinite Wisdom—and know that He is, and ever will be. If God and Jesus ever existed, They exist now and ever will. If They are perpetually existent, They are knowable—barriers between heaven and earth do not obtain in Their Omnipresence. The truth of Their Ever-Existence and Ever-Presence must be verified in the lived lives and personal realization of Their congregation of Truth-loving devotees.

~

> *"Therefore whosoever heareth these sayings of mine, and doeth them, I will liken him unto a wise man, which built his house upon a rock: And the rain descended, and the floods came, and the winds blew, and beat upon that house; and it fell not: for it was founded upon a rock.*
>
> *"And every one that heareth these sayings of mine, and doeth them not, shall be likened unto a foolish man, which built his house upon the sand: And the rain descended, and the floods came, and the winds blew, and beat upon that house; and it fell: and great was the fall of it"* (Matthew 7:24–27).

Parallel reference:

> *"And why call ye me, 'Lord, Lord,' and do not the things which I say? Whosoever cometh to me, and heareth my sayings, and doeth them, I will shew you to whom he is like: He is like a man which built an house, and digged deep, and laid the foundation on a rock: and when the flood arose, the stream beat vehemently upon that house, and could not shake it: for it was founded upon a rock.*

"But he that heareth, and doeth not, is like a man that without a foundation built an house upon the earth; against which the stream did beat vehemently, and immediately it fell; and the ruin of that house was great" (Luke 6:46–49, Sermon on the Plain). *

Jesus spoke: "And why call ye me Lord, without knowing my oneness with the Christ Intelligence, the Lord of all creation, and how my omnipresent Self manifests Itself in creation and in your consciousness? Because you call me Christ but do not feel my presence in your consciousness, you do not lead your life as I say unto you, or as my consciousness signifies by its Christ vibrations upholding the superconsciousness of your soul, your true Self. When you will be able to feel my Christ consciousness by awakening your superconsciousness, then you will follow the wisdom-righteousness I signify through your inner perception, but not before, when you still heed the instigations of delusion."

Anchoring one's life in the unshakable security of God-contact

The devotee who forsakes the compelling influence of matter and sensations and seeks the hidden Christ in the temple of superconsciousness can listen to the silent vibrations of that Infinite Christ; that devotee's nervous system—with its sensate, kinetic, emotional, and rational instrumentalities—will then automatically respond and act according to the perceptions of the inner divine propensities. That devotee, as the soul, builds his house of consciousness not on the shifting sands of earthly pleasures; but with the pickax of meditation and God-communion he digs deep to reach the bedrock of intuitive wisdom, and builds his house of bliss on the everlasting rock of God's Cosmic Consciousness. When the rains of difficult spiritual trials or the flood of accumulated sorrowful events or the mighty wind of death threatens with vehemence and impetuosity, the wise man's house of intuitive cosmic perception and bliss stands unshaken. The wisdom and bliss acquired by meditation becomes a permanent abode of the consciousness, which not even the most-dreaded event of death can destroy. The

---

* In the Bhagavad Gita, the Lord voices a similar admonition: "Men, devotion-filled, who ceaselessly practice My precepts, without fault-finding, they too become free from all karma. But those who denounce this teaching of Mine and do not live according to it, wholly deluded in regard to true wisdom, know them, devoid of understanding, to be doomed" (*God Talks With Arjuna: The Bhagavad Gita* III:31–32).

devotee whose consciousness does not rest on the frangible foundation of material desires will not be carried away into the plights of new incarnations. The consciousness built on the rock of God-consciousness shall not lose its divine contact in life or death, but will forever be housed in blissful immortality.

But he who gives only token praise to the Christ in Jesus, without heeding the voice of his inner higher consciousness and its intuitive wisdom-perceptions and acting according to those uplifting inspirations, is a man who has built his consciousness on a precarious foundation of earthly habits. When temptations will come to him, his house of self-control will break up and be swept away by the tide of ignorance, his temporary shelter of spiritual discipline thus devastated.

Whosoever leads a careless life patterned after the dictates of his impulsive desires and habits, and who tries to feel security in financial acquirement and sense pleasures, will lose his happiness during the trials of life.* Like a house built upon treacherous sand, earthly happiness cannot prevail against the rain, floods, and wind of physical disease and mental troubles, the changes of fortune, or the ultimate storm of death. Foolish is the man who lives for earthly happiness only, for at the time of death everything he loved and considered to be everlastingly his own will be taken away from him.

The Bhagavad Gita teaches that not even the direst suffering can cause ruin to the equanimity of the wise man. Having established his happiness not on the temporal pleasures of life, but in God as perceived in meditation, he stands unshaken amidst the crash of breaking worlds. His joy is both enduring and everlasting.†

---

* "He who ignores the scriptural commands and who follows his own foolish desires does not find happiness or perfection or the Infinite Goal. Therefore, take the scriptures as your guide in determining what should be done and what should be avoided. With intuitive understanding of the injunctions declared in holy writ, be pleased to perform thy duties here" (*God Talks With Arjuna: The Bhagavad Gita* XVI:23–24).

† "The relativities of existence (birth and death, pleasure and pain) have been overcome, even here in this world, by those of fixed equal-mindedness. Thereby are they enthroned in Spirit—verily, the taintless, the perfectly balanced Spirit.

"The knower of Spirit, abiding in the Supreme Being, with unswerving discrimination, free from delusion, is thus neither jubilant at pleasant experiences nor downcast by unpleasant experiences.

"Unattracted to the sensory world, the yogi experiences the ever new joy inherent in the Self. Engaged in divine union of the soul with Spirit, he attains bliss indestructible....

"Only that yogi who possesses the inner Bliss, who rests on the inner Foundation, who is one with the inner Light, becomes one with Spirit (after attaining freedom from

~

And it came to pass, when Jesus had ended these sayings, the peo-
ple were astonished at his doctrine: for he taught them as one
having authority, and not as the scribes. When he was come down
from the mountain, great multitudes followed him (Matthew
7:28 — 8:1).

---

karma connected with the physical, astral, and ideational bodies). He attains complete
liberation in Spirit (even while living in the body)" (*God Talks With Arjuna: The Bha-*
gavad Gita v:19–21, 24).

DISCOURSE 31

Why Jesus Mixed With "Publicans and Sinners"

Power of Human Will United to God's Will

❖

"Thy Sins Be Forgiven": Removing by Divine Fiat
the Karmic Effects of Past Wrong Actions

❖

How Man Can Be Freed From the Results of His Misdeeds

❖

The Qualitative and Quantitative Mission of a World Savior

❖

A Compassionate Message of God's Mercy and Forgiveness
for the Repentant

*"I will have mercy and compassion on the spiritually sick and I will
not forsake them; I will try to heal and save them, rather than let them
be sacrificed on the altar of their karmic destiny."*

*A*nd there came a leper to him, *beseeching him, and kneeling down to him, and saying unto him, "If thou wilt, thou canst make me clean." And Jesus, moved with compassion, put forth his hand, and touched him, and saith unto him, "I will; be thou clean."*

And as soon as he had spoken, immediately the leprosy departed from him, and he was cleansed. And he straitly charged him, and forthwith sent him away; and saith unto him, "See thou say nothing to any man: but go thy way, shew thyself to the priest, and offer for thy cleansing those things which Moses commanded, for a testimony unto them."

But he went out, and began to publish it much, and to blaze abroad the matter, insomuch that Jesus could no more openly enter into the city, but was without in desert places: and they came to him from every quarter.

And again he entered into Capernaum after some days; and it was noised that he was in the house. And straightway many were gathered together, insomuch that there was no room to receive them, no, not so much as about the door: and he preached the word unto them.

And they come unto him, bringing one sick of the palsy, which was borne of four. And when they could not come nigh unto him for the press, they uncovered the roof where he was: and when they had broken it up, they let down the bed wherein the sick of the palsy lay.

When Jesus saw their faith, he said unto the sick of the palsy, "Son, thy sins be forgiven thee."

But there was certain of the scribes sitting there, and reasoning in their hearts, "Why doth this man thus speak blasphemies? Who can forgive sins but God only?"

And immediately when Jesus perceived in his spirit that they so reasoned within themselves, he said unto them, "Why reason ye these things in your hearts? Whether is it easier to say to the sick of the palsy, 'Thy sins be forgiven thee'; or to say, 'Arise, and take up thy bed, and walk'? But that ye may know that the Son of man hath power on earth to forgive sins, (he saith to the sick of the palsy,) I say unto thee, arise, and take up thy bed, and go thy way into thine house."

And immediately he arose, took up the bed, and went forth before them all; insomuch that they were all amazed, and glorified God, saying, "We never saw it on this fashion."

And he went forth again by the sea side; and all the multitude resorted unto him, and he taught them.

And as he passed by, he saw Levi the son of Alphaeus sitting at the receipt of custom, and said unto him, "Follow me." And he arose and followed him.

And it came to pass, that, as Jesus sat at meat in his house, many publicans and sinners sat also together with Jesus and his disciples: for there were many, and they followed him. And when the scribes and Pharisees saw him eat with publicans and sinners, they said unto his disciples, "How is it that he eateth and drinketh with publicans and sinners?"

When Jesus heard it, he saith unto them, "They that are whole have no need of the physician, but they that are sick: I came not to call the righteous, but sinners to repentance."

—Mark 1:40—2:17

Why Jesus Mixed With "Publicans and Sinners"

꧁

And there came a leper to him, beseeching him, and kneeling down to him, and saying unto him, "If thou wilt, thou canst make me clean." And Jesus, moved with compassion, put forth his hand, and touched him, and saith unto him, "I will; be thou clean."

And as soon as he had spoken, immediately the leprosy departed from him, and he was cleansed (Mark 1:40–42). *

"I will," spoken by Jesus in response to the leper's prayer, signifies the human will attuned to God's omnipotent will. Human will is circumscribed by the body. It can keep the body well or plunge it into the abyss of disease or suffering, even destroying it. It can wield the bodily instrument to work changes in the world, more or less ac-

Power of human will united to God's will

cording to the degree of one's mental development, but always in a limited way. But when by ecstatic meditation the human will identifies itself with God's omnipresent will, it is able to work in all channels of cosmic forces and intelligences which govern the universe. The Self-realized devotee with his magnified will can effect any change in his extended cosmic body of the universe as naturally as an ordinary human being can will into activity his life force, nerves, and muscles to initiate desired effects in the physical body or its environs.

---

* Cf. parallel references in Matthew 8:1–3 and Luke 5:12–13.

Jesus, being one with the omnipresent Father and all-pervading Intelligent Cosmic Energy, felt himself not only in his own little body but in all bodies, including that of the leper. He willed the cosmic energy in that body to clean out the imperfections of illness, rearranging the life vibrations to effect atomic changes in the diseased tissues and cells. The healing was instantaneous.

And he straitly charged him, and forthwith sent him away; and saith unto him, "See thou say nothing to any man: but go thy way, shew thyself to the priest, and offer for thy cleansing those things which Moses commanded, for a testimony unto them." *

But he went out, and began to publish it much, and to blaze abroad the matter, insomuch that Jesus could no more openly enter into the city, but was without in desert places: and they came to him from every quarter (Mark 1:43–45).

Parallel reference:

But so much the more went there a fame abroad of him: and great multitudes came together to hear, and to be healed by him of their infirmities. And he withdrew himself into the wilderness, and prayed (Luke 5:15–16).

Jesus, as similarly do all great prophets, came to deliver the word of God to heal the deluded soul of man; and so did not want that focus to be diminished by his compassionate phenomenal feats of physical healings. He thus enjoined the leper not to draw unwarranted attention to his miraculous cure, but to give testimony of God's power only to the priestly authority who doubted the divine commission of Jesus. To further alleviate the doubts of the spiritual hierarchy, Jesus showed his belief in the greatness of Moses and his respect for the belief of those accustomed to the practice of Mosaic law, by instructing the leper to offer in the synagogue "for thy cleansing those things which Moses commanded."

The healed leper, however, understandably could not restrain his rejoicing and became an effective, though unsought, publicist for

---

* Cf. parallel references in Matthew 8:4 and Luke 5:14.

Jesus, so that great multitudes sought to be healed by him and to hear his holy word, making it impossible for Jesus to move about openly in the city environs. He withdrew from the pressing throng into the wilderness of the desert—and into the silent realm of his inner being, where no restless thoughts ever dared to impose upon him—and there he communed with God to renew himself in body and in spirit.

∾

And again he entered into Capernaum after some days; and it was noised that he was in the house. And straightway many were gathered together, insomuch that there was no room to receive them, no, not so much as about the door: and he preached the word unto them.

And they come unto him, bringing one sick of the palsy, which was borne of four. And when they could not come nigh unto him for the press, they uncovered the roof where he was: and when they had broken it up, they let down the bed wherein the sick of the palsy lay.

When Jesus saw their faith, he said unto the sick of the palsy, "Son, thy sins be forgiven thee" (Mark 2:1–5).

Parallel reference:

And, behold, they brought to him a man sick of the palsy, lying on a bed: and Jesus seeing their faith said unto the sick of the palsy; "Son, be of good cheer; thy sins be forgiven thee" (Matthew 9:2). *

While Jesus was again preaching to a multitude in Capernaum, a paralyzed man, lying helpless on a cot, was lowered before Jesus through the roof of the dwelling where the gathering was taking place—the only means of reaching Jesus' healing presence because of the crowd.† Seeing the undiscourageable persistence and the great faith in God of the palsied man and those who brought him for

---

* Cf. additional parallel reference in Luke 5:17–20.

† Luke 5:17 records that "there were Pharisees and doctors of the law sitting by, which were come out of every town of Galilee, and Judea, and Jerusalem."

healing, Jesus addressed him who lay stricken on his bed, forgiving his sins. The words of Jesus betokened removal of the karmic effects of the man's past wrong actions that had become manifested in his present condition: "Son, be delighted in Spirit, for thy sins, which were consciously or unconsciously committed by thee in the past but are unknown to thee now, are forgiven by the mercy of God; and thereby thy sickness, the karmic effect of those sins, is healed."

"Thy sins be forgiven": removing by divine fiat the karmic effects of past wrong actions

Divine channels of God, such as Jesus, can with will and cosmic energy remove from receptive persons the karmic residue of incarnations that is astrally impinged in their brains—mental and physical recordings of sin that keep on singing the evil refrain of mental and physical calamities. As acids can dissolve the grooves in a phonograph record, rendering it unplayable, so the mental and physiological "grooves" of stored karmic tracings in the brain cells can be obliterated by transmission of life force. With the burning of the inner sinful records, the misery-producing songs of evil experience cease also. The bad karma from the past that had produced in the stricken man the physical affliction of paralysis was removed by divine fiat through Jesus' words, "thy sins are forgiven thee."

∼

But there was certain of the scribes sitting there, and reasoning in their hearts, "Why doth this man thus speak blasphemies? Who can forgive sins but God only?"

And immediately when Jesus perceived in his spirit that they so reasoned within themselves, he said unto them, "Why reason ye these things in your hearts? Whether is it easier to say to the sick of the palsy, 'Thy sins be forgiven thee'; or to say, 'Arise, and take up thy bed, and walk'? But that ye may know that the Son of man hath power on earth to forgive sins," (he saith to the sick of the palsy,) "I say unto thee, arise, and take up thy bed, and go thy way into thine house."

And immediately he arose, took up the bed, and went forth before them all; insomuch that they were all amazed, and glorified God, saying, "We never saw it on this fashion" (Mark 2:6–12).

Parallel reference:

> *And, behold, certain of the scribes said within themselves, "This man blasphemeth."*
>
> *And Jesus knowing their thoughts said, "Wherefore think ye evil in your hearts? For whether is easier, to say, 'Thy sins be forgiven thee'; or to say, 'Arise, and walk'? But that ye may know that the Son of man hath power on earth to forgive sins," (then saith he to the sick of the palsy,) "Arise, take up thy bed, and go unto thine house."*
>
> *And he arose, and departed to his house. But when the multitudes saw it, they marvelled, and glorified God, which had given such power unto men (Matthew 9:3–8).* *

The Pharisees and doctors of the law, materially minded intellectuals, blind to Jesus' divine stature, could not understand his right and power to forgive sins. If one human being could absolve another of reaping the self-created results of evil actions, with lawful recompense set at naught, then by "forgiveness" a person would be able to relieve another from suffering the effects of swallowing poison. When a glutton eats too much and suffers from acute indigestion, it requires more than a word of forgiveness to ameliorate the painful reaction caused by his greed.

However, if that sufferer avails himself of a doctor's specialized knowledge and skill, and follows his prescription, he can relieve himself

How man can be freed from the results of his misdeeds

of the digestive distress. Likewise in the spiritual world, the psychologically sick person can be forgiven —freed from the painful results of his actions—if he follows the advice of a true teacher of wisdom, to whom he discloses his errors (confession) for the sake

of spiritual diagnosis and the finding and prescribing of the proper remedy. The healing of physiological ills by a spiritual specialist—maladies whose karmic instigation is hidden in forgotten sins of the past—requires not only spiritual diagnosis and prescribed remedial actions, but also the exercise of faith in God on the part of the sufferer and the bestowal of healing blessings, forgiveness of karmic sins, by one who serves as a channel of God's grace.

---

* Cf. additional parallel reference in Luke 5:21–26.

Sin consists of pursuing erroneous ways. Human beings, originally patterned by the Almighty Maker after His Perfect Image, chose to desecrate and distort their individuality into a flawed mortal image by the misuse of God-given independence. They themselves rectify their misdeeds by suffering the consequences or nullifying evil karma by righteous actions. Or God, their Creator, can change a repentant ignorance-distorted mortal by the deserved grace of His transmuting forgiveness. Or Sons of God can act on behalf of God to relieve others from their sufferings of body, mind, and soul. A spiritual and mental healing current can be offered invisibly to offset the effects of evil karma, past bad actions, lodged in the brain cells. Erroneous habits in individuals can be changed to good habits. Therefore, Jesus explained why he could say to the sick either, "Thy sins be forgiven thee by God," or, "I (as the conscious reflection of the power and true image of the Heavenly Father) say unto thee, 'Thy sins be forgiven thee,'" or, "Arise, and take up thy bed, and walk (thy karmic debt has been forgiven)."

The omnipresent consciousness of Jesus felt the thoughts of the doubting scribes and Pharisees and replied to their critical feelings: "Why are you concerned about my forgiving the sins of men? Wherein is there any difference whether I relieve people of their miseries by the power of God acting through me, or by my power given unto me by God?"

Jesus spoke from his absolute unity with God, free from all illusive egotism. Clerics or other spiritual teachers who have not found forgiveness or relief from their own sins, negating their perfect attunement with God, cannot possibly forgive or relieve other error-makers. For someone to serve as a channel of God's grace to remove karma from others, there must be no obstruction of identity with one's egoic nature. True devotees, even when fully awakened, never think of themselves as gurus or saviors of others. They behold as the Sole Doer in themselves none other than the pure God. The guru is the awakened God, awakening the sleeping God in the disciple.

The crowd of onlookers "marvelled, and glorified God, which had given such power unto men," uplifted and overjoyed to witness that Jesus, in form like themselves, could manifest the powers of the Almighty. They were filled with awe and reverential attention at these demonstrations, lessons of hope that all human children of God, including themselves, could attain God's blessing of divine transformation.

∾

And he went forth again by the sea side; and all the multitude resorted unto him, and he taught them.

And as he passed by, he saw Levi the son of Alphaeus sitting at the receipt of custom, and said unto him, "Follow me." And he arose and followed him (Mark 2:14). *

At the sight of Matthew, Jesus intuitively recognized a disciple whom he had known in many past incarnations. Matthew had been born at that time and place in order that God might be glorified through the apostolic assistance he was to render in the divine dispensation of Jesus. Even though Matthew was a publican (tax collector), his inner consciousness, which had been spiritually developed in a previous incarnation, remained unchanged. Jesus knew Matthew as a divine son, high in the path of Spirit, in spite of his lowly occupation, and called him with a firm, confident voice that bespoke recognition of his disciple from the past.

Physical scientists expose Nature's truth of the evolution of matter; but spiritual masters, sometimes dramatically, reveal the subtler truth of the soul's evolution through successive incarnations. Think what it means that out of the multitude of people surrounding him, Jesus glimpsed the publican Matthew, whom he had not seen before in that particular body, and immediately commanded: "Follow me." And equally remarkable—as though moments, not a lifetime, had passed—Matthew followed, not from any hypnotic spell, but because he too felt the call of past recognition. Great masters draw followers by rousing and stimulating the dormant soul discrimination and divine will in devotees by the consciousness-expanding spiritual magnetism emanating from the masters.

≈

And it came to pass, that, as Jesus sat at meat in his house, many publicans and sinners sat also together with Jesus and his disciples: for there were many, and they followed him. And when the scribes and Pharisees saw him eat with publicans and sinners, they said unto his disciples, "How is it that he eateth and drinketh with publicans and sinners?"

---

* Levi was also known as Matthew. Cf. parallel references in Matthew 9:9 and Luke 5:27–28.

When Jesus heard it, he saith unto them, "They that are whole have no need of the physician, but they that are sick: I came not to call the righteous, but sinners to repentance" (Mark 2:15–17).

Parallel references:

And Levi made him a great feast in his own house: and there was a great company of publicans and of others that sat down with them (Luke 5:29).

* * *

And it came to pass, as Jesus sat at meat in the house, behold, many publicans and sinners came and sat down with him and his disciples. And when the Pharisees saw it, they said unto his disciples, "Why eateth your Master with publicans and sinners?"

But when Jesus heard that, he said unto them, "They that be whole need not a physician, but they that are sick. But go ye and learn what that meaneth, 'I will have mercy, and not sacrifice': for I am not come to call the righteous, but sinners to repentance" (Matthew 9:10–13).

Offering food to holy personages is an ancient devotional tradition in the Orient. Most spiritual observances are customarily attended by feasts. All peoples—Christians, Hindus, Jews, Muslims—have feasts in connection with certain of their holy days. Though these feasts often become the occasion in themselves, overshadowing the ceremonial purpose, they were necessary when holy persons and their disciples gathered from far and near. In the time of Christ, journey was usually by foot with little accommodation along the way. It was not only a courtesy but a blessing to offer food to a traveler, especially to a holy man. Matthew, no doubt, felt doubly blessed to fete in his home his rediscovered Master from lives past.

The soul doctor Jesus, ate, drank, and associated with the socially outcast "publicans and sinners" who needed him to cure their spiritual sickness of material habits.* When the caste-conscious Pharisees and scribes, accustomed to associating with the upper classes and the

---

* "In Judea, under the Roman system, all circumstances combined to make the publican the object of bitter hatred. He represented and exercised in immediate contact, at a

devoutly orthodox, criticized Jesus for mixing with such untoward company, his reply signified:

"It is the sick in body who need the aid of a doctor, not those who are physically well. The same holds true for spiritually stricken souls. I love to be welcomed into their midst because they need mental, moral, and spiritual divine healing through the godly life manifesting through me."

Great masters open the door to soul liberation for those righteous persons moving steadily toward God; but they also bless the world at large by sowing seeds of enlightenment in the minds of those who need to turn toward better ways. What more convincing demonstration of God's love over evil than its power to win conversion of a wicked heart?

Spiritually virtuous people act properly and ideally in the various situations in life, in harmony with the laws of righteousness. They move along the path toward redemption through their right actions performed at the inner prompting of conscience, rewarded by a silent satisfaction from their soul. Righteous people need little or no corrective discipline, because their innate spiritual sense keeps them on the right path and prevents them from wandering into the temptations of ignorance.

"Sinners" are those who have defective discrimination and lack the conscience of soul attunement; they thus misuse their God-given reason to do that which is wrong. By the repetition of wrong actions, evil habits are developed, which guide sinners into inextricable labyrinthine

The qualitative and quantitative mission of a world savior

ways of error. It is they who need the prescriptions of a Christlike spiritual doctor to help them control themselves and to restore their ravaged conscience.

The metaphysical context of these verses enunciates the God-appointed role of Jesus as a world savior. As a personal savior, he bestows qualitative, or liberating, blessings and grace on his contemporary disciples and on those of all suc-

---

sore spot with individuals, the hated power of Rome. The tax itself was looked upon as an inherent religious wrong, as well as civil imposition, and by many the payment of it was considered a sinful act of disloyalty to God. The tax-gatherer, if a Jew, was a renegade in the eyes of his patriotic fellows. He paid a fixed sum for the taxes, and received for himself what he could over and above that amount. The ancient and widespread curse of arbitrariness was in the system. The tariff rates were vague and indefinite. The collector was thus always under the suspicion of being an extortioner." — *International Standard Bible Encyclopedia*

ceeding generations who look to him for salvation. But additionally, he came to fulfill the more universal dispensation, the quantitative good, of establishing a moral and spiritual standard for all mankind — "to call sinners to repentance." To that end, he mixed with those persons in need of healing from evil to demonstrate personally, by way of example, his quantitative ministry to the masses — to show the transforming power of righteousness that brings response from the forgiving heart of God.

Only a highly evolved soul can actually cure the soul sickness of delusive ignorance in others — and that only with their participation. In associating with sinners and publicans as well as with religious and cultured intellectual persons, and healing the physical and mental maladies of many of them, Jesus' main purpose was to rouse in them the healing process of spiritual awakening. Each benefited according to his or her present capacity; but by contact with the holy presence and blessing of Jesus, the healing had begun. In associating with his disciples, Jesus greatly magnified their spiritual advancement; and in keeping company with sinners he worked his healing powers on their soul sickness and started them on the path of redemption.

Jesus goes on to say to the intellectually self-important scribes and Pharisees, "Learn what it means, 'I will have mercy and not sacrifice'* — to care for the spiritually sick and needy, instead of catering only to the spiritually and morally healthy who make no uncomfortable demands on you. I will have mercy and compassion on the spiritually sick and I will not forsake them; I will try to heal and save them, rather than let them be sacri-

A compassionate message of God's mercy and forgiveness for the repentant

ficed on the altar of their karmic destiny. I am here to call not only those who are already redeemed — those who have shunned evil to embrace righteousness — but especially all manner of sinners from all walks of life who in their worldly-wise ignorant conceptions of the true meaning of life remain tenaciously identified with the body and its agonies and worries. If they are not helped to see their mistakes, they will not repent, but will settle for their motley existence of pleasure and pain, unaware of the saving grace of God-contact in the unqualified bliss of inner divine communion."

---

* Jesus was quoting from the Old Testament Book of Hosea (6:6): "For I desired mercy, and not sacrifice; and the knowledge of God more than burnt offerings."

To awaken repentance in those inured to evil is to show them the way to redeem themselves. The free will irrevocably endowed to all souls enjoins on them personal responsibility for their choices. Jesus knew that to penetrate the implacable nature of inveterate malefactors he had first to awaken their spiritual reason to make them sorry for their evil actions, and thereby ultimately cause them to redress their evil with a preference for righteousness. Redemption is not forthcoming until the wrongdoer is convinced of the error of his ways. Persons who repeat evil actions usually begin to develop a strong compulsive liking for that behavior, in spite of any consequent suffering. Without an understanding and acknowledgment of the inimical nature of sorrow-producing sinful actions, those who succumb to temptation can never find in themselves the will to repent. The error-prone must first be reasoned with, so that their paralyzed discrimination may be brought back to life.

Once discriminative reason is awakened, repentance usually follows; when people feel sorry for their evil actions, they want freedom from those habits. Without repentance, those in delusion make no effort to liberate themselves spiritually. Therefore, when one sees the inanity of his evil actions, he must repent and use his free will repeatedly to perform redeeming actions that reinforce his liberating good karma.

Great spiritual teachers never claim to forgive unrepentant offenders; their work is to awaken the natural righteousness in wrongdoers to the point where they will make an effort to free themselves. No one can prevent confirmed evildoers from reaping the effects of their evil actions; but if they rouse themselves to righteous efforts, the effects of their past evil actions can be neutralized by the effects of their good actions and by the intercession of divine grace.*

Repentance is the forerunner of spiritual liberation. It necessarily precedes any sincere and continuous effort to free oneself from evil. Great doctors of souls can inspire metaphysical truants to retrace their footsteps Godward, and support them in the journey; but the actual walking must be done by the error-stricken themselves. By convincing the heart of the folly and misery involved in delusion's nightmares of evil actions, the penitent arouses his soul, long held in that nonsensical somnolence, and with that awakening power makes a dash for spiritual liberty.

---

* Remission of sins by the grace of God or a God-knowing saint is discussed in Discourse 35.

572

DISCOURSE 32

"The Sabbath Was Made for Man, and Not Man for the Sabbath"

The Expansion of Consciousness Felt in the Presence of a Master

❖

Spiritual Consciousness Is Incompatible
With Small-Minded Dogmatism

❖

The Spirit of the Sabbath Observed Throughout Cosmic Creation

❖

Religious Rules Are to Be Followed With Wisdom,
Not Literalistic Blindness

❖

Sabbath Is a Necessary Observance for a Peaceful, Balanced Life

❖

Real Observance of the Sabbath:
Feeling God's Presence Through Inner Communion

"Jesus sometimes flouted 'the letter of the law' to demonstrate its inner spirit, as in his several clashes with the Pharisees over the proper observance of the Sabbath."

*A*nd the disciples of John and of the Pharisees used to fast: and they come and say unto him, "Why do the disciples of John and of the Pharisees fast, but thy disciples fast not?"

And Jesus said unto them, "Can the children of the bridechamber fast, while the bridegroom is with them? As long as they have the bridegroom with them, they cannot fast. But the days will come, when the bridegroom shall be taken away from them, and then shall they fast in those days.

"No man also seweth a piece of new cloth on an old garment: else the new piece that filled it up taketh away from the old, and the rent is made worse. And no man putteth new wine into old bottles: else the new wine doth burst the bottles, and the wine is spilled, and the bottles will be marred: but new wine must be put into new bottles."

And it came to pass, that he went through the corn fields on the Sabbath day; and his disciples began, as they went, to pluck the ears of corn. And the Pharisees said unto him, "Behold, why do they on the Sabbath day that which is not lawful?"

And he said unto them, "Have ye never read what David did, when he had need, and was an hungred, he, and they that were with him? How he went into the house of God in the days of Abiathar the high priest, and did eat the shewbread, which is not lawful to eat but for the priests, and gave also to them which were with him?"

And he said unto them, "The Sabbath was made for man, and not man for the Sabbath: Therefore the Son of man is Lord also of the Sabbath."

And he entered again into the synagogue; and there was a man there which had a withered hand. And they watched him, whether he would heal him on the Sabbath day; that they might accuse him.

And he saith unto the man which had the withered hand, "Stand forth." And he saith unto them, "Is it lawful to do good on the Sabbath days, or to do evil? to save life, or to kill?" But they held their peace.

And when he had looked round about on them with anger, being grieved for the hardness of their hearts, he saith unto the man, "Stretch forth thine hand." And he stretched it out: and his hand was restored whole as the other.

And the Pharisees went forth, and straightway took counsel with the Herodians against him, how they might destroy him.

But Jesus withdrew himself with his disciples to the sea: and a great multitude from Galilee followed him, and from Judea, and from Jerusalem, and from Idumaea, and from beyond Jordan; and they about Tyre and Sidon, a great multitude, when they had heard what great things he did, came unto him.

And he spake to his disciples, that a small ship should wait on him because of the multitude, lest they should throng him. For he had healed many; insomuch that they pressed upon him for to touch him, as many as had plagues.

And unclean spirits, when they saw him, fell down before him, and cried, saying, "Thou art the Son of God." And he straitly charged them that they should not make him known.

—Mark 2:18—3:12

"The Sabbath Was Made for Man, and Not Man for the Sabbath"

And the disciples of John and of the Pharisees used to fast: and they come and say unto him, "Why do the disciples of John and of the Pharisees fast, but thy disciples fast not?"

And Jesus said unto them, "Can the children of the bride-chamber fast, while the bridegroom is with them? As long as they have the bridegroom with them, they cannot fast. But the days will come, when the bridegroom shall be taken away from them, and then shall they fast in those days" (Mark 2:18–20).

Parallel reference:

Then came to him the disciples of John, saying, "Why do we and the Pharisees fast oft, but thy disciples fast not?"

And Jesus said unto them, "Can the children of the bride-chamber mourn, as long as the bridegroom is with them? But the days will come, when the bridegroom shall be taken from them, and then shall they fast" (Matthew 9:14–15).*

Jesus, characteristically, answered metaphorically the judgmental query put to him, but the meaning of his retort was plain: "Would it not be unseemly for the children of the bridechamber to engage in

---

* Cf. additional parallel reference in Luke 5:33–35.

mournful austerities rather than in rejoicing in the presence of the
bridegroom? Correspondingly, in the company of a master (the bridegroom), his disciples, his spiritual children, abiding
in his divine consciousness (the bridechamber) are   *The expansion of con-*
thereby joyously uplifted and purified in a measure   *sciousness felt in the*
exceeding that afforded by any austere ritual in-   *presence of a master*
junctions, such as disciplinary fasting." By virtue of
being near Jesus, his disciples automatically feasted on the bliss of
God-contact, manifested through the "bridegroom," Jesus' oneness
with the universal Christ Spirit wedded to universal Creative Spirit in
Nature.* His very presence among his disciples was sufficient, through
the exchange of vibrations and their receptivity to his limitless store
of spiritual power, to keep his disciples wrapped in the consciousness
of God.

Jesus did not dismiss the value of fasting with its spiritualizing influence on the minds of men. Periodic fasting, if properly done, not
only promotes health of the body and clarity of the mind, but helps to
free the soul from the bondage of body consciousness. It impresses the
consciousness with the knowledge that the body is not dependent on
food alone for sustenance, but on the Divine Spirit.† Fasting and meditation are thus effective aids in realizing one's connection with God.
But mental and bodily discipline are not an end in themselves; they are
a means to achieve God-consciousness, necessary only until one
reaches that goal. Jesus was a supreme exemplar of divine attainment,
and every receptive person fortunate enough to have contact with him
felt the emanations of his spiritual freedom automatically uplifting
them, if even momentarily, by a grace that transcended austerities.

Jesus went on to specify, however, that more would be required
of his disciples when his divinely magnetic incarnate personality would
be withdrawn from earthly manifestation into the heavenly realms.
They would then have to make greater personal effort in meditation
and in following the spiritual mandates of fasting and other disciplines
in order to retain their freedom from bodily attachment, and to maintain and heighten the elevated state of God-consciousness they had enjoyed in their Master's presence.

---

* See Discourse 16.

† "Man shall not live by bread alone, but by every word that proceedeth out of the
mouth of God" (Matthew 4:4; see Discourse 8).

All true masters are "living" even after discarding their mortal bodies. Their blessings are omnipresent, available to the ardent devotee whether or not disciple and master are incarnate on the same plane.

Disciples are those who strive for attunement with the teacher—to remain always in his spiritual "presence" whether their physical forms are proximate or apart. A vibratory blessing is actuated in the disciple who with reverent devotion makes that inward contact with his God-knowing guru. The magnetism of that subtle current helps to neutralize delusion's effects of karma and habits, allowing a fresh influx of insightful wisdom. The "same-old-me" consciousness is nudged aside to reveal the soul potential that the Lord created him to manifest.

It is the receptivity of the disciple that facilitates and ultimately makes permanent the transference of divine consciousness from the master who is in touch with God. The guru offers the same spiritual wealth to all students; but according to their receptivity, they absorb to greater or lesser degree. Those who are already rigidly habit-formed when they come to the teacher are always dissembling and questioning the master's wisdom, assertively defensive of the rightness of clinging to their accustomed second nature. But those who can put aside their obstinacy will find themselves wondrously reborn in spirit. Thus Jesus differentiated the responsive attitude of his close disciples, open to new revelations and bliss through direct perception, from the skeptics' fault-finding when his ways deviated from the hand-me-down dogmas, unaccommodative to any new infusion of vitalizing truth.

～

> "No man also seweth a piece of new cloth on an old garment: else the new piece that filled it up taketh away from the old, and the rent is made worse. And no man putteth new wine into old bottles: else the new wine doth burst the bottles, and the wine is spilled, and the bottles will be marred: but new wine must be put into new bottles" (Mark 2:21–23).

Parallel reference:

> And he spake also a parable unto them; "No man putteth a piece of a new garment upon an old; if otherwise, then both the new maketh a rent, and the piece that was taken out of the new

*agreeth not with the old. And no man putteth new wine into old
bottles; else the new wine will burst the bottles, and be spilled,
and the bottles shall perish. But new wine must be put into new
bottles; and both are preserved. No man also having drunk old
wine straightway desireth new: for he saith, 'The old is better'"
(Luke 5:36–39).**

J esus characterized as imprudent the use of the new inspiration emanating directly from his spirit for mending the fusty garment of
spiritual customs. Patches of new cloth cannot be
well-matched to worn fabric; too, the strong new   *Spiritual consciousness*
pieces would pull at the old material, rending it,   *is incompatible with*
making it even less useful than before. Jesus was liv-   *small-minded*
ing in Truth. He was emancipating the spirit of the   *dogmatism*
disciples who understood him through a dynamic
revelation of truth-consciousness that was incompatible with the prevailing religious stereotypes. No patchwork grafting of new perceptions
onto the threadbare cloak of dogma worn by the general populace
would suffice for the robes of realization he would offer to his followers. New inspiration, new ways of living truth, replaced the superficially interpreted theology of spiritual codes, rituals, and observances.

As new wine put into old containers may well burst the fragile
vessels by its expanding power, so new, powerful inspiration poured
into dogma-worn minds is sure to shatter old beliefs and cause mental rebellion. Jesus' new inspirations needed receptacles of newly enthusiastic, spiritually powerful souls capable of being filled brimful
with the divine revelations of Spirit.

So Jesus signified: "It would be foolish for my disciples to bottle up
their divine wisdom of new revelations of truth in an old atmosphere of
mechanical rules of popular superstitions and dogmatic codes of conduct.
As new wine should be kept in new bottles, so my disciples have been
given a new consciousness, a new atmosphere of spiritual living, within
which to preserve their new realizations. In their God-intoxication, they
are already experiencing that for which rules were made."

Jesus further noted that persons used to the wine of old dogma
would not have a taste for new revelations of truth. They would say,
"Oh, I know it all. The customary practices of the forefathers (no mat-

---

* Cf. additional parallel reference in Matthew 9:16–17.

ter how antiquated) were good enough for them, so they are good enough for me." Through force of habit they would prefer the old ways of dogmatic living to new habits of spiritual emancipation.

Jesus brought a new dispensation, and trained his disciples accordingly. "God hath made us able ministers of the new testament," wrote Saint Paul, "not of the letter, but of the spirit: for the letter killeth, but the spirit giveth life."* Jesus sometimes flouted "the letter of the law" to demonstrate its inner spirit, as in his several clashes with the Pharisees over the proper observance of the Sabbath.

~

And it came to pass, that he went through the corn fields on the Sabbath day; and his disciples began, as they went, to pluck the ears of corn. And the Pharisees said unto him, "Behold, why do they on the Sabbath day that which is not lawful?"

And he said unto them, "Have ye never read what David did, when he had need, and was an hungred, he, and they that were with him? How he went into the house of God in the days of Abiathar the high priest, and did eat the shewbread, which is not lawful to eat but for the priests, and gave also to them which were with him?" (Mark 2:23–26).

Parallel reference:

At that time Jesus went on the Sabbath day through the corn; and his disciples were an hungred, and began to pluck the ears of corn, and to eat. But when the Pharisees saw it, they said unto him, "Behold, thy disciples do that which is not lawful to do upon the Sabbath day."

But he said unto them, "Have ye not read what David did, when he was an hungred, and they that were with him; How he entered into the house of God, and did eat the shewbread, which was not lawful for him to eat, neither for them which were with him, but only for the priests?

"Or have ye not read in the law, how that on the Sabbath days the priests in the temple profane the Sabbath, and are

---

* II Corinthians 3:6.

blameless? But I say unto you, that in this place is one greater than the temple. But if ye had known what this meaneth, 'I will have mercy, and not sacrifice,' ye would not have condemned the guiltless" (Matthew 12:1–7). *

Through Moses came the scriptural command: "Remember the Sabbath day, to keep it holy. Six days shalt thou labour, and do all thy work: But the seventh day is the Sabbath of the Lord thy God: in it thou shalt not do any work, thou, nor thy son, nor thy daughter, thy manservant, nor thy maidservant, nor thy cattle, nor thy stranger that is within the gates: For in six days the Lord made heaven and earth, the sea, and all that in them is, and rested the seventh day: wherefore the Lord blessed the Sabbath day, and hallowed it" (Exodus 20: 8–11).

The spirit of the Sabbath observed throughout cosmic creation

The Sabbath day is meant to be a time of rest and repose, to balance man's outwardly active nature by contact with the transcendental stillness at the core of his being. It is the seventh day, or day of rest, following six days of hard material activity, in imitation of God's supposedly six days of creative activity followed by a seventh day of rest.† (Of course, the seven days were not solar days, but consisted of aeonic cycles.) The creation of the earth, as also its galactic neighborhood, took untold measures of time to make it habitable for man. When the divine schema and its operational laws and the ideations of forms and beings had been brought into existence under the direction of the active intelligence of God, the Father of creation, the directly active intelligence of God became inactive or indirectly active, allowing His reflection as the Universal Christ Intelligence, and His active Cosmic Creative Vibration of Holy Ghost (Mother Nature), to continue the process of evolving the cosmic plans. Thus, when most of the desires of God to create had been ideated, His will and intelligence could take a rest while the universe continued under its own momentum of cosmic law and His divine agencies of Reflective Intelligence and Creative Vibration. All creation has inherited the pattern of a rest period after

---

* Cf. additional parallel reference in Luke 6:1–4.

† "Thus the heavens and the earth were finished, and all the host of them. And on the seventh day God ended His work which He had made; and He rested on the seventh day from all His work which He had made" (Genesis 2:1–2).

581

intense creative activity. It is evident in the birth and death of stars, the solar and lunar cycles, the seasons, plant life, and in animals and man. It seems as if we and the universe in which we are situated share a kindred vibration in which rest is needed after activity. Therefore was the Sabbath made for man—a time not just for physical relaxation, but a transcendent spiritual rest for the rejuvenation of the indwelling spirit.

Jesus upheld the scriptural commandments given by the prophets; but he taught that it is the spirit of the laws laid down in the holy books that is to be followed, lest a literal following of a rule lead to perversion of its purpose.

The dogmatic priest of ancient times might be so fanatical about observing the Sabbath day that he would not leave his home and take

Religious rules are to be followed with wisdom, not literalistic blindness

a carriage to bring a doctor for his dying brother, servant, or guest.* To follow the Sabbath law while forswearing justified and critical needs, such as to ignore giving aid to a helpless person, is a sin, for it breaks a higher law of divine love and service and disregards the dictates of conscience, which in turn

disturbs inner harmony with God. To take rest on the Sabbath for communion with God, occasionally breaking the vow of interiorization for a legitimate purpose, would not contradict the spirit of observing that holy day. That is why Jesus taught his disciples that rules of conduct are for their betterment and thus should not be followed blindly, but may be modified with strict reason (though not license) when necessary.

Jesus defended his disciples who were inwardly observing the Sabbath in his holy company and service, even though from hunger they had plucked and eaten a few ears of grain as a matter of necessity. Jesus thereto reminded the critics about the story of David, who lived in the grace of God, and who, when he was in need and hungry, went into the house of God and asked of the priest the sacred shewbread for himself and his companions, even though it was contrary to the

---

* *Smith's Bible Dictionary* notes: "[Jesus'] Pharisaic adversaries...had invented many prohibitions respecting the Sabbath of which we find nothing in the original institution. Some of these prohibitions were fantastic and arbitrary....That this perversion of the Sabbath had become very general in our Saviour's time is apparent both from the recorded objections to acts of his on that day, and from his marked conduct on occasions to which those objections were sure to be urged."

law for anyone to eat it but priests in God's service.* If a literal adherence to scriptural injunction could be set aside for spiritual David in order to serve a higher purpose, how much more did Jesus, who was one with God, have the right to disregard outward nuances of the law when he saw that its spirit was truly fulfilled.

Jesus then also cites the priests who were exonerated from the sin of activity on the Sabbath in regard to work done by them in the environs and service of the temple. The transmuting spiritual vibration of Jesus, in whom the Holy Spirit was incarnate, was greater than the exculpatory sanctity of the temple; that is why he said to the Pharisees: "If you knew that the Spirit within me has made my body temple holier by far than the atmosphere of the ancient temple, and that the wisdom of Spirit guides all my actions and through me the actions of those who are with me, you would not condemn my disciples who stand faultless in the eyes of God and in the judgment of His eternal laws. Understand that God seeks not your rituals and sacrificial judgment of human behavior, but rather your compassionate wisdom and divine understanding. Then would I return your mercy, and wisdom would not be sacrificed on the altar of your ignorance."†

∿

And he said unto them, "The Sabbath was made for man, and not man for the Sabbath: Therefore the Son of man is Lord also of the Sabbath" (Mark 2:27–28).‡

The spiritual code of conduct for observance of the Sabbath, especially as a day of divine communion, was created for the advantage and spiritual upliftment of man; the Sabbath was not created as some special entity that man is bound to observe blindly, without

---

* The incident is recorded in I Samuel 21:1–6. The shewbread was a ritual offering of twelve newly baked loaves placed each Sabbath on a table in the temple sanctuary and sprinkled with incense. They were left there until the following Sabbath, when the incense was burned and they were eaten by the priests and replaced by twelve new loaves. It was forbidden to remove them from the sanctuary.

† As he did in Matthew 9:13 (Discourse 31), Jesus again quoted from Hosea 6:6: "For I desired mercy, and not sacrifice; and the knowledge of God more than burnt offerings."

‡ Cf. parallel references in Matthew 12:8 and Luke 6:5.

rhyme or reason. Indeed, an unenlightened following of a dogmatically delineated Sabbath may at times, contrarily, be disadvantageous.

Thus Jesus declared that the Son of man, his physical incarnation with its discriminative wisdom, was the determinative Lord as to the application of the Sabbath injunctions. The Sabbath well serves busy worldly people, giving them one day out of each seven days for freedom from busy-ness, that their outwardly active material nature may be replenished from within by soul calmness and bliss. Sunday (Sun's day, or Wisdom's day) should be spent in God-awakening activities, in keeping with the true purpose of the Sabbath.* To perform distracting material work on the Sabbath day instead of engaging in spiritual contemplation and communion with God may be in nonconformance with the Sabbath; but equally so if the businessman compliantly remains outwardly inactive yet is inwardly engrossed with business thoughts. A spiritual man who meditates every day, and fasts regularly, and who strives to remain conscious of God during every activity, and yet may be occasionally lax on the so-called one-day Sabbath, may apparently transgress the law, but in spirit he does not. The Sabbath is serving him; not he the Sabbath.

A rule consists of a system of mandated actions initiated to produce certain physical or mental results. For the most part, they are conditioned by time and the social and evolutionary state of man. Hence they are variable in accordance with man's environmental changes. Physical, hygienic, social, mental, and spiritual disciplines were temporarily or permanently engendered to suit the development of man and civilization. With due regard to the implacable essence of truth in God's universal laws of righteousness that rules are formulated to uphold, dictums may have to be modified and diversely applied according to the changing needs of man with changing times and cultures.

Jesus points out that if ordinary men can, without transgression, modify rules of conduct on the Sabbath, certainly the Son of man (his spirit within his body) was also master of the Sabbath day and could adapt its observance to accommodate the physical and spiritual needs of himself and his disciples with no diminution of the spirit of the law.

---

* Saturday was the customary Sabbath day during Jesus' time, and remains so in the Jewish religion. Though most modern Christian denominations use Sunday for that purpose, the Sabbath may be beneficially observed on any day suited to one's circumstances or community tradition.

Jesus upheld the Sabbath as essential for man to recharge his vitality by the restful silence of interiorization. The worldly person saturates himself with worries and bombardments of sensory stimuli throughout the week, and loads his body with excessive ill-chosen foods and their unassimilated poisons. A day of fasting and introspective silence, tapping the peaceful wisdom reservoir of the soul, gives each individual a chance to think things over and reorganize his life into a balanced mode. Sermons and periods of silence and meditation on the Sabbath recharge body, mind, and soul. This peace, if deeply infused into the consciousness, may last throughout the whole week, helping man to battle his restless moods, temptations, and financial worries. If the worldly person gives six days of the week to moneymaking pursuits, eating, and amusements, should he not give at least one day to the thought of God, without whom his very life, brain function, physical activity, feeling, and enjoyment of entertainments are impossible?

Sabbath is a necessary observance for a peaceful, balanced life

Observance of the Sabbath as a day given to God and spiritual culture signifies the willing cessation of all activities that scatter and divert the mind into material channels. To close theaters and other venues of entertainment on the Sabbath would be only a token formality, meaningless unless religionists willingly stay away from materialistic diversions to spend the day in God-reminding, spiritually rejuvenating activities. With so many material enticements kept alive on Sabbath days, the minds of people run riot. Where is the time for restorative calmness, introspection, and creative thinking to adopt the best actions for an all-round existence during the coming week? A Sabbath well spent in silence, meditation, and creative thinking (not frantic reasonings but a stilling of thoughts, which are then replaced with intuitive perception) affords the soul reinforcement with harmony, peace, and mental and physical strength to use discrimination to develop physically, mentally, and spiritually in the best possible way. The inveterate worker who goes at it nonstop seven days a week lets his soul become subject to mechanical activity. Such a person loses his ability to govern his activity by free will, discrimination, and peace. He becomes a physical and mental wreck, shorn of spiritual happiness. Activity and calmness both must be cultivated and kept in balance, one with the other, in order to produce peace and happiness during periods of activity as well as silence.

The reader may say that to observe the real spirit of the Sabbath by spending it in seclusion, fasting, introspection, and meditation is impossible in modern times. I would reply: "You might just as well say that it is impossible to be peaceful in modern times." Peace and God-realization come with a price: giving the time necessary to their cultivation. Mahatma Gandhi, one of the great modern spiritual and political reformers, a man of intense activity, nevertheless spent one day a week in complete silence. From this he drew power to lead the whole nation of India to freedom.

One reason why the modern generation is so restless is because children are not nurtured in spiritual ideals and practices. Instead, to get them out of the house they are sent off to the movies or other restless activities following a short, uninteresting Sunday School class in the morning. Spirituality needs to be encouraged (not forced as a discipline) from an early age. The example should be set in every home.

Spiritual endeavor in the beginning seems difficult unless approached with enthusiastic anticipation that generates a perpetual motion of divine ardor. The time comes when one's Sabbath becomes the most interesting and desirable experience by complete ecstatic communion with God. There is no happiness that excels the joy contact of God in deep meditation.

In my classes and lessons I have urged Self-Realization Fellowship students and disciples to celebrate the true spirit of the Sabbath, on

Real observance of the Sabbath: feeling God's presence through inner communion

whatever day of the week possible commensurate with their responsibilities. Even if they cannot devote the whole day to silence and divine communion, I suggest they give at least six hours solely to spiritual contemplation and deep meditation. God does not keep a calendar and make Himself available on only a specific day of the week. There are no time slots in eternity. So neither does He keep a clock to determine when the Sabbath begins and ends. The Sabbath is any day or hours of the day of interior communion with God, no matter what one is doing exteriorly, so that other days or hours of the day, though filled with life's responsibilities, may be inwardly converted into a Sabbath by feeling the presence of God during all activity. This is the spirit of the Sabbath law about which Jesus spoke, in contrast to the rigid literal interpretation simply involving cessation of work. In any case, physical inactivity does not stop the functional work of the body or control its involuntary movements or still the racing of inner thoughts, all of which involve activity that ties man's consciousness to the world.

The science of yoga defines the true meaning of the actionless state that lifts the soul to God-communion. The teaching of the Bhagavad Gita about action and nonaction—the "workless" state of union with Spirit in the vibrationless realm beyond active creation—parallels the true understanding of inner versus outer observance of the Sabbath:* "Actionlessness is not attained simply by avoiding actions. By forsaking work no one reaches perfection. Verily, no one can stay for even a moment without working; all are indeed compelled to perform actions willy-nilly, prodded by the qualities (*gunas*) born of Nature (Prakriti). The individual who forcibly controls the organs of action, but whose mind rotates around thoughts of sense objects, is said to be a hypocrite, deluding himself. But that man succeeds supremely, O Arjuna, who, disciplining the senses by the mind, unattached, keeps his organs of activity steadfast on the path of God-uniting actions [yoga meditation]."†

So long as man's mind and life force are tied to the senses, he is at work. It is when he learns to switch off the life-force currents in the nerves that connect the mind to the senses that he attains the true inactive state of transcendental Spirit. If "inactivity" is the measure of proper Sabbath observance, therefore, only the yogi who has reached the *savikalpa samadhi* state, wherein all bodily activity is suspended in the ecstatic trance of God-union, can be truly said to honor that commandment.

The Gita points out an even higher state: the ultimate stage of divine communion, *nirvikalpa samadhi,* in which the yogi retains his conscious oneness with Spirit without necessarily suspending outer activity. Perfectly identified with God as the Sole Doer, he is said to be "inactively active"—his outer bodily instrument engaged in doing the Lord's will, his inner being free of all desire-born entanglement in the world:

"He is a yogi, discriminative among men, who beholds inactivity in action and action in inaction. He has attained the goal of all actions (and is free)." And, "Like unto the lotus leaf that remains unsullied by water, the yogi who performs actions, forswearing attachment and surrendering his actions to the Infinite, remains unbound by entanglement in the senses."‡

---

* The word derives from Hebrew *shabath,* "to cease to do; to rest."

† *God Talks With Arjuna: The Bhagavad Gita* III:4–7.

‡ *God Talks With Arjuna: The Bhagavad Gita* IV:18 and V:10.
    In her masterworks *The Way of Perfection* and *The Interior Castle,* the renowned mystic Saint Teresa of Avila gives a systematic description, from her own personal ex-

Special Sabbath days are necessary for people who are continuously entangled in material affairs and who do not take any time for God. Jesus was always filled with the Spirit; to him every minute of every day was a Sabbath, whether he moved in the marts of men or retired into transcendent stillness. Hence, on any day of the week he could perform legitimate action, such as appeasing hunger or healing, without violating the spirit of the Sabbath.

~

perience, of the interiorized states of God-communion. These in essence correspond exactly with the progressively higher states of consciousness expounded in India's centuried, universal soul-science of yoga.

The saint describes deepening degrees of God-communion as beginning with the various forms of vocal and mental prayer, and progressing through the interiorized states of "infused recollection," "prayer of quiet," and "prayer of union" which culminates in perfect oneness with God or "spiritual marriage."

Of "the prayer of quiet," she writes in *The Way of Perfection*, trans. E. Allison Peers (Garden City, New York: Image Books, 1991): "In this state all the faculties are stilled. The soul, in a way which has nothing to do with the outward senses, realizes that it is now very close to its God, and that, if it were but a little closer, it would become one with Him through union....

"The body experiences the greatest delight and the soul is conscious of a deep satisfaction. So glad is it merely to find itself near the fountain that, even before it has begun to drink, it has had its fill. There seems nothing left for it to desire. The faculties are stilled and have no wish to move, for any movement they may make appears to hinder the soul from loving God."

She goes on to describe three distinct stages of union: simple union, ecstatic union, and perfect union (spiritual marriage). Saint Teresa's writings on these exalted states have been summarized as follows by Catholic scholar Albert Farges, in *Mystical Phenomena* (London: Burns, Oates, and Washbourne, 1926), who writes: "Whilst in simple union the senses are more or less asleep, and awake if disturbed; in ecstasy, on the contrary, they are totally suspended, or rather in a state of anaesthesia, to such an extent that even violent disturbance will not arouse them. The hand of an ecstatic engaged in prayer may be approached with the flame of a candle, without his feeling the least pain....[It] is as though the soul were no longer in the body: to such an extent that philosophers and theologians have asked themselves whether, for example, the soul of St. Paul, during his ecstasy, did really cease to animate his body....

"All mystical theologians are agreed in placing, above ecstatic union, a still more perfect degree of union, the height of earthly contemplation and a foretaste of eternal beatitude....In it ecstasy may become very rare....As Suarez has remarked, our Lord, during his mortal life, was able to enjoy the beatific vision without ever falling into the swoon of ecstasy....The highest summit of contemplative life here below seems, then, to coincide with freedom from this weakness and natural imperfection of the life of the senses; that is to say, with rarity and even complete absence of the swoons of ecstasy." *(Publisher's Note)*

*And he entered again into the synagogue; and there was a man
there which had a withered hand. And they watched him,
whether he would heal him on the Sabbath day; that they might
accuse him.*

*And he saith unto the man which had the withered hand,
"Stand forth." And he saith unto them, "Is it lawful to do good
on the Sabbath days, or to do evil? to save life, or to kill?" But
they held their peace (Mark 3:1–4).*

Parallel reference:

*And when he was departed thence, he went into their synagogue:
And, behold, there was a man which had his hand withered. And
they asked him, saying, "Is it lawful to heal on the Sabbath
days?" that they might accuse him.*

*And he said unto them, "What man shall there be among
you, that shall have one sheep, and if it fall into a pit on the Sabbath day, will he not lay hold on it, and lift it out? How much
then is a man better than a sheep? Wherefore it is lawful to do
well on the Sabbath days" (Matthew 12:9–12).**

Jesus knew the thoughts of the Pharisees, that they wanted to entrap him. Yet he boldly commanded the afflicted man: "Rise up
and stand forth in the midst of the throng in full view so that they can
behold the good works of God of healing on the Sabbath day."

And when the man stood up, Jesus addressed the throng as to
whether observing the Sabbath day precluded the performing of good
actions. Jesus, by his question, implied that since observing the Sabbath day was itself a good action, it was contradictory to outlaw other
good actions on Sabbath days. The Pharisees could not answer him
without entrapping themselves, and so remained quiet.

Jesus made his point that none soever among that throng would
refrain from rescuing his one valuable sheep fallen into a pit on the
Sabbath day; how much greater the necessity, then, to lift an even
more precious man from the pit of trouble. As the Sabbath was made
to increase man's spiritual consciousness, how can it be anything but
lawful to do any activity that enhances that consciousness?

---

* Cf. additional parallel reference in Luke 6:6–9.

~

*And when he looked round about on them with anger, being
grieved for the hardness of their hearts, he saith unto the man,
"Stretch forth thine hand." And he stretched it out and his hand
was restored whole as the other (Mark 3:5).**

Ignorance is regrettable; ignorance that hardens the heart is despicable. The callousness that obliterated compassion roused in Jesus
spiritual indignation—not base anger, but the will force of righteousness. He said to the man whose hand was withered, "Stretch forth
thine hand."

A person to be healed must do something to make his mind and
spirit receptive. The man's volition of putting forth his hand was an
act of faith in the divine healing power coming from Jesus. The command of Jesus signified: "Make an effort of your will to stretch forth
your heretofore useless hand and send the all-healing energy there. If
you do so and are in tune with me, my divine will, controlling the cosmic energy of the universe, also present in your will and your bodily
energy, will heal you."

~

Jesus reiterated his point about good works on the Sabbath on another occasion, as related in the Gospel According to St. Luke:

*And he was teaching in one of the synagogues on the Sabbath.
And, behold there was a woman which had a spirit of infirmity
eighteen years, and was bowed together, and could in no wise lift
up herself.*

*And when Jesus saw her, he called her to him, and said unto
her, "Woman, thou art loosed from thine infirmity." And he laid
his hands on her: and immediately she was made straight, and
glorified God.*

*And the ruler of the synagogue answered with indignation,
because that Jesus had healed on the Sabbath day, and said unto*

---

* Cf. parallel references in Matthew 12:13 and Luke 6:10.

the people, "There are six days in which men ought to work: in
them therefore come and be healed, and not on the Sabbath day."

The Lord then answered him, and said, "Thou hypocrite,
doth not each one of you on the Sabbath loose his ox or his ass
from the stall, and lead him away to watering? And ought not
this woman, being a daughter of Abraham, whom Satan hath
bound, lo, these eighteen years, be loosed from this bond on the
Sabbath day?" And when he had said these things, all his ad-
versaries were ashamed: and all the people rejoiced for all the
glorious things that were done by him (Luke 13:10–17).

~

After Jesus had healed the withered hand of the afflicted man, the
temple authorities were outraged at what they perceived as
Jesus' defiance of scriptural law:

And the Pharisees went forth, and straightway took counsel with
the Herodians against him, how they might destroy him.

But Jesus withdrew himself with his disciples to the sea: and
a great multitude from Galilee followed him, and from Judea,
and from Jerusalem, and from Idumaea, and from beyond Jor-
dan; and they about Tyre and Sidon, a great multitude, when
they had heard what great things he did, came unto him.

And he spake to his disciples, that a small ship should wait
on him because of the multitude, lest they should throng him.
For he had healed many; insomuch that they pressed upon him
for to touch him, as many as had plagues.

And unclean spirits, when they saw him, fell down before
him, and cried, saying, "Thou art the Son of God." And he
straitly charged them that they should not make him known
(Mark 3:6–12).

Parallel reference:

Then the Pharisees went out, and held a council against him,
how they might destroy him.

But when Jesus knew it, he withdrew himself from thence: and
great multitudes followed him, and he healed them all; and

591

charged them that they should not make him known: That it
might be fulfilled which was spoken by Isaiah the prophet, saying,
    "Behold My servant, whom I have chosen; My beloved, in
whom My soul is well pleased: I will put My spirit upon him,
and he shall shew judgment to the Gentiles. He shall not strive,
nor cry; neither shall any man hear his voice in the streets.
    "A bruised reed shall he not break, and smoking flax shall he
not quench, till he send forth judgment unto victory. And in his
name shall the Gentiles trust" (Matthew 12:14–21).

With plots brewing to destroy him, Jesus did not want to rouse
further excitement about his ability to perform spiritual miracles lest
the overwrought inimical forces feel threatened by his powers. So, prudently, he withdrew with his disciples to the sea, removing himself for
a time from the proximity of the controversy. But as a great multitude
had followed him, Jesus told his disciples to have a ship ready onto
which he could retire from the press of the throng. After he had ministered to the crowd and healed the many, he wanted to have refuge
in solitude. Even the greatest of the great, who serve mankind with
their spirit wholly united to God, never forget their highest duty and
joy of solitary ecstatic communion. From the adulation of crowds,
Jesus turned away to bask in the sole meaningful approbation of the
Heavenly Father—without whose power he could not heal the afflicted, and from whom he derived the grace of his strength, love, and
inspiration.

Understanding
Isaiah's prophecy
about Jesus' mission
and dispensation

With his very life in danger and his mission yet
to be consummated, Jesus asked those who were
healed and who were witnesses to his miraculous
powers to keep those blessings to themselves, lest
they only increase the ire of his enemies. Matthew
elaborates on the unfolding events by citing the ancient prophecy of Isaiah enunciating the future conditions surrounding the appearance and dispensation of Jesus on earth.* God speaks

---

* "Behold My servant, whom I uphold; Mine elect, in whom My soul delighteth; I have
put My spirit upon him: he shall bring forth judgment to the Gentiles. He shall not cry,
nor lift up, nor cause his voice to be heard in the street. A bruised reed shall he not
break, and the smoking flax shall he not quench: he shall bring forth judgment unto
truth. He shall not fail nor be discouraged, till he have set judgment in the earth: and
the isles shall wait for his law" (Isaiah 42:1–4).

to the prophet Isaiah that He will send His servant, "My beloved in whom My soul is well pleased"—God's beloved child Jesus, of divine stature, chosen by God to act as His servant in bringing to the world a great message that will redeem many souls. God also promised, "I will put My spirit upon him"—God's will and blessings and wisdom will grace the harmony-tuned soul of Jesus, that he might show to the people of the world divine judgment of salvation bestowed by wisdom and righteous living.

God signified further to Isaiah that this messenger would be no ordinary saintly soul still having to "strive" for spirituality and to "cry" in the darkness of delusion for wisdom, but that Jesus, in his coming Christ-consciousness incarnation, will be already spiritually reinforced with the will and wisdom of God. Even so, "neither shall any man hear his voice in the streets"—the divinity of Jesus, cloaked in mortal garb, will not be obvious to ordinary human beings, walking the streets of matter; they would not be able to hear the voice of the cosmic vibration of the Spirit of God encased in the body of Jesus.

"A bruised reed shall he not break"—the transcendent consciousness of Jesus as the Son of God would not be at all affected, even though his spirit was encased in the fragile reed of a body that might be bruised, or crucified. "Smoking flax shall he not quench"—his spirit, burning with wisdom like smoking flax, would not be quenched or suppressed by the persecution of the flesh. "Till he send forth judgment unto victory"—though reviled and threatened, he would not give up the body until he had sent forth, or expressed, his judgment of the soul-liberating justice of wisdom in complete victory of the fulfillment of his God-given dispensation. The triumph of Jesus would be punctuated with his return to earth after death, declaring the ultimate victory of Spirit over matter. He would not leave his incarnation on earth until he had declared to the world that he, even during crucifixion of his body, could retain the magnanimity and the God-conscious qualities of the soul untouched by the tortures of flesh and the hatred of man—and the final insult of death.

Isaiah prophesied that "the Gentiles," the world at large outside of Israel, would in a far-reaching measure come to accept Jesus as their guru or savior. Even when he was no longer incarnate, they would intuitively realize Spirit as the Christ in Jesus. The concluding words of the prophecy (Isaiah 42:4) confirm this stature of Jesus as a world savior: "He shall not fail nor be discouraged, till he have set judgment (the codes of righteousness) in the earth: and the isles (all continents) shall wait for his law."

Prophecies of the great ones can be understood and correctly interpreted only through the Self-realization and developed intuition of true devotees. Intellectuals write philosophical discourses that can be understood by all intelligent people. But the sayings of Jesus and the utterances of prophets are born of their pure Self-realization, not from the uncertain meanderings of reason. As such, they can never be grasped fully by the mere intellect of man; their meaning can be only inferred by reason. The Self-realization revelations of saints and prophets become fully meaningful only when intuitively felt and understood by those who have meditated and developed their own Self-realization with its direct perception of truth.

DISCOURSE 33

Ordination of the Twelve Apostles and Sermon on the Plain

A God-realized Master's "Spiritual Children":
The Inner Circle of Disciples

❖

Why Did Jesus Include the Traitor Judas
in the Select Group of Apostles?

❖

Jesus' Warnings to Those Who Shun the Wisdom of Seeking God

❖

Restoring Spiritual Sight to Those Whose Discrimination
Is Blinded by Ego

❖

How Man's Tree of Life Grows Good and Evil Fruits
of Sensations and Desires

❖

The Yoga Science of Freeing the Heart From Evil

"The disciples chosen by the guru become his expanded family responsibility until all are liberated in God. Jesus followed this tradition. And though one betrayed him, eleven carried on his work."

*A*nd it came to pass in those days, that he went out into a mountain to pray, and continued all night in prayer to God.

And when it was day, he called unto him his disciples: and of them he chose twelve, whom also he named apostles; Simon, (whom he also named Peter,) and Andrew his brother, James and John, Philip and Bartholomew, Matthew and Thomas, James the son of Alphaeus, and Simon called Zelotes, and Judas the brother of James, and Judas Iscariot, which also was the traitor.

And he came down with them, and stood in the plain, and the company of his disciples, and a great multitude of people out of all Judea and Jerusalem, and from the sea coast of Tyre and Sidon, which came to hear him, and to be healed of their diseases; and they that were vexed with unclean spirits: and they were healed.

And the whole multitude sought to touch him: for there went virtue out of him, and healed them all.

And he lifted up his eyes on his disciples, and said, "Blessed be ye poor: for yours is the kingdom of God. Blessed are ye that hunger now: for ye shall be filled. Blessed are ye that weep now: for ye shall laugh.

"Blessed are ye, when men shall hate you, and when they shall separate you from their company, and shall reproach you, and cast out your name as evil, for the Son of man's sake. Rejoice ye in that day, and leap for joy: for, behold, your reward is great in heaven: for in the like manner did their fathers unto the prophets.

"But woe unto you that are rich! for ye have received your consolation. Woe unto you that are full! for ye shall hunger. Woe unto you that laugh now! for ye shall mourn and weep. Woe unto you, when all men shall speak well of you! for so did their fathers to the false prophets.

"But I say unto you which hear, love your enemies, do good to them which hate you, bless them that curse you, and pray for them which despitefully use you.

"And unto him that smiteth thee on the one cheek offer also the other; and him that taketh away thy cloak forbid not to take thy coat also. Give to every man that asketh of thee; and of him that taketh away thy goods ask them not again.

"And as ye would that men should do to you, do ye also to them likewise.

"For if ye love them which love you, what thank have ye? for sinners also love those that love them. And if ye do good to them which do good to you, what thank have ye? for sinners also do even the same. And if ye lend to them of whom ye hope to receive, what thank have ye? for sinners also lend to sinners, to receive as much again.

"But love ye your enemies, and do good, and lend, hoping for nothing again; and your reward shall be great, and ye shall be the children of the Highest: for He is kind unto the unthankful and to the evil.

"Be ye therefore merciful, as your Father also is merciful.

"Judge not, and ye shall not be judged: condemn not, and ye shall not be condemned: forgive, and ye shall be forgiven:

"Give, and it shall be given unto you; good measure, pressed down, and shaken together, and running over, shall men give into your bosom. For with the same measure that ye mete withal it shall be measured to you again."

And he spake a parable unto them, "Can the blind lead the blind? Shall they not both fall into the ditch?

"The disciple is not above his master: but every one that is perfect shall be as his master.

"And why beholdest thou the mote that is in thy brother's eye, but perceivest not the beam that is in thine own eye? Either how canst thou say to thy brother, 'Brother, let me pull out the mote that is in thine eye,' when thou thyself beholdest not the beam that is in thine own eye? Thou hypocrite, cast out first the beam out of thine own eye, and then shalt thou see clearly to pull out the mote that is in thy brother's eye.

"For a good tree bringeth not forth corrupt fruit; neither doth a corrupt tree bring forth good fruit. For every tree is known by his own fruit. For of thorns men do not gather figs, nor of a bramble bush gather they grapes.

"A good man out of the good treasure of his heart bringeth forth that which is good; and an evil man out of the evil treasure of his heart bringeth forth that which is evil: for of the abundance of the heart his mouth speaketh.

"And why call ye me, 'Lord, Lord,' and do not the things which I say? Whosoever cometh to me, and heareth my sayings, and doeth them, I will shew you to whom he is like: He is like a man which built an house, and digged deep, and laid the foundation on a rock: and when the flood arose, the stream beat vehemently upon that house, and could not shake it: for it was founded upon a rock.

"But he that heareth, and doeth not, is like a man that without a foundation built an house upon the earth; against which the stream did beat vehemently, and immediately it fell; and the ruin of that house was great."

—Luke 6:12–49*

---

* Many of Jesus' sayings in verses 20–49, known as the Sermon on the Plain, parallel verses in the Sermon on the Mount in St. Matthew's Gospel. See Discourses 26–30 for corresponding commentary.

DISCOURSE 33

Ordination of the Twelve Apostles and Sermon on the Plain

And it came to pass in those days, that he went out into a mountain to pray, and continued all night in prayer to God.

And when it was day, he called unto him his disciples: and of them he chose twelve, whom also he named apostles; Simon, (whom he also named Peter,) and Andrew his brother, James and John, Philip and Bartholomew, Matthew and Thomas, James the son of Alphaeus, and Simon called Zelotes, and Judas the brother of James, and Judas Iscariot, which also was the traitor (Luke 6:12–16).

Parallel reference:

And he goeth up into a mountain, and calleth unto him whom he would: and they came unto him. And he ordained twelve, that they should be with him, and that he might send them forth to preach, and to have power to heal sicknesses, and to cast out devils:

And Simon he surnamed Peter; and James the son of Zebedee, and John the brother of James; and he surnamed them Boanerges, which is, The sons of thunder: And Andrew, and Philip, and Bartholomew, and Matthew, and Thomas, and James the son of Alphaeus, and Thaddaeus, and Simon the Canaanite, and

Judas Iscariot, which also betrayed him: and they went into an house (Mark 3:13–19). *

It was time for Jesus to choose from among his disciples the twelve whom he would "send forth" as apostles to spread his message.† Preliminarily ensconced in the solitary high reaches of the nearby mountains, Jesus passed the night in ecstatic prayer and God-communion, so deeply engrossed in his union and joy with God that he did not notice the silent passage of the hours into dawn. Ordinary worshipers engage in their devotions with their minds marking the measured pace of time, but Jesus prayed with his mind concentrated in the eternity of the Infinite Bliss of Spirit.

Mountaintops and caves are always sanctioned by the masters as quiet places for meditation. Legendary are the Himalayan yogis whose endeavors, lofty in clime and spirit, silently bless the world with their holy vibrations of God-communion. The Biblical history of the Holy Land refers often to sacred mountains frequented by the prophets. God first spoke to Moses on Mount Horeb (Exodus 3:1 ff.), and gave to him the Ten Commandments on Mount Sinai (Exodus 19:15 ff.). Mount Carmel is referenced in association with Elijah and Elisha and other prophets. And Mount Gerizim and the worship thereon of the forefathers is cited in the story of the woman of Samaria [Discourse 18].

Persons who seek opportunity to meditate in sequestered mountains find that locale free not only from the noise but also from the noxious vapors of the city. A high elevation assists the meditator with a rarefied atmosphere that is freer from gross gases. The physical and astral bodies of man become harmoniously adapted to a finer atmosphere than the denser air of low elevations. Highly charged oxygen in the mountains helps the practice of breathing exercises calculated to remove carbon waste from the system, quiet the heart, and switch off the life current from the five senses so that sensory stimuli cannot cause mental restlessness and distract the meditative attention from God.‡ Aesthetically, mountains have a spiritualizing effect as they lift

---

* See also additional parallel reference in Matthew 10:1–4 (Discourse 40).

† The word *apostle* comes from a Greek term meaning "to send forth."

‡ Scientists have shown that the air at higher elevations, because of greater exposure to solar and other radiation, contains a larger number of "negative ions"—molecules that have acquired an extra electron, giving them a negative electrical charge. Negative ions

the vision of man from the confinements of man-made edifices to the vast, limitless sky, the spacial physical embodiment of the Infinite.

The choosing of the twelve apostles by Jesus from among his disciples has a very significant meaning. In the guru-disciple tradition in India, each great master who attains God-consciousness has two kinds of devotees who come to him for spiritual training. Those, married or unmarried, who come for general instruction are called students; but those students who dedicate their entire lives to the pursuit of God-realization and who are thereby enjoined to propagate the teaching of the master to the world through the example of their spiritual development as manifested in their lives are called disciples.* From among the disciples are those who, in many orders, renounce the world in a single-hearted divine quest within a structured spiritual life and service to the work of the master. They help to disseminate his teachings not only through the example of their lives but also as ordained teachers, whether serving behind the scenes in the ashram or in public. The very act of living for God alone is in itself a sermon to the world, eloquent beyond the finest oratory. The duly ordained teacher who possesses both a holy life and a clarity in conveying truth is a true "apostle" of the master, "sent forth" to serve for him as a pure voice of his God-given message.

A God-realized master's "spiritual children": the inner circle of disciples

As worthy children endeavor to add to their family name prestige in the world, so disciples as the spiritual children of a master seek to extol his name by the virtue of their lives. When a father brings forth a son into the world, the child inherits by nature and environment the family traits, good or bad. Even if a child turns out to be problematic, or a criminal, he has still to be contended with by the family. Parents have no choice as to the kind of children they bring on earth (unless they know the spiritual art of procreation by which a good soul from the astral world can be invited to be born into their family by an act of super-will power and meditation). A master, on the other hand, has the advantage

---

of oxygen bond more readily to the hemoglobin in the blood, and thus more oxygen is assimilated with each breath. This accounts for the feeling of increased vitality produced by fresh mountain air (and by the ocean breeze and waterfalls and air just after a lightning storm, all of which generate negative ions). A summary of research on ions in the air and their effect on physical and mental well-being is found in *The Ion Effect* by Fred Soyka with Alan Edmonds (New York: Bantam Books, 1977). *(Publisher's Note)*

* See also Discourse 9.

of being able to select qualified disciples, his spiritual children, from a vast number of followers, and to implant in them the seed of his spiritual vitality so that they can perpetuate the influence of the master's life.

In the case of Jesus, he not only selected a particular group as his inner circle of disciples, but he chose them from among those souls he had known in a previous incarnation. That is why Jesus, on seeing Simon, told him, "Follow me," and without hesitation Simon followed him.* Jesus selected his disciples for three reasons: First, because they had not reached, but were near, the final state of realization; and therefore he wanted to assist them in the attainment of perfection. Second, after reawakening their past spiritual potential for reaching the final state of emancipation, Jesus required their assistance as apostles or model disciples who could be pioneers to propagate the message of Christhood to the masses through ideal living. Last of all, Jesus knew, according to the plan of the Heavenly Father, that he would have twelve disciples, these particular twelve, to carry out his message to the world. His mission as a world savior, assisted by twelve apostles, had been symbolically foreshadowed in his previous incarnation, when as Elisha he was the chosen disciple of the prophet Elijah: "So he [Elijah] departed thence, and found Elisha the son of Shaphat, who was plowing with twelve yoke of oxen before him, and he with the twelfth: and Elijah passed by him, and cast his mantle upon him" (I Kings 19:19).† The twelve yoke of oxen with which Elisha was plowing symbolized the twelve disciples whom Jesus was to bring under the yoke of spiritual discipline for the sake of their own perfection and to make them fit instruments to inaugurate the spread of Jesus' message to all lands.

When accepting a disciple for spiritual training, a master sometimes changes that individual's family name, which perpetuates a worldly lineage and kinship, to one signifying the disciple's new role in helping to perpetuate the master's spiritual lineage and the life of his ideals and teachings. Simon, whom Jesus renamed Peter, "the rock," was to represent the adamantine faith that would be the foundation of Jesus' ongoing mission; that is why later Peter was taken to task for denying Jesus three times under the impulse of fear.‡ Jesus changed the surnames of James and John, the sons of Zebedee, to

---

* See Discourse 23.

† See Discourse 2.

‡ See Discourse 73.

Boanerges ("the sons of thunder"), to denote their power to fulfill their apostolic roles as disciples of their omnipotent master.

There is a popular adage that says, "blood is thicker than water"; it was once quoted to me as a purported reminder that one should think first of one's family's wishes in preference to giving one's life to God. I say that is not true. Blood may be thicker than water, but spiritual blood is thicker still. The spiritual relation of souls united in seeking God is stronger and more binding than any other relation. Each person is born into a particular family for one lifetime only; but he or she who forms a spiritual bond with kindred souls will walk together the path to God through many lifetimes. Out of numerous children of numerous families, the disciples chosen by the guru become his expanded family responsibility until all are liberated in God. Jesus followed this tradition. And though one betrayed him, eleven carried on his work.

The coming of Judas into the company of the chosen of Christ distinctly shows that a disciple is given every spiritual opportunity of a master's blessings, yet has independence to work against the will of God. The omniscience of God surely has at least presumptive knowledge according to a person's karmic inclinations as to how that person is going to use his free will—whether he will exercise it properly or misuse it. Jesus knew the law of cause and effect and the evil propensities of the karma of Judas, so he could predict the probability of his betrayal;* and still Jesus chose him as a disciple. It should be clearly understood that it was not the God-ordained fate of Judas to betray Jesus; rather that Judas insinuated himself into that villainous role according to the lawful effects of his prenatal actions that predisposed him to be the cause of the betrayal of Christ, which set the stage for Jesus' test and sacrifice on the cross. Under the divine influence of Jesus, Judas had the opportunity to change his karmic pattern; but he heeded the voice of his egoic satanic ignorance rather than the guidance of Christ-wisdom. God puts his devotees through great tests, and Judas failed this one miserably. Yet, such is the paradox that it was Judas who precipitated the culminating victory of Jesus' life that showed to the world for the ages to come Christ's

Why did Jesus include the traitor Judas in the select group of apostles?

---

* Jesus' foreknowledge of Judas's treachery is apparent in many Gospel verses, such as John 6:71 [Discourse 43]; John 13:21–27 [Discourse 70]; and Matthew 26:46–47 [Discourse 73].

immortality as a world savior and eminent exemplar of the love and forgiveness of God. For his ill-chosen part in the drama of Christ's crucifixion and resurrection, Judas became his foremost publicity agent; but woe unto Judas for his perfidious act of betrayal.

~

And he came down with them, and stood in the plain, and the company of his disciples, and a great multitude of people out of all Judea and Jerusalem, and from the sea coast of Tyre and Sidon, which came to hear him, and to be healed of their diseases; and they that were vexed with unclean spirits: and they were healed.

And the whole multitude sought to touch him: for there went virtue out of him, and healed them all (Luke 6:17–19).

And Jesus, in divine glory, with his twelve disciples, stood in the plains amidst a great multitude of people, gathered to hear the gospel and to be healed. The crowd thronged to touch Jesus, for virtue, or life force, went out from his body, drawn by the faith of the sick. The all-healing energy, dormantly present in the afflicted, was roused by their faith and reinforced with the power coming from Jesus. That energy, finer than the finest of gross rays, emanates from the cosmic energy of God with power to destroy not only physical germs and physiological malfunctions, but mental bacteria of evil tendencies, and spiritual infectious agents of ignorance.

~

And he lifted up his eyes on his disciples, and said, "Blessed be ye poor: for yours is the kingdom of God. Blessed are ye that hunger now: for ye shall be filled. Blessed are ye that weep now: for ye shall laugh.

"Blessed are ye, when men shall hate you, and when they shall separate you from their company, and shall reproach you, and cast out your name as evil, for the Son of man's sake. Rejoice ye in that day, and leap for joy: for, behold, your reward is great in heaven: for in the like manner did their fathers unto the prophets.

"But woe unto you that are rich! for ye have received your consolation. Woe unto you that are full! for ye shall hunger. Woe unto you that laugh now! for ye shall mourn and weep. Woe unto you, when all men shall speak well of you! for so did their fathers to the false prophets" (Luke 6:20–26).

The Beatitudes, the enunciation of those who are blessed, are enumerated more extensively in the Gospel of St. Matthew, already commented on.* Having pointed out in The Beatitudes the practical behavior requisite on the path to heavenly bliss, Jesus' words in the "Sermon on the Plain" then gave warning to those who would shun that counsel. In contrast to the blessed ones who seek the rewards of heaven, woe unto those who are so satisfied with their material rewards that they foolishly do not seek the all-misery-quenching fountainhead of Everlasting Bliss.

Jesus' warnings to those who shun the wisdom of seeking God

Jesus had some rich followers. By his words, "Woe unto you that are rich," he condemned not the possession of wealth but attachment to earthly treasure, and selfish hoarding without sharing with others in need. Possessiveness makes one callous to the sufferings of others and gives one a false sense of security. Riches cannot prevent the advent of disease or catastrophe or death. To be satisfied with wealth gives one the false consolation that he has everything, whereas he really has very little—and even that is only given to him for his temporary use, to be instantly taken away when the time comes to leave this world. The only prosperity one takes with him is his treasure trove of wisdom and bliss from the realization of truth in meditation. Hence, Jesus warns man to beware of material wealth that it not act as an opiate to deaden the desire for God, who alone can give eternal satisfaction and security.†

Woe unto those who are content with material offerings and earthly pleasures, feeling no real hunger for God and truth. Someday with the approach of death, or through loss before death, there will

---

* See Discourse 26 for commentary on The Beatitudes according to the Gospel of St. Matthew, with parallel references from the above verses of Luke 6:20–23.

† Cf. Discourse 56: "Take heed, and beware of covetousness: for a man's life consisteth not in the abundance of the things which he possesseth" (Luke 12:15); and Discourse 63: "Children, how hard it is for them that trust in riches to enter into the kingdom of God! It is easier for a camel to go through the eye of a needle, than for a rich man to enter into the kingdom of God" (Mark 10:24–25).

605

be pangs of hunger for security and for alleviation of helplessness or innumerable wants.

Woe unto those who are smiling in satisfaction with material pleasure, for that will be short-lasting, followed by regret that precious time was lost in evanescent follies instead of being well spent in seeking the everlasting rejoicing of the soul.*

It was not to threaten or condemn that Jesus gave voice to his Father's loving wisdom-admonitions, but to help man to avoid the ignorant behavior that ends in suffering. Lord Krishna too in the Bhagavad Gita describes the woeful self-determined fate wrought by one who worships not God and His expression in the soul, but material wealth, power, and pleasures:

> Believing that fulfillment of bodily desires is man's highest aim, confident that this world is "all," such persons are engrossed till the moment of death in earthly cares and concerns. Bound by hundreds of fetters of selfish hopes and expectations, enslaved by wrath and passion, they strive to provide for physical enjoyments by amassing wealth dishonestly.
>
> "This I have acquired today; now another desire I shall satisfy. This is my present wealth; however, more shall also be mine. I have killed this enemy; and the others also I will slay. I am the ruler among men; I enjoy all possessions; I am successful, strong, and happy. I am rich and well-born; can any other be compared with me? Ostentatiously I will give alms and make formal sacrifices; I will rejoice."
>
> Thus they speak, led astray by lack of wisdom. Harboring bewildering thoughts, caught in the net of delusion, craving only sensual delights, they sink into a foul hell.†

A deluded individual, trying to the end of life to fulfill his numerous unslakable desires, is a victim of endless worries and frustrations. Such a person builds castles in the air, acquiring and maintaining a surfeit of possessions, vainly anticipating a continuity of happiness from sense enjoyments.

---

* "Because thou sayest, I am rich, and increased with goods, and have need of nothing; and knowest not that thou art wretched, and miserable, and poor, and blind, and naked: I counsel thee to buy of me gold tried in the fire, that thou mayest be rich; and white raiment, that thou mayest be clothed, and that the shame of thy nakedness do not appear; and anoint thine eyes with eyesalve, that thou mayest see" (Revelation 3:17–18).

† *God Talks With Arjuna: The Bhagavad Gita* XVI:11–16.

Driving the Money Changers Out of the Temple

And Jesus went into the temple of God, and cast out all them that sold and bought in the temple, and overthrew the tables of the moneychangers, and the seats of them that sold doves, and said unto them, "It is written, 'My house shall be called the house of prayer; but ye have made it a den of thieves.'"

—Matthew 21:12–13

A true exemplar of peace is centered in his divine Self. All actions arising therefrom are imbued with the soul's nonpareil vibratory power—whether issuing forth as a calm command or a strong volition....The actions of divine personalities, however, are sometimes willfully startling to shake complacent minds out of their vacuous acceptance of the commonplace. An accurate sense of spiritual propriety in a world of relativity requires a ready wit and a steady wisdom....

Spirituality abhors spinelessness. One should always have the moral courage and backbone to show strength when the occasion calls for it.

—Paramahansa Yogananda

Drawing by Heinrich Hofmann

The desire alcoholic, besotted with one draught of longings after another, is never appeased. His ever-gorged but still unquenched thirst receives respite only temporarily in death. He is soon reborn with his insatiable material desires intact, bringing in their wake new sufferings and cares. The one-track-minded individual, worshiping the gratification of human lusts, moves deeper and deeper into the mire of miseries.

Good activities and right behavior are the direct way to happiness. The pathways of desires and sensory gratifications are a confounding maze of troubles. Pursuit of material goals as the be-all and end-all of life takes man farther and farther from true soul happiness; he carries a self-created portable hades of misery within himself wherever he goes. Pursuit of divine activities leads straightway to the recovery of man's lost blessedness.

Jesus was not counseling a doleful existence when he said: "Woe unto you that laugh now." It is not that one should not laugh at all: Righteousness is the crucible of joy. But material pleasures must not counteract desire for spiritual pleasures; in fact, material enjoyments should be governed by spiritual standards. Unless enjoyment of the good and beauty in the world is spiritualized with right behavior, one becomes satiated with the intoxication of sense pleasures. The heart, so sated, all the more feels the contrast of pain at the loss of enjoyment. It is a psychological fact that pleasure is born of a desire fulfilled and pain is born of a desire unfulfilled. Both are crests of waves. Man is constantly tossing atop these contrasting extremes. In the hollow between the two waves is the state of indifference or boredom. He who rides on the crest of material pleasure must also invariably ride on the crest of pain, since relativity is the law of the physical world. Man must neutralize these relativities within himself by mental transcendence. Those who float on the still waters of inner peace never have to undergo the pain of unfulfillment. "He who is everywhere nonattached, neither joyously excited by encountering good nor disturbed by evil, has an established wisdom."*

Woe unto those of whom men of worldly standards speak well, acclaiming them for their material wealth and hedonistic life. Such commendation drowns one's conscience and power of judgment. Evil people encourage with praise those who glorify and prosper in evil; worldly people praise those who are engrossed in materialism; fanat-

---

* *God Talks With Arjuna: The Bhagavad Gita* II:57.

ics praise false prophets who speak not truth but what followers want to hear. All these are steeped in ignorance, like blind men leading blind men, stumbling into a common pit of error. Praise is harmful when it colors a person's perception of himself so that he does not recognize his faults. Praise is pernicious when it overestimates the good in a man, cloaking him in a false and hypocritical image. But praise is good when it correctly estimates one's virtues and inspires him to be even more virtuous. Praise in itself does not make anyone better and blame does not make anyone less than what he is in reality. Blame is helpful if it spurs one to correct himself; and praise is beneficial when it injects enthusiasm to be worthy.

⁓

[Verses 27–38 omitted here, as they are commented on in Discourses 27 and 30 as parallel to those in the Sermon on the Mount.]

And he spake a parable unto them, "Can the blind lead the blind? Shall they not both fall into the ditch?

"The disciple is not above his master: but every one that is perfect shall be as his master.*

"And why beholdest thou the mote that is in thy brother's eye, but perceivest not the beam that is in thine own eye? Either how canst thou say to thy brother, 'Brother, let me pull out the mote that is in thine eye,' when thou thyself beholdest not the beam that is in thine own eye? Thou hypocrite, cast out first the beam out of thine own eye, and then shalt thou see clearly to pull out the mote that is in thy brother's eye" (Luke 6:39–42).†

If persons who are physically or mentally or spiritually blind try to lead others who walk in similar darkness, all will fall into the same ditch of physical, or mental, or spiritual ruin. A master has intuitive divine sight and safeguards his disciples by guiding them around pitfalls and obstacles on the path of their progress. The soulfully diligent disciple in time finds discriminative sight returning to his ego-blinded

---

* Cf. Matthew 10:24–25, wherein Jesus repeated this counsel (Discourse 41).

† Verses 41–42 also appear in Matthew 7:3–5; they are commented on in Discourse 30 with a different emphasis consistent with the Matthew context.

vision. But he does not all at once become like the master, as is too often prematurely assumed from brief flashes of insight. A master is he who is perfected in the art of contacting God. Only when an advanced disciple similarly attains God-realization does he become "not above his master" but "as his master."* Even so,

an advanced disciple always gives reverential def- *Restoring spiritual* erence to his master who has been for him a mes- *sight to those whose* senger of God and the portal to soul freedom. Jesus *discrimination is* so honored John the Baptist as his guru of former *blinded by ego* incarnations.

How can a self-elected spiritual guide justify saying to his brothers, "I know the art of pulling out ignorance from your soul," when he has not rid himself of ignorance? Dislodging *maya's* deeply embedded ignorance is not an easy job. It requires practical realization and practical living of the life divine. If one is not a qualified jeweler, how can he accurately teach others to distinguish between good and faulty jewels or detect imitations mixed up with authentic gems? Similarly, how can one who has no direct experience of truth teach others to distinguish between ignorance and wisdom?

To pull out the "motes" of ignorance from others' souls presupposes that one has to some successful degree qualified himself by having pulled ignorance out from his own soul first. Jesus castigates as a "hypocrite"—one who is insincere in his actions—one whose own vision is befogged by ignorance yet who presumes with that blurred understanding to be a guide and healer of others suffering from inner blindness.

≈

"For a good tree bringeth not forth corrupt fruit; neither doth a corrupt tree bring forth good fruit. For every tree is known by his own fruit. For of thorns men do not gather figs, nor of a bramble bush gather they grapes" (Luke 6:43–44).

---

* The illumined master Swami Shankara, father of India's ancient monastic Swami Order, wrote: "No known comparison exists in the three worlds for a true guru. If the philosophers' stone be assumed as truly such, it can only turn iron into gold, not into another philosophers' stone. The venerated teacher, on the other hand, creates equality with himself in the disciple who takes refuge at his feet. The guru is therefore peerless, nay, transcendental" (*Century of Verses,* 1).

The reference to a tree and its fruit has not only a literal connotation, as already explained [in Discourse 10], but a metaphysical meaning as well. A human being is a composite of three kinds of trees: (1) The physical nervous system with its roots in the brain and the trunk in the spine (the cerebrospinal axis) and efferent and afferent nerves branching out from it, with the senses and their sensations at the end of the nerve branches as the fruits.* (2) An astral tree of life with its roots as the thousand-petaled rays in the brain, its trunk of life force in the *sushumna,* the astral spine, and burgeoning branches of life force with their life-giving fruits of vitality and subtle perceptions. (3) The tree of consciousness, which has its roots in the intelligence in the brain; its trunk consists of the mind, and its branches consist of reason, will, and feeling; it bears fruits of evil and good desires. As an aggregate, these three systems of nerves, life energy, and consciousness constitute the tree of life in man.†

How man's tree of life grows good and evil fruits of sensations and desires

The human tree of nerves yields good or bad sensations according to the nature of the individual who owns and tends the tree of the nervous system. When an individual administers polluted waters of evil stimuli to the roots in his brain of this tree of life, he produces fruits of evil sensations hanging from the branches of different nerves. That is, when a person feeds his brain with evil thoughts, howsoever aroused, that stimulus in the consciousness creates desire for evil sensations. When those desires are acted upon by the will, the endings of the optical branch nerves, or the auditory, or tactual, or olfactory, or gustatory branches of the nervous system become laden with fruits of evil sensations in response to contact with desired objects, such as the wish to see unwholesome sights, listen to words of flattery or evil gossip, engage in lustful sensations of touch or smell, or indulge an unbridled appetite. Conversely, a brain that is fed with good thoughts produces good fruit on the tree of life, from good habits and cravings for good sensations.

The roots of every tree of life grow deep in the soil of consciousness to tap the wellspring of Cosmic Consciousness. As such, the hu-

---

* Yoga science identifies ten "senses" with which the physical body is endowed: five instruments of knowledge (sight, hearing, taste, smell, and touch) and five instruments of action (the subtle powers behind the bodily faculties of manual skill, locomotion, speech, procreation, and elimination).

† See also Discourse 7, the tree of life in the Garden of Eden; and Discourse 10, Nathanael sitting under fig tree.

man nervous system was originally created by God to attract and enjoy good sensations only. But man, through misuse of his freedom of will, has converted his tree of life into a bearer of fruits of evil sensations. Once a nervous system is conditioned to producing desire for evil sensations, it is very hard to change its character. A good nervous system will not easily produce fruits of desire for evil sensations, nor will an evil-inclined tree of life produce of itself fruits in the form of desires for good sensations.

The astral tree, whose branches spread subtly throughout the physical nervous system, is fed by Cosmic Energy. If this astral tree is not impacted by vitiating evil physical habits, it produces fruits of fine inner perception which the advanced devotee can pluck and enjoy. As a person cannot partake of the fruits of an undiscovered mango tree hidden in a garden, so a devotee who is yet to see with the light of ecstasy this astral tree of life cannot even imagine the enjoyment to be had from its Elysian fruits: perceptions of subtle forces; possession of miraculous powers; seeing visions, which are true to life; listening to the celestial sounds beyond the reach of human ears, feeling sensations of the bodies of others, inhaling astral fragrance, savoring astral taste; and possession of the power to dislodge the astral body from the physical body (and to return at will), to magnify or decrease the size of the astral body—these are but a few of the wonders of having discovered one's heavenly astral body.

Behind the tree of astral life is the tree of consciousness. When this tree of consciousness is fed with the water of divine thoughts and intuition springing from the fountain of meditation, it becomes an entirely good tree bearing only fruits of good desires, spiritual aspirations, and wisdom.

Hidden beneath these three trees of the physical nervous system, of astral life, and of consciousness, is their creator and upholder, the superconsciousness of the soul.

Superconsciousness is rooted in the Cosmic Consciousness of God. It sustains the trunk of the threefold tree of life, as also its branches of superconscious perception, subconscious perception, and conscious perception. Superconsciousness, when perceived, will be found to be the source of the fruits of superconscious intuition and of subconscious spiritual dreams and of all good sensations and sentiments.

On a macrocosmic scale, God can be spoken of as the root of the universal tree of life; the Cosmic Energy can be spoken of as the trunk; and all rays shooting out of this Cosmic Energy for the creation of universes can be called the branches. The worlds and universes of causal, astral, and physical constitution are the fruits of the tree of Cosmic Consciousness.

God originally planned that this tree of Cosmic Consciousness should bear only fruits of good vibrations; but through *maya,* or cosmic delusion, Satan put some poison of his evil desires in the life-giving sap of Cosmic Energy. That is why we find earthquakes, dissolutions of planetary systems, and all manner of harsh collisions marring the harmony of matter, including the devastations of the evils in man.

~

"A good man out of the good treasure of his heart bringeth forth that which is good; and an evil man out of the evil treasure of his heart bringeth forth that which is evil: for of the abundance of the heart his mouth speaketh" (Luke 6:45).

A good heart will express itself in good actions; evil feelings will express themselves in an evil way. The use of the word *heart* by Jesus is esoterically significant here. The great master and exponent of Yoga, Patanjali, says that it is the heart, or *chitta,* the feeling aspect of man's consciousness, that has to be controlled in order to attain God-realization.* As the moon reflected in a pot of whirling water looks distorted, so also the blessed image of man's true nature as the soul is distorted when reflected in the sensation-disturbed mental waters of the bodily consciousness. Patanjali says that when, by meditation, the waves of sensations are stilled, then the pure blessedness of the soul can be perceived.

The yoga science of freeing the heart from evil

Experiences invading the mind do not create disturbance of restlessness until the heart, or feeling, is touched. If all experiences remained within an individual as academical knowledge, they could not hurt or bind him. It is the heart, with its duality, that becomes intimate with all experiences by having feelings of attraction or repulsion for them. If an individual observed his life's experiences as one unaffect-

---

* *Yoga Sutras* I:2: "*Yoga chitta vritti nirodha*—Yoga (scientific union with God) is the neutralization of the modifications of *chitta.*" See Discourse 26, where this *sutra* is discussed in the context of "Blessed are the pure in heart: for they shall see God."

edly watches motion pictures, he would go from this earth a free master. Instead, the heart through likes and dislikes binds an individual to the wheel of birth and death and mortal suffering. The heart therefore is the archives of an individual's life in which he stores his treasure of good or evil. The good person who is accustomed to do good actions and have good thoughts stores good habits in his heart, and his words and actions reflect that goodness. An evil individual, by evil actions, creates evil habits and a liking for evil in his heart; and when he speaks or acts, evil is expressed therein.

Thus, the good or evil entering a man's brain does not automatically make him good or bad; but when that stimulus lodges as feelings of attraction or repulsion within his heart, then it will manifest accordingly as good or evil. Man lives in an atmosphere fraught with evil, but no evil experience or perception can influence him to evil unless he absorbs the evil as a liking for it in his heart. That which comes out of the heart of man declares and affects him rather than that which merely goes into his brain as knowledge.*

---

* "Our research and that of others indicate that the heart is far more than a simple pump. The heart is, in fact, a highly complex, self-organized information processing center," report Rollin McCraty, Ph.D., and his associates in *Science of the Heart: Exploring the Role of the Heart in Human Performance* (Boulder Creek, California: Institute of HeartMath, 2001).

"Traditionally, the study of communication pathways between the 'head' and heart has been approached from a rather one-sided perspective, with scientists focusing primarily on the heart's responses to the brain's commands. However, we have now learned that communication between the heart and brain is actually a dynamic, ongoing, two-way dialogue, with each organ continuously influencing the other's function. Research has shown that the heart communicates to the brain in four major ways: *neurologically* (through the transmission of nerve impulses), *biochemically* (via hormones and neurotransmitters), *biophysically* (through pressure waves) and *energetically* (through electromagnetic field interactions). Communication along all these conduits significantly affects the brain's activity."

"Neurocardiologists have found that 60 to 65% of the cells of the heart are actually neural cells, not muscle cells as was previously believed," explains child-development expert Joseph Chilton Pearce in a 1999 interview in *Journal of Family Life* (Volume 5, Number 1). "They are identical to the neural cells in the brain, operating through the same connecting links called ganglia, with the same axonal and dendritic connections that take place in the brain, as well as through the very same kinds of neurotransmitters found in the brain. Quite literally, in other words, there is a 'brain' in the heart, whose ganglia are linked to every major organ in the body, to the entire muscle spindle system that uniquely enables humans to express their emotions."

"Our emotional-cognitive brain has direct, unmediated neural connections with the heart," Pearce reports. He explains that the brain "makes a qualitative evaluation of our experience of this world and sends that information instant-by-instant down to

When Jesus said, "Out of the abundance of the heart the mouth speaketh," he meant that speech is an index to the contents of the heart. The vibrations of the heart reverberate in the vibration of the voice. An individual's speech, no matter how dressed up with polished language, resonates with the inner tendencies abiding in that person's heart. In the tone and vibration of the voice is the echo of one's heart-experiences. A bad man may imitate the voice of a good person, but the evil in his heart will certainly vibrate in his pretending voice.

Through the tone and vibrations of mildness or harshness of an individual's voice one can recognize the nature of the hidden feelings in that person's heart. The whole history of an individual as to how he lives his life within himself and with his family and associates is revealed in his voice. The prenatal and postnatal story of one's life is written also in the eyes of an individual; but those who cannot read those signs in the eyes of others can, with the perception of calmness, intuit the evil or good hidden in the vibratory nature of an individual's voice.

~

For commentary on verses of Luke 6:46–49, see parallel verses in the Sermon on the Mount according to the Gospel of St. Matthew [Discourse 30].

---

the heart. In return, the heart exhorts the brain to make the appropriate response....In other words, the responses that the heart makes affect the entire human system." Thus, these scientists conclude, though the brain supplies the heart with perceptions, it is the heart, responding to the reports from the brain, that sends positive or negative instructions back to the emotional reactive centers in the brain (and, through hormones released into the bloodstream, to the entire body). *(Publisher's Note)*

Jesus Cites His Wondrous Works in Testimony to John the Baptist and Extols John's Greatness

"Jesus honored John with highest acclaim—he who had appeared in his previous incarnation as the God-realized Elijah."

Now when he had ended all his sayings in the audience of the people, he entered into Capernaum. And a certain centurion's servant, who was dear unto him, was sick, and ready to die. And when he heard of Jesus, he sent unto him the elders of the Jews, beseeching him that he would come and heal his servant.

And when they came to Jesus, they besought him instantly, saying, that he was worthy for whom he should do this: For he loveth our nation, and he hath built us a synagogue. Then Jesus went with them.

And when he was now not far from the house, the centurion sent friends to him, saying unto him, "Lord, trouble not thyself: for I am not worthy that thou shouldest enter under my roof: Wherefore neither thought I myself worthy to come unto thee: but say in a word, and my servant shall be healed. For I also am a man set under authority, having under me soldiers, and I say unto one, 'Go,' and he goeth; and to another, 'Come,' and he cometh; and to my servant, 'Do this,' and he doeth it."

When Jesus heard these things, he marvelled at him, and turned him about, and said unto the people that followed him, "I say unto you, I have not found so great faith, no, not in Israel."

And they that were sent, returning to the house, found the servant whole that had been sick.

And it came to pass the day after, that he went into a city called Nain; and many of his disciples went with him, and much people. Now when he came nigh to the gate of the city, behold, there was a dead man carried out, the only son of his mother, and she was a widow: and much people of the city was with her.

And when the Lord saw her, he had compassion on her, and said unto her, "Weep not." And he came and touched the bier: and they that bare him stood still. And he said, "Young man, I say unto thee, arise." And he that was dead sat up, and began to speak. And he delivered him to his mother.

And there came a fear on all: and they glorified God, saying, that a great prophet is risen up among us; and, that God hath visited His people. And this rumour of him went forth throughout all Judea, and throughout all the region round about.

And the disciples of John shewed him of all these things.

And John calling unto him two of his disciples sent them to Jesus, saying, "Art thou he that should come? or look we for another?"

When the men were come unto him, they said, "John the Baptist hath sent us unto thee, saying, 'Art thou he that should come? or look we for another?'"

And in that same hour he cured many of their infirmities and plagues, and of evil spirits; and unto many that were blind he gave sight. Then Jesus answering said unto them, "Go your way, and tell John what things ye have seen and heard; how that the blind see, the lame walk, the lepers are cleansed, the deaf hear, the dead are raised, to the poor the gospel is preached. And blessed is he, whosoever shall not be offended in me."

And when the messengers of John were departed, he began to speak unto the people concerning John, "What went ye out into the wilderness for to see? A reed shaken with the wind? But what went ye out for to see? A man clothed in soft raiment? Behold, they which are gorgeously apparelled, and live delicately, are in kings' courts.

"But what went ye out for to see? A prophet? Yea, I say unto you, and much more than a prophet. This is he, of whom it is written, 'Behold, I send My messenger before thy face, which shall prepare thy way before thee.'

"For I say unto you, among those that are born of women there is not a greater prophet than John the Baptist: but he that is least in the kingdom of God is greater than he."

And all the people that heard him, and the publicans, justified God, being baptized with the baptism of John. But the Pharisees and lawyers rejected the counsel of God against themselves, being not baptized of him.

And the Lord said, "Whereunto then shall I liken the men of this generation? And to what are they like? They are like unto children sitting in the marketplace, and calling one to another, and saying, 'We have piped unto you, and ye have not danced; we have mourned to you, and ye have not wept.'

"For John the Baptist came neither eating bread nor drinking wine; and ye say, 'He hath a devil.' The Son of man is come eating and drinking; and ye say, 'Behold a gluttonous man, and a winebibber, a friend of publicans and sinners!' But wisdom is justified of all her children."

—Luke 7:1–35

Then began he to upbraid the cities wherein most of his mighty works were done, because they repented not:

"Woe unto thee, Chorazin! Woe unto thee, Bethsaida! For if the mighty works, which were done in you, had been done in Tyre and Sidon, they would have repented long ago in sackcloth and ashes. But I say unto you, it shall be more tolerable for Tyre and Sidon at the day of judgment, than for you.

"And thou, Capernaum, which are exalted unto heaven, shalt be brought down to hell: For if the mighty works, which have been done in thee, had been done in Sodom, it would have remained until this day. But I say unto you, that it shall be more tolerable for the land of Sodom in the day of judgment, than for thee."

—Matthew 11:20–24

618

Jesus Cites His Wondrous Works in Testimony to John the Baptist and Extols John's Greatness

Now when he had ended all his sayings in the audience of the people, he entered into Capernaum. And a certain centurion's servant, who was dear unto him, was sick, and ready to die. And when he heard of Jesus, he sent unto him the elders of the Jews, beseeching him that he would come and heal his servant.

And when they came to Jesus, they besought him instantly, saying, that he was worthy for whom he should do this: For he loveth our nation, and he hath built us a synagogue. Then Jesus went with them.

And when he was now not far from the house, the centurion sent friends to him, saying unto him, "Lord, trouble not thyself: for I am not worthy that thou shouldest enter under my roof: Wherefore neither thought I myself worthy to come unto thee: but say in a word, and my servant shall be healed. For I also am a man set under authority, having under me soldiers, and I say unto one, 'Go,' and he goeth; and to another, 'Come,' and he cometh; and to my servant, 'Do this,' and he doeth it."

When Jesus heard these things, he marvelled at him, and turned him about, and said unto the people that followed him, "I say unto you, I have not found so great faith, no, not in Israel."

*And they that were sent, returning to the house, found the
servant whole that had been sick (Luke 7:1–10).*

Parallel reference:

*And Jesus said unto the centurion, "Go thy way; and as thou
hast believed, so be it done unto thee." And his servant was
healed in the selfsame hour (Matthew 8:13).* *

To heal the near-fatal affliction of his well-loved servant, which
would not yield to application of physical methods of healing,
the Roman centurion sought the superphysical help of a master. A man
acquainted with authority, he appealed to Jesus as being one who
could command the very laws governing heaven and earth. In rever-

---

*The dynamics of
faith: connecting one's
life with an unseen
Higher Power*

ent awe of Jesus' sovereign power, the centurion felt
himself unworthy even to have the Lord enter his
home. Jesus, being deeply moved by the humility
and great faith of this man outside the Hebrew congregation, commanded the instantaneous healing
that the centurion sought.

A Sanskrit name for the Lord in His aspect of Cosmic Ruler is Ishvara (from the root *is*, "to rule"), the Universal Spirit who holds the universes on a pinpoint of thought, revolving their workings on the spindle
of His will. The Roman officer, in addressing Jesus as "Lord," spoke with
intuitive certainty of Jesus' manifest divinity. He knew that Jesus had only
to "say in a word, and my servant shall be healed." A command from
Jesus, being united to the Word, cosmic *Aum* or Amen, carried the manifesting power of Omnipotence. In the *Yoga Sutras* of Patanjali, *Aum* (the
Word) is spoken of as the "symbol" (manifestation) of Ishvara, the creative power by which the entire cosmos of matter and energy is brought
into being.† At one with the omnipotent Lord, Jesus surcharged his word
with the cosmic vibratory Word, which endowed him with the authority
to heal, or to manifest any other condition in the material world.

God as the Ruler of Creation originally brought forth all phenomena by direct command of His will. He is the supreme sovereign au-

---

* The full context of this story is told, with slight variations from the Gospel According to St. Luke, in Matthew 8:5–13.

† *Yoga Sutras* 1:27.

thority; yet having manifested from His ideations the multifarious cosmic dream creation, He cedes the tedious governing authority to His universal laws. The power of *maya*, delusion, makes possible the effective operation of law, and by its very nature obscures the underlying and all-pervasive Sovereign Spirit. The Sole Reality, the Doer behind all cosmic happenings, seems absent from His universe. But with the eyes of faith, intuitive knowing, He can be espied, immanent and responsive.

Faith reveals a God who is intimately near, just behind the throb of the heart, a God who listens to every word of prayer. His eyes and ears are everywhere, His consciousness attuned to every particular of thought and condition. In His good time He will respond to every sincere entreaty—faster than one may think, when He is appealed to with implicit faith. It is doubt that makes Him seem far away. Offering half-hearted prayers, with the mind in the octopus-clutches of doubt, counteracts receptivity with an undercurrent of "Oh, He will probably not even hear me, let alone respond to my needs." His help is virtually obstructed by that kind of prayer! He must let the karmic law work its impartial justice for good or ill. But appeals made with love, confidence, and faith can transcend law and bring results that astonish. Faith means total trust—intuitive conviction, a knowing from the soul, that God is real and that His help is ever ready to flow into man's life. That is the faith extolled by Jesus, the open channel through which he could heal many of the afflicted, and change the lives of countless believers.

Despite man's vaunted advances in science and the healing arts, he cannot get away from the fact that in every department of life he is ultimately dependent on a Power higher than himself. In some respects, modern man enjoys a more secure existence than his ancestors; but still his days are fraught with terrible uncertainties. One never knows when accident or disease, financial failure or natural disaster will strike. Sooner or later, a time arrives in every person's life when a connection with that Higher Power suddenly becomes of utmost urgency, bringing him to his knees through painful desperation or worshipful devotion—the choice is his—in recognition that not a beat of the heart nor an inspiration of breath transpires without the supportive will of the Lord. That consciousness of total dependence on God is the power behind the dynamics of faith. Such reliance is not a submissive cowardice that paralyzes one's own constructive will, but an act of consecrated deference to God through love for Him and veneration of His supremacy.

Thus Jesus cited the exceptional faith of the Roman centurion over the rational skepticism among his own people. The soldier had the humility to bow to an authority superior to his own intellect and station, and the faith to recognize divine power and higher laws, unseen though they were, so that Jesus could say to him, "As thou hast believed, so be it done unto thee."

All creation operates under the law that the effect is equal to the cause. The faith of the centurion was great enough to act as sufficient cause to result in the healing of his servant—through the help of Jesus, who quickened the fruition of the above-mentioned cause. According to metaphysical law, healing power can be transferred from one soul to a consonant soul.* In this case, the centurion's faith was a conduit

---

* See also Discourse 20, commentary on John 4:45–54, in which Jesus heals the nobleman's son by operation of the same principle.

Spirituality and medicine researcher Larry Dossey, M.D., reports experimental verification of the mechanism behind this form of "distant healing" in his book, *Be Careful What You Pray For...You Just Might Get It* (New York: HarperCollins, 1997): "For a decade, a research team led by Jacobo Grinberg-Zylberbaum at the Universidad Nacional Autónoma de México in Mexico City, has performed experiments examining the electroencephalograms (EEGs or brain wave tracings) of subjects who are far removed from each other....While the distant subjects are sitting quietly, there is no correlation in the pattern of their respective EEGs. But when they allow a feeling of emotional closeness or empathy to develop between them, the EEGs begin to resemble each other, often to a striking degree. No type of energy or signal can be detected to pass between the distant individuals. Moreover, the statistical correlations between the distant EEG patterns do not diminish when the subjects are moved farther apart. This defies one of the hallmarks of energy as defined in physics—its decrease in strength with increasing distance from its source. Also, the EEGs remain equally correlated if the subjects are placed in metal-lined boxes, which block ambient electromagnetic energy....

"Grinberg-Zylberbaum's team, along with physicist Amit Goswami, of the Department of Physics and the Institute of Theoretical Science at the University of Oregon, propose that these 'transferred potentials' between brains demonstrate 'brain-to-brain nonlocal...correlations....' Nonlocal correlations have been a concern of physicists since they were proposed by Einstein, Rosen, and Podolsky in 1935....They were demonstrated experimentally in a celebrated study in 1982 by physicist Alain Aspect and his colleagues. Physicists assumed that nonlocal connections exist only between subatomic particles such as electrons and photons. But the pioneering work of Grinberg-Zylberbaum, Goswami, and their colleagues, which they have replicated, strongly suggests that nonlocal events occur also between human beings....

"But the connections between distant humans are not automatic. The researchers asked the subjects to try deliberately to 'feel each other's presence even at a distance.' If they did not, the distant EEG correlations were totally absent. This implies that love and empathy are required for distant connections between people to take place, and it is consistent with the universal belief that distant healing depends on love, caring, and compassion." *(Publisher's Note)*

through which the healing power of Jesus was received and transferred through the centurion's soul to his servant with whom he shared a warm affinity.

Depending on the development of his faculties of perception, man cognizes to greater or lesser degree the gross and subtle workings of cosmic law. A rank materialist acknowledges the physical operation of cause and effect: he knows that if he puts his hand in a fire, he will be painfully burned. Yet he tends arrogantly to disavow the subtler workings of moral laws of right action that would hedge the indulgence of his sense-bound desires; and scoffs at the suggestion that there are even higher laws of thought, free will, and expansion of consciousness that give spiritual purpose to his life. Knowledge of the Transcendent Author of all material, moral, and spiritual governance, the Law Framer, is utterly beyond his ken. Unlike the centurion, he egotistically proclaims himself —either overtly by his disrespect or tacitly by his indifference—unsubject to divine authority.

Materialists perceive the working of natural laws, but deny their Author

One Sankhya* aphorism reads: *Ishvar asiddhe* ("A Lord of Creation cannot be deduced" or "God is not proved"). My guru, Sri Yukteswar, explained: "The verse is not atheistical. It merely signifies that to the unenlightened man, dependent on his senses for all final judgments, proof of God must remain unknown and therefore non-existent."

Materialists, accustomed to rationalizing all phenomena in terms of cause and effect, often find no place in their philosophy for a God who transcends the lawful workings of creation. It is irony that rational man distrusts God because of the manifest workings of God's own law of cause and effect! Even a little reflection on the fact that there must be an Author of that law would suffice to start man on the quest for Ultimate Truth.

To accept nothing beyond the laws that govern *maya* is to remain bound in that realm of delusion—to become subject to rather than a ruler of the law of cause and effect. By identifying himself with creation rather than with the Transcendent Creator, man abdicates the authority given to him with his soul to have dominion over the cosmic phenomena. During sleep man cognizes himself as free from physical constraints; in his dreams he does not need to eat anything, nor

---

* One of the six classical systems of Hindu philosophy. See pages 625–26.

earn money, nor go to the doctor, nor experience birth and death, because (subconsciously at least) he is contacting the all-sufficient, ever-living soul. But immediately upon awakening he regains the consciousness of having a body, which is either young or old, sick or healthy, wealthy or poor. He limits himself so convincingly that those perceptions begin to make him what he is.

The phenomena imposed on man's belief are demarcated by the forces of causation he is capable of understanding—unless, like the centurion, he possesses faith in that which exists beyond the annals of intellect. Scientists have probed the causes of many wonders in creation that previous generations regarded as unexplainable; their application of that understanding has given us such modern "miracles" as radar, atomic energy, television, supersonic travel. Yet because they are unable to identify any known causality in the miracles performed by saints and masters, they deem them to be preposterous superstition.

Men of deeper insight, such as Einstein, James, Bose, and Jeans—all those who have intuitively touched the ultimate science and philosophy—realize that there is a supreme Power or Intelligence behind the varied forms of matter. What is preposterous is the assumption that the various forms of life and the grand potentials of the consciousness in man are just accidents of nature. It is by understanding the laws of life and of our individuality, which are invariably linked, that we find the homogeneity and harmony among all forces. The body is nothing but materialized life. Life is materialized consciousness. Consciousness comes from God.

How yoga frees man from subjection to the law of cause and effect (karma)

This world, existing in God's suggestion of a relativity of time and space, is merely a condensed thought of God. The wonder I behold is that everything in this universe God has created out of nothing but His own dream, His own ideations. Man's difficulty is that this dream is imposed upon him, like a cosmic hypnosis. When he supinely surrenders his own will to delusive somnolence, he has little or no control over the dream happenings.

Under *maya's* laws of causation, so many operations are necessary in order to achieve something. For us to have bread to eat, a farmer must plant the wheat and water it and tend its growth; then thresh it, grind it, and deliver it to a store. Then the baker has to buy it from the store, make it into dough, and put it in the oven to bake. Man thinks that by applying the material laws of cause and effect he has been able to produce that bread. But who created the life in the grain that makes the wheat? And who created the earth in which the wheat grew; and who created the heat in the fuel that stokes the oven?

It is God's consciousness that has given life to everything. It is the vibration of His thought that has been condensed into light; and that light has been condensed into life force; and that life force has been condensed into electrons and protons; and they have been condensed into molecules and atoms out of which the earth and man's body and everything in this universe is composed. When one, like Jesus, realizes the unity of the Self with God, and that Self as a manifestation of the one Cosmic Light, and beholds everything as a manifestation of that Light, one can control these cosmic radiations, even as God does. Jesus demonstrated that power and proclaimed: "Ye shall do even greater things than these I do."* By deeper and deeper meditation, the aspirant frees himself from *maya* in the Light beyond the atoms. Only by thus awakening from this daydream of delusion will man know he has been dreaming. When he can dissolve this dream in the ecstasy of God, he will be able to command the universal order to perform any miracle.

The Roman officer recognized in Jesus the divine authority to make matter obey his will—to supersede the processes that under the physical law of cause and effect would be necessary to heal the servant. Only supremely God-realized masters, as was Jesus Christ, can operate in a sphere unconditioned by any constraints of causality. United to the omnipotence of the Creator, they can bring into being any object or condition by direct materialization, with no precedent cause other than their act of divine will.

There is no law of causation when one knows the law of the Infinite. He who is in tune with God's mind can do anything.† As an earthly emperor may cause all his subjects to obey the laws of his kingdom without himself being bound by them, so the Absolute Monarch of the realm of manifestation has made all the laws needed for the orderly operation of His finite creation, including the law of cause and effect, but He is not subject to them.

That is how Lord Krishna counseled his disciple Arjuna: "The ultimate wisdom of Sankhya I have explained to thee. But now thou

---

* Paraphrase of John 14:12 (see Discourse 70).

† See Discourse 11, discussion of how Jesus changed water into wine through control of the creative thought-matrix underlying all materializations of energy and form.

must hear about the wisdom of Yoga, equipped with which, O Arjuna, thou shalt shatter the bonds of karma."*

Sankhya philosophy explains the orderly principles by which God's cause-and-effect creation is evolved from His undifferentiated Being and maintained as an objective (though delusive) dream reality.† Yoga science gives man the key to freeing himself from subjection to those laws: The way out of the prison of karma consists in banishing —through definite techniques of soul-awakening meditation—the delusion of being a mortal whose actions are governed by creation's law of karma.

So long as man considers himself a created being, he is servile to all the companionate forces of cause and effect. As a mortal man he is a creation made by God; as an immortal being of realization, he will know himself as a part of God, possessed of the Father's creative will and lordship over the cosmos.

Once having awakened to the truth that mortal enslavement is not his true lot, the prayer of every prodigal child of God should be to try to realize:

> "Thou art my Father, I am Thine offspring. Thou art Spirit; I am made in Thine image. Thou art Creator and Owner of the universe. Good or naughty, I am Thy child, with the right to command the cosmos....
>
> "By Thy grace I shall rediscover my true nature, that of omnipresent Spirit, and have dominion‡ over the world of matter."§

In the ecstasy of meditation, God makes the humblest of His servants to sit on a sovereign throne.

~

And it came to pass the day after, that he went into a city called Nain; and many of his disciples went with him, and much peo-

---

* *God Talks With Arjuna: The Bhagavad Gita* II:39.

† The twenty-four principles of cosmic creation—beginning with Prakriti (creative Mother Nature or Holy Ghost) and ending in the five elemental forms of gross matter —are explained in *God Talks With Arjuna: The Bhagavad Gita*, commentary on II:39.

‡ "And God said, 'Let us make man in our image, after our likeness: and let them have dominion over...all the earth'" (Genesis 1:26).

§ From *Whispers from Eternity* by Paramahansa Yogananda (published by Self-Realization Fellowship).

ple. Now when he came nigh to the gate of the city, behold, there
was a dead man carried out, the only son of his mother, and she
was a widow: and much people of the city was with her.

And when the Lord saw her, he had compassion on her, and
said unto her, "Weep not." And he came and touched the bier:
and they that bare him stood still. And he said, "Young man, I
say unto thee, arise." And he that was dead sat up, and began to
speak. And he delivered him to his mother.

And there came a fear on all: and they glorified God, saying,
that a great prophet is risen up among us; and, that God hath
visited His people. And this rumour of him went forth through-
out all Judea, and throughout all the region round about (Luke
7:11–17).

The power to restore life to the dead was with Jesus in his incarnation as Elisha, as recounted in II Kings 4:8–37:

"And it fell on a day, that Elisha passed to Shunem, where was a
great woman; and she constrained him to eat bread. And so it was,
that as oft as he passed by, he turned in thither to eat bread. And she
said unto her husband, 'Behold now, I perceive that this is an holy man
of God, which passeth by us continually. Let us
make a little chamber, I pray thee, on the wall; and   *Parallels between*
let us set for him there a bed, and a table, and a   *Jesus' miracles and*
stool, and a candlestick: and it shall be, when he   *those of his past life*
cometh to us, that he shall turn in thither.'   *as Elijah's disciple*

"And it fell on a day, that he came thither, and
he turned into the chamber, and lay there. And he said to Gehazi his servant, 'Call this Shunammite.' And when he had called her, she stood before him. And he said unto him, 'Say now unto her, "Behold, thou hast
been careful for us with all this care; what is to be done for thee?"'...
And Gehazi answered, 'Verily she hath no child, and her husband is
old.'...And he said, 'About this season, according to the time of life,
thou shalt embrace a son.'...And the woman conceived, and bare a son
at that season that Elisha had said unto her, according to the time of life.

"And when the child was grown, it fell on a day, that he went out
to his father to the reapers. And he said unto his father, 'My head, my
head.' And he said to a lad, 'Carry him to his mother.' And when he
had taken him, and brought him to his mother, he sat on her knees till
noon, and then died.

"And she went up, and laid him on the bed of the man of God, and shut the door upon him, and went out. And she called unto her husband, and said, 'Send me, I pray thee, one of the young men, and one of the asses, that I may run to the man of God, and come again.'...So she went and came unto the man of God to mount Carmel....

"And when Elisha was come into the house, behold, the child was dead, and laid upon his bed. He went in therefore, and shut the door upon them twain, and prayed unto the Lord.

"And he went up, and lay upon the child, and put his mouth upon his mouth, and his eyes upon his eyes, and his hands upon his hands: and stretched himself upon the child; and the flesh of the child waxed warm.

"Then he returned, and walked in the house to and fro; and went up, and stretched himself upon him: and the child sneezed seven times, and the child opened his eyes.

"And he called Gehazi, and said, 'Call this Shunammite.' So he called her. And when she was come in unto him, he said, 'Take up thy son.'

"Then she went in, and fell at his feet, and bowed herself to the ground, and took up her son, and went out."

~

John the Baptist, even after being imprisoned, followed the ministry of Jesus with keen interest.*

And the disciples of John shewed him of all these things.

And John calling unto him two of his disciples sent them to Jesus, saying, "Art thou he that should come? or look we for another?"

When the men were come unto him, they said, "John the Baptist hath sent us unto thee, saying, 'Art thou he that should come? or look we for another?'"

And in that same hour he cured many of their infirmities and plagues, and of evil spirits; and unto many that were blind he

---

* John the Baptist also, in his incarnation as Elijah, had raised a widow's son from the dead. Indeed, when Jesus as Elisha resurrected a dead child by laying his own body over the corpse, as described above, he was reenacting the same method previously used by his guru Elijah in bringing the widow's son back to life (see I Kings 17:17–24, cited in Discourse 39).

gave sight. Then Jesus answering said unto them, "Go your way, and tell John what things ye have seen and heard; how that the blind see, the lame walk, the lepers are cleansed, the deaf hear, the dead are raised, to the poor the gospel is preached" (Luke 7:18–22).

Parallel reference:

Now when John had heard in the prison the works of Christ, he sent two of his disciples, and said unto him, "Art thou he that should come, or do we look for another?"

Jesus answered and said unto them, "Go and shew John again those things which ye do hear and see: The blind receive their sight, and the lame walk, the lepers are cleansed, and the deaf hear, the dead are raised up, and the poor have the gospel preached to them" (Matthew 11:2–5).

John in no wise questioned or doubted that Jesus was the savior prophesied to incarnate in that era. John had already proclaimed this to his disciples and the masses. But in the brutal confines of prison, John's mortal nature reached out for the solace of confirmation from Jesus' own lips. Further, he sought this testimony to be heard directly by his disciples for their own spiritual continuity. John faced certain death, and he desired that the faith of his followers be strengthened in God's word through Jesus.*

---

* The death of John is recorded later, in the Gospel of Mark 6:14–29 (and in a parallel reference in Matthew 14:3–12): "And king Herod heard of him [Jesus]; (for his name was spread abroad:) and he said, that John the Baptist was risen from the dead, and therefore mighty works do shew forth themselves in him. Others said, that it is Elijah. And others said, that it is a prophet, or as one of the prophets. But when Herod heard thereof, he said, 'It is John, whom I beheaded: he is risen from the dead.'

"For Herod himself had sent forth and laid hold upon John, and bound him in prison for Herodias' sake, his brother Philip's wife: for he had married her. For John had said unto Herod, 'It is not lawful for thee to have thy brother's wife.'

"Therefore Herodias had a quarrel against him, and would have killed him; but she could not: For Herod feared John, knowing that he was a just man and an holy, and observed him; and when he heard him, he did many things, and heard him gladly.

"And when a convenient day was come, that Herod on his birthday made a supper to his lords, high captains, and chief estates of Galilee; and when the daughter of the said Herodias came in, and danced, and pleased Herod and them that sat with him, the king said unto the damsel, 'Ask of me whatsoever thou wilt, and I will give it thee.' And

The answer Jesus gave to the disciples of John the Baptist, to be relayed to the imprisoned prophet, verified by example of his godly works his Christ incarnation. "Relate all you have seen and heard about the demonstrations of God through me: The physically and spiritually blind receive physically sighted eyes or spiritual inner sight. The lame walk; physical, moral, and spiritual lepers are physically healed and inwardly cleansed by wisdom. The physically deaf get back their hearing; the spiritually deaf hear the voice of wisdom. The physically dead are enlivened again through cosmic energy; the spiritually dead are resurrected by wisdom and spiritual baptism. The poor in spirit receive the living contact of God-wisdom and God-vibration."

Why John the Baptist asked Jesus to confirm that he was the prophesied savior

Jesus speaks of his message vibrating with God-consciousness ("the gospel"—God's vibration of Truth).* No one can preach God-vibrating truth unless he experiences it within himself. Ordinary spiritual teachers speak from book-learning and rote, but masters such as Jesus speak truth that is vibrantly alive with the wisdom of God within their consciousness.

◦

"And blessed is he, whosoever shall not be offended in me"
(Luke 7:23 and Matthew 11:6).

"And blessed is he who does not misjudge my exceptional works as blasphemy, finding fault with me in accusations that I perform miracles to serve my own purposes and egotistically extol my

---

he sware unto her, 'Whatsoever thou shalt ask of me, I will give it thee, unto the half of my kingdom.'

"And she went forth, and said unto her mother, 'What shall I ask?' And she said, 'The head of John the Baptist.' And she came in straightway with haste unto the king, and asked, saying, 'I will that thou give me by and by in a charger the head of John the Baptist.'

"And the king was exceeding sorry; yet for his oath's sake, and for their sakes which sat with him, he would not reject her. And immediately the king sent an executioner, and commanded his head to be brought: and he went and beheaded him in the prison, and brought his head in a charger, and gave it to the damsel: and the damsel gave it to her mother. And when his disciples heard of it, they came and took up his corpse, and laid it in a tomb." (See also Discourse 42.)

* See Discourse 22.

own glory. Blessed is he who instead appreciates the spiritual miracles I perform through the sanction and will of God to alleviate suffering and bring deluded souls unto Him."

Phenomenal powers possessed by semi-developed souls might well delude their yet immature spiritual consciousness, which is easily spoiled by the praise of admirers. They begin to see themselves as the doers of holy works, forgetting that all glory and honor belong to God alone. Phenomenal powers exert some influence on the operation of natural laws, but no miracles that transcend such laws can be performed without God-consciousness. So it is foolish to revel in self-laudation.* The devotee in the course of his higher spiritual development receives the gift of miracles, but to use that God-given divine power without the sanction of God is sin and involves spiritual degradation.

Jesus saw how the display of miracles was looked upon by the priestly caste as a divine offense; but whosoever recognized that his performance of miracles was to declare the glory of God was blessed, for that inner perception of Jesus as a channel of God was the awakening in them of divine realization.

~

And when the messengers of John were departed, he began to speak unto the people concerning John, "What went ye out into the wilderness for to see? A reed shaken with the wind? But what went ye out for to see? A man clothed in soft raiment? Behold, they which are gorgeously apparelled, and live delicately, are in kings' courts.

"But what went ye out for to see? A prophet? Yea, I say unto you, and much more than a prophet. This is he, of whom it is written, 'Behold, I send My messenger before thy face, which shall prepare thy way before thee'" (Luke 7:24–27).†

In commendation of John the Baptist, Jesus addressed the crowd — many of whom were followers of John who had sought him out in his ascetic haunts in the wilderness:

"When you went out into the wilderness, it was not to see the reeds along the riverbank, or in anticipation of finding a man clothed

---

* "Not unto us, O Lord, not unto us, but unto Thy name give glory" (Psalms 115:1).

† Parallel verses in Matthew 11:7–10.

with soft silk garments, but to seek John the Baptist, nature-clad only in skins, a divine reed vibrating with the wind of God. You did not expect him to be gorgeously attired as a man of political authority such as could be found in a king's court. You went to see a spiritual man of greater authority than possessed by any in earthly courts of kings.* Yea, you went to see a prophet who declares God. But he is much more than an ordinary prophet, for he was specially ordained by God (not only to be my preceptor in a former incarnation, but also) to perform an eminent and predestined part in the divine plan, to come on earth at this time to declare the Son of God in me."

In confirmation, Jesus quotes from the scriptures, "Behold, I (God) send My messenger (John the Baptist) before thy face (in advance of thee), which shall prepare thy way before thee (and it is ordained that My divine messenger John shall open the minds of the people to recognize the Christ in thee, O My son Jesus)."†

Even though God has given independence to all creation, yet in this Satan-disordered cosmos God has implanted certain patterns to defeat the influence of Satan and reestablish His kingdom. Prophets from time to time give foreknowledge of those plans. Hence Jesus declares that the appearance of John the Baptist to introduce him to the world was ordained by God long before, as expressed in the Scriptures, and therefore John was "much more than a prophet"; he was God-blessed and chosen as a part of God's grand scheme.

~

> "For I say unto you, among those that are born of women there is not a greater prophet than John the Baptist: but he that is least in the kingdom of God is greater than he."
>
> And all the people that heard him, and the publicans, justi-fied God, being baptized with the baptism of John. But the Phar-

---

* Cf. Gospel According to Thomas, verse 78: "Why have you come into the field? To see a reed tremble in the wind? To observe a man wearing soft cloth? Your kings and great men all wear soft clothes, and yet they cannot see the truth."

† Cf. Mark 1:2: "As it is written in the prophets, 'Behold, I send My messenger before thy face, which shall prepare thy way before thee.'" The reference is to the Old Testament book of the prophet Malachi: "Behold, I will send My messenger, and he shall prepare the way before Me" (Malachi 3:1). That the promised messenger would be the reincarnation of the prophet Elijah is declared in a later passage, Malachi 4:5 (see page 634).

isees and lawyers rejected the counsel of God against themselves, being not baptized of him (Luke 7:28–30).

Parallel references:

"Verily I say unto you, among them that are born of women there hath not risen a greater than John the Baptist: notwithstanding he that is least in the kingdom of Heaven is greater than he. And from the days of John the Baptist until now the kingdom of Heaven suffereth violence, and the violent take it by force. For all the prophets and the law prophesied until John. And if ye will receive it, this is Elijah which was for to come. He that hath ears to hear, let him hear" (Matthew 11:11–15).

***

"The law and the prophets were until John: since that time the kingdom of God is preached, and every man presseth into it" (Luke 16:16).

"Verily, I say unto you all that among the lineage of holy prophets, there has been none greater than John the Baptist." Jesus therewith honored John with highest acclaim —he who had appeared in his previous incarnation as the God-realized Elijah, and who was in his present role selected by God to baptize in Spirit Christ Jesus, reformer of a world cycle.

Jesus positively identifies John as the reincarnation of Elijah

Jesus then distinguishes—with no intended denigration of John's greatness—between John the Baptist's Self-realization in earth life and the Self-realized state of the individual soul when it is fully liberated in the kingdom of God—one with the Absolute Spirit—with no necessary submission to the cosmic compulsories of habitation in any of the three bodily confines and their interaction with the manifestations of God's threefold dream creation.

From the time preceding John the Baptist "the prophets and the law prophesied," enunciated God's will in law and prophecy. "Since that time, the kingdom of God is preached," when John proclaimed, "The kingdom of God is at hand," and Jesus followed after in preaching, "The kingdom of God is within you." From then until this present time and all future times "the kingdom of heaven suffereth violence (allows itself to be seized by will and determination)," and every true man has sought entry into that kingdom. Jesus says with the great yogi Patanjali that the "violent take it by force," that determined devotees achieve salvation and the heavenly blissful state by throwing their vision, life force, and concentration on God. As stated by Patanjali: "The attainment [of the goal of yoga—divine union with God] is nearest to those possessing *tivra-samvega*, divine ardor (fervent devotion and striving for God, and extreme dispassion toward the world of the senses)."*

One who deeply, intensely, and continuously meditates, being guided by one's guru, or savior, knows how with divine will-force to release quickly his consciousness from the body through the gates of the inner heavenly kingdom and allow it to join the cosmic life present in all space. The soul is thus freed from the bodily prison and unites with the omnipresence of the Universal Christ Consciousness in the realization, "I and my Father are one." The expeditious attainment of the heavenly kingdom by spiritually ardent aspirants was fully characterized in John the Baptist, who seized the kingdom of God by his extreme asceticism and the vehemence of his will.†

Then Jesus again confirms that the incarnation of John the Baptist was no fortuitous happening, but that in truth it was the fulfillment of the prophecy: "Behold, I will send you Elijah the prophet before the coming of the great and dreadful day of the Lord."‡ Jesus unequivocally proclaims: "And if ye will receive it, this is Elijah which was for to come. He that has ears to hear, let him hear." That is, "All those who have the power of understanding, let them hear, receive, and realize the truth that John the Baptist is none other than Elijah of a former incarnation."

Jesus here definitely acknowledges reincarnation. This grand philosophy alone explains how souls who are taken by death and leave the shores of life without attaining salvation can again strive and attain final emancipation through a succession of other human incarnations. Liberated souls or those liberated from mortal karma but still advancing in the astral or causal worlds reincarnate on earth not from karmic compulsion but with a special God-ordained mission for the blessing of mankind.

---

* *Yoga Sutras* I:21.

† Cf. Luke 10:27: "Thou shalt love the Lord thy God...with all thy strength." (See commentary in Discourse 53.)

‡ Malachi 4:5.

The return to earth life of the soul of Elijah in a body called John the Baptist was to perform those activities in support and declaration of the divine plan made manifest in the tremendous world mission of Jesus.

When Jesus addressed the receptive souls in the crowd, "He that hath spiritual ears to hear and feel the vibration of truth, let them realize the truth behind my words," he knew that many others present were nonbelievers seeking cause to condemn him. Most of the people who heard Jesus justified the word of God proclaimed by him because they had received baptism and spiritual preparation from John the Baptist. But the nonbelievers, "the Pharisees and lawyers" who were not among the avowed followers or initiates of John, rejected outright the revelations of God coming through Jesus, counsel that would have awakened their torpid consciousness.

~

And the Lord said, "Whereunto then shall I liken the men of this generation? And to what are they like? They are like unto children sitting in the marketplace, and calling one to another, and saying, 'We have piped unto you, and ye have not danced; we have mourned to you, and ye have not wept.'

"For John the Baptist came neither eating bread nor drinking wine; and ye say, 'He hath a devil.' The Son of man is come eating and drinking; and ye say, 'Behold a gluttonous man, and a winebibber, a friend of publicans and sinners!' But wisdom is justified of all her children" (Luke 7:31–35).*

The purveyors of wisdom, whose minds access the graduate tomes of truth, must perforce view the spiritually unlettered masses as children, their understanding and behavior con-strained within their accustomed, often petty, ways. Jesus so likens those of his unenlightened genera-tion. He compared spiritually vacuous men to chil-dren sitting idly in a marketplace, neither engaged in acquiring useful commodities nor busy with joyous play, nor feeling repentant for whiling away uselessly the valuable, evanescent moments of time. Metaphorically, Jesus described the world as a mar-

Jesus' analogy of the childishness of the spiritually idle

---

* Cf. parallel reference Matthew 11:16–19.

ketplace where people choose from its variety and acquire with their labors things material or spiritual. But all too few heed the exhortation of those who are wiser to be engrossed in what is truly worthwhile. The industrious accuse the lazy for their fault in not being progressive, saying, "We played the flute of opportunity, but you didn't dance to its tune of offerings." Jesus came and offered the way to the kingdom of heaven; but ignorant people, instead of busying themselves with spiritual endeavor, continue to while away their time in physical and mental laziness. Some casually mourn for the careless loss of life's treasured time, while others, not learning from any example of remorse, never shed a tear for fruitlessly idling away their life.

Conscientious devotees, realizing the worth of that something else that exists beyond the norm, are busy investing in spiritual qualities; some persons superficially revel in spiritual matters; some do not rejoice in spiritual culture at all. Some whose deeper thoughts are stirred by suffering or a sense of emptiness mourn for not finding the truth of existence; others never weep for not perceiving truth because they do not connect life's miseries with their spiritual ignorance.

Jesus' analogy also alludes to the childishness of persons who set expectations for the behavior and beliefs of others, accusing the non-responsive for not being spiritually progressive according to those standards. Jesus by inference cites the nonbelievers and skeptics, themselves spiritually indolent, yet accusing one another about their faults of omission. Being thus engrossed in the foolishness of false superiority, and pomposity rather than religiosity, they failed to recognize and take advantage of the wisdom and grace brought to them by God through the Christ in Jesus.

Jesus went on to point out the flawed reasoning of those nonunderstanding minds: "You who are busy whiling away your time in life's marketplace, where you could find God, have shown yourselves to be ignorant, indifferent, blind, and so mentally scattered that you could not recognize the spiritual greatness of John the Baptist and the inestimable good he could do unto you. You foolishly judged him to be possessed of a devil, because unlike your comfort-loving selves he is austerely self-controlled and abstemious in food and drink. If you can think of his holy asceticism as indicative of being possessed, then how can you justify by that standard your criticism of one who comes amongst you eating and drinking and socializing in the manner of the times? Yet you malign me as a greedy man, a wine taster, and one who consorts with publicans and sinners. No doubt you could not recognize in me the son of God hidden behind the son of man, or human nature. You know not that all children of God's wisdom, whatever they do, even though outwardly not understood, are justified by the subtle and immutable laws of their God-realization."

In the dark era of Jesus' time, scientific techniques for attaining God-communion and God-union were hidden from the masses. Those who reached that spiritual pinnacle found the way to interiorization primarily through intense devotion and discipline of the body and mind. In portraying his less advanced role as John the Baptist, the prophet set the severe standard of devout self-discipline of fasting and observance of certain physical laws and spiritual rites. Jesus, however, came exemplifying God-consciousness; his participation in the normal social customs involved only his physical nature (son of man) and did not touch his spiritual nature as manifested in him as the Son of God. The Son of God, the inner Christ, was completely detached from the actions of the son of man, the external personality of Jesus. Jesus signified that the critics of both himself and John the Baptist were so spiritually blind that they could not recognize either the spirituality of the outwardly ascetic nature of John the Baptist, nor the Christ in Jesus hidden behind the apparently unmodified ordinary habits of his simple life.

Jesus supported his actions of association with "publicans and sinners" as being guided by wisdom. His sociability was to break down caste barriers; and to minister, without reservation, to all those who needed him; to show how the redeeming power of God could help and uplift the error-stricken by their confidence in his instrumentality, born of his compatibility and compassion.

~

Then began he to upbraid the cities wherein most of his mighty works were done, because they repented not:

"Woe unto thee, Chorazin! Woe unto thee, Bethsaida! For if the mighty works, which were done in you, had been done in Tyre and Sidon, they would have repented long ago in sackcloth and ashes. But I say unto you, it shall be more tolerable for Tyre and Sidon at the day of judgment, than for you.*

---

* The town of Chorazin is no longer extant; it is thought to have been about two miles

"And thou, Capernaum, which are exalted unto heaven, shalt be brought down to hell: For if the mighty works, which have been done in thee, had been done in Sodom, it would have remained until this day. But I say unto you, that it shall be more tolerable for the land of Sodom in the day of judgment, than for thee" (Matthew 11:20–24). *

66 "O ye inhabitants of Chorazin and Bethsaida, you were favored to have seen the mighty works of God's power, you witnessed spiritual demonstrations of what God's grace and blessings could do for you; but you have failed to profit enough to change your ways.

What is the real "day of judgment"?

Your unreceptive attitude will ultimately lead you on paths of error into pits of misery. Even the people of ancient Tyre and Sidon, though not of your spiritual heritage, would have been more receptive than you have been. Had they witnessed such divine demonstrations, they would have deeply repented their evil ways in acts of penance. I prophesy unto you that when I will leave this body and am in my Christ Consciousness I shall watch the souls of the deceased inhabitants of Tyre and Sidon lifted to a higher region of vibratory existence than shall be your lot when you are judged by your actions."

The "day of judgment" is not fixed by God at a certain period of eternity, but in general is the period after death when a disembodied soul receives the judgment or fruits of actions according to the accumulated actions of previous lives.

All of life is a school, and whether he knows it or not, each person is preparing for a "final examination" on the last day of his earthly incarnation. In social life it may be difficult to judge a person's character by his outward appearance (unless one knows the intuitive art of reading personality); but at death the facade of pretenses is

---

north of Capernaum. Bethsaida, home of Peter, Andrew, and Philip, was situated on the Sea of Galilee where the Jordan River enters it. Tyre and Sidon were wealthy trading cities on the Mediterranean coast in Phoenicia (modern Lebanon), with whom the Jews had occasionally been enemies; see, for example, Joel 3:4–6: "Yea, and what have ye to do with Me, O Tyre, and Zidon, and all the coasts of Palestine?…Because ye have taken My silver and My gold, and have carried into your temples My goodly pleasant things: The children also of Judah and the children of Jerusalem have ye sold unto the Grecians, that ye might remove them far from their border."

* Cf. parallel verses in Luke 10:13–15.

The Woman Taken in Adultery

And the scribes and Pharisees brought unto him a woman taken in adultery; and when they had set her in the midst, they say unto him, "Master, this woman was taken in adultery, in the very act. Now Moses in the law commanded us, that such should be stoned: but what sayest thou?"...

When they continued asking him, he lifted up himself, and said unto them, "He that is without sin among you, let him first cast a stone at her."

—John 8:3–5, 7

Jesus threw an explosive countercharge amidst the sanctimonious hypocrites who hid their own sins and came to condemn the guilty woman and also to implicate Jesus in lawbreaking if he dared to show mercy to her and thus ignore the law of Moses. Jesus shamed them by suggesting, "No one among you is free from sin; should you not cast aspersions of guilt and stones of condemnation first at yourselves?"...

Jesus understood human nature and its weakness of yielding to sex transgressions. He knew that social or religious persecution cannot stamp out unhealthy sex habits deep-rooted in the brain and the mind; but that these detrimental compulsions can be overcome by a repentant individual who thoroughly impresses the mind with understanding of the destructive effects of those habits on himself, and who adopts the proper measures of self-control, will power, good company, and meditation to eliminate them. ...Thus the blessing and admonition of Jesus: "Neither do I condemn thee. Go and sin no more."

—Paramahansa Yogananda

Drawing by Heinrich Hofmann

stripped away from every man and he stands utterly revealed before the self-administering tribunal of "the last judgment."

"For as he thinketh in his heart, so is he."* Each soul, though in essence purely divine, has put on a mask of outer personality and character—a vibratory encasement that is the composite of all thoughts, feelings, sensory experiences, desires, and habits a person has harbored in his life. Every individual is unique unto himself; no two vibratory expressions are identical, for each one's thoughts, choices, and reactions in the school of life are his own. From childhood until his last breath, all these experiences are stored as vibratory patterns, tabloid records, in the brain. These karmic tendencies influence each person's behavior, personality, and life experiences.

Most people have difficulty remembering even major happenings of daily life after sufficient time has passed; the conscious mind usually begins to forget the details of events after a few minutes, and most of them wholly vanish over the course of a few days, months, or years. But behind the conscious mind is the subconscious mind; there all outstanding experiences of one's life are registered and can be recalled with the proper stimulus. Even deeper is the superconscious mind, which never forgets anything a person ever does, in this or prior incarnations. Body-bound man, in ordinary waking consciousness, usually has no access to the superconscious realm. But at the time of death, when life force and consciousness are withdrawn into the spine and brain in order to leave the mortal frame, the tabloid karmic "recordings" of every act, thought, feeling, and desire since childhood are activated and made visible. In a flash, the soul is presented with a review of that entire incarnation—all of the good and all of the evil that person has done, no matter how thoroughly he has "forgotten."

Viewing the sum total of the use he has made of that incarnation, the dying person is overwhelmed by a concentrated composite of his predominant feelings and desires. If he has led a basically good life, there will be consciousness of happiness or satisfaction; if the primary "accomplishment" of his life has been to cause pain to himself or others, his mind will be overcome by great remorse or guilt. The overriding impression—whether strongly positive or negative or somewhere in between—created by this life review is the "judgment" that deter-

---

* Proverbs 23:7.

mines where he will go in the astral interlude between incarnations as well as the conditions of his rebirth in a physical body.*

The overall tenor of a person's thoughts and feelings during his earth life thus renders the "verdict" on "the day of judgment." The final impression left in one's consciousness, the distilled essence of his predominant habits of a lifetime, is thus the karmic judge that at the sound of "Gabriel's trumpet" announces a man's next destination.†

The day of judgment, therefore, is a time after death when souls, according to their individual karma, receive judgment from the cosmic law as to what kind of rebirth or spiritual promotion they should have on earth or another higher sphere of existence.

"And that is why I know and can foretell to you, O inhabitants of Chorazin and Bethsaida, that because of your spiritual indifference you will reap poor fruits on the day of judgment of your karma after death. My consciousness—which is omniscient, perpetual, and uninterrupted by death—now sees all that will happen in future to you for the spiritual opportunity you scorned. I prophesy that I surely shall grieve on your day of judgment for your folly."

Jesus speaks similarly concerning Capernaum (his stated abode during his public life—thus the city most favored by God, "exalted unto heaven") as to how she will suffer in the future because of the individual and mass karma of her spiritually unappreciative inhabitants. Had the peoples of even the condemned Sodom seen such demonstration of the glorification of God in the life and works of Christ, their better response would have resulted in the continued preservation of the city and secured her inhabitants a better state in the hereafter.‡

---

* "That thought with which a dying man leaves the body determines—through his long persistence in it—his next state of being" (*God Talks With Arjuna: The Bhagavad Gita* VIII:6).

† See Discourse 21.

‡ "Though India possesses a civilization more ancient than that of any other country, few historians have noted that her feat of survival is by no means an accident, but a logical incident in the record of devotion to the eternal verities that India has offered through her best men in every generation. By sheer continuity of being, by intransitivity before the ages (can dusty scholars truly tell us how many?), India has given the worthiest answer of any people to the challenge of time.

"The Biblical story of Abraham's plea to the Lord that the city of Sodom be spared if ten righteous men could be found therein, and the Divine Reply: 'I will not destroy it for ten's sake,' gains new meaning in the light of India's escape from oblivion. Gone

The point is made that the Cosmic Law dispenses karmic effects commensurate with causative actions; but in addition to the action itself is motivation. Ignorance does not stay the law; but a willful and knowing rejection of a righteous course once it has been made evident increases the resultant karmic burden. Thus the judgment of the Cosmic Law against the ignorant evildoers of Sodom would be less severe than the judgment of that Law against those spiritual offenders in Capernaum who blaspheme God by rejecting and vilifying a supreme representative of Christ Intelligence sent to them by God.

---

are the empires of mighty nations, skilled in the arts of war, that once were India's contemporaries: ancient Egypt, Babylonia, Greece, Rome.

"The Lord's answer clearly shows that a land lives, not in its material achievements, but in its masterpieces of man." — *Autobiography of a Yogi*

The Forgiveness of Sins

Biblical Concept of Sin Has Been Misunderstood for Centuries

❖

Realization of the Soul's Divinity
Frees One From Effects of All Past Wrongs

❖

How Pure Love for God Brings Forgiveness of Sins

❖

Jesus' Compassion and Wisdom
in Dealing With the Woman Taken in Adultery

❖

A Forgiving Attitude Toward Others
Attracts God's Forgiveness for Oneself

❖

When One Forgives a Hurt,
Does It Free the Offender From Karmic Consequences?

❖

Five Methods for Obtaining Absolution
From Karmic Effects of Wrong Actions

"Man is essentially and eternally made in the image of God; the sins of a million lives cannot erase the perfection of his soul."

*A*nd one of the Pharisees desired him that he would eat with him. And he went into the Pharisee's house, and sat down to meat. And, behold, a woman in the city, which was a sinner, when she knew that Jesus sat at meat in the Pharisee's house, brought an alabaster box of ointment, and stood at his feet behind him weeping, and began to wash his feet with tears, and did wipe them with the hairs of her head, and kissed his feet, and anointed them with the ointment.

Now when the Pharisee which had bidden him saw it, he spake within himself, saying, "This man, if he were a prophet, would have known who and what manner of woman this is that toucheth him: for she is a sinner."

And Jesus answering said unto him, "Simon, I have somewhat to say unto thee." And he saith, "Master, say on."

"There was a certain creditor which had two debtors: the one owed five hundred pence, and the other fifty. And when they had nothing to pay, he frankly forgave them both. Tell me, therefore, which of them will love him most?"

Simon answered and said, "I suppose that he, to whom he forgave most." And he said unto him, "Thou hast rightly judged."

And he turned to the woman, and said unto Simon, "Seest thou this woman? I entered into thine house, thou gavest me no water for my feet: but she hath washed my feet with tears, and wiped them with the hairs of her head. Thou gavest me no kiss: but this woman since the time I came in hath not ceased to kiss my feet. My head with oil thou didst not anoint: but this woman hath anointed my feet with ointment. Wherefore I say unto thee, her sins, which are many, are forgiven; for she loved much: but to whom little is forgiven, the same loveth little."

And he said unto her, "Thy sins are forgiven."

And they that sat at meat with him began to say within themselves, "Who is this that forgiveth sins also?"

And he said to the woman, "Thy faith hath saved thee; go in peace."

—Luke 7:36–50*

---

* Other passages about the forgiveness of sins are also covered in this Discourse: John 8:3–11, Mark 11:25–26, Luke 17:3–4, and Matthew 18:21–35.

The Forgiveness of Sins

❦

The all-forgivingness of divine love was demonstrated time and again in those who made themselves devotionally receptive to the Christ in Jesus. His words to the woman of sinful repute gave voice to the redeeming compassion of God that responds in full measure to a devotee's heart-offering that is singularly replete with love. This freely given grace is similarly expressed by the Lord in the Bhagavad Gita: "Even a consummate evildoer who turns away from all else to worship Me exclusively may be counted among the good, because of his righteous resolve. He will fast become a virtuous man and obtain unending peace."*

Reigning over every action of an individual is the law of karma. Good begets good results; evil begets evil consequences. An evil action against society is a crime; an evil action against the welfare of the soul is a sin. The operation of cosmic law in regard to human actions differs from the operation of human law. A criminal is punished by the human law if and when detected and properly convicted; but if undetected he is able to go free. But the law of karma works unfailingly; it knows all and metes out its judgment accordingly. "Be not deceived; God is not mocked: for whatsoever a man soweth, that shall he also reap."†

Centuries of misunderstanding of Biblical concepts of sin and its supposed abomination in the sight of God have created a popularly

Biblical concept of sin has been misunderstood for centuries

---

* *God Talks With Arjuna: The Bhagavad Gita* IX:30–31.

† Galatians 6:7.

accepted image of the Almighty whose wrath against sinners is heartless, exactingly and vengefully severe. Intimidated man is made to cower before the judgment of his Maker. But saints of all religious persuasions who have entered the Divine Presence in interiorized personal communion universally declare that His omnipotence is expressed not as vengeance but as compassion, love, and goodness.

Though God is the Creator and Sustainer of man, He has ordained the law of cause and effect, or karma, to govern life so that man himself is the judge of his own actions. By good action he compels the law of karma to reward him. When he chooses to act evilly, it is then according to his own decree and invitation to the law of karma that he creates his own suffering.*

When a man works evil there is no conscious force ready to pounce upon and destroy him. The cosmic law makes no conscious decisions regarding an individual's fortune or misfortune. "The All-Pervading takes no account of anyone's virtue or sin. Wisdom is eclipsed by cosmic delusion; mankind is thereby bewildered."† As man gropes his way through the bewildering offerings of delusive creation, he fashions his own rewards from virtuous decisions or punishments from sinful choices inasmuch as his acts are in consonance with or contrary to cosmic law.

When a soul is identified with the body and its sense pleasures, it forgets its divine nature. This forgetfulness in the throes of indiscriminate indulgences is sinful, because the consciousness turns away from God and follows the path of ignorance. Man thereby sins by acting against the interest of his own true Self. Hence, when a child of God chooses to be identified with the senses and sensory happiness, he is a sinner against his soul, a violator of his soul's divine happiness. To love sensual pleasures to the exclusion of the blissful contact of the God-knowing soul in meditation is the basic sin that begets, through ignorance, all other manner of sinful behavior. He who fails to seek and find the superior happiness of ever new bliss present in the soul, which can be experienced in meditation, will forget his divine Self in the material lusts of the ego, the delusive pseudoself. If a prince squanders all his treasury on wining and dining his wicked, pleasure-mad friends,

---

* "Crime and punishment grow out of one stem. Punishment is a fruit that unsuspected ripens within the flower of the pleasure which concealed it."—Emerson, in *Compensation*.

† *God Talks With Arjuna: The Bhagavad Gita* v:15.

then he sins against his own interest. Similarly, when man forgets his princely soul-nature and caters to the temporary pleasures of the egoistically controlled body, he loses his right and ability to access the innate wealth of everlasting ever new bliss kept hidden from him in his sovereign Self.

When afflicted with the painful consequences of his errors, sin-beset man cries pitifully for God's mercy. That mercy has been given to each soul, but man's egoic individualism enshrouded in ignorance prevents him from accepting it. The *Why God seems so* worldly man thus thinks that God has forgotten him *remotely distant from* —or that He is so remotely distant from human af- *human affairs* fairs that man's travails are of no account to Him. The opposite is true: God is the nearest of the near, ever lovingly concerned and working silently for the welfare of His children; it is man who maintains a distant aloofness from God by forsaking Him in preoccupation with material pursuits. And when man then suddenly and urgently needs God's help, he no longer recalls how to make connection with that Divine Immanence.

Originally, when God created man He did not deny him the knowledge or revelation about Himself. As recounted in scripture, communion between God and man in primeval creation was natural and fraught with no obstruction. But man transgressed the law of God and thereby raised the walls of sin and ignorance, shutting out his perception of God. Adam and Eve in the beginning met the Beneficent Creator in their daily walks of life. The Lord never denied them His visit, until they knowingly transgressed His code of conduct. In point of fact, God did not drive them away; Adam and Eve drove themselves out of Paradise by their disobedience. Their own action created around themselves the walls of sinful transgression, through the opacity of which they could no longer view the Resplendent Spirit.

Man's persistence in error is why he is ostracized, banished from God-consciousness. But it would be wrong to blame God as being selfish, sitting on a celestial golden throne, enjoying the cream of His creation, while consigning the earth's poor fellows to till the hard soil of life. The truth is, if God is omnipresent, then He suffers in those who weep, toils in those who labor, rejoices in those who realize the bliss of the soul. The Great Spirit wished Himself to be many, hence He has become the many; but the many acknowledge Him not. They have segregated themselves by their individualism. Clinging to the delusion of separate ego-existence, they are utterly forgetful that their individuality is but a bubble upon the Cosmic Sea. Salvation lies in breaking that delusion of individualism, so that the little bubble may merge itself in the ocean of Spirit.

Each soul, pristinely fashioned after its Creator, remains ever immutable no matter how apparently sinful the externalized ego consciousness as expressed through the instruments of body and mind. Sin only acts like a crust that encapsulates the soul and prevents its manifestation of oneness with Spirit. When that crust of sin is broken, the ever pure soul becomes the predominating consciousness as it reexpresses the realization of its identity with God.

When the soul again realizes itself as a son of God, a true child of the Immaculate Infinite, and that through dream delusion it only temporarily imagined itself to be a sinner, then the consciousness feels an engrossing faith in that reality. The conviction of being a sinner is imaginary and changeable; the latent conviction that the soul is a son of God is permanent and unchangeable, even though temporarily hidden in a mortal matrix of

Realization of the soul's divinity frees one from effects of all past wrongs

sin. When one has faith in the divinity of his soul and its all-powerful God-attuned nature, he finds quick freedom from the results of past sinful actions.

If a chamber is dark for a thousand years, that darkness cannot be driven away by beating it with a stick. But if a light is brought in, the aeonic blackness is dispelled at once. Similarly, when a soul is in the darkness of incarnations of ignorance and evil actions, if the light of wisdom and faith in the soul and God is introduced, then all that delusive obscurity vanishes instantly.

Thus the consummate way that human beings can escape reaping the results of their past wrong actions is to change their status from a human being to that of a divine child. The evil actions of a soul identified with the body (that is, as the ego) will have to suffer punishment according to the law of karma. But if the soul, by ecstatic meditation, becomes fully liberated from its identification with the body and beholds itself as a pure image of Spirit, it is no longer subject to punishment for any mistakes it made in its human state.

Consider the postulate that a powerful monarch of a country disguised himself, went into a tavern belonging to his estate, got drunk, quite forgetting his status, and started a vicious brawl with one of the patrons. The innkeepers took him to a judge, appointed to that post by the king. As the judge was about to sentence the monarch, he came to his senses, threw off his disguise, and exclaimed: "I am the king who appointed you as the judge, and I have the power to cast you into prison. How dare you presume to convict me?" Similarly, the ever perfect kingly soul during its identification with the body may commit an evil and may be convicted as guilty according to the judge of karma; but when that soul identifies its consciousness with God, the Creator of the karmic judge, that royal soul is no longer under the jurisdiction of such judgment regarding its past dereliction.

The more one establishes one's identity with the Absolute and never deems himself a sinner, the more he will feel God's mercy.

Love for God, surrender to God, will destroy in man the karma of ignorance. Pure love, divine love, removes the barriers between man and his Maker. The sinful woman who "loved much" found herself transformed by its sanctifying touch.

How pure love for God brings forgiveness of sins

"I am impartial toward all beings," the Lord declares in the Bhagavad Gita. "To Me none is hateful, none is dear. But those who give Me their heart's love are in Me, as I am in them."*

God is love. Every soul, even when the outward consciousness is deluded or in a wicked state, is a holy receptacle filled with this divine love. No matter how deeply error-stricken man is identified with sensuous pleasures, when by meditation he consciously feels the love of God within himself, he begins to rise above his bad habits. Regardless of the intensity of his sins, when man turns his mind within and sincerely seeks and finally attains God's bliss and love templed in the soul, he does not have to undergo the suffering linked to his previous sense attachment. This is the grace that was bestowed on the woman who loved much. With her own consciousness permeated with the love of God within herself, and with the help of Jesus Christ, her consciousness became free from her habit of sin, of being identified with the compulsive pleasures of the flesh.

Jesus forgave her as a potential divine child made in the image of God. In spite of her many sins, she realized from the teachings of Jesus that the power of God was within herself, and that the power of Jesus could awaken within her that God-consciousness which would release

* *God Talks With Arjuna: The Bhagavad Gita* IX:29.

her from the consequences of those past transgressions. This is what is meant by the forgiving of sins.

When a criminal breaks a city ordinance, he is condemned according to the provisions of that law. But the governor of the state is empowered in extenuating circumstances to pardon the offender. Likewise, God, being all-powerful, and also His saints who are tuned with Him and who exercise their divine will force, can stop the fruition of evil karma in any individual. Only God and realized sons of God can completely or partially forgive an individual's sins against his soul, provided that person is devotedly sincere in seeking forgiveness, not through mere supplication, but through divine love.

Shallow prayer and selfish fear of consequences will not cause God arbitrarily to contradict the just and sanctioned working of His karmic law. This would in effect permit man to continue in error without consequences. Nor can God be moved by fitful emotions of praise or bartered deals of good behavior for past misdeeds. Man's recourse to the intercession of the grace and forgiveness of God, saving him from his self-created fate at the merciless bar of law, is that God is both law and love. The devotee who seeks redemption by attuning his actions to the righteous guidance of divine law and also implores with pure devotion and faith the unconditional love of God, will be transformed in God's light of forgiveness. There is no doubt about this divine assurance: Any sin, and its consequence, can be forgiven the repentant devotee who loves God deeply enough, and thereby puts his life in tune with the all-compassionate Lord.

Love is greater than law; it is the unifying thread that attaches the devotee's heart to the unconditional heart of God. Law is based upon impersonal justice weighed according to the principle of cause and effect; but love claims God as our own forgiving Father-Mother whose all-embracing mercy abides whether or not the full measure of the law has been met.*

The sinful woman forgiven by Jesus loved much because despite the magnitude of her sins, in the presence of divine love she felt no condemnation but rather faith in its redeeming power. And like the man in the parable who was forgiven his greater debt relative to the

---

* "All the wickedness in the world that man might work or think is no more to the mercy of God than a live coal in the sea." — William Langland, fourteenth-century English mystical poet.

debtor forgiven little, her love was magnified by the awesome forgiveness she received through the medium of her devotion and faith and the blessing of the Christ in Jesus.*

The removal by God's grace of a small karmic debt may be less noticed and responded to by a complacent righteous man secure in his love for God, whereas the effect of overwhelming love and gratitude is roused in a man whose devotion and faith has merited a divine reprieve from some dire karmic consequence of his own sinful making.

Thus one who loves much is forgiven much; and one who is forgiven much, loves even more.

~

And he said unto her, "Thy sins are forgiven."

And they that sat at meat with him began to say within themselves, "Who is this that forgiveth sins also?"

And he said to the woman, "Thy faith hath saved thee; go in peace" (Luke 7:48–50).

Jesus' several pronouncements of his forgiveness of sins was a source of consternation to the people of his time who believed that only God could forgive the sins of an individual. They could little understand the power of Jesus as manifesting his oneness with God, enabling him to do all wonders sanctioned by the Divine Will.

As stated previously, only God and the highly advanced saints can forgive others and free them from suffering the results of their transgressions; this is because they understand the exact relation of mind, habits, and the brain of individuals and can change the nature of a person's brain cells and mind, favorably altering karmic patterns.† Some credulous wrongdoers consider it sufficient to confess their sins to an ordinary cleric to receive divine amnesty from their evil deeds. Because

Forgiveness of sins means erasing karmic patterns left in the brain by wrong actions

---

* Saint Teresa wrote: "There are souls whom the certain conviction that God is with them benefits more than all the fear they may ever have. If a soul love greatly, and is thankful naturally, the remembrance of the mercies of God makes it turn to Him more effectually than all the chastisements of hell it can ever picture to itself—at least, it was so with me." —*Life of St. Teresa of Jesus* (New York: Benziger Bros., 1904), Chapter xv.

† See Discourses 13, 25, and 31.

confession confers on them a sort of mental consolation and because they cannot see the subtle operation of the law of karma—whose punitive judgments may not be discernibly linked in time or condition to their cause—they deem themselves forgiven.

The idea of confession provides some measure of restraint and unity of moral purpose, but even better than confessing to human beings is confession to the Lord in a contrite surrender of pure love. It is unseemly to say to God "I am a sinner." What God wants to hear is that man remembers his true relationship with his Heavenly Father-Mother: "Lord, I am Thy child. You brought me into a world that is fraught with delusion and temptations. Though I might have made mistakes, I am Thy child just the same." We came from God, fashioned from His own One Being, and in Him we will ultimately merge again. Faith in this belief, this conviction, alone can bring soul freedom.

Jesus said to the woman who was forgiven of many sins that it was her faith that saved her. Her faith, made strong by the humble deference of her love, released her mind from the grip of her senses and focused it within on her true Self. When Jesus found that she was willing to quit her identification with her dissolute behavior, he stimulated with his cosmic energy the life energy concentrated in her brain and erased or "forgave" the evil tendencies with which her mind had become saturated.

In Jesus' pronouncement, "Thy sins are forgiven," he emphasized that God's energy passing through him into the woman had been the principal factor in the healing. He then said, "Thy faith hath saved thee," emphasizing that her receptivity, her conviction in the unlimited power of God, was the second requisite.

The divine power of Jesus roused the omnipresent Divine Will to send the healing cosmic energy to the brain cells of the sinful woman. The concomitant release of the latent healing life energy in her brain cells was due to her "faith," the revival of her sin-paralyzed will in response to the divine will of God through Jesus.

"O woman, thy faith in the infinite power of divine healing charged your sin-paralyzed will with Divine Will, causing a release of stored-up energy in the brain which, reinforced with the cosmic energy from me, has cauterized the sinful tendencies lodged in your brain cells. Now, freed from the automatic reaction and compulsion of evil habits and sense slavery, you can be conscious of the revived peace of your soul—'Go in peace.'"

~

In another incident, recounted in the Gospel According to St. John, Jesus dramatically illustrated the divine attitude toward erring children of God:

> *And the scribes and Pharisees brought unto him a woman taken in adultery; and when they had set her in the midst, they say unto him, "Master, this woman was taken in adultery, in the very act. Now Moses in the law commanded us, that such should be stoned: but what sayest thou?" This they said, tempting him, that they might have to accuse him. But Jesus stooped down, and with his finger wrote on the ground, as though he heard them not.*
>
> *So when they continued asking him, he lifted up himself, and said unto them, "He that is without sin among you, let him first cast a stone at her." And again he stooped down, and wrote on the ground. And they which heard it, being convicted by their own conscience, went out one by one, beginning at the eldest, even unto the last: and Jesus was left alone, and the woman standing in the midst.*
>
> *When Jesus had lifted up himself, and saw none but the woman, he said unto her, "Woman, where are those thine accusers? Hath no man condemned thee?"*
>
> *She said, "No man, Lord." And Jesus said unto her, "Neither do I condemn thee: go, and sin no more"* (John 8:3–11).

In this highly charged confrontation, Jesus displays divine wisdom, compassion, and spiritual skill in handling a most difficult situation. He threw an explosive countercharge amidst the sanctimonious hypocrites who hid their own sins and came to condemn the guilty woman and also to implicate Jesus in lawbreaking if he dared to show mercy to her and thus ignore the law of Moses. Jesus shamed them by suggesting, "No one among you is free from sin; should you not cast aspersions of guilt and stones of condemnation first at yourselves?"

Jesus' compassion and wisdom in dealing with the woman taken in adultery

The words of Jesus are variously applicable in the practical affairs of life: (1) Only the highly spiritual man who is free from sin himself is justified in casting the stone of criticism at the materially minded man in order to awaken him. (2) Any person who is successfully rein-

653

ing in with self-control his own sin may cast a stone of helpful warning at an unrestrained sinful individual. (3) Stones of criticism should not be cast at anyone for any fault if the accuser also harbors that fault within himself. The spiritually ignorant have no right to criticize others about their spiritual ignorance. Individuals with specific sense attachments ought not to criticize others who possess that same weakness. Only persons who do not make social mistakes themselves are justified in critiquing others' social errors.

Jesus said in effect: "No one in the crowd was sinless and therefore could not with a clear conscience condemn you. Nor do I, with my divine perception and wisdom, condemn you before God, even though you have ignorantly sinned. Henceforth, follow the path of righteousness. The Christ Consciousness in me has saved you from reaping the consequences of your past adulterous actions. Never again identify your mind with those insatiable lusts that were devastating to your true soul joy. If you repeat your sinful actions, they will fast become a habit again that will compel you to act sinfully, even against your will. In that hapless slavery, you will suffer dire social, mental, moral, spiritual, and physical condemnation from which it will be very difficult for you to be forgiven, or freed through your own efforts or the help of others."

Adultery is not only a social crime but also a sin against divine happiness. Adulterous behavior leads to marital disruptions, social disharmony, and loss of the true values of love. Those who engage in sexual promiscuity rather than transmuting sex energy into constructive purposes devitalize their body of energy, their minds of peace and happiness, their souls of divine bliss and wisdom.

Jesus understood human nature and its weakness of yielding to sex transgressions. He knew that social or religious persecution cannot stamp out unhealthy sex habits deep-rooted in the brain and the mind; but that these detrimental compulsions can be overcome by a repentant individual who thoroughly impresses the mind with understanding of the destructive effects of those habits on himself, and who adopts the proper measures of self-control, will power, good company, and meditation to eliminate them. Once such a repentant individual becomes free from the enthrallment of sex habits by accumulation of life energy in the brain through deep meditation, which also summons the intercession of one's guru, or savior, and the redeeming grace of God, the penitent should not revive those habits and their attendant miseries by sowing fresh seeds of illicit sex activities on the tender soil of his mind. Thus the blessing and admonition of Jesus: "Neither do I condemn thee. Go and sin no more."

The law of karma should not make people fatalists, but should enable them to diagnose scientifically all the hidden seeds of self-created potential miseries, that they may in time be properly destroyed or at least their growth mitigated by physical, mental, and spiritual means. Seeds of evil actions that have been de-powered cannot suddenly germinate to cause suffering in one who is unprepared.

According to the legal statutes of a country, a judge might sentence a young criminal to three years in a reformatory school. But the judge usually has the privilege to commute that sentence to probation if the young offender repents and promises good behavior. So, according to the law of karma, a person who acts evilly must reap the consequences of his actions. But if that evildoer corrects his misbehavior and by intense devotion, prayer, and meditation appeals to God for pardon, then God, being the Maker of the law of karma, can grant him amnesty from punishment, allowing him instead to work out his sentence through the amelioration of such counteracting ways as righteous actions and consciousness-transforming meditation.

～

"And when ye stand praying, forgive, if ye have ought against any: that your Father also which is in heaven may forgive you your trespasses. But if ye do not forgive, neither will your Father which is in heaven forgive your trespasses" (Mark 11:25–26).

Here Jesus points out another truth pertinent to the devotee seeking forgiveness from past wrong actions: If one is forgiving toward those who have offended him, then the omniscient Father, the invisible but ever present Cosmic Consciousness, which enfolds the devotee as he prays for redemption, will also forgive that petitioner's spiritual offenses. But if the omniscient Father finds an unforgiving attitude toward those who have offended His child, then He, likewise, may withhold forgiveness for that child's own spiritual sins. It is not that God whimsically plays tit for tat

A forgiving attitude toward others attracts God's forgiveness for oneself

---

* See parallel passage in Matthew 6:14–15, Discourse 28.

with His children. Rather the cosmic law of cause and effect is active even in man's relationship with God, particularly in the beginning stages when divine union has not been irrevocably established. Man begets the causes that bring forth God's response.

Man's soul is a reflection of God, and when he misuses his free will to behave contrary to his divine soul-image, he creates a distortion in his consciousness in which God reflects to him a response of his own making. It is the nature of the soul to express unconditional love. When connate forgiveness is withheld by resentment and ill will toward an offender, God likewise does not show Himself as forgiveness to that person of vengeful disposition. But when soul-forgiveness is beneficently manifested outwardly to one's fellow beings, no matter how they have offended him, then he is imbued with the corresponding reflection of God's redemptive forgiveness.

Jesus is pointing out that the code of human conduct should not be enforced by justice alone, but be tempered by forgiveness and love —a plea the devotee would be wise to heed. It is the duty of federal or civil law to deal with crime; it is not for an individual to try to punish a person who has offended him—even if it is obvious that he justly merits it. The divine way is to try to forgive him, because he is a child of God, although an erring brother, whose immutable soul has no part in man's mischief. No doubt, a wronged person, also, is responsible for many offenses toward God and man. But if the omniscient Father finds that one of His sons forgives an offending brother, then because of that mitigating divine love He will relax the determinate law of cause and effect and forgive some of the forgiver's spiritual offenses, even as he forgave his errant brother.

～

"Take heed to yourselves: If thy brother trespass against thee, rebuke him; and if he repent, forgive him. And if he trespasses against thee seven times in a day, and seven times in a day turn again to thee, saying, 'I repent'; thou shalt forgive him" (Luke 17:3–4).

"Take heed of the following truths: If your brother acts against your noble wishes and good principles, discipline him by telling him the effects of his evil actions; and if he truly repents of his evil ways, forgive him—even if he repeats his offense seven times in a day."

This is an affirmation by Jesus that no matter how many times a man falls prey to evil, the divine image within him remains untarnished and is worthy of consideration. As soon as the evildoer repents, the covering of evil is pushed aside to reveal the shining true Self. When an evildoer repents, but is not forgiven and is still accused and made to feel guilty of his forsaken error, the consciousness of wrongdoing is replanted in him. If his will is weakened by discouragement and absorbs that suggestion, he may again succumb to error. Therefore the psychology of forgiveness consists in helping the wrongdoer to remove permanently the mask of evil from his soul by encouraging in him the cultivation of good karma.

Though one should not hold unforgiving feelings in his heart, neither should he express forgiveness to a wrongdoer who does not truly repent of his evil actions; otherwise it would only justify to him deliberate repetition of his evil behavior. But a brother should forgive an error-stricken brother as many times as possible if the offender really tries to forsake his evil ways yet falls occasionally due to weakness of will and strength of fleshly physical habit. To extend repeatedly the hand of forgiveness to a repentant brother is to mirror the example of the Heavenly Father who forgives us all countless, infinite, times.

~

Then came Peter to him, and said, "Lord, how oft shall my brother sin against me, and I forgive him? till seven times?" Jesus saith unto him, "I say not unto thee, until seven times: but, until seventy times seven.

"Therefore is the kingdom of heaven likened unto a certain king, which would take account of his servants. And when he had begun to reckon, one was brought unto him, which owed him ten thousand talents. But forasmuch as he had not to pay, his lord commanded him to be sold, and his wife, and children, and all that he had, and payment to be made. The servant therefore fell down, and worshipped him, saying, 'Lord, have patience with me, and I will pay thee all.' Then the lord of that servant was moved with compassion, and loosed him, and forgave him the debt.

"But the same servant went out, and found one of his fellowservants, which owed him an hundred pence: and he laid

hands on him, and took him by the throat, saying, 'Pay me that thou owest.' And his fellowservant fell down at his feet, and besought him, saying, 'Have patience with me, and I will pay thee all.' And he would not: but went and cast him into prison, till he should pay the debt.

"So when his fellowservants saw what was done, they were very sorry, and came and told unto their lord all that was done. Then his lord, after that he had called him, said unto him, 'O thou wicked servant, I forgave thee all that debt, because thou desiredst me: shouldest not thou also have had compassion on thy fellowservant, even as I had pity on thee?' And his lord was wroth, and delivered him to the tormentors, till he should pay all that was due unto him.

"So likewise shall my heavenly Father do also unto you, if ye from your hearts forgive not every one his brother their trespasses" (Matthew 18:21–35).

The above story of the king and his servants is yet another illustration of the operation of the law of karma, cause and effect, in which Jesus points out that the effects of already performed evil actions can be modified by the neutralizing power of prayer and good actions. But along with receiving the mitigating grace of divine help and forgiveness, the recipient also incurs an obligation to learn to forgive the sins against him of his repentant brothers.

When human beings tune themselves to God by deep prayer in meditation and realize their divinity, the perfect soul-image within them, they need not suffer for their past human errors. But if after this ecstatic experience their consciousness reverts to mortal habits, they lose that freedom from karma and again subject themselves to be governed by the exacting law of cause and effect.

Jesus used the example of forgiveness of one's debts to indicate the wiping away of karmic debt—that one can escape the law of karma by identifying himself with God through faith, love, and ecstatic prayer, even as the servant was forgiven his debt when he petitioned his king. But if after finding divine forgiveness from one's own karma by meditation, one again becomes meanly human by unforgiveness toward his brothers who sin against him, his reidentification with human life and behavior binds him again to the inexorable laws of limiting karma. Having been forgiven as a divine child of God, the devotee should conscientiously strive to retain his identity with his true soul-image, remaining continuously forgiving and loving like his Father-God.

The question arises: If a man performs an evil action against his brother and repents and is forgiven by him "until seventy times seven," then is the transgressor free also from the operation of the law of karma? The answer is very complicated. One must consider the mechanism by which man is bound by his karma.

When one forgives a hurt, does it free the offender from karmic consequences?

Persons who think that repentance alone will atone for their evil habits, and who keep repenting after each repetition of the evil deed, will not thereby receive amnesty from their sinful behavior, no matter how often they are forgiven by man. Repentance is not a cure for the consequences of evil actions. It serves only to keep the mind consciously acquainted with the painful results of evil deeds, with the hope of preventing further repetition of evil experiences. After repentance, one must forever relinquish the evil habit.

Repentance is not accomplished by beating one's breast in self-condemnation or uselessly "crying over spilled milk"; it means to so impregnate the mind with the consciousness of the repugnance of evil that one will automatically shrink from even the thought of evil deeds, not to speak of the evil deeds themselves. Unless the mind learns to abhor evil actions, it is very difficult to keep it proof against the allurements of temptation.

Basically, if a guilty man, being forgiven, repents and does not repeat his evil actions, then he may eventually be free from acting erroneously again through the influence of subconscious traces left by the evil activity. He thereby incurs no further bad karma from repetition of that action, and the resulting good karma from improved behavior may at least partially lessen the effects of his past wrong actions. But it is evident that if a man finds forgiveness for his evil actions from his fellow being, that may not necessarily assure exemption from suffering from the law of karma which governs his past misbehavior.

The only sure way for a person to find freedom from the effects of his bad actions is to strike at them at their roots. The karmic patterns of evil consequences one has created in his brain cells and mind must be cauterized either by divine intervention or by consciously engaging one's will power and life force to erase therein all traces left by evil activities.

In addition to faith, devotion, intense prayer, and good actions—as already explained—scientific techniques of meditation are the

659

surest way that man can help himself to burn up all traces of his past evil actions. In deep meditation the mind becomes interiorized and contacts the superconsciousness of the soul. This stimulates the impressions of good actions stored up in the consciousness and subconsciousness of the brain and counteracts the traces of evil actions there.

Attention and life energy are inseparable forces working in the brain and the nervous system during all physical and mental activities of man. When the attention is centralized on a particular sense attraction, then energy goes outward and becomes identified with that specific sense pleasure. But by deep concentration, whether on a good or an evil thought, the attention becomes interiorized. When an evil thought becomes interiorized by concentration—such as when one broods on a lustful desire, or on a vengeful feeling—it stimulates the impressions of evil actions in the brain, invigorating their fruition while diminishing the effectiveness of good karmic patterns. When a good thought becomes interiorized by deep meditation, the inwardly focused mind withdraws life force from the nervous system and centralizes it in the brain cells; the peaceful, powerful character of the concentrated life force stimulates the harmonious traces of good actions and burns up at the roots the inharmonious traces of evil actions.

In summary, there are several methods of overcoming the effects of past evil actions, of receiving "forgiveness of one's sins," absolution from the karmic effects of actions contrary to the welfare of one's true Self or that otherwise in any manner bring untoward consequences:

1. Divine meditation—especially as the devotee advances to the higher states of soul-realization and God-consciousness—is the surest

Five methods for obtaining absolution from karmic effects of wrong actions

way of burning up the prenatal and postnatal traces of all evil actions and of stimulating the traces of good actions.

2. An effective though slower way to neutralize bad karma gradually is to bring all of one's physical and mental actions into harmony with the eternal laws of righteous behavior, including the practice of deep prayer, devotion, and faith.

3. An advanced soul, or an emissary of God as was Jesus, has the power by will force to charge the brain of the receptive devotee with cosmic energy, which cauterizes the roots of past karmic evils and of wicked habits lodged in the brain cells and saturated in the mind.

4. There is an exceptional metaphysical technique by which great masters and advanced yogis can do away with the accumulated traces of many, many lives of binding karmic actions. When such an advanced soul in the ecstasy of deep meditation identifies his consciousness with God, he changes his status from a human being with karma to a perfect image of God or divine soul. But unless he is completely liberated, he has to revert to human status when he comes down from his meditative ecstasy. So the law of karma with its determinative judgment comes to bring punishment to the temporarily changed individual. But that individual says to the intelligent law: "You can't punish me for the faults of a human being who through delusion I dreamed I was before. By wisdom I have regained consciousness of my true Self, a perfect image of God free from the chains of karma." But the law of karma insists: "Whether you are a master now or were an ordinary human being before, you are still the same individualized being and therefore must pay for your uncompensated past human karma."

The master, finding himself thus confronted, adopts an ingenious method to "pay up" and satisfy all karmic debt against himself. The master or yogi enters a state of soul realization and finds in the archives of his superconsciousness exactly all binding karmic traces of his past actions. He then proceeds to work them out in one or two or many bodies, which he creates in a vision—a true-to-life experience. For example, if for five incarnations the yogi led a worldly life in which material habits were not overcome or desires were yet unfulfilled, in his vision he creates five bodies which undergo the necessary experiences and play out the parts of those five different lives in a matter of hours. Then the master says to the law of karma: "There in the vision, by the intensity of my concentration and divine consciousness, I have experienced in the materialized five lives all results of my karma; now I am free."

As soon as the karmic effects of evil actions have been manifested and experienced, whether in a self-created conscious dream or vision in a few minutes or hours, or in the ordinary events of life in a number of years, the karmic law has been satisfied and the penitent man is "forgiven," freed from that particular karmic debt.

Souls who are bound by ignorance do not learn the redeeming lesson of an experience even when it is repeated several times during many years—or lives! But the wise man by deep concentration attains realization of the truth in an experience in a few minutes.

This unique vision-method of working out one's karma is not an option available to the ordinary aspiring devotee; it can be performed only by the highly advanced who are in tune with the Cosmic Consciousness and thus have complete control over the all-creative Cosmic Energy, by which they can materialize visions or copies of actualities by the power of will. Occasionally, highly developed souls, by the same method, can offer their advanced consciousness to work out karma of others in a condensed, accelerated, manner.

5. There is a fifth way by which great masters can work out the traces of their actions when they have also taken onto themselves the karma of others. Masters and saviors such as Jesus can offer their bodies to experience not only their own karma but also the karma of others to help them toward liberation. The crucifixion of Jesus informs us of one such example. Jesus was not crucified by the will of God to fulfill some dramatic cosmic plan. His suffering on the cross was due to some of his own actions and the taking onto himself of some of the consequences of the sinful actions of his disciples and followers. Jesus knew that his preaching the truth in defiance of political authority and against the canons and traditions of religion would inevitably attract the karma of death; in his incarnate work, he had created a cause that would by the law and purview of the times command a fatal consequence. He also knew that by forgiving the evil actions of his disciples and others he had taken on their karmic debt which he would have to pay with suffering in his own body. He consciously, for the sake of highest gain in God-consciousness for himself and others and for working out the karma of himself and others, permitted his body to be crucified. By that supreme sacrifice, he was freed from the cosmic constraints of his mortal incarnation and regained immortality for himself and others. On the higher plane of his immortality and omnipresence, Jesus, as a world savior, as with other saviors and great masters, continues his mission of redeeming souls.

It is evident there is much involved regarding the forgiving of sins by God and by the advanced consciousness of man.

The salient consolation is that every human being has absolute surety about his final emancipation if he tries his utmost to help redeem himself. Man is essentially and eternally made in the image of God; the sins of a million lives cannot erase the perfection of his soul. There is no reason why he should continue an existence of ignorance and suffering. In the Bhagavad Gita the Lord declares: "To those thus

ever attached to Me, and who worship Me with love, I impart that discriminative wisdom (*buddhi yoga*) by which they attain Me utterly.
From sheer compassion I, the Divine Indweller, set alight in them the
radiant lamp of wisdom which banishes the darkness that is born of
ignorance."* By the methods of advanced meditation and the grace of
divine forgiveness man can quickly work out the errors of his many
past lives and become free, regaining the lost and forgotten perfection
of his soul and its immortality in God.

---

* *God Talks With Arjuna: The Bhagavad Gita* x:10–11.

What Is Blasphemy Against the Holy Ghost?

Angelic and Devilish Spirits Both Influence Man's Life

❖

The Evil Works of Satan in Conflict
With the Redeeming Works of the Holy Ghost

❖

Reverent Contact With the Holy Ghost
Frees One From Delusion and Suffering

❖

"The Sign of Jonah": Jesus Predicts the Miracle
of His Resurrection

❖

Spiritual Dangers of Arrogant Self-Sufficiency and Pride

❖

Jesus Upholds Love for God Above Attachment to Family

"One who never meditates rejects the prime means of attuning his life with the saving Christ Consciousness inherent in the Cosmic Aum Vibration. By deliberate deeper acts of meditation...regain bliss consciousness through vibratory contact of God as Holy Ghost."

*A*nd it came to pass afterward, that he went throughout every city and village, preaching and shewing the glad tidings of the kingdom of God: and the twelve were with him, and certain women, which had been healed of evil spirits and infirmities, Mary called Magdalene, out of whom went seven devils, and Joanna the wife of Chuza Herod's steward, and Susanna, and many others, which ministered unto him of their substance.

—Luke 8:1–3

Then was brought unto him one possessed with a devil, blind, and dumb: and he healed him, insomuch that the blind and dumb both spake and saw. And all the people were amazed, and said, "Is not this the son of David?" But when the Pharisees heard it, they said, "This fellow doth not cast out devils, but by Beelzebub the prince of the devils."

And Jesus knew their thoughts, and said unto them, "Every kingdom divided against itself is brought to desolation; and every city or house divided against itself shall not stand: And if Satan cast out Satan, he is divided against himself; how shall then his kingdom stand? And if I by Beelzebub cast out devils, by whom do your children cast them out? Therefore they shall be your judges. But if I cast out devils by the Spirit of God, then the kingdom of God is come unto you.

"Or else how can one enter into a strong man's house, and spoil his goods, except he first bind the strong man? and then he will spoil his house. He that is not with me is against me; and he that gathereth not with me scattereth abroad.

"Wherefore I say unto you, all manner of sin and blasphemy shall be forgiven unto men: but the blasphemy against the Holy Ghost shall not be forgiven unto men. And whosoever speaketh a word against the Son of man, it shall be forgiven him: but whosoever speaketh against the Holy Ghost, it shall not be forgiven him, neither in this world, neither in the world to come.

"Either make the tree good, and his fruit good; or else make the tree corrupt, and his fruit corrupt: for the tree is known by his fruit. O generation of vipers, how can ye, being evil, speak good things? for out of the abundance of the heart the mouth speaketh. A good man out of the good treasure of the heart bringeth forth good things: and an evil man out of the evil treasure bringeth forth evil things. But I say unto you, that every idle word that men shall speak, they shall give account thereof in the day of judgment. For by thy words thou shalt be justified, and by thy words thou shalt be condemned."

Then certain of the scribes and of the Pharisees answered, saying, "Master, we would see a sign from thee."

But he answered and said unto them, "An evil and adulterous generation seeketh after a sign; and there shall no sign be given to it, but the sign of the prophet Jonah: For as Jonah was three days and three nights in the whale's belly; so shall the Son of man be three days and three nights in the heart of the earth. The men of Nineveh shall rise in judgment with this generation, and shall condemn it: because they repented at the preaching of Jonah; and, behold, a greater than Jonah is here.

"The queen of the south shall rise up in the judgment with this generation, and shall condemn it: for she came from the uttermost parts of the earth to hear the wisdom of Solomon; and, behold, a greater than Solomon is here.

"When the unclean spirit is gone out of a man, he walketh through dry places, seeking rest, and findeth none. Then he saith, 'I will return into my house from whence I came out'; and when he is come, he findeth it empty, swept, and garnished. Then goeth he, and taketh with himself seven other spirits more wicked than himself, and they enter in and dwell there: and the last state of that man is worse than the first. Even so shall it be also unto this wicked generation."

While he yet talked to the people, behold, his mother and his brethren stood without, desiring to speak with him. Then one said unto him, "Behold, thy mother and thy brethren stand without, desiring to speak with thee."

But he answered and said unto him that told him, "Who is my mother? and who are my brethren?" And he stretched forth his hand toward his disciples, and said, "Behold my mother and my brethren! For whosoever shall do the will of my Father which is in heaven, the same is my brother, and sister, and mother."

—Matthew 12:22–50*

---

*Cf. parallel references in Luke 11:14–32.

What Is Blasphemy
Against the Holy Ghost?

And it came to pass afterward, that he went throughout every city and village, preaching and shewing the glad tidings of the kingdom of God: and the twelve were with him, and certain women, which had been healed of evil spirits and infirmities, Mary called Magdalene, out of whom went seven devils, and Joanna the wife of Chuza Herod's steward, and Suzanna, and many others, which ministered unto him of their substance (Luke 8:1–3).

Jesus' preaching manifested the divine inspiration and authority of his God-realization, distinct from pedantic theology. His consciousness at one with the consciousness of God transcended every thought of selfish personal comfort in his itinerant life devoted to revealing the ever-newly joyous state attainable in the kingdom of God —in the inner meditative state of Cosmic Consciousness. The holy company that journeyed with Jesus included the twelve apostles and some of the devout women who had been healed by him, including Mary Magdalene, who had been relieved of seven devils—seven evil forces that had obsessed her at different times.*

---

* See Discourse 24 for detailed discussion of possession by evil spirits.

Then was brought unto him one possessed with a devil, blind, and dumb; and he healed him, insomuch that the blind and dumb both spake and saw. And all the people were amazed, and said, "Is not this the son of David?" But when the Pharisees heard it, they said, "This fellow doth not cast out devils, but by Beelzebub the prince of the devils" (Matthew 12:22–24).

Parallel reference:

And the scribes which came down from Jerusalem said, "He hath Beelzebub, and by the prince of the devils casteth he out devils" (Mark 3:22).

When Jesus healed the possessed person, restoring his sight and speech, the people were amazed and said, "Is this the son of David? One with the power to perform such divine works can be no ordinary man, belonging to an ordinary human family." Supported by scripture, they conjectured whether indeed this was the one prophesied to come out of the house of King David, born of his seed, or lineage.* Notwithstanding the popular acclaim, Jesus' adversaries (commonly denoted as the Pharisees and scribes) accused him of casting out devils, evil spirits, not by divine fiat but by the power of Beelzebub, the prince of the devils.†

Angelic and devilish spirits both influence man's life

---

* See II Samuel 7:12: [God speaking to David] "And when thy days be fulfilled, and thou shalt sleep with thy fathers, I will set up thy seed after thee, which shall proceed out of thy bowels, and I will establish his kingdom."

Isaiah 11:1–2: "And there shall come forth a rod out of the stem of Jesse [father of David], and a branch shall grow out of his roots: And the spirit of the Lord shall rest upon him, the spirit of wisdom and understanding, the spirit of counsel and might, the spirit of knowledge and of the fear of the Lord."

Jeremiah 23:5–6: "Behold, the days come," saith the Lord, "that I will raise unto David a righteous branch, and a King shall reign and prosper, and shall execute judgment and justice in the earth. In his days Judah shall be saved, and Israel shall dwell safely: and this is his name whereby he shall be called, The Lord Our Righteousness."

† Hebrew *Ba'al zebhubh*, a Canaanite deity ("lord of flies"); in some translations rendered as Beelzebul, "lord of dung."

The *Encyclopaedia Britannica* gives this brief summary of the concept of devils as expressed in principal world religions:

"In Zoroastrianism, a religion founded by the 6th-century-BC Persian prophet Zoroaster, the hierarchy of demons (daevas) is headed by Angra Mainyu (later called

The ensuing discourse by Jesus contrasts the unseen intelligent evil force, or Satan, with God's omnipresent invisible power in creation, the Holy Ghost.

As explained [see Discourses 1 and 7], by the command of the Holy Ghost—Cosmic Vibratory Force; the Word, *Aum* or Amen—all things are created. Immanent in the Holy Ghost is the conscious reflection of Deity, the Christ Intelligence, by which that Cosmic Vibratory Power is guided to evolve all manifestations of goodness in the world. The conscious Satanic Power spawns and directs the evil forces of the world, fight-

---

Ahriman), the Evil, or Destructive, Spirit. The demons are in constant battle with Ahura Mazda (later called Ormazd), the Good Lord.

"The hierarchy of demons in Judaism, which is rooted in ancient Middle Eastern and Zoroastrian demonology after the postexilic period (after 538 BC), is quite varied. The prince of the forces of evil (Hebrew *shedim,* meaning 'demons' and applied to foreign gods, or *se'irim,* meaning 'hairy demons'), who often were believed to inhabit desert wastes, ruins, and graves and to inflict humanity with various physical, psychological, and spiritual disorders, was called by different names: Satan (the Antagonist), Belial (the spirit of perversion, darkness, and destruction), Mastema (Enmity, or Opposition), and other names. Though the Old Testament refers to Satan as the prosecutor of God's celestial court (Zech. 3; Job 1–2), a hierarchy of demons under Satan or other princes of evil was developed in intertestamental literature and later Judaism.

"The hierarchy of demons in Christianity is based on various sources: Jewish, Zoroastrian, Gnostic (a syncretistic religious dualistic-belief system in which matter is viewed as evil, the spirit good, and salvation as being attainable through esoteric knowledge, or *gnosis*), and the indigenous religions that succumbed to Christian missionizing. In the New Testament, Jesus speaks of Beelzebub as the chief of demons and equates him with Satan. In the European Middle Ages and the Reformation period, various hierarchies of demons were developed, such as that associated with the seven deadly sins: Lucifer (pride), Mammon (avarice), Asmodeus (lechery), Satan (anger), Beelzebub (gluttony), Leviathan (envy), and Belphegor (sloth).

"The Islamic hierarchy of demons is headed by Iblis (the devil), who also is called *Shaytan* (Satan) or *'aduw Allah* ('Enemy of God'). Based to a great extent on Jewish and Christian demonology, Iblis became the leader of a host of *jinn,* spiritual beings that generally bode evil.

"In Hinduism, the *asuras* are the demons who oppose the *devas* (the gods). Among the various classes of *asuras* are *nagas* (serpent demons), Ahi (the demon of drought), and Kamsa (an archdemon). Demons that afflict humans include the *raksasas* (grotesque beings who haunt cemeteries, impel the performance of foolish acts, and attack *sadhus* (saintly men) and *pishacas* (beings who haunt places where violent deaths have occurred).

"Buddhists often view their demons as forces that inhibit the achievement of Nirvana (bliss, or the extinction of desire); an important example is Mara, an arch tempter, who, with his daughters, Rati (Desire), Raga (Pleasure), and Tanha (Restlessness), attempted to dissuade Siddhartha Gautama, the Buddha, from achieving his enlightenment. As Mahayana (Greater Vehicle) Buddhism spread to Tibet, China, and Japan, many of the demons of the folk religions of these areas (e.g., the Chinese *kuei-shen;* the Japanese *oni*) were incorporated into Buddhist beliefs."

ing to obstruct the pattern of Holy Ghost and using the enticements of delusion in order to keep finite creation from dissolving back into Spirit.

Though God is the Aggregate Creator—nothing can exist outside His consciousness—still He has given man freedom to align himself with either the divine Christ Intelligence in creation or the demonic intelligence of Satan. In that sense, man participates actively in the perpetuation of evil. The lives of individuals declare their good or evil nature by the degree of their seeming separation from blissful immortal Spirit—that is, the degree to which they respond to and absorb the redeeming power of Holy Ghost or the outgoing force of cosmic delusion. Through gradual evolution in repeated incarnations on earth and in the heavenly astral spheres, souls who respond to the divine-love pulls of Christ-imbued Holy Ghost progress to ultimate Self-realization, the perfect manifestation of the image of the Divine within them.

Increase of delusive separation from God, and consequent evils of suffering manifesting from the bad karma created by an individual's careless or willful wrong choices and actions, are the fate of those who attune their lives with the outgoing satanic force. Extremely evil individuals, who continue to pull to the farthest depths away from God, karmically draw themselves after death to dark astral spheres of nightmarish demonic horrors and conflicts—or in rare cases reincarnate on earth for one lifetime in animal forms of suitable expression for their self-chosen evils. As animals have no free will, being guided primarily by instinct, they accrue no karma for their actions; therefore, this temporary devolution of a degraded soul burns out some of its evil karma without the acquirement of further sin.

As there are various kinds of angelic beings in the astral world due to souls' different degrees of Self-realization attained during earth existence, so also there are various kinds of degraded astral beings: petty evil spirits and powerful evil spirits, whose wicked behavior has consigned them—for a karmically determined span of time—to a hellish after-death state. Both angelic beings and devilish spirits do at times come to aid or to harm, respectively, virtuous or misbehaving persons on earth. Jesus' detractors, unable to deny his manifest supernatural power to relieve the afflicted from evil, yet being unwilling to credit it to the intervention of God's grace, defamed his works as being in collusion with "the prince of the devils."

~

And Jesus knew their thoughts, and said unto them, "Every king-dom divided against itself is brought to desolation; and every city or house divided against itself shall not stand: and if Satan cast out Satan, he is divided against himself; how shall then his kingdom stand? And if I by Beelzebub cast out devils, by whom do your children cast them out? Therefore they shall be your judges. But if I cast out devils by the Spirit of God, then the king-dom of God is come unto you" (Matthew 12:25–28). *

Why would Satan, the Cosmic Evil, cast out the devil entities and forces which were under his influence, and which were carry-ing out his nefarious wishes in the cosmos? If the controlling powers in a kingdom are divided in their aims and act contradictorily, their domain would disintegrate. It is Satan who, working on the evil karma of individuals, plagues them with bacteria and intelligent agents of sickness and infirmity.† How could Jesus use the same satanic or Beelzebub force to destroy Satan-produced devil-possession and dis-eases? This view is untenable and unreasonable.

It is similarly indefensible that God, the Source of all good and who is Goodness itself, could send, in any way—no matter what the offense—disease and suffering to human beings. It is not God but Satan who bedevils this relativistic world with every form of evil. Good health, reason, self-control, peace, desire to meditate, every thought of welfare for the body, mind, and soul come from God. And every physical, mental, or spiritual ail-ment that infects the well-being of man comes from Satan. Satan is try-ing to perpetuate the separation of finite creation from Spirit by evil; God is trying to redeem all creatures by good. It is owing to the evil temptations of Satan that souls come back to material existence again and again until they divest themselves, through wisdom, of all imper-fect desires and karmic consequences of misuse of their free will in choosing evil. The Archangel of God, the outgoing cosmic delusive force endowed to create the dream spectacle of the cosmos, became the rebellious perpetuator of finitude, Satan, by engendering reincarnation,

The evil works of Satan in conflict with the redeeming works of the Holy Ghost

---

* Cf. parallel reference in Mark 3:23–26.

† See also Discourse 24, page 405, discussion of Jesus' "rebuking the fever" that af-flicted Peter's mother-in-law.

determined by the law of cause and effect, which dictates that every earthbound desire and attachment produces an earth-reincarnating effect. By succumbing to the compelling temptations of physicality, deluded man is kept imprisoned by Satan behind the bars of flesh. But all the while, God is opening door after door of goodness and righteousness that beckons souls to enter their native kingdom of omnipresence in Spirit. The life of Jesus demonstrated the constant choices that man must make between good and evil; as when he was mercilessly cursed and abused by evil people, he nevertheless did not use his divine force to destroy them. Instead, he summoned his love and infinite divine compassion to say, "Father, forgive them, for they know not what they do."

Jesus pointed out the obvious flaw in the accusation that he used the power of Satan to cast out from persons the evils of Satan; such a divided purpose, working against itself, could not long endure. Beelzebub certainly does not want individuals to be free from the miseries perpetrated by his evil forces, which in effect makes his palliative offerings of material gains and pleasures all the more tempting and desirable.

Jesus further cautions that if they impute to him the casting out of devils by Beelzebub, then they imply the same must be true of other healers; those wise persons belonging to their community who have healed others and cast out devils must likewise have done so by the power of the prince of devils. When these doers of good works hear this, they will certainly condemn those accusers who maintained that devils are cast out and sickness healed by the power of Beelzebub. Jesus then avers: "But if I cast out evil disembodied souls or heal other afflictions caused by the evil force by awakening the invisible all-flowing power of the spiritual presence of God, then those so healed will feel in their consciousness not only release from evil, but the presence of the Almighty Cosmic Consciousness."

Jesus' pronouncement that "Every kingdom...city or house divided against itself shall not stand" is a great law that governs all successful households, cities, business and religious organizations, nations, and races. If a group of people wants to retain its individuality and achieve its goals, each one should act in agreement with the collective aims. When there is division among those members, there is trouble, disharmony, and disintegration. Harmony even amidst differences should be the breath of life governing all communities of individuals, all secular and religious organizations, and all nations.

~

"Or else how can one enter into a strong man's house, and spoil his goods, except he first bind the strong man? and then he will spoil his house. He that is not with me is against me; and he that gathereth not with me scattereth abroad.

"Wherefore I say unto you, all manner of sin and blasphemy shall be forgiven unto men: but the blasphemy against the Holy Ghost shall not be forgiven unto men" (Matthew 12:29–31). *

Jesus elaborates on his God-given power and the reverence owed to the Holy Ghost manifestation of God: "How else can I enter into the strong organization of Satan in the cosmos and destroy his evil works in nature and wicked influence in men except that I bind Satan by my wisdom? It is because I consciously behold Satan and use my will against him that I am able to cast out from possessed persons his evil spirits and temptation-entities. Beelzebub, not being with me, is against me. Likewise are all souls who are not in harmony with the Christ Consciousness in me; they act against the laws of that Omnipresent Intelligent Harmony, and thereby suffer.

"Every soul who does not know how to gather wisdom by contacting that Christ in meditation scatters his concentration in the antics of the body and remains distracted, suffering from restlessness. He who has interiorized his consciousness by meditation gathers wisdom and bliss with the help of my Christ Consciousness within his soul. But he who is not identified with that indwelling Divine Presence diffuses his consciousness in the flesh and sense pleasures and is full of disquiet and trouble.

"That is why I declare the truth unto you that all kinds of errors —physical, mental, and moral—belonging to those who in body-identified spiritual blindness unknowingly act against God will be forgiven, when by repentance and awakening soul wisdom they receive the inner realization of God's all-pervading, karma-dissolving presence in the Holy Ghost.

"But those who have consciously felt the holy cosmic vibration of *Aum* (Holy Ghost) in meditation and ridicule it as a physical sound, or deliberately ignore its transforming power and regress into worldly

---

* Cf. parallel reference in Mark 3:27–28.

consciousness, will not be forgiven the effects resulting from their errors—that is, their karma of ignorance will not be washed away by the healing blessings of God flowing through that Divine Vibration."

When one contacts the Holy Vibration and feels the ever new joy in it, and then wantonly rejects that joy by reverting to an inharmonious

Reverent contact with the Holy Ghost frees one from delusion and suffering

life, he "blasphemes against the Holy Ghost" and cannot be saved from reaping the results of his bad karma. This presupposes that no one can commit blasphemy against the Holy Ghost who does not first know that manifestation of God as the Cosmic Sound heard in meditation or as the Infinite Peace or Joy subtly vibrating within the God-tuned consciousness. If one willfully chooses the worldly offerings of the senses after having had the comparison of finer joys through this inner communion, he will have to endure the consequences of his actions. He will have to work out by his own effort the karma of his bad-habit–controlled life and distracted mind, having shut himself off from the uplifting grace of God and Christ flowing freely into the consciousness of those who are attuned to the Holy Ghost. By ignoring the intuitional guidance of this cosmic sound in meditation—"the Comforter, which is the Holy Ghost,...shall teach you all things"*—he sentences himself to inner restlessness and to continued witless entrapments in delusion and suffering.

All manner of physical and mental errors can be forgiven, and their karmic fruits modified or destroyed altogether, by the blessings of great souls; but no one can remove the restlessness of a distracted devotee who blasphemes against his perception of Cosmic Vibration and bliss. Not even a master can give the contact of Cosmic Vibration and joy of meditation unless the devotee forsakes his restlessness by his own effort of will. Those who are indolent in seeking the vibratory contact of God through the Holy Ghost must make the effort in deep meditation to remove their irreverence of indifference toward this divine manifestation of the Infinite Creator.

Restlessness, the outgoing dissipation of the soul's attention, is the most disabling weapon employed by the Evil Perpetuator of changeful delusion. A restless body and mind are the playground of Satan, who loves to perform there his wily dance of distraction to divert man's consciousness from the Immutable Spirit and Its calm reflection

---

* John 14:26 (see Discourse 70).

676

in the depths of the soul. But one who regularly and deeply interior-
izes the mind through devotional meditation is aided by the uplifting
vibrations of the Holy Ghost and finds himself immersed in God all
the time—in the redemptive grace of divine peace, love, and joy.

Unwillingness to meditate should be recognized as among the foremost enemies of man's physical, mental, and spiritual well-being; that
"blasphemy" against the inner magnetic pull of the Holy Ghost should
be consciously excised from the mind. One who never meditates rejects
the prime means of attuning his life with the saving Christ Consciousness
inherent in the Cosmic *Aum* Vibration. By deliberate deeper acts of meditation each seeker must remove his restlessness in order to regain bliss
consciousness through vibratory contact of God as Holy Ghost, his introduction to the Infinite Christ and the cosmic consciousness of Spirit.

~

*"And whosoever speaketh a word against the Son of man, it shall
be forgiven him: but whosoever speaketh against the Holy
Ghost, it shall not be forgiven him, neither in this world, neither
in the world to come" (Matthew 12:32).* *

W hosoever uses wrong language against the "son of man" (the
bodily manifestation of any individual, by which Jesus included
himself) will find forgiveness from God and the masters if he seeks it
and is repentant. But anyone who contacts the inner peace and joy of
the Holy Ghost in meditation but then thinks or talks in a way that vibrates evilly in contradiction to that spiritually harmonious vibration
will forego that meditative state and set up an inner conflict from which
he will suffer restlessness and inner turmoil in this world and in his next
incarnation as well. The outer man must be disciplined to conform to
his harmonious inner spirit. If he persists in his contradictory behavior,
he will form the habit of mental restlessness so deep in his "son of
man" consciousness that he will feel as if eternally condemned to be
restless and to be denied recovery of the ever-new blessed contact of the
Holy Vibration of Spirit in his soul consciousness.

~

---

* Cf. parallel references in Mark 3:29–30 and Luke 12:10.

> *"Either make the tree good, and his fruit good; or else make the tree corrupt, and his fruit corrupt: for the tree is known by his fruit. O generation of vipers, how can ye, being evil, speak good things? for out of the abundance of the heart the mouth speaketh. A good man out of the good treasure of the heart bringeth forth good things: and an evil man out of the evil treasure bringeth forth evil things" (Matthew 12:33–35).*

Because the Pharisees insinuated that the good works of Jesus were performed by the power of evil, he countered with the argument, "If you admit that the results of my healing actions are good, then you must also concede that I work with the power of goodness. If, as you say, I am evil, then how could I produce these good fruits of divine healing? Evil can only bring forth evil. As a tree is known by its fruit, so you must discern by my actions that within me is the spiritually laden tree of divine knowledge. O ye human vipers filled with the poison of ignorance and self-created evil karma, how can you rightly declare what is true? According to the contents of your heart your mouth speaks.* You bring forth from that evil hoard that which is evil, rather than bringing forth from the treasure of goodness that lies within your soul, hidden under the debris of your evil actions."

∾

> *"But I say unto you, that every idle word that men shall speak, they shall give account thereof in the day of judgment. For by thy words thou shalt be justified, and by thy words thou shalt be condemned" (Matthew 12:36–37).*

A spoken word is a threefold composite of vibrations, consisting of physical energy (sound), life force activated by the speaker's will, and thought. Man's every utterance leaves good or evil vibrational traces in his physical body and brain; in his astral body of life energy, which mediates between flesh and consciousness; and in his mind, his consciousness, as tabloid tendencies. The sum total of all mental tendencies resulting from evil thoughts and good thoughts determines a good or bad rebirth for a soul after death.

---

* See also commentary in Discourse 33 on parallel verses (Luke 6:43–45).

Thus Jesus' meaning: "I declare unto you that every useless word (heedlessly spoken without regard to truth and righteousness) that men will speak will retain its effect in the brain and the mind; and when the soul leaves the body, its existence in the astral world and eventual reentry into another life on earth will be modified and governed by the judgment of his evil karma resulting from those damaging words. By good words expressed by a good mind you will store good results to be reaped by your soul, and by evil words actuated by an evil mind you will amass evil effects that will return to you in lives to come."

~

Then certain of the scribes and of the Pharisees answered, saying, "Master, we would see a sign from thee."

But he answered and said unto them, "An evil and adulterous generation seeketh after a sign; and there shall no sign be given to it, but the sign of the prophet Jonah: For as Jonah was three days and three nights in the whale's belly; so shall the Son of man be three days and three nights in the heart of the earth"

(Matthew 12:38–40).

The all-powerful Heavenly Father, being endowed with all grace, is infinitely humble. So also are His devotees who manifest His perfect image. Divine souls such as Jesus do not demonstrate miracles or signs to oppose man's wickedness or to satisfy the unthinking curiosity of disbelieving people, but use their powers only as a benign helping force humbly expressing the hidden mightiness of God.

"The sign of Jonah": Jesus predicts the miracle of his resurrection

When the Pharisees sought from Jesus a sign of his divine authority, he retorted, "O ye generation who are addicted to the evils of ignorance and sensual habits, what right have you to seek a miraculous sign, which is merited only by virtuous and deserving souls? No sign will be given to you except what has been already given by the prophet Jonah, who showed that he had attained God-consciousness and thereby his life, saturated with immortal life, could remain in a state of suspended animation in the belly of a whale."*

---

* Recounted in the Old Testament book of Jonah, chapters 1 and 2.

679

Whether the tale of Jonah is literally or metaphorically true, there are numerous records in India of yogis or ecstasy-tuned souls who were known to have remained buried alive in a suspended state under water or the earth. Two well-known cases concern Trailanga Swami of India, who periodically used to remain for very long periods beneath the waters of the Ganges;* and the well-documented case of the eighteenth-century Sadhu Haridas, who placed his body in suspended animation and was buried for several weeks, and then revived himself when disinterred [cited earlier in Discourse 8].

Such feats are not intended by God to be commonplace in an age yet reaching for enlightenment, but they are evidence of the ability to live in a breathless state and thereby to master life and conquer death. Jesus related that the story of Jonah—"Now the Lord had prepared a great fish to swallow up Jonah. And Jonah was in the belly of the fish three days and three nights"†—was prophetically analogous to Jesus' crucified body remaining entombed in the earth three days and nights and then coming forth alive. Jesus foretells that the greatest sign he would give to the world would be the resurrection of his physical body—his demonstration of complete victory over death.

Jesus speaks of his entombment as referring to his body, the "son of man"—a body connected with a generation of human beings or family tree. The Son of God, which was encased in the body of Jesus but also omnipresent, certainly could not be buried in the heart of the earth. It was the physical body of Jesus and its resurrection after three days that would declare to mankind the almighty power of God.‡

By material science man builds wondrously fast and serviceful airplanes; but when a plane crashes, and passengers are horribly converted into a broken mass of bones and flesh, science cannot tell man how to conquer his ultimate weakness—the Satan-imposed delusion of death and physical destruction. By the higher science of God-realization, man can know that body and soul, both being the reflections of Spirit Immortal, are immortal too. Jesus showed that by following the laws of superphysical existence and understanding the relation of matter and mind, the soul could conquer the delusion of

---

* Many miraculous incidents from the life of Trailanga Swami are recounted in *Autobiography of a Yogi*, Chapter 31.

† Jonah 1:17.

‡ Jesus repeats his words about the "sign of Jonah" in Matthew 16:4. (See Discourse 44.)

body consciousness, or, if desired, register its immortality in its phys-ical vehicle. When man fully realizes the relation between conscious-ness and the body, he will understand why the separation of con-sciousness and life from the body disintegrates the bodily cells, and will know how to remodel the body by introducing life and mind into it at will, even if it has undergone physical death. The attainment of conscious immortality as evidenced in the resurrection of his physical body is the foremost "sign" and metaphysical demonstration that Jesus has shown to the world for all times, to awaken faith and give courage and hope to those who would strive and earn by meditation their own immortality in the kingdom of God.

∾

> "The men of Nineveh shall rise in judgment with this generation, and shall condemn it: because they repented at the preaching of Jonah; and, behold, a greater than Jonah is here.
>
> "The queen of the south shall rise up in the judgment with this generation, and shall condemn it: for she came from the ut-termost parts of the earth to hear the wisdom of Solomon; and, behold, a greater than Solomon is here" (Matthew 12:41–42).

Jesus emphasized that the men of Nineveh who repented of their material habits and awakened their spirituality in response to the preaching of Jonah would judge and condemn the generation of Jesus for not appreciating the Christ amongst them, greater than Jonah, fully awakened in Spirit. The Queen of Sheba who came from a dis-tant land to hear the wisdom of Solomon* would likewise condemn Jesus' generation for not responding to the Christ whose wisdom out-shone even that of the proverbially wise Solomon. Though all souls, ordinary laymen and masters alike, are potentially the same perfect images of God, their differences are manifestations of the degree of their realization and expression of soul qualities. Jesus Christ fully manifested all the qualities of soul and Spirit; the spiritual conscious-ness of Solomon and Jonah had yet to attain that perfection.

∾

---

* I Kings 10:1–10.

"When the unclean spirit is gone out of a man, he walketh through dry places, seeking rest, and findeth none. Then he saith, 'I will return into my house from whence I came out'; and when he is come, he findeth it empty, swept, and garnished. Then goeth he, and taketh with himself seven other spirits more wicked than himself, and they enter in and dwell there: and the last state of that man is worse than the first. Even so shall it be also unto this wicked generation" (Matthew 12:43–45).

Jesus here is referring to tenuous spiritual gains that degenerate into the arrogance of a false superiority. He saw that some souls among the people of his time had attained sufficient spiritual development to contact the inner vibratory blessing of the Holy Ghost, which re-

Spiritual dangers of arrogant self-sufficiency and pride

moved some of their spiritual blemishes and cast out the inner devil of sense attachment. But Jesus notes that although they had temporarily exorcised the devil of material attachment, their egregious attitude toward him, and prejudicial failure to recognize the Spirit in him, would bring back not only their material consciousness but even greater devils of ignorance, sense attachment, pride, self-sufficiency, spiritual indifference, and lack of spiritual appreciation and spiritual judgment, when by spiritual receptivity they could instead have transformed themselves with the enlightening help of Jesus.

Jesus admonishes: "O ye people of this generation, your erstwhile spiritual development has made you self-complacent and stagnant so that you do not avail yourselves of the God-sent opportunity of redeeming your souls by attunement with the Christ-manifestation within me. Because of your ill-conceived arrogance, you will suffer even greater ignorance from its possessing devils than you had before."

Jesus points out that man is a free agent and that by appreciation and contact of great masters he can develop himself; or, by spiritual indifference to God's emissaries and their teachings, he can remain as ignorant as ever; or, by becoming hidebound in narrow theological beliefs and traditions, he can imagine himself to be self-sufficient, ignoring the salvation-yielding teachings of great masters.

≈

While he yet talked to the people, behold, his mother and his brethren stood without, desiring to speak with him. Then one said unto him, "Behold, thy mother and thy brethren stand without, desiring to speak with thee."

But he answered and said unto him that told him, "Who is my mother? and who are my brethren?" And he stretched forth his hand toward his disciples, and said, "Behold my mother and my brethren! For whosoever shall do the will of my Father which is in heaven, the same is my brother, and sister, and mother" (Matthew 12:46–50). *

Parallel reference:

Then came to him his mother and his brethren, and could not come at him for the press. And it was told him by certain which said, "Thy mother and thy brethren stand without, desiring to see thee." And he answered and said unto them, "My mother and my brethren are these which hear the word of God, and do it" (Luke 8:19–21).

66"Those devotees who are receptive to the inspiration of God as coming through me and who act accordingly, and who feel God-consciousness manifested as the Word or ever-new-bliss-saturated Cosmic Sound heard in meditation, are tuned to my one Father, the one Cosmic Consciousness; because of sharing this common perception with me, they are my real relatives. All women with God-consciousness are my mothers and sisters, and all men with God-consciousness are my brethren."

Jesus did not teach disrespect to parents; elsewhere (Matthew 15:4) he cited the divine commandment "Honor thy father and mother."† His point was that while everyone should give due respect to parents, honoring in them the Divine Father-Mother's

Jesus upholds love for God above attachment to family

gifts of protecting wisdom and love, one should not be so attached to them that if they blaspheme and ask him to desist from his sincere spiritual aspirations—whether in following the path of renunciation or in

---

* Cf. parallel reference in Mark 3:31–35.

† See Discourse 44.

meditation on God—he would submissively obey them and forsake God. The teaching of Jesus, and all great masters, is that God should come first, before every desire and before everyone. The engagement with God in meditation must be one's most important consideration, for no one can keep any other engagement in life without borrowing brain activity and energy, mental and muscular power, from God.

No human love should be held as greater than love for God; for it is God who is the Giver of all those we love. If we love our relatives dearly for their lovable natures, how much more should we love God who wisely selected for us those loving parents, brothers, and sisters. We should not forget that God is our perpetual Parent in the past, present, and future times, who during many incarnations looks after us through the instrumentality of countless parents and other familial relations. Those who adore family in utter forgetfulness of God within those persons will be disillusioned when death will sever those family ties. It is the tie with God, invisible but invulnerable, that is everlasting.

Jesus wanted to emphasize in the minds of the multitude his realization of this truth when they cried out, "Behold, thy mother and thy brethren." God alone, whom he perceived everywhere, was his real and only Relative behind all incarnation-imposed family relations.

Reflect, if one dies and is reborn to the family next door to his previous home, his dearly beloved former family would treat him as a stranger. The mysterious workings of reincarnation are meant to make it absolutely evident that it is God alone who, by instilling instincts of affection in the earthly mother and father, Himself looks after the baby through that parental affinity. And by extension, when one is attuned to God one will find again in Him all those soul-expressions of God whom he thought were lost to him.

Jesus wanted to express his consciousness that he could consider none other than God Himself as his Heavenly Father-Mother, and that whosoever lived in tune with God he considered as his divine relative. Jesus thereby affirmed not only the Fatherhood of God but also the brotherhood of man. All devotees who feel God as their own common Heavenly Father find themselves united by the familial divine cord of lasting universal brotherhood.

"And He Spake Many Things Unto Them in Parables"

Jesus' Sermon About the Kingdom of Heaven

Parable of the Sower:
Spiritual Truths Bless Man to the Degree of His Mental Receptivity

❖

Jesus' Deeper Explanation:
The Vibratory Seed of Wisdom Received Through Contact With Aum

❖

The Wheat and the Tares:
Destroying the Weeds of Bad Habits in the Subconscious Mind

❖

The "Leaven" of Meditative Joy
Uplifts the Conscious, Subconscious, and Superconscious Minds

❖

The "Harvest" of Good and Bad Karma
Reaped at "the End of the World"

"Unto those souls that are yet wholly identified with their physical bodies, all these subtle perceptions about the states of heaven, Christ Consciousness, and Cosmic Consciousness are explained in coverings of parables, lest those persons scorn, for lack of understanding, that sacred knowledge of fully revealed truth."

*T*he same day went Jesus out of the house, and sat by the sea side. And great multitudes were gathered together unto him, so that he went into a ship, and sat; and the whole multitude stood on the shore. And he spake many things unto them in parables, saying, "Behold, a sower went forth to sow; and when he sowed, some seeds fell by the way side, and the fowls came and devoured them up: Some fell upon stony places, where they had not much earth: and forthwith they sprung up, because they had no deepness of earth: And when the sun was up, they were scorched; and because they had no root, they withered away. And some fell among thorns; and the thorns sprung up, and choked them: But other fell into good ground, and brought forth fruit, some an hundredfold, some sixtyfold, some thirtyfold.

"Who hath ears to hear, let him hear."

And the disciples came, and said unto him, "Why speakest thou unto them in parables?"

He answered and said unto them, "Because it is given unto you to know the mysteries of the kingdom of heaven, but to them it is not given. For whosoever hath, to him shall be given, and he shall have more abundance: but whosoever hath not, from him shall be taken away even that he hath.

"Therefore speak I to them in parables: because they seeing see not; and hearing they hear not, neither do they understand. And in them is fulfilled the prophecy of Isaiah, which saith, 'By hearing ye shall hear, and shall not understand; and seeing ye shall see, and shall not perceive:

"'For this people's heart is waxed gross, and their ears are dull of hearing, and their eyes they have closed; lest at any time they should see with their eyes, and hear with their ears, and should understand with their heart, and should be converted, and I should heal them.'

"But blessed are your eyes, for they see: and your ears, for they hear. For verily I say unto you, that many prophets and righteous men have desired to see those things which ye see, and have not seen them; and to hear those things which ye hear, and have not heard them.

"Hear ye therefore the parable of the sower. When any one heareth the word of the kingdom, and understandeth it not, then cometh the wicked one, and catcheth away that which was sown in his heart. This is he which received seed by the way side. But he that received the seed into stony places, the same is he that heareth the word, and anon with joy receiveth it; yet hath he not root in himself, but dureth for a while: for when tribulation or persecution ariseth because of the word, by and by he is offended.

"He also that received seed among the thorns is he that heareth the word; and the care of this world, and the deceitfulness of riches, choke the word, and he becometh unfruitful. But he that received seed into the good ground is he that heareth the word, and understandeth it; which also beareth fruit, and bringeth forth, some an hundredfold, some sixty, some thirty."

Another parable put he forth unto them, saying, "The kingdom of heaven is likened unto a man which sowed good seed in his field: But while men slept, his enemy came and sowed tares among the wheat, and went his way. But when the blade was sprung up, and brought forth fruit, then appeared the tares also.

"So the servants of the householder came and said unto him, 'Sir, didst not thou sow good seed in thy field? From whence then hath it tares?' He said unto them, 'An enemy hath done this.' The servants said unto him, 'Wilt thou then that we go and gather them up?' But he said, 'Nay; lest while ye gather up the tares, ye root up also the wheat with them. Let both grow together until the harvest: and in the time of harvest I will say to the reapers, "Gather ye together first the tares, and bind them in bundles to burn them: but gather the wheat into my barn."'"

Another parable put he forth unto them, saying, "The kingdom of heaven is like to a grain of mustard seed, which a man took, and sowed in his field: Which indeed is the least of all seeds: but when it is grown, it is the greatest among herbs, and becometh a tree, so that the birds of the air come and lodge in the branches thereof."

Another parable spake he unto them: "The kingdom of heaven is like unto leaven, which a woman took, and hid in three measures of meal, till the whole was leavened."

All these things spake Jesus unto the multitude in parables; and without a parable spake he not unto them: That it might be fulfilled which was spoken by the prophet, saying, "I will open my mouth in parables; I will utter things which have been kept secret from the foundation of the world."

Then Jesus sent the multitude away, and went into the house: and his disciples came unto him, saying, "Declare unto us the parable of the tares of the field." He answered and said unto them, "He that soweth the good seed is the Son of man; the field is the world; the good seed are the children of the kingdom; but the tares are the children of the wicked one; the enemy that sowed them is the devil; the harvest is the end of the world; and the reapers are the angels. As therefore the tares are gathered and burned in the fire; so shall it be in the end of this world. The Son of man shall send forth his angels, and they shall gather out of his kingdom all things that offend, and them which do iniquity; and shall cast them into a furnace of fire: there shall be wailing and gnashing of teeth. Then shall the righteous shine forth as the sun in the kingdom of their Father. Who hath ears to hear, let him hear.

"Again, the kingdom of heaven is like unto treasure hid in a field; the which when a man hath found, he hideth, and for joy thereof goeth and selleth all that he hath, and buyeth that field.

"Again, the kingdom of heaven is like unto a merchant man, seeking goodly pearls: who, when he had found one pearl of great price, went and sold all that he had, and bought it.

"Again, the kingdom of heaven is like unto a net, that was cast into the sea, and gathered of every kind: which, when it was full, they drew to shore, and sat down, and gathered the good into vessels, but cast the bad away. So shall it be at the end of the world: the angels shall come forth, and sever the wicked from among the just, and shall cast them into the furnace of fire: there shall be wailing and gnashing of teeth."

Jesus saith unto them, "Have ye understood all these things?" They say unto him, "Yea, Lord." Then said he unto them, "Therefore every scribe which is instructed unto the kingdom of heaven is like unto a man that is an householder, which bringeth forth out of his treasure things new and old."

And it came to pass, that when Jesus had finished these parables, he departed thence.

—*Matthew 13:1–53*

"And He Spake Many Things Unto Them in Parables"

Jesus' Sermon About the Kingdom of Heaven

The same day went Jesus out of the house, and sat by the sea side. And great multitudes were gathered together unto him, so that he went into a ship, and sat; and the whole multitude stood on the shore. And he spake many things unto them in parables, saying, "Behold, a sower went forth to sow; and when he sowed, some seeds fell by the way side, and the fowls came and devoured them up: Some fell upon stony places, where they had not much earth: and forthwith they sprung up, because they had no deepness of earth: And when the sun was up, they were scorched; and because they had no root, they withered away. And some fell among thorns; and the thorns sprung up, and choked them: But others fell into good ground, and brought forth fruit, some an hundredfold, some sixtyfold, some thirtyfold.

"Who hath ears to hear, let him hear" (Matthew 13:1–9).*

In the well-known parable of the sower, the seed, and the ground, Jesus illustrates how divine seeds of truth grow or perish according to the mental soil, or faith and receptivity, of the spiritual aspirants on whom the seeds have been sown: "Hearken attentively, with wisdom,

---

* Cf. parallel passages in Mark 4:1–9 and Luke 8:4–8.

to the truth that here among you are devotees with varying degrees of receptive minds on which have been sown the seeds of my teachings.

"Some seeds of truth fell by the wayside of the spiritual indifference of curiosity seekers. Those seeds of potentially enlightening intuitional experiences were trodden by the animals of material habits and devoured by the fowls of doubts flying in the atmosphere of the mind.

Parable of the sower: Spiritual truths bless man to the degree of his mental receptivity

"Some seeds of my teachings fell upon the rocky terrain of materially crude minds with only a little soil of skin-deep spiritual perception and appreciation. In such persons, the teachings sprouted into some short-lived, but not deep-rooted, spiritual experiences. When the sun of daily material habits rose, those experiences were fatally scorched. Because they did not form deep-rooted habits in the superconsciousness of the soul, they withered away due to the lack of nourishment of continued devotion and spiritual aspiration in new acts of meditation and fervent effort.

"And some seeds of my teachings were sown on the mental soil of persons filled with prolific thorns of spiritual distrust and theological doubts. Thus, though those seeds sprouted somewhat in such theoretically inquisitive minds, those spiritual inspirations could not survive when choked by the overwhelmingly predominant thorns of theological skepticism. The ill-fated plants of inspiration could bear no fruits of divine wisdom or God-contact.

"Other seeds of my teachings fell on the soil of mentalities furrowed and ploughed by receptivity, watered with continuous goodness and regular, deep spiritual effort at meditation, and hedged in by good company so that the animals and birds of material minds and doubts could not invade and destroy the burgeoning garden of soul qualities. In those protected, receptive minds, the seeds of truth grew into trees laden with the fruits of Self-realization. These human trees, strong and sturdy, could withstand any onslaughts while providing an increasing yield of wisdom, ever new bliss, and advancement in divine attainment of spiritual qualities—thirty, sixty, one hundredfold."

Jesus' analogy makes it plain that a true disciple, by virtue of a dedicated spiritual life, is fertile ground in which a God-sent guru's teachings can be successfully sown. When the proper seed of instruction is planted in the receptive heart-soil of a sincere, determined student who nurtures it with deep daily meditation, devotion, and self-discipline in following the *sadhana,* spiritual practices, prescribed by the guru, that seed will sprout and grow into the infinity-branched tree of God-realization.

What makes the difference in receptivity is whether one's desire and effort to know truth are strong. The most responsive are those who have an ardent desire for God.

The parable of the sower and the seed points out how the various good or bad habits of persons affect whether the soil of their minds is fertile or stony. Even if one feels thwarted by bad habits that are already formed, that opposition can be overcome by one's strong spiritual desire and faithful adherence to the guru's teachings. The highest intelligence is to be able to change what needs to be changed in one's life so that continual soul progress is possible.

Receptive students will definitely make progress with the help of the guru. Resistance from bad habits of the past may make it difficult to obey the divine teachings, but if sincere students make the effort in spite of the inclination to resist, they change. Resistance is formidable if they listen to their moods; but if instead they listen receptively to the wisdom of their guru, who wants for them only their highest good, every seed of divine awakening he plants within them will take root in their fertile consciousness.

"*Who hath ears to hear, let him hear.*" Jesus meant: "He who is receptive and hears with spiritual understanding what I say, let him appreciate the truth in my words and live by them for complete soul-emancipation." It is useless to listen haphazardly to the teachings of Jesus or give them only scant attention. A follower of Christ should be earnest and diligent like a spiritual husbandman, employing the art of growing plants of Self-realization by plowing and seeding the consciousness with the proper technique of meditation and moral and spiritual living. The yield will be the fruits of divine wisdom, bliss, and complete spiritual liberation.

~

And the disciples came, and said unto him, "Why speakest thou unto them in parables?"

He answered and said unto them, "Because it is given unto you to know the mysteries of the kingdom of heaven, but to them it is not given. For whosoever hath, to him shall be given,

and he shall have more abundance: but whosoever hath not,
from him shall be taken away even that he hath.

"Therefore speak I to them in parables: because they seeing
see not; and hearing they hear not, neither do they understand"
(Matthew 13:10–13). *

Parallel reference:

And when he was alone, they that were about him with the
twelve asked of him the parable. And he said unto them, "Unto
you it is given to know the mystery of the kingdom of God: but
unto them that are without, all these things are done in parables:
That seeing they may see, and not perceive; and hearing they may
hear, and not understand; lest at any time they should be con-
verted, and their sins should be forgiven them" (Mark 4:10–12).

When Jesus was asked by his disciples why he taught the people
in the subtle illustrations of parables, he answered, "Because it
is so ordained that you who are my real disciples,
living a spiritualized life and disciplining your actions according to my teachings, deserve by virtue
of your inner awakening in your meditations to understand the truth of the arcane mysteries of heaven
and how to attain the kingdom of God, Cosmic
Consciousness hidden behind the vibratory creation

To the receptive, Jesus
revealed heavenly
truth; for the masses
he cloaked it in
parables

of cosmic delusion. But ordinary people, unprepared in their receptivity, are not able either to comprehend or to practice the deeper
wisdom-truths. From parables, they glean according to their understanding simpler truths from the wisdom I send out to them. By practical application of what they are able to receive, they make some progress toward redemption.

"Because you are receptive and advanced in spiritual thought, the
expanded cup of your understanding can hold the oceanic revelations
of truth which I have poured into you from my own realization in the
state of Christ Consciousness and Cosmic Consciousness, the kingdom
of heaven and the kingdom of God."

---

* Cf. parallel references in Mark 4:25 and Luke 8:9–10 and 8:18. See also Discourse
63, commentary on Luke 19:26, in which Jesus repeats this saying.

The state of Cosmic Consciousness is called the kingdom of God because it is the infinite kingdom of the one King of Absolute Existence, Absolute Consciousness, and Absolute Bliss untouched by vibratory manifestations. The kingdom of heaven is the wondrous astral realm of heavenly forces and beings, imbued with the omnipresent Christ Consciousness. The state of Cosmic Consciousness can be felt by souls who in meditation have withdrawn their minds from the region of the body and gone beyond the subconscious and concentration on the superconscious bliss perceptions of the astral kingdom of heaven and the immanent Christ state. But unto those souls that are yet wholly identified with their physical bodies, all these subtle perceptions about the states of heaven, Christ Consciousness, and Cosmic Consciousness are explained in coverings of parables, lest those persons scorn, for lack of understanding, that sacred knowledge of fully revealed truth. Unreceptive persons would not even try to fathom the deeper truths by which they could be free from their bad habits of materiality, "lest they should be converted" from body-identified souls into spiritual beings, through the grace of God and their own effort.

Jesus then cites an exact law that governs all habits. "Whosoever hath" created a habit of spirituality shall attract perceptions of Self-realization from within himself; and having the taste of soul wisdom and bliss, shall grow more spiritual habits, attracting greater manifestations of soul unfoldment. "But whosoever hath not" — that is, cares not to possess or create spiritual habits of meditation and living — must lose, owing to the lack of tasting the spiritual joy of Self-realization felt in meditation, any spiritual habit that might be latent within him.*

How do the receptive perceive truth, whereas the unreceptive "seeing see not; and hearing they hear not, neither do they understand"? The ultimate truths of heaven and the kingdom of God, the reality that lies behind sensory perception and beyond the cogitations of the rationalizing mind, can only be grasped by intuition — awakening the intuitive knowing, the pure comprehension, of the soul.

"Therefore, O ye my disciples, I speak in parables, covering the meat of truth with the shell of mystical words, esoteric illustrations. Just as a bird does not know the use of a nutcracker to get at the ker-

---

* Jesus repeats this saying in Luke 19:26 in a different parable; it is discussed in more detail in that context in Discourse 63.

nel within the nutshell, so ordinary minds do not see the way of using intuition to break through the shells of the parables and get at the wisdom hidden therein. Such persons, lacking intuitive inner perception, do not hear the revelations of truth accompanying my words, even though they hear that wisdom falling from my lips. It is as though they never heard it at all."

~

"And in them is fulfilled the prophecy of Isaiah, which saith, 'By hearing ye shall hear, and shalt not understand; and seeing ye shall see, and shall not perceive:

"'For this people's heart is waxed gross, and their ears are dull of hearing, and their eyes they have closed; lest at any time they should see with their eyes, and hear with their ears, and should understand with their heart, and should be converted, and I should heal them.'*

"But blessed are your eyes, for they see: and your ears, for they hear. For verily I say unto you, that many prophets and righteous men have desired to see those things which ye see, and have not seen them; and to hear those things which ye hear, and have not heard them" (Matthew 13:14–17).

Parallel reference:

And he turned him unto his disciples, and said privately, "Blessed are the eyes which see the things that ye see: For I tell you, that many prophets and kings have desired to see those things which ye see, and have not seen them; and to hear those things which ye hear, and have not heard them" (Luke 10:23–24).

Jesus alludes to the divine perception of the prophet Isaiah, who foresaw how the law of cause and effect would govern those whose spiritual perceptions were uncultivated over many incarnations. Even as they were in his own time, the souls of those people in the large gatherings who listened to the words of Jesus remained unreceptive. Though hearing the words of Jesus, they could understand them only

---

* Isaiah 6:9–10.

superficially. Though they saw the awesome powers manifested by
Jesus, they remained spiritually blind to his divine stature. Their hearts,

A consciousness dark-
ened by materiality is
blind and deaf to
spiritual perceptions

their inner feelings or consciousness (*chitta*), for incarnations inured to the inharmonious vibrations of
materiality, could not resonate to the ring of truth
vibrating in the words of Jesus. Because the minds
of such persons are habitually responsive to the restlessness and desires of the senses, their inner sight of
spiritual receptivity and desire to meditate is confined to darkness, their
ears deafened to the Christ teachings. They will not open their eyes of
insight or hear with spiritual reason or receive the pure feeling of intuition in the heart lest at some time they see truth with their eyes of wisdom, and understand truth by listening to the words of Jesus, and realize truth with the intuitive feeling of their hearts and be transformed
from material beings groveling in misery into spiritual beings engrossed
in the unending joy of ecstasy. They are so enamored of their material
delusion that they fear the message of Jesus, which proposes to take
them out of their long-lived familiar existence in ignorance.*

Jesus praised, in contrast, the consciousness of his disciples:
"Blessed are your eyes of wisdom, for they see the truth; and blessed
are your ears of receptivity, for you listen understandingly to truth.
Verily the Christ Consciousness within me declares unto you that in
many ages numerous prophets who have seen and foretold the plan of
God, and numerous kingly men, powerful in morality and righteousness, have desired to see those divine demonstrations which, because
of your good karma, you are now seeing in my life; but they have not
been fortunate enough to observe such miracles of God, or to hear as
you have heard the liberating wisdom words of the silent God as are
coming directly through my Christ Consciousness."

It is rare to witness the living God made manifest in the life and
wisdom of a God-knowing soul. Many devotees have longed for such
an opportunity, but relatively few have been able to have that privilege. It is only from time to time, in select ages, that great souls are
sent by God with a special mission to declare His glory. That is why
Jesus reminded his disciples that they were extraordinarily blessed to
behold the manifestation of God's divine love and powers, which are

---

* See also Discourse 66, commentary on John 12:37–43, in which these verses from
Isaiah are repeated.

696

seldom demonstrated as openly as in the life of Jesus—and of a few great masters of India.

⁓

"Hear ye therefore the parable of the sower. When any one heareth the word of the kingdom, and understandeth it not, then cometh the wicked one, and catcheth away that which was sown in his heart. This is he which received seed by the way side. But he that received the seed into stony places, the same is he that heareth the word, and anon with joy receiveth it; yet hath he not root in himself, but dureth for a while: for when tribulation or persecution ariseth because of the word, by and by he is offended.

"He also that received seed among the thorns is he that heareth the word; and the care of this world, and the deceitfulness of riches, choke the word, and he becometh unfruitful. But he that received seed into the good ground is he that heareth the word, and understandeth it; which also beareth fruit, and bringeth forth, some an hundredfold, some sixty, some thirty" (Matthew 13:18–23).

Parallel reference:

And when he was alone, they that were about him with the twelve asked of him the parable....And he said unto them, "Know ye not this parable? And how then will ye know all parables?

"The sower soweth the word. And these are they by the way side, where the word is sown; but when they have heard, Satan cometh immediately, and taketh away the word that was sown in their hearts. And these are they likewise which are sown on stony ground; who, when they have heard the word, immediately receive it with gladness; and have no root in themselves, and so endure but for a time: afterward, when affliction or persecution ariseth for the word's sake, immediately they are offended.

"And these are they which are sown among thorns; such as hear the word. And the cares of this world, and the deceitfulness of riches, and the lusts of other things entering in, choke the word, and it becometh unfruitful.

"And these are they which are sown on good ground; such as hear the word, and receive it, and bring forth fruit, some thirtyfold, some sixty, and some an hundred" (Mark 4:10, 13–20). *

Having conveyed to the crowd the parable of the sower and the seed in words of easily discerned interpretation applicable to their mentality, Jesus later explained the parable to his disciples as denoting a deeper metaphysical concept, which they had inferred but not grasped—thus their request for elaboration.

Jesus' deeper explanation: the vibratory seed of wisdom received through contact with Aum

Jesus mildly remonstrated: "Do you not understand this parable? Then how will you understand the subtle teachings I am giving to you in all of the other parables spoken by me? Hear ye, now, the parable of the sower explained in a new way for you.

"The seed is the 'word,' the vibration of wisdom and cosmic sound coming from Cosmic Consciousness as felt by the devotee through his intuition in meditation.† Only those who have experienced the ecstasy of an interiorized consciousness by deep meditation on the holy sound of the *Aum*, or Amen, can feel the vibratory wisdom of God and hear His Cosmic Vibration thrumming throughout the universe. God as Spirit, formless and infinite, does not commonly speak in words but vibrates His consciousness as perceptions through intelligible vibratory sound understood only by devotees with developed intuition.

"The sower, the advanced devotee, is one who has attained contact with the Cosmic Sound and Wisdom in meditation. Those by the wayside where the word is sown are devotees who have temporarily meditated deeply and for a little while have received in their consciousness through the intuition-permeated feelings of the heart, the Vibratory Wisdom and Cosmic Sound proceeding from within. But after a time, not fully realizing those perceptions as the vibrations of

---

* Cf. parallel reference in Luke 8:11–15. (Mark 4:11–12 are commented on with their parallel in Matthew, earlier in this Discourse; see page 693.)

† "In the beginning was the Word (the holy *Aum* or Amen Vibration imbued with divine Christ Intelligence) and the Word was with God, and the Word was God" (John 1:1; see Discourse 1). In the original Greek text the term *logos* is used consistently for the verse in John and in these verses in Matthew and Mark, implying the same intended meaning.

God Himself, they became spiritually indifferent in maintaining that contact. Then Satan as cosmic delusion came to them, immediately bringing back the consciousness of the body and taking away from within them the perception of that Vibratory Wisdom and Cosmic Sound, which had come to free them, but which they had failed to appreciate as a manifestation of the blessed Cosmic Consciousness of God.

"When the seed of Cosmic Vibration was first perceived by less prepared devotees in whose minds were stony-hard material habits, contact with the strange wisdom-vibrations and cosmic sound in meditation gave delight to those devotees. But they did not meditate long enough and continuously enough so that they could feel the Cosmic Vibration not only in their conscious mind but in the deeper levels of their subconscious and superconscious minds.

"Such devotees, meditating for a relatively little while on the vibratory manifestation of God, find that afterward, when tempted by their habits of material pleasures, or when afflicted with diseases of the body, or persecuted by poverty or spiritual tests, they ceased to meditate, and the diverse sprouts of inner vibratory communion, having formed no deep roots, withered and fell away."

Those devotees who hear the Cosmic Vibration and experience temporarily the pleasure in it, often undergo a mental comparison between the joy of meditation and the pleasures and habits of the body; but uncommitted devotees, not persevering long enough to become strongly accustomed to the perception of God as the Cosmic Wisdom and Cosmic Bliss of meditation, succumb to the long-familiar sensory demands and pleasures of the body.

"And there are some devotees whose mental field is filled with the thorns of temporal interests and worries. These devotees who succeed in contacting the cosmic vibratory manifestation of God in meditation are subject to being gradually overwhelmed by the influences of the world, with its concerns and lures of happiness promised by wealth and the pleasure-giving lusts of life. Those devotees who succumb, kill their meditation perceptions of the vibratory peace-manifestations of God before they can become fruitful with ultimate wisdom and emancipation.

"Lastly, there are those supremely successful devotees whose mental ground is made fertile and tilled by good company and good thoughts and consistency in deep meditation. Their contact with the sacred vibratory manifestation of God in meditation, with honest sincerity and pure intuitive perception of the heart, becomes a continuing experience of the ecstasy of divine communion. By patient perseverance in contacting God as the joy of His vibratory presence in the ecstasy of meditation, these devotees reap the harvest of manifold wisdom and conscious immortality, far beyond their dreams."

~

In the verses recorded in the Gospels According to St. Mark and St. Luke, Jesus goes on to emphasize in additional metaphors how important it was for his disciples to understand, through their own intuitive Self-realization, the deeper truths hidden in his parables:

> And he said unto them, "Is a candle brought to be put under a bushel, or under a bed? and not to be set on a candlestick? For there is nothing hid, which shall not be manifested; neither was any thing kept secret, but that it should come abroad. If any man have ears to hear, let him hear."
> And he said unto them, "Take heed what ye hear: with what measure ye mete, it shall be measured to you: and unto you that hear shall more be given. For he that hath, to him shall be given: and he that hath not, from him shall be taken even that which he hath" (Mark 4:21–25).

Parallel reference:

> "No man, when he hath lighted a candle, covereth it with a vessel, or putteth it under a bed; but setteth it on a candlestick, that they which enter in may see the light. For nothing is secret, that shall not be made manifest; neither any thing hid, that shall not be known and come abroad. Take heed therefore how ye hear: for whosoever hath, to him shall be given; and whosoever hath not, from him shall be taken even that which he seemeth to have" (Luke 8:16–18).

66 No devotee who has kindled the candle of intuitive perception of truth by the taper of meditation keeps it ignorantly hidden under a bushel of restless thoughts, or obscured by forgetfulness under the bed of his subconsciousness. Rather, he keeps that flame of

Self-realization burning constantly on the candlestick of his conscious mind, so that all the thoughts that enter his consciousness are illumined by his light of inner realization. One who continuously keeps his candle of Self-realization burning on the candlesticks of his consciousness and memory will find that no truth will remain hidden from him; all will be manifested or revealed in the perception of inner illumination. A devotee of advanced realization, through telepathy and feeling the presence of God everywhere, can feel all secrets of human hearts and nature vibrating in the ether. There is nothing concealed in the universe that will not be known to a devotee with inner light. Every truth hidden in the deepest bowels of mysteries will perforce be brought out in the devotee's illuminating inner vision.

No truth is hidden from one who kindles the inner light of intuitive Self-realization

"If anyone has a keen perception and receptive ears of spirituality, let him hear these truths of awakening Self-realization and live them.

"Take care to practice the truths you hear from me and meditate upon them. As much as will be your efforts to know the truth, so much wisdom will you receive from my words. Those of you who will meditate deeply and live by my sermons will receive greater Self-realization; and those who will pay less attention to practicing my teachings will receive commensurately less.

"That willing devotee who thus grows in Self-realization shall, because of his receptivity, receive ever more truth, given unto him through his inner superconscious contact with Cosmic Consciousness. But he who does not care to be receptive and is negligent in applying my teachings will find that even those spiritual tendencies he now possesses, brought over from past incarnations, will erode away."

～

Another parable put he forth unto them, saying, "The kingdom of heaven is likened unto a man which sowed good seed in his field: but while men slept, his enemy came and sowed tares among the wheat, and went his way. But when the blade was sprung up, and brought forth fruit, then appeared the tares also.

"So the servants of the householder came and said unto him, 'Sir, didst not thou sow good seed in thy field? From whence then hath it tares?' He said unto them, 'An enemy hath done

this.' The servants said unto him, 'Wilt thou then that we go and gather them up?' But he said, 'Nay; lest while ye gather up the tares, ye root up also the wheat with them. Let both grow together until the harvest: and in the time of harvest I will say to the reapers, "Gather ye together first the tares, and bind them in bundles to burn them: but gather the wheat into my barn"'" (Matthew 13:24–30).*

The kingdom of heaven, the perceptions and realizations of God in superconsciousness, can be compared to a man who by daily deep meditation sowed and cultivated good seeds of spiritual experiences in the field of his consciousness; but while he slept (that is, while his "men"

The wheat and the tares: destroying the weeds of bad habits in the subconscious mind

or physical abilities were rapt in their daily active dreams of delusion, unmindful of his spiritual perceptions) his enemy of subconscious materialistic habits sowed weeds of materiality among the wheat seeds of Self-realization. This enemy emerged from and then secretly disappeared again within his subconscious mind. In the course of time when the blades of spiritual development grew appreciably, beginning to produce fruits of divine bliss and wisdom, there appeared concurrently an abundance of tares of inner doubts, vexations, fears, and a sense of hopelessness about being able to attain God-communion and solve the mysteries of life.

So the servants of self-control and spiritual discipline belonging to the household or consciousness of the devotee arose within him and vibrated their question unto him, "O devotee, did you think that you sowed only seeds of Self-realization in your field of consciousness? Then whence did these weeds of spiritual obstacles arise in you?" The devotee, in introspection, spoke unto his spiritual self-control and divine aspiration: "An enemy of subconscious bad habits has secretly grown these weeds along with the crop of my spiritual habits."

Through introspection, the spiritual servants, with their desire to meditate, intimated unto the devotee: "O master of the household of your consciousness and thoughts, do you desire us to busy ourselves in weeding out from the subconscious mind the deep-rooted tares?"

---

* Tares: "This bearded darnel, *lolium temulentum,* is common in Palestine and resembles wheat except that the grains are black. In its earlier stages it is indistinguishable from the wheat stalks so that it has to remain till near the harvest." — *Robertson's Word Pictures of the New Testament.*

Jesus Forgives the Sinful Woman

"Her sins, which are many, are forgiven; for she loved much...."

And they that sat at meat with him began to say within themselves, "Who is this that forgiveth sins also?"

And he said to the woman, "Thy faith hath saved thee; go in peace."

—Luke 7:47, 49−50

The all-forgivingness of divine love was demonstrated time and again in those who made themselves devotionally receptive to the Christ in Jesus. His words to the woman of sinful repute gave voice to the redeeming compassion of God that responds in full measure to a devotee's heart-offering that is singularly replete with love....

Centuries of misunderstanding of Biblical concepts of sin and its supposed abomination in the sight of God have created a popularly accepted image of the Almighty whose wrath against sinners is heartless, exactingly and vengefully severe....But saints of all religious persuasions who have entered the Divine Presence in interiorized personal communion universally declare that His omnipotence is expressed not as vengeance but as compassion, love, and goodness....

There is no doubt about this divine assurance: Any sin, and its consequence, can be forgiven the repentant devotee who loves God deeply enough, and thereby puts his life in tune with the all-compassionate Lord.

—Paramahansa Yogananda

Drawing by Heinrich Hofmann

The devotee responded: "O ye, my servants, do not waste time in concentrating on the negative habits, which engender discouragement, for in doing so you might uproot some spiritual habits as well for lack of attention to their growth. Cultivate the spiritual habits; when the harvest of divine ecstasy arrives with its joy and wisdom contact of God, I will ask the expert reapers of spiritual perception and realization to go deep into my subconscious mind and gather up the weeds of bad habits of all past incarnations and consign them to the fire of the instantaneously annihilating power of wisdom and of the life energy accumulated in the brain through the interiorization of the mind."

In meditation and sleep the mind and energy retire into the spine and brain cells and obliterate habits of worries and disquietude. In sleep, the subconscious mind, being mechanical, uses the retired energy to dispel only temporarily the troublesome mental aberrations. In deep meditation the superconscious mind uses the relaxed energy concentrated in the brain to penetrate into the brain grooves where habits are secreted, consciously seeking out and cauterizing the unwanted evil proclivities.

"O ye divine perceptions, having separated out and destroyed all the tares of spiritual obstruction, gather up the wheat of divine wisdom and bliss grown in the field of consciousness and store it in the expansive receptacle of my superconsciousness."

～

Additional correlative parable included in the Gospel According to St. Mark:

> *And he said, "So is the kingdom of God, as if a man should cast seed into the ground; and should sleep, and rise night and day, and the seed should spring and grow up, he knoweth not how. For the earth bringeth forth fruit of herself; first the blade, then the ear, after that the full corn in the ear. But when the fruit is brought forth, immediately he putteth in the sickle, because the harvest is come" (Mark 4:26–29).*

The kingdom of God is the region of Cosmic Consciousness where God the Father dwells beyond the precincts of vibratory creation wherein the sole reflection of God the Father inheres as the universal Christ Consciousness. The kingdom of heaven, situated within the astral vibratory region of pure manifestations, hidden behind the physical vibrations of electrons, protons, and matter, is a lesser state realized by the devotee than that of the kingdom of God.

How seeds of heavenly astral perceptions grow into full realization of Cosmic Consciousness

In the foregoing parable of the wheat and the tares likened unto the kingdom of heaven, Jesus speaks of the devotee who can feel the subtle vibrations of the astral world in superconscious ecstasy, but who has a mixed consciousness of both heavenly perceptions and material attachments. But in the mention of the kingdom of God in this present verse, Jesus speaks of the advancement of those devotees who go beyond the heavenly contact of vibratory creation to become one with God the Father Consciousness, Cosmic Consciousness, the Blissful Infinity beyond all creation.

Jesus relates metaphorically how the kingdom of God is attained. When the spiritual man sows the seeds of superconscious ecstasy — oneness with the supersensory realizations of the heavenly forces of the astral regions — into the soil of his consciousness, and feels that state of astral ecstasy equally during sleep and wakefulness, he will find that the astral ecstasy will mature into contact with the Christ Intelligence hidden in all vibratory creation and only thinly veiled in the manifestations of Heaven. Automatically, the Christ state will grow into the cosmic consciousness of God the Father lying beyond creation; for the "earth," or astral perception within the body, brings forth by astral ecstasy the fruit of the consciousness of Christ Intelligence and gradually of the consciousness of Cosmic Consciousness beyond vibratory creation.

The devotee develops through various stages, just as a seed of corn develops into the blade, then the ear, and then the full corn. The blade refers to the superconsciousness of astral ecstasy with its perception of divine lights and vibrations, the first manifestations in the consciousness of the advancing devotee.

The second stage is marked by the contact of Christ Intelligence in all vibration, which is referred to in the parable of the corn as "the ear."

In the third state, the devotee contacts God's consciousness beyond creation, which is the "full corn" in Jesus' metaphor.

When the fruit of the highest ecstasy of God-consciousness is harvested in the consciousness of the devotee, he uses his "sickle" of wisdom to sever his human consciousness from finite perception and to commingle his human consciousness, filled with the harvest of vibratory astral ecstasies and ecstasies in Christ Consciousness, with the ecstasy of the Blissful Absolute, the God the Father consciousness of vibrationless infinitude.

~

Another parable put he forth unto them, saying, "The kingdom of heaven is like to a grain of mustard seed, which a man took, and sowed in his field: Which indeed is the least of all seeds: but when it is grown, it is the greatest among herbs, and becometh a tree, so that the birds of the air come and lodge in the branches thereof" (Matthew 13:31–32).

Parallel reference:

And he said, "Whereunto shall we liken the kingdom of God? Or with what comparison shall we compare it? It is like a grain of mustard seed, which, when it is sown in the earth, is less than all the seeds that be in the earth: but when it is sown, it groweth up, and becometh greater than all herbs, and shooteth out great branches; so that the fowls of the air may lodge under the shadow of it" (Mark 4:30–32).*

"The kingdom of heaven, the ecstasy of superconsciousness with its perceptions of the heavenly vibrations of the divine astral regions, is as a mustard seed of ever new happiness when sown in the field of one's consciousness. These nascent ecstasies of superconsciousness, becoming firmly rooted in the 'earth' of daily ecstatic meditation, begin to grow and become a potentially effectual part of the conscious and subconscious makeup of the physical body. Such perceptions may seem preliminarily to be less significant than all other seeds of sense happiness or material experiences, but when the tiny 'mustard seed' of the inspiration and joy felt in daily meditation matures within the soil of human consciousness, it becomes supremely predominant in its influence over all other herbs of human sense perceptions.

---

* Cf. parallel reference in Luke 13:18–19.

"It shoots its superconscious branches of joy into the conscious and subconscious perceptions and experiences of one's everyday existence, proliferating until it becomes 'a tree' of cosmic joy and wisdom. The 'birds of the air,' the thoughts and perceptions of one's mental atmosphere, converge in the branches of this ecstatic joy, which spreads throughout the entire consciousness of man.

"In time, the superconscious perceptions expand into Christ Consciousness, and ultimately into Cosmic Consciousness, the kingdom of God. There is nothing similar with which to compare that state, except to say that its potential realization lies as if in a relatively infinitesimal spiritual 'mustard seed' with its burgeoning power of proliferation. He who has attained the supreme ecstasy of Cosmic Consciousness in the kingdom of God the Father, transcending all vibratory creation, he alone knows. No one else can know. The human mind, with its limitation, cannot comprehend that state of ecstasy. The mind and human consciousness must become expanded into oneness with Cosmic Consciousness in order to realize the kingdom of God."

～

Another parable spake he unto them: "The kingdom of heaven is like unto leaven, which a woman took, and hid in three measures of meal, till the whole was leavened" (Matthew 13:33). *

"The kingdom of astral ecstasy and superconscious joy of meditation is like unto 'leaven' which the devotee introduces into the 'three measures of meal,' the three divisions of consciousness—conscious, subconscious, and superconscious. As leaven raises or increases the three measures of meal, so the leaven of the ecstatic astral bliss of meditation, when experienced daily, spreads throughout the entire consciousness, subconsciousness, and superconsciousness—thence expanding the body-confined consciousness into the experience of Cosmic Vibration, Christ Consciousness, and the Cosmic Consciousness kingdom of God."

The "leaven" of meditative joy uplifts the conscious, subconscious, and superconscious minds

In the "kingdom of heaven" ecstasy, the astral forces that govern creation are perceived; initially in this superconscious ecstasy one per-

---

* Cf. parallel reference in Luke 13:20–21.

ceives occasional lights and sounds and bliss—the most significant being the variations of the light of the spiritual eye and of the sound of the holy *Aum* vibration with their effusion of peace and joy. In subconscious "ecstasy," as in the state of sleep, the devotee experiences an imaginary or pseudo state of unconscious joy. In cosmic ecstasy, the ecstasy of Cosmic Vibration, the devotee joyously feels all vibratory creation as his own body. In Christ ecstasy, the devotee feels himself merged in the transcendent reflected image of God's Intelligence as Christ Consciousness omnipresent in creation. In God the Father ecstasy the devotee feels one with the infinity of Cosmic Consciousness beyond vibratory creation, with its indescribable state of joy: "He who knows, knows. Naught else knows."

$\sim$

All these things spake Jesus unto the multitude in parables; and without a parable spake he not unto them: That it might be fulfilled which was spoken by the prophet, saying, "I will open my mouth in parables; I will utter things which have been kept secret from the foundation of the world" (Matthew 13:34–35).

Parallel reference:

And with many such parables spake he the word unto them, as they were able to hear it. But without a parable spake he not unto them: and when they were alone, he expounded all things to his disciples (Mark 4:33–34).

These spiritual interpretations as they have come to me through the inspiration of Jesus Christ convince me that some of the most profound truths he expounded to the world have not been given in such simple terminology since the beginning of the whirl of this world cycle, or *yuga*.

Jesus conveyed in terms and illustrations familiar to his generation the eternal verities he received directly from God. The ordinary people of his time could not understand, for example, the differences between the kingdom of heaven attained by superconscious ecstasy

---

* "Spoken by the prophet" refers to Psalms 78:2.

and the transcendent kingdom of God-consciousness. Jesus taught the deeper truths to his disciples when they were alone with him, the same truths he guarded with parables when given to the nonunderstanding masses, but discernable to all deserving advanced souls who could hear the underlying wisdom with ears of intuition.

Ordinary people, to whom deep metaphysical truths were unintelligible, received the parables as simple illustrations from which guid-

Without soul intui-
tion, the ultimate
truths remain a mys-
tery to man

ance they could better their lives and rouse their faith in God. To this day, the words of Christ are received similarly, with varying literal and theological interpretations around which have grown so many denominations and sects. The reference of Matthew to "things which have been kept secret from the foundation of the world" declares the ultimate nature of truth as provable only by the infallible perception of soul intuition, the direct experience of truth by becoming one with it. Without this inner realization, truth remains a mystery to man, only dimly imagined or otherwise surmised by the intellect. Thus, to understand the one and only one perception of Jesus Christ behind the words of his teachings, devotees must be able to perceive through their intuition in the sanctuary of meditation the revealed mysteries of which he spoke in parables.

The very fact that it was to his close disciples alone that Jesus "expounded all things" of those truths he had hidden in the parables given to the multitudes tells modern would-be disciples of Christ that they need not be satisfied with receiving the same revamped superficial sermons at Sunday morning church services. A minister with mere theoretical knowledge of the scriptures is gratified if he can momentarily inspire his congregation with what he infers or imagines to be the truth taught by Jesus Christ. But a real divine spokesman, meditating to become imbued with Christ Consciousness, inspires others to become with him a disciplined band of truth demonstrators who by meditation congregate in the inner sanctuary of silence to learn from God, who speaks through the lips of the devotee's intuition, the mysteries of life and soul liberation.

A true house of God will not be satisfied only with preaching theories about God; it will teach the art of God-contact, of how to make the soul of man an illuminated temple wherein God Himself will come and deliver sermons through His voice of intuition to the sincerely seeking devotional thoughts of the devotee.

~

Then Jesus sent the multitude away, and went into the house: and his disciples came unto him, saying, "Declare unto us the parable of the tares of the field." He answered and said unto them, "He that soweth the good seed is the Son of man; the field is the world; the good seed are the children of the kingdom; but the tares are the children of the wicked one; the enemy that soweth them is the devil; the harvest is the end of the world; and the reapers are the angels. As therefore the tares are gathered and burned in the fire; so shall it be in the end of this world. The Son of man shall send forth his angels, and they shall gather out of his kingdom all things that offend, and them which do iniquity; and shall cast them into a furnace of fire: there shall be wailing and gnashing of teeth. Then shall the righteous shine forth as the sun in the kingdom of their Father. Who hath ears to hear, let him hear" (Matthew 13:36–43).

The parable of the tares is explained to his close disciples by Jesus in an expanded metaphorical imagery: "He who cultivates the good seed of God-wisdom (the good children) in his own consciousness (the world) finds the body (son of man) attuned with Cosmic Consciousness (the kingdom); even as my body (the Son of man) is attuned, and as I have come to sow my teachings and my life in the field of the world consciousness.

The "harvest" of good and bad karma reaped at "the end of the world"

"But the cosmic delusion of Satan implants ignorance, the weeds of worries, anger, fear, mental darkness, in the minds of evil-bent individuals.

"The inimical cosmic ignorance is the devil, the archangel of God who misused his independence and created the seeds of all evils to entrap man in delusion. When souls leave this earth at the 'end of the world'—after finishing earthly existence at the time of death, or by otherwise transcending worldly consciousness—they reap the harvest of their good or bad karma. The reapers are the truth-revealing bright angels of soul intuition.

"In the after-death state, the astral-bodied consciousness of souls with evil karma, gathered together in the astral world, will burn in the fire of sorrows resulting from their own ignorance. The Son of man, the visible form of Jesus or any being with Christ Consciousness, will

709

send forth angelic messengers of light, or come themselves, to receive souls in their after-death state. They will gather the astral-bodied souls who offend or create wrong vibrations wherever they are and who are full of iniquity or bad karma, and these astral beings shall be made to realize consciously that the searing fire of their misery is their self-created conflagration of evil and ignorance. They will wail and remonstrate about their errors and the sad state of their astral existence. Those that can draw on their store of subverted good karma and spiritual desire, and will repent and consciously try to embrace righteousness, will shine forth as the sun of wisdom manifested in their soul through contact with the consciousness of God.* Those who have ears to hear, let them hear; God is not a God of vengeance but of redemption, who aids souls whether they punish or reward themselves according to their own activities."

A kind and merciful God would never throw a sinner into an eternally tormenting furnace of fire; even the greatest sinner in the after-death state is an immutable, immortal soul and has a luminous astral body that cannot be burned by any physical fire.† Souls encrusted with wicked karma not only can repent and heal the burns of their evil ways in this life by the salve of wisdom and peace found in meditation, but also, in the after-death state, they can find redemption when they are awakened by the angels of God and are given the opportunity in their astral existence to repent and resurrect their buried good karma. Evil-bound souls usually die in an unconscious transition from the body, but the after-death unconscious state is temporarily removed by angels of God to give souls suffering subconsciously in the fire of their own wicked tendencies a chance to strive toward God-consciousness by astral meditation. If they are overwhelmed by their habitual preference for ungodly mortal ways, that door of opportunity is quickly closed, leaving them closeted in their karmic destiny.

This parable is ambiguously complex in its broad scope of meaning of "the end of the world," as intended by Jesus. The literal end of the world could refer either to the extinction of the earth after it has

---

* "In those who have banished ignorance by Self-knowledge, their wisdom, like the illuminating sun, makes manifest the Supreme Self" (*God Talks With Arjuna: The Bhagavad Gita* v:16).

† The true meaning of the various Biblical references to "hellfire" is explained in Discourses 48 and 68.

completed its aeonic cycles of usefulness to creation; or further, to the dissolution of the entire universe when Spirit ceases Its creative dreamings after trillions of years of manifestation. The vast extent of these two possibilities is hardly relevant, though true in principle, to the warning given by Jesus to evildoers to change their ways.

The "end of the world" is more usefully understood as applied to that time when the world ends in the consciousness of each individual, temporarily or permanently, as the case may be. This occurs in the following ways: In deep sleep when the superconsciousness of the soul becomes semiconscious, reminding the subconscious of man's essential perfection hidden in the tares of worldly consciousness; in righteous freedom from earthly desires and attachments, breaking karmic bonds that tie man to the world; in death, when the world recedes from one's consciousness, being replaced by astral perceptions; in *samadhi* meditation when God alone is experienced as the Sole Reality; and in the highest *nirvikalpa samadhi* state in which one transcends delusion even while engaged in material activities. The metaphor given by Jesus applies to any and all of these ways to experience the end of the world, and to the condition of man pertinent to each.

In consequence, the above parable can also be explained as follows: The devotee who sows the good seeds of wisdom in his consciousness and in his bodily activities becomes a good example in the world, and all his children of good tendencies are saturated with the blissful state of the soul's intrinsic contact with Cosmic Consciousness. And the tares or weeds are those mental tendencies of selfishness, greed, lust that spring up as children of wicked ignorance born of sense contact with Satan's delusive temptations; they arise in the consciousness of man without his participation in creating them, only in succumbing to them. In creating these evils, Satan fights God everywhere, in man and in nature, resisting and marring God's perfection and harmony at every opportunity. At the end of worldly consciousness, the devotee will gather in his divine harvest through his reapers of angelic intuition, Self-realization and wisdom. He will burn in the newly kindled fire of his wisdom the tares or weeds of accumulated karmic effects of his past evil actions.

The God-saturated son of man, the devotee, will send his angels of intuitive perceptions deep into the subconscious and superconscious minds to gather all hidden offending and sinning tendencies of past lives and these will be burned in the flames of the devotee's fiery wisdom spread throughout his conscious and subconscious and superconscious minds. His evil inner tendencies will wail and rebel at being consumed in the fire of wisdom. Then the pure righteousness of the devotee will come out from behind the clouds of all past evil karma and shine forth as the sun of cosmic wisdom, ablaze with pure transcendental consciousness in the kingdom of God the Father, felt in the union of the body, mind, and soul with Christ Intelligence in creation and Cosmic Consciousness beyond creation.* Those who have spiritual ears, let them hear and absorb into their consciousness through direct experience the truth of these words.

☙

"Again, the kingdom of heaven is like unto treasure hid in a field; the which when a man hath found, he hideth, and for joy thereof goeth and selleth all that he hath, and buyeth that field.
"Again, the kingdom of heaven is like unto a merchant man, seeking goodly pearls: who, when he had found one pearl of great price, went and sold all that he had, and bought it"
(Matthew 13:44–46).

66   T**he astral kingdom of heavenly forces and heavenly perception, experienced by the devotee in superconscious ecstasy, is filled with rich spiritual treasure, angels of God, departed saintly souls and masters, revelations of the mysteries of life and death and of the

God-realization: the "pearl of great price"

comings and goings of all manifestations, hidden behind the field of material consciousness and sense perception. When the physical consciousness of man finds these truths revealed, he secretes these treasures deep within his consciousness and in great joy disposes of all his material desires and by the power of his deep devotion and good karma he secures the possession of that superconscious field of truth.

---

* "O Arjuna, by the knowers of truth, this body is called *kshetra* ('the field' where good and evil karma is sown and reaped); likewise, that which cognizes the field they call *kshetrajna* (the soul)....As the one sun illumines the entire world, so does the Lord of the Field (God and His reflection as the soul) illumine the whole field (Nature and the bodily 'little nature'). They enter the Supreme who perceive with the eye of wisdom the distinction between the *Kshetra* and the *Kshetrajna* and who also perceive the method of liberation of beings from Prakriti (delusive Nature)" (*God Talks With Arjuna: The Bhagavad Gita* XIII:1, 33–34).

"Yet again, when the heavenly kingdom of the astral forces is revealed unto a devotee, he becomes a divine merchantman of these prized pearls of truth, seeking until he finds the one peerless pearl of God-wisdom in divine realization, of priceless value. When his consciousness goes out again into the world after this discovery, he forsakes all his material desires and with accumulated power of desire-free transcendent meditation, he possesses that all-surpassing pearl of God-wisdom."

≈

"Again, the kingdom of heaven is like unto a net, that was cast into the sea, and gathered of every kind: which, when it was full, they drew to shore, and sat down, and gathered the good into vessels, but cast the bad away. So shall it be at the end of the world: the angels shall come forth, and sever the wicked from among the just, and shall cast them into the furnace of fire: there shall be wailing and gnashing of teeth" (Matthew 13:47–50).

"The devotee, with his net of Self-realization cast into the sea of meditation, gathers astral perceptions and also insight into the proclivities of his bad karma. When he finds in the net of his introspection this mixed catch, which he has pulled onto the shores of his outer mind, he sits down to the task in meditation of gathering up the good things which he found in the net of his devotion, and casting out by the force of wisdom all hidden evil tendencies.

"All devotees will find this experience at 'the end of the world,' that is, when they have finished their earthly desires. Those devotees will find the angels of intuition and Self-realization come out of the depths of their consciousness to sever all wicked karma from their acquired good tendencies, casting the evil propensities into the utterly consuming fire of inner wisdom. These die-hard evil karmic predispositions, born of bad habits, offer woeful inner resistance; but in spite of their remonstrances, they will surely be consumed by the fire of wisdom kindled by the devotee."

≈

Jesus saith unto them, "Have ye understood all these things?" They say unto him, "Yea, Lord." Then said he unto them, "There-

fore every scribe which is instructed unto the kingdom of heaven is like unto a man that is an householder, which bringeth forth out of his treasure things new and old" (Matthew 13:51–52).

"Therefore, every person who finds the heavenly kingdom of astral superconsciousness by meditation is an accomplished devotee, a divine householder of his bodily existence, with precious treasure from which he brings forth out of this spiritual acquisition new revelations of truth and old truths expressed newly."

DISCOURSE 38

"Thy Faith Hath Made Thee Whole"

Storm, Disease, Devils, Death, Bow to the Will of Jesus

The Ever-Wakeful Omniscience of Illumined Masters

❖

All Forces of Nature Subject to the God-Given Power in Man's Soul

❖

A Remarkable Exorcism of "Unclean Spirits" or "Tramp Souls"

❖

How Faith Can Draw "Virtue" or Healing Energy
From Divine Personages

❖

Jesus Raises Jairus' Daughter From the Dead

❖

How Spiritual "Laborers" Can Reap
the "Plenteous Harvest" of God-realization

"Wondrous was the love and compassion of Jesus as he journeyed through the busy cities and villages teaching in the synagogues the gospel, God's vibratory truth, and giving forth of his divine power to heal all manner of suffering."

Now it came to pass on a certain day, that he went into a ship with his disciples: and he said unto them, "Let us go over unto the other side of the lake." And they launched forth. But as they sailed he fell asleep: and there came down a storm of wind on the lake; and they were filled with water, and were in jeopardy. And they came to him, and awoke him, saying, "Master, master, we perish."

Then he arose, and rebuked the wind and the raging of the water: and they ceased, and there was a calm.

And he said unto them, "Where is your faith?" And they being afraid wondered, saying one to another, "What manner of man is this! for he commandeth even the winds and water, and they obey him."

And they arrived at the country of the Gadarenes, which is over against Galilee. And when he went forth to land, there met him out of the city a certain man, which had devils long time, and ware no clothes, neither abode in any house, but in the tombs.

When he saw Jesus, he cried out, and fell down before him, and with a loud voice said, "What have I to do with thee, Jesus, thou Son of God most high? I beseech thee, torment me not." (For he had commanded the unclean spirit to come out of the man. For oftentimes it had caught him: and he was kept bound with chains and in fetters; and he brake the bands, and was driven of the devil into the wilderness.)

And Jesus asked him, saying, "What is thy name?" And he said, "Legion": because many devils were entered into him. And they besought him that he would not command them to go out into the deep.

And there was there an herd of many swine feeding on the mountain: and they besought him that he would suffer them to enter into them. And he suffered them. Then went the devils out of the man, and entered into the swine: and the herd ran violently down a steep place into the lake, and were choked.

When they that fed them saw what was done, they fled, and went and told it in the city and in the country.

Then they went out to see what was done; and came to Jesus, and found the man, out of whom the devils were departed, sitting at the feet of Jesus, clothed, and in his right mind: and they were afraid. They also which saw it told them by what means he that was possessed of the devils was healed. Then the whole multitude of the country of the Gadarenes round about besought him to depart from them; for they were taken with great fear: and he went up into the ship, and returned back again.

Now the man out of whom the devils were departed besought him that he might be with him: but Jesus sent him away, saying, "Return to thine own house, and shew how great things God hath done unto thee." And he went his way, and published throughout the whole city how great things Jesus had done unto him.

And it came to pass, that, when Jesus was returned, the people gladly received him: for they were all waiting for him. And, behold, there came a man named Jairus, and he was a ruler of the synagogue: and he fell down at Jesus' feet, and besought him that he would come into his house: for he had one only daughter, about twelve years of age, and she lay a dying.

But as he went the people thronged him. And a woman having an issue of blood twelve years, which had spent all her living upon physicians, neither could be healed of any, came behind him, and touched the border of his garment: and immediately her issue of blood stanched.

And Jesus said, "Who touched me?" When all denied, Peter and they that were with him said, "Master, the multitude throng thee and press thee, and sayest thou, 'Who touched me?'"

And Jesus said, "Somebody hath touched me: for I perceive that virtue is gone out of me."

And when the woman saw that she was not hid, she came trembling, and falling down before him, she declared unto him before all the people for what cause she had touched him, and how she was healed immediately. And he said unto her, "Daughter, be of good comfort: thy faith hath made thee whole; go in peace."

While he yet spake, there cometh one from the ruler of the synagogue's house, saying to him, "Thy daughter is dead; trouble not the Master."

But when Jesus heard it, he answered him, saying, "Fear not: believe only, and she shall be made whole." And when he came into the house, he suffered no man to go in, save Peter, and James, and John, and the father and the mother of the maiden. And all wept, and bewailed her: but he said, "Weep not; she is not dead, but sleepeth."

And they laughed him to scorn, knowing that she was dead. And he put them all out, and took her by the hand, and called, saying, "Maid, arise." And her spirit came again, and she arose straightway: and he commanded to give her meat.

And her parents were astonished: but he charged them that they should tell no man what was done.

—Luke 8:22–56

And when Jesus departed thence, two blind men followed him, crying, and saying, "Thou son of David, have mercy on us."

And when he was come into the house, the blind men came to him: and Jesus saith unto them, "Believe ye that I am able to do this?"

They said unto him, "Yea, Lord."

Then touched he their eyes, saying, "According to your faith be it unto you." And their eyes were opened; and Jesus straitly charged them, saying, "See that no man know it." But they, when they were departed, spread abroad his fame in all that country.

As they went out, behold, they brought to him a dumb man possessed with a devil. And when the devil was cast out, the dumb spake: and the multitudes marvelled, saying, "It was never so seen in Israel." But the Pharisees said, "He casteth out devils through the prince of the devils."

And Jesus went about all the cities and villages, teaching in their synagogues, and preaching the gospel of the kingdom, and healing every sickness and every disease among the people. But when he saw the multitudes, he was moved with compassion on them, because they fainted, and were scattered abroad, as sheep having no shepherd.

Then saith he unto his disciples, "The harvest truly is plenteous, but the labourers are few; pray ye therefore the Lord of the harvest, that he will send forth labourers into his harvest."

—Matthew 9:27–38

"Thy Faith Hath Made Thee Whole"

Storm, Disease, Devils, Death, Bow to the Will of Jesus

Now it came to pass on a certain day, that he went into a ship with his disciples: and he said unto them, "Let us go over unto the other side of the lake." And they launched forth. But as they sailed he fell asleep: and there came down a storm of wind on the lake; and they were filled with water, and were in jeopardy. And they came to him, and awoke him, saying, "Master, master, we perish."

Then he arose, and rebuked the wind and the raging of the water: and they ceased, and there was a calm.

And he said unto them, "Where is your faith?" And they being afraid wondered, saying one to another, "What manner of man is this! for he commandeth even the winds and water, and they obey him" (Luke 8:22–25).

Parallel reference:

And the same day, when the even was come, he saith unto them, "Let us pass over unto the other side." And when they had sent away the multitude, they took him even as he was in the ship. And there were also with him other little ships. And there arose a great storm of wind, and the waves beat into the ship, so that it was now full.

720

> *And he was in the hinder part of the ship, asleep on a pillow:*
> *and they awake him, and say unto him, "Master, carest thou not*
> *that we perish?"*
>
> *And he arose, and rebuked the wind, and said unto the sea,*
> *"Peace, be still." And the wind ceased, and there was a great calm.*
>
> *And he said unto them, "Why are ye so fearful? How is it*
> *that ye have no faith?" And they feared exceedingly, and said one*
> *to another, "What manner of man is this, that even the wind and*
> *the sea obey him?" (Mark 4:35–41).**

Although the body of Jesus was asleep, his inner consciousness was awake in the ever-knowingness of God's omnipresence. The center of an individual's consciousness is in the con-

The ever-wakeful om-niscience of illumined masters

scious mind during wakefulness, the subconscious mind during sleep, and in superconsciousness during deep meditation. When an individual is concentrated in the state of wakefulness, his subconsciousness and superconsciousness remain in the background. When he is asleep, his consciousness and superconsciousness remain in the background. But a master like Jesus, whose center of consciousness is Cosmic Consciousness, is omniscient in Spirit whether his body is awake or asleep. He is able to watch his body sleeping and to be aware of any present or far-flung condition or circumstance, even as God watches all human beings and notes equally the grandeur of evolving universes and the fall of a single sparrow.

God's omnipresent consciousness knows the life and death, the sleep and wakeful activities, of all creatures present in Him, even as we know all our thoughts within our one mind. A human being with his one self-contained life is conscious of the sensations of his body or of pain that may occur in any conglomerate of the twenty-seven thousand billion cells of his body; God's consciousness, encompassing all space, knows every happening, even in any one of the tiniest atoms among the multitudinous creations in the cosmos.

Jesus questioned his disciples' faith because they did not realize that, even though his body slept, his consciousness was awake with the Father in the storm, in the boat, in the disciples—in everything. If the disciples had had faith in the omnipresent consciousness of Jesus,

---

* Cf. additional parallel reference in Matthew 8:23–27.

they would have known his inner consciousness was aware of their plight and that he was, even in that dire moment, protecting them.

To reanimate their paralyzed trust, Jesus admonished: "Why do you permit ignorance to assault you with fear and steal away your faith in the all-protecting omnipresent power and consciousness within me?" With the sanction of the Divine Will to prove the omnipotence of God within him, Jesus rose and addressed the sea, commanding the forces of nature, winds and water: "O ye boisterous wind and tumultuous sea, governed by cosmic forces, you who are created and active according to the will of God, the Father with whom I am One, I command you to change your vibration and be peaceful and quiet."

"Peace, be still." As soon as Jesus, with his omnipresent consciousness and the omnipotent will of God within him, vibrated peace,

All forces of nature subject to the God-given power in man's soul

the God-guided forces of nature immediately followed his example, becoming still in vibrations of calmness. It seems to ordinary persons that the elemental processes of nature are the result of the workings of coincidental blind forces without any plan. But it is evident that the harmony in nature, the routine of seasons, the mathematics of planetary order, the sustenance of life, reveal an intelligent law and cosmic plan of God by which they are governed. Only an obstinate rationalist ascribes to chance the law and order in the universe and in the tidy life-supporting generosity of this earth; the divine man consciously perceives God in everything upholding by His divine will the scrupulous laws and forces of His wonderworks.

Hence, Jesus, being a master, not in imagination but by Self-realization of his oneness with Spirit, could evoke the will of God manifested in his own will to control the raging storm and waves.

I was blessed to witness the control of nature by my great master, Swami Sri Yukteswarji. Once when I was with Master at his seaside ashram in Puri on the Bay of Bengal, he asked me to lead his students in a summer solstice procession along the beach and through the streets of the town. The weather boded the expected seasonal heat, with not the slightest prospect of rain or clouds. I remonstrated with Master that it would be next to impossible for the disciples to maintain any decorum while walking barefoot on the fiery sands and city streets. Master replied, "I will tell you a secret. The Lord shall send an umbrella of clouds; you all shall walk in comfort."

As soon as the religious procession started, the entire sky became overcast as though by magic, and a very light rain fell, cooling the streets and scorching seashore. To the astonishment and immense gratitude of all, the comforting rain continued throughout the two-hour procession; but the instant we returned to the hermitage, the sky burned again with the oriental sun and the parade route seared with hostile intent. Master ascribed no personal credit to his part in the many miracles I saw him perform. As to taming the relentless Indian sun, he remarked simply, as was his wont: "You see how God feels for us. The Lord responds to all and works for all. Just as He sent rain at my plea, so He fulfills any sincere desire of the devotee. Seldom do men realize how often God heeds their prayers. He is not partial to a few, but listens to everyone who approaches Him trustfully. His children should ever have implicit faith in the loving-kindness of their Omnipresent Father."

Whether a master prays for a specific response from God, or in divine attunement with God wills that desired effect, he activates the manifesting power of the Lord's creative vibration. Long before Western science recognized the vibratory essence of matter, the *rishis* of ancient India spoke of the whole spectrum of nature as an objectification of *Aum*, the Primal Sound or Vibratory Word. They showed that all natural phenomena can be controlled by the manipulation of vibration through the use of certain mantras or chants.* Historical documents tell of the remarkable powers possessed by Miyan Tan Sen, sixteenth-century court musician for Akbar the Great. When ordered by the Emperor to sing a night raga at midday, Tan Sen intoned a mantra that instantly caused the whole palace precincts to become enveloped in darkness.

Man was made to be lord over nature, and the forces of nature in turn work together to serve man. Man negates his lordship by faulty, self-serving stewardship of his earthly environment. He guides nature, though usually unknowingly, not only by his actions but also by the vibrations of his thoughts. The calamitous effects of floods, tornadoes, earthquakes, and all other natural disasters are results of the cumulative evil actions and thoughts of earth's human beings. The evils of war, for example, create tremendous negative vibrations that unbalance the

---

* Folklore of all peoples contains references to incantations with power over nature. The American Indians developed effective sound rituals for rain and wind. Tan Sen, the great Hindu musician, was able to quench fire by the power of his song.

forces of nature and release unrestrained energy. Conversely, man's goodness promotes peace, prosperity, well-being. When man becomes master of himself, sublimating the evil vibrations within himself, he reclaims the God-given power in his soul by which he can command from servant Nature—with God's sanction—whatever he so wills.

Several thousand years hence in the fourth *yuga*, the spiritual age of this present world cycle, there will be greater control of the elemental processes of nature, both in the earth's environment and in people's lives in general. In the heavenly spheres of the astral world, it is common to control the atmosphere and one's individual state of being. (The astral beings in the lower strata have no such control.) In the higher regions they can manipulate the lifetronic light-images and forces according to the power of their will. In the gross material world when one doesn't want rain, it rains; and when the earth needs rain, the sun shines. Imagine living in a world where you can command the storm to come and snow to melt. By control of the astral forces that empower nature, Jesus could calm the ravaging storm and Sri Yukteswarji could cool with clouds the searing rays of the sun. While there is a certain degree of uniformity in nature, there is also tremendous vagrancy—unpredictable extremes meant to bring out the conqueror in man, to encourage him to look behind the apparent disorder and to spiritualize his will with God's will in the malleable heavenly astral forces that activate the workings of the material universe.

〜

> *And they arrived at the country of the Gadarenes, which is over against Galilee. And when he went forth to land, there met him out of the city a certain man, which had devils long time, and ware no clothes, neither abode in any house, but in the tombs.*
>
> *When he saw Jesus, he cried out, and fell down before him, and with a loud voice said, "What have I to do with thee, Jesus, thou Son of God most high? I beseech thee, torment me not." (For he had commanded the unclean spirit to come out of the man. For oftentimes it had caught him: and he was kept bound with chains and in fetters; and he brake the bands, and was driven of the devil into the wilderness) (Luke 8:26–29).* *

----

* Cf. parallel references in Matthew 8:28–34 and Mark 5:1–20.

I n rare cases, lunacy is not due to some derangement in the brain, but to possession by tramp souls, some of which are demonic evil spirits, which can be exorcised or driven out by healers like Christ. Thus Jesus had commanded: "O   *A remarkable exor-* thou disembodied soul, an erstwhile reflection of   *cism of "unclean spir-* Spirit now vile with unclean evil karma, you must   *its" or "tramp souls"* give up your unlawful possession of this man's body; you have tormented him and deprived him of all sane sensibilities." When Jesus so spoke, an evil spirit in the madman fearfully implored Christ not to dispossess it from its now-accustomed habitat.

As previously explained, a tramp soul of demonic nature is often a disembodied spirit of a murderer or other such vicious criminal or licentious person, a "devil."* Because of a profane disregard for the sanctity of life, his own karma condemns his spirit to a nightmarish existence in the lower spheres of the astral world, where he remains "earthbound," roaming disconsolately in the dark regions of astral etheric space. Such spirits, not finding a much-desired quick rebirth, seek out and possess demented minds of persons whose bad karma attracts that particular fate. Masters who can distinguish between spirit possession and ordinary mental disorders have the power to consciously evict tramp souls from the human bodies they have seized.

~

And Jesus asked him, saying, "What is thy name?" And he said, "Legion": because many devils were entered into him. And they besought him that he would not command them to go out into the deep (Luke 8:30–31).

E vil spirits in the astral world are controlled by Satan, with each having a distinctive name and features. That is why Jesus asked the spirit that addressed him to identify itself. The leader of the agglomerated spirits in the madman replied that his name was Legion, which signified that many devils, wicked disembodied spirits, were crowding and disordering the one mental house of this madman. As many thoughts can remain in one mind, and various moods and various personalities can be displayed by the same actor, so various dis-

---

* See Discourse 24.

embodied spirits, being subtle, not physical, could occupy the same one mind and body of the possessed Gadarene.

These disembodied astral beings knew the influence of Jesus Christ's consciousness in the astral world. They knew of his power over evil spirits; so they begged him not to condemn them to roam again, without the consciousness of a physical body, in the oceanic depths of black space where they were trammeled in the torments of their own visions of a nightmare existence without a light to guide them.

These diabolical spirits crowding the brain of their host were highly delighted with their freedom to run riot among the perceptions of a world full of definite objects, enjoying through the brain of this possessed individual the sensations of sound, light, taste, smell, and touch. They feared being denied a further joyride in the fleshly vehicle, which they sent careening through a land of physical sensations and sceneries, and being thrown back into the Hades and nightmare of dark subconscious existence, "the deep."

~

And there was there an herd of many swine feeding on the mountain: and they besought him that he would suffer them to enter into them. And he suffered them. Then went the devils out of the man, and entered into the swine: and the herd ran violently down a steep place into the lake, and were choked (Luke 8:32–33).

Since Jesus Christ, by his divine power, was compelling the unclean spirits to leave the body of the madman, they implored him to let them enjoy instead the lesser sensibilities in the bodies of a nearby herd of swine, preferring a transition from the feeling of human sensations to the feeling of animal sensations rather than suddenly to be whirled back into the dark subconscious Hades to which they were condemned by their evil karma.

Jesus acquiesced. Through his help, the unclean spirits then left the brain of the possessed individual and entered the bodies of the herd of swine. The takeover by the evil spirits, and their wanton excitement in experiencing the perceptions of animal pleasure, deranged the normal instinctive behavior of the swine. In maniacal behavior, they ran violently into the lake and were drowned. The unclean spirits, along with the souls (the individualized evolving consciousness) of the swine, were driven back into the dark astral region of undeveloped beings—the wicked spirits were thrust again into their subconscious state of self-created nightmares; the souls of the swine were soon to incarnate in higher life-forms according to the natural order of upward evolution.

~

When they that fed them saw what was done, they fled, and went and told it in the city and in the country.

Then they went out to see what was done; and came to Jesus, and found the man, out of whom the devils were departed, sitting at the feet of Jesus, clothed, and in his right mind: and they were afraid. They also which saw it told them by what means he that was possessed of the devils was healed. Then the whole multitude of the country of the Gadarenes round about besought him to depart from them; for they were taken with great fear: and he went up into the ship, and returned back again (Luke 8:34–37).

It was foolish of the people of Gadara to be afraid of Jesus because of their nonunderstanding. What they should have feared was their own ignorance. Had they realized the redeeming power of Jesus, they would have asked him how they could be free from being possessed by ignorance, the devil of devils.

Circumspection in spiritual matters is wise, but closed minds are deplorable. Even in modern times, in the absence of many once-prevalent bizarre superstitions, there are still otherwise educated people who remain skeptical, even fearful, of a true master who can demonstrate as well as teach the art of attaining advanced states of consciousness in ecstatic meditation—as also the God-given powers accompanying those elevated states. There is nothing akin to superstition, magic, self-hypnosis, mediumistic spiritualism, witchcraft, or any such practices in the spiritual science of God-realization and God-union—yoga—as taught by a God-knowing master. It is the purest of sciences, for it opens naturally all inner doors for the expression of the potentials innate in the soul, the image of God in man, his true Self.

Fixity in spiritual ignorance is the cause of lost opportunity for soul progress, just as the uncomprehending fears of the Gadarenes two thousand years ago incited them to command Jesus to depart from their shores instead of asking from him the way to salvation.

~

Now the man out of whom the devils were departed besought him that he might be with him: but Jesus sent him away, saying, "Return to thine own house, and shew how great things God hath done unto thee." And he went his way, and published throughout the whole city how great things Jesus had done unto him (Luke 8:38–39).

Jesus was without ego—the remarkable hallmark of true masters. He spoke not of his own powers of healing, but of the Divine Power that manifested through him: "how great things God hath done." Jesus asked the man dispossessed of the legion of devils to serve as living publicity, that other afflicted souls might be encouraged to seek help from the unlimited divine power. Publicity used for material gain yields material results. Publicity for spiritual purposes is useful to broadcast truth and divine demonstrations for the inspiration and guidance of souls; but its use for self-laudation and personal material gain is pernicious and repugnant to the spiritual man.

~

And it came to pass, that, when Jesus was returned, the people gladly received him: for they were all waiting for him. And, behold, there came a man named Jairus, and he was a ruler of the synagogue: and he fell down at Jesus' feet, and besought him that he would come into his house: for he had one only daughter, about twelve years of age, and she lay a dying.

But as he went the people thronged him. And a woman having an issue of blood twelve years, which had spent all her living upon physicians, neither could be healed of any, came behind him, and touched the border of his garment: and immediately her issue of blood stanched.

And Jesus said, "Who touched me?" When all denied, Peter and they that were with him said, "Master, the multitude throng thee and press thee, and sayest thou, 'Who touched me?'"

And Jesus said, "Somebody hath touched me: for I perceive that virtue is gone out of me."

And when the woman saw that she was not hid, she came trembling, and falling down before him, she declared unto him before all the people for what cause she had touched him, and how she was healed immediately. And he said unto her, "Daughter, be of good comfort: thy faith hath made thee whole; go in peace" (Luke 8:40–48).*

The omnipresent Christ Consciousness in Jesus, being conscious of the astral world and its subsistent life force in all bodies, knew that among the throng pressing upon him, one particular woman, by her faith-enhanced will power, through her hands reverently contacting the hem of his garment, had drawn some life force from his body into her body. Like a powerful X-ray of energy, it had burned out her pernicious disease. As a diseased person touching the electrodes of an electrical medical apparatus may be benefited by the stimulus of the current, so the woman desiring healing made contact with the magnetism of Jesus and reinforced the impaired life force in her own body with the subtle aura, or astral current, emanating from and surrounding his body.

How faith can draw "virtue" or healing energy from divine personages

In the cure of every diseased human body, medicine or mental healing only rouses and supplements the inert life force, the direct cause of healing. A sick person can energize his healing life force by his will power revived by the strong will of a healer, or the sick person may by faith draw life force from a divinely magnetic individual's body and thereby rouse and reinforce his own all-healing life force to effect the healing. It was the latter case that caused Jesus to say, "Some subtle faith, seeking healing, has touched my astral emanation by an astral hand and has withdrawn virtue, or life force, from me."

---

* Cf. parallel references in Matthew 9:18–22 and Mark 5:21–34.

See also Mark 6:53–56 (and its parallel in Matthew 14:34–36), which cite similar instances of healing: "And when they had passed over, they came into the land of Gennesaret, and drew to the shore. And when they were come out of the ship, straightway they knew him, and ran through that whole region round about, and began to carry about in beds those that were sick, where they heard he was. And whithersoever he entered, into villages, or cities, or country, they laid the sick in the streets, and besought him that they might touch if it were but the border of his garment: and as many as touched him were made whole."

When Jesus said, "Virtue is gone out of me," he emphasized the healing power that went out of him; when he said, "Thy faith hath made thee whole," he emphasized the receptivity of the woman who was healed. Both are necessary. Healers must be sure of the presence of these two factors in divine healing—the faith of the person desiring to be healed and the ability of the healer to charge himself with divine healing power by daily deep God-contact in meditation. The virtue, or conscious cosmic energy that Jesus always felt within himself and that emanated from him, was absorbed by the faith of the woman, producing healing in her. It is noted in the Gospel that in Jesus' own country, some people could not be healed of their sickness because they were too material to receive the blessing of the omnipotent consciousness of God manifested in him.*

When Jesus felt "virtue is gone out of me," he expressed the principle of *darshan* in which a divine personage, with or without conscious intention, bestows blessings on those who approach the indwelling Divinity with a pure heart and mind. Receptive devotees thereby attract instant blessings from the mere sight or touch of a holy person.

Doubt is insidious static that disturbs the reception of the vibration of healing, no matter how strong the power of the healer. An individual must tune his consciousness, radio-like, with faith and proper mental attitude in order to receive the broadcastings of distant or direct healing vibrations from the healer. Jesus' words, "Thy faith hath made thee whole," signified, "Thy mental receptivity to the divine power in me has made it possible to produce the desired healing."

~

While he yet spake, there cometh one from the ruler of the synagogue's house, saying to him, "Thy daughter is dead; trouble not the Master."

But when Jesus heard it, he answered him, saying, "Fear not: believe only, and she shall be made whole." And when he came into the house, he suffered no man to go in, save Peter, and James, and John, and the father and the mother of the maiden. And all wept, and bewailed her: but he said, "Weep not; she is not dead, but sleepeth" (Luke 8:49–52).

---

* See Discourse 39.

730

Parallel reference:

> *While he yet spake, there came from the ruler of the synagogue's house certain which said, "Thy daughter is dead: why troublest thou the Master any further?" As soon as Jesus heard the word that was spoken, he saith unto the ruler of the synagogue, "Be not afraid, only believe."*
>
> *And he suffered no man to follow him, save Peter, and James, and John the brother of James. And he cometh to the house of the ruler of the synagogue, and seeth the tumult, and them that wept and wailed greatly. And when he was come in, he saith unto them, "Why make ye this ado, and weep? The damsel is not dead, but sleepeth" (Mark 5:35–39).*

Jesus was admonishing: "Do not fill your mind with the fear of hopelessness, but believe in the all-powerful divine will within me, and your daughter shall awake from her death sleep."

Owing to the serious condition of the maiden, in which the grip of death itself was to be loosened, Jesus did not want his mind to be intruded upon by any inharmonious thoughts from the crowd; so he asked only his advanced disciples, Peter, James, and John, to follow him into the home of Jairus. To those in the household who were weeping and wailing, he said, "Why are you making such a fuss and show of despair? Although your physical eyes behold the child as dead, I see that she is only sleeping in God and that she can be awakened through His will."

Jesus raises Jairus' daughter from the dead

∼

> *And they laughed him to scorn, knowing that she was dead. And he put them all out, and took her by the hand, and called, saying, "Maid, arise." And her spirit came again, and she arose straightway: and he commanded to give her meat.*
>
> *And her parents were astonished: but he charged them that they should tell no man what was done (Luke 8:53–56).*

Parallel reference:

> *And they laughed him to scorn. But when he had put them all*

out, he taketh the father and the mother of the damsel, and them that were with him, and entereth in where the damsel was lying.

And he took the damsel by the hand, and said unto her, "Talitha cumi"; which is, being interpreted, "Damsel, I say unto thee, arise."

And straightway the damsel arose, and walked; for she was of the age of twelve years. And they were astonished with a great astonishment. And he charged them straitly that no man should know it; and commanded that something should be given her to eat (Mark 5:40–43). *

Jesus freed himself from all occlusive vibrations of doubt by sending away from his environment those who had surrendered their thoughts to the testament of death. Then, with his body filled with dynamic cosmic energy, Jesus took the hand of the dead damsel in his right hand and vibrated his life-giving power within her, commanding, "Damsel, by the God-consciousness and cosmic vibration that are equally present within me and your dead body, I vibrate and will with my cosmic will that you be conscious of this life-giving cosmic energy and forsake your deathly sleep. Awake!"

Jesus, through the Christ Intelligence, which governs all astral forces and beings, commanded by his universal will the astral-bodied soul of the damsel to reenter her physical body, which he had recharged with life force from cosmic energy. The child was healed instantly and arose from her bed. The parents were at once elated and in awe as they witnessed the reanimation of their lifeless daughter. Jesus, in respecting the secrecy and seriousness of divine healing of the dead, sanctioned only rarely by God, asked those present not to discuss the matter with others.

Jesus then instructed that the girl be given something to eat to help her consciousness reaccustom itself to the feel of her physical body after her brief experience as an astral being in the astral world of light and vibratory energy. Saints, after coming out of a deep ecstasy, often drink water or take light nourishment in order to revive the consciousness of the body.

Awakening the physically dead by recalling the soul to reenter its discarded body and awakening the spiritually dead by bestowing God-

---

* Cf. additional parallel reference in Matthew 9:23–26.

consciousness are considered the highest forms of healing performed by a God-realized master. Greater even than healing the physically dead is the changing of a person who is materially minded into a God-minded soul. By a special technique of will, and with divine permission, great masters can transmit God-consciousness into advanced disciples.*

≈

And when Jesus departed thence, two blind men followed him, crying, and saying, "Thou son of David, have mercy on us."

And when he was come into the house, the blind men came to him: and Jesus saith unto them, "Believe ye that I am able to do this?"

They said unto him, "Yea, Lord."

Then touched he their eyes, saying, "According to your faith be it unto you." And their eyes were opened; and Jesus straitly charged them, saying, "See that no man know it." But they, when they were departed, spread abroad his fame in all that country (Matthew 9:27–31).†

The cosmic energy sent by the will and the touch of Jesus into the eyes of the blind men, being an intelligent, all-powerful, all-creative force, rearranged the astral lifetrons and the atomic electrons and protons—which had been deranged in the diseased eyes—and brought about the required healing, so ordered by the command: "According to your faith be it unto you."

After they had received the healing Jesus said, "Take care that no materially minded men hear about your healing; for such persons, no matter what spiritual demonstrations they behold, habitually cherish their disbelief in the almighty power of God that can work contrary to their concepts of the norms of nature."

---

* One among many examples that might be cited is recorded in Deuteronomy 34:9: "And Joshua the son of Nun was full of the spirit of wisdom; for Moses had laid his hands upon him: and the children of Israel hearkened unto him, and did as the Lord commanded Moses."

† This story is repeated, with slight variations, in Matthew 20:29–34. Cf. parallel references in Luke 18:35–43 and Mark 10:46–52 (in the latter passages, only one blind man is cited; Mark's rendering names him as "blind Bartimaeus, the son of Timaeus").

733

~

As they went out, behold, they brought to him a dumb man pos-
sessed with a devil. And when the devil was cast out, the dumb
spake: and the multitudes marvelled, saying, "It was never so
seen in Israel." But the Pharisees said, "He casteth out devils
through the prince of the devils." *

And Jesus went about all the cities and villages, teaching in
their synagogues, and preaching the gospel of the kingdom, and
healing every sickness and every disease among the people. But
when he saw the multitudes, he was moved with compassion on
them, because they fainted, and were scattered abroad, as sheep
having no shepherd (Matthew 9:32–36).†

Wondrous was the love and compassion of Jesus as he journeyed through the busy cities and villages teaching in the synagogues the gospel, God's vibratory truth, and giving forth of his divine power to heal all manner of suffering. His universal heart felt for
the multitude of scattered lives pursuing their moment-by-moment
mechanical busy-ness of existence in a delusion-imposed stupor. Like
sheep without a shepherd, they had no spiritual guide or guru to lead
them through the wilderness of the world to the kingdom of Cosmic
Consciousness.

~

Then saith he unto his disciples, "The harvest truly is plenteous,
but the labourers are few; pray ye therefore the Lord of the har-
vest, that he will send forth labourers into his harvest" (Matthew
9:37–38).‡

"The harvest of cosmic consciousness is plenteous, nay endless,
but very few are the devotees who will labor in meditation to
sow the seeds of this harvest in order to reap its fruits. Pray therefore
that God, the giver of cosmic consciousness, may bless you to become

---

* Cf. Matthew 12:22–24 (commented on in Discourse 36).

† Cf. parallel reference in Mark 6:6, 34.

‡ Cf. parallel reference in Luke 10:2 (Discourse 40).

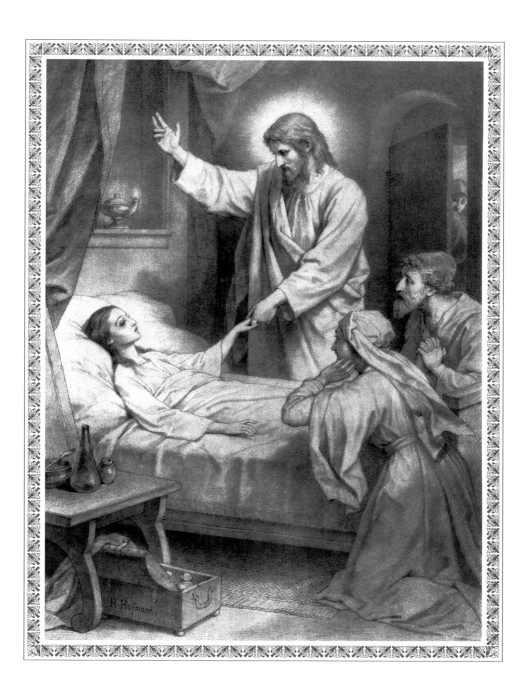

Jesus Raises Jairus's Daughter From the Dead

And he took the damsel by the hand, and said unto her, "Talitha cumi"; which is, being interpreted, "Damsel, I say unto thee, arise."

And straightway the damsel arose, and walked.

—Mark 5:41–42

Part of Jesus' mission was to make visible God's healing mercy. Through his public miracles, Jesus demonstrated that even "incurable" diseases and "insoluble" problems can be surmounted, sometimes instantly, by attunement with Divine Will. The purpose of these miraculous healings was not to glorify the perishable body, but to rouse faith in the omnipresence of God and in man's innate ability to contact and personally know his Heavenly Father....

Jesus showed what it is to be in touch with the Cosmic Dynamo. When one feels God's presence, His vibratory energy, the strength of His infinite power, any thought he declares will materialize.

—Paramahansa Yogananda

Drawing by Heinrich Hofmann

true aspiring devotees that through His grace and your spiritual efforts you may attain the full measure of that divine harvest."

The harvest of God-realization is abundant beyond measure: eternal wisdom, eternal ever new bliss, eternal consciousness and immortality. But there are very few human beings who will live a life of discipline and continuity in meditation from which they may reap in the short season of life the everlasting harvest of God-contact.

How spiritual "laborers" can reap the "plenteous harvest" of God-realization

God-realization comes to the devotee not only owing to his efforts to manifest Self-realization, but also because of the Lord's divine compassion. That grace is withheld from the devotee who with pride by reason of his spiritual realizations demands of God to surrender Himself. Egotism is the cause of many difficulties in reaching the ultimate spiritual goal; even though one may attain phenomenal powers, there is certain danger of falling from grace without the support of humility.

Neither does a devotee receive divine mercy if he blindly professes belief in God but deliberately breaks the spiritual laws voiced by God's prophets. To scorn the eternal verities in a desultory life on the assumption that God's mercy will save an unreformed sinner anyway is a false hope indeed. That is why Jesus expressed that God is the Lord who grants the final harvests, but it is for the devotee laborers to grow their spirituality on the soil of their meditative life.

Christ, in concert with the masters of India, taught that each devotee should regularly practice all the step-by-step methods of higher realization, and at the same time with deepest devotion pray unto his own Father-God to grant him final liberation. "Pray unto God, who can grant salvation, to give His blessings that you may become divine laborers tilling the soil of your consciousness with meditation and sowing in it the seeds of wisdom and Self-realization, that in the end you may reap the richest harvest of liberating God-contact." The Lord of the harvest can be attained not by proxy, blind beliefs, nor a sudden unmerited divine visitation of enlightenment, nor by expecting to be in His presence by the virtue of death, but by the spiritual labor of scientific meditation, righteous living, and the Lord's bestowal of divine grace.

"A Prophet Hath No Honor in His Own Country"

The Value of Establishing Regular Times for Communion With God

❖

The Christ in Jesus Fulfilled Isaiah's Prophecy
of Healing and Salvation

❖

Without the Receptivity of Faith,
Man Shuts Divine Power out of His Life

❖

Reverent Devotion, Avoiding Overfamiliarity,
Makes One Receptive to a Master's Blessings

❖

Jesus Cites From His Past-Life Experience
the Divine Laws Governing Miracles

❖

True Devotees Win Honor in the Heart of God

"Vision clouded by familiarity cannot pierce to the celestial expanses of a godly soul. Devotion is required to apprehend the measureless reaches of a master's consciousness."

*A*nd he came to Nazareth, where he had been brought up: and, as his custom was, he went into the synagogue on the Sabbath day, and stood up for to read. And there was delivered unto him the book of the prophet Isaiah. And when he had opened the book, he found the place where it was written,

"The Spirit of the Lord is upon me, because He hath anointed me to preach the gospel to the poor; He hath sent me to heal the brokenhearted, to preach deliverance to the captives, and recovering of sight to the blind, to set at liberty them that are bruised, to preach the acceptable year of the Lord."

And he closed the book, and he gave it again to the minister, and sat down. And the eyes of all them that were in the synagogue were fastened on him. And he began to say unto them, "This day is this scripture fulfilled in your ears."

And all bare him witness, and wondered at the gracious words which proceeded out of his mouth. And they said, "Is not this Joseph's son?"

And he said unto them, "Ye will surely say unto me this proverb, 'Physician, heal thyself: whatsoever we have heard done in Capernaum, do also here in thy country.'" And he said, "Verily I say unto you, no prophet is accepted in his own country.

"But I tell you of a truth, many widows were in Israel in the days of Elijah, when the heaven was shut up three years and six months, when great famine was throughout all the land; but unto none of them was Elijah sent, save unto Sarepta, a city of Sidon, unto a woman that was a widow. And many lepers were in Israel in the time of Elisha the prophet; and none of them was cleansed, saving Naaman the Syrian."

And all they in the synagogue, when they heard these things, were filled with wrath, and rose up, and thrust him out of the city, and led him unto the brow of the hill whereon their city was built, that they might cast him down headlong. But he passing through the midst of them went his way.

—Luke 4:16–30

"A Prophet Hath No Honor in His Own Country"

🌿

And he came to Nazareth, where he had been brought up: and, as his custom was, he went into the synagogue on the Sabbath day (Luke 4:16). *

Though Jesus taught that the consummate worship of God is in the inner temple of silent meditative communion, it was "his custom" to go to the synagogue on the Sabbath day, upholding by his example the value of congregational worship. "Whatever a superior being does, inferior persons imitate," the Bhagavad Gita points out. "His actions set a standard for people of the world."† Though Sabbath observances at the synagogue were unnecessary for Jesus, whose consciousness was united to Spirit every mo-

The value of establishing regular times for communion with God

---

*This story of Jesus' preaching in Nazareth, and being rejected by the people of his hometown, is recounted in greater or lesser detail in the Gospels of Matthew, Mark, and Luke. Each of them places the story at a different time in the chronology of Jesus' life: In Luke, the event occurs just after the beginning of Jesus' public preaching in Galilee; Matthew (13:54–58) and Mark (6:1–6) describe it as taking place later in Jesus' ministry. Luke has the most detailed account of the story, but most scholars acknowledge that this gospel narrates it out of sequence, since there is reference to the healing miracles that Jesus performed in Capernaum, and Luke relates this before Jesus' visit to Capernaum (Discourses 23, 24, and 25). Thus, the commentary in this Discourse is based primarily on Luke's detailed telling, though not his chronology.

†*God Talks With Arjuna: The Bhagavad Gita* III:21.

ment of every day, weekly church or temple worship provides for the sense-habit-driven masses a vitally needed soul-recharging respite from their environment of materialistic concerns and pursuits. By joining the congregation for scripture reading and prayer, Jesus signified that all human beings should set aside definite times—at the very least once each week—for God-reminding worship that will revivify in their lives the peace and wisdom of their souls.

The average churchgoer, for whom worship is a Sunday-only affair, usually finds the eroding influence of material habits predominant on the remaining six days, and can seldom retain sufficient of the sacred influences of the worship service to keep his consciousness spiritualized until the following Sunday. Of course, a dime is better than no money at all. Even once-weekly Sunday sermons help the materially minded person acquire some spiritual ballast from the peaceful effects of scriptural wisdom, prayer, and silence. However, to feel appreciably throughout the week an undiminished inspiration of Sunday peace one ought to make each day a real "Sun's Day" or Wisdom's Day by basking in the light of the Sun of Wisdom and cultivating a regenerating inner peace through a regular habit of meditation in the early morning, at noontime before lunch, in the evening before dinner, and especially during the quiet time before sleep. The true peace-church into which Jesus sought to lead his followers is the inner sanctuary of silence wherein one is spiritually restored in the obliging wisdom and joy of the soul. If anyone, even twice daily, during the hours of dawn and in the depth of night, worships God in the temple of meditation for fifteen minutes to one hour, he will find the spiritual habit of peace diminishing his worry-producing material habits.

But there will be those who cannot bring themselves to set aside even a half hour out of twenty-four to meditate: the so-called too-busy person—busy until death with a myopic foolish pursuit of perishable treasure to satisfy unsatisfying desires. Stocks and bonds and vain accumulations cannot pass through the pearly gates of the afterlife, leaving the astral being to rue its paucity of spiritual wealth. Such persons ought at least to make their best effort weekly to commune with God at church or temple or other place of worship—not merely bringing the body to services while the heart and mind are rehashing the worries of the business week, but giving one's devotion to God with attentive sincerity, a calm body, and a quiet mind. The temporary upliftment brought by this minimal fulfillment of the divine command to "remember the Sabbath day"* may eventually incline the worshiper to make his Sunday peace more lasting by devoting a time to meditation every day.

Scheduling the important things in one's life creates the willingness and facilitates the ability to perform those actions. The body assimilates food more equably when breakfast, lunch, and dinner are partaken at the same hours each day. Consistency in worshiping on the Sabbath develops the habit of thinking of God and spiritual cultivation at least once a week. Regularity in the repetition of any material or spiritual action—eating, efforts at business success, churchgoing, meditation—is bound to create a physiological, and consequently psychological, habit.

In general, people are ruled by their habits. When their bad material habits hold sway, they may wonder why, in spite of their continued willingness to get rid of these despots, they are still dragged by them into undesirable behavior. Bad habits cannot be stopped by merely wanting to eradicate them, but only by reconditioning oneself physiologically and psychologically with contravening good habits. Willingness is not enough. One must act according to that willingness, not only once or a few times, but repeatedly and continuously until the opposite good habit is installed. Only then can one expect the demise of the tyrannical bad habit. Achievement lies in continued regularity of activity. Knowing the law of habit that governs human nature, Jesus set the example by his customary attendance at the synagogue on the Sabbath day.

～

He went into the synagogue on the Sabbath day, and stood up for to read. And there was delivered unto him the book of the prophet Isaiah. And when he had opened the book, he found the place where it was written,

"The Spirit of the Lord is upon me, because He hath anointed me to preach the gospel to the poor; He hath sent me to heal the brokenhearted, to preach deliverance to the captives, and recovering of sight to the blind, to set at liberty them that are bruised, to preach the acceptable year of the Lord."†

---

* Exodus 20:8. See Discourse 32 for additional commentary on the spiritual purpose of the Sabbath.

† Isaiah 61:1–2.

*And he closed the book, and he gave it again to the minister,
and sat down. And the eyes of all them that were in the synagogue were fastened on him. And he began to say unto them,
"This day is this scripture fulfilled in your ears" (Luke 4:16–21).*

Jesus used the medium of a passage from the book of Isaiah that tal-
lied with the works of his divinely ordained mission to proclaim distinctly thereby that his coming had been foretold in the Hebrew scriptures. Of course, charlatans may quote scripture to serve their own
nefarious ends; but Jesus knew he was the promised Messiah, the Christ,

*The Christ in Jesus ful-
filled Isaiah's prophecy
of healing and
salvation*

spoken of by the holy ones of centuries past. In his
meek way, Jesus read the words of Isaiah to declare
that he was not an ordinary religious teacher, but
was chosen and empowered by the Lord, "He hath
anointed me," for a preordained mission.*

"The Spirit of the Lord (the Infinite Intelligence
of Christ Consciousness, which directs all creation) is upon my soul," not
through symbolical baptism with water by man, but through immersion
in the Ocean of Spirit. When one restores his mortally identified soul to
union with the infinite Spirit, he is baptized with illimitable spiritual wisdom and thus can ably and fittingly "preach the Gospel," the intuitively
perceived truths of God, "to the poor," to humble recipient minds.

Likewise, only God-saturated souls can permanently "heal the
brokenhearted"—human hearts sorely wounded with disillusionment
and despair by dependence on treacherous expectations of material
satisfaction. As immortals, souls are sent on earth to be entertained by
the Lord's cosmic drama; but when delusion captures and holds man's
consciousness with its subtle nuances of pretense, the divine nature
loses itself in identification with the physical form and its love of material pleasures. Matter can never satisfy spirit; sooner or later this is
a hard-won realization. Then God-knowing souls come to the rescue
of the brokenhearted by illuminating the way of return to the imperishable happiness of Spirit hidden within one's own soul.

God-empowered souls, attuned with the Source of all power, can
restore sight to the sightless, by exercising matter-controlling Divine
Will to remodel the disorganized atoms in a blind man's eyes, and also
bring "recovery of sight" to the spiritually blind.

---

* The word *Christ* (as also *Messiah*) literally means "the Anointed."

God-perceiving souls alone can offer "deliverance to the captives" of mortal bondage, and "set at liberty" those who have been long bruised by woes, worries, and the faithlessness of inconstant friends. None but God-sent saviors can forgive those who are willing to repent, and to them impart assurance of salvation in the here and now ("the acceptable year of the Lord").*

The human race goes through repeated fourfold cycles of evolution and degeneration, its mental and moral capacities developing gradually from the darkness of the material age to the enlightenment of the spiritual age, and then falling through long decline back to the material again.† Though the Lord works through His God-realized devotees at all times, in all ages, to redeem His erring children, from time to time during dire periods of world civilization when the misery of ignorance envelops man's existence in darkness, God sends a special manifestation of Himself, an incarnate emissary of the divine Christ Consciousness, or Son, to redeem the faithful and reestablish the divine pattern of reformation. Jesus, knowing the prevalence of false prophets, wanted the people to know that he was not a self-elected, self-serving teacher but the God-ordained Christ-messenger promised in the scriptures long before, evidenced in his bringing divine healing of body, mind, and soul to God's children as prophesied in the book of Isaiah. That is why he declared: "This day is this scripture fulfilled in your ears."

~

And all bare him witness, and wondered at the gracious words which proceeded out of his mouth. And they said, "Is not this Joseph's son?"

---

* Translations other than the wording given in the King James Version as "the acceptable year of the Lord" show that the meaning intended is "the year of the Lord's favor or amnesty."

† The scriptures of India identify these four stages as Kali Yuga (the age in which humanity comprehends only the grossest physical aspects of creation), Dwapara Yuga (in which the human intellect develops enough to understand and harness the finer atomic and electromagnetic forces), Treta Yuga (the mental age, in which the dormant powers of the mind become highly developed), and Satya Yuga (the spiritually enlightened age, during which humanity as a whole lives in attunement with God and His laws and purposes in creation). See *yugas* in glossary.

And he said unto them, "Ye will surely say unto me this proverb, 'Physician, heal thyself: whatsoever we have heard done in Capernaum, do also here in thy country.'" And he said, "Verily I say unto you, no prophet is accepted in his own country" (Luke 4:22–24).

Parallel reference:

And many hearing him were astonished, saying, "From whence hath this man these things? And what wisdom is this which is given unto him, that even such mighty works are wrought by his hands? Is not this the carpenter, the son of Mary, the brother of James, and Joses, and of Juda, and Simon? And are not his sisters here with us?" And they were offended at him.

But Jesus said unto them, "A prophet is not without honour, but in his own country, and among his own kin, and in his own house."

And he could there do no mighty work, save that he laid his hands upon a few sick folk, and healed them. And he marvelled because of their unbelief (Mark 6:2–6). *

All those who heard the words of Jesus and felt the magnetism of the sacred power with which he spoke of the fulfillment of prophecy perceived the ring of truth in his gently delivered profound utterances. Yet even while they sat in wonderment, their human habit of familiarity consciousness returned with discrediting doubts: "Oh, how could the son of our Joseph, someone from our own community whom we have known since childhood, be anything other than an ordinary person like the rest of us? Though he is reputed to perform mighty works, is it not audacious, if not blasphemous, for him to claim power to interpret scripture as a prophecy applicable to himself?"

When prophets incarnate in this world, though they are usually born in a good, devout family, it is often in an environment that is less than receptive, even rebellious, because they come to bring light to those who are in the darkness of delusion. That is why in the Bhagavad Gita, the Lord says: "Whenever there is a decline of virtue and a predominance of evildoing, I incarnate to give help to the virtuous and protect

---

* Cf. additional parallel reference in Matthew 13:54–58.

them from the wicked."* So it is that Jesus came to minister in a dark
time amidst ignorance and corrupted religiosity. He performed only
good works, but his spiritual reforms met with a
nonunderstanding populace that led to his cruel cru-   *Without the receptiv-*
cifixion—and it seems that those in his own home-   *ity of faith, man shuts*
town have been cited as among the least receptive.†   *divine power out of*
                                                         his life
Replying to their unvoiced challenge, Jesus sig-
nified: "My dear people, you expect me to furnish
you with proof of my words by performing divine healings here just as
I healed the sick at Capernaum. You wonder why, as a spiritual physician, I heal people in other towns, but not those of my own community.
It is because you do not accept that God's power works through me. Acceptance signifies faith; and without the good soil of faith, no healing
seed can be brought to fruition even by a man of God. The Almighty
subjects His prophets to His inculcated spiritual laws. We are constrained to honor the code that gives man free will, which God Himself
does not contradict. There can be no greater healer than omnipotent
God. He is trying to heal His mortal children from all troubles; but since
He gave independence to man, man is free to shut divine power out of
his life or to allow it to shine through the window of faith.

"Divine healing is based on the law of reciprocity. Here in my own
town you are used to thinking of me as an ordinary mortal man; and
consequently you have no faith in the Divine in me. Without your faith,
I cannot heal you. The irrevocable gift of free will permits man successfully to resist divine influences, including the intercession of saints."

A street lamp sheds light in all directions except directly beneath
its housing, where there is shadow. Similarly, a prophet illumined with
God sheds light unto all and is widely appreciated except, often, by
those who are near to him in a family or social, but not devotional,
relationship. Shortsighted overemphasis on the human relationship
blinds them to the spiritual greatness in a divine personage.

A judge whose authority and admonitions are feared or admired
in the courtroom is divested of that power at home with his wife; indeed, subject to admonishment by her! It is a psychological fact that
familiarity without respect breeds contempt. It is a natural worldly

---

* Paraphrase of IV:7–8.

† Nathanael was perhaps referring to this when he asked Philip, in John 1:45: "Can
there any good thing come out of Nazareth?" (Discourse 10).

tendency for persons living in close relationships to evaluate each
other not as souls but in terms of one's own expectations, resulting in

Reverent devotion,
avoiding overfamiliar-
ity, makes one recep-
tive to a master's
blessings

erosion of mutual regard, lack of courtesy, overfamiliarity, suspiciousness, insulting speech or acts. In
distant closeness love lives. In wrong familiarity
love dies.

One should never take others for granted and
thereby fail to appreciate the divine uniqueness of
every soul. Persons who live amidst the scenic
grandeur of the magnificent Himalayas little appreciate the uplifting
vistas because their attention is on their home life; they become so
used to their extraordinary venue that they consider it as "nothing special." But to visitors who come from distant lands with an eager attitude of mind, the majestic vastness of the lofty peaks are an awesome
experience. Similarly, the family members of a prophet, or his com-
munal associates, accustomed to relating to him as one of their own
among the many, lack the respectful attention that would perceive the
greatness hidden behind his human personality that merits their regard
and honor. Vision clouded by familiarity cannot pierce to the celestial
expanses of a godly soul. Devotion is required to apprehend the measureless reaches of a master's consciousness.

Sincerely seeking devotees, whether from nearby or afar, come to
associate with a holy person not in the casual way of human relatives
or social acquaintances, but to absorb with reverent attention the presence of God within him. Their devotion imbues them with the proper
appreciation for their master, and hence, full receptivity to his blessings.

Because of the unbelief of the people of his own town, Jesus
"could there do no mighty work, save that he laid his hands on a few
sick folk, and healed them"—he used the positive-negative poles of
his hands to send forth the cosmic energy to heal those few who had
faith in God's power in him. Divine law did not sanction miracles for
the benefit of the many in the place where Jesus had grown up because, even as powerful as he was, the seed of healing could not sprout
on the rocky soil of disbelieving minds.

Jesus observed that since his reputation of performing miraculous
cures had preceded him, most persons in the gathering around him
were little more than spiritual thrill-seekers who wanted him to
demonstrate his fabled feats as if he were a spectacle in a circus. He
wanted them to understand that the miracles of prophets are sacred

and are enacted not to satisfy their own or others' whims, but only according to the will of God. He cited from his previous-life experience that the works of the prophets Elijah and Elisha were governed strictly by what God directed them to do, not necessarily what they were capable of doing. His past-life guru, Elijah, and himself, as Elisha, had been supremely endowed with healing power and could have cured thousands, yet they healed only those God commanded them to heal, in accordance with His divine laws.

~

"But I tell you of a truth, many widows were in Israel in the days of Elijah, when the heaven was shut up three years and six months, when great famine was throughout all the land; but unto none of them was Elijah sent, save unto Sarepta, a city of Sidon, unto a woman that was a widow. And many lepers were in Israel in the time of Elisha the prophet; and none of them was cleansed, saving Naaman the Syrian" (Luke 4:25–27).

S incerity of faith and devotion, not presumed obligation to family or community, is the sufficient condition for divine intercession— as illustrated when God permitted Elijah to bring no miraculous aid to the many suffering in his own country, but only to a spiritually deserving widow of a foreign land.* Similarly with the many lepers in Israel during the time of Elisha: He bestowed divine healing only on one from another country.†

Jesus cites from his past-life experience the divine laws governing miracles

The crowd at the Nazareth synagogue was unknowingly tempting Jesus to go against the will of the Father in order to prove himself. Giving no countenance to any special claim on him as being one of their own, he cut them short by his reference to the honored prophets Elijah and Elisha. He spoke truthfully from the memory of his past incarnation, that when the accumulated destructive vibrations of evil actions of the masses prevented the harmonious functioning of the heav-

---

* Sarepta (Zarephath) was in or near the prominent city of Sidon, in Phoenicia, not in Elijah's native country of Israel. The story of the widow whose meager store of meal and oil was miraculously replenished for many days till the end of the drought, and whose son was raised from the dead by Elijah, is told in I Kings 17:8–24.

† II Kings 5:1–14.

enly laws controlling all forces of nature, resulting in devastating drought and famine, there were many needy widows in Israel, but Elijah worked no miracles for them. Only one—a foreigner—because of her faith received God-ordained spiritual aid from Elijah.

Without directly accusing the cynics at Nazareth, Jesus indicated that he would perform for them no feats of divine healing, for the same reason that Elijah brought no aid to his famine-stricken country. Even the God-illumined prophet, with all his power, was helpless to stop the devastation caused by mass karma, the willful misdeeds of the people.*

Jesus was not speaking fatalistically: Widespread human evils such as wars, moral iniquity, or spiritual degeneration disrupt the subtle astral forces behind the physical mechanisms governing earth's climate and other environmental conditions, wreaking so-called natural disasters on good and evil persons alike. These are not "fate" or "acts of God," but the outcome of the karmic law, that man must suffer the consequences of his actions if he does not invoke and make himself receptive to the intercession of God's aid and forgiveness when he has fallen. The masses of people in Elijah's time did not exercise their free choice to cultivate repentance and faith, and therefore had to undergo the ravages of three-and-a-half years of famine.

Then Jesus, with subtle insinuation, spoke of himself as the Elisha of yore, who was similarly constrained from healing the many lepers of his time, with the exception, at God's command, of one honorable Syrian named Naaman. By citing these stories from the scriptures, Jesus elucidated the divine laws that work in justice and secrecy, producing both karmic consequences of man's actions and the intervention of God's contravening mercy if man is receptive through repentance, devotion, and faith:

"My dear countrymen, you do not understand how divine laws operate; you yourselves by your irreverent faithlessness have decreed that I cannot work multiple wonders of healing in my own country. As the prophet Elisha healed one Syrian leper but not the multitude of lepers in Israel, so also I do only what God's will operating through His spiritual laws influences me to do."

---

* It was during this time that Elijah said to God: "The children of Israel have forsaken Thy covenant, thrown down Thine altars, and slain Thy prophets with the sword; and I, even I only, am left" (I Kings 19:14).

～

And all they in the synagogue, when they heard these things,
were filled with wrath, and rose up, and thrust him out of the
city, and led him unto the brow of the hill whereon their city was
built, that they might cast him down headlong. But he passing
through the midst of them went his way (Luke 4:28–30).

The congregation in the synagogue became irate at the intransigent words of Jesus spoken by him in scriptural affirmation of his God-ordained mission, and in condemnation of their unreceptive consciousness. In wrathful frustration that Jesus would exhibit no phenomenal feats to prove himself, they rose up as a murderous mob, desirous of his death for blasphemy in proclaiming himself the chosen one of God prophesied in the scripture. They led him to a high precipice to throw him down to his death; but strange as are the decrees of God, Jesus was protected by Invisible Divine Power. God cast oblivion in the hearts of these adversaries of Jesus, allowing him to walk right through their midst before they could regain the presence of mind to carry out their violent intent.*

True devotees win honor in the heart of God

Though "a prophet hath no honor in his own country,"† he has the blessing of God to accomplish his work according to the will of God. He is moved neither by the accord nor condemnation of man. Whosoever seeks honor from man or is self-aggrandizing inevitably reaps dishonor; but one who unconditionally loves and obeys God, and serves God in all, receives immortal honor. Human fame elicits only empty words of praise, and perhaps a statue for the passing birds to roost on and soil. The God-known devotee secures a living monument in people's hearts. That is the true shrine of honor for every great one of God who has graced this world. In the heart of God, and in the hearts of millions down the centuries—that is where Jesus Christ is enshrined.

---

* One of the powers possessed by a great master is the ability to prevent any specific thought from arising in the mind of others. The God in Jesus communicated with the God present in the souls of the Nazarenes to induce a momentary lapse of their evil intent.

† John 4:44.

Jesus' Counsel to Ministers of God's Word

(Part I)

A True Minister Teaches Actual Contact of God to His Congregation

❖

Churches Should Emphasize Inner Development
More Than Oratory and Social Activities

❖

The Difference Between Christianity and Churchianity

❖

"Hives" of Organized Churches Should Be Filled
With the Honey of God's Presence

❖

The Paths of Outer and Inner Renunciation

❖

Avoiding Commercialism in Religion:
Jesus' Instructions on Money in the Ministry

"Jesus did not send out his disciples with theological degrees, but equipped them to preach the gospel through the example of their spiritual lives and with power born of God-contact felt in meditation."

*A*nd **when he had called** unto him his twelve disciples, he gave them power against unclean spirits, to cast them out, and to heal all manner of sickness and all manner of disease.

Now the names of the twelve apostles are these; the first, Simon, who is called Peter, and Andrew his brother; James the son of Zebedee, and John his brother; Philip, and Bartholomew; Thomas, and Matthew the publican; James the son of Alphaeus, and Lebbaeus, whose surname was Thaddaeus; Simon the Canaanite, and Judas Iscariot, who also betrayed him.

These twelve Jesus sent forth, and commanded them, saying, "Go not into the way of the Gentiles, and into any city of the Samaritans enter ye not: but go rather to the lost sheep of the house of Israel. And as ye go, preach, saying, 'The kingdom of heaven is at hand.' Heal the sick, cleanse the lepers, raise the dead, cast out devils: freely ye have received, freely give.

"Provide neither gold, nor silver, nor brass in your purses, nor scrip for your journey, neither two coats, neither shoes, nor yet staves: for the workman is worthy of his meat.

"And into whatsoever city or town ye shall enter, enquire who in it is worthy; and there abide till ye go thence. And when ye come into an house, salute it. And if the house be worthy, let your peace come upon it: but if it be not worthy, let your peace return to you. And whosoever shall not receive you, nor hear your words, when ye depart out of that house or city, shake off the dust of your feet. Verily I say unto you, it shall be more tolerable for the land of Sodom and Gomorrha in the day of judgment, than for that city."

—Matthew 10:1–15

After these things the Lord appointed other seventy also, and sent them two and two before his face into every city and place, whither he himself would come. Therefore said he unto them, "The harvest truly is great, but the labourers are few:

pray ye therefore the Lord of the harvest, that he would send forth labourers into his harvest.

"Go your ways: behold, I send you forth as lambs among wolves. Carry neither purse, nor scrip, nor shoes: and salute no man by the way.

"And into whatsoever house ye enter, first say, 'Peace be to this house.' And if the son of peace be there, your peace shall rest upon it: if not, it shall turn to you again.

"And in the same house remain, eating and drinking such things as they give: for the labourer is worthy of his hire. Go not from house to house. And into whatsoever city ye enter, and they receive you, eat such things as are set before you: And heal the sick that are therein, and say unto them, 'The kingdom of God is come nigh unto you.'

"But into whatsoever city ye enter, and they receive you not, go your ways out into the streets of the same, and say, 'Even the very dust of your city, which cleaveth on us, we do wipe off against you: notwithstanding be ye sure of this, that the kingdom of God is come nigh unto you.' But I say unto you, that it shall be more tolerable in that day for Sodom, than for that city."

—Luke 10:1–12 *

---

* Luke 10:1–16 consists of Jesus' instructions to the seventy disciples he sent out in addition to the twelve apostles, at a later time in his mission according to the story as told by Luke. (Luke is the only one of the four gospels that describes the sending out of the seventy.) Much of Jesus' counsel to the seventy is identical to that he gave to the twelve apostles as recorded in Matthew and Mark; therefore the sending out of the twelve and of the seventy are treated together in this and the next Discourse. (Luke 10:13–15 are omitted here, as they are commented on in Discourse 34 with the parallel verses from Matthew 11:20–24.)

Jesus' Counsel to Ministers of God's Word

(Part I)

𝒴

And when he had called unto him his twelve disciples, he gave them power against unclean spirits, to cast them out, and to heal all manner of sickness and all manner of disease (Matthew 10:1).*

As wealthy people can transfer their funds during their lifetime or after they are gone to anyone they choose, so also great prophets of Self-realization can by certain techniques transfer at will their spiritual ecstasies, God-wisdom, and healing power unto their true disciples. Jesus did not send out his disciples with theological degrees, but equipped them to preach the gospel through the example of their spiritual lives and with power born of God-contact felt in meditation, and the blessing of the grace he bestowed upon them.

∼

Now the names of the twelve apostles are these; the first, Simon, who is called Peter, and Andrew his brother; James the son of Zebedee, and John his brother; Philip, and Bartholomew; Thomas,

---

* Cf. parallel references in Mark 6:7 and Luke 9:1.

754

and Matthew the publican; James the son of Alphaeus, and Leb-
baeus, whose surname was Thaddaeus; Simon the Canaanite, and
Judas Iscariot, who also betrayed him (Matthew 10:2–4).*

Jesus gave his divine power to Judas along with the other eleven; but instead of using his free will to take advantage of his spiritual opportunity, Judas succumbed to delusion and became an instrument of evil. Even though Jesus gave to his disciples in equal measure, they each received and manifested his teachings differently according to their various degrees of spirituality and good and bad karma. The advanced disciples, such as Saint John, were completely liberated during the lifetime of Jesus; but Judas had to work out through many incarnations the evil karma of his act of betrayal of Jesus. According to certain great masters in India, Judas has been working out his sins for twenty centuries and was finally liberated in India in this twentieth century. The bad karma of Judas was prodigious because he not only sinned through an act of treachery against his Master, but also blasphemed against the Holy Ghost and God the Father (Cosmic Consciousness) manifest within the Christ in Jesus.

≈

These twelve Jesus sent forth, and commanded them, saying, "Go
not into the way of the Gentiles and into any city of the Samari-
tans enter ye not: but go rather to the lost sheep of the house of
Israel. And as ye go, preach, saying, 'The kingdom of heaven is at
hand.' Heal the sick, cleanse the lepers, raise the dead, cast out
devils: freely ye have received, freely give" (Matthew 10:5–8).†

Jesus knew he had come on earth to establish a great movement to uplift mankind. To disseminate his message, he chose twelve disciples to be apostles who could go forth to preach the truth and declare it by example. He blessed them with his spirit to demonstrate God's power by healing sickness of the body resulting from bad phys-

---

* Cf. parallel references in Mark 3:14–19 and Luke 6:13–16, in which Jesus ordains the twelve apostles (commented on in Discourse 33).

† Cf. parallel reference in Luke 9:2. See also Discourse 44 re "lost sheep of the house of Israel" (Matthew 15:24).

ical habits, mental sickness due to psychological errors and wrong thinking, and soul sickness effected by delusive ignorance; and to cast

Jesus endowed his disciples with divine power

out devils and banish metaphysical ignorance lodged in the three bodies of man, and also to free souls from the possession of Satan's evil agents.

In the modern world, preaching only in theory the staid dogma of theology or one's own imaginations about truth is quite the vogue. There are few real teachers left in the world who live the life—those who are in tune with God and who know how to heal physical, mental, and soul sickness by God's power, and who can cast out Satan's satellites present in the ignorance engulfing man's soul, in the psychological aberrations of anger, greed, lust, and other bad habits, and in the karma-engendered ailments of the body.

Jesus endowed his disciples with divine power so that they in turn could instill that power in true, receptive devotees to heal them, first and foremost, of ignorance, the primal cause of all human misery. Jesus also taught his apostles the art of developing dynamic will power for healing by cosmic energy and innate life force the afflicted bodies and minds of people who above all wanted spiritual awakening, but found themselves too enervated by their physical and psychological defects.

Jesus counseled his apostles as he prepared to send them out to serve other souls: "Do not follow after the Gentiles ('heathens or pagans,' being interpreted as spiritually indifferent worldly people), nor enter into any city of the rigid-minded Samaritans, but rather go to the shepherdless, truth-seeking, innocent souls of the true Israel, those who are pure lovers of God. Preach that the blissful kingdom of heaven is within every soul, and thus within reach of everyone. Heal the spiritually sick as well as the physically sick. Cleanse the lepers and those who are unclean with sinful habits. Raise the spiritually dead; and raise also, after you have judged their good and bad karma, any whom the Heavenly Father tells you should be brought back to life from physical death. Cast out Satan and his satellites from obsessed souls. You have received truth through the eagerness of your free will and by my free will; give this truth freely to those who spontaneously, without persuasion or compulsion, are willing to receive it."

The succeeding generations of Christian denominations and teachers have done much good in keeping alive the thought of Jesus

by recitation of his life and words, but rarely have they given actual God-contact to their congregations. For the most part, ministers and religious leaders are chosen according to their physical personality, oratorical power, organizing abil-   *A true minister teaches*
ity, or theological degrees, and not according to the   *actual contact of God*
quality of their Self-realization. Jesus and his disci- *to his congregation*
ples, possessing no theological degrees or intellec-
tual college education, nor instruction in elocution, preached what they knew from direct God-contact: "We speak that we do know, and testify that we have seen" (John 3:11).

How different are those who speak from realization from the many missionary types, both in the Orient and the Occident, who come forth from theological training to preach to others with the purpose of converting and holding followers with dogma. Appointed or self-elected soap-box orators can create intellectual or emotional upheavals in the minds of listeners to be sufficiently convincing, but they cannot save or uplift souls. To save others, one must first save oneself. To heal others, one must have healing power. Only those who are thoroughly grounded in meditation so that there is real contact of their hearts, minds, and souls with God (whether or not they have book learning) are qualified to teach. Intellectual or emotional preaching through the power of a good memory or creative imagination bears no comparison with spiritual preaching through example of a God-attuned life and consciousness.

Contact with God is evidenced in a holy life. The ego is diminished and replaced with an ever-increasing love for God and desire to follow His will alone. A truly holy person touches one's whole being with a "peace which passeth all understanding"* and radiates to all as kindness and goodwill. God-contact in deep meditation opens the channel of soul intuition and speaks through the inner guiding voice of conscience. God uses His great prophets to proclaim revelations; He speaks personally to His true devotees those revelations that will change them into God-loving beings who inspire others to become likewise. The exultations, visions, and divine oneness of God-contact come in good time to the advanced devotee who perseveres in deepening meditation; but God's presence is no less real in its subtle transforming power of inner peace, joy, understanding, and divine love.

* Philippians 4:7.

A true minister of truth hears the voice of God as inner intuitive inspiration and does not depend solely on running to a library to prepare undigested, unlived sermons. Jesus preached extensively to the masses; and in between gatherings, he retired to the seclusion of the desert or mountaintops to commune with God. Renewed in body and spirit, he came back to give his reinforced God-consciousness to the true seekers.

Ministers of churches and leaders of religious organizations should be selected according to their devotion to God and Self-realization attained through meditation. Persons of shallow spirituality, whose lives and understanding lack at least some degree of actual God-contact, can do little more than lead their followers down the path of ignorance; their ministry consists primarily of worrying themselves with the financial problems and fund-raisings of their organizations. But those who are themselves settled in God are the true ministers who can successfully transmit God to other souls.

Even business ethics demand that one should not attempt to sell a product without a thorough acquaintance with the article and a sincere belief in its usefulness. How unethical it is, then, to try to sell God to others without an inner intuitive perception of God and faith in what God is, and how in a supreme way He is essential to all.

The age-old tradition of India is that every would-be spiritual teacher must first learn to contact God and live a life of discipline under the tutelage of a divine teacher. They must be worthy disciples before they can be teachers of others. Any accredited disciple of a great teacher who lives and upholds his master's ideals is a person considered fit to teach.

It is exemplary when great teachers not only instruct their disciples in the ways of physical and mental healing by the system of dietetics and methods of concentration and prayer, but also initiate them in the highest technique of meditation to cure spiritual sickness by driving away the ignorance of delusion. Real divine ministers can teach spiritually advanced devotees more advancement and spiritually sick true seekers the art of healing themselves.

Religious denominations, in their modern form, do well in reminding people of the necessity of knowing God and truth; but to really serve, they should be universities of spiritual discipline and offer comprehensive practical training in God-contact as well as in spiritual living. A house of God should not be a social and moral organization only, but primarily a spiritual academy for training in actual God-perception.

Realization of God is the true and only purpose of churches and temples; all activities should be subservient to that cause. Genuine seekers fall away from congregational worship if they do not receive a real experience of God.

The usual method of most religious denominations has been to hold their people by inbred churchgoing habits, or by dogma and threats of eternal perdition, or by stimulating lectures and musical or festive entertainments. Congregations are often built on the personalities of oratorical ministers, trained like actors to effectively deliver the lines of their theoretical sermons. In the absence of that intellectual or emotional oratory, as also practiced musical performances and supplemental socials, the members in time lose interest if they have not received fulfillment in an inner experience of God-contact in meditation. The church cannot compete with professional entertainment and should not try to do so; the temple of God is a unique place where souls should come together to share the joy of God-communion.

Nor should huge sums of money be tied up in church edifices just to attract class-conscious persons with the grandeur of architecture, offering scarcely more than a place to see and be seen. There is nothing wrong in dedicating to God beautiful places of worship. But structural hives, regardless of their magnificence, are useless unless they are filled with the honey of God's presence.

As with churches in the West, many elaborate Hindu temples in India have become places of mechanical chanting and ritualism. Holy temples at first were places of meditation and worship for saintly souls and those who came for their blessings; but after their passing, priests or trustees with ambition for power and financial gain seized control and desecrated the sacred sanctuaries with their unspiritual commercial methods. Owing to this monopoly, great masters now avoid the temples in favor of sequestered nooks and simple *mandirs* where they teach the methods of attaining Self-realization to selected students, less by preaching and more by meditating with them in the inner temple of God-contact. Sermons may create the desire to know God, but meditation with great saints or according to their methods gives one the knowledge and bliss of actual God-communion.

Holy ones of God illumine the way, but ascendancy to God is through the eager striving of the devotee, along with divine blessings. As one cannot satisfy his hunger if somebody else eats for him, so a master's intercession and guidance prepares the divine feast of God-realization,

Teach universal moral and spiritual truths instead of untested dogmas

but it is for the devotee to partake of the blessed manna. What is the use of unqualified teachers of religion coercing followers to believe blindly in untested dogmas which the propounders themselves have not assimilated and proven within their own experience to be true? Instead of stuffing dogma into the trusting minds of their congregations, religious leaders should nourish those minds with greater love and eagerness for God-realization, and with stimulating truths of universal wisdom. Rather than conducting only stilted services and scripture classes in which the members are passive recipients, the congregation should be reorganized to do more of their own introspective thinking and silent prayer and meditation.

It would be a more peaceful, harmonious world if the various religions and religious denominations ceased condemnation of paths different from their own. Instead of fighting about the infallibility and exclusivity of their respective dogmas, they should foster a spirit of unity based on the commonality of the real meaning of life and man's relationship with his Creator. The universal moral and spiritual codes of discipline for right human behavior that are basic to all true religions would be found to be a universal spiritual treatise on the art of moral and spiritual living. It would be a "Code Book of All Religions," of the psycho-ethical laws that can really daily uplift and help humanity to come together in brotherhood under the one Fatherhood-Motherhood of God.

Sankhya, Yoga, and Vedanta, three comprehensive philosophies of India, are pragmatic and meant directly to discipline human activity so that it will yield the highest wisdom and final emancipation. The Sankhya philosophy teaches that the cardinal necessity of man consists in destroying the roots of the threefold suffering of body, mind, and soul so that there is no possibility of recurrence. It describes the spiritual cosmology of creation and man's place in the divine schema. Yoga is the science of the step-by-step-methods of progressive Self-realization that lead directly to God. According to the highest Hindu scripture, the Bhagavad Gita, Yoga is the supreme way, for it is the science of salvation. Vedanta is the doctrine of the Ultimate; it describes the goal of God-realization and the singularity of Spirit—of the One in the many and the many as naught else than the One. Yoga provides the technique by which the Ultimate Goal is realized. Vedanta describes the contents of the mine of divine wisdom; Yoga is the way to mine that knowledge for human use. In the combined religious experiences of these three philosophies, humanity will find the highest standard of right living that alone can produce ideal citizens of the world and of the kingdom of God.*

The purpose of a church is to give God-contact. If it claims to meet that criterion, then it must do so or it will cease to exist as a spiritual force. Toward this end, it is the paramount duty of all clerics to improve themselves by daily deep scientific meditation for communion with God, and to reform their congregations likewise with spiritual habits and the joy of divine communion. The Self-realization of true seekers would spontaneously,

External forms of congregational worship are of limited value for God-communion

without urging, hold those members to their respective path that is leading them to God. A strong congregation is united in uncoerced loyalty born of each member's Self-realization garnered from the inner discipline and meditation taught by the church or temple.

Services should not consist so much of various rituals of the body and mind required in chanting and choirs, standing up and kneeling down, intoned prayer, scripture recital, and other external ceremonial practices. Congregational worship should stress primarily meditation, interiorization with cessation of bodily motions, absence of mental restlessness, and the presence of God-contact. When bodily motions cease and thoughts become quiet, God begins to appear as the blessedness of stillness and divine bliss on the altar of peace and changelessness.

Congregational recitation of chants and prayers keeps the mind external. They may do some good, no doubt, to those whose concentration on the meaning is sincere and devout. But the effect remains limited unless supplemented by deep, secreted, soul-loving prayers in the quietness of solitude. The lack of individual prayer and communion with God has divorced modern Christians and Christian sects from Jesus' teaching of the real perception of God, as is true also of all religious paths inaugurated by God-sent prophets whose followers drift

---

* A synthesis of these three philosophies is provided in Paramahansa Yogananda's comprehensive commentary on the Bhagavad Gita, *God Talks With Arjuna.* Explaining the mysticism of Hindu thought, Paramahansaji shows the universality of the yoga science. *(Publisher's Note)*

into byways of dogma and ritual rather than actual God-communion. Those paths that have no esoteric soul-lifting training busy themselves with dogma and building walls to exclude people with different ideas. Divine persons who really perceive God include everybody within the path of their love, not in the concept of an eclectic congregation but in respectful divine friendship toward all true lovers of God and the saints of all religions.*

When church paraphernalia creates a top-heavy, scantily useful organization, it loses the spirit of Christ. His teaching emphasizes universal love and brotherhood; but that is not what one thinks of when one sees Christian sects disparaging one another over contradictory doctrines, or maligning non-Christian denominations as heathen. Where is Christ's ideal of deeds of mercy and goodness? Sermons *about* Jesus, but without the revealed essence of the *message* of the great Master, make the house of God just a place for worshiping the personality of God's earthly representative, or just a refuge from mundane responsibilities where one can soothe his worries in intellectual

---

* In *Lost Christianity* (New York: Jeremy P. Tarcher/Penguin, 2003), Dr. Jacob Needleman, professor of philosophy at San Francisco State University and former director of the Center for the Study of New Religions at the Graduate Theological Union in Berkeley, writes: "In my own academic work as a professor of philosophy and religion....it became increasingly clear to me that were Christianity actually to recover its own esoteric tradition, it would be a development of immense significance. In using this term, 'esoteric,' I mean to say the Christianity that works, that actually produces real change in human nature, real transformation....

"Weren't Westerners now being attracted to Oriental religions because they could find in them the sort of methods for inner work that may have been predominant among the early Fathers?...Where did [those methods] come from? Where have they gone? The whole modern world is beginning to look for them as an indispensable element of what has been lost from the Christian path."

Professor Needleman cites the work of Dom Aelred Graham, a pioneering Catholic monk and prior of a Benedictine monastery in England: "The very future of the Christian tradition may depend, according to Dom Aelred, 'on reviewing its basic doctrines in the light of religious insights now being made available from the East.'...Dom Aelred therefore urges that the contemporary Christian seek after the attainment of a transformed quality of consciousness in himself, 'the God-centered consciousness of Jesus,' just as the Mahayana Buddhist strives to attain for himself the same level of being as the Buddha."

"That this happens to be what Christianity is all about is rather more than hinted at in passages from both the Pauline epistles and the Fourth Gospel," writes Aelred Graham in *Contemplative Christianity* (New York: Seabury Press, 1974). "Could it be that in striving to attain the Christ-consciousness we have the only effective foundation for Christian renewal? To achieve 'the mind of Christ' may well demand a profound rethinking of Christianity's prayer life." *(Publisher's Note)*

or emotional sermons, or a comfortable place to be temporarily stirred by ritual and good music without any self-effort to center one's thoughts upon God. Whatever be the practices in the Lord's house, they should not be to the neglect of direct individual communion with God. Otherwise, the holy precincts are changed into a den where thieves of restless material thoughts and vibrations of dogmatic bigotry disguised in holy robes hold supreme sway. "It is written, 'My house shall be called the house of prayer; but ye have made it a den of thieves.'"* Silent inner prayer of pure devotion to God is the common denominator that can unite the denominations of all religions in the love of God.

In the hermitages of India where great masters live, there is very little of that form of preaching in which the master does most of the thinking for the disciples—as it is done in the Western churches. Instead, in India's hermitages that follow the ancient tradition of her lineage of saints, the master and the disciple often sit together to discuss spiritual principles; and then together, or individually, through proven techniques of concentration and meditation, they try to commune with God and to realize truth through the direct experience of soul intuition.

Western churches will profit spiritually when they have become temples where both leaders and members in unison can commune with God and with the Christ Consciousness that was manifest in Jesus. Therein is where Christianity is different from churchianity. Establish Christ first in the hearts of men, then he will reign in the church also.

The difference between Christianity and churchianity

"In the churches, temples, tabernacles, mosques, the realization of Christ Consciousness is with me; no limitations bind me. I am of the Infinite Christ, the blissful *Kutastha Chaitanya*." That is the chord of unity around which all melodies of life can be played in harmony. "I want to pray to God with the language of the soul and the yearning of all hearts. Then, O Lord, thousands will hearken and follow Thee." Christ cannot be monopolized by any self-selected group claiming to be the only true followers. Christ belongs to all, regardless of religion, race, or generation. Every devotee of Jesus should ask himself if he is truly a modern-day Christian. Those who are sincere should discipline

---

* Matthew 21:13 (see Discourse 64).

763

the body and soul with divine communion. In the morning and in the darkest, quietest hours of night in meditation, they should open the soul as a lotus bud. Then they can say, "Come! Him whom I feel in my heart, of him I preach. Come, follow the Christ which is in my heart and in my actions."

In the West, one who aspires to be a spiritual teacher by virtue of his personality or intellect often starts his career by first desiring to build a church and a denomination of his own. From the beginning he involves and entangles himself in financial difficulties, obliging him to concentrate primarily on fund-raising. Money and desire for the fame and false glory of claiming many followers have kept the churches and temples in spiritual stagnation. Instead of first concentrating on the building of ornate edifices with heavy mortgages, teachers should establish the temples of Self-realization in the souls of their followers.

What is necessary for the revival of true churches of Christ is not new denominations, but the real teachings of Christ and the living of those teachings, improving the quality of church members by meditation, and the selection of God-known, God-contacting ministers. The failings of churchianity can be abolished and real Christianity be brought back into the church if the churches are made places of worship by members who practice meditation in their homes and also as part of their congregational services. The atmosphere of nonsectarian meditation for deep inner God-communion would change churches from the divisiveness of churchianity into the heaven of Christ Consciousness or Christ-ianity.

Every spiritual teacher should pass his life more in meditation, and in order to be able to transmit spirituality to real seekers—those whom he meets through the will of God and proper moral publicity—regularly meditate with them whenever he can, in small groups, preferably in quiet or secluded centrally located places. If churches get together and follow the above practice they will bring about a real revival of Christ Consciousness in the hearts of true worshipers. In deeply meditating together in small sincere groups, such seekers will find that the Christ Consciousness which was in Jesus will manifest in them and bring about in their consciousness the Second Coming of Christ.

"Hives" of organized churches should be filled with the honey of God's presence

If this spiritual nucleus of devout devotees then wants to build a church, it is commendable; for they will then be qualified to fill that hive with the honey of God's presence. The leader should be under no constraint to cater to or flatter others for monetary gain. He must faithfully make time daily to keep his most important engagement with God in meditation. The pure vibrations of a true minister draw those devotees who really seek God. Such souls, by receiving the blessing of their own realization, will give loyal support to a leader whose spiritual demeanor and moral behavior give sincere evidence of his communion with God.

God makes no distinction between rich and poor, fame or no fame. A successful minister is often equated with an elaborate church in an aristocratic neighborhood, attended by a rich, influential congregation. In sending forth his first apostles, Jesus gave a hint to all generations as to where churches should be built and to whom the teachings should be given. Suitable areas, aristocratic or poor, are those in which there is spiritual interest. That is where to build a foundation, wherever people repent of their earthly folly and like lost sheep are sincerely seeking return to the fold of God-consciousness.

Thus did Jesus command his disciples that they should not go to the self-satisfied worldly people, "the Gentiles," worshipers of gods of fame and fortune, or to the Samaritans, fixed in their convictions, but rather to the truth-seekers who are repentant for having strayed away from God. "Vibrate into them your God-realization and show them that the kingdom of heaven, the state of attunement with the heavenly powers of astral vibration, wisdom, bliss, and God-consciousness, lies within their reach, just behind the human consciousness of wakefulness and subconsciousness, in the state of superconsciousness and God-contact as realized in deep meditation. As you heal the soul of material consciousness by establishing the kingdom of heaven or God-consciousness there, so also heal the ailments of the bodily instrument of the soul.

"Free the truly repentant God-seekers not only from physical sickness but also from mental, moral, and spiritual sickness. Raise spiritually dead people into the consciousness of God; and by transmitting your God-power, release them from devils and obsessions of cosmic delusion and Satanic ignorance and evil disembodied souls. Bring to life the good departed souls who have more good than evil karma, or at least equal good and bad karma, because such acts are now sanctioned by the Heavenly Father to assure benighted mankind that all things are possible with God's true devotees and followers of the path of goodness. The worthy souls you resurrect will do much good on earth.

"You have received by your own free accord, through your uninfluenced, spontaneously spiritual free will, and through my own free will and God's divine compassion, the God-consciousness transmitted into your self-disciplined meditating lives. In the way you have grasped God-consciousness, teach the same to the people. You exercised your divine ardor, reason, and free will to meditate and advance spiritually, and so you awakened the spontaneous response in God and desire in me to transmit into you Our divine consciousness. Likewise teach other devotees to rouse their free will and to meditate and thereby receive the God-consciousness freely available to them."

Truth cannot be received just by listening to dogmatic, moral, or scriptural sermons, but must come by the above law of the spontaneous, uncoaxed spiritual ardor and spiritual labor of the devotees and the responding divine compassion of God in granting them Self-realization.

~

"Provide neither gold, nor silver, nor brass in your purses, nor scrip for your journey, neither two coats, neither shoes, nor yet staves: for the workman is worthy of his meat.

"And into whatsoever city or town ye shall enter, inquire who in it is worthy; and there abide till ye go thence. And when ye come into an house, salute it. And if the house be worthy, let your peace be upon it: but if it be not worthy, let your peace return to you" (Matthew 10:9–13).

Parallel references:

And commanded them that they should take nothing for their journey, save a staff only; no scrip, no bread, no money in their purse: but be shod with sandals; and not put on two coats. And he said unto them, "In what place soever ye enter into an house, there abide till ye depart from that place" (Mark 6:8–10).

---

* Cf. additional parallel reference in Luke 9:3–4.

* * *

After these things the Lord appointed other seventy also, and sent them two and two before his face into every city and place, whither he himself would come. Therefore said he unto them, "The harvest truly is great, but the labourers are few: pray ye therefore the Lord of the harvest, that he would send forth labourers into his harvest.

"Go your ways: behold, I send you forth as lambs among wolves. Carry neither purse, nor scrip, nor shoes: and salute no man by the way.

"And into whatsoever house ye enter, first say, 'Peace be to this house.' And if the son of peace be there, your peace shall rest upon it: if not, it shall turn to you again.

"And in the same house remain, eating and drinking such things as they give: for the labourer is worthy of his hire. Go not from house to house. And into whatsoever city ye enter, and they receive you, eat such things as are set before you: And heal the sick that are therein, and say unto them, 'The kingdom of God is come nigh unto you'" (Luke 10:1–9).

J esus was saddened that most people were satisfied just to join the services in the synagogue, but there were few spiritual laborers who deserved to reap the rich harvest of eternal abundance in God's kingdom.* To awaken the people from their doldrums of delusion, he sent his disciples before him to preach the gospel, not as salaried missionaries, but as selfless adepts who would live the life as preached by Christ, and similarly preach the truth in word and deed. Under whatever conditions one speaks the word of God, what matters most is the example of a holy life.

Jesus sent out his disciples not as salaried preachers but as selfless renunciants

"After being true devotee-laborers who have reaped the harvest of wisdom and God-contact, go forth to the world to share your divine realization with others. In your travels, do not burden your consciousness with dependence on material things; take no monies in your purse nor extra clothing. Do not salute any man on the way, tarrying

---

* For commentary on "the harvest truly is great, but the labourers are few," see Discourse 38.

in useless conversations; keep your mind within on thoughts of God, giving Him the highest respect of your undivided attention.

"Into whatever city or town you enter, find out who are spiritual and worthiest to receive your message of salvation; there abide in the harmonious vibration of that household, accepting their hospitality as your ministerial wage, until you have finished your counsel in that area and are ready to go elsewhere to help others. Into whatever house you enter, salute its inhabitants humbly as manifestations of God. If that house be spiritually deserving, then bless it to feel your soul's peace. But if you find it unreceptive and unappreciative, pray for those who dwell therein, but let your rejected gift of peace return into your soul.

"Wheresoever they receive you, eat and drink whatever is given you, heal the sick, and tell them God's kingdom of heavenly bliss lies hidden very near, just behind their waking consciousness. Teach them by meditation to enter into the Cosmic Consciousness of that divine kingdom."

In the above verses, Jesus tells the way his disciples should live in the world during the time they preach his gospel to his people. It parallels the uniting of the two distinct paths followed in India by spiritually aspiring devotees. First, the school of outer renunciation; second, the school of yoga, which enjoins mental renunciation and nonattachment while living in the world.

A follower of the path of outer renunciation leaves the world, does not marry, divests himself of personal possessions and human re-

The paths of outer and inner renunciation

lations, and seeks a secluded place, such as an ashram, where undisturbed by worldly intrusions, the devotee can pursue his *sadhana* for attaining God-realization. The Order of Swamis belongs to the path of renunciation, akin to monastic orders in the West.*

The path of yoga, the uniting of the soul with Spirit through the practice of scientific meditation techniques of God-contact, can be followed by devotees in all walks of life. A yogi does not necessarily have

---

* Speaking of the first Christian monastic communities (the Desert Fathers), which were formed in Egypt in the early centuries following the life of Jesus, British historian Sir Charles Eliot writes: "Egypt was a most religious country, but it does not appear that asceticism, celibacy, or meditation formed part of its older religious life, and their appearance in Hellenistic times may be due to a wave of Asian influence starting originally from India." —*Hinduism and Buddhism,* Volume III.

to be in the world as a householder or to leave the world as a monastic. Whether yogis live in the civilized jungle of physical luxury or in the primitive conditions away from material influences and comforts, by tuning in with the Infinite they seek to become so concentrated on divine bliss that automatically their minds will rise above and inwardly renounce the desire for material fulfillments.

A true yogi is a practitioner of real renunciation, even if he lives in the world and to outer appearances looks like any ordinary person of the world. The advanced yogi, having inwardly renounced all desires and attachments, remains intoxicated with God. Such yogis do not mind obeying fastidiously, as well, the laws of outward renunciation. Lahiri Mahasaya was a sublime exemplar of a householder yogi; he took no formal vows of renunciation but no taint of worldly consciousness dared touch his sanctity.

The devotee of outer renunciation, on the other hand, forswears all material luxuries in the beginning to accustom his consciousness to the simple life and the nonattachment native to his soul—the prerequisite renunciation of worldly pleasures and worldly ways of living before one can know God. But though an aspirant renounce everything outwardly, he may yet remain inwardly attached to mundane objects and be haunted by sensual desires. The yogi says, "Have God-contact first through meditation; and then through attachment to God the attachment to material objects will drop away." The yogi who practices the scientific meditation technique of actual God-contact belongs to the highest spiritual path. The physical austerities of renunciation alone without the yoga of God-union is unnecessarily arduous. Therefore, even the devout renunciant ought to be a yogi as well.

The path of outer renunciation is successfully followed only by the few; the path of yoga can be followed by all. Devotees may choose the path of renunciation or the path of yoga as suitable according to their differing temperaments; but to be a yogi as well as a renunciant is wonderful. Outward as well as inward renunciation is ideal for those with a single-hearted yearning for God—for those devotees of God who, without the obligations and entanglements of a family, can give their full time to seeking God through yoga and unreserved service to God and all mankind.

Jesus was a yogi, constantly engaged in divine union, and a man of renunciation as well. He not only contacted God in his spirit and inwardly rose above all material attachments, but he also practiced nonattachment to material things in his outward life. He instructed his apostles likewise to be men of renunciation along with the inner wisdom and Self-realization they possessed. Jesus Christ first empowered his disciples with God-consciousness and then advised them: "O my disciples, who are divinely charged and permeated with God and His healing powers, show your exalted spiritual example of having overcome the world by taking nothing for your journey that would indicate a sense of luxury for the body or dependence on material security for your needs."

As similarly advocated by Jesus, the Buddhist monks of India from pre-Christian times and the members of the Swami Order in India confined their possessions chiefly to a staff and simple dress; and most of the time they went barefoot or wore wooden or woven-straw sandals —shoes made from the hides of slaughtered animals being considered unclean and unholy.

Jesus' instructions to his disciples were apropos to the times and climate, presenting a truly holy example for the people of his country. I am sure Jesus, or any Oriental teacher, would greatly modify the dress code and other rules of renunciation to be followed by those disciples who live under different conditions or in cold countries.

Barefooted or sandal-shod swamis in India who are clad only in simple cotton *dhotis* when in the warm regions dress sensibly in warmer attire when they go to the cold regions of the Himalayas. Even so, I have seen some great swamis and yogis in secluded haunts of the frigid mountain regions bare-bodied without suffering from cold or any effects of exposure to extreme weather. The garb one wears, or the lack of it, and other external expressions of renunciation do not necessarily make one spiritual. I have always stressed to the monks and nuns of Self-Realization Fellowship who have chosen to follow the path of renunciation I have embraced: "First make your heart a hermitage and your robe the love of God."

Avoiding commercialism in religion: Jesus' instructions on money in the ministry

Jesus further instructs his disciples as to how they should maintain themselves: "O ye divine renunciants, remember that just as the skilled workman earns his honest livelihood by his labor, so you, as divine workmen giving to people the highest spiritual service and salvation, deserve to receive your bodily maintenance from those you help. Even though I ask you to live humbly by the grateful charity of the people you serve, always retain the consciousness that you are not beggars, but divine children made in the almighty image of God." A spiritual man who is sincerely engaged in offering the public the highest service, that of saving souls, lives very honorably even though he exists by alms and the goodwill of those he serves.

In the West, owing to the high cost of living, ministers receive salaries. But the one baneful result of this subsistence is that the minister is often thereby controlled by the trustees or board of a church; and if he, as an employee, does not agree to the course outlined by his "employers," he runs the chance of being discharged, just as a clerk in an office may be discharged for refusal to obey his superior.

In the centers of religious concentration in India, there are institutions where swamis and yogis may freely board without any obligations whatsoever. This arrangement is intended to foster the growth of real teachers who want to devote themselves exclusively to the cause of spiritual welfare, without the time-devouring distractions of gainful ordinary employment. The concomitant evil that arises is from abuse of this beneficence by persons who simply do not care to put forth the effort to maintain themselves; they don the garb of renunciants to enjoy free board and lodging from such religious institutions. Nevertheless, this provision for real spiritual teachers immensely helps the growth of advanced souls by freeing them from the control of a board of trustees or philanthropic gifts compromised with conditions.

In the Western world, sometimes religious teachers who are not satisfied with their limited ministerial salary try to utilize various other means of fund-raising in the guise of providing for God's work, but from which they personally benefit. There is no sin for ministers or religious teachers to arrange to maintain themselves financially so that they can be free to help without interruption the growth of spirituality in the world, provided that neither God nor their followers are exploited for that purpose. I have always maintained that it is all right in the modern world to use business methods in religion, but that it is blasphemy and a grievous spiritual sin to use religion for business or to trade upon the sacred name of God or dupe sincere devotees to satisfy one's personal ambition for financial gain and luxurious habits.

Teachers who promote their self-envisioned greatness by publicizing falsehoods claiming contact with God and that they have been commissioned by masters and saints are no more than metaphysical racketeers. If truth-seekers of the West followed the discriminating method of India, that only those teachers are qualified who truly live the spiritual life and who are definitely known to have practiced and achieved self-mastery under a great living master or bona fide lineage established by such a master, they would avoid being disillusioned by the antics of self-elected pseudoprophets.

The aim of false prophets is always the same, to gratify their ego with the adoration of a large following and to reap financial gain from their trusting flock. Maintaining a church or religious organization by freewill offerings received at services and religious meetings and from funds received from book sales and other media of disseminating truth is spiritually legitimate if the money is used for propagating the spiritual cause and for the reasonable livelihood of the teacher who gives all his life to the spreading of the divine work. However, it is condemnable if such funds are diverted to line the pockets of unscrupulous pseudoprophets and their acolytes.

The instruction of Jesus to the apostles he sent forth made these spiritual ideals of ministry unequivocally clear. Times change, as well as the external modes of expression; but the ideals are invariable. A teacher of God's word must be an exemplar of the highest ideals of self-abnegation for the greater love of serving God and truth-seeking souls. Concentration was to be on those who were "worthy," receptive, regardless of their station—high or low, rich or poor, certainly not just the wealthy or influential from which favors can be sought.

The commercial religious teacher uses his students to further his own ends; the true spiritual teacher guides the attention of devotees to bring them unto God.

~

"And whosoever shall not receive you, nor hear your words, when ye depart out of that house or city, shake off the dust of your feet. Verily I say unto you, it shall be more tolerable for the land of Sodom and Gomorrha in the day of judgment, than for that city" (Matthew 10:14–15).

Parallel reference:

"But into whatsoever city ye enter, and they receive you not, go your ways out into the streets of the same, and say, 'Even the

very dust of your city, which cleaveth on us, we do wipe off against you: notwithstanding be ye sure of this, that the kingdom of God is come nigh unto you.' But I say unto you, that it shall be more tolerable in that day for Sodom, than for that city" (Luke *10:10–12*).*

"And whosoever will not appreciate your exemplary lives, nor receive your message of divine liberation, nor listen to your words of wisdom, depart you, without anger or arrogance, from that house or city and shake off the dust of their disbelief and disdain; let not their evil vibrations cling to you. Let your humble act of response to their rejection and scorn be a testament before their own conscience of the folly of the ignorance of their evil natures. Verily I say unto you that the law of karma will record and punish that city or home that refused your soul-liberating message — in which you demonstrated 'that the kingdom of God is come nigh unto you' — even more than Sodom or Gomorrha suffered due to the effects of their ignorance-induced misdeeds. The judgment of the Cosmic Law will be severe against those spiritual offenders who blaspheme against God by not recognizing you who are divine representatives of the Christ Intelligence and God the Father."

---

* Cf. additional parallel references in Mark 6:11 and Luke 9:5.

DISCOURSE 41

Jesus' Counsel to Ministers of God's Word

(Part II)

The Wisdom and Peace Bestowed
by Awakening of Kundalini and the Spiritual Eye

❖

Overcoming Trials and Persecutions in the Spiritual Path

❖

The Sword of Wisdom and Self-Control
to Fight Unspiritual Temptations and Influences

❖

Conquering Satan Who Fell Like Lightning From Heaven

❖

God Is Revealed Not by Intellectuality,
but by Pure and Guileless Devotion

---

*"Jesus lovingly urged all spiritual aspirants to 'Come unto me' (the
Christ Consciousness) and 'Take my yoke upon you' — follow the step-
by-step methods of self-discipline that lead to Christ Consciousness
and that assure ultimate liberation in God's kingdom."*

"**Behold, I send you forth** as sheep in the midst of wolves: be ye therefore wise as serpents, and harmless as doves. But beware of men: for they will deliver you up to the councils, and they will scourge you in their synagogues; and ye shall be brought before governors and kings for my sake, for a testimony against them and the Gentiles. But when they deliver you up, take no thought how or what ye shall speak: for it shall be given you in that same hour what ye shall speak. For it is not ye that speak, but the Spirit of your Father which speaketh in you.

"And the brother shall deliver up the brother to death, and the father the child: and the children shall rise up against their parents, and cause them to be put to death. And ye shall be hated of all men for my name's sake: but he that endureth to the end shall be saved.

"But when they persecute you in this city, flee ye into another: for verily I say unto you, ye shall not have gone over the cities of Israel, till the Son of man be come. The disciple is not above his master, nor the servant above his lord. It is enough for the disciple that he be as his master, and the servant as his lord. If they have called the master of the house Beelzebub, how much more shall they call them of his household?

"Fear them not therefore: for there is nothing covered, that shall not be revealed; and hid, that shall not be known. What I tell you in darkness, that speak ye in light: and what ye hear in the ear, that preach ye upon the housetops.

"And fear not them which kill the body, but are not able to kill the soul: but rather fear Him which is able to destroy both soul and body in hell.

"Are not two sparrows sold for a farthing? and one of them shall not fall on the ground without your Father. But the very hairs of your head are all numbered. Fear ye not therefore, ye are of more value than many sparrows.

"Whosoever therefore shall confess me before men, him will I confess also before my Father which is in heaven. But *whosoever shall deny me before men, him will I also deny before my Father which is in heaven.*

"Think not that I am come to send peace on earth: I came not to send peace, but a sword. For I am come to set a man at variance against his father, and the daughter against her mother, and the daughter in law against her mother in law. And a man's foes shall be they of his own household. He that loveth father or mother more than me is not worthy of me: and he that loveth son or daughter more than me is not worthy of me. And he that taketh not his cross, and followeth after me, is not worthy of me. He that findeth his life shall lose it: and he that loseth his life for my sake shall find it.

"He that receiveth you receiveth me, and he that receiveth me receiveth Him that sent me. He that receiveth a prophet in the name of a prophet shall receive a prophet's reward; and he that receiveth a righteous man in the name of a righteous man shall receive a righteous man's reward.

"And whosoever shall give to drink unto one of these little ones a cup of cold water only in the name of a disciple, verily I say unto you, he shall in no wise lose his reward."

And it came to pass, when Jesus had made an end of commanding his twelve disciples, he departed thence to teach and to preach in their cities.

—Matthew 10:16—11:1

And they went out, and preached that men should repent. And they cast out many devils, and anointed with oil many that were sick, and healed them.... *

And the apostles gathered themselves together unto Jesus, and told him all things, both what they had done, and what they had taught. And he said unto them, "Come ye yourselves apart into a desert place, and rest a while": for there were many coming and going, and they had no leisure so much as to eat.

—Mark 6:12–13, 30–31

––––––––––

* Mark 6:14–29 (as also Matthew 14:3–12) recounts the death of John the Baptist, covered in Discourse 34.

"He that heareth you heareth me; and he that despiseth you despiseth me; and he that despiseth me despiseth Him that sent me."

And the seventy returned again with joy, saying, "Lord, even the devils are subject unto us through thy name."

And he said unto them, "I beheld Satan as lightning fall from heaven. Behold, I give unto you power to tread on serpents and scorpions, and over all the power of the enemy; and nothing shall by any means hurt you. Notwithstanding in this rejoice not, that the spirits are subject unto you; but rather rejoice, because your names are written in heaven."

In that hour Jesus rejoiced in spirit, and said, "I thank Thee, O Father, Lord of heaven and earth, that Thou hast hid these things from the wise and prudent, and hast revealed them unto babes: even so, Father; for so it seemed good in Thy sight.

"All things are delivered to me of my Father: and no man knoweth who the Son is, but the Father; and who the Father is, but the Son, and he to whom the Son will reveal Him."

And he turned him unto his disciples, and said privately, "Blessed are the eyes which see the things that ye see: For I tell you, that many prophets and kings have desired to see those things which ye see, and have not seen them; and to hear those things which ye hear, and have not heard them."

—Luke 10:16—24 *

[Matthew 11:25—27 parallels Luke 10:21—22, but in a slightly different context of time and place, concluding with:]

"Come unto me, all ye that labour and are heavy laden, and I will give you rest. Take my yoke upon you, and learn of me; for I am meek and lowly in heart: and ye shall find rest unto your souls. For my yoke is easy, and my burden is light."

—Matthew 11:28—30

---

* See footnote in Discourse 40, page 753, about the seventy disciples whom Jesus sent out to preach in addition to the twelve apostles.

Jesus' Counsel to Ministers of God's Word

(Part II)

꿏

"Behold, I send you forth as sheep in the midst of wolves: be ye therefore wise as serpents and harmless as doves" (Matthew 10:16).

Parallel reference:

"Go your ways: behold, I send you forth as lambs among wolves" (Luke 10:3).

"Wherever you go, my consciousness must be manifest in you; keep yourselves always humble, inoffensive, unrevengeful, like meek lambs, even when you are surrounded by ravenous wolves of ruthless, conscienceless people and predacious satanic sense temptations that are everywhere present in worldly environments. Abide at all times in great wisdom and calmness born of the divine realization you have received by awakening your serpent force (the coiled divine energy that rises up in the spine and opens the astral cerebrospinal centers of spiritual perception) and in the peace you have acquired by concentrating your consciousness in the peace-producing, dovelike spiritual eye."

The wisdom and peace bestowed by awakening of kundalini and the spiritual eye

779

It is not generally understood what Jesus meant when he spoke of being wise as serpents and harmless as doves. Ordinary serpents have no wisdom, are quick to anger, and are stupid enough to court their own death by biting people. Doves are not altogether harmless, for they can spread mites and disease. Even though the dove might be traditionally a symbol of peace for its peaceful looks and behavior, the serpent certainly does not look wise or inspiring. Since Jesus was addressing his advanced disciples, he used these words metaphorically, in an esoteric sense.

As previously explained [in Discourse 14], the Oriental scriptures employ the simile of a serpent to illustrate the *kundalini* or astral life force in the body, which, when awakened with the help of an advanced technique of Self-realization, passes through a serpentine coiled passage at the base of the spine upward to the highest spiritual centers in the brain, bestowing divine consciousness. The dove symbolizes the tricolored spiritual eye—the mouth of the dove representing the white star in the middle of the spiritual eye; the blue and gold spherical rings surrounding the star symbolizing the wings of the dove.*

A person in ordinary consciousness, identified with the minutiae of his little ego's senses, reason, and feeling, perceives himself circumscribed by his body, family, society, country, world, and a certain portion of space. But when by scientific meditation he awakens his serpent force, he reverses the searchlight of his awareness from physical sense consciousness to divine consciousness. Taking his *kundalini* force upward through the cerebrospinal centers and penetrating his life and consciousness through the spiritual eye, he beholds himself as omnipresent. His perception is restricted no longer to a limited sphere of matter and the sensations in one body, but expands into perception of the infinite reaches of space and awareness of the sensations of all beings.

The devotee who perceives through his spiritual eye his omnipresent existence, who feels an ineffable peace and attunement with every thing and every living creature, and who beholds all selves as manifestations of his own being, becomes harmless to all, equally loving the different parts of his own cosmic body. Awakened in eternal wisdom, the realization of his true Self, he cannot in any wise be in-

---

* See Discourse 6, commentary on declaration of John the Baptist when he baptized Jesus: "I saw the Spirit descending from heaven like a dove, and it abode upon him" (John 1:32).

wardly disturbed or incited to evil actions no matter how provoked by trials and temptations.

Jesus knew that his advanced disciples had awakened their higher consciousness by rousing the *kundalini* divine life energy through practice of the methods of meditation he had taught them. Therefore he reminded them to retain the deep wisdom and calmness bestowed by *kundalini* awakening when confronted with opposition and persecution. Anyone who has lifted up this coiled life energy and thereby elevated his human consciousness into Christ Consciousness by penetrating through the spiritual eye has acquired tremendous miraculous power; such a one could destroy by divine will force his would-be enemies, as well as satanic temptations.* That is why Jesus warned his disciples not to use their powerful awakened energy in vengeful retaliation when confronted by the wickedness of erring children of God; but rather to overcome enemies with the celestial power of God's infinite peace and love, with which they were blessed in the baptism of their consciousness by the spiritual eye, the dove of light.†

All Christlike souls aspiring to attain the kingdom of God must behave divinely and resist evil only by soul force, even as God resists Satan by divine forces of goodness. Evil cannot be conquered by the evil use of spiritual power. To use divine power for evil purposes is blasphemy and conducive to spiritual downfall. The soul force acquired by arduous meditative effort is quickly lost if one employs it under the influence of the intoxication of delusion to wreak vengeance against one's own divine brethren.‡

---

* See also pages 798 ff. of this Discourse, where Jesus tells the disciples he has given them "power to tread on serpents," i.e., power over all satanic material temptations engendered by the outgoing life force and consciousness.

† Saint Paul emphasized this teaching of Jesus in letters he wrote to those in his ministry:

"Stand therefore, having your loins girt about with truth, and having on the breastplate of righteousness; and your feet shod with the preparation of the gospel of peace; above all, taking the shield of faith, wherewith ye shall be able to quench all the fiery darts of the wicked. And take the helmet of salvation, and the sword of the Spirit, which is the word of God" (Ephesians 6:14–17).

"For the weapons of our warfare are not carnal, but mighty through God to the pulling down of strong holds; casting down imaginations, and every high thing that exalteth itself against the knowledge of God, and bringing into captivity every thought to the obedience of Christ" (II Corinthians 10:4–5).

‡ Jesus emphasizes this even more in Luke 9:54–56, when the disciples ask him if they should call fire from heaven to destroy those who opposed them. (See Discourse 49.)

Jesus wanted his disciples to set a different example for habitually belligerent human beings, that the indomitable wisdom and peace of the meditation-awakened soul is stronger than the mightiest forces of evil.

∽

"But beware of men: for they will deliver you up to the councils, and they will scourge you in their synagogues; and ye shall be brought before governors and kings for my sake, for a testimony against them and the Gentiles" (Matthew 10:17–18).*

J esus prophesied as to the persecutions his disciples would meet at the hands of uncomprehending men: "You will be delivered up to the judges and be whipped in the synagogues for preaching the gospel of divine freedom. You shall be taken to task before governors and kings for living the principles of my path of truth. Materially minded men, 'the Gentiles,' and the political forces who thus oppose you will themselves be condemned before a higher tribunal. Their evil treatment of you, when for my sake you will give testimony to the truth in me, will remain as evidence that will testify against them during the judgment delivered by Cosmic Law."

∽

"But when they deliver you up, take no thought how or what ye shall speak: for it shall be given you in that same hour what ye shall speak. For it is not ye that speak, but the Spirit of your Father which speaketh in you" (Matthew 10:19–20).

Parallel references:

"But when they shall lead you, and deliver you up, take no thought beforehand what ye shall speak, neither do ye premeditate: but whatsoever shall be given you in that hour, that speak ye: for it is not ye that speak, but the Holy Ghost" (Mark 13:11).

* * *

---

* Cf. parallel references in Mark 13:9 and Luke 21:12–13.

*"And when they bring you into the synagogues, and unto mag-
istrates, and powers, take ye no thought how or what thing ye
shall answer, or what ye shall say: for the Holy Ghost shall teach
you in the same hour what ye ought to say" (Luke 12:11–12).*

* * *

*"Settle it therefore in your hearts, not to meditate before what
ye shall answer: for I will give you a mouth and wisdom, which
all your adversaries shall not be able to gainsay nor resist" (Luke
21:14–15).*

Jesus tells advanced devotees to use their attunement with the Holy
Ghost Cosmic Vibration and its wisdom, and not the ego with its
limitations, for general guidance of conduct in crit-
ical moments. The speech of most persons in such   *Be guided not by ego*
situations is guided by selfishness, fear, and pen-   *but by intuitive di-*
chants of their ego. Hence the effect of their words   *rections from God-*
often brings disaster to them. Advanced souls guide   *contact*
their intelligence and free will and speech by the wisdom in the Holy Ghost. All true devotees who have felt in meditation
this Cosmic Vibration, the *Aum* sound of the Holy Ghost, can in all
problems of life fruitfully guide their actions according to the intuition-
bestowed direction of infinite wisdom.

"When they arrest you, do not use your calculating human reason, but let God speak through your intuition and the instrument of
your voice. Let not your human ego speak, for its tongue is tied with
rationalizations of personal motives; but let the wisdom of your Father speak through your inner surrender to Him. The intelligent Cosmic Vibration, the materializing manifestation of God, will drop the
specific needed wisdom within your developed intuition at the time
you are required to speak in defense of truth and of yourself, living for
its cause."

Here Jesus is outlining how God-guided people should act when
confronted with persecution. In such matters as business and lawsuits,
people plan with definite self-interest their activities and their words
in all transactions; but Jesus points out that souls who are in tune with
"the Spirit of your Father," Cosmic Consciousness vibrating through
the Holy Ghost, are guided by higher wisdom and all-seeing intelli-

gence in their senses, thoughts, feelings, intellect, and intuitions, instead of depending only on the studied preparedness of limited reason.

Cosmic Consciousness does not reason with devotees, it rather drops truths in their intuitions. Intuition is the father of reason and can satisfy all the demands of reason.

Reason is based on sense experience and is limited by it. If the sense experience is misinterpreted, reason proves to be erroneous. A person beholding wind-blown dust on a distant hill might be led to think that the hill is on fire and emanating a cloud of smoke. Sensory-dependent reason from immediate observation or from memory conditioned by repeated past experiences can blunder if the sensory observation or experience is faulty or incomplete.

God has no senses, nor reason dependent on sensory perceptions; He Himself is the Knower, the process of knowing, and the wisdom to be known. He knows the truth about all things through His cosmic intuition, His feeling present in everything. Likewise do His true devotees, being in tune with the Spirit of their Heavenly Father, depend on the unlimited power and guidance of intuitive God-perception and not on limited reason when confronted with persecutions or human problems.

In the context of the reference in Luke cited above (21:14–15), as also in St. John (14:26), Jesus assures his disciples of his intercession in times of need: "'I will give you a mouth and wisdom'—you will feel my spirit of Christ Consciousness with you, manifesting in 'the Comforter, which is the Holy Ghost...he shall teach you all things.'"

～

> "And the brother shall deliver up the brother to death, and the father the child: and the children shall rise up against their parents, and cause them to be put to death. And ye shall be hated of all men for my name's sake: but he that endureth to the end shall be saved" (Matthew 10:21–22).*

Parallel reference:

> "And ye shall be betrayed both by parents, and brethren, and kinsfolks, and friends; and some of you shall they cause to be

---

* Cf. parallel reference in Mark 13:12–13.

put to death. And ye shall be hated of all men for my name's sake. But there shall not an hair of your head perish. In your patience possess ye your souls" (Luke 21:16–19).

J esus further prophesied of those who would live and preach his truth: "Satan will create great mischief and will rouse a material brother to persecute a spiritual brother and the un-

spiritual father to persecute the spiritual child. The

unspiritual children will rise up against their par-

ents who believe my truth and will put them into

Overcoming trials and persecutions in the spiritual path

trouble and be the cause of their great suffering and death. And for manifesting the subtle pure light of Christ Consciousness in your actions, you will be scorned by materially minded men who are used to living in the darkness of ignorance. And some of you shall be condemned to death, but not a hair of realization of your head of wisdom shall perish or be lost sight of in the eyes of God.

"That devotee who overcomes trials and persecutions in the spiritual path, not only for a little while, but to the end of life—who is patient and endures difficulties, temptations, and spiritual disappointments of not finding God by ardent prayers or years of meditation— shall possess the eternal life of the immortal soul. He shall be permanently saved from enforced trialsome reincarnations that are the lot of desire-bound individuals."

≈

"But when they persecute you in this city, flee ye into another: for verily I say unto you, ye shall not have gone over the cities of Israel, till the Son of man be come" (Matthew 10:23).

66 B ut when they persecute you in one city for preaching God's message, waste not your time and counsel in resisting the unreceptive. Use common sense, and in divine meekness seek out another city in which to preach His word. Verily, by the all-seeing power of spiritual vision, I declare and prophesy that you will not have finished preaching in the cities of Israel until the works and message delivered through my body (Son of man) have become fully known throughout the world."

≈

"The disciple is not above his master, nor the servant above his lord. It is enough for the disciple that he be as his master, and the servant as his lord. If they have called the master of the house Beelzebub, how much more shall they call them of his household?" (Matthew 10:24–25).*

Jesus emphasizes that the persecution of his disciples would be as flagrant if not more so than he himself would endure. "Beloved ones, you know that even a masterful disciple is not honored like his master, no matter how spiritually advanced the disciple is; nor is a glorified servant ever regarded more highly than his lord. It is sufficient before the eyes of God that the disciple become equal to his master and that the servant develop inner lordly qualities akin to his lord; but the same evaluation is not true in the eyes of the people. Thus, when the materially minded people and the Pharisees have called the Master of the house of Christ teachings "Beelzebub" (Prince of Devils),† then how much more shall they condemn you all whom they regard as less than myself, as being followers rather than originators of the truth that has been revealed through my Christ Consciousness?"

∼

"Fear them not therefore: for there is nothing covered, that shall not be revealed; and hid, that shall not be known. What I tell you in darkness, that speak ye in light: and what ye hear in the ear, that preach ye upon the housetops" (Matthew 10:26–27).‡

"O ye, my beloved ones, though I ask you to be meek and humble when subjected to maltreatment, and to follow the course of least resistance during your preaching campaigns, fear not your critics, that you may serve the true seekers to whose receptive consciousness all truth covered from the gaze of the spiritually ignorant must be

---

* Jesus repeated this guidance to his disciples at the Last Supper (John 15:20). See Discourse 71.

† Reference to the Pharisees' slander of Jesus in Matthew 12:24. (See Discourse 36.)

‡ These sayings of Jesus are repeated in Luke 12:2–3 as part of another speech, and are also commented on in that context in Discourse 55.

uncovered. There is no wisdom that will remain forever hidden from the awakened consciousness and spiritual hunger of those devotees. All things that the spiritually dark, ignorant people cannot perceive will be perceived by those who are developed in intuitional Self-realization. The esoteric truths that I convey to you in the darkness of secrecy, which are hidden from the gaze of the unregenerate masses, and that I vibrate within you in the secrecy of your souls, I ask you to reveal with the light of your Self-knowledge to others who are in light, highly advanced due to their past good karma, that they may understandingly perceive those truths. And the truths that you have heard me speak openly, and those that I shall reveal in your intuitional ears within through my Christ Intelligence, for public dissemination, you can proclaim loudly to all without distinction."

It is here noted that Jesus asks his disciples to spread two kinds of teaching—first, the hidden higher teachings to the selected spiritually refined people; second, the general teachings for the public at large.

~

> *"And fear not them which kill the body, but are not able to kill the soul: but rather fear Him, which is able to destroy both body and soul in hell.*
>
> *"Are not two sparrows sold for a farthing? and one of them shall not fall on the ground without your Father. But the very hairs of your head are all numbered. Fear ye not therefore, ye are of more value than many sparrows" (Matthew 10:28–31).*

Parallel reference:

> *"And I say unto you, my friends, be not afraid of them that kill the body, and after that have no more that they can do. But I will forewarn you whom ye shall fear: Fear Him, which after he hath killed hath power to cast into hell; yea, I say unto you, fear Him.*
>
> *"Are not five sparrows sold for two farthings, and not one of them is forgotten before God? But even the very hairs of your head are all numbered. Fear not therefore: ye are of more value than many sparrows" (Luke 12:4–7).*

"I vehemently declare unto you, my friends (friends elected through the choice of my Father's love in my heart and not imposed upon me by nature, as are relatives), do not fear those who would threaten you with death, for they who would kill your body would have no further

Moral and spiritual courage to uphold divine principles

power over you. They cannot destroy or cause grief to your divine consciousness nor dissolve your indestructible, immutable soul. But I warn you, and all who are wicked, that you must learn to stand in respectful and loving awe before God—the Almighty One who through His law of cause and effect evolved your soul and body from His own Self, and who alone upholds your existence and perpetuates by His divine will the immortality of your soul. His divine law of karma is empowered, after the death of your body, to prevent the expression of your soul's peace and joy and to make your astral-bodied consciousness suffer your accumulated wickedness of one life or many lives. Therefore, rather fear your wicked actions, which can compel the divine law to make you conscious of a self-created after-death hell of the effects of your burning conscience and wicked tendencies, which even in life will torment with its fires the inner being as well as the outer health and other conditions necessary to a happy existence.

"Fear not, therefore, even if you have to sacrifice the body. That sacrifice will not bring destruction to the soul, but the sacrifice of a spiritual principle might bring disaster to the soul as well as to the body."

Jesus is emphasizing to his disciples the necessity of moral and spiritual courage, that it is a great sin if one, for fear of man, acts against the cosmic law. Persecution may destroy the body, but acting against the laws of truth affects both the body and the soul. The miseries of the body end in death, but the agonies accruing out of an individual's evil actions continue to confine the soul in the sufferings of its astral body in the after-death state.

The conception of hell as a place where souls are literally burned everlastingly with fire and brimstone is ridiculous. It is the propensity for vindictiveness in man's own heart that assumes such awful cruelty as the revenge of a Creator offended by the misdeeds of man. Poor God! That is a terrible declaration against Him—the Father-Mother who created all things in love, sustains them on the Infinite Bosom of love, and draws them back to Everlasting Bliss by the forgiveness of love. The transmigration of the soul through the matrix of reincarnation with its transforming opportunities for better efforts precludes any justification for an everlasting punishment meted out for man's temporary lapses into ignorance and evil. The evil man in time becomes again the perfect soul. At what point would a just God suddenly cancel an individual's divine birthright to keep striving toward the potentials of his true Self, to suffer instead an everlasting hell? It is untenable that Jesus, who was love, mercy, forgiveness incarnate, would support and preach such a doctrine. The context of his whole life and teachings forbids a literal reading of references to hell as a place of eternal fiery torment.

Concept of "hellfire and brimstone" created by man's own vindictiveness

Material fire can produce sensations of burning on the physical body, but the soul itself is incorporeal and cannot be tortured by physical sensations. Its astral-bodied consciousness, however, if afflicted with hellish wicked tendencies acquired in earth life, can undergo for a time a mental hell of torture that who can gainsay might be worse than a physical fiery hell.

The mental hell of wickedness can persist in the after-death state indefinitely until one gains a new opportunity to improve himself in a new incarnation, or otherwise repents and prays for release. An individual's stubbornness and doggedness to be wicked, even in the after-death state, can make his self-created mental hell as everlasting as he permits it to be.

Jesus continues: "Beloved ones, remember your eternal connection with the ever watchful Heavenly Father. God, being omniscient and omnipresent, does not fail to direct the destiny of insignificant sparrows—'one of them shall not fall on the ground without (the consciousness of) your Father.' How much more does He protect and appreciate the work of the devotees who are self-sacrificing, even martyred, for the sake of truth.

"God is conscious of all things throughout the present, past, and future, even of every hair on your head. Therefore, fear not for your life and actions, as the children of God are of more concern to the Father than the mechanical life of the sparrows who, insignificant though they are, are lovingly attended to by Him."

These high expectations Jesus placed before his disciples are absolutes of faith and surrender to God, lofty above the uncomprehending common man's compliance. The devotee is asked to embrace unconditionally the truth that this universe with all its detail is planned by the intelligence of the Cosmic Father. When man will know Him, he will understand the why of all inexplicable circumstances and happenings and will marvel at the wisdom of the Father, whose love, present in everything, tries to foil the inharmonious doings of Satan's cosmic delusion. Man, being made in the image of God, has no cause to fear negligence on the part of the Divine; with surety He will help the efforts of every soul to retrace its footsteps to His Kingdom of Eternal Bliss.

~

> *"Whosoever therefore shall confess me before men, him will I confess also before my Father which is in heaven. But whosoever shall deny me before men, him will I also deny before my Father which is in heaven" (Matthew 10:32–33).*

Parallel reference:

> *"Also I say unto you, whosoever shall confess me before men, him shall the Son of man also confess before the angels of God. But he that denieth me before men shall be denied before the angels of God" (Luke 12:8–9).* *

"Whoever shall avow before materially minded people and persecutors that he is in tune with my consciousness and my teachings shall find me also in tune with him; and I shall intercede with the Father about taking him into His kingdom of luminous infinity, even though he may have sins of evil karma. Every soul who will suffer physical death as the consequence for teaching my truth will find his sins expiated thereby; his consciousness will pass through the Christ Intelligence in Cosmic Vibration to the transcendent sphere of Cosmic Consciousness.

Receiving the blessing of the guru's divine intercession

"That individual of little faith and devotion who, for fear of persecution, will deny before materially minded people his attunement with the Christ Consciousness in me, or will deviate or desist from Christ living, will find, when he reaches the blissful Christ Intelligence state after death, that consciousness weakening within him (due to his weakness of denial), preventing him from remaining in the Christ In-

---

* Cf. additional parallel references in Mark 8:38 and Luke 9:26 (Discourse 45).

telligence and from ascending higher into the God-the-Father state of Cosmic Consciousness."

Jesus here speaks to his disciples of the importance of his divine intercession—the blessing of the guru—that will strengthen the nascent experience of the Christ Consciousness within them. He then cautions that they must not lose that blessing by diminishment of their attunement with the Christ Consciousness in him, under duress of obstacles or spiritual persecution, or through succumbing to selfish motives. The fortitude of faith and of perseverance in divine attunement brings forth upon the devotee the liberating grace of the "Father which is in heaven," and the assistance of the heavenly forces of "the angels of God." But Jesus warns that devotees who are deterred from their course of personal advancement and of helping to uplift the consciousness of others, intimidated by fear of worldly condemnation or cowed by temptation, will forfeit divine aid, suffer loss of their contact with Christ Consciousness, and be unable to advance further.

~

"Think not that I am come to send peace on earth: I came not to send peace, but a sword. For I am come to set a man at variance against his father, and the daughter against her mother, and the daughter in law against her mother in law. And a man's foes shall be they of his own household. He that loveth father or mother more than me is not worthy of me: and he that loveth son or daughter more than me is not worthy of me. And he that taketh not his cross, and followeth after me, is not worthy of me. He that findeth his life shall lose it: and he that loseth his life for my sake shall find it" (Matthew 10:34–39).*

J esus speaks to his disciples not only of the divisive conditions that will accompany the establishment of his message of spiritual reformation, but also of the inevitable obstacles faced by those who seek to tread the single-hearted path to God in a world intent on human relations and material values.

---

* Cf. parallel reference in Luke 12:51–53, Discourse 56.

Jesus repeats the last two sentences of this counsel in another context in Matthew 16:24–25. (See Discourse 45 for commentary.)

"Think not that I came to bring material peace for souls to be settled complacently in earthly life. I came not to offer short-lasting material happiness, but to give to the valiant spiritual soul a two-edged

The sword of wisdom and self-control to fight unspiritual temptations and influences

sword of wisdom and self-control, divine strength and determination by which he can sever the compulsions of material passions and temptations and successfully resist any unspiritual familial influence that might obstruct his attainment of everlasting happiness and freedom.

"The eternal truth that I preach and that is manifested within you will variously affect people according to their various good and bad karma: A spiritually inclined devotee of mine might not agree with his materially minded father, or a daughter attuned to Christ Consciousness might not be in harmony with her unspiritual mother, and the spiritual daughter-in-law might act against the material wishes of her mother-in-law, and a man enjoying the ecstasy of Christ Consciousness in his meditations might find the members of his material family inimical to him owing to their own contrary karmic tendencies.

"Since parents are given by God through His laws of nature, the devotee's love for them must not be in forgetfulness of the greater love he owes to his Heavenly Parent. Similarly with attachment to son or daughter; to be worthy of God is to meditate upon Him until one knows Him as the supreme Cosmic Lover—the Love behind all human loves."

Jesus certainly does not mean that his teachings will not bring peace in family life amidst truth-seeking family members. Rather, he is admonishing all who set their sights on the kingdom of God not to remain steeped in the ignorance of a material life, but to use the sword of wisdom he brought to them to destroy their delusions of earthliness.

Family environment and familial love exert a strong force on even the most stalwart devotee. Jesus therefore stresses that if a devotee finds his family members dissuading him or trying to obstruct his efforts to cultivate God-consciousness, he should not yield but continue undeterred and undismayed. The devotee should remember that he alone has to reap the consequences of his actions; he should not let any perversity on the part of his earthly family turn him against his Heavenly Father. The firm words of Jesus point out that those who overcome all obstacles create good karma and tendencies that will automatically lead them to the attainment of Cosmic Consciousness, the kingdom of God.

Jesus was unequivocal; on another occasion, he said, "If any man come to me, and hate not his father, and mother, and wife, and children, and brethren, and sisters, yea, and his own life also, he cannot be my disciple" (Luke 14:26). He does not mean literally that all devotees should hate their parents and relatives or detest their own life. As he pointed out elsewhere: "Who is my mother and who are my brethren?...Whosoever shall do the will of my Father which is in heaven."* And also, "Take no thought for your life, what ye shall eat, or what ye shall drink; nor yet for your body, what ye shall put on....But seek ye first the kingdom of God, and His righteousness; and all these things shall be added unto you."† Jesus is citing the truth that no one can perform his duties to his parents, spouse, or other relatives, or to his own body and life, without the gifts of understanding, life, and action, which come from God alone. Anyone seeking God must be able to forsake the inordinate human love for God-given gifts, for the sake of attainment of God Himself. The price of material attachment is usually forgetfulness of God accompanied by unending miseries; the price of God-realization is primarily absolute mental renunciation and secondarily, in apt cases, renunciation of all material possessions and bodily attachments as well. In the Bhagavad Gita, Lord Krishna speaks similarly: "Forsaking all duties, think of Me alone. As no duties can be performed without the human faculties borrowed from Me, I will forgive you the sins of nonperformance of lesser duties provided they are forsworn in order to seek Me alone."‡

"He that taketh not his cross and followeth after me" — who fights not temptations with self-discipline and in meditation uplifts his mind from the plane of senses to enter the star door in the spiritual eye that leads to Christ Consciousness — "is not worthy of me," of my divine Christ-kingdom. He who in daily life is not prepared to hold his Christ-peace of meditation at all times — during the crucifixion of calmness by restlessness, of self-control by temptation, of divine loyalty by persecution — does not merit the attainment of Christ Con-

---

* Matthew 12:48, 50 (see Discourse 36).

† Matthew 6:25, 33 (see Discourse 29).

‡ Paraphrase of XVIII:66: "Forsaking all other *dharmas* (duties), remember Me alone; I will free thee from all sins (accruing from nonperformance of those lesser duties). Do not grieve!"

sciousness, and to pass from the painful repetitions of incarnate earth life into the eternal life of ever new bliss.

"He that findeth his life"—puts material happiness as the goal of his life—"shall lose it"—shall perforce lose whatever temporary satisfactions he has garnered when death dissolves his tenuous hold on material existence. "He that loseth his life for my sake"—sacrifices his desires for material pleasures to purify his consciousness for contact with the blissful Christ Consciousness in meditation—"shall find" the everlasting happiness of the divine life.

"O ye disciples, remember that he who discovers only the material pleasures of his mundane life will lose the divine joys hidden behind that externalized consciousness. He who finds and establishes the cosmic joy of meditation in his life loses the hankering that compels attachment to the passing fancies of material life. He finds the Christ Consciousness within, and with it the everlasting joys hidden behind the facades of materiality. That devotee, divested of desires for the pleasures of the body, will find in the ever new joy of ecstasy in Christ Consciousness in meditation that material prosperity and earthly happiness will be added unto him; but he who seeks material happiness only will lose it because of the rudeness of its short-lasting nature."

~

"He that receiveth you receiveth me, and he that receiveth me receiveth Him that sent me. He that receiveth a prophet in the name of a prophet shall receive a prophet's reward; and he that receiveth a righteous man in the name of a righteous man shall receive a righteous man's reward. And whosoever shall give to drink unto one of these little ones a cup of cold water only in the name of a disciple, verily I say unto you, he shall in no wise lose his reward" (Matthew 10:40–42).

"He that heareth you heareth me; and he that despiseth you despiseth me; and he that despiseth me despiseth Him that sent me" (Luke 10:16).

"To receive" and "to hear" denote the ability to absorb the God-wisdom transmitted by a true divine guru, or a disciple in tune with him, by expanding the capacity of one's own consciousness and inner attunement with the guru's God-consciousness.

"O ye disciples, any devotee who listens to your teachings as I have imparted them to you, and who follows you, follows me. My Christ Consciousness is with you through your devotion and meditation, and anyone who will be in tune with you will be in tune with my Christ Con-
sciousness. Those devotees who receive of your consciousness through their intuition and attunement, my beloved disciples, will gradually, through your aid and the spiritual vibrations emanating from your meditations, contact the Christ Consciousness within themselves. Those who will be able by deep meditation to be one with the Christ Conscious-
ness in all vibratory creation (the Son) and will discipline their lives under your tutelage, will ultimately be able to be one with Cosmic Consciousness beyond creation (God the Father), whose reflection is present in the Christ Intelligence within me.

*Blessings of attune-
ment with a God-
realized master or his
faithful disciples*

"He who is in tune with Christ-tuned disciples is automatically in tune with Christ Consciousness. And he who can receive Christ Intelligence in his expanded consciousness is in tune with the Cosmic Con-
sciousness out of which Christ Consciousness emanates. Anyone who hates you who faithfully represent me hates my Christ Consciousness, ignorantly rebelling against it; he is further out of tune with Him who sent me, the Cosmic Consciousness whose reflection I am."

Jesus is emphasizing how truth-seekers can reach the Cosmic Consciousness of God by tuning in their consciousness with true God-realized gurus, who in turn have been trained by their Christlike teachers. Through the hierarchy and lineage (*guru-parampara*)* of true gu-
rus, a truth-seeker is properly introduced to God.

Jesus continues: "A person in tune with the spiritual vibrations ('the name') of a prophet, or of a righteous man, or of the serviceful acts of mercy of a faithful disciple will receive the prophetic qualities and wisdom accorded to a prophet, or the reward of happiness reaped by the virtues of a righteous man, or divine mercy, respectively, according to the merits of his actions.

"The devotee who has supremely expanded his consciousness by meditation in order to receive Christ Consciousness, a prophet's consciousness, will be in tune with the Cosmic Intelligence in all vibra-

---

* The holy succession of a line of gurus, by which a master appoints his spiritual successor. (See "Gurus of Self-Realization Fellowship" in glossary.)

tory creation; and he who tunes himself with the consciousness of a righteous individual, and lives his own life righteously, according to the law of cause and effect will be a righteous man. And he who thoughtfully gives drink to the thirsty—or who offers a cup of the cool waters of wisdom or uplifting truth vibrations in the selfless spirit of a disciple, to quench the thirst of the 'little ones,' beginners on the path of God who seek relief from the thirst of unslaked material desires—'shall in no wise lose his reward'; he will acquire good karma and heavenly tendencies that will eventually lift him toward Christ Consciousness."

The above words of Jesus Christ have a distinct parallelism with some verses in the Bhagavad Gita: "Those individuals who worship different deities and different embodiments of the qualities of God attain what they desire, but those devotees who want Me (God) come unto Me."* Jesus similarly pointed out that all good actions are rewarded, and followers of different forms of virtue attain their objectives according to the focus of their innate desires. But those who strive for attunement with the God-realization of a prophet, who want to achieve Christhood, attain their goal and become Christlike, according to their heart's desire.

～

And they went out, and preached that men should repent. And they cast out many devils, and anointed with oil many that were sick, and healed them (Mark 6:12–13).

Having instructed his disciples in the proper dispensation of their ministry, Jesus sent them forth. Accordingly, they preached about the vibrations of God-consciousness emanating from Jesus and echoed his call for people to repent and forsake their material attachments in order to attain God-consciousness, the kingdom of God, through spiritual awakening. By the power of their developed will, the

---

* VII:21–23: "Whatever embodiment (a God-incarnate, a saint, or a deity) a devotee strives faithfully to worship, it is I who make his devotion unflinching. Absorbed in that devotion, intent on the worship of that embodiment, the devotee thus gains the fruits of his longings. Yet those fulfillments are verily granted by Me alone. But men of scant knowledge (worshiping lesser gods) receive limited results. The devotees of the deities go unto them; My devotees come unto Me."

disciples freed many people from obsessions and healed many of the sick of their various diseases—anointing them with oil blessed by the rites of prayer, even as people in India are anointed with drops of holy water from the sacred rivers or otherwise blessed in spiritual rites. The disciples by their services akin to those of their Master proved themselves as far more than products of a theological school. They actually lived the truth, and thus by their spiritual examples and instrumentality did great good to mankind by healing bodies of physical and mental diseases and souls of ignorance.

∼

And the apostles gathered themselves together unto Jesus, and told him all things, both what they had done, and what they had taught. And he said unto them, "Come ye yourselves apart into a desert place, and rest a while": for there were many coming and going, and they had no leisure so much as to eat (Mark 6:30–31).

On the return of the apostles from their successful journeys, Jesus pointed out that preachers of truth should always be equipped with divine consciousness. They should condition themselves in meditation so that they are steeped in God before going out to spread the gospel; and when they feel themselves spiritually depleted after active periods of teaching others, they should again retire to quiet places and recharge themselves through God-contact in meditation before they resume their ministry.

∼

And the seventy returned again with joy, saying, "Lord, even the devils are subject unto us through thy name."

And he said unto them, "I beheld Satan as lightning fall from heaven. Behold, I give unto you power to tread on serpents and scorpions, and over all the power of the enemy: and nothing shall by any means hurt you. Notwithstanding in this rejoice not, that the spirits are subject unto you; but rather rejoice, because your names are written in heaven" (Luke 10:17–20).

The seventy disciples, also, which Jesus had sent out at a later time to teach, returned and reported to their Master, marveling at the powers expressed through them in his name. When citing especially their command over devils, Jesus spoke to them of Satan as the source of evil, and of how the evil force can be conquered within oneself.

Conquering Satan who fell like lightning from heaven

"While I was in my omnipresent Christ Consciousness, I beheld satanic delusion as a conscious cosmic force, a lightning-like creative energy, repulsed out of heavenly Cosmic Consciousness. Behold, I give you divine power by which you will be able to conquer Satan and his minions; by overcoming delusion, nothing shall in any way harm you. Through my Christ Consciousness, I will give you the will power by which you shall be able to control the coiled serpent force at the base of the spine. The creative life force flowing outward into the body feeds sexual desires and 'scorpions' of tormenting, poisonous, evil instincts. When you master the technique of withdrawing the coiled serpent force upward through the awakened astral centers in the spine to the celestial astral region in the cerebrum, then you will have full self-control over the unruly passions of sex and all evil desires that obstruct the attainment of divine bliss. Be less elated that you have power to control evil spirits and evil forces in healing others, and rather rejoice more that your souls have attained a sufficient degree of Self-realization to access the heavenly region of Cosmic Consciousness."

As was explained in previous verses,* Satan was originally an archangel, an intelligent force of God's creative cosmic energy, endowed with power to create in tune with Divine Intelligence perfect heavenly manifestations in material creation. This force came out of Maha-Prakriti, Great Nature, the Holy Ghost, the primal creative aspect of Spirit. The informing power of the Mother of Creation is *maya,* cosmic delusion, that transforms the One Spirit into myriad manifestations. With a thin veil of *maya,* Prakriti's pure nature, Para-Prakriti, works in harmony with God's reflected Christ-*Kutastha* Intelligence to produce the divine laws and forces informing all manifestations of the heavenly astral-causal realms. A denser pall of cosmic delusion was required to generate the gross vibrations necessary to beget a sustained material creation from this underlying astral-causal

_____

* See Discourse 7.

matrix. Because these gross vibrations of cosmic delusion distort and eclipse the true nature of matter as made of God's consciousness, this outflowing creative power is referred to as Prakriti's impure nature, Apara-Prakriti. It is this aspect to which Satan is equated, depicted as an archangel fallen from divine grace, a creative force not guided by heavenly vibrations—a force that rebelled against God-consciousness, obscuring the Innate Divinity, in order to preserve his own kingdom of humankind through self-perpetuating misuse of free will.

Thus, heaven is not only transcendental Cosmic Consciousness, but also that region of manifestation in which the pure Cosmic Intelligent Energy works in tune with the creative will of Cosmic Consciousness, God the Father of Creation. And the sphere of space in which there is the creation and presence of imperfect manifestations is the field wherein the conscious cosmic force of Satan, the energy fallen from heavenly attunement into deception, spawns tantalizing delusions of bondage to oppose the hidden essence of the intercessional, liberating works of the pure Divine Intelligence.

Similarly, in the human body there is the transcendent and heavenly region and the region of delusion or satanic influence. The heavenly region extends from the astral dorsal or heart center up to the transcendental cerebral center of Spirit. The region of satanic influence and the receptacle of baser instincts extends from below the heart, through the lumbar, sacral, and coccygeal centers (notwithstanding that when these very centers are spiritualized by meditation and righteous action, their soul-attuned functions then aid the devotee, respectively, with self-control, adherence to spiritual observances, and resistance to untoward sensory temptations).* When the energy from the senses is concentrated by meditation in the divine astral center in the brain, the devotee is spoken of as having attained heaven. But in most people, those who do not meditate nor behave in harmony with their soul qualities, their consciousness is tied to the life force flowing downwards, falling from the heavenly astral cerebral region to the region of the senses.

The satanic or delusive force in every human being keeps the lightning-like life force continuously descending toward the senses, allowing the searchlight of sensory perceptions to reveal the attraction of sense objects only. This, Jesus also observed in the seventy disciples he was addressing. Unlike the more advanced among his twelve apos-

---

* See also commentary in *God Talks With Arjuna: The Bhagavad Gita* I:II.

799

tles, they had yet to master fully the art of *pranayama,* life-force control. So Jesus taught them — "I give unto you the power" — by meditation and will power to reverse the life force — "to tread on serpents and scorpions" of sensory passions — and thereby enjoy the heavenly consciousness and divine perceptions of the kingdom of God within them.

Thus Jesus said to these disciples that they should rejoice, not only for being able to control the devils or evil passions aroused when the force at the base of the spine flows outward to stimulate lust and other sensory passions, but for the power they had been given to withdraw the energy upward, through the coiled serpent-like passage at the base of the spine into the cerebrospinal region of heavenly forces and heavenly bliss.

By self-mastery "over all power of the enemy," acquired by obedience and meditation, Jesus assured them, "Your names are written in heaven" — having secured their consciousness in the kingdom of heaven within, they would be qualified to be recalled to the infinite wall-less mansion of the blissful Cosmic Consciousness of the Heavenly Father.

~

*In that hour Jesus rejoiced in spirit, and said, "I thank Thee, O Father, Lord of heaven and earth, that Thou hast hid these things from the wise and prudent, and hast revealed them unto babes: even so, Father; for so it seemed good in Thy sight" (Luke 10:21).** *

6 6 I thank Thee, O Heavenly Father, Thou Infinite Lord pervading as Cosmic Consciousness behind all heavenly manifestations and in the vibrationless region beyond creation ('Lord of heaven') and as Christ Consciousness existing in all vibratory creation ('Lord of...earth'), that although You have hidden Yourself and Your omniscience from egotistically wise and theoretically prudent individuals, You have revealed the mystery of truth unto Your simple, guileless children, even though they are but babes in wisdom before Your incomparable Infinite Mind. Heavenly Father, the revealing of Yourself and

---

* Cf. parallel reference in Matthew 11:25–26.

ultimate truth unto Your devotees who are humbly simple and sincere —spiritual babes who surrender their sensate intelligence unto the unlimited intuitional inspiration that comes from Thee —is in accord with Thy proper judgment."

God is revealed not by intellectuality, but by pure and guileless devotion

Though Jesus' disciples were mostly uneducated in scholarly matters, he found them receptive to a higher knowledge than that of the rationalizing intellect. Divine realization, perception of the Infinite, is unrelated to academic degrees. It is good to have knowledge befitting a professor in preference to a doltish brain of an ignorant man; but if one's intellect is so complacent in its scholastic distinction that one feels no need to seek wisdom in God, the evolution of that soul is laggardly compared to an illiterate who has devotion to the Lord. By drawing his disciples from among the common populace —even "publicans and sinners" and unlettered fishermen such as Peter, James, and John—Jesus showed that it was possible for any devotee to attain divine realization, for God is not a respecter of persons as to their status. As the little and big fingers equally belong to one's hand, so all souls—whether or not they are significant in the eyes of the world—belong to God. Whoever approaches Him with pure devotion will attain Him.

God reveals Himself unto those who completely surrender themselves unto Him, those who have no intellectual or emotional resistance to Him. Before God, the most accomplished of humans is but a child; even the most brilliant scientist does not know why or how God created this world. The Lord is not interested in how much one knows, but in how much one loves Him. The only way to touch Him is by the ardent devotion of the heart.

Jesus lauded the childlike qualities of his disciples over the "wise and prudent" who loved to use their erudition and logic to find fault with his teachings. A closed-minded critical attitude is spiritually stultifying. Attunement with the guru through devotion enables the devotee to progress steadily toward God-realization; doubters and habitual criticizers fall by the wayside. A guru does not seek to silence the disciple's reason; but he can only help those who are willing to be taught, not those who self-assertively "know it all." That devotee becomes filled with intuitive wisdom who is childlike in guilelessness, free of presumption and doubt, full of sincerity, humble and receptive. That devotee finds God.

≈

> *"All things are delivered to me of my Father: and no man knoweth who the Son is, but the Father; and who the Father is, but the Son, and he to whom the Son will reveal Him."*
>
> *And he turned him unto his disciples, and said privately, "Blessed are the eyes which see the things that ye see: For I tell you, that many prophets and kings have desired to see those things which ye see, and have not seen them; and to hear those things which ye hear, and have not heard them" (Luke 10:22–24).* *

"The omniscience and omnipotence of Cosmic Consciousness, God the Father of creation, are transmitted to the omnipresent reflected Christ Consciousness so that the laws of all manifestation can be intelligently governed by truth and wisdom. No materially minded man knows the Christ Consciousness (Son); only the Cosmic Consciousness, which is the Father of Christ Consciousness. And no one knows the Cosmic Consciousness (Father) except through the Christ Consciousness (Son). Devotees realize Cosmic Consciousness only by first experiencing Christ Consciousness in meditation."

Freedom from body consciousness necessary to know Christ and Cosmic Consciousness

Jesus elsewhere said: "I and my Father are one." He realized the Christ Consciousness within his consciousness as perfectly united with the Cosmic Consciousness. As the reflection of the moon in the lake and the moon in the sky are essentially the same image, so Cosmic Consciousness mirrored in all cosmic vibration as Christ Consciousness is the same as the Cosmic Consciousness existing beyond the vibratory realm.

The ordinary man is bound by the consciousness of the body and its relation to the material world, but by advancement in meditation he does away with the circumscriptions of bodily attachments and realizes an unfathomable depth of bliss, which lies beyond his conscious and subconscious experiences in the superconsciousness of the soul.

When the devotee, through protractive devout endeavor, is able to enter the ecstasy of meditation and become one with the supercon-

---

* Cf. parallel reference to verse 22 in Matthew 11:27. Verses 23–24 were commented on in Discourse 37 with their parallels in Matthew 13:16–17.

scious state, he then attains, with the help of his guru and advanced techniques, an expanded ecstasy in which he perceives himself as a vast light and endless consciousness in which he finds all galaxies, star rivers, and vibratory objects glimmering like glowworms within his omnipresent Self. When the devotee by passing his consciousness through his inner spiritual eye experiences this vast cosmic vision, he is spoken of as having attained Christ Consciousness. The whole vibratory universe, and everything in it, is felt as his own Self, just as he feels all the cells and the different parts of his own physical body.

After attaining Christ Consciousness, the devotee goes further, beyond all vibratory space, into an indescribable state of Cosmic Consciousness of pure ever new Joy, Consciousness, and Existence. Here in this Cosmic Consciousness no eddies of vibration or change can disturb the absolute bliss of the consciousness of the devotee merged in divine union with God.

In the very highest ecstasy that an incarnate soul can experience, *nirvikalpa samadhi,* the supremely advanced devotee finds his consciousness simultaneously merged in the vibrationless Cosmic Consciousness and the ocean of Cosmic Vibration with its bubbles of planets, nebulae, comets, stars, and universes. Jesus attained this state; hence he said, "The Father (Cosmic Consciousness) knows the Son (Christ Consciousness), and the Son knows the Father."

No one can suddenly jump from limited body-consciousness and its attachment to earthly surroundings directly to realization of the Transcendental Infinite, God the Father. Even though man's soul itself is an individualized reflection of the Christ Intelligence, the soul consciousness is entangled in a cluster of electronic and lifetronic vibrations of the physical and astral bodies. The soul consciousness of man must first leave the limited region of the senses and bodily consciousness. Like a little wave being reabsorbed into the sea, the consciousness then encounters expansion in the vast Holy Ghost Cosmic Vibration. As the expanded soul is baptized in that sacred Vibration of Spirit, it experiences the immanent Christ Intelligence. Only then, blessed by this Reflected Presence, does the consciousness go beyond to the vibrationless infinitude, the kingdom of God the Father, Cosmic Consciousness.

If Jesus were speaking of his body as the Son of God, one would have to conclude that no souls were ever redeemed before the birth of Jesus—neither Abraham, Jacob, Moses, Elijah, nor any of the prophets. The true meaning of this verse (and similar ones*) is that spiritually evolved souls, of whom many existed before the time of Jesus and would continue to be born after him, have to pass their consciousness through the Holy Ghost Cosmic Vibration and the Son or Christ Intelligence existing in it before they can ascend to the transcendent kingdom of His Heavenly Majesty, God. Thus the emphasis of Jesus that it is the Son or Christ Consciousness alone that can reveal God the Father to any soul.

∽

> *"Come unto me, all ye that labour and are heavy laden, and I will give you rest. Take my yoke upon you, and learn of me; for I am meek and lowly in heart: and ye shall find rest unto your souls. For my yoke is easy, and my burden is light" (Matthew 11:28–30).*

In oneness with the infinite Christ Intelligence, Jesus lovingly urged all spiritual aspirants to "Come unto me" (the Christ Consciousness) and "Take my yoke upon you"—follow the step-by-step methods of self-discipline that lead to Christ Consciousness and that assure ultimate liberation in God's kingdom:†

"O ye aspiring souls who are heavily laden with bad karma and are struggling to free yourselves from the self-created prison of evil actions: Tune your consciousness in deep meditation with the all-pervading, ever new bliss of Christ Consciousness, which surpasses the semijoyous state

---

* For example, John 14:6: "...no man cometh unto the Father, but by me." (See Discourse 70.)

† Yoke (*zugo* in the original Greek of the Gospel) and *yoga* are etymologically related, all deriving from the Sanskrit root *yuj*, signifying union. (See also Discourse 5, page 84 n.) Even as Jesus in these verses promises his disciples that the transcendent, all-liberating Cosmic Consciousness will be revealed to those who attune themselves with the immanent Christ Consciousness by taking up his "easy" yoke of spiritual discipline, so does Bhagavan Krishna declare to his disciple Arjuna in the Bhagavad Gita:

"To thee, the uncarping one, I shall now reveal the sublime mystery (the immanent-transcendent nature of Spirit). Possessing intuitive realization of this wisdom, thou shalt escape from evil. This intuitive realization is the king of sciences, the royal secret, the peerless purifier, the essence of *dharma* (man's righteous duty); it is the direct perception of truth—the imperishable enlightenment—attained through ways (of yoga) very easy to perform" (*God Talks With Arjuna: The Bhagavad Gita* IX:1–2).

of subconsciousness in sleep and the ever new joyous state of superconsciousness beyond the state of deep sleep. Then you will forever rest in my Infinite Consciousness, never again to be forced to reincarnate on the misery-making earth. Take upon your consciousness my consciousness and expand your consciousness to Christ Consciousness. The materially proud concentrate on physical experiences and do not perceive my Christ Intelligence

The yoga of self-discipline that most easily brings liberation to the soul

meekly and humbly lying within the hearts of all souls; but those who know me and my way rest their souls in the depths of inner concentration and find me as the Infinite Christ which has abided always within themselves, never demanding recognition or advertising my own being.

"Those who are yoked to material consciousness find their burden of karma very heavy, to be worked out through copious struggles of many incarnations. But those who attune their consciousness to Christ Consciousness discover that the burden of my Consciousness on their consciousness is not heavy with suffering but light with freedom and joy everlasting. They find the spiritual ease and freedom of a consciousness no longer weighed down with materiality, and a baptism of their soul in the all-freeing light of the Holy Ghost vibration, Christ-wisdom, and the Father's Eternal Bliss."